Years of Weimar, the Reich and Post-War Germany

second edition

DAVID EVANS & JANE JENKINS

HODDER
EDUCATION
PART OF HACHETTE LIVRE UK

Hachette's policy is to use papers that are natural, renewable and recyclable products and made from wood grown in sustainable forests. The logging and manufacturing processes are expected to conform to the environmental regulations of the country of origin.

Orders: please contact Bookpoint Ltd, 130 Milton Park, Abingdon, Oxon OX14 4SB. Telephone: +44 (0)1235 827720. Fax: +44 (0)1235 400454. Lines are open 9.00a.m.–5.00p.m., Monday to Saturday, with a 24-hour message answering service. Visit our website at www.hoddereducation.co.uk

© David Evans and Jane Jenkins 1999, additional material © David Evans 2008.

First published in 1999 by
Hodder Education,
part of Hachette Livre UK,
338 Euston Road,
London NW1 3BH.

This second edition first published 2008.

Impression number   5 4 3 2 1
Year   2012 2011 2010 2009 2008

Typeset in 10pt Minion by Fakenham Photosetting Limited, Fakenham, Norfolk
Printed in Malta

A catalogue record for this title is available from the British Library.

ISBN 978 0 340 96660 0

Contents

⌁ LIST OF TABLES ⌁

✺ LIST OF MAPS ✺

✺ LIST OF DIAGRAMS ✺

⤳ LIST OF ILLUSTRATIONS ⤳

❧ LIST OF PROFILES ❧

⌁ ACKNOWLEDGEMENTS ⌁

The Publishers would like to thank the following for permission to reproduce material in this book:
Berlin Wall Online, for an extract from "Berlin Memories" by Ger Tillekens, from www.dailysoft.com/berlinwall/memories (November 14, 2002) used on page 484; **Blackwell Publishing**, for Table 25 from *The Nazi Party: A Social Profile of Members and Leaders 1919–1945* by Michael Kater (Blackwell, 1983) used on page 126, **Cambridge University Press**, for extracts from *A Concise History of Germany* by Mary Fulbrook (Cambridge University Press, 1990) used on pages 460, 467; **T & T Clark Ltd**, for extracts from *The Third Reich and the Christian Churches* by Peter Matheson (T & T Clark, 1983) used on pages 228, 229, 230; **Hamlyn/Octopus Publishing**, for extracts from *Hitler: A Study in Tyranny* by Alan Bullock (Odhams, 1952) used on pages 42, 320, 373; **HarperCollins Publishers**, for extracts from *The Fontana History of Germany, 1918–1990: the Divided Nation* by Mary Fulbrook (Fontana, 1991) used on pages 391, 437; for an extract from *The World At War* by Mark Arnold-Foster (Collins, 1974) used on page 446; **HarperCollins Publishers Inc**, for an extract from *Inside Europe* by John Gunther (Harper & Brothers, 1936) used on page 371; **Orion Publishing Group**, for extracts from *Hitler* by J. C. Fest (Weidenfeld & Nicolson, 1974) used on pages 141, 147, 316; for extracts from *Inside the Third Reich* by Albert Speer (Weidenfeld & Nicolson, 1970) used on pages 159, 171, 189–190, 223, 224; for extracts from *Account Settled* by Hjalmar Schacht (Weidenfeld & Nicolson, 1949) used on pages 344, 345–346; **Palgrave Macmillan**, for extracts from *Hindenburg, the Wooden Titan* by John W. Wheeler-Bennett (Macmillan, 1936) used on pages 7–8, 9, 94–95, 97; for an extract from *Weimar and the Rise of Hitler* by A. J. Nicholls (Macmillan, 2000) used on page 75; for extracts from *The Last Days of Hitler* by Hugh Trevor-Roper (Macmillan, 1947) used on pages 188–189, 417; for Table 43 and Table 51 adapted from *The Nazi Economic Recovery 1932–1938* by R. J. Overy (Macmillan, 1982) used on pages 351, 366, 371; **Penguin Books Ltd**, for extracts from *The Origins of the Second World War* by A. J. P. Taylor (Penguin Books, 1964), © A. J. P. Taylor, 1961, 1963, used on pages 377, 381–382, 389–390; **The Random House Group Ltd**, for extracts from *Mein Kampf* by Adolf Hitler, originally published by Hurst & Blackett (1939) used on pages 244, 248, 250, 254–255; **University of Exeter Press**, for extracts from *Nazism 1919–1945, A Documentary Reader,* edited by Jeremy Noakes and Geoffrey Pridham (University of Exeter Press, 1983): Volume 1 – *The Rise to Power 1919–1934*, used on pages 141, 145; Volume 2 – *State, Economy and Society 1933–1939* used on pages 169, 192, 193, 292, 293, 294, 296, 353–354, 365; Volume 3 – *Foreign Policy, War and Racial Extermination*, used on pages 208–209, 224, 284, 424, 428.

The Publishers would like to thank the following for permission to reproduce the following copyright illustrations in this book:
AKG-images page 40; The Art Archive/German Poster Museum, Essen/Marc Charmet page 121 **al**; © Bettman/CORBIS pages 451, 469, 478; Bildarchiv Preußischer Kulturbesitz pages 82, 270, 312, 317; Central Press/Hulton Archive/Getty Images page 444; David Evans pages 41, 441; Daniel Fitzpatrick, St Louis Post-Dispatch, used by permission, State Historical Society of Missouri, Columbia, pages 401, 457; Galerie der Stadt Stuttgart/AKG-Images © Dacs London 2008 page 79; Bert Hardy/Picture Post/Getty Images page 450; Hulton Archive/Getty Images page 24; Illustrated London News page 166 **a**; Imperial War Museum pages 3, 115, 56 **c**, 121 **br**, 164, 165, 166 **b**, 167, 168 **a** and **b**, 215, 290, 291, 383; Imperial War Museum Hulton page 46; © Jacques Langevin/CORBIS SYGMA page 480 **a**; Library of Congress, Prints & Photographs Division, Clifford Berryman Collection © 2008 The Washington Post Company page 398; David Low, Evening Standard/Solo Syndication/Associated Newspapers Ltd page 149; Keystone/Hulton Archive/Getty Images pages 112, 315; Chris Niedenthal/Time Life Pictures/Getty Images page 480 **b**; Popperfoto/Getty Images page 56 l; Punch Ltd, www.punch.co.uk pages 39, 410; Roger-Violett/Topfoto page 333; © 2001 Topham/AP/Topfoto page 472; St Louis Post-Dispatch, used by permission, State Historical Society of Missouri, Columbia page 453; Image from FV Grunfeld 'The Hitler File', with kind permission of Weidenfeld and Nicolson, a division of The Orion Publishing Group, page 270; Wiener Library pages 56 **r**, 63, 247, 326.

(**a** above; **b** below; **r** right; **l** left)

Every effort has been made to trace and acknowledge ownership of copyright. The Publishers will be glad to make suitable arrangements with any copyright holders whom it has not been possible to contact.

Preface: How to use this book

This book covers a period in the history of one country, Germany, during the period 1918–1945. Emerging from defeat in the First World War and the humiliation of the treaty that followed, the German people struggled to survive the political and economic chaos that was part of the upheavals of the 1920s, the years of the Weimar Republic. In 1933, they finally gave their support to one of the most evil men in history, Adolf Hitler, and for the next twelve years lived under his Nazi regime. For many Germans, the period began as a time of fulfilment that brought a restoration of national pride but by the early 1940s Hitler's Third Reich had degenerated into racialist tyranny and faced the prospect of defeat in another war. The book considers many issues and raises many questions. Whilst some are explained, others are still under review with a final judgment yet to be reached. Some are so complex and contradictory they may never be satisfactorily answered.

Although the introduction of a two-tier system of examinations, Advanced Subsidiary and Advanced Level (AS and A2) have brought some changes in syllabus content and methods of assessment, the historical skills required to succeed in the examinations remain largely the same. These are the skills needed to analyse, evaluate, interpret and use different types of historical sources, the ability to use historical concepts to develop an argument, to communicate clearly and write concisely and with relevance. To these has been added a synoptic dimension and the ability to prepare well-planned coursework which we will consider later.

1 ⌐ USING SOURCES

We study history in order to find out about the past. It is necessary to discover not merely what happened but also to consider why it happened, who was responsible and what were the consequences. To do this it is necessary to find evidence. On almost every historical topic there is a vast amount of source material that can be used to build up an overall and balanced picture. It is not therefore surprising that the use of sources in A-level examining has increased considerably. Sources may be primary or secondary. Primary sources may take the form of written documents, eye-witness accounts, films and photographs; secondary sources may be written accounts based on research, interpretations and opinions, illustrations, maps, diagrams, cartoons and sometimes statistics. Different sources provide different types of evidence and the first task of an historian is to assess their usefulness by judging their reliability. Is the source genuine? To what extent is it biased?

Many types of sources are used in AS and A1 examinations. Questions may be based on a single source, two sources or many (multi-) sources. Some may be original or primary sources written or photographed by people who witnessed the event at first hand. Others may represent the views of historians who, after completing their research and enjoying the advantages of hindsight, will detail their conclusions in books. Historians often disagree with each other and will challenge interpretations, evaluations and conclusions reached. They will point out errors, inconsistencies and conflicting points of view. The documentary exercises that accompany the chapters in the book are of the types currently used by the examination boards. They are designed to help you develop the skills needed to assess evidence and help you comment on their value and reliability. The questions have been chosen to test your ability to:

- demonstrate understanding by showing your ability to recall/select the most relevant historical knowledge and apt terminology needed to answer questions based on sources
- evaluate and interpret primary and secondary source material of various types
- extract the relevant information needed to answer the question
- distinguish between fact, opinion and fiction
- detect bias, be aware of gaps and inconsistencies in the source material, place it in context
- compare and reach conclusions based on the evidence provided by the sources
- draw conclusions about the value of the sources based on the academic expertise of their authors

2 ⌐ ANSWERING SOURCE BASED QUESTIONS

The documents you may be asked to consider may be extracts from books and documents as well as visual material such as pictures, illustrations, maps, cartoons and statistics. The books may be academic texts, memoirs, or diaries. Pictures may take the form of photographs or artists' impressions. Statistics may appear in numerical form or in graphics such as column graphs, bar graphs and pie charts. If the questions are structured, presented as a series of questions, the chances are that the marks for the questions will be progressive with the highest mark reserved for the last, usually most demanding question. You will need to consider the mark allocation and provide lengthier and more detailed answers as the questions become more difficult. Take care to note if your answer has to be derived from the source only or if you are invited to use your own background knowledge.

UNDERSTANDING THE SOURCE

Before you begin to answer the questions read the source(s) carefully. If there are words you do not understand, you may be able to work out their meaning from the contexts of the text. You may be asked to explain a particular word of phrase. If this is the case, a simple dictionary definition may or may not be sufficient. It is usually necessary to explain the meaning within the context of the source. Keep your answer as brief as possible and if the question can be answered with one or two words, there is no need to write a whole sentence. Unless you are specifically asked to do so, do not include your own additional background knowledge. This type of questions can be time-consuming since there is a temptation to waste a great deal of time providing unnecessary detail.

CONSIDERING THE ATTRIBUTION OR AUTHORSHIP OF A SOURCE

In considering the authorship of a source, or provenance as it is sometimes called, you should bear in mind:

● who actually wrote the source. Did he actually witness the events himself or did he produce the work as a result of consulting other peoples' works – research?
● was the author a knowledgeable person. Was he possibly an academic with a reputation for his existing work in that particular field. Is the information provided reliable and well-founded or the author merely expressing a personal opinion possibly based on guesswork?
● did the author have a particular reason or motive for writing in that way? In other words, was he biased or even possibly lying. Remember, authors write for money (royalties) and the more sensational or controversial they are the more likely it is that their books will sell well!

COMPARING SOURCES

Some questions will require you to compare sources and comment on their similarities and differences. The sources may be taken from the works of authors who share the same view but more likely from the works of authors who have differing views or place differing emphasis on aspects of an historical topic. Here it is essential that you understand what the authors are getting at so that you can identify the differences in their viewpoints and arguments. Often such differences will be immediately obvious but sometimes it is necessary to 'read between the lines' in order to discover a meaning that is not immediately obvious. More difficult is the ability to detect a nuance – a very slight degree or shade of difference. Here again, consider the attributions to the sources since these may make the reasons for the differing views and emphasis immediately obvious.

TESTING THE RELIABILITY OF A SOURCE

Sources will usually reflect the opinions of their authors – their bias and prejudices. Some sources will be propaganda clearly designed to make a specific impression on the reader and influence his thinking. Remember that propaganda often includes blatant and intended falsehoods. Photograph-type sources should be considered similarly. It used to be claimed that 'the camera does not lie' but today we are aware that photographs can be faked and that cameramen can give a false impression simply by altering the angle of their camera. Of course, cartoons are almost inevitably biased since they are intended to represent the view of the newspapers in which they appear.

EVALUATING A SOURCE

When it comes to finally evaluating a source, ask yourself the following questions.

- Is the source of significant or only limited value?
- Is the source the produce of genuine academic research or is it mere trivia?
- Does the source show deficiencies – are there gaps in the detail provided, are there obvious errors or inconsistencies?
- To what extent does the source show bias or merely represent the unsubstantiated views and opinions of the author? Is the source blatant propaganda?
- Just how valuable is the source to an historian studying that particular topic?

3 ⌐ ANSWERING ESSAY QUESTIONS

TYPES OF QUESTIONS

Most history essay questions fall into one of three categories. These are:

- questions that require you to investigate the causes, events and consequences that will tend to start with phrases such as 'Account for. . .' and 'For what reasons. . .'
- questions that require you to consider the relative importance of factors. These will be introduced by such phrases as 'How important. . .,' and 'To what extent. . .'
- questions that require you to discuss issues or develop an argument. These are likely to begin with such phrases as 'Do you agree that. . .', 'With what justification can it be claimed that. . .' and 'Comment on the view that. . .'. They may also end with 'How valid is this assessment of. . .' or simply 'Discuss.'

Examples of all the questions detailed above are provided at the end of the chapters.

REQUIREMENTS OF A GOOD ESSAY ANSWER

It is essential that before you start answering a question you make absolutely sure that you have read the question correctly and decide upon your approach. Failure to do this is one of the main reasons why students fail to achieve their expected grades. You may be advised to prepare an outline or skeleton answer. This is sound advice but remember that it can be very time consuming. A good answer should aim to achieve:

● balance – you should make sure that you are aware of all aspects of the question and do not emphasise some to the detriment of others.
● breadth – you should show a sound depth of knowledge based on your recall of your lesson notes and your own reading.
● depth – you should provide support for your argument and make sure that it is based on accurate and relevant factual evidence.

It is usual to divide an essay into three parts – introduction, development and conclusion.

1 **Introduction.** This is really where you set the scene. Your introduction should outline your intended approach and briefly state your argument. Try to relate your introduction to the wording of the question. A word of warning, some feel that writing the introduction is a good opportunity to impress the examiner with a fine turn of phrase which takes the form of a dramatic or flamboyant statement. This can be overdone and may prove counter-productive!

2 **Development.** This is the main section or body of your answer. In it you refer to the points mentioned in your introduction, develop your argument and provide explanations with supporting evidence. Make sure that the factual detail you include is accurate and avoid irrelevance or flannel. Sometimes good answers can be surprisingly short whilst, on the other hand, lengthy answers can be repetitive and lacking in focus. Take the trouble to write paragraphs that are well constructed and correctly spelt and punctuated. In spite of the shortage of time, try to avoid allowing your handwriting developing into an illegible scribble.

3 **Conclusion.** Once again refer to your plan or introduction and make sure that all the points you intended to raise have been adequately dealt with. This is an opportunity to bring together the factual content, issues and argument used and reach a conclusion. This should be brief and should not merely be a summary of what you have already stated in the development of your answer. You should make the examiner aware that your argument is complete and that you have reached a conclusion.

An essay likely to gain high marks should:

● use accurate and relevant historical knowledge
● be well-focused throughout
● follow an evaluative/analytical approach
● include evidence of a developed and well-supported argument
● contain a reasonable number of accurate dates
● be clearly written using sentences and paragraphs
● contain few spelling mistakes and errors in punctuation and grammar.

Examiners are not impressed by:

- irrelevance, verbiage, flannel and chatty-type answers
- answers that merely repeat notes
- 'I'll tell you all I know'-type answers. Such answers are badly-focused, largely narrative in content and cover all aspects of the topic being considered whether they are relevant or not
- answers in which the essential issues raised by the question are dealt with in the final paragraph
- answers that contain significant omissions
- inaccurate or generalised dates such as 'In the 1930s. . .'
- poor standards of literacy and slovenly and sometimes near illegible hand-writing
- the incorrect spelling of frequently used historical terms – *Anschluss, Gleichschaltung, Lebensraum, Luftwaffe, Volksgemeinschaft* – or historical names – Goebbels, Heydrich, Rathenau, Schuschnigg.
- the use of slang or witticisms.

4 ⤶ SYNOPTIC QUESTIONS

The word synoptic comes from the Greek synopsis and means to take an overall or general view. Synoptic-type questions will require you to draw together your knowledge of an extended period of time, usually a hundred years, and be able to show your understanding of the political, economic, cultural, social and religious characteristics of the period. Of necessity, such questions tend to be very broad-based and may follow an on-going theme. You will be required to use a range of historical skills and concepts in order to present an argument. To do this, you will need to:

- **recall** – identify from the broad factual content of your study that which is relevant to the questions
- **communicate** – show clearly your mastery of that knowledge and that you can explain it in a clear manner
- **understand** – indicate that you have a clear understanding of the important developments of the period
- **interpret** – provide evidence of your ability to evaluate different types of sources
- **explain** – evaluate different interpretations of historical events
- **identify** – show evidence of your ability to recognise cause, change and continuity
- **access** – indicate the importance of events, individuals, ideas and attitudes in their historical setting
- **make judgements** – provide historical explanations and evaluate evidence (see above under 'USING SOURCES')

The questions may be structured, take the form of an open-ended essay or be based on a range of sources. The sources may be primary or secondary and cover many areas of historical debate. Topics covered in this book may be used for synoptic questions and are mentioned at the end of Chapter 15 (page 447).

In your examination, it is absolutely essential that you allow yourself sufficient time to answer the required number of questions. Rushed final answers and answers written in outline do not earn high marks!

5 ↶ COURSEWORK ASSIGNMENTS

Coursework requirements and the nature of assignments vary from one examination board to another. With some, it is possible for students to undertake an assignment decided and marked by the centre but moderated by the examination board. Alternatively, it is possible to work on an assignment based on a topic nominated by the examination board. The assignment is then marked and moderated by the examination board concerned. The usual objectives to be examined are:

● the ability to recall, select and deploy historical knowledge and communicate that knowledge in a clear and efficient way
● the ability to present historical explanations that show an understanding of appropriate concepts and arrive at substantiated judgements
● the ability to evaluate and use a range of sources
● the ability to explain and interpret historical events
● an awareness of historiography – a knowledge of differing interpretations of historical events and development by leading historians.

6 ↶ MAKING NOTES

Advice sections that appear at the end of each chapter are intended to help you develop your skills of research and analysis based upon the content and themes explored in the chapters. The guidelines below will help you break down the information by asking questions about the various elements –

● locate the relevant section of the chapter and refer to the written or visual evidence provided
● skim-read the section in order to gain an overall picture of the main areas of argument or interpretation. This focuses your attention on the relevant material and ensures an effective understanding
● using the questions, organise your notes on the main themes covered in the chapters, leaving out the detail that adds nothing to your understanding of the main points identified.

You are also encouraged to make use of the bibliographies (see at the end of most chapters) in order to carry out further research and so develop your own ideas and form judgements.

The Birth of the Weimar Republic

INTRODUCTION

At the start of the twentieth century, Germany was a major military power and well on the way to outstripping its rivals to become the greatest industrial nation in Europe. This progress was interrupted in August 1914 with the outbreak of a great European war.

From the German viewpoint, entry into the war was justified. War promised to remove the threat of Russian aggression; end once and for all the possibility of French retaliation for humiliation during the Franco-Prussian War of 1870 and loss of the provinces of Alsace and Lorraine; challenge the naval supremacy of its greatest commercial rival, imperialist Britain, and end the danger of encirclement by those same three hostile powers. Some also saw it as an opportunity for territorial expansion and the chance to further the cause of Pan-Germanism, the union of all German peoples. Kaiser Wilhelm II told the nation that God was on their side and promised his troops that they would be home 'before the leaves fell from the trees'. His son, the Crown Prince, even spoke of 'a gay and jolly little war'. In fact, the war was to drag on for four costly years. Largely a **war of attrition**, it was fought on several fronts, with German resources being additionally drained by the need to support unreliable allies. The war was to claim millions of lives, cause incalculable material damage and bring economic hardship and political bitterness which was to threaten the very fabric of German society. Finally, it was to rob Germany of territory, valuable resources, all its overseas colonies and, for a time, even its self-respect.

war of attrition a war in which the opposed sides try to wear each other down

1 ⌐ EARLY PROGRESS

On the face of it, Germany was led into the war by the Kaiser and the Imperial Chancellor, Theobald von Bethmann Hollweg, but behind the scenes the military leaders carried most influence and dictated the course of events. Earlier, German socialists had called for a general strike in the event of war but, in 1914, such divisions disappeared as people demonstrated their patriotism and rallied to support the war effort. The Kaiser could justifiably say, 'I see no parties any more, I only see Germans'.

To start with, the war went well for Germany, particularly on the Eastern Front where armies under Field Marshals Hindenburg and Ludendorff won spectacular victories against the Russians, but, on the

Western Front, it was a different story. Here the position rapidly deteriorated into stalemate as the opposing armies became bogged down and experienced the harsh realities of trench warfare. Late in 1916, Hindenburg and Ludendorff were transferred to the Western Front in the hope that they could repeat their earlier successes against the Russians.

During the months which followed, this partnership was to determine not only military strategy but was also to have a major say in political policy. With the aristocratic Hindenburg acting as a figurehead, the more dynamic Ludendorff became effectively the country's military dictator. The Kaiser, now a political nonentity, accepted their decisions and agreed to appoint and dismiss ministers at their direction. Both men had significant roles to play in the post-war history of Germany.

THE KAISER'S WARLORDS – HINDENBURG (1847–1934) AND LUDENDORFF (1865–1937)

Paul von Hindenburg was born in Posen into a Prussian land-owning family which could trace its aristocratic and military traditions back to the thirteenth century. As a young officer, he had fought with distinction against the Austrians at Sadowa (Königgrätz) in 1866 and against the French in 1870. He won promotion by 'the ordinary process, not brilliance' and, unlike most of his class, lacked both influence and money. He retired from the army in 1911 but, at the outbreak of war in 1914, was recalled and sent to defend East Prussia against the invading Russians.

Erich von Ludendorff was a man of much more modest origins. Son of an impoverished landowner, he was commissioned into one of the less fashionable infantry regiments. Nearly 20 years Hindenburg's junior, he was an ambitious man with immense mental and physical energy. His hard work and mastery of detail attracted attention and he was appointed to the general staff where he worked with the younger von Moltke and von Schlieffen. In 1914, he was sent to the Eastern Front as Hindenburg's Chief-of-Staff.

---

2 ⌐ A FAILED PEACE INITIATIVE AND THE FIRST SIGNS OF UNREST

At the end of 1916 when there seemed a chance that a negotiated peace might be possible, Woodrow Wilson, the American President, called upon the warring nations to state their terms. The Allies demanded the evacuation of all territory occupied by the Germans, including Belgium,

PICTURE 1

The Kaiser (centre) with Field Marshals Hindenburg and Ludendorff walking through a captured French village in 1917

and the return to France of Alsace-Lorraine; Ludendorff, however, insisted that Germany should be allowed to retain Belgium and all the lands gained at the expense of Russia. So the opportunity to bring about a reasonable peace was lost and the war was set to become a fight to the finish. At the same time, Ludendorff chose to ignore the views of Bethmann Hollweg and with only the half-hearted support of the Kaiser declared Germany's intention of resuming unrestricted submarine warfare – the sinking of neutral shipping bound for allied ports. His decision was largely responsible for the American entry into the war in April 1917 on the side of the Allies. Within three months, Bethmann Hollweg, who had played a major role in bringing about the peace initiative, was forced to resign and was replaced by a Prussian civil servant, Georg Michaelis. Unknown, apart from the fact that his signature appeared on German ration cards, Michaelis was described by Ludendorff as 'the right man in the right place'. The new Chancellor, who was no more than a puppet and invariably backed the military, was disliked and failed to win the support of the *Reichstag*. After only 100 days in office, he resigned. His successor was the Bavarian aristocrat, Count Georg von Hertling. Although an experienced politician, he was old, half blind and lacked the vigour to challenge the military. With the morale of the people boosted by constant promises of final victory, the vast majority of Germans continued to support Ludendorff's military dictatorship.

On the home-front, a successful Allied blockade meant that the German people had suffered economic shortages since the first months of the war. Bread had been rationed since January 1915 and food became particularly scarce during the severe winter of 1916–17, the so-called 'turnip winter' since people had little else to eat. In 1917, the grain harvest was only half that of 1913 whilst across the country generally, clothing, fuel and other necessities were in increasingly short supply. Even so, the German High Command had some cause to believe that the war could still be won. In April 1917, they schemed to neu-

1914	August	Start of the First World War; German successes on the Eastern Front
1916	Feb–Dec	Heavy casualties during Battles of Verdun and Somme; Hindenburg and Ludendorff transferred to the Western Front
1916–17	April	Acute shortages of the 'turnip winter'
1917	April	American entry into the war
	November	Start of Bolshevik revolution in Russia
1918	March	Treaty of Brest-Litovsk
	September	Ludendorff accepts war is lost, calls for an armistice
	October	Prince Max of Baden appointed German Chancellor; resignation of Hindenberg; naval mutinies at Wilhelmshaven and Kiel
	November	Mutinies at other major German North Sea ports; 'German Revolution' begins; Eisner proclaims Bavarian Socialist Republic; abdication of Kaiser Wilhelm II; Ebert becomes Chancellor; Gröner-Ebert agreement; Armistice signed at Compiègne
1919	January	Spartacist uprising in Berlin; murder of Liebknecht and Luxemburg; election of Constituent Assembly
	February	National Assembly gathers at Weimar; Ebert becomes provisional President; Scheidemann becomes Chancellor; assassination of Eisner
	April	Communist republic declared in Bavaria
	May	Bavaria's Communist regime crushed
	June	Bauer replaces Scheidemann as Chancellor; Treaty of Versailles signed

tralise Russia by allowing the revolutionary, Lenin, to leave his place of exile in Switzerland, travel across Germany and be smuggled into Russia. The revolution which Lenin masterminded eventually led to the Russian withdrawal from the war in December 1917 and, afterwards, to the Treaty of Brest-Litovsk. The terms imposed on Russia's Bolshevik government were harsh and ensured that much of the country's industrial capacity as well as the important grain producing region, the Ukraine, passed under German control. The Bolsheviks also had to pay a considerable sum in reparations. Meanwhile, on the Western Front, the advantages to the Allies of American entry into the war were slow to materialise.

As shortages worsened and the numbers of dead and wounded spiralled into millions, more and more Germans began to question the wisdom of continuing with an indefinite war. In the German parliament, the *Reichstag*, there was a marked change in the attitude of the country's left-wing political parties. The traditionally moderate and largely popular SPD, the German Social Democratic Party (*Sozialdemokratische Partei Deutschlands*) had supported the war from the outset but now some within the Party began to see things differently. Before the end of 1915, a minority had voted against the massive expenditure on the war. Internal differences led to a split with some members breaking away to form a new, more radical left-wing party,

Q

Why did some German political parties change their attitude to the war?

the USPD, the Independent German Social Democratic Party (*Unabhängige Sozialdemokratische Partei Deutschlands*). Far more extreme was the Spartacist League (*Spartakusbund*) which had its origins as a pressure group within the USPD. Encouraged by the success of the Bolsheviks in Russia, it aimed to bring an end to Germany's old imperial and capitalist order and replace it with a communist system. More immediately, it wanted to end the suffering of the people and bring an end to the war. The League urged the war-weary German people to protest more vigorously and organised anti-war demonstrations and strikes. The first signs of unrest occurred in April 1917, when a wave of unrest swept the country as workers protested against their conditions. Two months later there was a mutiny in the German fleet based at Kiel and this was vigorously suppressed. In the *Reichstag*, a resolution was passed in favour of seeking a negotiated peace but this was ignored by the High Command. In January 1918, 400,000 Berliners went on strike. This unrest spread rapidly to other towns and cities until the number involved in industrial action exceeded a million. In spite of this, the majority of influential Germans refused to believe that the war was lost or to think that the old imperial system was under threat.

3 ⌁ THE EVENTS OF 1918 AND THE END OF THE WAR

During the spring of 1918, Ludendorff launched a new offensive on the Western Front. In a bold gamble, he risked the bulk of his reserves in one final attempt to land a decisive blow before the deployment of American forces finally swung the balance of the war in favour of the Allies. Although the German armies gained some initial success, they did not have the military strength to exploit their breakthrough and the offensive ground to a standstill. By July, a million American soldiers had arrived in France and, on 8 August, the Allies launched a counter-offensive which forced the Germans into headlong retreat. With his army demoralised and units surrendering without a fight, Ludendorff's gamble had failed. The disillusioned Field-Marshal offered to resign and later wrote: 'The 8th August was the black day of the German army in the history of this war ... Everything I had feared and of which I had given warning, had here, in one place become a reality. Our war machine was no longer efficient.'

> **Q**
>
> *To what extent might Ludendorff's decision to risk all in a final offensive be considered a blunder?*

On 6 October, the last major German defensive positions, the Hindenburg Line, were breached. At army headquarters in Spa, the German High Command appeared to have lost its nerve. In angry outbursts, Ludendorff blamed his failures on a lack of reserves, a shortage of munitions and the defeatist attitude of the *Reichstag*.

Not only were the German armies close to defeat but, on the home front, the country was near to total economic collapse. In addition, in common with the rest of Europe, Germany was in the grip of an influenza epidemic. Spanish influenza, so-called because the King of

Spain was one of its early victims, was causing more deaths than the battlefield! Desperately short of medicines and with malnutrition rampant, on one day alone 1,700 Berliners died of the virus, and even the Chancellor was infected. By the time it had run its course, the epidemic had claimed the lives of over a million Germans.

On 29 September, Ludendorff advised the government that the war was lost and called for an armistice. Four days later, Prince Max of Baden, a liberal known for his democratic views and a man who had earned international respect for his work with the Red Cross, was asked to form a government. His cabinet was made up of representatives of the majority parties in the *Reichstag*, including leading SPD members Philipp Scheidemann and Gustav Bauer. It was the first parliamentary cabinet in German history. The Prince, an experienced negotiator, thought it best not to appear too eager and wanted to wait a month before seeking terms for an armistice. Both Hindenburg and Ludendorff were against this. When he did make his first approaches, they were to the American President, Woodrow Wilson. He realised that terms based on the President's own ideas, his 'Fourteen Points', would be more lenient than any he could expect from the Anglo-French Allies. Wilson's response was first to demand the withdrawal of German troops from all occupied territory, an immediate end to submarine warfare and the dismissal of Germany's 'undemocratic rulers' – the Kaiser and his **military clique**. Ludendorff was against the acceptance of such terms and went as far as to urge the military to continue the war and make one last desperate stand to save the honour of the army. On 27 October, the Field Marshal avoided the humiliation of dismissal by tendering his resignation and, disguised in blue spectacles and false whiskers, quietly made his way to Sweden. Prince Max begged the Kaiser to abdicate, but he refused.

military clique the group of senior officers close to the Kaiser

KEY ISSUE

The need of Germany to bring the war to an end.

4 ↩ THE START OF THE 'GERMAN REVOLUTION'

The period of turmoil, which some historians have referred to as the 'German Revolution', began towards the end of October 1918. News that Germany was suing for an armistice led to a further increase in revolutionary activity, much of it encouraged by Bolshevik propaganda. On 29 October, sailors mutinied at Wilhelmshaven and then, far more seriously, at Kiel when they were ordered to put to sea and engage in one last futile act of defiance against the Royal Navy. Possibly a ploy by fanatical German naval officers to wreck the armistice negotiations, the mutiny resulted in shots being fired and the deaths of eight sailors. This led to a more general mutiny, with the sailors setting up councils on all their ships. Three days later, soviet-style councils of workers and sailors took control of the ports of Cuxhaven, Bremen, Hamburg, Lubeck and Rostock. On 8 November, Kurt Eisner, a former journalist and a leading member of the USPD (see page 14), led a demonstration in Munich which ended with his supporters taking over the main public

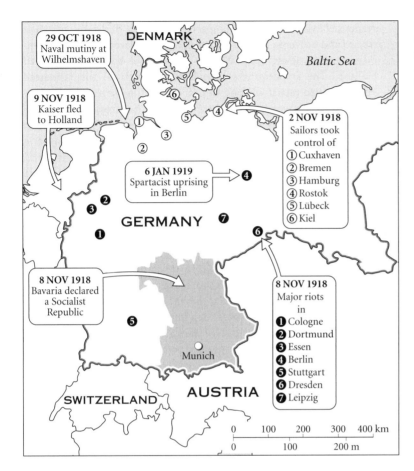

MAP 1

Germany in revolution – the mutinies and riots of October 1918 – January 1919

29 OCT 1918
Naval mutiny at Wilhelmshaven

9 NOV 1918
Kaiser fled to Holland

2 NOV 1918
Sailors took control of
① Cuxhaven
② Bremen
③ Hamburg
④ Rostok
⑤ Lübeck
⑥ Kiel

6 JAN 1919
Spartacist uprising in Berlin

8 NOV 1918
Bavaria declared a Socialist Republic

8 NOV 1918
Major riots in
❶ Cologne
❷ Dortmund
❸ Essen
❹ Berlin
❺ Stuttgart
❻ Dresden
❼ Leipzig

DENMARK

Baltic Sea

GERMANY

Munich

SWITZERLAND   AUSTRIA

0   100   200   300   400 km
0   100   200 m

buildings. Later Eisner, whose real name was Salomon Kosnowsky and who was of Jewish descent, proclaimed a Bavarian Democratic and Socialist Republic with himself as Prime Minister. There were also widespread riots in the Ruhr as well as disturbances in Berlin, Cologne, Dresden, Leipzig, Stuttgart and elsewhere across Germany. With the country already in chaos, the situation worsened when on 7 November the SPD advised Prince Max that they might withdraw from his coalition if the Kaiser did not abdicate within 48 hours. Wilhelm II, confident that he still commanded the support of the army, once again refused to give up his throne. In *Hindenburg, the Wooden Titan*, J.W. Wheeler-Bennett described the final emotive meeting between a deputation, which included Hindenburg, and the Kaiser:

> **KEY ISSUE**
>
> *Crisis point – German revolutionaries take advantage of the chaos and attempt to seize power.*

Standing before his Emperor, Hindenburg made his report. He was calm now and had overcome the emotion of the morning. Lucidly he set forth the reasons why he was no longer able to guarantee the Emperor's safety at Spa. In conclusion he said, 'I cannot accept the

> responsibility of seeing the Emperor hauled to Berlin by insurgent troops and delivered over as a prisoner to the Revolutionary Government. I must advise Your Majesty to abdicate and to proceed to Holland.' The Emperor was convulsed with rage ... and requested Hindenburg to repeat what he had reported. The Marshal did so, concluding with the words: 'Would to God, Sire, it were otherwise.' For the remaining sixteen years of his life, Hindenburg was to be haunted by memories of these November days and the part he had played in them.

On 9 November, Prince Max announced the Kaiser's abdication, even though the Kaiser had not formally agreed to it. That night, Wilhelm left Germany and crossed into Holland where he was to spend the remainder of his life in exile. When the Germans invaded Holland in 1940, the British government offered the ex-Kaiser safe refuge in Britain. Commenting 'Old trees cannot be transplanted', he declined the invitation with thanks. He died the following year.

In spite of Wilhelm's abdication, the SPD still went ahead and withdrew from the government. Prince Max had no choice but to hand over the chancellorship to the leader of the Social Democrats, Friedrich Ebert. His government, which contained only socialists drawn from the SPD and USPD, was backed by the workers' and soldiers' councils. It was agreed to hold elections for a constituent National Assembly on the 19 January. Earlier, on 7 November, German delegates had passed through the Allied lines to begin the negotiation of an armistice. In the forest of Compiègne, they assembled in a railway carriage to agree terms which finally came into effect at 11 am on the morning of 11 November 1918. The wild scenes of rejoicing in the streets of London, Paris and New York were not repeated in Berlin, where the city was the scene of disturbances and was under threat of a major uprising.

5 ⌐ THE ORIGIN OF *DOLCHSTOSSTHEORIE* (THE 'STAB-IN-THE-BACK' THEORY)

Even as the war ended, there were Germans already prepared to find excuses for their defeat. The military spoke of betrayal and claimed that the army had been 'stabbed in the back' by traitors at home. The newspaper *Neue Zürcher Zeitung* was the first to use the term when it reported, 'As far as the German army is concerned, the general view is summarised in these words: It was stabbed in the back by the civilian population'. Those who stood accused of disloyalty were pacifists, socialists and communists who had agitated for an end to the war and had been responsible for organising strikes and mutinies, and those who had finally negotiated an armistice. To these so-called *Novemberverbrecher* – November criminals – Hitler was to add the Jews.

A German army officer (quoted in F.L. Carsten, *The Reichswehr and Politics 1918–1933*) said:

> At the most difficult moment of the war, the long prepared revolution attacked our rear...I do not know of any revolution in history that has been undertaken in such a cowardly manner... It was the poison of the people in the rear, most of whom have never heard a shot. . .

Field Marshal Hindenburg claimed (quoted in J.W. Wheeler-Bennett, *Hindenburg, the Wooden Titan*):

> In spite of the superiority of the enemy in men and materials, we could have brought the struggle to a favourable conclusion if determined and unanimous co-operation had existed between the army and those at home. But while the enemy showed an even greater will for victory, divergent party interests began to show themselves to us.

In *Mein Kampf*, Adolf Hitler was more direct when he later wrote:

> Emperor Wilhelm II was the first to offer the hand of friendship to the Marxist leaders, not suspecting that they were scoundrels without any sense of honour. While they held the imperial hand in theirs, the other hand was already feeling for the dagger.

Support for the 'stab-in-the-back' theory was to become a main theme of the military and those on the political right. Since it **absolved** the German army of the disgrace of defeat and transferred the blame to other more acceptable scapegoats, it was to gain wide acceptance nationally.

absolved set free from any responsibility for

6 ↷ GERMANY UNDER THREAT

A *The Ebert-Gröner Agreement*

At the same time as German delegates were negotiating an armistice at Compiègne, Ebert was in the chancellery building in Berlin considering how best to deal with the upheavals which were threatening his government.

On the centre-right of the party and a patriot, Ebert had prevailed upon the SPD to support the German war effort and had himself lost two sons in the war. He would have been prepared to support the continuation of the Hohenzollern line had Wilhelm been willing to abdicate in order to allow his grandson to rule as a **constitutional monarch**. Ebert distrusted the extreme left and wanted to oversee Germany's peaceful transition to democratic government.

On 9 November, he received a telephone call from Wilhelm Gröner, a general who had served Germany with distinction during the war and had replaced his rival, Ludendorff. During their conversation, the two men came to an agreement aimed to save Germany from the clutches of

constitutional monarch a king or emperor whose powers are limited to those granted by the constitution

Bolshevism. On the one hand Ebert promised to maintain the status of the army against the revolutionary soldiers' councils and to guarantee it adequate supplies; on the other, Gröner undertook to use the army to support the government and maintain law and order by suppressing revolutionary activity. The agreement between the leader of the SPD and a general who, until recently, had been associated with the now dis-credited military regime, was to lay Ebert open to the charge that he had betrayed the socialist revolution.

B *Ebert's predicament*

At the beginning of 1919, Ebert found himself caught in the crossfire between extremists of both left and right. Most troublesome were the Spartacists who, in December 1918, had ceased to be a faction within the USPD and had formed the KPD, the German Communist Party (*Kommunistische Partei Deutschlands*). Following the example of Lenin's Bolsheviks, they worked to infiltrate and gain control of the workers' councils as a prelude to a revolution which would eliminate capitalism in Germany. Although they claimed widespread support, the Spartacists remained a relatively small revolutionary group but with formidable and charismatic leaders. Sympathy for their cause was localised, spasmodic and lacked the backing needed to sustain a national uprising. They combined with other left-wing groups to organ-ise demonstrations and appeared quite formidable but, when it came to direct action, the number of Spartacists prepared to take up arms and contest the streets was limited to hundreds. Not all were politically motivated, some joined in simply for the enjoyment of violence. Even so, Spartacist activities were a matter of concern. To German conserva-tives – the military, the landowners, industrialists, those engaged in business, commerce and finance and the professional upper and middle classes – left-wing agitation in the form of demonstrations, riots and strikes was invariably seen as Bolshevik-inspired. It had to be outlawed and crushed.

It was a counter-balance to the militant left that the *Freikorps* first appeared. Recruited from among the ranks of demoralised ex-servicemen, embittered nationalists and adventurers of all kinds, the movement also appealed to the unemployed who were attracted by food, clothing and pay provided at government expense. *Freikorps* units, many of them with distinctive names and uniforms, sprang up all over Germany. They were led by former army officers determined to keep alive the old traditions and wartime spirit and preach the legend of the 'stab in the back'. They were opposed to both socialism and com-munism and any advance towards democratic government. Their immediate priority was to stamp out left-wing subversion and win control of the streets.

KEY ISSUE

The emergence of the Freikorps.

C *The Spartacist uprising of January 1919*

The Spartacists, who took their name from Spartacus the leader of the slave revolt against Rome in 73 BC, were led by a group of middle-class intellectuals, including Karl Liebknecht, Rosa Luxemburg, Clara Zetkin and Franz Mehring.

The son of the founder of the SPD and close friend of Karl Marx, Karl Liebknecht (1871–1919) became a barrister and politician but his anti-militarist views led to his expulsion from the *Reichstag* in 1916. Sentenced to a term of imprisonment for treason, he was released in 1918 following an amnesty granted by Prince Max. Polish-born Rosa Luxemburg (1871–1919), who held a doctorate in law and economics, married Gustav Lubeck in order to gain German citizenship. She had already been imprisoned in Russia for her involvement in the revolution of 1905. Championing the cause of revolution rather than a gradual approach, she earned the nickname *Blutige Rose* – Bloody Rosa.

During the war, Spartacist agitation achieved little, but towards the end of 1918 Liebknecht used his considerable skills as an orator to urge the masses to reject Ebert's moderation and support what he referred to as the 'real revolution'. In December, 16 Spartacists were killed in Berlin when soldiers opened fire on demonstrators. Early in 1919 the movement decided to boycott the elections for the new constituent assembly. On 6 January, they staged an uprising in Berlin, declaring that a new revolutionary government had been set up to replace that of Ebert. At

PICTURE 2

A satirical cartoon by the German artist George Grosz shows the savagery of the Freikorps

the request of Gustav Noske, a defence expert and the acknowledged hard man of the SPD, units of *Freikorps* rather than the military were sent to deal with the Spartacists. Led by General Walter von Lüttwitz, it took the *Freikorps* three days of savage street fighting to crush the uprising. Afterwards, Spartacist sympathisers were rounded up and, together with their leaders, brought to summary justice. Liebknecht was badly beaten before being shot 'while attempting to escape'; Luxemburg, who declined an opportunity to flee the city, was shot and her body thrown into a canal. The historian, Harold Kutz, has written, 'the workers who wanted a real revolution were swept under the carpet with a broom unhesitatingly provided by the army command'. The irony was that both Liebknecht and Luxemburg had been against the coup. Bloody Rosa, who had quarrelled with Lenin, had turned against the idea of a communist-inspired revolution and had urged the movement to accept more gradual reform backed by the support of the masses. The Spartacist threat may have been over but *Freikorps* terror had only just begun.

D *How close had Germany been to revolution?*

Bearing in mind the condition of Germany towards the end of 1918 when set against the general European background, it is easy to understand why some thought the country 'ripe for revolution'. The nation's morale had been shattered by defeat in war, shortages remained acute, demobilisation was slow and disorganised, and the country was awash with arms. With the Hohenzollerns out of the way, there was a feeling that it was time to make a break with Germany's imperial past and create a more just society. On the face of it, events in Germany seemed about to follow a close parallel with those in Russia a year earlier. The nation was in a state of turmoil, the monarchy had been overthrown and a provisional government set up, a network of workers' and soldiers' councils was widespread across the country, and left-wing extremists were actively planning a coup in Berlin similar to that engineered by the Bolsheviks in St. Petersburg in October 1917.

However, there were also major differences in the comparative situations. Germany was an advanced industrial nation with a powerful capitalist class backed by a substantial and influential middle class. The condition of the German working classes, who since the 1880s had benefited from a range of welfare measures, was in no way similar to that of their Russian counterparts who for generations had suffered tsarist indignity and oppression. Unlike the Russian army, which, humiliated time and again, had been driven to mutiny, the German army could still reflect on the glorious achievements of Prussian militarism in bringing about the nation's unification. Hindenburg, in common with other Germans of his age, had fought at the Battle of Sadowa in 1866 and taken part in the victorious campaign against France in 1870 – both still within living memory. Even with the Kaiser gone, there were still powerful conservative forces in position in the civil service, the judiciary and the professions and the old class structure remained intact.

Hindenburg and Ludendorff may have passed from the scene temporarily but High Command influence was still in place in the form of General Gröner and others.

The political left, whose whole-hearted commitment to revolution was essential, was divided in both policy aims and strategy. The majority SPD was far from revolutionary and more dedicated to the introduction of social reform and the promotion of democratic government. Whilst Hugo Hasse's Independent Socialists of the USPD were more radical, they certainly did not envisage a revolutionary solution to the nation's problems. The Spartacists and other minority extremist groups did preach revolution but the threat they presented to the stability of Ebert's government proved to be exaggerated. In 1918, there was widespread discontent which resulted in demonstrations and strikes but these were aimed more at the Kaiser and his discredited military clique than the capitalists and upper classes. With the socialists disunited and lacking in revolutionary intent, anarchy on a grand scale never really occurred. Ebert's pact with Gröner was also born of the fear that left-wing militancy might threaten German stability, possibly lead to civil war and jeopardise the peace talks about to start in Paris. The fact that the revolutionaries stood no chance against the military and *Freikorps* was not clear to Ebert at the time and consequently he was judged to have over-reacted. It was certainly true that the willingness shown by the SPD leadership to collaborate with the military was not a good omen for the future. In a situation of relative calm, the nation elected its first constituent assembly.

7 ⟿ THE ELECTION OF THE FIRST CONSTITUENT ASSEMBLY

A *German political parties in 1919*

The election of the constituent assembly, which took place on 19 January 1919, was based on a system of proportional representation, with women enjoying the rights of franchise for the first time. With the Communists boycotting the election, seven major and a number of minor parties were left to contest the 421 seats in the *Reichstag*. Long-established parties such as the SPD and the Catholic Centre Party, *Zentrum*, were joined by a number of newcomers, mainly renamed versions of former conservative and liberal parties which had existed in imperial days.

Other minor political parties included the BVP, the Bavarian People's Party (*Bayerische Volkspartei*), the Bavarian wing of the Centre Party, and a little known fringe party of the extreme right, the DAP, the German Workers' Party (*Deutsche Arbeiterpartei*) founded by Anton Drexler in Munich on 9 January 1919. The Party did not contest the election. Three months later, it was renamed the NSDAP, the National Socialist German Workers' Party (*Nationalsozialistische Deutsche Arbeiterpartei*).

DIAGRAM 1

The political outlook of the parties

Political parties of the left tend to favour more radical and socialist policies. Communists, those who support the political and economic theories of Karl Marx, represent the extreme left in politics. Centre parties support liberal ideals and prefer moderate political and social reform. Parties to the right are conservative in outlook and opposed to socialism. Those on the extreme right tend to hold strong nationalist and racist views and are often referred to as fascists. In Germany, the National Socialists represented the extreme right in politics. After the war, the Communists (KPD) won their first seats in the *Reichstag* in 1920. The first Nazis (NSDAP) appeared four years later in 1924.

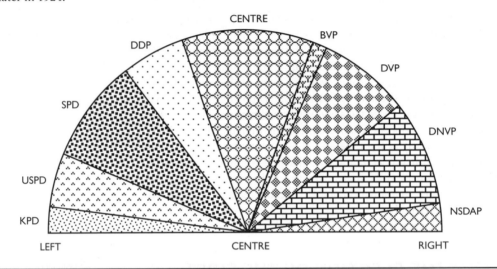

	Political parties	Main features
KPD	German Communist Party (*Kommunistische Partei Deutschlands*)	Representing the extreme left in German politics, the Party was formed in 1918 by members of the Spartacist League. Although support declined after the attempted coup of 1919, it recovered and during the late 1920s again became a major political force in Germany
USPD	German Independent Social Democratic Party (*Unabhängige Sozialdemokratische Partei Deutschlands*)	In 1917, personal and policy differences led to the rise of a splinter group of more radical socialists within the SPD which broke away from the main party. This independent group disapproved of Ebert's moderate line and was strongly anti-war. It was short-lived and by 1924 had virtually disappeared
SPD	German Social Democratic Party (*Sozialdemokratische Partei Deutschlands*)	Founded in 1875 by August Bebel and Wilhelm Liebknecht, the Party survived the hostility of Bismarck to become, by 1914, the largest in the *Reichstag*. A moderate socialist party, it drew its support from the working and lower middle classes. It maintained a high level of support throughout the 1920s and early 1930s
DDP	German Democratic Party (*Deutsche Demokratische Partei*)	Really the left-wing of the former National Liberals, the Party was formed in 1918 by a group of businessmen and intellectuals. Of the non-socialist parties, it was the one most committed to constitutional reform

	Political parties	Main features
Z	Catholic Centre Party (*Zentrum*)	A Party originally established in 1870 to defend Roman Catholic interests during the Church's struggle with Bismarck, the *Kulturkampf*. Politically to the right of the DDP, it continued to attract the support of working and middle class Catholics
DVP	German People's Party (*Deutsche Volkspartei*)	The right-wing of the former National Liberals, the Party was largely supported by the better-off professional upper and middle classes. It was nationalist and anti-republican. After 1928, it lost out when many of its members switched to the DNVP
DNVP	German National People's Party (*Deutschnationale Volkspartei*)	In 1919 the most right-wing of the parties to contest the election. Founded a year earlier, it was nationalist in outlook and hostile to the Republic. It had monarchist sympathies and longed for a return to former imperialist ways. The Party was supported by landowners and industrialists and had strong upper middle class backing

B *The election of January 1919*

With 38 per cent of the vote and 163 seats in the *Reichstag*, the SPD won easily but, against the expectations of many, failed to win an overall majority. Some supporters may have been upset by the Spartacist uprising and it is possible that extending the vote to women may have influenced the outcome. The USPD fared badly and won only 22 seats. The second largest party was the Centre Party with 91 seats and third, the liberal DDP with 75. Most surprising was the showing of the extreme right DNVP with 44 seats.

		Number of seats
Social Democrats	(SPD)	163
Democratic Party	(DDP)	75
Catholic Centre	(Zentrum)	71
Nationalist Party	(DNVP)	44
Independent Socialists	(USPD)	22
Bavarian Party	(BVP)	20
People's Party	(DVP)	19
Independents and others		7

TABLE 2
The Reichstag *election of January 1919*

By an overwhelming majority, the new assembly elected Friedrich Ebert to be the new Republic's first President. He immediately asked fellow socialist, Philipp Scheidemann to become Chancellor and form a government. With the USPD refusing to join the majority socialists, the SPD instead formed a coalition with Zentrum and the DDP. The first task of the government was to draw up a new constitution.

8 ◦ THE CONSTITUTION OF THE WEIMAR REPUBLIC

With Berlin and other major German cities still considered unsafe, on 11 February representatives of the assembly gathered at a new theatre in the market town of Weimar. The town, once the home of the literary figures Goethe and Schiller, was to give its name to both the new constitution and future governments based on it. To start with, discussions centred on the draft proposals of Hugo Preuß, a liberal and legal scholar. There was much argument about the extent to which the 18 individual German states, the *Länder* (plural of *Land* meaning region), should surrender their authority to a single state with all power vested in the constituent assembly. Once a compromise settlement had been agreed, details of the new Constitution were made known.

A *The Constitution*

The first clause began, 'The German *Reich* is a republic. Political authority is derived from the people.' The main points of the Constitution were that the head of state would be a President to be elected every seven years. His powers were far reaching – he would be supreme commander of the armed services and appoint all important officials, both civilian and military; he would nominate the Chancellor and alone have the power to summon and dissolve the *Reichstag*. In the event of an emergency, Article 48 of the Constitution allowed the President to suspend civil liberties, take emergency powers and rule by decree, stating:

> In the case of a State not fulfilling the duties imposed on it by the Federal Constitution of the Federal laws, the President of the Federation may enforce their fulfilment with the help of the armed forces. Where public security and order are seriously disturbed or endangered within the Federation, the President of the Federation may take the measures necessary for their restoration, intervening in case of need with the help of armed forces. For this purpose he is permitted, for the time being to cancel, either wholly or partially, the fundamental laws laid down in articles 114, 115, 117, 118, 123, 124 and 153.
>
> The President of the Federation must, without delay, inform the *Reichstag* of any measures taken in accordance with...this Article. Such measures shall be withdrawn upon the demand of the *Reichstag*.
>
> Where there is danger in delay, the State Government may take provisional measures of the kind described...for its own territory. Such measures shall be withdrawn upon the demand of the President of the Federation or the *Reichstag*.

The situations during which such powers could be taken were never clearly defined; it was just assumed they would be at a time of crisis or national emergency. On the face of it, it seemed that a system of checks and balances involving the President, Chancellor and *Reichstag* would prevent any misuse of Article 48 but, as later events proved, it was not that simple.

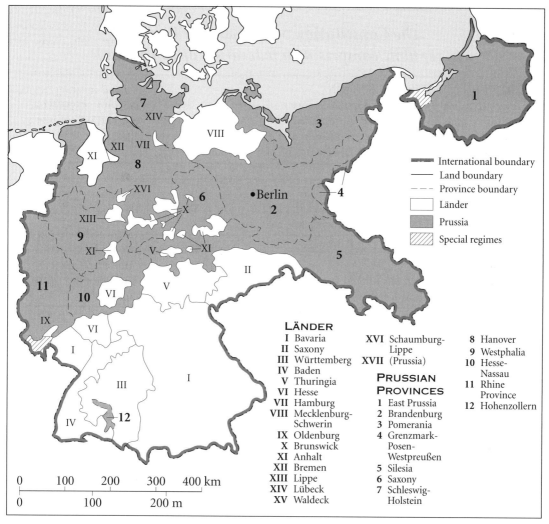

MAP 2
The Länder, *and Prussia and its provinces under Weimar*

LÄNDER
I Bavaria
II Saxony
III Württemberg
IV Baden
V Thuringia
VI Hesse
VII Hamburg
VIII Mecklenburg-
　　Schwerin
IX Oldenburg
X Brunswick
XI Anhalt
XII Bremen
XIII Lippe
XIV Lübeck
XV Waldeck
XVI Schaumburg-
　　　Lippe
XVII (Prussia)

PRUSSIAN PROVINCES
1 East Prussia
2 Brandenburg
3 Pomerania
4 Grenzmark-
　Posen-
　Westpreußen
5 Silesia
6 Saxony
7 Schleswig-
　Holstein
8 Hanover
9 Westphalia
10 Hesse-
　　Nassau
11 Rhine
　　Province
12 Hohenzollern

The **Reich**, or Republic, was to be a federation of the 18 *Länder*. The chancellor (whose role was similar to that of a British prime minister) would normally be the leader of the largest party in the *Reichstag*, although this soon proved to be not always the case. For the *Reichstag* to function, the chancellor would have to negotiate with leaders of other parties in order to create a workable coalition from which he could form a government. The two parliamentary institutions were to be the *Reichstag* and *Reichsrat*. The *Reichstag* contained the elected deputies and alone had the authority to introduce and approve legislation. The *Reichsrat*, largely an advisory body, was of far less importance and only had the power to delay. Deputies to the *Reichstag* would be elected every four years by a system of proportional representation which allocated each party one deputy for every 60,000 votes cast for it. The franchise

Reich means empire, so German Reich refers specifically to the German Empire

Third Reich, page 110

The Constitution of the German Reich
(a republic comprising a federation of 18 Länder)

PRESIDENT OF THE FEDERATION

A non-political figure. Presidential elections occurred every seven years. Main **executive** authority and responsible for nominating the Chancellor. Supreme commander of the German armed forces. Powers to summon and dissolve the *Reichstag*. Under Article 48 of the Constitution, power to rule by decree at a time of national emergency.

CHANCELLOR

Usually though not always the leader of the largest party in the *Reichstag*. Negotiated with other party leaders in order to form workable coalitions.

REICHSRAT

Consisted of delegates nominated by the parliaments of the *Länder*. An advisory body with the power only to delay legislation.

REICHSTAG

Consisted of deputies elected every four years by a system of **proportional representation**. The **legislature** or law-making body within the German Parliament.

Proportional representation is a system of voting by which seats in the *Reichstag* were allocated in proportion to the total number of votes cast for each party. According to the Constitution, each party received one seat for every 60,000 votes cast. PR is considered a very democratic system since it ensures that all but the smallest parties are represented in the Parliament and have a say in the nation's affairs. It also leads to a multi-party system of government with no single party holding an overall majority. Governments elected by proportional representation will therefore tend to be coalitions made up of several parties. This can lead to political instability.

The legislature, executive and judiciary represent the three main functions of government. The legislature is the law-making body with the power to pass, amend and repeal laws. In Germany, this power was vested in the *Reichstag*; in Britain, the House of Commons. The executive is the body which sees to it that the laws are properly executed or put into operation. In Germany, this was the President's responsibility; in Britain, it is the role of government departments and the Civil Service. The judiciary sees to it that the laws are fairly applied and punishes those who break them. In both Germany and Britain, this is the function of the judges and courts. In a democracy, it is essential that the three functions are kept separate. In Germany, at times of national emergency, it was possible for the President to exercise executive power and assume the role of law maker. As we shall see, in a dictatorship all three powers become vested in the same person, the dictator.

was extended to all males and females over the age of 20. For the first time German women had the right to vote. The *Reichsrat* would consist of delegates nominated by the parliaments of the federal states, the *Länder*.

B *The new Constitution – some considerations*

The Constitution of the Weimar Republic, on the face of it an attempt to combine aspects of the institutions of Britain and the United States, was a sincere attempt to introduce democratic government in Germany. In the broadest sense it was far from revolutionary but, from a German viewpoint, it represented a major break with the former imperial regime which had always been far more authoritarian than democratic. Pressure from those demanding constitutional reform and truly democratic institutions backed by the threat of revolution made such a step impossible to resist. Even so, those who had enjoyed privilege and status under the old regime were not going to give ground easily. From the very start they worked to undermine the authority of the new Republic. The introduction of proportional representation created a multi-party system of government which ensured that the Weimar Republic would inevitably be ruled by a series of coalition governments. Such governments were often short-lived and brought with them the risk of political instability.

Whilst power appeared to be concentrated with law makers in the legislature, the elected deputies of the *Reichstag*, considerable authority was also placed in the hands of the executive, those responsible for seeing that the laws were put into effect, the president. In certain circumstances, the president had the power to rule by decree and govern the Republic directly. He could also impose his own rule on troublesome *Länder*. The *Länder*, working within the framework of a federal system, could always create problems and this was most likely to happen when the political make-up of an individual state *Land* was different from that of the national government. During the presidency of Friedrich Ebert, over 130 emergency decrees were issued to deal with economic and law and order issues.

Later, as we shall see, Article 48 was abused and became a permanent way of governing. Although the Constitution introduced political changes designed to provide Germany with a democratic form of government, within the new Republic much remained unchanged. With no change in the structure of German society, the ruling elite of imperial times were still in position in the civil service, diplomatic corps, in the management of industry and commerce and, more widely, in the churches and universities. Unwilling to transfer their loyalty from an imperialist kaiser to the democratically elected president of a republic, they were to prove a dangerous and subversive influence. In the election of January 1919, they gave their representatives, the DVP and DNVP, a foothold in the *Reichstag*.

C *A bill of rights*

The Constitution of the Weimar Republic also included a bill of rights, intended to protect the interests of individual citizens, extracts from which are shown below:

114	Personal liberty is guaranteed. No intrusion on, or denial of, personal liberty by public authority is allowed, unless supported by law.
115	The home of every German is a sanctuary for him, and this is guaranteed; exceptions allowed only for legal reasons...
117	Every German has the right, within the limits of the law, to express himself freely by word, writing, printed matter or picture, or in any other manner...
123	All Germans have the right, without notification or special permission to assemble peacefully and without arms.
124	All Germans have the right to form unions and societies, provided their objects do not run counter to the law...
151	The organisation of economic life must correspond to the principles of justice, with the aim of ensuring for all conditions worthy of a human being.
153	Property is guaranteed by the Constitution...

Again, the rights provided by the bill could be withdrawn by the president acting under Article 48 of the Constitution. The lofty ideals of the bill were to endure for as long as the Weimar Republic could withstand the pressure and hostility of reactionary elements dedicated to its downfall.

On 1 May, at a time when delegates were still finalising details of the Constitution, details of the terms demanded by the Allies were released.

9 ∽ THE TREATY OF VERSAILLES

The Germans agreed to an armistice in November 1918 largely because they believed that the terms imposed by the Allies would be similar to those outlined by the American President, Woodrow Wilson, in his Fourteen Points. These points, the basis of a peace programme outlined by Wilson in an address to the United States Congress in January 1918, included the restoration of all land occupied by Germany, the drawing up of new national boundaries based on the principle of self-determination and proposals intended to encourage post-war reconciliation. In his speech, the American President said, 'Peoples are not to be handed about from one sovereignty to another by an international conference...national aspirations must be respected, peoples may now be dominated and governed only by their own consent. Self-determination is not a mere phrase but a principle of action which statesmen will ignore at their peril.' Unfortunately his views did not coincide with those of the other allied leaders. Georges Clemenceau, the French Prime

Minister, wanted revenge for the nightmare of the previous five years during which his country had been part-occupied by the Germans and suffered over 1,358,000 dead. He was determined to make sure that Germany would never be in a position to threaten France again. 'Mr Wilson bores me with his Fourteen Points', he said, 'Why, God Almighty only has ten'. Although Britain had not suffered the devastation of France, her dead totalled a million and the German submarine campaign had led to the loss of over seven million tonnes of merchant shipping. The financial cost of the war to the British people was an estimated £75 billion. Prime Minister, David Lloyd George, himself facing the challenge of a general election, promised that he would squeeze the German orange 'until the pips squeaked'. In reality, he took a more moderate line, stating that his aim was 'not to gratify vengeance, but to vindicate justice'.

Q Account for the differing attitudes of the Allied delegates at Versailles.

A *Territorial terms of the Treaty*

1. Alsace-Lorraine was to be returned to France.
2. The Rhineland, although to remain German, was to be demilitarised and occupied by allied troops for fifteen years.
3. The coal-rich Saar Basin was to be administered by the League of Nations for fifteen years before a **plebiscite** decided the region's future.
4. Eupen and Malmedy were to pass to Belgium.
5. Northern Schleswig was to become a part of Denmark.
6. Recreated Poland was to be given access to the Baltic Sea by means of a strip of territory, the 'Polish Corridor'. Danzig, at the end of the 'corridor', was to be a Free City within the customs frontier of Poland and placed under the control of the League of Nations.
7. Posen was to pass to Poland whilst the future of Silesia was to be decided by a plebiscite.
8. Memel was to be placed under international control.
9. The Kiel Canal, the River Rhine and other German rivers and waterways were to be internationalised.
10. Germany had to give up all her overseas colonies. They were to become mandates of the League of Nations.
11. Clause 80 of the Treaty stated that any future union of Germany and Austria was forbidden.

plebiscite a direct vote of all electors on an issue of national importance, such as a change in the constitution

As a result of these changes, Germany lost 13 per cent of her land and 12 per cent of her population. The land lost represented 48 per cent of her iron production and a sizeable amount of her coal resources. It was claimed that since millions of Germans were forced to live as minorities under foreign rule, as far as Germany was concerned the principle of self-determination was not applied. This is only true in part. Whilst in Danzig, an entirely German city, the people not only had to accept Polish rule but also forfeit their German nationality, elsewhere, when plebiscites were held, regions which voted overwhelmingly to remain German had their wishes respected. In Silesia, where a

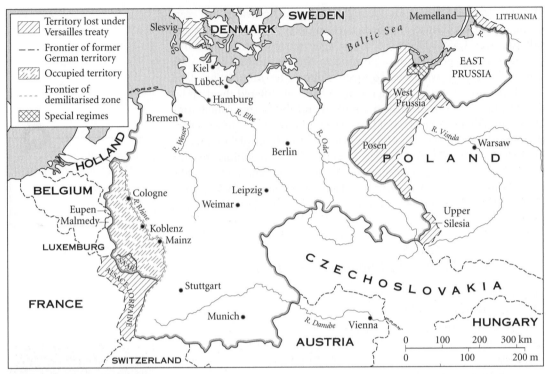

MAP 3
Germany and the Treaty of Versailles, 1919

plebiscite proved indecisive, an unsatisfactory compromise allowed the region to be divided between Germany and Poland. Lloyd George, who seemed more aware than others of creating German minorities, wrote:

> I cannot conceive any greater cause of future war than that the German people, who have certainly proved themselves one of the most vigorous and powerful nations in the world, should be surrounded by small states, many of them consisting of people who have never set up a stable government for themselves but each of them containing large masses of Germans clamouring for reunion with their native land. These proposals must, in my judgement, lead sooner or later to a new war...

B *Military terms of the Treaty*

1 The German army was to be reduced to 100,000 men. It was to be without tanks and heavy guns.

2 The import of arms and munitions was to be forbidden.

3 Sports clubs and universities were no longer allowed to provide training 'in the profession or use of arms'.

4 The German navy was to be limited to 15,000 men and was to consist of only six battleships, six cruisers and 24 smaller vessels.

No submarines were allowed. The remainder of the fleet was to make its way to Scapa Flow in readiness to surrender to the Allies.

5 Germany was not allowed to possess any military aircraft.

C *The issues of war guilt and reparations*

The extent to which different nations were responsible for the war which began in 1914 has long been debated among historians. It is now generally accepted that several countries, for different reasons and in varying degrees, contributed, but that was not the feeling among the victors in 1919. In Paris, Germany was made to accept blame for the war. Article 231 of the treaty read, 'The Allied and Associated Governments affirm and Germany accepts the responsibility of Germany and her allies for causing all loss and damage to which the Allied and Associated Governments and their nationals have been subjected as a consequence of the war imposed on them by the aggression of Germany and her allies.'

The amount to be paid was to be decided later by a Reparations Committee. The payment of reparations by the vanquished to the victors was far from being a new idea. In 1871, at the end of the Franco-Prussian War, France had to pay an indemnity of five billion francs to Germany; in 1918, at Brest-Litovsk, the Germans had demanded six **milliards** of marks from Russia's new Bolshevik government as compensation to 'those who had suffered damage by reason of Russian measures'. Also controversial was Article 227 which contained proposals for the trial of the German Kaiser as a war criminal.

> **milliards** a milliard is a thousand million

D *The Treaty signed*

On 16 June, the German delegates led by Count Brockdorff-Rantzau were formally presented with details of the terms. The Treaty, which included some 440 Articles, was not as vindictive as Clemenceau had wanted nor as moderate as Lloyd George would have wished. It certainly fell far short of the conciliatory features of Wilson's Fourteen Point proposals. The German delegates were given 14 days, later extended to 21, to consider the terms and respond.

In Germany, there was indignation and outrage as Chancellor Scheidemann denounced the terms in the *Reichstag*; on 19 June, when the cabinet rejected the terms by eight votes to six, he resigned. President Ebert also offered to go declaring the treaty 'a peace of violence'. As a symbol of the grief felt at what was considered a national injustice, he went as far as to order the suspension of public amusements for a week! Although the Allied blockade had been lifted, shortages remained acute and a resumption of the war would be a futile gesture likely to encourage further revolutionary activity and endanger the republic. In a final attempt to reach a more acceptable compromise, the government agreed to accept all the terms apart from those demanding the trial of the Kaiser as a war criminal and the admission of war guilt. The offer was rejected and the Allies responded with an ultimatum demanding the unconditional acceptance of the terms within 48 hours or face the

PICTURE 3

The German delegation at Versailles. They played no part in the negotiations and were presented with the terms as a fait accompli

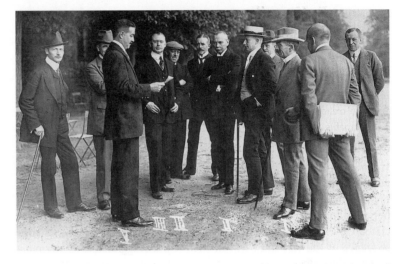

Q

Did the German delegates at Versailles have any choice other than to accept the terms demanded by the Allies?

renewal of hostilities. The new Chancellor, Gustav Bauer, who had formed a coalition of the SPD, Centre and DDP, struggled to win over waverers before putting the issue to the *Reichstag* where acceptance of the terms was finally agreed by 237 votes to 138. When news of this reached the German fleet interned at Scapa Flow, the crews opted to scuttle their vessels rather than surrender them as had been agreed. The Allies were angered by what they considered a show of bad faith.

The Treaty of Versailles was finally signed on behalf of Germany by representatives of the SPD and Centre Party, Hermann Müller and Johannes Bell, on 28 June 1919 in the Hall of Mirrors – the very same room in which 48 years earlier Bismarck had first proclaimed the German Empire. That same day, the German newspaper, *Deutsche Zeitung*, carried banner headlines and bitterly denounced the terms:

> VENGEANCE! GERMAN NATION
> Today in the Hall of Mirrors, the disgraceful treaty is being signed. Do not forget it. The German people will with unceasing labour press forward to reconquer the place among nations to which it is entitled. Then will come vengeance for the shame of 1919.

As Hindenburg retired for a second time, he wrote a final farewell to the men who had served under him. It concluded:

> Whatever you may think as individuals about recent events is entirely your own affair; but as regards your actions I would beg each one of you to be guided solely by the interests of your country... It is only by the united efforts of all of us that we can hope, with God's help, to raise our unhappy German Fatherland from its present depths of degradation and restore its former prosperity. Farewell. I shall never forget you!

That done, the old Field Marshal retired to his estate at Hanover.

E *Versailles – was it a just peace?*

The Treaty of Versailles may be regarded from different viewpoints. In 1920, Philip Gibbs, a journalist and front-line newspaper correspondent during the war, wrote in *Now It Can Be Told*:

> The treaty was…a piece of vengeance. It reeked with injustice. It was incapable of fulfilment. It sowed a thousand seeds from which wars might spring… The ideals for which millions of men had fought and died – liberty, fair play, a war to end war, justice – were mocked and outraged, not by men of evil but by man of good, not by foul design but with loyalty to national interests. Something blinded them…

The historian Anthony Wood, writing in 1964 (*Europe 1815–1945*), totally disagreed:

> In fact, any defeated country, whether it negotiates or not, has to accept the conditions the victor demands. Great Britain and France both had reservations over the Fourteen Points, and in any case, the terms which Germany imposed on Russia at Brest-Litovsk, in March 1918, deprived her of any moral right to complain of Versailles; indeed, in comparison with her allies, Austria-Hungary and Turkey, Germany had kept the bulk of her territory intact and those regions which had been removed from her were of a mixed population and had mostly been the fruit of conquest.

From the German viewpoint, their delegates had been ignored and, with the terms imposed and not negotiated, the Treaty was nothing more than a humiliating *Diktat*. From the start, many Germans felt no moral obligation to maintain the Treaty. They were convinced that it would continue for only as long as the victors were sufficiently united and strong enough to endorse it or, alternatively, until such time as they had a leader bold enough to challenge it. Why were the Allies so determined to make Germany accept responsibility for the war? The reason was that it would be easier to justify the payment of reparations if guilt for starting the war was self-confessed. Meanwhile, the Germans continued to deny vigorously their responsibility for the war and argued that their declaration of war on Russia and the invasion of Belgium and France in 1914 had been acts of self-defence.

At first, the Allies were unable to agree a level of reparations which would both satisfy their own expectations and still be within Germany's ability to pay. During a period when a series of conferences were called to discuss the issue, the Germans were ordered to make substantial deliveries of gold, currency, goods and raw materials to the Allies and were also asked to submit their own proposals. At a conference held in London during March 1921, the Allies were not impressed when the Germans tried to reduce the amount then being considered and made a counter offer which was conditional on the return of both the

Rhineland and Upper Silesia. A month later, the Inter-Allied Reparations Committee finally presented its report. It recommended that Germany should pay £6,600 million (132,000 million marks), plus interest as it accrued, in annual instalments of £100 million. National outrage led to a political crisis in Berlin and the resignation of the government. One final humiliation remained. Although, in 1920, Germany had earnestly sought to be one of the founder members of the new post-war international organisation, the League of Nations, the bitterness of the war years ensured that its request was denied. Germany was not yet considered sufficiently respectable to be brought back into normal relations with the rest of the world.

KEY ISSUE

Deciding how much Germany should pay.

10 ∽ BIBLIOGRAPHY

A bibliography for Chapters 1–4 appears on pages 107–8.

11 ∽ TOPICS FOR DISCUSSION AND TWO-PART ESSAY QUESTIONS

A *This section consists of questions that might be used for discussion (or written answers) as a way of expanding on the chapter and testing understanding of it.*

1. To what extent was the Kaiser still in a position to influence policy decisions in 1918?
2. Account for the change in the attitude of the German Socialist Party to the war during 1917 and 1918.
3. In your view, does the 'stab-in-the-back' theory have any credibility?
4. What do you understand by the term 'extremist' in politics?
5. Did Ebert have any choice but to accept the backing of the military in 1919?
6. Would you agree that the Spartacist uprising of January 1919 was doomed from the start?
7. What are the weaknesses of an electoral system based on proportional representation?
8. Which was the more important – *Reichsrat* or the *Reichstag*? Give reasons for your answer.
9. Explain the significance of Clause 48 of the Constitution.

B *Two-part essay questions.*
1. (a) What were the reasons for the mutinies and riots that led to a period of turmoil in Germany during 1918 and 1918?
   (b) Describe how Ebert managed to restore and maintain law and order in Germany during this period.

2. (a) Describe the extent of the powers granted to the President by the German constitution of 1919.

(b) Explain the reasons for the popularity of the Social Democrats (SPD) in the elections of 1919.

3. (a) Why did Article 231, the War Guilt Clause, prove offensive to so many Germans?

(b) Describe the extent to which the Treaty of Versailles limited Germany's industrial and military potential.

12 ⤶ MAKING NOTES

Read the advice section about making notes on page xx of Preface: how to use this book, and then make your own notes based on the following headings and questions.

1. *Why were German revolutionaries so active during 1918–19?*
Read the relevant sections of the chapter dealing with the unrest during the final stages of the war and immediately afterwards.
(a) Identify the reasons for the discontent:

Events	Causes
i mutinies in the German fleet	
ii widespread rioting across Germany	
iii Bavaria declared a socialist republic	
iv dissatisfaction in German army	
v Spartacist uprising in Berlin	
vi emergence of the *Freikorps*	

(b) Why did the threat of revolution come to nothing?
(c) What part was played by military and paramilitary units in these events?
(d) What was the reaction of the major political parties and German society to these upheavals?

2. *What were the strengths and weaknesses of the Weimar Constitution?*
Study the section of the chapter dealing with the Weimar Constitution.
(a) Identify the similarities of the new German Constitution with the systems of government of Britain and the United States.
(b) To what extent might the new system of government be considered truly democratic?
(c) What weaknesses might exist because of
   (i) the intention to use an electoral system based on proportional representation?
   (ii) the powers vested in the President by Article 48?

3. *Account for the German reaction to the terms of the Treaty of Versailles* Read the relevant sections of the chapter dealing with the terms imposed on the Germans at Versailles.

(a) Consider the impact of the terms on Germany.

(b) Consider the German reaction:

	Reasons for German indignation
Territorial losses in Europe	
Loss of colonies	
Regions whose future was to be decided by plebiscite	
Clause 80 and the union of Germany and Austria	
Military clauses	
War guilt	
Reparations	

(c) Why did Germany accept the terms?

The Weimar Republic – The Early Years 1920–3

2

INTRODUCTION

The Weimar Republic which came into existence in 1919 was to last until 1933. It was to govern Germany for a period longer than the life-span of Hitler's Third Reich. Faced with enormous difficulties and undermined by those who held democratic government in contempt, it was, many would argue, doomed from the start. Even so, it survived its early troublesome years and, in the mid-1920s, enjoyed a period of relative prosperity. Finally it was to be destroyed by economic circumstances and a right-wing conspiracy planned by those who had worked to subvert it. What started as a bold experiment in democracy by honest and well intentioned politicians was betrayed and made to give way to the nightmare of Nazism. As the years of the Weimar Republic unfold consider if it really was doomed from the start. Did its leaders make irreparable errors or did it fall victim to unforeseeable circumstances? Is it possible that with other leaders, different policies and the greater understanding of other nations, it might have survived to thwart the ambitions of Adolf Hitler?

1 ∽ AN OMINOUS BEGINNING

As Hannah Vogt has written of the Weimar politicians who took office in 1919, 'the men who were to pick up the reins of government faced a tremendous, thankless task'. From the outset, Philipp Scheidemann's coalition of Socialists (SPD), left-wing liberals (DDP) and Centre Party members faced a backlash of resentment over a lost war and disappointing peace. Most damning was the hostility of the extreme left and extreme right. The Communists accused them of disloyalty for failing to back them during the upheavals of the previous twelve months. To the nationalists they represented both the 'November traitors' and those responsible for their country's humiliation at Versailles. The new government's standing in public opinion was further undermined by influential conservative forces. Still firmly in place, they showed only

TABLE 3

Date chart of the domestic history of the Weimar Republic, 1920–3

1920	March	Attempted Kapp *Putsch*; Communist uprising in the Ruhr; Hermann Müller forms a new government
	June	*Reichstag* election, Coalition parties (SPD–Centre–DDP) suffer heavy losses; new Coalition formed by Fehrenbach
	October	Differences lead to split in USPD
1921	Jan–Feb	Paris and London Conferences on reparations
	April	Reparations Committee sets payment at £6,600 million
	May	Resignation of Fehrenbach government; Josef Wirth becomes Chancellor
	August	Assassination of Matthias Erzberger
1922	April	Genoa Conference
	June	Assassination of Walther Rathenau
	November	Resignation of Wirth government; Wilhelm Cuno becomes Chancellor
1923	January	Occupation of Ruhr by French and Belgian troops
	August	Hyperinflation and collapse of the German mark; resignation of Cuno government; Gustav Stresemann becomes Chancellor
	September	Unrest in Bavaria, Saxony and Thuringia; President Ebert declares state of emergency under Clause 48 of the Constitution
	November	Attempted Munich *Putsch*; Stresemann resigns; Wilhelm Marx becomes Chancellor

progressive system of taxation the percentage of tax paid increases according to the size of income

superficial loyalty to the Republic and were ever willing to undermine its authority. Neither was the popularity of the government increased by the economic policies of its Finance Minister, Matthias Erzberger. In order to cope with pressing financial problems inherited from the war years and worsened by the terms imposed at Versailles as well as post-war uncertainty, Erzberger imposed taxes on profits and inherited wealth. He also introduced a **progressive system of taxation** which fell most heavily on the wealthy. Consequently, government leaders were accused of acting in bad faith and working in the interests of Germany's former enemies. Ebert, as well as Chancellor Bauer and his ministers, were continually criticised. In January 1920, public interest was aroused when Karl Helfferich, a former imperial Vice-Chancellor, accused Erzberger of earlier using his position to gain personal financial advantage. During the libel action which followed, the charges against Erzberger were proved largely false but even so, he was discredited and forced into retirement. The trial ended on 12 March 1920, the day before the Republic faced its first major challenge from the right.

2 ⌐ THE KAPP *PUTSCH*, MARCH 1920

A *Background*

In addition to the widespread hostility shown to the government and the sniping of the German extremist parties, Bauer's administration

WOLFGANG KAPP (1858–1922)

Kapp's father, who had been involved in revolutionary activity in Germany in 1848, emigrated to the United States the following year. His son, Wolfgang, was born in New York in 1858 and the family returned to Germany in 1870. Young Kapp, a doctor of law, spent some years working for the Prussian Ministry of Agriculture and, in 1906, became director general of an agricultural credit bank. During the 1914–18 war, he worked with Admiral Von Tirpitz to found the extreme right-wing *Vaterlandspartei* (Fatherland Party). After the upheavals of 1918, he was elected to the *Reichstag* where he campaigned for the restoration of the monarchy.

faced another major problem. In order to bring about the reductions in the armed services imposed at Versailles, swingeing cuts had to be made in manpower – an army of 650,000 had to be cut to 200,000 by November 1919 and, thereafter, to only 100,000. A group of officers led by General von Lüttwitz denounced the proposed cuts and demanded the dissolution of the *Reichstag* and the calling of elections. Together with Wolfgang Kapp, he made plans to overthrow the government. Their scheming had the implied support of Ludendorff.

Matters finally came to a head when the government's Defence Minister, Gustav Noske, ordered a number of units to disband. These included the Baltikum Brigade, which had recently returned from service in the Baltic provinces, and a brigade commanded by Hermann Ehrhardt which had earlier been responsible for crushing the Spartacist uprising and suppressing the communist republic in Bavaria.

B *The attempted* Putsch

On the night of 12/13 March, the men of the two brigades left their barracks on the outskirts of Berlin and moved into the city. The following morning, they marched triumphantly through the Brandenburg Gates into the city centre. Joined by other units of *Freikorps*, their numbers rose to over 12,000. Kapp's plan was to seize Berlin with their aid and then set up a right-wing government with himself as Chancellor. Noske ordered the *Reichswehr*, the new professional army allowed under the Treaty of Versailles, to act against the putschists but army leaders, previously willing to move against left-wing militants, could not be persuaded. Although the army commander, General von Seeckt, did not support Lüttwitz, he nevertheless refused to act declaring that '*Reichswehr* does not fire on *Reichswehr*'. Under threat, members of the government left Berlin. They moved first to Dresden, where the local army commander was unable to guarantee their safety, and then on to Stuttgart. Before leaving the capital, they called upon German workers

KEY ISSUE

The first right-wing move against the new Republic.

to defend the Republic and register their opposition to Kapp and his insurgents by supporting a general strike. A proclamation signed by Ebert and Bauer went out to workers:

> Workers, Party Comrades! The military putsch has started. The Baltic mercenaries, fearing the command to dissolve, are trying to remove the republic and form a military dictatorship. Lüttwitz and Kapp are at their head... The achievements of a whole year are to be smashed, your dearly fought freedom is to be destroyed. Everything is at stake! The strongest action is required. No factory must work while the military dictatorship of Ludendorff and the others rules. Down your tools! Come out on strike! Fight with all means for the republic. Therefore down tools! There is only one way against the dictatorship...paralysis of all economic life! No hand must move! General strike all along the line! Workers unite! Down with the counter-revolution.

Beyond Berlin, Germany's military leaders acted cautiously and appeared largely uncommitted. Although Walther Reinhardt, commander of the *Reichswehr*, remained loyal to the government and was prepared to take action, others were reluctant to become directly involved. Significantly, from a distance, Hindenburg remained an impassive spectator of these events. Abroad, there was concern at events in Germany and foreign governments refused to recognise Kapp's authority.

C *The collapse of the* Putsch *and the aftermath*

The strike quickly proved effective. Without water, gas, electricity and public transport, Berlin was paralysed as everyday life came to a standstill. When national and regional newspapers failed to appear, Kapp's supporters tried to promote their views by handing out printed newssheets and propaganda leaflets. To make matters worse, civil servants refused to follow Kapp's orders and the *Reichsbank* refused him any financial support. In reality, the *Putsch* had been mistimed, badly planned and had failed to muster anything like the expected support. Apart from a general desire to overthrow the Republic, the leaders of the *Putsch* had no worthwhile policies and lacked the means to establish effective government. Although some right-wing parties had a measure of sympathy for the putschists, some openly supported them. In desperation Kapp made exaggerated promises in an effort to win public support. Typically, he hoped that an undertaking to cancel examinations would at least find favour with Berlin students. Kapp's attempt to govern became increasingly frustrated and, as his position weakened, so clashes between hostile crowds of workers and supporters of the *Putsch* increased. After four days the *Putsch* finally collapsed and Kapp resigned. Together with Lüttwitz, he fled abroad to join Ludendorff in Sweden. Of the 412 officers implicated in the insurrection, only 48 were relieved of their duties and just one was sentenced to a term of imprisonment!

The left-wingers and trade unionists, concerned at the re-emergence of militarism, were furious at the government's inept handling of the affair. Calling for another national strike, they put forward a nine-point plan which included demands for a truly socialist government, the removal of anti-republican elements in the administration, the creation of a new republican army and a range of major economic reforms. President Ebert resisted most of these demands but could not prevent the resignation of Chancellor Bauer and Defence Minister Noske. On 15 March, a communist uprising began in the Ruhr. As arms were issued to a so-called Red Army, barricades were raised in the streets. A government was set up at Essen with the aim of establishing an independent soviet republic. This time the army, which had stubbornly declined to take action against Kapp, had no qualms about dealing with the insurgents. Hundreds were killed and executed as the *Reichswehr* restored normality.

Fiasco as it may have appeared, the attempted *Putsch* of March 1920 was significant. It indicated that disgruntled German nationalists were as ready to act against the Weimar government as their left-wing counterparts. It also showed that German workers were prepared to resist attempted military coups. It made clear that the government could not in all circumstances rely on the support of the *Reichswehr*.

The legacy of Kapp's *Putsch* was an even greater hatred of Weimar democracy by the militarists and nationalists and a new determination to destroy what they saw as Bolshevik-backed republicanism by any means possible. On the other hand, left-wing extremists were embittered by what they considered to be the 'treachery of the Ebert, Noske, Bauer clique'. Interestingly, Lenin considered the failure of the Kapp *Putsch* to be as significant as the defeat of the Kornilov uprising in August 1917. In Russia, this event had contributed greatly to the success of Bolsheviks and Lenin thought that the defeat of Kapp might have similar consequences in Germany.

3 ⌐ MOB VIOLENCE AND POLITICAL SLAYINGS

A *The 'White Terror'*

During the following months, Germany witnessed an orgy of mob violence and assassinations as left- and right-wing extremists took matters into their own hands. Some atrocities were carried out by the left but the vast majority were part of a 'White Terror' orchestrated by the right. *Freikorps* violence was **arbitrary** and their attitude at the time is best summed up in an instruction given by a leader to his men, 'It is a lot better to kill a few innocent people than let one guilty person escape'. In his *History of the SS*, G.S. Graber described a *Freikorps* atrocity:

arbitrary not bound by any rules

Ehrhardt a particularly vicious unit of *Freikorps*

Nothing could be heard but the sound of marching boots. A small boy in the crowd of onlookers laughed. . .two members of the ***Ehrhardt*** broke ranks, knocked the boy down and beat him with their rifle butts until he was quite still. Nobody else moved, though someone had the courage to hiss. An officer barked a command and machine guns opened fire on the crowd.

Few of those responsible for such crimes were brought to justice. Among the victims of the 'White Terror' were Matthias Erzberger, Walther Rathenau and several other leading left-wing leaders. Erzberger, the leader of the Centre Party, had served as deputy in the *Reichstag* since 1903. He had been amongst those who had negotiated the armistice conditions in 1918. A year later, he was appointed Finance Minister in Bauer's administration. He had already survived one assassination attempt during his libel action in 1920 and, on 26 August 1921, was murdered by members of the *Organisation Consul*, a group of political activists which largely comprised young ex-officers with a reputation for violence.

B *The murder of Walther Rathenau*

Walther Rathenau was the son of a wealthy Jewish industrialist who had founded the immense Allgemeine Elektrizitäts-Gesellschaft combine (AEG). During the war, he had played a crucial role in maintaining war production and countering the effects of the Allied naval blockade. After the war he joined the DDP and served as Minister for Reconstruction, and it fell to him to fulfil the economic obligations imposed on Germany at Versailles. He had strongly-held democratic convictions and worked to encourage international co-operation. In 1922, he became Foreign Secretary and was largely responsible for negotiating the Treaty of Rapallo that same year (see page 45) which restored normal relations between Weimar Germany and Communist Russia. In spite of his achievements, the highly-regarded statesman was not popular with right-wing nationalists who accused him of encouraging 'creeping Communism'. Always a likely target for assassins, he refused to take any precautions to ensure his safety. On 24 June 1922 he was gunned down as he drove to his office in an open car.

The men responsible for the outrage were again members of the *Organisation Consul*. The motive of the assassins remains uncertain. It may have been just the random murder of a leading member of the government or, possibly, a retaliatory strike against the man responsible for restoring diplomatic relations with Soviet Russia. The fact that he was a Jew may have been a contributory factor and some have even gone as far as to suggest that his disregard for his own safety indicated that he sought martyrdom.

C *Reaction to Rathenau's murder*

Rathenau's murder led to a wave of revulsion among the German people who were angry at the government's failure to counter right-wing outrages. A Law to Defend the Republic was passed which gave the authorities far-reaching powers and set up special courts to deal with those responsible for acts of terrorism. It is estimated that during this period there were 376 political murders – 354 committed by the right compared with 22 by the left. Of those responsible, only ten, all of them from the left, were brought to trial and sentenced to death. The average prison sentence imposed on right-wing assassins was four months and the average fine per murder just two marks!

D *The* **Stahlhelm** *and other private armies*

In such a tense atmosphere, it was inevitable that a number of paramilitary-type, private armies should appear. The *Stahlhelm* (Steel Helmet) was a right-wing organisation made up of army veterans. Founded by Franz Seldte and Theodor Duesterberg, two former army officers, it was strongly monarchist and nationalist. Its main aim was to guard against any left-wing revolution. The movement was destined to play a prominent role in German politics during the 1920s and early 1930s. Opposed to the *Stahlhelm* were the *Reichsbanner* and the *Rotfrontkämpferbund* (Red Front Fighters). The *Reichsbanner* attracted SPD members and trade unionists who were ex-servicemen. It was a uniformed but unarmed organisation. The *Rotfrontkämpferbund* was the unofficial army of the Communists. Ex-*Freikorps* men and others who had failed to adjust to civilian life joined the *Sturmabteilung*. These were the streetwise stormtroopers of the emerging Nazi Party who accepted violence as a way of life.

	Chancellor	Composition of the Coalition
Feb 1919 – Jun 1919	Philipp Scheidemann	SPD/Centre/DDP
Jun 1919 – Mar 1920	Gustav Bauer	SPD/Centre/DDP
Mar 1920 – Jun 1920	Hermann Müller	SPD/Centre/DDP

TABLE 4
Governments of the Weimar Republic February, 1919 – June 1920

The frailty of multi-party governments based on uneasy coalitions became apparent early in the life of the Weimar Republic. During the 18 turbulent months between February 1919 and June 1920, three governments fell. With more troubles looming, the situation was not going to improve.

TABLE 5

The Reichstag *election of June 1920*

		Number of seats
Social Democrats	SPD)	102
Independent Socialists	(USPD)	84
Nationalist Party	(DNVP)	71
People's Party	(DVP)	65
Catholic Centre	(Zentrum)	64
Democratic Party	(DDP)	39
Bavarian Party	(BVP)	16
Communists	(KPD)	4
Independents and others		26

4 ↶ YEARS OF ONGOING CRISES, 1920–4

A *The* Reichstag *Election of June 1920*

Although the SPD remained the largest party, it lost 61 seats and 16 per cent of its vote. The result showed the first move towards the polarisation of public opinion with more people voting for the extremist parties. The nationalist parties, the DNVP and DVP, did well and the Communists, now back in the political arena, won four seats. The new government, a centre-right coalition, was led by Konstantin Fehrenbach of the Centre Party.

B *A period of failed coalitions*

Konstantin Fehrenbach, an outstanding criminal lawyer and one of the *Reichstag*'s most gifted speakers, formed a coalition which comprised his own Centre Party and the DVP but with the SPD excluded. During this time, a split among the Independent Socialists of the USPD began a break-up which was to lead to the virtual disappearance of the Party. Whilst a few opted to return to the SPD, the majority switched to the Communist KPD. Fehrenbach's government lasted only nine months before failure to win any concessions from the Allies on the issue of reparations prompted its resignation.

Following Fehrenbach's resignation, it fell to Joseph Wirth to form a new government. Another Centre Party politician, he reshuffled the coalition and moved it more to the left by including the SPD and DDP and dropping the DVP. Then later, in order to bring about a more equitable left–right balance, he carried out another shake-up and brought

TABLE 6

Governments of the Weimar Republic, June 1920 – August 1923

	Chancellor	Composition of the Coalition
Jun 1920 – May 1921	Konstantin Fehrenbach	Centre/DDP/DVP
May 1921 – Nov 1922	Josef Wirth	Centre/DDP/SPD
Nov 1922 – Aug 1923	Wilhelm Cuno	Centre/DDP/DVP

DVP members back into his cabinet. It was Wirth who had to deal with the aftermath of the assassinations of Erzberger and Rathenau and continue the search for a satisfactory solution to the reparations problem. In 1922, the German government asked for a moratorium – a temporary suspension of the next payment. At the same time, they failed to make delivery of timber and telegraph posts already due. At a conference called at Cannes to consider the German request, Raymond Poincaré, the French Prime Minister, made his country's position very clear. France, he said, wanted 'her due, all her due'. He warned that if it was not forthcoming, 'a firm hand would fall on her [Germany's] neck'. The Germans claimed that for them it was simply a matter of 'First bread, then reparations'. On 14 November 1922, following the withdrawal of the SPD from Wirth's coalition, the Chancellor resigned and was replaced by Wilhelm Cuno.

A highly respected businessman with an international reputation, Wilhelm Cuno belonged to no political party. As a director of the Hamburg-America Shipping Line, he had twice refused cabinet appointments. A known supporter of business and industrial interests, he formed a centre-right coalition of the DDP, Centre and DVP. By comparison with Fehrenbach and Wirth, the economic and political problems Cuno was about to face were enormous. Although the German request for a moratorium was received favourably by the British government, the French remained adamant. Poincaré was convinced that the German government was making excuses to avoid payment that it could afford. When in January 1923 the Germans failed to deliver the quota of reparations due, he decided it was time to act.

> **KEY ISSUE**
>
> *Difficulties over reparations.*

C *The issue of reparations*

The total amount of reparations to be paid was not decided at Versailles but was to be calculated by a specially appointed Reparations Committee. In the meantime, Germany was required to make an interim payment of £1,000 million. In March 1921, they failed to make the payment due and, as a result, Allied troops crossed the River Rhine and occupied Dusseldorf, Duisburg and Ruhrort. The following month, the Reparations Committee announced that the amount of compensation to be paid by Germany had been fixed at 132,000 million gold marks – the equivalent of £6,600 million. An astronomical sum, but a considerable reduction on the 269,000 million gold marks (over £14,000 million) first suggested! The amount was to be paid in annual instalments of £100 million, some in cash and some in goods such as coal and shipping.

There was no greater critic of the reparations demanded of Germany than the eminent British economist, John Maynard Keynes. In his book, *The Economic Consequences of the Peace*, he condemned the treaty and expressed the view that the amount demanded of Germany was totally unrealistic and went well beyond that country's ability to pay. He urged the Allies to cancel all the existing debts between themselves and reduce German reparations to a more reasonable level. His proposals did not appeal to either the USA or France. During the war, the United States had loaned Britain a staggering £959 million, with smaller but still substantial sums going to France and Italy. The Americans were not prepared to consider any reduction and wanted the debts repaid in full. 'They hired the money, didn't they?' said President Calvin Coolidge. France was not interested in Germany's ability to pay but only in ensuring that the severity of the terms would cripple Germany's economy and hinder its recovery. The prospect of paying such a huge sum was greeted with dismay by the Germans. The Chancellor and Finance Minister, Josef Wirth, tried to persuade the Allies to modify their demands and, when this was turned down, requested the postponement of payments for two years. When this was also refused, Germany made a first payment of £50 million.

> **Q**
>
> *To what extent was Keynes's view of German reparations justified?*

D *An exercise on the fall of the early Weimar governments*

Between 1919 and 1923, the various coalitions of the Weimar Republic were all short-lived. Read through the chapter again and give the reasons for the collapse of the six governments prior to August 1923.

Date	Chancellor	Reason for the fall of the Government
Feb 1919 – Jun 1919	Philipp Scheidemann	
Jun 1919 – Mar 1920	Gustav Bauer	
Mar 1920 – Jun 1920	Hermann Müller	
Jun 1920 – May 1921	Konstantin Fehrenbach	
May 1921 – Nov 1922	Josef Wirth	
Nov 1922 – Aug 1923	Wilhelm Cuno	

5 ⤷ THE OCCUPATION OF THE RUHR

On 11 January 1923, Poincaré sent 60,000 French and Belgian troops across the River Rhine to occupy the Ruhr. The region, the industrial heartland of Germany, not only produced 80 per cent of the nation's steel and 71 per cent of its coal but it also supplied the resources essential to industrial production elsewhere in the country. It was the region on which the whole German economy was dependent. The occupying force included teams of French, Belgian and Italian engineers sent to supervise the running of the Ruhr's factories and mines. A report in *The Times* of 12 January 1923 described the scene:

THE RECKONING.

Pan-German. "MONSTROUS, I CALL IT. WHY, IT'S FULLY A QUARTER OF WHAT WE SHOULD HAVE MADE *THEM* PAY, IF *WE'D* WON."

PICTURE 4
A Punch cartoon of 1920 ridicules the German reaction to the Allied demand for reparations

...the main body of French forces came down the hill... At the head rode a party of cyclists in dark blue uniform and steel helmets... Many took no trouble to hide the hatred in their hearts... I saw a man turn aside and sob and mutter, 'The swine... May God pay them out for this cruel outrage.' The French...halted before the door of the Council Chamber.

'General Rampon, commanding the French troops who are occupying Essen, requests the presence of the Mayor.'

'I am his deputy', was the reply.

'Then will you please come here.'

'Pardon, Monsieur – I can only receive official visitors.'

As the issue escalated into a trial of strength between France and Germany, the Weimar government ordered an indefinite suspension of all reparations payments and instructed German workers not to co-operate but to engage in a campaign of passive resistance. Some went further and became involved in acts of sabotage. Confrontation became inevitable once French soldiers attempted to round up and deport strikers. During a number of clashes some 150 Germans were killed. In Essen Krupp workers tried to stop soldiers requisitioning lorries; in Mülheim workers tried to form a militia to oppose the French. One man, Albert Schlaggeter, a local *Freikorps* officer, was executed for being involved in the derailment of trains. Later he was to become a Nazi folk hero. Abroad, the French action was criticised by both the British and American governments. Hitler later commented in *Mein Kampf* on the significance of the event:

the French occupation of the Ruhr opened up great possibilities for the future not only in Germany's foreign politics but also in her internal politics. A considerable section of people who had looked upon France as the champion of progress and liberty were suddenly cured of this illusion... When the French put their threats into effect...it was a great and decisive moment. If at that moment our people had changed not only their frame of mind but also their conduct, the Ruhr district would have made for France what Moscow turned out for Napoleon.

PICTURE 5

A German cartoon of 1923 with the caption 'Hands off the Ruhr' shows France with her hand impaled on Ruhr factory chimneys

What were the consequences? Whilst the French did achieve some success in managing the Ruhr factories and mines, their action further embittered Franco-German relations and put at risk the continuation of the Anglo-French *entente*. More seriously, it accelerated the collapse of the German economy by triggering a massive rise in inflation which was to have quite staggering economic and political repercussions for Germany.

6 ↜ GERMAN ECONOMIC COLLAPSE – THE TRAGEDY OF HYPERINFLATION

The German mark had been declining in value since 1914. In 1914 the British pound (£) could be exchanged for 20 marks but, by 1919, this had risen sharply to 250 marks. The loss of the war and the humiliation of defeat caused the mark to fall further and the situation was not helped by the German government's failure to balance its budget and live within its means. The Weimar government also showed an unhealthy willingness to issue large amounts of paper money. Even so, it was the occupation of the Ruhr which finally sent the value of the mark plummeting out of control. The result was raging **hyperinflation** as the nation became flooded with worthless paper money which had lost virtually all its purchasing power. At one stage the *Reichsbank* was using 300 paper factories and 150 printing works to supply Germany with the necessary money.

Amusing stories abound of a time when a single egg cost millions of marks, wages were taken home in wheelbarrows and meals increased in price as they were being eaten, but for most Germans the situation was

hyperinflation as the amount of money in circulation increases so prices rise. When the situation gets out of hand it is referred to as hyperinflation

PICTURE 6
German banknotes and stamps of the period of hyperinflation

TABLE 7
The decline in the value of the German mark

Marks to the £		
	1914	20
	1919	250
early	1921	500
late	1921	1,000
	1922	35,000
late	1923	16,000,000,000,000

TABLE 8

The price of a loaf of bread in Germany

Marks	
1918	.63
Jan 1923	250
July 1923	3,465
Sept 1923	1,500,000,000
Nov 1923	201,000,000,000

anything but humorous. Working-class wage earners, their living standards already cut to the bone, simply became poorer and then finally destitute; the well-off, the capitalist and land-owning classes with their wealth held largely in land and buildings or in overseas investments, were far better able to survive with some even doing well out of the crisis. Industrialists, with their manufacturing empires built on credit, were able to pay off their debts with near worthless paper marks. Those, like Thyssen, Krupp and Stinnes, still able to export, earned valuable foreign currency which they used to buy up businesses and factories and amass fortunes. The section of society which really suffered were the German middle classes. Living largely on fixed incomes, not only did the purchasing power of their salaries fall, but family savings put aside to finance their retirement became worthless. A person who had put aside 100,000 marks in 1913 found that, by the end of 1923, those savings would not have bought a postcard. With the value of the mark changing several times a day people rushed to the shops to spend their wages immediately they were paid. Many survived by scrimping, bartering and selling their treasured possessions and family heirlooms; some turned to theft and violence. Alan Bullock, in *Hitler, A Study in Tyranny* wrote:

> The savings of the middle classes and working classes were wiped out at a single blow which no revolution could ever equal; at the same time the purchasing power of wages was reduced to nothing. Even if a man worked until he dropped, it was impossible to buy enough for his family – and work, in any case, was not to be found. Whatever the cause of the phenomenon...the cause of the inflation was to undermine German society in a way which war, nor the revolution of 1918, nor the Treaty of Versailles had ever done.

It was a time when poverty gave way first to hopelessness and then to anger. The unemployed, impoverished families with children to clothe and feed, the elderly reduced to pauperism and those cheated of their savings became increasingly desperate. They also became more prepared to listen to the firebrand orators of the extremist parties who raged at the government's incompetence and offered their own plausible solutions. The Communists urged people to follow the example of the Russian Bolsheviks and unite in a proletariat revolution to overthrow the discredited Weimar regime, while the leadership of a little-known party of the extreme right, the National Socialist German Workers' Party, saw the crisis as a God-sent opportunity to steal the limelight. By mid-1923, it was abundantly clear that the government's policy of passive resistance to the French occupation of the Ruhr and their attempts to cope with the still accelerating hyperinflation were failing hopelessly. On 12 August Cuno and his cabinet resigned to make way for Gustav Stresemann.

KEY ISSUE

The plight of the German middle classes.

7 ✍ FOREIGN POLICY

Those responsible for the direction of German foreign policy during the early years of the Republic certainly had their work cut out. From the start the major issues which dominated European politics were the implications of the territorial changes brought about by the post-war peace treaties, the burden of reparations and relations between the victor and vanquished nations.

A *Reparations and international relations*

Most of the governments of the Weimar Republic made efforts to bring about some revision of the Treaty of Versailles and, in particular, lessen the economic burden imposed by the funding of reparations. To start with German strategy was mainly prevarication – shifting position, constant quibbling and evading the truth. This was more than matched by allied, mainly French, obstinacy. The creation of a **buffer state** by the occupation and demilitarisation of the Rhineland did little to allay French fears of a future German revival and Prime Minister Poincaré remained unhappy with the security offered to his country by the terms agreed at Versailles. His concern over French vulnerability was heightened when the United States refused to ratify the Treaty and then lapsed into isolation. As a consequence, he worked to create a network of defensive alliances with Czechoslovakia, Romania and Yugoslavia, the so called Little Entente. As far as the payment of reparations was concerned, Poincaré remained totally intractable – Germany was not to escape the shackles of its debts.

From a German viewpoint, the issue of reparations closely linked its foreign policy with its domestic economic policy. A number of conferences had already taken place even before the Reparations Committee had finalised the amount to be paid. At Spa in 1920, the Allies proposed a total of 269 billion marks as Germany's total liability to be paid off in 42 annual instalments. The Germans responded with vague counter-proposals which related to the method of payment and the extent to which payment could be made in goods. Essential issues were put to one side and left unresolved. Further conferences held in Paris and London in 1921 proved equally unproductive. The whole issue finally came to a head in April 1921 when the Reparations Committee made its report fixing reparations at £6,600 million. The signs were ominous when, the following month, the first payment due was only received after the Allies had threatened to occupy the Ruhr. During 1922, Wirth's centre-left coalition followed a seemingly more conciliatory line by adopting a policy of 'fulfilment'. The government undertook to try and fulfil the terms imposed on Germany with the underlying aim of proving to the Allies just how impossible this was. German nationalists were indignant and the newspaper *Deutsche Zeitung* accused the Chancellor of 'boasting to the world how obediently he has done everything, how punctually he is paying the billion marks...how he is turning us

buffer state a neutral state lying between two hostile powers.

into slaves'. In April 1922, a conference was called at Genoa to consider the overall European economic situation.

B *The Genoa Conference, 1922*

Called at the recommendation of the British Prime Minister, David Lloyd George, and with representatives of Germany and Soviet Russia in attendance, the conference was to consider how 'to remedy the paralysis of the European system'. Behind the scenes there had been much **wheeler-dealing** which left the German representative, Rathenau, undecided whether to make deals with the Allies or the Russians. He did not wish to offend either and the situation was made more complex when the Russians hinted that they too might demand reparations from Germany.

The atmosphere was soured when the French again refused to reduce the financial demands on Germany and then went as far as to insist that Russia's Communist regime should honour the debts of the former tsarist government! In spite of the furore, a decision was made to postpone the remainder of Germany's payments for that year. In addition and quite unexpectedly, German and Russian delegates agreed to meet again separately at Rapallo. Seven months later, another international conference was held in London. This time a British undertaking to cancel all France's war-time debts failed to make Poincaré any more amenable and he remained totally adamant that Germany should pay its reparations in full. On 9 January 1923, when the Cuno's government requested a moratorium, the French responded by occupying the Ruhr. Although the burden of reparations was later moderated by the Dawes Plan (1924), the issue was far from settled.

C *Russo-German relations*

There is some anomaly in the fact that whilst the Weimar Republic was constantly struggling to contain communist-inspired insurrections in Germany, a facet of its foreign policy was to try and establish better relations with the Soviet Union. The two countries had a great deal in common – both were outcast nations considered unfit for involvement in mainstream European affairs, both were hostile to Polish nationalism and had suffered territorial losses in 1919 in order to reconstitute an independent Poland, both had been denied membership of the League of Nations. In 1920, many Germans would not have been disappointed if the Soviet Union had been successful during the Russo-Polish War since this would have demolished the territorial changes relating to Poland agreed at Versailles and made a reconsideration of the whole Treaty a possibility. A year later Germany was further displeased by the outcome of the plebiscite in Upper Silesia which resulted in the division of the region, with Germany retaining the bulk of the land and Poland holding on to the main industrial areas. Secret collaboration between Germany and Russia had already proved beneficial to both countries. General Hans von Seeckt, head of the *Reichswehr*, had no scruples about

wheeler-dealing
bargaining to get the best advantage before making a deal

KEY ISSUE

Secret collaboration between Germany and the Soviet Union.

arranging for arms, forbidden to the German army, to be manufactured and then tested in distant and inaccessible regions of Russia. In Berlin, a company was formed as cover for this illicit arms trade. In return, German engineers and army officers were sent to help develop the Russian armaments industry and instruct the Red Army.

D *The Treaty of Rapallo, 1922*

A Russo-German agreement was finally signed at Rapallo on 16 April 1922. Under its terms, diplomatic relations were restored between the two countries and Russian claims to reparations from Germany and German claims for compensation for property confiscated at the time of the revolution were waived. Henceforward, the two countries agreed to 'co-operate in a spirit of goodwill in meeting the economic needs of both countries'. The treaty marked a defeat for Rathenau, who did not want to go this far with Russo-German emergence from diplomatic isolation, and further increased French concern, particularly since there were rumours of secret military clauses. Generally, the Allies regarded it as evidence of German double-dealing and of Russian scheming to keep the capitalist countries divided. The show of friendship did not prevent Moscow from encouraging German Communists to work for a national revolution when, only a year later, the country was close to economic collapse.

(Take care not to confuse the Treaty of Rapallo of April 1922 with a similarly named Treaty of Rapallo which was concluded in November 1920 and settled differences between Italy and Yugoslavia.)

8 ⌁ THE CHANCELLORSHIP OF GUSTAV STRESEMANN

In August 1923, at a time of crisis when the future of Weimar Germany seemed at risk, Gustav Stresemann became Chancellor, the Republic's seventh in a little under four years. Certainly a controversial politician, he is considered by some historians to have been the outstanding German statesman of the 1920s.

The problems the new Chancellor and his cabinet faced were enormous. German industry was at a standstill, the economy had collapsed under a mountain of worthless banknotes and the people, driven to the limits of their endurance, were threatening levels of unrest more severe than anything yet experienced by the Republic. In spite of strong opposition, he abandoned the policy of passive resistance to the French occupation of the Ruhr and resumed the payment of reparations. He also appointed Hjalmar Schacht, a highly respected banker, as special currency commissioner with responsibility for tackling the disastrous hyperinflation.

Imperial War Museum Hulton
01921754

PICTURE 7
Gustav Stresemann

GUSTAV STRESEMANN (1878–1929)

Born in Berlin, the son of a publican and brewer, Gustav Streseman was an accomplished academic who attended universities in Berlin and Leipzig and afterwards earned a reputation as an organiser and negotiator whilst working for various trade associations. His wife was the daughter of a well-to-do Jewish businessman and one of the leading hostesses in Berlin society. He joined the *Deutsche Volkspartei*, the German People's Party or DVP, and was elected to the *Reichstag* in 1907. An out-and-out monarchist, he believed in the 'spiritual, military and economic superiority of the German Empire'. His commitment to Pan-Germanism caused him to champion Germany's claim for Polish and Russian territory. Although unfit for military service, he proved himself an uncompromising patriot during the war. He worked closely with Hindenburg and Ludendorff and was their mouthpiece in the *Reichstag*. After the war, he denounced the armistice, the Weimar Republic and the Treaty of Versailles. He approved of the action taken against left-wing activists but was in two minds at the time of the Kapp *Putsch*. The turning point came when he recognised the reality that the future of Germany depended on the survival of the Weimar Republic and was converted to 'realistic republicanism'.

In August 1923, Stresemann formed a 'Grand Coalition' of DVP, SPD, DDP, and Centre members to face the challenge of Germany's daunting political willingness to adjust his policies to the needs of the day. He was also an optimist with the courage to swim against the tide of public opinion.

> An old Jewish story tells of a man who, sentenced to death, pleaded for a year's reprieve during which time he promised to teach the King's horse to fly. When his wife asked how he could dream of making such an impossible promise, he replied 'Before the year is up the King can die, or I can die or the horse can die. And who knows, perhaps the horse will learn to fly after all!' This story is an apt description of the character and behaviour of Gustav Stresemann. (Annelise Thimme, *Germany to 1929*)

A *The 'Miracle of the Rentenmark'*

Without loss of time, Schacht established a new currency, the *Rentenmark*. Based on land values and foreign loans, each *Rentenmark* was worth 10,000,000,000,000 million old marks. The 'miracle of the *Rentenmark*' came about because people had confidence in the new currency even though it was far from soundly based. In truth, it was an illusion and, had it failed, there was no realistic way that the value of the land backing the currency could have been converted into cash. In addition, the Finance Minister, Hans Luther, took urgent measures to curb inflation and **balance the budget**, which included the sacking of 900,000 civil servants and public employees. In 1924, the *Rentenmark* was replaced by the *Reichsmark* and this remained German currency until 1945.

> **balance the budget** ensuring that a country's spending is balanced by its income

B *Restoration of law and order*

Some saw Stresemann's decision to abandon passive resistance as a surrender to the French. In nationalist Bavaria, a stronghold of the patriotic *völkisch* movement, there was a strong reaction. The right-wing *Land* called a state of emergency and appointed Gustav von Kahr as State Commissioner with dictatorial powers. Kahr, a bitter opponent of the Republic, had long supported calls for Bavarian independence. He ordered the Bavarian military to ignore orders from Berlin and made them swear an oath of loyalty to his government. As relations between the Bavarian *Land* and the national government worsened, there seemed a real chance of open rebellion. Troubles were not limited to Bavaria. At Kustrin and Spandau, close to Berlin, there was a mutiny amongst renegade *Freikorps* units known as the *Fehme* or 'Black Reichswehr'. In Socialist-governed Saxony and Thuringia, the SPD accepted Communist ministers into their cabinets. In both states, paramilitary units were made ready as money and advisers arrived from Russia to prepare for the struggle ahead. In the Rhineland, the French mischievously did their best to encourage people to set up their own independent Rhenish Republic. In September 1923, Stresemann, recognising the need to restore law and order and maintain national unity, asked President Ebert to use the authority allowed by Article 48 of the Constitution to declare a state of national emergency. This done, he empowered his Defence Minister, Otto Gessler, and head of the army, Hans von Seeckt, to restore the government's authority. Regular units of *Reichswehr* easily dealt with the undisciplined 'Black Reichswehr' before being sent to depose the governments of Saxony and Thuringia. Impressed by Stresemann's firm handling of the situation in the two Socialist states, the Bavarian nationalists moderated their tone and showed greater restraint. Even so, it was in the Bavarian state capital, Munich, that the most serious disturbance occurred when, on 8 November 1923, a group of right-wing extremists attempted a *Putsch* (see pages 58–60). The group, the National Socialists, was led by a little-known Austrian, Adolf Hitler.

By the end of the year, Stresemann's decision to use a presidential decree to declare a state of emergency, suppress political activity and ban political parties, had so offended the SPD that they withdrew from his coalition and forced his resignation. Although only in office for a few months, Stresemann was not lost to politics since, as we shall see, he remained influential in framing German foreign policy until his death in 1929.

> **Q**
>
> *Was Stresemann justified in bringing Article 48 of the Constitution into play in 1923?*

9 ↫ BIBLIOGRAPHY

A bibliography for Chapters 1–4 appears on pages 107–8.

10 ↫ DISCUSSION TOPICS AND TWO-PART ESSAY QUESTIONS

A *This section consists of questions that might be used for discussion (or written answers) as a way of expanding on the chapter and testing understanding of it.*

1. Explain the attitude of Germany's military leaders to the Kapp *Putsch* in 1920.
2. What do you consider to be the most likely motive for the murder of Rathenau in 1922?
3. Examine the reasons for the growth of paramilitary private armies in Germany during the early 1920s.
4. To what extent was Poincaré's decision to occupy the Ruhr in 1923 justified?
5. During the period of hyperinflation, why were some sections of German society more severely affected than others?
6. Would you agree that although Stresemann was only Chancellor for three months, he achieved a great deal?

B *Two-part essay questions.*

1. (a) To what extent would it be true to say that the payment of reparations was the main cause of Germany's post-war economic problems?
   (b) 'Between 1918 and 1923, the governments of the Weimar Republic were largely successful in coping with Germany's economic problems. How far would you agree with this view?
2. (a) How far would it be true to say that the German economic collapse in 1923 was self-inflicted?
   (b) Examine the view that, in 1923, Gustav Stresemann was 'the saviour of Germany'.

11 ➣ SINGLE SOURCE DOCUMENTARY EXERCISE ON THE IMPACT OF HYPERINFLATION ON GERMANY

Study the following source carefully and then answer the questions based on it.

Unfortunately, this picture of accelerating and shocking decline in health conditions applies to the whole Reich. In rural areas where many <u>self-sufficient farmers</u> are able to feed themselves...conditions seem to be better. But in the towns and heavily populated industrial areas, there has been a decided deterioration. Especially hard hit are the middle class, those <u>living on small annuities</u>, the widows and the pensioners, who with their modest incomes can no longer afford the most basic necessities at present day prices. It is going just as badly for those who cannot yet earn. I mention students only as an example. The expense of even the most basic foodstuffs – I need only indicate fats, meat and bread – and the want of coal, linen, clothing and soap prevent any improvement in living conditions. The height to which prices have climbed may be shown by the fact that...wholesale prices have risen on the average to 5,967 times their peacetime level, those of foodstuffs to 4,902 times... Meat consumption has fallen from 52 kilograms per person in 1912 to 26 kilograms per person in 1922. For many people, meat has become a rarity. A million and a half German families are inadequately provided with fuel. Thousands upon thousands of people spend their lives jammed together in the most primitive dwellings... There are complaints of the appearance of scurvy, which is the result of an unbalanced and improper diet. From various parts of the Reich, reports are coming in about an increase in suicides. More and more often one finds old age and weakness listed as the causes of death in the official records; these are equivalent to death through hunger.

From a speech made on 20 February 1923 by the President of the Reich Department of Health, quoted in The German Inflation of 1923 *by F.K. Ringer.*

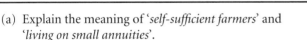

(a) Explain the meaning of '*self-sufficient farmers*' and '*living on small annuities*'.
(b) What can be inferred from the source about the reasons for the '*shocking decline in the health conditions*' of the German people?
(c) How valuable is the source to an understanding of the effects of hyperinflation on the German people? (In your answer use relevant background knowledge as well as information derived from the source.)

3

The Weimar Republic – Years of Challenge 1924–8

INTRODUCTION

At the end of 1918 much of Europe lay devastated and exhausted. In several countries, extremist political parties took advantage of the chaos and tried to seize power. Earlier, in 1917, disillusionment with the war had led to a revolution in Russia and, twelve months later, in other countries there were several attempted left-wing coups by groups seeking to copy the example set by Lenin's Bolsheviks. Left-wing agitation almost invariably led to a right-wing backlash. Most spectacular was that staged by Mussolini in Italy in 1922. There it was the consequence of the failure of numerous short-lived governments to cope with the country's economic problems and deal with left-wing inspired strikes and demonstrations. As we have seen, the drift towards dictatorship might well have extended to post-war Germany but there the Weimar Republic survived attempts to overthrow it. Among the fiercest opponents of the Republic were the National Socialists or Nazis. In this chapter we will examine the origins and the rise of the Nazi Party. We will need to consider if it could truly claim that, unlike Mussolini's Fascists, it gained power legally and with the backing of the German people.

1 ⌐ THE NATIONAL SOCIALIST MOVEMENT

A *Origins*

In March 1918, Anton Drexler, together with Karl Harrer, formed the *Freier-Arbeiter-Ausschuss*, the Committee for Independent Workmen.

The group, which consisted mainly of artisans and people from the lower middle class, met regularly to discuss political matters. Drexler's stated aim was to build 'a bridge between the masses and the nationalist right'. In January 1919, Drexler decided to go it alone and founded his own *Deutsche Arbeiterpartei* (DAP), the German Workers' Party. Members of the new Party met once a week in the Sternecker Brau, a beer hall. The topics they discussed included Germany's shame, concern about the breakdown of law and order and the nation's moral standards. They were openly hostile to the wealth and privileges of the upper classes and were strongly anti-Semitic. They called for quite unusual reforms, such as limiting the annual profits of firms to 10,000 marks and the right of skilled workers to be considered middle class. Drexler shrewdly noted that happiness lay not 'in talk and empty phrases at meetings, demonstrations and elections but in good work, a full cookpot and a fair chance for the children'. He described his party as being 'a classless socialist organisation led only by German leaders'. Other members of Drexler's group were Ernst Röhm, Dietrich Eckart, Ritter von Epp and Gottfried Feder.

B *Hitler's involvement with the movement*

At this time, Adolf Hitler, who was still serving in the German army, had been appointed a *Bildungsoffizier*, an instruction officer with the political department of the army's district command in Munich. His job was to see that young Germans were not easily indoctrinated with ideas such as socialism and pacifism. In September, he was ordered to attend a meeting of the German Workers' Party and report on its activities. As usual, the meeting took place in the Sternecker Brau and, on that particular evening, members had gathered to hear a talk by Gottfried Feder. Feder, a political and economic theorist, was later to make an important contribution to the planning of Nazi Party policy. That evening, he spoke of the means by which capitalism could be eliminated. Hitler, impressed by what he heard, rose frequently to question the speaker. Drexler is said to have whispered to his neighbour, 'Man, he has a big mouth; we could use him'. As Hitler left, Drexler handed him a copy of his pamphlet, *Mein Politisches Erwachen* (My Political Awakening). Hitler later recalled the meeting:

> After I had heard Feder's first lecture, the thought flashed through my head that I had found the essential suppositions for the founding of a new party... The development of Germany was clear enough to show me that the hardest battles of the future were to be fought not against enemy nations, but against international capital. I felt a powerful prophecy of this coming battle in Feder's lecture.

C *Hitler, leader of the Party*

Shortly afterwards, Hitler received an unsolicited membership card with an invitation to the Party's next committee meeting. After some thought, he joined the German Workers' Party as its 55th member. Co-opted on to the Party's committee, he was given responsibility for recruitment and propaganda. He enthusiastically organised gatherings and recruiting campaigns and, as the Party grew, he took to addressing the meetings himself. Early in 1920, 2,000 attended the Party's first rally. Adolf Hitler had found an outlet for his talents as an organiser and political agitator. Beyond Drexler's control, within a year he was leader of the Party and immediately set about giving it a fresh impetus and a keener cutting edge. Using his undoubted skills as a rabble-rouser, he found that he was able to sway large audiences. The main objects of his outbursts were the 'stab in the back' in 1918, the betrayal of the nation at Versailles, the policies of the Weimar government and the existence of a Marxist-Jewish plot to undermine and subvert the German people. He spoke of a need for strong national leadership to deal with the problems facing Germany. In 1920, as the *Deutsche Arbeiterpartei* put forward a new Twenty-five Point Programme, Hitler made plans to further reorganise the Party.

D *The Twenty-five Point Programme*

The programme gave a very clear indication of the Party's main objectives. These included demands for:

1. the union of all Germans to form a Greater Germany on the basis of the right of self-determination;
2. the Treaties of Versailles and St. Germain to be scrapped (the Treaty of St. Germain was the post-war settlement agreed with Austria);
3. sufficient land and colonies to feed the German people as well as the provision of adequate room for the resettlement of any surplus German population;
4. citizenship of the State to be granted only to people of German blood. Accordingly, no Jew was to be a member of the nation;
5. non-Germans to live in Germany only as guests;
6. the right to vote in elections to be allowed only to German citizens. All official appointments to be filled by Germans;
7. the first duty of the government to be to provide work for all its citizens. Foreign nationals (non-Germans) to be deported if it should become impossible to feed the entire population;
8. all non-German immigration to cease. All non-Germans who entered the country after 2 August 1914 to be required to leave;
9. all German citizens to have equal rights and duties;
10. all German citizens to undertake physical or mental work and that such work must be for the general good;
11. the abolition of all incomes unearned by work and an end to the slavery of having to pay high interest charges;
12. personal enrichment from war to be regarded as a crime and such profits to be confiscated;
13. the nationalisation of all businesses which had been formed into corporations;
14. profit-sharing in major industrial enterprises;
15. adequate insurance cover for the old;
16. large department stores to be divided up and leased to small traders;

17 an end to all speculation in land and the seizure of land needed for communal purposes without compensation;

18 the ruthless prosecution of criminals whose activities were against the public interest (to include punishment by death of common criminals, money-lenders and profiteers);

19 the practice of using Roman Law to be replaced by German common law;

20 higher education to be available to every 'able and hardworking German'. School curricula to be 'brought into line with the requirements of practical life'. All pupils to be taught civic affairs. The gifted children of poor parents to be educated at the expense of the State;

21 health standards to be raised by protecting mothers and infants and banning child labour. Gymnastics and sports to be compulsory;

22 the abolition of mercenary armies and the formation of a people's army;

23 all newspaper editors and contributors to be German, and non-German newspapers only to appear with the permission of the government. Newspapers which publish material liable to undermine the national interest to be banned;

24 religious freedom for all – providing the views expressed by denominations did not threaten or offend the German people;

25 the creation of a strong central government for the Reich to put the new programme into effect. The government to have unconditional authority over the entire Reich.

Whilst provision for the young and old, a crackdown on crime and other features of the programme might appear in the manifesto of any present-day British political party, the stated aims of the German Workers' Party included a hidden agenda. In addition to being openly racist and anti-capitalist, it also included numerous limitations on civil liberties essential to the establishment of a dictatorship.

E *An exercise on the Twenty-five Point Programme*

Examine Hitler's Twenty-five Point Programme and consider which of the points might be classified as:

Points in the Party's Programme
seeking to revise the terms of the Treaty of Versailles
aimed at bringing about an improvement in the country's economic condition
intended to improve standards of education

	Points in the Party's Programme
aimed at restricting civil liberties	
anti-capitalist	
nationalist	
anti-Semitic	

F *The formation of the* Sturmabteilung *and other changes*

Hitler needed personal protection and a means of ensuring security at his meetings and disrupting those of his rivals. It was with these aims in mind that, in 1921, he took steps towards creating a force of stormtroopers, the *Sturmabteilung*. Generally known by the abbreviation SA or, from the colour of their uniform, the Brownshirts, they were recruited from among disgruntled ex-*Freikorps* members, the unemployed and the criminal classes. Much feared and a law unto themselves, their rowdy gangs roamed the streets offloading Nazi propaganda and threatening to beat up those who gave offence, real or imagined. In order not to raise the suspicion of the allied Control Commission, they claimed to be the 'Gymnastic and Sports Section' of the movement! From the start, they showed greater allegiance to their own leaders than senior Party officials.

Hitler also appreciated the propaganda value of using symbols, salutes and slogans and of attracting to the Party nationally known figures and celebrities. He adopted the swastika (the *Hakenkreuz* or crooked cross) as the Party emblem and introduced the raised arm salute. He changed the name of the Party to the *Nationalsozialistische Deutsche Arbeiterpartei*, the National Socialist German Workers' Party or NSDAP. The term Nazi is an acronym of N*ationalsozialistische*.

Among new converts to the Nazi cause were several high-ranking soldiers, including Ludendorff. Hermann Göring, a combat pilot who had taken over command of Richthofen's squadron after the death of the Red Baron, was another who joined the Nazis.

Across Germany there were numerous other groups which shared aspects of Hitler's ideology. The *völkisch* movement, which had developed after the war, consisted of people eager to cultivate and exploit nationalist extremism and racial awareness. They emphasised the features that were distinctive of the German race and the need to eliminate the corrupting influence of others. The most prominent of several small political parties based on ex-servicemen's organisations was the *Kampfbund*, the Militant Association, a Bavarian rightist group. The Nazi leader, unwilling to compromise or tolerate the interference of others, made no attempt to bring these right-wing elements together. Just who was Adolf Hitler, the charismatic orator who had hijacked Drexler's party and remodelled it to his own requirements?

KEY ISSUE

Hitler's need to reorganise the Party.

1889	Adolf Hitler born at Braunau-am-Inn in Austria
1903	After father's death went to live in Linz
1905	Moved to Vienna and failed to gain place in Academy of Arts
1909	After a period of homelessness, lived in a home for the destitute
1913	Moved to Munich
1914	Served in the German army
1916	Wounded during the Battle of the Somme
1918	Awarded Iron Cross (First Class); Hitler in hospital when armistice agreed and war ends
1919	German Workers' Party founded in Munich by Anton Drexler; Hitler first attended meeting of the Party
1920	Hitler appointed leader of the Party; Twenty-five Point Programme proposed
1921	First steps taken to create *Sturmabteilung* (SA)
1923	Failure of attempted *putsch* in Munich
1924	Hitler tried for treason and imprisoned at Landsberg am Lech; began work on *Mein Kampf*; first Nazis elected to the *Reichstag*

TABLE 9
Date chart: Hitler and the Nazi Party – the early years

2 ⌒ ADOLF HITLER

A *Childhood*

Adolf Hitler was born on 20 April 1889 at the Gasthof zum Pommer, a guesthouse in the small Austrian town of Braunau-am-Inn. Some mystery surrounds his family background and Hitler later went to great lengths to hide the truth. His grandmother, Maria Anna Schicklgrüber, had once worked as a domestic servant. Whilst still unmarried, she gave birth to a son, Alois. Sometime afterwards, she married Georg Heidler who agreed to bring up the child as his own. It is claimed that the child's real father was a Graz Jew named Frankenberger who had been employed in the same house as young Maria. For some reason, possibly because he was better able to care for the child, the boy was turned over to Georg Heidler's brother. Alois Schicklgrüber was first apprenticed to a shoemaker in Vienna but, at the age of 18 became a customs officer. During his career with the Austrian Customs Service, he was promoted to the highest level his educational qualifications would allow. In 1877, he changed his name from Schicklgrüber to Hitler. Alois Hitler was married three times – to Anna Glasl-Horer, Franzisca Matelsberger, by whom he had two children, and finally Klara Polzi. Twenty-three years her husband's junior, she was to bear him five children, the third of which was named Adolf. Three years after Adolf Hitler was born, his father retired to a small farm in Lambach. The young Adolf was brought up strictly. At the local school he was described as lazy and something of a loner. In spite of his genuine interest in art and history, he failed his examinations and left school with 'an elemental hatred of teachers and the education system to which he had been subjected'. In *Mein Kampf*, Hitler quite dishonestly claimed that he had been brought up in dire poverty and that, at school, he had been looked upon as a leader. His school years certainly left him with a loathing of those he

KEY ISSUE

Hitler – the influence of his adolescent years.

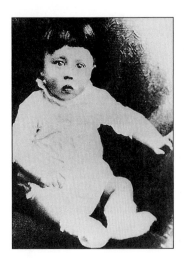  

Imperial War Museum HU3338

PICTURES 8–10
Adolf Hitler as a baby; (centre and right) Hitler's parents, Alois and Klara Hitler

considered to be educated. When his father urged him to enter the civil service, he refused saying that he did not want to work in 'a government cage'.

B *Early years*

After his father's death, Hitler left home and lived in Linz. He didn't work but lived on an allowance made by his mother. People who knew him at this time say that he seemed to live in a fantasy world. It was during this period that he first became infatuated with the music of Richard Wagner. Wagner's music, he claimed, charged him emotionally. There were certainly similarities between the two men – both came from uncertain backgrounds, both failed at school, both displayed an abnormal hatred of the Jews and both were vegetarians!

In 1905, Hitler, now aged 16, went to Vienna for the first time – a city where Jews formed a third of the total population. There, still living in a dream world, he wasted his time and made no effort to find work. He made several applications for admission to the Academy of Arts but was rejected each time. He was later to blame his failure on the prejudice of influential Jewish academics at the Academy. In 1907, his mother died. Of Hitler, overcome with grief, it is said that with her death 'whatever affection he had for any human being came to an end'. Hitler's behaviour became truly bizarre. He attacked the bourgeois world which had rejected him and claimed that around him there was only 'injustice, hatred and hostility'. Humiliated, he lived as a recluse and began to show an interest in the views of outlandish philosophers. He became fascinated by the writing of Lanz von Liebenfels who edited the magazine *Ostara*. A disgraced monk, Liebenfels wrote articles on the supremacy of the Aryan race and was strongly anti-Semitic. Hitler also read the works of Charles Darwin and was impressed by his theory of **natural selection**. Another man whose views appealed was the raving anti-Semitist Georg von Schonerer. Schonerer warned of a time when the Germans would be a minority in their own country and wanted bounties to be given to those who murdered Jews.

natural selection
survival of the fittest

C *Years of poverty and the coming of war*

In 1909, Hitler's money finally ran out. Homeless, he roamed the streets and slept rough before being taken into a home for the destitute in a Vienna suburb. Brooding and in the depths of despair, he later boasted that even then 'in my imagination, I lived in palaces'. Still refusing to find regular work, he wrote poetry and completed some paintings which he sold. In 1912, his circumstances improved when he inherited some money from an aunt. The following year, the 24-year-old Hitler finally left Vienna and moved to Munich in Germany. It is said that he left the Austrian capital in order to escape military service. In Munich, he continued his **bohemian** lifestyle until the Austrian authorities caught up with him. He was charged with avoiding military service and taken to Salzburg for a medical examination which he failed! He was back in Munich when war was declared in August 1914. Among the first to enlist, he joined the 16th Bavarian Reserve Infantry Regiment and served as a runner. According to his commanding officer, he lacked leadership qualities and consequently he never rose above the rank of corporal. He was a brave and dedicated soldier and was twice wounded and twice awarded the Iron Cross. He was in hospital recovering from the effects of poison gas when he first heard the news that the German High Command had asked for an armistice. In *Mein Kampf*, Hitler recalled his feelings:

bohemian an unconventional person who rejects a normal way of life

> They wanted to capitulate. Was such a thing really possible?. . .I tottered and groped my way back to the dormitory, threw myself on my bunk and dug my burning head into my blanket and pillow. . .And so it had all been in vain. In vain all the sacrifices and privations, in vain the hunger and thirst of months which seemed endless; in vain the hours in which, with mortal fear clutching at our hearts, we nevertheless did our duty; and in vain the deaths of millions who died. Would not the graves open of those, who with faith in the fatherland, had marched forth never to return. Would they not open and send the silent mud and blood covered heroes back as spirits of vengeance to the homeland which had cheated them with such mockery. . .Did all this happen only so that a gang of wretched criminals could lay hands on the fatherland?

3 ↬ THE MUNICH *PUTSCH*, NOVEMBER 1923

A *Background*

Bavaria and its state capital, Munich, already had a reputation for political extremism. In November 1918 Kurt Eisner attempted to set up a council of workers and soldiers to run Bavarian affairs. This was followed by months of confusion during which Eisner was murdered, then, in April 1919, Ernst Toller proclaimed a Communist-type republic in Munich. After a week of fighting, Toller's regime was crushed. As fear of yet another left-wing coup persisted, so right-wing groups became increasingly active in Bavaria. In 1921, Gustav von Kahr became head of a right-wing government. Behaving increasingly like a dictator, he openly resisted control from Berlin, encouraged **Bavarian separatism** and refused a Berlin demand that Bavarians should surrender all their weapons. During this period, Bavaria became a known refuge for right-wing extremists dedicated to the overthrow of the Weimar Republic. Hitler and the Nazis were against Kahr's separatist policies. In October 1922, Benito Mussolini, leader of the Italian Fascists, successfully organised a 'March on Rome' which led to the fall of the Italian government and his appointment as Prime Minister. Hitler spoke of repeating Mussolini's achievement by leading a 'March on Berlin' but Kahr and other Bavarian ministers thought his idea harebrained and refused to back his plan. Consequently, the Nazi leader plotted to out-manoeuvre them and leave them with no choice.

> **Bavarian separatism**
> the demand for Bavaria to become an independent state

B *The events of 8/9 November 1923*

On the evening of 8 November 1923, Kahr was due to address a political gathering at the Bürgerbräukeller, a beer hall in Munich. With General Otto von Lossow, the army commander in Bavaria, Hans von Seisser, head of the Bavarian state police and other prominent men in attendance, the hall was packed to capacity. Strategically placed among the audience were Nazis who had managed to smuggle arms into the hall. Kahr was well into his speech when Hitler arrived with lorries of SA and *Kampfbund* supporters. They sealed off the building before the Nazi leader, surrounded by men brandishing rifles, entered the room. To get attention, a man climbed onto a table and fired his revolver into the ceiling. Hitler then spoke to his bewildered audience:

> A national revolution has started...the hall is surrounded...no one may leave the premises. The Bavarian government and the national government have been overthrown and a provisional government is being set up. The barracks of the *Reichswehr* and the state police have been occupied; the *Reichswehr* and state police are approaching under the swastika flag.

SA men ushered Kahr and the two other Bavarian state ministers into an adjoining room where Hitler tried to cajole them into joining him. He promised them positions in his new administration but warned, 'I know that you will find this step difficult... Each one of you must assume his allotted position; whoever fails has forfeited his right to live. You must fight with me, triumph with me or die with me'. The three men, Kahr especially, reacted bravely and argued with the Nazi leader. Hitler, nevertheless, returned to the hall and told the people, quite falsely, that the three Bavarian ministers had agreed to join him. Back in the side room, he then misled Kahr by advising him that the people had indicated their willingness to 'stand behind him if he joined in'. In the end, Hitler's double-dealing paid off and the three men gave way. In the meantime, Ludendorff had arrived dressed in his Field Marshal's uniform and immediately demanded to know why Hitler had acted without keeping him fully informed. The Nazi leader once again returned to the hall and addressed his audience in a voice charged with emotion:

> Now I am going to carry out what I swore to myself five years ago when I lay crippled in an army hospital; neither to rest nor sleep until...the present pitiful Germany had been raised to a Germany of power and greatness, of freedom and glory. Amen.

In the morning, the three Bavarians were released. Kahr immediately broke the promises made to Hitler and used the local radio station to disassociate himself from the Nazi leader's actions. He also declared the National Socialist Party to be dissolved. Hitler's confidence seemed affected by the betrayal of Kahr. He also knew that, without the backing of Lossow and Seisser, he could expect no support from the army or police. Even so, he pressed ahead with his plans to mobilise his supporters in readiness to march into the centre of Munich. Led by Hitler, Ludendorff and Göring, the 3,000 Nazis easily swept aside a police cordon as they made their way towards the Odeonplatz close to the offices of the Bavarian War Ministry. Here they were confronted by a more determined and better armed detachment of police who called upon them to end their demonstration and surrender. As they converged a shot rang out and a policeman fell dead. Immediately his comrades responded by firing into the demonstrators. Some of those close to Hitler fell whilst others scattered and fled. Ludendorff alone refused to run for cover and marched boldly through the line of policemen to be placed under house arrest. Some of the Nazi leaders were immediately taken into custody whilst others were rounded up later. Sixteen Nazi demonstrators died whilst Göring, one of those at Hitler's side, was shot in the thigh. He was taken to a Munich hospital and later made his way to Austria. Hitler escaped but was captured two days later. The historian, Joachim Fest, in *The Face of the Third Reich*, described what actually happened to Hitler:

KEY ISSUE

Ludendorff's involvement.

Hitler fled, leaving behind a few thousand followers and sixteen dead. The legend, obviously put about later by himself, that he carried a helpless child out of the firing line – he even produced the child in support of his statement – has been proved false. Whilst he was hiding at Uffing am Staffelsee, in a house belonging to the Hanfstaengl family, he declared that he must end it all and shoot himself but the family succeeded in making him change his mind. Soon after he was arrested and taken to prison 'with a pale harassed face over which fell a tangled strand of hair'.

C *A failed* Putsch – *the consequences*

Many of those who took part in the *Putsch* were later destined to win high office in the Nazi leadership. These included Wilhelm Frick, Rudolf Hess, Heinrich Himmler, Ernst Röhm, Alfred Rosenberg and Julius Streicher. Gregor Strasser, travelling from Landshut, arrived too late. On the other hand, Hitler was not going to forget the betrayal of Kahr, Lossow and Seisser.

Was the 'Beer Hall *Putsch*' merely a demonstration which got out of hand or was it a genuine attempt by Hitler to use Munich as a springboard from which to win control of Bavaria and then Germany? If the latter was the case, the odds would certainly have been stacked against him. In addition to the Bavarian authorities, he would have had to face the opposition of the government in Berlin and the possible involvement of the *Reichswehr*. His action might have even triggered French intervention. Whatever, the attempted *Putsch* did serve some purpose. It provided Hitler with much needed publicity and a certain amount of prestige and the Nazi Party was now recognised as being in the forefront of German right-wing politics. The Nazi leader also learned some important lessons. The German people would not follow the Italian example, and the road to office lay through legal methods via the ballot box. To win power, he first had to gain the popular support of the masses. Still, overall the episode was quite an achievement for a man who, up to that time, had been a political nobody and whose Party had yet to make a political show in the *Reichstag* elections.

> **KEY ISSUE**
>
> *Advantages gained and lessons learned from a failed* Putsch.

4 ⌐ AFTERMATH OF MUNICH – CHARGES OF HIGH TREASON

The publicity gained by the Nazis at the time of the Munich *Putsch* was further enhanced when Hitler, Ludendorff, Röhm, Frick and four other defendants were brought to trial on charges of conspiracy to commit treason.

A *The trial*

The trial, which was held at the Infantry Officers' School in Munich, began on 24 February 1924 and lasted for 24 days. The Nazi leader was in sparkling form and dominated proceedings from the start. With the courtroom packed with journalists and with Kahr, Lossow and Seisser set to give evidence against him, he used the occasion to every advantage. With his Iron Cross pinned to his coat, Hitler began by admitting his part in the *putsch* but totally rejected the charge of high treason levelled against him:

> I cannot declare myself guilty. True, I confess to the deed but I do not confess to the crime of high treason. There is no question of treason in an action which aims to undo the betrayal of this country in 1918. Besides, by no definition can the deed of 8th and 9th November be called treason...And if we were committing treason, I am surprised that those who, at that time, had the same aims as I, are not standing beside me now... There was no such thing as high treason against the traitors of 1918. I feel myself the best of Germans who desired what was best for his people.

PICTURE 11

A cartoon of 1924 shows Ludendorff and Hitler ranting from Munich beer-mugs. A judge argues, 'High treason? Rubbish! The worst we can charge them with is breaking bye-laws about entertaining in public.'

More accuser than accused, he spoke with great fervour as he charged Ebert and Scheidemann with being the real traitors and then shouted down those who tried to give evidence against him. The judges, clearly sympathetic to his case, did not even intervene when many of those in court stood to cheer and applaud. Hitler concluded:

> Then gentlemen, [you will not] be the ones to deliver the verdict over us, but that verdict will be given by the eternal judgement of history, which will speak out against the accusation that has been made against us... You might just as well find us guilty a thousand times, but the goddess of the eternal court of history will smile and tear up the motions of the state's attorney and the judgement of this court: for she finds us not guilty.

At the end of the trial the presiding judges had difficulty in persuading the three lay members of the court (two insurance agents and a stationer) to pass a guilty verdict. They did so in the end but only on the understanding that Hitler would serve only part of any sentence passed. After taking into consideration that 'the defendants' motives were patriotic and honourable', Hitler was sentenced to five years fortress arrest, whilst Ludendorff was acquitted. The press, which allocated many columns to the courtroom drama and gave verbatim reports of Hitler's speeches, provided the Nazi leader with an excellent propaganda platform. Many Germans were impressed by the hero's role he had played so effectively.

> **KEY ISSUE**
>
> *Hitler's defence – its propaganda value.*

B *Imprisonment at Landsberg am Lech*

Hitler was sent to the old fortress prison at Landsberg, a town on the River Lech in southern Bavaria. Fortress arrest was the most lenient form of detention and, making the most of his privileges allowed by the easygoing regime, the Nazi leader enjoyed celebrity status. Hitler found time to read, write and receive unlimited visitors and, on the occasion of his 35th birthday, the gifts he received reportedly filled several rooms. Even more important, it gave him time to take stock of the situation and in his cell, which he shared with Rudolf Hess, he began work on his biography. The book, *Mein Kampf* (My Struggle), was to become the best-selling bible of the National Socialist movement.

5 ⌐ *MEIN KAMPF*

A *The writing of* Mein Kampf

Only the first volume of *Mein Kampf* was written whilst Hitler was in Landsberg prison. He dictated a draft of its content to two fellow prisoners, Rudolf Hess (see pages 166–7) and Emile Maurice, who later became Hitler's personal bodyguard and chauffeur. The remainder of *Mein Kampf* was written between 1925 and 1929 following Hitler's release from prison. He first intended to call the book *Four and a Half Years of Struggle Against Lies, Stupidity and Cowardice*, but his publisher advised him to use a shorter title.

B *The contents of* Mein Kampf

Mein Kampf is dedicated to the 16 men who lost their lives at the time of the Munich *Putsch*. In the author's preface, Hitler states that his reason for writing the book is to 'destroy the legendary fabrications which the Jewish press have circulated about me'.

Mein Kampf is not an easy book to read. As for Hitler's literary style and views, judge for yourself from the extracts which follow on next pages.

Author's Preface

ON April 1st, 1924, I began to serve my sentence of detention in the Fortress of Landsberg am Lech, following the verdict of the Munich People's Court of that time.

After years of uninterrupted labour it was now possible for the first time to begin a work which many had asked for and which I myself felt would be profitable for the Movement. So I decided to devote two volumes to a description not only of the aims of our Movement but also of its development. There is more to be learned from this than from any purely doctrinaire treatise.

This has also given me the opportunity of describing my own development in so far as such a description is necessary to the understanding of the first as well as the second volume and to destroy the legendary fabrications which the Jewish Press have circulated about me.

In this work I turn not to strangers but to those followers of the Movement whose hearts belong to it and who wish to study it more profoundly. I know that fewer people are won over by the written word than by the spoken word and that every great movement on this earth owes its growth to great speakers and not to great writers.

Nevertheless, in order to produce more equality and uniformity in the defence of any doctrine, its fundamental principles must be committed to writing. May these two volumes therefore serve as the building stones which I contribute to the joint work.

[signature: Adolf Hitler]

The Fortress,
Landsberg am Lech.

AT half-past twelve in the afternoon of November 9th, 1923, those whose names are given below fell in front of the *Feldherrnhalle* and in the forecourt of the former War Ministry in Munich for their loyal faith in the resurrection of their people :

Alfarth Felix, Merchant, born July 5th, 1901

Bauriedl Andreas, Hatmaker, born May 4th, 1879

Casella Theodor, Bank Official, born August 8th, 1900

Ehrlich Wilhelm, Bank Official, born August 19th, 1894

Faust Martin, Bank Official, born January 27th, 1901

Hechenberger Ant, Locksmith, born September 28th, 1902

Koerner Oskar, Merchant, born January 4th, 1875

Kuhn Karl, Head Waiter, born July 26th, 1897

Laforce Karl, Student of Engineering, born October 28th, 1904

Neubauer Kurt, Waiter, born March 27th, 1899

Pape, Claus von, Merchant, born August 16th, 1904

Pfordten Theodor von der, Councillor to the Superior Provincial Court, born May 14th, 1873

Rickmers Joh., retired Cavalry Captain, born May 7th, 1881

Scheubner-Richter, Max Erwin von, Dr. of Engineering, born January 9th, 1884

Stransky Lorenz Rittern von, Engineer, born March 14th, 1899

Wolf, Wilhelm, Merchant, born October 19th, 1898

So-called national officials refused to allow the dead heroes a common burial. So I dedicate the first volume of this work to them as a common memorial, that the memory of those martyrs may be a permanent source of light for the followers of our Movement.

The Fortress, Landsberg a/L., October 16th, 1924,

[signature: Adolf Hitler]

PICTURE 12
The Author's Preface to Mein Kampf

On racial purity and natural selection:

> The fox remains always a fox, the goose remains a goose, and the tiger will retain the character of a tiger. The only difference that can exist within the species must be in the various degrees of structural strength and active power, in the intelligence, efficiency, endurance, etc. with which the individual specimens are endowed. It would be impossible to find a fox which has a kindly and protective disposition towards geese, just as no cat exists which has a friendly disposition towards mice.
>
> The stronger must dominate and not mate with the weaker, which would signify the sacrifice of its own higher nature. Only the born weakling can look upon this principle as cruel, and if he does so it is merely because he is of a feebler nature and narrower mind; for if such a law did not direct the process of evolution then the higher development of organic life would not be conceivable at all.

On the Jews:

> If the Jews were the only people in the world they would be wallowing in filth and mire and would exploit one another and try to exterminate one another in a bitter struggle, except in so far as their utter lack of the ideal of sacrifice, which shows itself in their cowardly spirit, would prevent this struggle from developing.
>
> The black-haired Jewish youth lies in wait for hours on end, satanically glaring at and spying on the unsuspicious girl whom he plans to seduce, adulterating her blood and removing her from the bosom of her own people. The Jew uses every possible means to undermine the racial foundations of a **subjugated** people. In his systematic efforts to ruin girls and women he strives to break down the last barriers of discrimination between him and other peoples. The Jews were responsible for bringing negroes into the Rhineland, with the ultimate idea of bastardising the white race which they hate and thus lowering its cultural and political level so that the Jew might dominate. For as long as a people remain racially pure and are conscious of the treasure of their blood, they can never be overcome by the Jew. Never in this world can the Jew become master of any people except a bastardised people.

subjugated brought under the power of or conquered

On the mentally and physically handicapped:

> Those who are physically and mentally unhealthy and unfit must not perpetuate their own suffering in the bodies of their children. From the educational point of view there is here a huge task for the People's State to accomplish. But in a future era this work will appear greater and more significant than the victorious wars of our present bourgeois epoch. Through educational means the State must teach

> individuals that illness is not a disgrace but an unfortunate accident which has to be pitied, yet that it is a crime and a disgrace to make this affliction all the worse by passing on disease and defects to innocent creatures, out of mere egotism.
>
> And the State must also teach the people that it is an expression of a really noble nature and that it is a humanitarian act worthy of admiration if a person who innocently suffers from hereditary disease refrains from having a child of his own but gives his love and affection to some unknown child who, through its health, promises to become a robust member of a healthy community.

On democracy:

> Democracy, as practised in Western Europe today, is the forerunner of Marxism. In fact the latter would not be conceivable without the former. Democracy is the breeding-ground in which the **bacilli** of the Marxist world pest can grow and spread. By the introduction of parliamentarianism democracy produced an abortion of filth and fire, the creative fire of which, however, seems to have died out.

bacilli a disease bearing germ

On the British nation:

> The British nation will therefore be considered as the most valuable ally in the world as long as it can be counted upon to show that brutality and tenacity in its government, as well as in the spirit of the broad masses, which enables it to carry through to victory any struggle that it once enters upon, no matter how long such a struggle may last or however great the sacrifice that may be necessary or whatever the means that have to be employed; and all this even though the actual military equipment at hand may be utterly inadequate when compared with that of other nations.

The first edition was full of grammatical mistakes and errors of punctuation which were later corrected. Although it has some autobiographical content, it is more a consideration of Hitler's views and future plans. Since the book was designed to appeal to dissatisfied elements in Germany, its content is strongly nationalistic and highly critical of the post-war settlement and the Weimar Republic. Throughout, its underlying theme is racial, emphasising the supremacy of the Aryan races, the need for racial purity and contempt for the Jews. It is also scornful of Marxists, Catholics, pacifists and those holding democratic and liberal ideals.

On publication, a Berlin newspaper critic described *Mein Kampf* as 'the ramblings of a lunatic' and historians have largely tended to agree with that original estimate of its worth. In *Hitler and Germany*, B.J. Elliott comments, 'If Hitler was a forceful speaker, he was certainly no writer'. The American historian Louis L. Snyder describes it as 'crudely written, turgid in style...filled with long words, awkward expressions and constant repetition, all reflecting a half-educated man' whilst Fest notes that 'the pages devoted to anti-Semitism give off a stench of naked obscenity'. Bullock's view is that 'as a political best seller it was a failure, with few, even among the Party members, having the patience to read it'. Whatever the book's literary merits, by 1939 it had sold over five million copies, been translated into 11 languages, provided Hitler with an income and eventually made him a rich man. In retrospect, it might also be claimed that had people spent more time studying *Mein Kampf* rather than debunking it, they might have been better prepared for events soon to unfold!

6 ⌐ THE NAZI PARTY DURING HITLER'S IMPRISONMENT

During the time Hitler was in prison planning his future strategy and dictating *Mein Kampf*, he appointed Alfred Rosenberg to manage the affairs of the Nazi Party.

ALFRED ROSENBERG (1893–1946)

Alfred Rosenberg was born in Tallinn in Estonia, then a province of Russia. For a time he lived in Paris where he studied architecture and taught art but in 1920 he emigrated to Germany. He became a German citizen, settled in Munich and soon afterwards joined the Nazi Party. A scholarly and outwardly cultured and respectable man, he disliked and was disliked by the rough element in the Party. An influential Party ideologist, he was first appointed by Hitler editor of the Nazi newspaper *Völkischer Beobachter* (Racial Observer). He used the paper to popularise Nazi racial theories. He wrote copiously and his works included *The Tracks of the Jew Through the Ages* and *The Crime of Freemasonry* (1921). In his most famous book *The Myth of the Twentieth Century* (1930), he urged Germans to reject Christianity in favour of pagan mythology. He denounced the Old Testament as being responsible for 'our present Jewish domination' and claimed that the Christian churches were based on 'prodigious, conscious and unconscious falsifications'. Hitler thought his book 'illogical rubbish' whilst Goebbels described it more crudely as an 'ideological belch'. Outspoken Max Amann, who became the Nazi Party's business manager, bluntly described him as 'a buffoon, the stuck-up crackpot ninny'. Fest's view is that the real tragedy of Rosenberg was that 'he really believed in National Socialism'. He was certainly a strange choice as temporary Party leader. Was it, as he himself thought, a move intended to hasten the break-up of the Party so that Hitler, on his release, could start again from scratch?

MAP 4
Hitler and the Nazi Party – the early years

Without Hitler at the helm, the Nazi Party, which had officially been dissolved, began to break up into warring factions. Personal rivalries developed and there were squabbles over ideological differences. In 1924, an alliance of extreme right-wing parties, the *Völkisch-Nationaler Block*, decided to contest the election. Several Nazis, including Ludendorff, Röhm and Rosenberg, put themselves forward as candidates. The *Block* received over two million votes and sent 32 deputies to the *Reichstag*. Of these, ten, including Feder, Frick, Ludendorff, Röhm and Strasser, were former members of the now dissolved Nazi Party. From his cell at Landsberg, Hitler fumed at their betrayal.

Q

To what extent did the Party decline during Hitler's imprisonment?

7 ⌁ WEIMAR POLITICS, 1923–8

A *Introduction*

The five and a half years which followed the collapse of Stresemann's 'Grand Coalition' was a period during which two men shared the German chancellorship six times. They were Wilhelm Marx, leader of the Centre Party, and Hans Luther, a non-party politician.

Still without the support of the SPD, Marx took over Stresemann's minority government operating under the state of emergency declared

TABLE 10
*Governments of the Weimar
Republic, November 1923 – June
1928*

	Chancellor	Composition of the Coalition
Nov 1923 – Jun 1924	Wilhelm Marx *(Reichstag elections of May 1924)*	Centre/DDP/DVP/BVP
Jun 1924 – Jan 1925	Wilhelm Marx *(Reichstag elections of Dec 1924)*	Centre/DDP/DVP
Jan 1925 – Dec 1925	Hans Luther	Centre/DVP/DNVP/BVP
Jan 1926 – May 1926	Hans Luther	Centre/DDP/DVP/BVP
May 1926 – Dec 1926	Wilhelm Marx	Centre/DDP/DVP/BVP
Jan 1927 – Jun 1928	Wilhelm Marx	Centre/DVP/DNVP/BVP

in October 1923. It was against this background that a plan intended to assist German economic recovery was approved by the *Reichstag* in April 1924.

B *The Dawes Plan, 1924*

The plight of the German economy had become a matter of worldwide concern and it was through the previous efforts of Stresemann that an international committee was set up to consider German finances and the ongoing problem of reparations. The committee, which sat under the chairmanship of the American financier, Charles G. Dawes, issued its report in April 1924. In order to balance the nation's budget and stabilise its currency, the Dawes Committee recommended that the national bank, the *Reichsbank*, should be reorganised under Allied supervision and that Germany should receive an international loan of 800 million gold marks. The loan was to be mainly financed by the United States. A new system for the payment of reparations was arranged so that the amount due annually was reduced and a longer period allowed for repayment. Germany was now to pay £50 million per annum for the following five years and then £125 million annually. Although the *Reichstag* approved the plan, it was far from popular with certain sections of the German people. The main advantage was that it provided a break from the massive payments previously expected but, since it fixed no final date for the end of payments, the total amount to be paid remained undecided. In addition, acceptance of the plan meant that, to some extent, control of the German central banking system passed into foreign hands. This point was hammered home by the enemies of the Republic, particularly the Nazis who claimed that the plan was 'a second Versailles'. Few seemed concerned that any recovery brought about by the Dawes Plan was dependent on American loans or seemed aware of the possible consequences of the United States finding itself in financial difficulties. In *Mein Kampf*, Hitler later reflected on the Plan:

Q

Why was German public opinion divided on the issue of the Dawes Plan?

> The result of all this was to create the mood which made many look upon the Dawes Plan as a blessing... From a higher point of view, we may speak of one sole blessing in the midst of so much misery. The blessing is that, though men may be fooled, Heaven can't be bribed. For Heaven withheld its blessing... It has given us our deserts... Now that the nation has learned to cry for bread, it may one day learn to pray for freedom.

The following month, Marx asked the *Reichstag* to extend the period of government by presidential decree. When it refused, he had no option but to resign and call for elections.

C *The coalitions of Marx and Luther*

Although the SPD just about managed to remain the largest party, the real victors were the parties of the extreme right and left where the DNVP, the various nationalist groups which made up the *Völkisch-Nationaler Block*, and the KPD made significant gains. The Communists emerged from nowhere to become a major party backed by mass support. As a result, Marx returned to lead another centre-right coalition made up of DDP, Centre and DVP members which differed little from its predecessor. Still in a minority and with divisions within his government, Marx's survival depended on the support of members of non-government parties, the SPD and the DNVP. Faced by an increasingly hopeless situation, he tried to strengthen his coalition by inviting the SPD back into government but the Centre and DVP would have none of it. In December, after just six months in office, Marx was forced to call a second *Reichstag* election in the same year for very much the same reasons as he had called the first – to find a way out of the political deadlock.

With 31 seats gained, the SPD retrieved much of the ground lost in the elections of 1920 and May 1924. In an atmosphere of greater polit-

TABLE 11
The Reichstag *election of May 1924*

		Number of seats
Social Democrats	(SPD)	100
Nationalist Party	(DNVP)	95
Catholic Centre	(Zentrum)	65
Communist Party	(KPD)	62
People's Party	(DVP)	45
* *Völkisch-Nationaler Block*		32
Democratic Party	(DDP)	28
Bavarian Party	(BVP)	26
Independent Socialists	(USPD)	0
Others		29

* The *Völkisch-Nationaler Block* included Nazi Party members (see page 67)

		Number of seats
Social Democrats	(SPD)	131
Nationalist Party	(DNVP)	103
Catholic Centre	(Zentrum)	69
People's Party	(DVP)	51
Communist Party	(KPD)	45
Democratic Party	(DDP)	32
Bavarian Party	(BVP)	16
* *Völkisch-Nationaler Block*		14
Independent Socialists	(USPD)	0
Others		29

* The *Völkisch-Nationaler Block* included Nazi Party members (see page 67)

ical stability and with the economic situation improving, extremist parties had lost their appeal. Although the Communists fared badly, it was the Nazis and their nationalist partners who lost most heavily. The new Chancellor was Hans Luther.

Although Luther was non-party, he was an experienced politician who had already served as Food Minister and Finance Minister under Cuno, Stresemann and Marx. He followed the practice of his predecessor and again formed a centre-right coalition which excluded the SPD. For the first time, he brought members of the DNVP into the government. Luther's first coalition had only been in office a month when Friedrich Ebert's death made the election of a new president necessary. Eight candidates stood in the first round of the election and Karl Jarrès, although only a compromise candidate, won over ten million votes but failed to gain the necessary overall majority. Otto Braun of the DDP was the second most popular choice with Wilhelm Marx, the former Chancellor, coming third. Ludendorff, with barely a quarter of a million votes, came last with the additional humiliation of being beaten by Ernst Thälmann, the Communist. The second round was contested by Marx, Thälmann and a new candidate, Paul von Hindenburg. Enticed out of retirement by the old navy chief, von Tirpitz, but with his candidature strongly opposed by Stresemann, the 76-year-old field marshal was still held in high regard by the nation. If nothing else, the upright and distinguished Prussian aristocrat certainly looked the part. A snob with no fondness of the Republic or its democratic institutions, he was most at home in the company of military figures and those of his own social class. Stresemann expressed the view that the German people would never be content with a head of state who was a 'civilian in a top hat but still longed for a military man with a chestful of medals.' So it turned out; Hindenburg won but by the narrowest of margins over Marx with Thälmann coming nowhere.

It was during Luther's first year-long administration that Stresemann successfully negotiated a series of agreements with Britain, France and other major European powers, the Locarno Pact (see page 74). Bitterly

First round (Votes in millions)		Second round (Votes in millions)		TABLE 13
Karl Jarrès	10.41	Paul von Hindenburg	14.55	*The Presidential election of March/April 1925*
Otto Braun	7.80	Wilhelm Marx	13.75	
Wilhelm Marx	3.89	Ernst Thälmann	1.93	
Ernst Thälmann	1.87			
Willy Hellpach	1.57			
Heinrich Herd	1.01			
Erich von Ludendorff	.29			

opposed to the Pact, the DNVP withdrew from the government and forced the resignation of Luther's cabinet. The ensuing crisis lasted a number of weeks before Hindenburg intervened. Showing his true colours, he insisted that if a centre-right coalition was impossible, a minority government was preferable to one which included Socialists! As a result, in January 1926, Luther formed a new minority government.

Luther's second coalition, which comprised the Centre, DDP and DVP, lasted only four months. This time the government was brought down by something seemingly quite insignificant, a disagreement over the colour of the Republic's flag! Prior to 1919, the German flag had carried the imperial colours of black, white and red but the Republic had replaced this with a tricolour of black, red and gold. An order that diplomatic and consular offices abroad should show both flags led to uproar amongst supporters of the Republic. When, in May 1926, DDP members voted against the government on an issue of no confidence, Luther resigned.

After 15 months out of office, Wilhelm Marx returned for his third stint as Reich Chancellor. His centre-right minority government which continued to exclude the SPD did not have long to run. After seven months the DNVP backed an SPD call for a no confidence vote and, in December 1926, the government was brought down. When Marx became Chancellor for a fourth time, he formed another coalition which was even more to the right. His government, which included Centre, DVP and DNVP members, not only excluded the Socialist SPD but the democrats of the DDP as well. This time the government survived for 18 months before party differences surfaced to shatter the fragile alliance. The first was quite trivial – criticism of measures taken against pornography. Intended to protect the young from 'literary rubbish and dirt', they were seen by some as forms of cultural censorship. More damaging was the disagreement over granting equal status to state and church schools. With no compromise possible between the secular DVP and the Catholics of the Centre Party, the defeat of the latter in May 1928 caused them to withdraw from the coalition and once again force Marx's resignation.

8 ⌐ TOWARDS ECONOMIC RECOVERY

Unpopular or not, acceptance of the Dawes Plan triggered a period of economic recovery. As Germany entered a period of greater stability and prosperity, resentment against the Republic faded and people became less interested in extremist politics. Although much of it was used to pay reparations, between 1924 and 1930 the country received 25.5 billion marks in American loans as well as substantial sums in the form of foreign investments. The inflow of foreign capital allowed the Weimar government to embark on a programme of public building which saw the constructions of new hospitals and schools. In addition, gas and electricity services were taken into public ownership. Big business and the nation's industrial giants flourished, with the coal, iron and steel industries attaining something approaching their pre-war levels of production. German workers benefited as real wages, the value of wages measured in terms of the goods and services they will buy, returned to their pre-war level and hours shortened and social insurance cover improved. As a result, strikes and working days lost fell dramatically. This new-found prosperity did not extend to everyone. Farming recovered slowly after the war and agricultural wages and living standards lagged behind that of the rest of the community. With 20 per cent of agricultural land belonging to less than 1 per cent of the population, land ownership was a major issue. In 1919, the *Reichssied-lungsgesetz*, the Reich Resettlement Law, undertook to confiscate large estates and make the land available for redistribution and resettlement. Due to the opposition of the landowners and **Junker**, very little progress was made so that by 1928 only 500,000 hectares of land had been made available to benefit less than 3 per cent of the farming community. It is important not to overestimate the extent of German economic recovery. Unemployment still stood at nearly two million and with the economy heavily dependent on loans, foreign indebtedness had risen to half the national income. In truth, the German people were enjoying 'borrowed prosperity' as Stresemann recognised when he said, 'Germany is dancing on a volcano. If the loans are called in a large section of our economy will collapse'.

Junker rich, landowning class, descended from the former militaristic Prussian nobility

KEY ISSUE

The German economy – 'Dancing on a volcano'?

9 ⌐ STRESEMANN AND GERMAN FOREIGN POLICY

Although Gustav Stresemann was German Chancellor for only five months in 1923, he was to serve as Foreign Secretary to successive Weimar governments for a further six years. During that time he worked to improve the nation's standing and restore Germany to its rightful place among European nations. To achieve this, he tried to bring about a better understanding with France and was prepared to collaborate with the allied governments by accepting the obligations

TABLE 14
The economics of the Weimar Republic, 1919–28

(To make it possible to compare the statistics of one year with another, measurements are made against a base year to which the figure 100 is allocated, as shown in the headings)

AVERAGE EARNINGS (1935 = 100)		
	Nominal Wages per week	*Real Wages per week*
1914	76.0	94.6
1926	93.4	83.2
1927	109.6	92.3
1928	124.5	102.2

POPULATION	
1914	66,790,000
1918	66,811,000
1919	62,897,000
1924	62,486,000
1928	64,393,000

COAL, IRON AND STEEL PRODUCTION (1913 = 100)			
	Coal	*Iron*	*Steel*
1918	83.2	61.4	68.6
1921	71.7	40.6	57.7
1923	32.8	25.6	36.0
1926	76.4	49.9	70.6
1928	79.4	61.1	84.8

COST OF LIVING (1914 = 100)	
1924	130.8
1925	141.8
1926	142.1
1927	147.9
1928	151.7

UNEMPLOYMENT		
	Total	*% of working population*
1921	346,000	1.8
1924	927,000	4.9
1926	2,025,000	10.0
1928	1,312,000	6.2

INDUSTRIAL PRODUCTION (1928 = 100)	
1918	55
1922	70
1923	46
1925	81
1928	100

INDUSTRIAL DISPUTES		
	Strikes and lockouts	*Working days lost*
1913	2,462	11,761
1918	532	1,453
1919	3,719	33,083
1921	4,485	15,874
1924	1,973	36,198
1926	351	1,222
1927	844	6,144
1928	739	20,399

imposed at Versailles. In July 1925 his efforts were rewarded when the French and Belgian governments agreed to withdraw their troops from the Ruhr. At the end of the year he travelled to Locarno to represent Germany at a major international conference.

A *The Locarno Pact, 1925*

The conference, called to consider the causes of international tension in Europe, opened at the Swiss town of Locarno on Lake Maggiore on 1 December 1925. It was attended by representatives of most major European powers, including Austen Chamberlain of Britain and Aristide Briand of France. Briand, apparently more agreeable than his predecessor Poincaré, was prepared to work for Franco-German reconciliation. At the conference Stresemann stated that, as far as Germany was concerned, its western frontiers with France and Belgium were final and to be maintained for all time. He also agreed that the Rhineland could remain permanently demilitarised. His attitude towards Germany's eastern frontiers was not so magnanimous. He refused to accept the existing frontiers with Poland and Czechoslovakia as final but undertook to negotiate future changes and not bring them about by force of arms. Stresemann declared, 'We are citizens each of his own country, but we are also citizens of Europe and we are joined together by a great conception of civilisation. We have the right to speak of a European idea'. The various treaties which made up the Locarno Pact were hailed as a major step towards the establishment of a lasting peace in Europe and afterwards statesmen spoke enthusiastically of a new understanding and a willingness to cooperate and work for peace, the 'Spirit of Locarno'. For their efforts, in 1926 Stresemann and Briand shared the Nobel Peace Prize. Stresemann had won quite a diplomatic triumph since he had assumed much, given away nothing and gained a great deal. Significantly, he had managed to reach agreements with both Germany's eastern and western neighbours without offending either. The Pact received a mixed reception nationally and the *Reichstag* only approved the Pact after much heated debate with 174 voting against acceptance. As acts of good faith, Britain withdrew her troops from the Rhineland and, in 1926, Germany was finally admitted to the League of Nations. Germany's membership of the League was not achieved without opposition. Spain, Portugal and Brazil were against Germany being immediately allocated a seat on the League's Council while, in Germany, some still bitterly resented the earlier Allied decision to refuse membership. Amidst the euphoria, French reaction was more muted and French troops did not leave the Rhineland until 1930. Of course old antagonisms did not disappear overnight, far from it. The following year President Hindenburg opened old wounds when, speaking publicly, he once again denied German responsibility for the outbreak of war in 1914.

B *Stresemann's motives*

Stresemann, seen by many as the man who helped stabilise European international relations, was regarded by the Communists as nothing more than a monopoly capitalist and the forerunner of Hitler. A.J. Nicholls, in *Weimar and the Rise of Hitler*, has written of his motives thus:

> Stresemann's own motives in concluding these treaties have been subject to much speculation... After his death, sections of his diaries and papers were published, and it is not surprising that the editors selected those which reinforced the picture of Stresemann the peace-maker, Stresemann the good European. With German defeat in the Second World War, a great deal more documentary evidence became available – much of it from the files of the German foreign office. It became clear that, at the same time as he was working for détente in the West, Stresemann was also expressing strongly nationalist points of view over such questions as the future of Germany's eastern fron-tiers and the possible union with Austria. In addition, there could no longer be any doubt that he knew of the secret military arrangements between Berlin and Moscow. There was nothing particularly surprising in these revelations...Stresemann had always been a German national-ist... His career in the war and after it had demonstrated this. He made few bones about the fact that it was German weakness, not a belief in pacific courses, which forced him to make concessions over such matters as passive resistance in the Ruhr, reparations or the recognition of Germany's western frontier.

10 ⌐ HITLER AND THE NAZI PARTY – 'THE WILDERNESS YEARS'

A *Difficult times*

In December 1924, a few months prior to the presidential election, Hitler was released from prison on parole. The Germany into which he re-emerged had undergone considerable change. The government had authority, order had been restored, the country had a more stable mon-etary system and the economy was starting to recover. In something approaching normality, there was less scope for political activists or even a gifted rabble-rouser such as Hitler. Some of his earlier associates were either dead or living in exile and many of his former patrons had turned their backs on him. The banned Nazi Party was no longer a credible force in German politics and the SA, although still in existence, had lost its fearsome image. To keep within the law, units had to mas-querade as sports and rifle clubs. Rosenberg, a poor stop-gap leader, had allowed the Party to disintegrate into factions which were ever at loggerheads. Julius Streicher had formed a nationalist-racist party in Bavaria while, in northern Germany, Gregor Strasser led a newly formed National Socialist Freedom Party. Supported by Röhm, it drew its support from the urban working classes and was most interested in furthering the socialist aspects of Nazi policy. Hitler had problems of his own. Austria had cancelled his citizenship and since Germany would not grant him naturalisation papers, he was stateless. Banned from political activities, he could not make speeches. There were moments when Hitler wondered if it was worth continuing and he even thought of emigrating to the United States. In 1925, he rented a house in Ober-salzberg where his widowed half-sister, Angela Raubal, kept house for him. During this time, he became infatuated with his niece, Geli. A 17-year-old blonde and 20 years his junior, she became his close companion for the next six years. (Their relationship was an embarrassment to the Party until, in September 1931, she was found dead in Hitler's Munich flat. Many rumours surround the circumstances of her death.) Gradually the Nazi leader pulled himself together and, in February 1926, called a meeting of Party leaders at Bamberg in southern Germany to try and sort matters out.

KEY ISSUE

The condition of the Nazi Party during the mid-1920s.

B *The Bamberg Conference, 1926*

Hitler's decision to call the meeting was something of a gamble. His aim was to restore some semblance of party unity and agree a future programme. He certainly did not want to encourage those who hankered after a more socialist programme. To achieve his aims, he had to stage-manage the proceedings and put pressure on Strasser's delegates to come into line. Bamberg was no random choice for a meeting place. It was the centre of a strongly nationalistic region of Germany where the majority of local people likely to attend would be sympathetic to Hitler's views. Skilfully manipulating the delegates, he dominated the conference and turned what should have been an open debate into a rasping five-hour monologue. Interrupted by bursts of loud applause, he challenged Strasser's views and pleaded with the delegates not to 'trample on the memory of the National Socialist dead'. Playing his hand cunningly, he found enough common ground to bring the two sides together and eventually won the day. Even so, deep differences remained and the conflict between the nationalists and socialists within the Party was far from settled. One of those converted to Hitler's view was 29-year-old Joseph Goebbels from Rheydt in the Rhineland. His decision was to have important repercussions for both himself and the Party.

Slowly Hitler began to recover lost ground and, by mid-1926, he was once again in control of the Party. Even so, and in spite of all his efforts, Party membership had fallen to only 35,000 and there was no rush of new recruits to join. Outside their heartland of Bavaria, the going was particularly hard with the Nazis unable to compete with the SPD and KPD in the industrial areas. Even when it came to street brawling, the SA was no match for the *Rotfrontkämpferbund*, the Communist Red

Front Fighters. The Brownshirts were undisciplined and inclined to go their own way, and Hitler was still far from certain he could even depend on their loyalty. He warned, 'We will have to teach Marxism that National Socialism is master of the streets' and ordered Ernst von Salomon to set about reviving the Party's image. It was at this time that he first set up an elite force responsible for his own personal safety. This bodyguard, the *Schutzstaffel* or SS, was to play a major role in securing Nazi rule over Germany. The reformed Party's first real trial of strength was to come in 1928 with the *Reichstag* election.

Q

To what extent was the Bamberg Conference a victory for Hitler?

C *Reorganising and rebuilding the Party*

Believing that the Republic's new-found stability would not last, Hitler worked to make sure that his Party would be in a position to exploit the situation once circumstances changed in his favour. From his Munich headquarters, he planned a new framework for the Nazi Party. For reasons of organisation, Germany was to be divided into *Gaue*, or regions. Each *Gau* had a leader, a **Gauleiter**, chosen for his commitment to the Party and his enthusiasm for Nazi policies. It was success as the Gauleiter of Berlin that helped Joseph Goebbels to progress to the highest ranks in the Party. To start with, the *Gaue* had no standard size but, in 1928, they were reorganised to correspond with the established 35 *Reichstag* electoral districts. Each *Gau* was subdivided into areas, each of which roughly corresponded to that of a British county. These districts, or *Kreise*, were under the control of *Kreisleiter*. Each *Kreis* was divided into even smaller units. Known as *Ortsgruppen* and supervised by an *Ortsgruppenleiter*, each covered a city or a town. Later, cities and towns were divided into districts known as *Zellen* under *Zellenleiter* and groups of houses and flats, *Blocks*, were placed under *Blockleiter*. Although the various units had some limited freedom to deal with matters relevant to their own areas, the structure was controlled from the top by Hitler. Even so, there were conflicts within the Party. To enforce discipline, the Party leader used a system of courts, *Uschla*, and, when necessary, leaders were replaced and members expelled. By 1929, the NSDAP was a well-run political party based on a sound nationwide structure. Another aspect of the reorganisation of the Party was the restructuring of the SA. Under a new leader, Franz von Salomon, it ceased to be a rabble of street hooligans and was given more clearly defined responsibilities. These included spreading Nazi propaganda and organising demonstrations against the Communists and Jews. They had to show more restraint in case their behaviour caused the Party to be banned again. The more elite SS, *Schutzstaffel*, formed in 1926, remained relatively unimportant until Heinrich Himmler became the organisation's leader in 1929. The *Hitler Jugend*, Hitler Youth, was formed in 1926 to rival other longer established German youth organisations. It was first placed under the leadership of Kurt Gruber. There were also professional groups established for doctors, lawyers and teachers. In 1927, the Nazis held their first rally in Nuremberg, a city

Gauleiter a regional Nazi Party leader responsible for all political and economic activities, civil defence and mobilisation of labour in his district

KEY ISSUE

The structure of the Nazi Party.

rich in historical tradition and where the Party was already extremely popular.

11 ⌐ WEIMAR SOCIETY AND CULTURE – YEARS OF ILLUSION

A *Weimar attitudes*

In Germany, as elsewhere in Europe, the 1920s saw long established social attitudes and values challenged as cracks appeared in what had been a traditionally authoritarian society. The influence of the landed aristocracy had been eroded and in part replaced by the dominance of the commercial and industrial moguls; the trade unions and left-wing political parties had provided the working classes with a platform from which to fight for improved conditions and greater political representation; as women became increasingly employed in white-collar occupations so they gained economic emancipation and, in contrast to the old fashioned and staid *Hausfrauen* (housewife-types), were increasingly prepared to reject former constraints and flaunt their sexuality; many of the young who thought themselves **avant-garde** sought to shock and give society a new face; religious teachings and traditional values were questioned. Many showed themselves eager to forget the horrors of war – 'after weeping for so many dead there came a period of happy-go-lucky gaiety'. At a time when there seemed no **parameters** of good taste, new provocative fashions, forms of entertainment and crazes reached Europe from America to contribute to what was already seen as a cigarette-smoking, fast car-driving, jazz-loving, glitzy and increasingly permissive society.

avant-garde favouring the newest ideas

parameters lines which mark limits

B *Cultural developments*

In an explosion of new forms of popular entertainment, the theatre and music hall began to be replaced by the cinema – silent films to begin with, but after 1929, 'talkies'. Some film makers have tried to portray this period in German history as totally a time of self-indulgence when people were preoccupied with café-life, bars, nightclubs and striptease. *Blue Angel* (1930), which told the story of a professor's love for a night-club singer, made Marlene Dietrich an international Hollywood star. She said of the film, 'At the time, I thought the film was awful and vulgar and I was shocked by the whole thing. I was a well brought up German girl.' More recently *Cabaret* (1972), in which Liza Minella played the part of a night club singer undecided between her English lover and a homosexual German baron, tried to capture the atmosphere of Berlin as a hot-bed of vice.

But this portrayal is something of a travesty for, in truth, the Weimar years produced a diversity of new creative talent and were a time of considerable cultural achievement in Germany. The author Thomas

Mann, best known for his novel *The Magic Mountain* (1924), won the Nobel Prize for literature in 1929; the Czech-born German Franz Kafka used his novels to depict horror and the uncertainty of human life; the poet Stefan George became something of a cult figure. Among those attracted to his circle was Claus von Stauffenburg, later to become famous for his involvement in a plot to kill Hitler. A greater truth in war novels was shown by Arnold Zweig and Erich Maria Remarque. The most remarkable book of the Weimar period, Remarque's *All Quiet on the Western Front* (1929), illustrates the futility of war. Written in only six weeks, it is considered to be among the greatest anti-war books ever written. Whilst back-street Berlin might have seemed the sleaze capital, Max Reinhardt's glittering productions attracted as large audiences as, for very different reasons, did Bertolt Brecht's *Die Dreigroschenoper*, The Threepenny Opera. Even though it had a left-wing bias and depicted the social evils which led people into crime, it was immensely popular. The author of *Mein Kampf* was soon to see that the works of Mann, Remarque, Reinhardt and Brecht were outlawed!

The Bauhaus movement was a school of architecture and design founded in 1919 by Walter Gropius. It aimed to bring together artistic skills and the technical skills of mass production by using basic materials and shapes to make furniture and a wide range of household decorations, fitments and handicrafts which were 'clear, mathematically precise, economical, pure and functional'.

Metropolis, 1927–1928 (Detail) by Otto Dix, Galerie der Stadt Stuttgart/AKG-Images©DACS London 2008

PICTURE 13

A painting by the German expressionist artist Otto Dix illustrates the high life and corruption of Weimar Germany

12 ❧ BIBLIOGRAPHY

A bibliography for Chapters 1–4 appears on pages 107–8.

13 ❧ DISCUSSION TOPICS AND ESSAY QUESTIONS

A *This section consists of questions that might be used for discussion (or written answers) as a way of expanding on the chapter and testing understanding of it.*

1. To what extent might the experiences of Hitler's adolescent years have influenced his attitudes in adult life?

2. 'A beer hall brawl which got out of hand.' How valid is this judgement of events in Munich in November 1923?

3. At his trial in 1924, how justified was Hitler in denying the charge of treason?

4. Explain why some Germans were against acceptance of the Dawes Plan.

5. How valid was Stresemann's view that, from the mid-1920s, Germany was 'dancing on a volcano'?

6. On what grounds might it be claimed that the Locarno Pact (1925) was a diplomatic triumph for Stresemann?

B *Essay questions.*

1. 'By far the greatest German politician of the 1920s.' How valid is this assessment of Gustav Stresemann?
2. To what extent did the attitudes of Weimar society represent a reaction against the past?

14 ⌁ MULTI-SOURCE DOCUMENTARY EXERCISE ON THE MUNICH *PUTSCH* OF NOVEMBER 1923

Study the following sources carefully and then answer the questions based on them.

Counting on a huge popular demonstration in their favour, they hoped that...the army and police would refuse to fire. In the hour before noon about 7,000 men, in files eight abreast, their rifles slung across their backs to proclaim their peaceful intentions, marched across the bridge into the inner city. The flood advanced. In its front line marched Hitler, Ludendorff and other leaders. Suddenly the police rushed forward, levelled their rifles and took aim... Streicher screamed, 'Ludendorff! Don't shoot your general!' It was too late. A volley rent the air, killing fourteen men... Then panic seized the street. In a desperate scramble for safety, everyone fled. The revolution was finished.

SOURCE A *From* I Knew Hitler *by Kurt Ludecke, a former close associate of Hitler.*

Hitler fled, leaving behind a few thousand followers and sixteen dead. The legend...that he carried a helpless child out of the firing line...has been proved false. Whilst he was hiding...he declared that he must end it all and shoot himself but the family succeeded in making him change his mind. Soon after he was arrested and taken to prison 'with a pale harassed face over which fell a tangled strand of hair'.

SOURCE B *From* The Face of the Third Reich *by Joachim Fest.*

I cannot declare myself guilty. True, I confess to the deed but I do not confess to the crime of high treason. There is no question of treason in an action which aims to undo the betrayal of this country in 1918. Besides, by no definition of treason can the deed of 8th and 9th November be called treason... And if we were committing treason, I am surprised that those who, at that time, had the same aims as I, are not standing beside me now... There is no such thing as high treason against the traitors of 1918.

SOURCE C *Hitler's response to charges at his trial in February 1924.*

SOURCE D (PICTURE 15)

A cartoon from the German satirical magazine Simplicissimus *showing Hitler riding into Berlin with President Ebert on foot and in chains, published on 1 April 1924.*

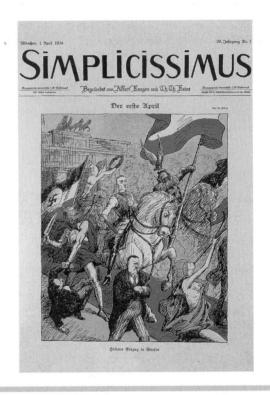

SOURCE E *From* The Munich Putsch *by A.J. Nicholls.*

The *Putsch* put an end to the hopes in Bavaria that the province could be used as the base for a right-wing assault on the Weimar Republic. It gave Hitler a great advantage from a political point of view for at his trial...he was able to claim the credit for having led the movement against the treasonable Weimar system in Berlin. Moreover, the imprisonment that followed allowed him to devote his attention to writing *Mein Kampf* in which he laid down the principles which were to guide him through the stormy years to come. His reputation among extreme nationalists was finally established throughout Germany.

Q

(a) Compare Sources A and B. To what extent do they agree the nature of Hitler's behaviour at the time of the Munich *Putsch*?

(b) To what extent do the views expressed in Sources A and E support Hitler's claim (Source C) that he was not guilty of treason?

(c) How useful are the sources to providing an understanding of the events and consequences of the Munich *Putsch*? (In your answer use your own relevant background knowledge as well as information derived from the sources.)

The Weimar Republic – Years of Crisis 1928–33

1 ⌁ AN ELECTORAL BLOW FOR THE NAZIS

In 1927 the ban on Hitler's involvement in political activities was officially lifted. The following year came the first real trial of strength of the
reformed Nazi Party in the *Reichstag* elections.

		Number of seats
Social Democrats	(SPD)	153
Nationalist Party	(DNVP)	73
Catholic Centre	(Zentrum)	62
Communist Party	(KPD)	54
People's Party	(DVP)	45
Democratic Party	(DDP)	25
Bavarian Party	(BVP)	19
Nazi Party	(NSDAP)	12
* Others		51

* Others included over 36 regional and small parties the largest of which was the Business Party (*Wirtschaftspartei*).

TABLE 15
The Reichstag *election of May 1928*

The election gave the left an impressive victory over the parties
which had previously formed Marx's centre-right coalition. The SPD
with a third of the votes cast won 153 seats in the *Reichstag*, only ten less
than in their heyday of 1919. The only others to gain significantly were
the Communists who were now the fourth largest political party in
Germany. With a meagre 12 seats and less than 3 per cent of the
popular vote, the Nazis suffered a severe blow. Hitler had spent his time
re-establishing his control over the Party rather than concentrating on
the election. In addition, the Party was not yet sufficiently well organised regionally to contest elections. Although some would have preferred Otto Braun, the SPD Prime Minister of Prussia, Hermann Müller
was appointed to lead the new coalition. Müller, who had earlier served
as Chancellor for four months in 1920, was a well-intentioned man of
great integrity but lacked the assertiveness and dynamism required of a
charismatic leader. He was far more inclined to conciliation than confrontation.

KEY ISSUE

The Nazis routed.

TABLE 16

Governments of the Weimar Republic, June 1928 – January 1933

	Chancellor	Composition of the Coalition
Jun 1928 – Mar 1930	Hermann Müller	SPD/DDP/Centre/BVP/DVP
Mar 1930 – Oct 1931	Heinrich Brüning	Rule by presidential decree
Oct 1931 – May 1932	Heinrich Brüning	Rule by presidential decree
Jun 1932 – Dec 1932	Franz von Papen	Rule by presidential decree
Dec 1932 – Jan 1933	Kurt von Schleicher	Rule by presidential decree

2 ↩ MÜLLER'S GRAND COALITION, 1928–30

Once appointed, Müller put together a Grand Coalition comprising members of the SPD, DDP, Centre and DVP. His cabinet included the ever-present Gustav Stresemann, who had served his country as Foreign Minister since 1923, and the old soldier Wilhelm Gröner as Defence Minister. With control of 301 of the 491 seats in the *Reichstag*, Müller's government should have been reasonably secure but, in reality, the coalition was flawed. From the start, the coalition partners seemed motivated more by party self-interest than the need to agree policies likely to guarantee the government's long-term survival. Plagued by internal dissent as ministers squabbled amongst themselves and with their own backbench supporters, Müller faced a vicious circle of inter-party disputes. Within the SPD, there were differences between the mainstream moderates and left-wing factions; the DVP, soon to lose the moderating influences of Stresemann, moved to the right. After Marx's resignation following his Party's poor showing in 1928, the leadership of the Centre passed to Monsignor Ludwig Kaas, a Roman Catholic priest whose main aim was to defend his Party's religious interests. With so many internal divisions and the prospect of a backlash orchestrated by the disgruntled and frustrated non-coalition parties of the right, Müller's coalition was in for a rough ride.

A *Unresolved issues*

Even before Müller took office, the issue of republic versus imperial flag still continued to simmer. In 1927, the flying of both flags at the opening of the Tannenberg Memorial so offended the republicans of the SPD that they boycotted the ceremony. An ongoing disagreement about the cost of building a new battle-cruiser, the *Panzerkreuzer A* also continued. Although previously sanctioned by Marx's government, the largely pacifist SPD were against financing what was to be the first of a series of modern German battleships. Government embarrassment was further increased when the Communists demanded a referendum on the issue.

In November 1928, the hostility of employers to state regulated compulsory arbitration in matters of pay and conditions came to a head. The owners of iron and steel works in the Ruhr finally refused to accept the pay award made by the official arbitrator and locked out their employees. Denied unemployment benefit, the plight of the workers attracted public sympathy until the government finally agreed to make payments to needy workers and their families. Behind the scenes, it took all the skills of the Interior Minister, Carl Severing, to work out a compromise solution which would keep the coalition intact. Even so, faced with a fall in tax revenue and an increase in unemployment, the issue of financing social security payments was far from settled. Above all others, the most serious problem faced by Müller's government was the future of the German economy once the provisions made by the Dawes Plan came to an end.

KEY ISSUE
Müller's difficulties.

3 ⤳ THE YOUNG PLAN, 1929

A *Background*

All arrangements made under the terms of the Dawes Plan were due to end in 1928. The Plan, which had contributed hugely to German economic recovery and provided the wherewithal for the payment of repa-

TABLE 17
Date chart of the domestic history of the Weimar Republic, 1929–33

1928	May	Electoral defeat for the Nazis
	June	Müller appointed Chancellor
1929	January	Himmler appointed head of the SS
	March	Young Plan agreed by *Reichstag*
	June	Proposals of the Young Plan made known
	July	DNVP and Nazis join forces to oppose the Young Plan
	October	Death of Gustav Stresemann; Wall Street stock market crash
1930	March	Resignation of Müller's government; Brüning takes office as leader of centre-right minority government
	July	Presidential decree used to introduce new economic measures; SPD protest over use of presidential decree leads to dissolution of the *Reichstag*
	September	Considerable Nazi gains in *Reichstag* elections (107 seats)
1931	May	Failure of leading German banks
	October	Formation of Harzburg Front alliance
1932	January	Hitler's speech to German industrialists at Dusseldorf
	April	Hindenburg re-elected President; ban on SA and SS imposed by Brüning government
	May	Resignation of Brüning's government
	June	Von Papen appointed Chancellor; ban on SA and SS lifted
	July	Elections. Nazis with 230 seats become the largest party in the *Reichstag*
	September	*Reichstag* dissolved
	November	Elections. Setback for Hitler as Nazis lose 34 seats
	December	Resignation of von Papen; von Schleicher appointed Chancellor
1933	January	Secret meeting between Hitler and von Papen; Hitler appointed German Chancellor

rations, was largely financed by foreign, almost entirely American, loans. Stresemann had warned of the vulnerability of the German economy and of the horrendous consequences of an end to the inflow of foreign loans. Uncertainty together with a steady rise in unemployment were already giving rise to serious misgivings about the future of the economy. At a meeting of the League of Nations it was announced that the Dawes Plan would be replaced by a new scheme which would arrange for the final settlement of the reparations issue. The search for a solution was entrusted to a committee of experts under the chairmanship of Owen D. Young, head of the American General Electric Company and a former member of the Dawes Committee. The leading German representatives on the Young Committee were *Reichsbank* president, Hjalmar Schacht, and the industrialist, Albert Vogler. Although the German economy was the main issue and it was essential for Germany that the committee reached a satisfactory conclusion, the German representatives took the opportunity to press for the revision of the Treaty of Versailles, the return of the Polish corridor and their former colonies.

The Young Committee finally concluded that Germany should continue to pay reparations averaging two billion marks annually for the next 59 years. Payments would rise from 1.7 billion marks in 1930 to 2.4 billion marks by 1966 and then gradually diminish. Payments would be supervised by the Bank for International Settlement and any future action taken against Germany in the event of non-payment would require the authority of the International Court of Justice at the Hague. On the credit side, Germany regained control of its banking system, knew the full extent of its reparations liability and the final date of settlement. On the debit side, the sum to be paid was still quite considerable and would remain a burden for the next 60 years, until 1988. All for a war which, they still insisted, was not solely their responsibility. The fact that a final date was agreed for the French withdrawal from the Rhineland in no way diminished the fury of the nationalists. Hitler made the point, 'Why should generations unborn be saddled with the debts of their elders?' Schacht resigned his presidency of the *Reichsbank* as a measure of his disgust but the most outspoken critic of the Young Plan was Alfred Hugenberg, the new leader of the Nationalist DNVP.

Why were some opposed to the acceptance of the Young Plan?

B *Opposition to the Plan*

Although still the second largest party in the *Reichstag*, the DNVP had lost ground in 1928. To that point, the Party had represented a broad band of right-wing opinion from middle-of-the-road conservatism to die-hard monarchism and there were times when serious differences threatened to split the party. In October 1928, when Hugenberg became leader, he set about recovering his Party's lost prestige and moved the Party decidedly to the right by rallying opposition against the Young Plan and Müller's government. At the other extreme, the third largest party, the KPD, abandoned whatever little understanding existed with the SPD and under Thälmann's leadership, became increasingly dominated by Moscow, referring to the SPD as 'social fascists' and 'the spear-head of bourgeois treason'. The bitterness between the two parties intensified after clashes during 'bloody May'. On May Day 1929, the KPD decided to ignore the ban imposed on demonstrations and took to the streets in Berlin. The authorities restored order but at a cost of 30 dead and 200 wounded.

Meanwhile, Hugenberg, leader of the DNVP, found new allies in his opposition to the Young Plan which he had now broadened to an all-out attack on the Republic. Hugenberg was one of those who made a fortune at the time of hyperflation in 1923–4 and created a great media empire. A man full of his own importance, he was described as 'an abrasive, stubborn, difficult personality, opinionated and confrontational.' Alan Bullock's assessment is no kinder – 'a bigoted German national-ist... An ambitious, domineering and unscrupulous man with large resources at his disposal.' He used the media to popularise his own views and to spread anti-government propaganda.

In his campaign against the Young Plan, Hugenberg worked closely with his Party, the DNVP, the *Stahlhelm*, the powerful, right-wing, ex-servicemen's organisation and the Pan-German League. He also had influential backers such as Schacht and Vogler. In 1929, he joined forces with Hitler and together they embarked on a scandalous attack on Müller's government. They drafted a Law Against the Enslavement of the German People which demanded a total denial of Germany's responsibility for the war, a final end to all reparations payments and charges of high treason levelled against Müller and his cabinet for their acceptance of the Young Plan. A propaganda campaign encouraged the German people to believe that they were the slaves of foreign capital. Defeated in the *Reichstag* by 311 to 60 votes, the measure was put to a national referendum where it gained less than six million votes, an unimpressive 13.8 per cent of the electorate. On 12 March 1930, the *Reichstag* finally accepted the Young Plan. Hugenberg and Hitler hoped that Hindenburg would still block the measure but, the following day, he behaved constitutionally and signed. Afterwards the right-wing press pilloried the old President. 'He has today forfeited the original unlim-ited confidence originally placed in him by every genuinely patriotic German' declared *Deutsche Zeitung* while in *Der Angriff* Goebbels scoffed, 'Is Hindenburg still alive?'

> **KEY ISSUE**
>
> *The influence of Hugenberg, the unscrupulous press baron.*

4 ⌐ GROWING ECONOMIC PROBLEMS AND THE FALL OF MÜLLER'S COALITION

As the aftermath of a collapse on the New York Stock Exchange (see pages 88–9) began to add to Germany's economic difficulties, the government found itself with a widening **trade gap**, a domestic budget deficit of 1,700 million marks and rapidly rising unemployment. The most immediate problem was the lack of financial reserves to provide benefit for the growing number out of work. To make matters worse, German industrialists were calling for a reduction of their tax burden

> **trade gap** the difference in the value of a nation's imports and exports

and less social spending. Schacht did further damage when he went as far as to warn foreign bankers not to provide loans needed by the German government to balance its budget! In December, Müller's coalition faced a vote of no confidence. Members of the *Reichstag*, aware that acceptance of the Young Plan was absolutely essential to deal with the growing economic crisis, ensured the government's survival by 222 votes to 156. Even so Müller's problems were not over. With the acceptance of the Young Plan, the historian E.J. Feuchtwanger's view was that 'the cement holding the coalition together had gone'. Within the government a rift between the SPD and the DVP led to yet another crisis. The issue was once again the financing of payments to the unemployed. With the SPD looking to reduce the budget deficit by increasing insurance contributions – from the 3 per cent fixed in 1927 to 3.5 per cent which the DVP, who represented employers' interests, resolutely opposed – a compromise deal seemed the only possible way out. When such an agreement proved impossible, the Chancellor made known his intention of asking the President to grant him emergency powers under Article 48 to introduce new social legislation. Hindenburg refused and, when Müller resigned on 27 March 1930, the last genuinely democratic government of the Weimar Republic came to an end. On the face of it, the immediate cause for the government's failure was a disagreement over a 0.5 per cent increase in insurance contributions but there were deep-rooted reasons – the failure to resolve the conflict between the SPD and DVP, fears for the future of the economy and the drift to the right in politics largely inspired by German capitalists and industrialists. No future coalition of parties was to command a majority in the *Reichstag*.

> ### KEY ISSUE
>
> *The beginning of the end for German democracy.*

5 ꙮ THE DEATH OF GUSTAV STRESEMANN, OCTOBER 1929

It was during the period of Stresemann's declining health that his People's Party (DVP) moved significantly to the right. Worn out by years of effort and increasing right-wing criticism of his policies, he died suddenly of a heart attack on 3 October 1929. He was only 51. Two months earlier, the first of the Hague Conferences agreed to the final evacuation of the Rhineland although the region was to remain demilitarised. This, together with his contribution to the Locarno Pact, were the main triumphs of Stresemann's foreign policy.

6 ꙮ THE COMING OF THE GREAT DEPRESSION

A *The Wall Street Crash, October 1929*

During the 1920s the American people enjoyed a period of unparalleled activity and prosperity. The American President, Herbert Hoover,

Differing views of Stresemann

Stresemann certainly made a major contribution to Germany's post-war rehabilitation and re-emergence as a European power but is Perry's estimate below an exaggeration? In a changing political climate, would Stresemann have successfully countered Hugenberg's influence in German politics let alone the advance of Hitler and the Nazis? Annelise Thimme gives a different view.

K. Perry, writing in *Modern European History*

Stresemann's death was a turning point in the history of the Republic largely because he had no successor. No later foreign minister contributed his unflagging pursuit of national aims with the diplomatic skill that won foreign confidence. His realism contributed to the one period of real peace in the inter-war years and, if he had lived to guide Germany through the approaching world depression, Hitler might never have come to power.

Annelise Thimme, writing in *Germany to 1929*

Stresemann could not have stopped the world economic crisis, nor could he have prevented the growth of German right-wing extremism. Good fortune allowed him to die at the peak of his success before events could vindicate the words 'the end of Germany' that he exclaimed of Hitler's putsch in 1923.

---

boasted that his country was 'nearer the final triumph over poverty than ever before'. These years of high living, the so-called 'Roaring Twenties', came to an end in October 1929. The United States economy had thriven on an artificial boom based on high profits from rash investments which had sent the price of stocks and shares soaring above their real value. In a get-rich-quick environment, everyone who speculated made money – then the bubble burst. As prices on Wall Street fell alarmingly, so Americans rushed to sell their shares whilst they still had some value. On 24 October 1929, 'Black Thursday', during panic selling on the New York stock exchange 13 million shares changed hands in one day. The heavy selling continued and reached a climax on 28 October when a further 16 million shares were sold. On 30 October the New York stock market collapsed totally. As the demand for goods and services fell, production slowed and factories were forced to lay off workers. Drained of investment, firms failed, businessmen went bankrupt and millions of American workers lost their jobs. The consequences of the crash have been likened to 'an economic blizzard' as its effects spread rapidly to Europe and the rest of the world. As international business and trade collapsed, what William Carr has called 'the tinsel prosperity of Western Europe' came to an end. In Germany, the weakness of the foundations on which German economic revival had

Q

Simply explained, what led to the collapse of the American stock market in 1929?

depended were exposed for all to see. The so-called 'golden years' of the Weimar Republic were nearly over.

B *The impact of the world recession on Germany*

As we have seen, German prosperity was largely dependent on American loans. In 1927 and 1928, Germany had borrowed almost five times the amount needed for reparations' payments. Now with support of the mark at an end, with loans drying up and American bankers calling in existing loans, Germany lurched into crisis. Mindful of what happened in 1923, people rushed to convert their savings into gold or a stronger foreign currency. So large quantities of gold and foreign exchange left the country and, in the first two weeks of June 1931 alone, foreign funds totalling 1,000 million marks went overseas. The clamour for gold led to a run on banks. In the summer of 1931, the Austrian *Kreditanstalt* failed and, soon afterwards, the German *Norddeutsche Wollkammerei* and *Darmstadterbank* collapsed. To counter this panic selling, the government ordered the banks to close and placed restrictions on the movement of money. The shortage of ready money caused inconvenience and hardship. German heavy industry was particularly badly hit. Between 1929 and 1932, the demand for steel, machine goods, shipping and chemicals fell rapidly and, as a result of the slump in world trade, the value of German exports fell by 55%, from £630 million in 1929 to £280 million in 1931. German agriculture was in difficulties before the Wall Street Crash. As a result of the harvest failure in 1928 and the collapse of world prices for agricultural products, so the plight of already hard-pressed German farmers further increased.

Unemployment, just 132,000 in 1929, rose to three million within a year and then leapt to over five million by the spring of 1931. By mid-1932, there were nearly six million registered unemployed with the real total nearer 8.5 million. Four out of every ten Germans were without jobs. As we shall see, the economic crisis which created armies of unemployed was also going to have major political consequences.

> **Q**
>
> ...and why did it have such an impact on Germany?

TABLE 18

The decline in exports and production, 1929–33

	German exports 1929–33 (1913 = 100)	Industrial production 1929–33 (1928 = 100)	
1929	98.0	1929	100
1930	92.2	1930	87
1931	82.7	1931	70
1932	55.6	1932	58
1933	50.7	1933	66

7 ↜ THE BRÜNING YEARS, MARCH 1930 — MAY 1932

The fall of Müller's coalition meant that, for the remaining years of the Weimar Republic, the SPD would be excluded from office. Although their support remained solid and, until July 1932, they continued to be the largest party in the *Reichstag*, they were destined to be permanently an opposition party though not without influence. On 28 March 1930, Hindenburg nominated Heinrich Brüning of the Centre Party to lead a new minority government. The President held Brüning in high esteem because of his impressive war record and devout Catholicism. So great was Hindenburg's admiration that he threatened to resign the presidency if Brüning refused the chancellorship. His choice was also supported by his confidantes, the military men Gröner and von Schleicher. At 45, Brüning became the youngest man to hold the office of Reich Chancellor.

HEINRICH BRÜNING (1885–1970)

Born in Münster into a middle-class family, Brüning was an educated man with a doctorate in economics. He also had a distinguished war record and, as a machine-gun officer, had been awarded the Iron Cross for bravery. After the war, he became involved in the Catholic trade union movement and, in 1924, was elected to the *Reichstag* as deputy for Silesia. By 1929, he had progressed to the leadership of the Catholic Centre Party. Although on the anti-socialist right of his party and a monarchist at heart, he was a democrat. Importantly, Brüning recognised and did not underestimate the growing threat of Hitler and the Nazi Party.

A *Brüning's first administration, March 1930 – October 1931*

Brüning's cabinet was made up of Centre, DVP, DNVP and non-party members. To start with, he tried to rule by arranging **ad hoc** alliances to back each piece of legislation but this proved time-consuming and made effective day-to-day government impossible. In July 1930, Finance Minister Hermann Dietrich put forward a number of financial proposals intended to tackle Germany's economic problems. When these deflationary measures, which included tax increases and reductions in government expenditure, were rejected by the *Reichstag*, Hindenburg brought into play Article 48 of the Weimar Constitution which allowed rule by presidential decree. Two days later, after an SPD motion calling for the withdrawal of the decree was narrowly approved, Hindenburg dissolved the *Reichstag* and called for an election. Many historians claim that it was Hindenburg's decision to by-pass the *Reichstag* and authorise rule by decree which ended parliamentary government and concluded the years of German democracy. The introduction of rule by presidential decree certainly made Brüning entirely dependent on Hindenburg and, as some have claimed, reduced the role of the Chancellor to that of merely being the President's yes-man in the *Reichstag*.

ad hoc made up for a special purpose

TABLE 19
The Reichstag *election of September 1930*

		Number of seats
Social Democrats	(SPD)	143
Nazi Party	(NSDAP)	107
Communist Party	(KPD)	77
Catholic Centre	(Zentrum)	68
Nationalist Party	(DNVP)	41
People's Party	(DVP)	30
Democratic Party	(DDP)	20
Bavarian Party	(BVP)	22
Others		72

The election held in September 1930 marked a significant swing to the parties of the extreme left and right. For the NSDAP, with 6.5 million votes and 107 deputies elected to the *Reichstag*, the result was more than impressive; the Communists, with their representation increased from 54 to 77, also had good cause to celebrate. With support for the SPD and Centre holding reasonably firm, the real losers were the other nationalist parties of the right, the DNVP and the DVP, with large numbers of their supporters switching to the Nazis. As William Carr states 'two out of every five Germans voted for parties bitterly opposed to the principles on which the Republic rested'.

Since the Bamberg conference in February 1926 (see pages 76–7), Hitler had kept a reasonably low profile as he worked to further develop and reconstruct his party. The showing of the Nazis in the election of May 1928 had come as a bitter disappointment. Once Hitler became associated with Hugenberg in opposition to the Young Plan, his fortunes began to pick up. Again the centre of media attention, he attracted the backing of leading German industrialists such as Emil Kirdorf and Fritz Thyssen and, with party membership beginning to increase, the Nazis made steady gains in the local government (*Landtag*)

KEY ISSUE

The recovery of Nazi fortunes.

elections. In the hope that the changed economic circumstances would signal his Party's take-off, in 1930 Hitler campaigned vigorously and to good effect. Afterwards, Hindenburg refused Hitler's demand for a position in the cabinet and is supposed to have jokingly said that he could be postmaster-general so that he could lick stamps!

B *Brüning's second administration, October 1931 – May 1932*

Now under pressure from parties on both the extreme left and right, and faced by a rapidly worsening economic situation, Brüning's position was even more hopeless than before. Rapidly rising unemployment and the stringent economic measures now passed by decree increased the suffering of millions of Germans. The economic chaos made it easy for the extremist parties to stir up popular discontent and this often spilt onto the streets as the unruly SA took on gangs of Communists. Hitler distanced himself from such activities and played his hand carefully. Realising that he had to win over the still largely unconvinced old conservative elite – the privileged upper class including landowners, industrialists, bankers and business men – he worked to cultivate an air of greater respectability. In January 1932 he used a meeting of the influential Düsseldorf Industry Club to present the capitalist-friendly face of National Socialism and convince those present that he represented their best interests.

With many despairing of Brüning's management of the economy, a growing number began to regard Hitler as an acceptable alternative. Brüning's situation was not helped by his plan to create an Austro-German customs union. The idea upset France and he was forced to back down and so further highlight the fact that in reaching foreign policy decisions Germany still had to appease its neighbour. In October 1931, Hitler and Hugenberg joined forces in an effort to oust Brüning.

C *The Harzburg Front*

On 11 October 1931 representatives of right-wing political parties and organisations met at Bad Harzburg. They included veterans of the *Stahlhelm*, other ex-military men, industrialists, members of the now depleted DNVP and Nazis. Among the eminent individuals present were Hjalmar Schacht, Fritz Thyssen, Alfred Hugenberg and Adolf Hitler. Hugenberg called for a united front to rescue Germany from 'Bolshevik peril and bankruptcy', demanded Brüning's resignation and called for new elections. Hitler warned that Germany had to choose between nationalism and communism. The Harzburg Front represented a powerful combination of industrial, financial and political interests and, with the backing of the NSDAP, could claim mass support. Against the Front, Brüning still had the backing of Hindenburg and the authority of presidential decree, Article 48. In the end, the Harzburg Front achieved little since Hitler, acting cagily, only gave it his half-hearted backing. He rightly suspected that Hugenberg was trying to use him and, with the Nazi Party in the ascendancy, he did not want to compromise his position.

In the spring of 1932, Hindenburg's seven-year term as President was due to come to an end. Although aged 85 and in declining health, he remained a respected figure and Brüning urged him to stand for re-election.

> **KEY ISSUE**
>
> *Article 48 and rule by presidential decree.*

8 ⌁ HINDENBURG VERSUS HITLER – THE PRESIDENTIAL ELECTION OF 1932

Hindenburg was upset since he felt that Brüning could have arranged for his continuation as President without the need for an election. Hitler, with so much at stake, dithered, uncertain whether to stand and risk the humiliation of defeat. Encouraged by Goebbels and other leading members of NSDAP, he finally decided to enter the race. The other candidates were the old campaigner and communist, Ernst Thälmann, and Theodor Duesterberg, one of the founders of *Stahlhelm*, a

TABLE 20

The Presidential election of 1932

MARCH 1932 First round		APRIL 1932 Second round	
Paul von Hindenburg	18,650,000	Paul von Hindenburg	19,360,000
Adolf Hitler	11,340,000	Adolf Hitler	13,420,000
Ernst Thälmann	4,980,000	Ernst Thälmann	3,710,000
Theodor Duesterberg	2,560,000		

member of the DNVP. With the Nazis making scurrilous remarks about the ageing Field Marshal and leaking the fact that Duesterberg had a Jewish grandfather, it was far from a clean fight.

In the first round, Hindenburg, with 49.6 per cent of the vote came desperately close to winning an overall majority, but had to face the humiliation of a second ballot. Hitler, with 30.1 per cent of the vote, also did remarkable well with Thälmann and Duesterberg trailing well behind. In the second round, the Nazi leader, who had rejected advice to stand down, did marginally better with 36.7 per cent of the vote but Hindenburg won quite easily. Hitler did not consider his showing to have been a success and was bitterly disappointed. Still, his priority was not to win the presidency but the chancellorship and control the *Reichstag*.

9 ⤺ THE FALL OF BRÜNING

Now distanced from Brüning because of the Chancellor's unwillingness to fix the presidential elections, Hindenburg was prepared to be part of a number of intrigues which would finally bring to an end the Weimar Republic's last democratic government and replace it with more authoritarian right-wing rule. In May 1932, he dismissed Wilhelm Gröner, non-party Defence Minister and strong man in Brüning's government, when Gröner placed a ban on the activities of the SA and SS. A month later, Brüning sought Hindenburg's signature on an emergency decree intended to turn the estates of former Prussian aristocrats, the East Elbian estates, into 600,000 allotments for the unemployed. The landowning class protested against the socialising of agriculture and put pressure on Hindenburg to get rid of the unpopular Chancellor. As a result, the President refused to authorise the decree and, at Schleicher's prompting, readily betrayed the man who had served him so loyally and well by demanding Brüning's resignation. Within a year, Brüning emigrated to the United States to become professor of political science at Havard University.

In *Hindenburg, the Wooden Titan*, J.W. Wheeler-Bennett says of this period:

Q

Why had Brüning's government become so unpopular by May 1932?

The tragedy of Brüning is the tragedy of Weimar. There was no greater believer in sound parliamentary institutions than he, yet under the irresistible pressure of events it was he who struck the first blow at their foundation. None desired more passionately the welfare and happiness of the German people, yet he became known as the 'Hunger Chancellor', and was forced to impose upon them the most crushing of burdens. It would have been hard to find a greater German patriot, yet he was hounded from office for 'lack of patriotism'. He played the game according to the rules and failed, but to his less scrupulous successors was conceded all that he sought to achieve and more. One fundamental error Brüning committed at the outset. He trusted Hindenburg.

10 ✑ THE *REICHSWEHR* AND THE REPUBLIC

A *The origins and the role of the* Reichswehr

The first association of the new Republic with the German military occurred in November 1919 when Friederich Ebert accepted General Gröner's offer to use the army to maintain law and order and suppress revolutionary activity (see page 10). Two months later, the army and units of the *Freikorps* joined together to put down the Spartacist uprising in Berlin (see page 11). For a time, paramilitary units of *Freikorps* existed side-by-side with the new standing army of the Republic, the *Reichswehr*. In fact, many of those recruited to serve in the army were former *Freikorps* members.

The *Reichswehr* was made up of men who had survived the rigorous cuts imposed on the army at Versailles and was officered by those who had formerly served in the imperial army. The *Reichswehr*, like the *Freikorps*, was monarchist and nationalist in outlook. It remained loyal to the memory of the Kaiser and those who had led them during the war years, particularly Hindenburg and Ludendorff. It believed that the 'stab-in-the-back' theory exonerated the army for defeat in 1918. Its attitude to the Weimar Republic was at best uneasy and uncertain and at worst hostile and unsupportive. Although it was unhesitatingly prepared to act against left-wing uprisings, its loyalty when dealing with nationalist instigated troubles was far less certain. The confusion resulting from this conflict of loyalties was evident in 1920 when General von Lüttwitz, commander of the *Reichswehr* in the Berlin region, joined with Wolfgang Kapp in a plot against the Republic (see pages 30–1). Called to put down the attempted *putsch*, General von Seeckt refused declaring that '*Reichswehr* does not fire on *Reichswehr*'. On the other hand, General Reinhardt, the first head of Army Command, remained loyal and proved himself to be 'the only general prepared to defend the Republic by force if necessary'.

According to the Constitution, the president was commander-in-chief of all the armed forces of the Reich but, within the government, army matters were handled by the defence minister. Between 1919 and 1932, three men shared the tricky responsibility of trying to integrate the *Reichswehr* and the Republic. They were the right-wing socialist,

Gustav Noske (1919–20), who was considered the SPD's military expert; Otto Gessler (1920–28), former mayor of Nuremberg and member of the liberal DDP who held the post for eight years; and non-party Wilhelm Gröner (1928–32), the general who had thrown his weight behind Ebert in 1919. The post-war German army was limited to 100,000 men and possessed no tanks, aeroplanes or other offensive weapons. Its role was limited to that of a police force and the maintenance of internal order.

B *The role of General Hans von Seeckt*

In 1919, Hans von Seeckt was appointed head of the *Truppenamt* (Troops Bureau) which had replaced the banned General Staff. Recognising the need for co-operation between the army and the Republic but strongly opposed to their integration, three months after his apparent disloyalty in 1920 Seeckt had regained the confidence of the government and was appointed army chief. Between 1920 and 1926 he worked to restructure and strengthen the *Reichswehr*. As William Carr says, he set out 'to create a superb fighting machine which would one day restore Germany to her former greatness'. Something of a **martinet**, he earned a reputation for his organisational skills and for his understanding of the difficult relationship between military planning on the one hand and political policy on the other.

> **martinet** a strict disciplinarian

Under him, the *Truppenamt* became a General Staff in all but name and he carefully selected his senior officers and warned them against becoming involved in politics. Although the *Reichswehr* was originally based on the *Freikorps*, Seeckt did not want to attract street rabble-type recruits but looked for men who had the makings of good and well-disciplined soldiers. There was no shortage of suitable recruits. In collaboration with the arms manufacturer, Alfred Krupp, he ignored the disarmament clauses imposed at Versailles; he increased the size of the *Reichswehr* and arranged a plentiful supply of modern weapons, and even imported armaments from abroad. Believing that a Russo-German alliance would be unbeatable in any future war, he approved of the 1922 Treaty of Rapallo (see page 45), and the arrangements made with the Soviet Union for the training of men of the *Reichswehr* and closer collaboration with the Red Army. Defence Minister, Otto Gessler, who allowed Seeckt to make all the important military decisions, certainly knew what was going on but turned a blind eye and even defended his activities in the *Reichstag*. To Seeckt must go the credit for re-establishing the professional German army which was to be the basis of Hitler's future *Wehrmacht* (as the army was known after 1935).

Suspicious of the Nazis, in 1924 he ordered the commander of the armed forces in Bavaria to resist Hitler's Beer Hall *Putsch*. The Nazis reacted by describing him as a 'lackey of the Weimar Republic' and 'a pawn of Jewish-Masonic elements'. He was even accused of being influenced by his Jewish wife. He was dismissed in 1926 following two ill-judged if trivial decisions. Many disapproved when he chose to allow duelling among army officers and republicans were upset when the press disclosed that he had allowed a Hohenzollern, Prince Wilhelm of Prussia, the son of the former Crown Prince, to take part in army manoeuvres in uniform. Some senior officers, infuriated by Seeckt's dismissal pressed for a military-backed *putsch*. Afterwards, Seeckt entered politics and in 1930 he was elected as a DVP deputy to the *Reichstag*. In an apparent change of heart, he tended to sympathise increasingly with Hitler. The importance of Seeckt lies in his efforts to define the relationship between the army and the state. In establishing the army's independence, he had turned the *Reichswehr* into 'a state within a state' and created a situation in which the allegiance of the army was to its commanders alone.

KEY ISSUE

Seeckt and the relationship between the army and the state.

C *The continuing influence of Hindenburg*

After Hindenburg became President in 1925, there was a marked improvement in relations between the army and the Republic. In addition to the fact that the President was nominally head of the German armed services, as the nation's former wartime military leader he still commanded the loyalty and respect of those who had served under him and those who were old enough to be aware of the glories of the Hindenburg legend. As none had managed before him, he was able to bring together the army and the Republic. In the words of J.W. Wheeler-Bennett in *Hindenburg, the Wooden Titan*:

> The army of which Hindenburg found himself Commander-in-Chief in 1925 resembled its Imperial predecessor in one particular aspect. It was above politics because it dominated them. With zealous care it had been removed from political control and no disruptive influences existed within its ranks. It never played politics but no government could stand a week without its support. In the words of Gröner, 'The Reichswehr had become a factor which no one could pass over in political decisions.'

Hindenburg's intention to introduce a far more authoritarian form of government was made easier by the fact that he could depend on the loyalty of the army. As we have seen, he was able to arrange first the appointment and then the dismissal of Brüning. One of those most able to influence the President's decision-making was Kurt von Schleicher, who had served in the same regiment as Hindenburg during the war. In 1929, Schleicher was appointed to a high administrative office in the *Reichswehr*. He had always dabbled in politics and now used his position to become a quite unscrupulous master of intrigue and double-dealing. Arrogant, self-opinionated and ambitious, Schleicher became the voice of the army in German politics. He quite unashamedly used his friendship with Hindenburg and his son, Oskar, to become a power-broker, firstly in the role of 'chancellor-maker' and then as a manipulator of chancellors. His aim, to establish a strong non-party government able to guarantee the well-being of the German people, may have appeared noble enough but his methods, deceit, dishonesty and duplicity, were totally ignoble.

11 ∽ DISASTER LOOMS – THE GOVERNMENTS OF VON PAPEN AND VON SCHLEICHER

Following the fall of Brüning's government in May 1932, Schleicher played a significant role in influencing the President to appoint Franz von Papen as Chancellor in preference to Hugenberg. He thought that Papen would be the more easy to manipulate.

FRANZ VON PAPEN (1879–1969)

Born into a wealthy and noble family, von Papen was to play an important role in Hitler's progress towards the chancellorship. At first, Papen followed a diplomatic career and was appointed military attaché at the German embassy in Washington. In 1916 he was expelled from the United States because of his involvement in espionage activities. Back in Europe, he was sent to serve as an adviser to the Turkish army. After the war, he joined the Centre Party. Better known for his talents as a horseman than a politician, he made little impression on his colleagues and failed in his first attempt to win a seat in the *Reichstag*. Papen's success lay, as Fest says, in the fact that 'he supplemented his personal inadequacies with a network of connections'. These connections included his close association with the aristocracy through his noble birth, his control of the newspaper, *Germania*, his friendship with German industrialists through his marriage to the daughter of a rich Saar magnate, his links with the hierarchy of the Roman Catholic Church and, of course, his association with Schleicher. His *Junker* background and his religion also made him acceptable to the class-conscious Hindenburg. A socialite and a man of great personal charm, he was never held in high regard or even taken seriously as a politician. To some, he was no more than a laughing stock. His appointment as Chancellor was greeted with both amazement and amusement. The French ambassador in Berlin wrote, 'Everyone smiled. There [is] something about von Papen that prevents either his friends or his enemies taking him entirely seriously. He bears the stamp of frivolity. He is not a person of the first rank.'

A Von Papen's administration, June–December 1932

Papen's cabinet, representing mainly landed and industrial interests, was known as 'the cabinet of the barons'. It was made up only of non-

party and Nationalist (DNVP) members, and included Schleicher as the Defence Minister and Konstantin von Neurath as Foreign Minister. Neurath, a career diplomat who had served in turn as German ambassador to Denmark, Italy and Britain, was later to join the Nazis and become Hitler's Reichsprotektor of Bohemia and Moravia.

Considered to be the best man to deal with the Nazis, Papen's first act was to remove the ban imposed on the SA and SS. This concession resulted in an immediate increase in violence. Even though the army tried to maintain order, furious street clashes between Nazis and Communists led to over 1,000 casualties. The bloodiest fighting occurred on 17 July, when 7,000 Nazis paraded provocatively through a working-class quarter of Hamburg and then had to fight their way through street barricades. Papen used the lawlessness as an excuse to dismiss the socialist government of Prussia on the grounds that it could not keep order. When Otto Braun, leader of the SPD in Prussia challenged the legality of the act, Hindenburg sent in the *Reichswehr* to settle the issue. Braun was ousted and replaced by a Reich Commissar. Prussia represented almost 60 per cent of Germany and had been a major stronghold of socialism in Germany and a pillar of support for the Republic. Hindenburg's takeover of the *Land* showed the Nazis just how easily a democratic system could be replaced by an autocratic regime.

> **KEY ISSUE**
>
> *The collapse of Papen's 'cabinet of barons'.*

B *The two Reichstag elections of 1932*

With the situation fast getting out of control, Papen dissolved the *Reichstag* and called for elections. This time Hitler made every effort and the Party campaigned as never before. Altogether, the Nazi leader travelled over 50,000 kilometres and addressed meetings in 50 different towns and cities. Everywhere was to be seen red bunting, swastika flags and the brown-shirted men of the SA. In *Hitler, A Study in Tyranny*, Alan Bullock comments on the impact of the Führer's electioneering:

The whole familiar apparatus of Nazi ballyhoo was brought into play – placards, press, sensational charges and counter charges, mass meetings, demonstrations, SA parades... this was more than clever electioneering. The Nazi campaign could not have succeeded as it did had it not at the same time corresponded and appealed to the mood of a considerable proportion of the German people.

At the time, in a report made to his Central Committee, a German Communist wrote (quoted in R. Sewell, *Germany from Revolution to Counter Revolution*):

The strength of the Nazis is sufficiently well known... The Fascists, who are protected by the state, are unleashing terror on a scale which has no parallel elsewhere in Germany. Even in the city there are streets in which our comrades hardly dare to be seen after dark... The police pay no attention to these events and avoid confrontation with the Nazis, even though they do not directly support these murderous bandits.

PICTURES 17–18

Electioneering posters of the Social Democrat and Nationalist parties. The SPD poster on the left states, 'Clear the way for List 1', and the DNVP poster on the right states, 'Against civil war and inflation', both parties indicating their intention of dealing with Nazis and communists

In something approaching a landslide victory, the Nazis gained 37 per cent of the vote and returned 230 deputies to become the largest party in the *Reichstag*. Although they only lost ten seats, the SPD with 133 deputies came a poor second. The Communists made further gains to come third whilst the DVP and former DDP virtually disappeared. In

TABLE 21
The Reichstag *election of July 1932*

		Number of seats
Nazi Party	(NSDAP)	230
Social Democrats	(SPD)	133
Communist Party	(KPD)	89
Catholic Centre	(Zentrum)	75
Nationalist Party	(DNVP)	37
Bavarian Party	(BVP)	20
People's Party	(DVP)	7
* Democratic Party	(DDP)	4
Others		11

* What remained of the DDP was called the *Deutsche Staatspartei* after July 1930

spite of their success, the Nazis had nothing like an overall majority but it seemed reasonable that Hitler, as leader of the largest party, might expect to be appointed Chancellor. However this was not the case. Hindenburg, who disliked the Nazis and thought the Austrian-born, ex-corporal unsuited to such high office, offered him only the vice-chancellorship under Papen. Not surprisingly, Hitler regarded the offer as a snub and declined. Uncertain of the reaction of the army, Hitler also resisted pressure from Röhm, leader of the SA, and others to seize power illegally.

Papen's new cabinet was virtually the same as the old. With the Nazis, SPD, Communists and the Centre Party all in opposition, the *Reichstag* could not properly function and Papen's government had no realistic chance of surviving. On 12 September, the Nazis joined with the Centre Party in a vote of no confidence and heavily defeated Papen's cabinet by 512 to 42. The *Reichstag* was again dissolved and for the second time in six months the German people went to the polls. Although money was scarce, Hitler roused himself for yet another round of frantic electioneering.

Even allowing for a slightly lower turnout, the loss of 34 seats came as a bitter blow to the Nazis. Many Germans had tired of Nazi-orchestrated street violence and, within the Party, there was a decline in momentum and morale suffered. Hitler was concerned that Nazi fortunes might have peaked too soon. The Nazi leader was also worried by

Q

Did Hitler have sound reasons for refusing the Vice-chancellorship in July 1932?

TABLE 22
The Reichstag *election of November 1932*

		Number of seats
Nazi Party	(NSDAP)	196
Social Democrats	(SPD)	121
Communist Party	(KPD)	100
Catholic Centre	(Zentrum)	70
Nationalist Party	(DNVP)	52
Bavarian Party	(BVP)	18
People's Party	(DVP)	11
Others		14

the increase in support for the Communists and the partial recovery in the fortunes of the DNVP. This time, Hindenburg had no choice but to offer Hitler the chancellorship but withdrew the right to rule by presidential decree. Determined to secure unconditional power, the Nazi leader again refused. Faced by a desperate situation, Papen even suggested abolishing the Weimar Constitution, setting up his own right-wing, elitist government and banning both the Communist and Nazi parties. Whilst Hindenburg pondered, Schleicher, the Defence Minister, spoke critically of Papen's plan. He feared that the army might be unable to contain both the Communists and the SA and that the situation would get out of control and end in civil war. Behind the scene, Schleicher took advantage of the Chancellor's difficulties and urged Hindenburg to drop Papen. His scheming worked and, on 3 December 1932, Schleicher himself was appointed Chancellor.

> **KEY ISSUE**
>
> *A landslide victory and then the Nazis lose ground.*

C Von Schleicher's administration, December 1932 – January 1933

In what might be described as a period of government by intrigue, Schleicher continued to plot and scheme. When his attempts to bargain with other political parties in order to form a workable coalition failed, he tried to create a division in the ranks of the Nazis by offering the vice-chancellorship to Gregor Strasser on the socialist left-wing of the Party. Hitler intervened to prevent it.

THE STRASSER BROTHERS – GREGOR (1892–1934) AND OTTO (1897–1974)

The Strassers were a middle-class Bavarian family, and Gregor was greatly affected by the misery he witnessed in post-war Germany. After joining the Nazis, he worked to win over lower middle- and working-class support for National Socialism and so helped to create a broad-based party backed by popular support. The growth of the Party and its gains in the 1928 election were largely due to his efforts. Together with his brother, Otto, and Joseph Goebbels, he represented the socialist aspirations of the movement. Much liked, he became second only to Hitler in popularity and, at one time, seemed a possible rival for the leadership. Even after the Bamberg Conference in 1926 (see pages 76–7), he continued to criticise aspects of Hitler's policies. He later spoke openly against Hitler's courtship of German industrialists and the severity of his anti-Semitic policies.

Younger brother, Otto, shared Gregor's views that working-class reforms were needed along socialist lines and thought that socialist principles should be the guiding influence in the Party. He founded and ran the newspaper *Berliner Arbeiter Zeitung* but became disillusioned with Hitler and as a result lost Hitler's support of his views. In 1930, Otto left the Party to organise the revolutionary *Schwarze Front* (Black Front) which Hitler quickly suppressed when he came to power.

Meanwhile Gregor Strasser continued to quarrel openly with Hitler and, in 1932, angered the Nazi leader when he hesitated before being forced to reject Schleicher's offer of the vice-chancellorship. Afterwards, he resigned and ceased to be politically active. In 1934, Gregor was murdered when Hitler took his revenge for his earlier disloyalty. Otto was more fortunate and escaped to Canada. He returned to Germany in 1955 but never again became involved in politics.

Q

Assess the significance of the role of Gregor Strasser to the events of 1932–3.

12 ⌐ VON PAPEN'S REVENGE – HITLER OFFERED THE CHANCELLORSHIP

Unable to govern effectively, Schleicher sought Hindenburg's permission to rule by decree, dismiss the *Reichstag* and govern without it. In effect, his aim was to set up a military dictatorship. Hindenburg, who had already lost faith in his new Chancellor, refused. It was now Papen's turn to scheme and avenge the earlier betrayal of Schleicher. Following a secret meeting with Hitler in Cologne during which he agreed to back the Nazi leader, Papen returned to Berlin and persuaded Hindenburg to remove Schleicher and appoint Hitler on his own terms. He told the ageing President that, in his view, Hitler could be more easily restrained once he was burdened with the responsibilities of the chancellorship. Papen told a friend, 'In two months' time, we'll have pushed him so far into the corner that he'll be squeaking.' At 11.20 on the morning of 30 January 1933, Adolf Hitler was sworn into office. That evening the SA organised a torchlight parade through the centre of Berlin to celebrate the triumph of their leader. Years later, Papen wrote in his *Memoirs*:

KEY ISSUE

The decision to offer Hitler the chancellorship.

> We were to learn in the course of time into what hands Germany had fallen... One thing must be understood. The first Hitler government was formed in strict accord with parliamentary procedure. He had been brought to power by the normal interplay of democratic processes. It must be realised that neither he nor his movement had acquired the character or carried out atrocities for which they were to be condemned fifteen years later... We believed Hitler when he said that once he was in a position of power and responsibility, he would steer his movement into more ordered channels.

13 ⌐ AN ISSUE CONSIDERED: HOW WAS IT POSSIBLE FOR THE NAZIS TO COME TO POWER IN GERMANY IN 1933?

A *Introduction*

The appointment of Hitler as Chancellor of Germany on 30 January 1933 is one of the most important events of the twentieth century. It led to the establishment of a Nazi dictatorship in Germany and monstrous acts of tyranny and genocide. Eventually, it brought about the Second World War which had far-reaching consequences for Europe and the world as a whole. The American historian John Snell asks, 'How was it possible for the Nazis to come to power in one of the most civilised countries of Europe just fourteen years after that country had thrown its monarchical armour on the slag heap of history and wrapped itself in the clothing of democratic republicanism.'

The years 1929 to 1933 were crucial in Hitler's rise to power. During that period, those who had so long undermined the Weimar Republic finally brought about its collapse. The major contributory factor to these events was the rise of the Nazi Party and its development into a mass movement. In 1932 more than a third of the German electorate voted for the Nazis. At the time, people were largely unaware of the possible disastrous consequences of their actions. After the Second World War, many Germans found it difficult to come to terms with the responsibility of the crimes committed during the Nazi era. It was only during the 1960s that the works of German historians attempted to bring a fresh insight into what exactly happened during this period. Joachim Fest, author of *The Face of the Third Reich* (Weidenfeld & Nicolson 1970) and *Hitler* (Weidenfeld & Nicolson 1974), is of the view that only a German historian can place Hitler in his true historical context and make an objective evaluation of him. British and American historians have also made major contributions to our understanding of this period of German history. Their work has been helped by documents made available after 1945 when German archives fell into Allied hands. During the immediate post-war period, they proved more willing than German historians to search out the truths about these terrible events. As a result, a mass of information has been gathered and there is much general agreement about what happened and why. Even so, historians differ in their interpretations of this knowledge, about the causes of these events and where the blame lay. These differences of opinion have led to an ongoing debate which continues to this day.

B *The debate*

THE ROLE OF HISTORY

One reason for the disagreement is the different timescale used by various historians. Some consider Hitler's appointment as Chancellor in January 1933 against a background of German and European history stretching back into the nineteenth century and well beyond. A good example of this approach is to be found in *The Rise and Fall of the Third Reich* (Secker & Warburg 1960) written by the American William L. Shirer. For some time European correspondent of the *Chicago Tribune*, during the 1930s he worked for the Columbia Broadcasting Service and experienced and reported on these events at first hand. Shirer traces the emergency of Nazism back to the sixteenth century. He sees it as the natural continuation of German history and the outcome of the autocratic rule and militarist policies of such as Frederick the Great, Bismarck and the imperial Kaisers Wilhelm I and Wilhelm II. He attributes much to the sixteenth century religious reformer, Martin Luther, the 'erratic genius' who aroused the German people to Protestantism and, at the same time, first fired their nationalist spirit. He also notes the influence of the German political thinkers Georg Wilhelm Hegel, Friedrich Neitzsche and Heinrich von Treitscke (see Chapter 9). Hegel, who glorified war and saw it as 'the great purifier' emphasised 'the supreme right of the state over the individual'. Neitzsche identified humanity as being composed of two types of people, the weak and slavish and the strong and masterful. He urged mankind to reject the slave morality of Christianity and aim to be the 'lords of the earth'. Like Hegel, Treitscke glorified the state and regarded war as the 'basis of all political virtues'. The French historian, Edmond Vermeil, supported this view when he wrote that Nazism 'was a simplified theology and crude caricature of German intellectual tradition'. Similarly, in *The Course of German History* (Methuen 1961), the Oxford don A.J.P. Taylor implied that German history was bound, in the end, to produce something like Nazism and that it grew inevitably from the German past.

Such interpretations tend towards determinism since they see the course of events decided beforehand by the progress of history. They regard the character of the German people as being conditioned by their history. Consequently, because of their national characteristics the German people must take the blame for what happened. Other historians have agreed that the German character is different from that of other European nations, such as Britain and France. It has been argued that Germany did not emerge as a full-blooded nation state until after the Franco-Prussian War of 1870 and, as a result, it has no longstanding traditions of democratic government. Again, unlike Britain and France, its industrial revolution came later and was more rapid. The weakness of liberalism in Germany and the stifling of the advance of socialism have also been mentioned. Interpretations of history can be more easily undertaken by hindsight.

THE ROLE OF POLITICAL INTRIGUE

Other writers follow a different approach to the determinists and explain the events which led to the rise of Hitler by closely examining the years of the Weimar Republic. In some cases they concentrate on the months, weeks and days immediately prior to 30 January 1933. Some accounts of this kind are available only in German but this approach is also used by Karl Bracher (*The German Dictatorship*, Weidenfeld & Nicolson 1971) and Martin Broszat (*Hitler and the Collapse of Weimar Germany*, Berg 1987). They consider the extent to which the outcome remained in the balance until the last moment and argue that, although it might have been difficult to save the Weimar Republic, the coming of Hitler was not inevitable. Historians like Bracher and Broszat emphasise the importance of developments that were likely but not certain to occur, including the impact of the personalities of those involved. They are less concerned with the underlying social and economic factors.

THE ROLE OF GERMAN CAPITALISTS

Marxist historians explain the rise of Hitler as being largely a product of the self-interest of German capitalists. Franz Neumann, a Marxist historian who left his homeland in 1936, questions if Hitler would have managed to come to power without the support of German industrialists, bankers and the middle-class bourgeoisie who feared and exaggerated the threat of communism. The German Communist Party was the largest in Europe outside the Soviet Union and was slavishly loyal to Moscow. Neumann argues that it was to the advantage of the unscrupulous businessmen, who had taken advantage of the economic chaos of the early 1920s to build large industrial empires, to back Hitler. Hitler may not have been their first choice but, at that time, he was the best available option. They supported and financed him hoping that, in the end, he would be their pawn.

THE ROLE OF PERSONALITY

One of the earliest books written about the Nazi leader was *Hitler, A Study in Tyranny* by the Oxford don, Alan Bullock. Of the view that the Nazis came to power by showing a deep conviction to a narrow range of principles (the aims of which were simple, popular and easy to understand), he also recognises the importance of the personality and charisma of Hitler. The success of the Nazis, he argues, was largely a product of Hitler's ability as an orator, propagandist and opportunist. Fest says of Hitler that no one in history produced so much hysteria, so much rejoicing and, in the end, so much hate. He reminds us that Hitler led Germany with such brilliance that it took a coalition of the world's greatest powers six years to bring about his defeat. Fest also holds him responsible for 'the most appalling times in history'.

THE ROLE OF PSYCHOLOGY

An alternative approach is to consider how Hitler and the Nazis managed to win the votes of such a large section of the German population. In their analysis, some historians have tried to find psychological reasons for the Nazi electoral success. They have considered long-term factors such as the German tendency to accept authority and domination by those considered to be their superiors. In Germany, this was usual in all levels of society and within the family. Short-term and more immediate factors would have been the stress and trauma caused by the humiliation of defeat in 1918 and the insecurity which was the result of the political and economic crises of the 1920s. Then, of course, there was the influence of Nazi propaganda (see below) and the magnetism and charisma of Hitler. Zevedei Barbu, the Romanian-born historian, explains the success of the Nazis by their ability to 'manipulate the social and psychological condition of the German people' and appeal to all classes and sections of the community. An analysis of electoral statistics shows which groups of Germans were attracted to Nazism but does not explain why. Some of those who wrote before and soon after the Second World War detected an irrational element in the voting pattern of the German electorate or an 'uprising of stupidity', as it was put at the time. Recent analysis has shown that in Germany various social groups voted for the Nazis for a host of different reasons. Reasons which seemed very valid, at least at the time (see page 117).

THE ROLE OF PROPAGANDA

In *Mein Kampf*, Hitler observed, 'The understanding of the masses is very limited, their intelligence is small... as a result, all effective propaganda must be limited to a few points and must harp on these in slogans until the last member of the public understands.' Prior to 1933, most forms of mass communication were unavailable to the Nazis. Propaganda techniques used by them were limited largely to speech-making, political rallies, the fear instilled by the slogan chanting SA and the opinions expressed by the Party newspapers, *Völkischer Beobachter* (People's Observer) and *Der Angriff* (The Attack). Nazi propaganda was adapted so that it appealed to all groups and, as a result, it attracted people from a wider range of social and economic backgrounds than any other party. In 1932, Joseph Goebbels was sufficiently confident that his propaganda had done its work to claim, 'The election campaign is ready in principle. We now only need to press the button in order to set the machine in action.' Is the explanation that the German people were simply duped too shallow?

14 ⌐ BIBLIOGRAPHY

There are a great many books written about all aspects of the history of the Weimar Republic. Among the books specific to this period of German history are the long-established *Weimar and the Rise of Hitler* by A.J. Nichols (Macmillan 1968). The most recent edition includes a review of recent research and interpretations of the period. The most thoroughly detailed is *From Weimar to Hitler, Germany 1918–1933* by E.J. Feuchtwanger (Macmillan 1995). This book includes appendices and essential statistics. Although they concentrate more on the rise of the Nazi Party than other developments, useful sections are to be found in more general texts covering the history of Germany during the inter-war years. These include such standard works as *Hitler, A Study in Tyranny* by Alan Bullock (Odhams Press 1952) and *Hitler* by Joachim C. Fest (Weidenfeld & Nicolson 1974). The first chapters of *Germany,*

1918–1990 by Mary Fulbrook (Fontana Press 1991) also provide a useful introduction to the Weimar years. William Carr's *A History of Germany 1815–1985* (Edward Arnold 1992) covers a much broader period. Along the lines of a traditional textbook, it is clearly written and accessible. The first section of *The Longman Companion to Nazi Germany* by Tim Kirk (Longman 1995) contains a wealth of information about society, economy and culture during the Weimar years. Volume 2 of *Nazism 1919–1945: A Documentary Reader* by J. Noakes and G. Pridham (Exeter UP 1983) contains many documents and a commentary of the period. Concise and analytical in approach are *From Bismarck to Hitler, Germany 1890–1933* by G. Layton (Access to History series, Hodder & Stoughton 1995), *Imperial and Weimar Germany 1890–1933* by John Laver (History at Source series, Hodder & Stoughton 1992) and John Hiden's *The Weimar Republic* (Seminar Series, Longman 1974). They all also provide helpful advice on examination technique. Interesting but with a strong political bias is *Germany From Revolution to Counter Revolution* by Rob Sewell (Fortress Books 1988).

Biographies and books dealing with specific events include *Hindenburg, the Wooden Titan* by J.W. Wheeler-Bennett (Macmillan 1967); *Versailles and After* by R. Henig (Methuen 1984); F.L. Carsten's *Revolution in Central Europe, 1918–1919* (Temple Smith 1972) and *The Reichswehr and Politics, 1918–1933* (Oxford UP 1966); *The Spartacist Uprising* by E. Waldmann (Marquette 1958); *The German Inflation of 1923*, F.K. Ringer (ed.) (OUP 1969); *Hitler and the Beerhall Putsch* by H.J. Gordon (Princeton UP 1972); *Gustav Stresemann and the Politics of the Weimar Republic* by H.A. Turner (Princeton UP 1963); *Culture and Society in the Weimar Republic* K. Bullivant (ed.) (Manchester UP 1977); *Hitler and the Collapse of the Weimar Germany* by M. Broszat (Oxford UP 1987).

15 ∽ DISCUSSION TOPICS AND INTERPRETATIVE ESSAY QUESTIONS

A *This section consists of questions that might be used for discussion (or written answers) as a way of expanding on the chapter and testing understanding of it.*

1. In what sense was Müller's Grand Coalition flawed from the outset?
2. Was the issue of financing social security the main reason for the collapse of Müller's government?
3. To what extent did Alfred Hugenberg influence German politics during the late 1920s?
4. (a) Why did a depression which began in the United States have such a catastrophic effect on Germany?
   (b) Give some examples of economic measures which might be considered deflationary.

5. 'Not a person of first rank.' Is this view of von Papen justified?
6. To what extent would you agree that, by 1932, a split between Hitler and the Strasser brothers had become inevitable?
7. After the election of November 1932, what options were available to Hindenburg?

B *Interpretative essay questions.*

1. 'In the end, it is hard to escape the conclusion that his chancellorship was a dismal failure.' (Geoff Layton, a specialist European historian, in *From Bismarck to Hitler: Germany 1890–1933*. 2002.)
    How valid is this interpretation of the chancellorship of Heinrich Brüning?
2. 'Hitler came to power legally and within the system. He used a system that was seriously flawed.' (Jackson J. Spielvogel, an American university lecturer in *Hitler and Nazi Germany*. 1922.)
    How valid is this interpretation of the means by which Hitler was appointed Chancellor of Germany?

16 ⌐ TWO SOURCE DOCUMENTARY EXERCISE ON THE INTRIGUE SURROUNDING THE EVENTS OF JANUARY 1933

Study the two sources carefully and then answer the questions based on them.

On 4th January 1933, Papen, Hess, Himmler and Keppler arrived at my house in Cologne... The negotiations took place exclusively between Hitler and Papen... Papen said that he thought it best to form a government in which the conservative and nationalist elements that had supported him were represented together with the Nazis. He suggested that the new government should, if possible be led by Hitler and himself together. Then Hitler made a long speech in which he said that, if he were elected Chancellor, Papen's followers could participate in his government as Ministers if they were willing to support his policy...including the removal of all Social Democrats, Communists and Jews from leading positions in Germany and the restoration of order in public life. Papen and Hitler reached agreement in principle...

SOURCE A *Evidence given by the German financier, Kurt Schroeder, at the Nuremberg trials,* Nuremberg Documents, 1946.

SOURCE B *Evidence given by Otto Meissner, a State Secretary in the Reich President's office, at the Nuremberg trials,* Nuremberg Documents, 1946.

Schleicher came to power because he believed he could form a government which would have the support of the National Socialists. When it became clear that Hitler was not willing to enter Schleicher's Cabinet and that Schleicher on his part was unable to split the National Socialist Party, as he had hoped to do with the help of Gregor Strasser, the policy for which Schleicher had been appointed Chancellor was wrecked. Schleicher was aware that Hitler was embittered against him because of his attempt to split the Party... So he now changed his mind and decided to fight against the Nazis – which meant that he now wanted to pursue the policy which he had opposed when Papen had suggested it a few weeks before. Schleicher went to Hindenburg with a demand for emergency powers needed for action against the Nazis. Furthermore, he believed it would be necessary to dissolve the *Reichstag*, and this was to be done by Presidential decrees on the basis of Article 48... In the middle of January, when Schleicher was asking for emergency powers, Hindenburg was not aware of the contact between Papen and Hitler...

See page 17 for further discussion of *Reich*

(a) What can be deduced from the sources about the relationship between Hitler and the former German Chancellors Papen and Schleicher?

(b) To what extent might it be claimed that Papen and Schleicher had similar attitudes towards Hitler and the Nazis?

(c) For what reasons might historians have reservations about accepting the sources as reliable?

(d) Based on the evidence of the sources and your own knowledge would it be correct to claim that Hitler came to power solely as a result of political intrigue?

Third Reich (Third Empire) name given to describe the system of government which ruled Germany from January 1933 to May 1945. The phrase, first used in 1923 by a German nationalist writer, was adopted by Hitler in the early 1920s to indicate his intention of establishing a new empire. He regarded his government as a logical extension of two previous German empires. The First Reich was the Holy Roman Empire of the German nation which lasted from AD 962 to 1806. The Second Reich was founded by Otto von Bismarck in 1871, which lasted until 1918. Hitler believed that his Reich would be the greatest of all German empires and would last for 1,000 years.

The Nazis Come to Power

5

INTRODUCTION

Hitler's accession to power on 30 January 1933 is one of the most important events of the twentieth century, but this was not immediately obvious to those who had handed him power. The position of Hitler was that he was one of three Nazis brought into a coalition government in which the Nationalists and Catholics were the dominant partners. In the year which followed his appointment, Hitler laid the foundations of the Nazi dictatorship which superseded the democratic constitution of Weimar though that process was not completed until 1938. Von Papen, as Vice-Chancellor (see page 98), believed that he could control and moderate Hitler who had not been able to secure a majority in the *Reichstag*. Prior to Hitler becoming Chancellor, the Nazi Party had never won more than 37 per cent of votes cast in a Weimar election.

Hitler had come to power chiefly as a result of the failure of the other political parties to combine against him. His left-wing opponents, the SPD and the KPD, failed to realise in time that their disagreements were small compared with the size of the Nazi threat which faced them. Besides Hitler, only two other Nazis were admitted into the Nationalist Coalition government, Frick as Minister of the Interior and Göring as

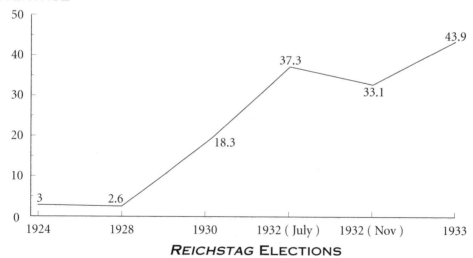

DIAGRAM 2
The NSDAP share of the vote in Reichstag *elections, 1924–33*

PICTURE 19

Hitler takes command: the Nazi Party leadership poses for a victory photograph

Minister without Portfolio, whilst the Party as a whole held 247 seats in the *Reichstag* out of the total 585.

This chapter provides an analysis of Hitler's support and examines his efforts to secure power.

1 ⌐ PRELUDE TO POWER

Hitler immediately introduced policies to consolidate his position within the *Reichstag* and the country. His first priority was to secure a parliamentary majority after he had rejected attempts to gain the support of the Catholic Centre Party. He sought to fight an election with State machinery on his side. He aimed not to revolt against the State, but to take over State machinery and use it to make the Nazi 'revolution'. He made his 'Appeal to the Nation' speech on the 31 January while von Papen persuaded Hindenburg into dissolving the *Reichstag* and holding new elections on 5 March. In his 'Appeal' Hitler presented the Nazi party as an alternative to the weakness of the old regime, and to the democratic system which had rested on the SPD and the Catholic Centre Party. The other parties, he argued, had failed in foreign policy and had brought economic ruin at home. His appeal to the German people was to 'give us four years and then judge us'.

KEY ISSUE

How did Hitler attempt to secure his power?

The Nazis had both the finance and the force to support the electoral campaign which followed this appeal. In the weeks, which followed they used violence and intimidation. Göring played a prominent part, since his office as Minister for Prussia gave him control of nearly two-thirds of Germany. He purged the Prussian civil service and police of people who were opposed to the NSDAP and replaced them with Nazis. Göring also recruited 50,000 'police' auxiliaries to help maintain law and order. These recruits were attached either to the SA or the SS and were used in the campaign to intimidate supporters of rival political parties, especially the Communist KPD.

In the five weeks which followed Hitler's appeal of 31 January the democratic parties which challenged the NSDAP met with increasing repression and intimidation:

● Göring issued the 'Shooting Decree' order that any policeman shooting someone engaged in activities considered hostile to the State had his support. As a result the democratic parties of Weimar could not rely on police protection. Their meetings were disrupted and their speakers attacked.
● Following a decree of 4 February, which gave Hitler the power to suppress newspapers hostile to the NSDAP, the media were prevented from reporting in favour of his political rivals.
● The Nazis' increasing intimidation of their opponents, particularly the left, had its effects; meetings were cancelled and party members resigned, particularly if they were government employees such as teachers and civil servants.

2 ↰ THE *REICHSTAG* FIRE

The climax to this electoral campaign came on the 27 February when the *Reichstag* building was burnt down. This event is one of the great 'whodunits' in history. Much has been written about the event, but the

1933	January	Hitler appointed Chancellor; delivers his 'Appeal to the Nation' speech
	February 1	Hindenburg dissolves the *Reichstag*
	4	Decree for the Protection of the German People gives Hitler power to ban political meetings and suppress newspapers and publications of rival parties
	17	Göring orders police to make 'concord' with SS, SA and *Stahlhelm*, and to make free use of their weapons against the left
	27	The *Reichstag* fire, claimed by the Nazi leadership to be the start of a Communist uprising
	28	Emergency decrees suspend civil rights, the left-wing press is banned, Communist and Socialist leaders are arrested
	March	*Reichstag* elections

TABLE 23
Date chart of chief events in Hitler's accession to power

full truth is not known. The deranged Dutchman, Van der Lubbe, who was accused and tried for the crime, was personally involved but it is not clear what his motives were or whether he acted alone or on the orders of others since the trial proved only his guilt. He was sentenced to death.

Joseph Goebbels, writing his account of these years, *My Part in Germany's Fight* (1935), claimed that when he heard of the fire he thought it was 'pure fantasy', though there could be no doubt that 'the Communists had made a final attempt to seize power by creating an atmosphere of panic and terror'. The Communists, however, had nothing to gain from this event and much to lose as subsequent events were to show. For this reason it is possible to blame the Nazi leadership and certainly many contemporaries, including those within the party, came to hold this view. Hermann Rauschning was at this time a trusted supporter of Hitler, President of the Danzig Senate and responsible for promoting Nazism in the Danzig Free State. After a quarrel with Hitler in 1936, he became one of the Nazi regime's leading critics in exile in America. His insight into the circumstances surrounding the *Reichstag* fire is quoted from *The Voice of Human Destruction*, which he wrote in 1940:

> Shortly after the *Reichstag* fire, Hitler asked me for a report on the Danzig situation, for there were to be elections in Danzig as in the Reich. Gauleiter Forster accompanied me. While waiting in the lobby of the Reich Chancellery, we got into conversation with some of the Nazi celebrities who were also waiting there. Göring, Himmler, Frick and a number of *Gauleiter* from the western provinces were talking together. Göring was giving details of the *Reichstag* fire, the secret of which was still being carefully guarded. I myself had unhesitatingly ascribed it to arson on the part of persons under Communist, or at any rate Comintern, influence. It was not until I heard this conversation that I discovered that the National Socialist leadership was solely responsible, and that Hitler knew of the plan and approved it.
>
> The complacency with which this close circle of the initiated discussed the deed was shattering. Gratified laughter, cynical jokes, boasting – these were the sentiments expressed by the 'conspirators'. Göring described how 'his boys' had entered the *Reichstag* building by a subterranean passage from the President's palace, and how they had only a few minutes at their disposal and were nearly discovered... Göring, who had taken a leading part in the conversation, closed with the significant words: 'I have no conscience, my conscience is Adolf Hitler'.

Q

What does this source reveal about the role of the Nazis in the Reichstag fire?

Rauschning revealed the ruthless character of Hitler and Nazism and was placed on Himmler's blacklist of enemies of Nazism. Given the circumstances of his background, his reliability may be questioned, but he is an important source on the early years of the regime. Much of what he has written about the era has been substantiated elsewhere. But con-

Imperial War Museum NYP 68046

PICTURE 20
The Reichstag *or parliament building in Berlin in flames on the night of 27 February 1933*

siderable doubts remain about the fire and the controversy has continued. Van der Lubbe was posthumously acquitted by a West Berlin court in 1980. The event was, however, of tremendous advantage to the Nazis. Hitler recognised the tactical and propaganda opportunities it presented to him to further his plans for dictatorship. On hearing news of the fire he is reported by the British journalist Sefton Delmer, writing in 1936 (*The Germans and I*), to have said to von Papen, 'This is a God-given signal. If this fire, as I believe, turns out to be the handiwork of the Communists, then there is nothing that shall stop us from crushing out the murderous pest with an iron fist.'

Göring reacted immediately and the police were put on an emergency alert. Writing in 1934, Göring proclaimed:

> I needed no pretext to strike against the Communists. Their crimes were so tremendous that without any further prompting I was determined to begin the most ruthless war of extermination against them... On the contrary, as I testified at the *Reichstag* Fire trial, the fire, which forced me to take measures so rapidly, was actually extremely awkward for me, since it compelled me to act faster than I had intended and to strike before my preparations were complete.

Q

How does Göring's account of the fire differ from Rauschning's?

Göring accused the Communists of planning a national uprising and 4,000 Communist Party members were arrested, including the leader of the Party, Thälmann. The day following the fire, Hitler got President Hindenburg to sign the Emergency Decree for the Protection of the German People which suspended the democratic freedoms provided by a bill of rights in the Weimar Constitution (see page 16). This emergency decree was the real significance of the fire because it became the legal basis of the Nazi dictatorship until that collapsed in 1945. It

- replaced a constitutional government by a permanent state of emergency;
- freed Hitler from dependence on his Nationalist allies and gave his regime a legal basis for persecution, terrorism and repression of all resistance and opposition;
- took away from the people their basic liberties such as a guarantee of their personal liberty and property, freedom of speech and assembly and freedom from arbitrary arrest and imprisonment without trial for an indefinite period.

Anti-Communist hysteria was whipped up by the whole propaganda apparatus of government and Party. The other political parties were also subjected to intimidation, while the police did nothing. SA troops marched throughout the country and by the time of the elections on the 5 March 51 opponents of the Nazis were dead and several hundred injured.

3 ⌁ 5 MARCH ELECTION

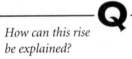

How can this rise be explained? **Q**

In the elections of 5 March nearly 89 per cent of the people voted, a very high number. Hitler increased the NSDAP vote by nearly 10 per cent more than it had secured in November 1932 (see page 111).

The fall in the NSDAP November vote was partly due to an improvement in economic conditions as a result of Brüning's public works programme, combined with a shortage of campaign money. Added to this, some supporters had become disillusioned at the failure of the negotiations after the July elections so that they drifted over to the extreme left.

apolitical someone who is not interested in politics

The increase in the 5 March vote was due in large measure to the 8% increase in the poll, which brought out **apolitical** voters anxious to climb on to the Nazi 'bandwagon'. The middle classes who were drifting away from Hitler in the autumn of 1932 rushed back again due to fear of the 'red peril' that was a Communist government. Others felt that a Nazi regime was inevitable and that it was time to make peace and accept the new order of things. Finally, those who would not have been expected to vote Nazi now did so, either out of self-preservation or fear or intimidation. This must be true for those Jews, Communists and Socialists who voted Nazi for the first time. Hitler also allowed the Communist candidates' names, including those in prison, to remain on the ballot papers. This split the left-wing vote.

TABLE 24
The Reichstag *election of 5 March 1933*

	Size of vote	Number of seats
NSDAP	43.9	288
DNVP	8.0	52
DVP	1.1	2
Zentrum/BVP	13.9	92
DDP	0.9	5
SPD	18.3	120
KPD	12.3	81
Others	1.6	7

Total number of seats: 647 (November 1932: 584)

Despite these tactics, Hitler remained disappointed. Although the Nazis increased their vote by 5.5 million, which gave them 288 out of 647 seats in the *Reichstag*, this was not the enormous victory which had been predicted. Hitler missed the majority he had hoped for by nearly 40 so that he was still dependent on the support of Papen and Hugenberg, the leader of the DNVP. The Nazis' Nationalist coalition partners gained 52 members, thereby giving Hitler a bare majority of 51.9 per cent; while not overwhelming, this was sufficient with the absence of the KPD. The detailed result is shown in Table 24.

> **Q**
> *To what extent would Hitler be satisfied with the results of the 5 March election?*

4 ⌁ ELECTORAL SUPPORT FOR THE NSDAP

Historians who have analysed the electoral statistics have paid special attention to the question 'Which sections of the population felt most attracted to the Nazis and which were most resistant to their appeal?' With the absence of an independent public opinion after March 1933, the available evidence on support for the Nazi party is highly subjective and suspect. A great deal of effort has, therefore, gone into analysing the Nazi electoral success. This can be done in two ways.

One approach is to examine socio-psychological factors, which emphasise the anxieties of a people defeated by the First World War and broken by the various crises of 1920 which saw many people's savings and employment destroyed. This produced a profound anxiety and disillusionment with democracy, especially as none of the constitutional parties of the Weimar Republic appeared prepared to take responsibility for pulling Germany out of depression. They feared that failure would result in having to take the blame. There was a breakdown of parliamentary government and electoral support for the moderate democratic parties passed to the Nazis and Communists.

The other kind of approach to the rise of the Nazi mass movement relies on detailed analysis of electoral statistics in order to verify which social groups were attracted to Nazism and why. Although it is not

> **KEY ISSUE**
> *Who voted Nazi?*

possible to conduct a retrospective opinion poll, the work of writers like T. Childers, *The Nazi Voter, The Social Foundations of German Fascism*, University of North Carolina Press, Chaple Hill, (1983), R. F. Hamilton, *Who Voted for Hitler*, Princeton University Press, (1983) and M. H. Kater, *The Nazi Party: A Social Profile of Members and Leaders 1919–1945*, Blackwell, (1983), have greatly strengthened our understanding of the sources and nature of the support the Nazis were able to mobilise. The social spectrum represented by the NSDAP was drawn from workers, aristocrats and academics, as well as rural and craft workers. This constituency made them the single largest popular party, but two thirds of Germany did not vote Nazi. The Catholic vote remained constant as did that for the Socialist and Communist parties. The views of historians on the electoral support for the NSDAP can be summarised in the chart below.

HISTORIANS' DEBATE

Historians' views on the electoral support for the NSDAP

Detlef Muhlberger, *The Sociology of the NSDAP, the Question of Working Class Membership*, (Journal of Contemporary History 1980):

He argues that the NSDAP made many converts among those sections of the working class in smaller towns or rural areas, that had not previously been effectively organised by the parties of the left. This group included the rural workers of E. Prussia, old fashioned craft workers (of toys and clocks) and state employees who had probably voted for the German Democratic Party (DDP) rather than for the Socialists (SPD). They were joined by the peasantry, a third of whom lived on small uneconomic farms, who were attracted to the promise of a system which protected their interests against a modern age of industry and trade unions. A half of Hitler's vote came from the villages. Hopes of a protection of their interests and an improvement in their conditions also attracted small businessmen who found demand for their products falling between 1929 and 1933. They, like so many others in society, had become disillusioned with democracy. Thus, the NSDAP not only had a disproportionately high following among the middle and even upper middle classes, but also had a considerable following among the working class, though not in proportion to their share of the total population. The NSDAP could therefore claim to be the only party cutting across the whole political spectrum, representing the Volksgemeinschaft as a whole and overcoming class divisions. Muhlberger concludes that by January 1933 all the evidence points to a 30 to 35 per cent membership of workers, a view shared by T. Childers in his 1983 study of the Nazi Voter.

T. Childers, *The Nazi Voter, The Social Foundations of German Fascism,* **University of North Carolina Press, Chaple Hill (1983):**
Using the elections results of the Weimar period, he charted not only the varying fortunes of the Nazis, but also the social composition of the vote from election to election (see Diagram 2 page 111). He concluded that, after 1928, the Nazis won over the old middle class, made up of small merchants, craftsmen, and farmers, who were being overtaken by the modern industrial state. They were also joined by the new middle class of small investors and pensioners, who were hit by the various economic crises which affected Weimar Germany, particularly that of 1929–33. These middle-class voters deserted the traditional democratic parties. Also to be found in the Nazi constituency were the elites, some blue-collar workers, the young and women. Where the young were concerned, they responded to the Nazi propaganda appeal of friendship and belonging to a movement which stressed the importance of their independence. Women were won over in large numbers by an appeal to support the family and provide *Arbeit und Brot* (Work and Bread). With some justification then, the Nazis could claim to be a *'Volkspartei'* though much of their support was unstable.

R. F. Hamilton, *Who Voted for Hitler,* **Princeton University Press (1983):**
His investigations were based on the July 1932 election in Berlin and Hamburg, Cologne and Munich; the Ruhr cities and a selection of five other towns. He criticised the lower middle-class party thesis of T. Childers and others, pointing out that the upper class and upper middle class voted disproportionately for the Nazis (see Table 26, page 126). His explanation is that the Nazis were better than other parties as they offered more attractive policies. This, together with the economic and political crisis, forced a change in voting patterns. He concluded that the further up the social scale the more support there was for the Nazis. There is no doubt that the elites had, by 1932–3, written off the Weimar Republic and did not want a return to parliamentary government. This was particularly true of the large landowners, especially in East Germany, whose organisation, the Reichslandbund, *had been heavily infiltrated by the Nazis. Hitler had directed his propaganda and electioneering tactics at the landed interest when he sought to use the agrarian depression to gain support in rural areas. The NSDAP were to benefit from the declining vote for the DNVP and other parties in the countryside. They were joined by many small and medium-sized enterprises at a regional level who expected, in return for their support of the Nazis, protection for their interests.*

5 ⌐ HITLER'S ATTRACTION TO THE GERMAN PEOPLE

Hitler had an acute awareness of the potential of a mass-media. He rose to power in a society suffering from a national humiliation caused by defeat in the First World War, followed by the imposition of an alien system of democracy on a people accustomed to the absolute rule of a monarch. To this was added all the effects of a social catastrophe caused by inflation, economic depression and mass unemployment. He recognised the importance of understanding the emotional ideas of the masses and finding a way to the hearts and minds of his audience. He was one of the greatest orators of the twentieth century. It is now recognised that Nazi propaganda and policies reflected the hopes and expectations of large sections of the population. His propaganda with its stirring messages of *Deutschland Erwacht* (Germany Awake), *Hitler, Unsere letzte Hoffnung* (Hitler, Our Last Hope) and *Nationalsozialismus, der Organisierte Wille der Nation* (National Socialism, The Organised Will of the Nation) gave many a sense of purpose and a feeling of power. Hitler presented himself as a man of the people who would save Germany from decline. He had two big advantages to his appeal. Firstly he was a figure from below, a man from outside of politics who was not tainted by the failure of the 1920s or even 1918–19. He was one of them, a frontline soldier, a victim. Many Germans identified with him because he could speak the language of the humble at his meetings. His second advantage was his messianic self-belief that he had been chosen by history, that he alone could save Germany. This was the origin of the Führer myth, that Hitler was a German messiah. Propaganda re-enforced this image. Hitler promised that he would heal all class rifts and bitter conflicts, that he would weld society together for the greater good. The notion of *Volksgemeinschaft* (community of the people) based on the principle laid down in the party programme of 1920 *Gemeinnutz geht vor Eigennutz* (Common good before the good of the individual) contained within it the promise of moral renewal and a restoration of public harmony. It would replace the divisive party system and class barriers of the Weimar Republic with national unity. The message was simple – vote Nazi for a reborn Germany. The context of the early 1930s, with 8.5 million unemployed people, favoured Hitler. There was a feeling that Germany needed a strong leader and people whether they were young or old, male or female, soldier or civilian, worker or peasant, landowner or business man, middle class or aristocrat, looked to Hitler as their saviour and redeemer. The staged political rallies with their marching columns of the SA and *Sieg Heil* shouts (Hail to Victory), their bands, uniforms, banners and flags combined with Hitler's speeches captured the imagination of the masses and gave the illusion of a nation's 'triumph of the will'. Hitler's presence meant that for many life took on a tremendous new significance.

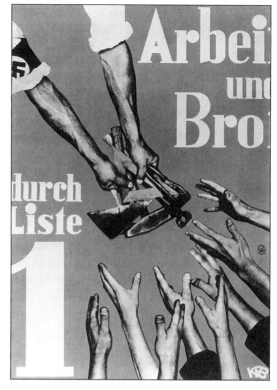

PICTURES 21–24

A series of Nazi election propaganda posters

A *The regional basis of the Nazi vote*

A study of the percentage of votes cast in the different electoral districts of Germany shows the significance of religion and industrialisation in determining support. The height of Nazi electoral popularity in 'free' elections, which came in July 1932, provides a clear picture of this. Catholic voters of all social classes remained loyal to the Centre (Zentrum) Party. This loyalty was also shown to the working class parties, for though the Social Democrats (SPD) generally lost to the Communists (KPD), the total socialist vote remained stable. This would suggest that support for the Nazis came from the Protestant middle class. The example of Lower Saxony would seem to support this statement for it was of mixed religion, mostly Protestant with some Catholic areas, but with the same social composition. In the July 1932 election, the Nazis won 55 per cent of the vote in Protestant East Friesland, but only 8 per cent in the Catholic district next door where the Catholic Centre won 81 per cent. The religious factor was crucial for Catholicism was a restriction on the growth of Nazism. Priests presented the Nazis as anti-religious whilst the Centre Party was the Catholic party and they remained loyal to it. This was particularly true of rural areas, though Catholics in towns were more exposed to Nazi appeal.

The relative strength of the Nazi Party was particularly evident in terms of its regional distribution:

KEY ISSUE

Did support for the Nazi Party vary between regions?

- The Party was weak in the industrial cities and in south Germany, despite the fact that the Party originated in Bavaria.
- The North German Plain was the area where the social and religious bases of support proved to be most crucial in the decisive period 1930–3. The Nazis could mobilise the population in the Protestant and predominantly rural areas of the North German Plain, stretching from East Prussia to Schleswig-Holstein, where their strong nationalism appealed to a population who resented the loss of territory through the Treaty of Versailles. Here nine out of ten districts were solidly Nazi.
- They were weakest in the big cities and in the industrial areas generally with their concentrations of workers who remained loyal either to the SPD or the KPD.

The voters most resistant to the Nazis were those who normally supported the Catholic Centre Party or its Bavarian counterpart, the BVP. While Catholics formed about 35 per cent of the German population, support for the two Catholic parties had settled down to around 15 per cent in the Weimar years. It did not drop materially below this level in the elections of the early 1930s, except for the last one in March 1933, when Hitler was already Chancellor. Centre Party and BVP voters were usually practising, church-going Roman Catholics, with women in the majority. The Catholic clergy preached from the pulpit that support for National Socialism was sinful, largely because of its racial doctrines which stressed the inequality of races. In the final months before Hitler's arrival in power, the leaders of the Centre Party unsuccessfully

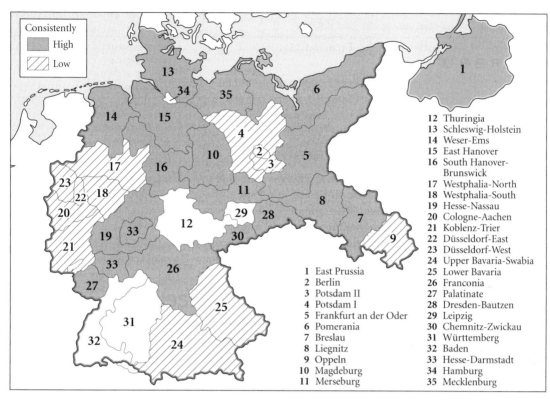

MAP 5
Analysis of the strength of support for the Nazi Party by electoral district in Reichstag *elections, 1924–32*

12 Thuringia
13 Schleswig-Holstein
14 Weser-Ems
15 East Hanover
16 South Hanover-
  Brunswick
17 Westphalia-North
18 Westphalia-South
19 Hesse-Nassau
20 Cologne-Aachen
21 Koblenz-Trier
22 Düsseldorf-East
23 Düsseldorf-West
24 Upper Bavaria-Swabia
25 Lower Bavaria
26 Franconia
27 Palatinate
28 Dresden-Bautzen
29 Leipzig
30 Chemnitz-Zwickau
31 Württemberg
32 Baden
33 Hesse-Darmstadt
34 Hamburg
35 Mecklenburg

1 East Prussia
2 Berlin
3 Potsdam II
4 Potsdam I
5 Frankfurt an der Oder
6 Pomerania
7 Breslau
8 Liegnitz
9 Oppeln
10 Magdeburg
11 Merseburg

negotiated with him about the formation of a coalition and this began to confuse Catholic voters. Nevertheless, the Nazi electoral performance in predominantly Catholic areas, like the Rhineland and Lower and Upper Bavaria, remained below the national average.

The significance of religion and of the rural/urban divide becomes obvious if we look at the percentage of votes cast for the Nazi Party in each of the elections between 1924 and 1932. There is a consistency in terms of those states which recorded a high, and those a low, vote for the NSDAP. This is summarised in Map 5 and in the chart on pages 124–5.

B *The social basis of the Nazi vote*

Between 1928 and 1930 the Nazi Party concentrated on winning over their voters who were drawn from sections of the middle class, small shop owners, peasantry and craftsmen. They met with success with these social groups so that the NSDAP came to have a disproportionately high following among the middle and even upper middle classes. After 1930 they directed their attention to winning over the workers, who were disillusioned with democracy under the impact of high unemployment. They set up a National Socialist Factory Cell Organization (NSBO), but it had limited success. The Nazis failed substantially in their efforts to

KEY ISSUE

The core of the Nazi vote.

Consistency of the Nazi vote in electoral districts		
Percentage of votes cast in favour of the NSDAP	*Electoral districts*	*Main economic/ social/religious features of the electoral district*
Consistently high	1 East Prussia 5 Frankfurt a.d. Oder 6 Pomerania 10 Magdeburg 13 Schleswig-Holstein 14 Weser-Ems 15 E Hanover 35 Mecklenburg	These eight districts lay in the Protestant and predominantly rural areas of the North German Plain stretching from (1) E Prussia to (13) Schleswig-Holstein
	7 Breslau 8 Liegnitz	These two states were exceptions – they were Catholic with a mixed economy. Border disputes with Poland made these states very nationalistic so that they responded to Nazi programme.
	16 S Hanover-Brunswick 19 Hesse-Nassau 33 Hesse-Darmstadt	Protestant with a mixed economy
	27 Palatinate	Catholic with a mainly rural economy – voted Nazi because of border disputes with France and their attempts to set up a separatist regime in 1920s
	11 Merseburg 30 Chemnitz-Zwickau	Protestant and industrial
	26 Franconia (Northern Bavaria)	Mixed in religion – Nazism united the previously politically divided Protestants against the dominance of the Catholic Centre/BVP parties

court the industrial working class traditionally mobilised by the left-wing parties and the trade union movement. Nevertheless, most commentators calculate that somewhere around 30 per cent of Nazi voters were blue-collar workers and some put it higher. The NSDAP made many converts among the craft sections of the working class employed in smaller firms and in less heavily industrialised smaller towns or rural areas. Such workers had not previously been effectively organised either by the parties of the left or trade unions. It is important to realise that it was the complexity of the German working class which explains the presence of a working-class Nazi vote. There is some evidence that the

Percentage of votes cast in favour of the NSDAP	Electoral districts		Main economic/ social/religious features of the electoral district
Consistently low	2	Berlin	Protestant, industrial cities
	3	Potsdam II	
	34	Hamburg	
	17	Westphalia-North	Nazism was particularly
	18	Westphalia-South	weak in these areas
	20	Cologne-Aachen	because they were both
	22	Düsseldorf-East	Catholic and industrial
	23	Düsseldorf-West	
	21	Koblenz-Trier	Nazism was weakest in
	24	Upper Bavaria-Swabia	Catholic and rural areas.
	25	Lower Bavaria	Upper and Lower Bavaria (South) were largely Catholic and illustrated the importance of the religious divide in comparison with the Protestant Nazi-dominated North.
	9	Oppeln	Catholic and mixed economy

decline of the SPD was not only to the benefit of the KPD, but also to the NSDAP. This still means that workers were under-represented in the Nazi movement in relation to their proportion in the population as a whole, around 45 per cent. It does, however, give some weight to Hitler's claim to be the leader of a mass movement whose broad-based support had risen above class barriers.

6 ᕃ WHO WERE THE NAZIS?

A *Size of the membership and types of members*

Historians have more reliable evidence on membership because of the availability of party membership records. At the time of Hitler's appointment as Chancellor in January 1933, membership numbered around 850,000, rising to over eight million by 1945 (the German population in 1933 was around 64 million, rising to around 70 million by 1940). By 1940 about 10 per cent of the population were party members. This small percentage was part of a deliberate policy to preserve an elite group, though many more Germans were associated with the Party through their organisations.

Various efforts have been made to identify the typical Nazi. A comprehensive survey of members and leaders of the Nazi Party for the

KEY ISSUE

The Nazi Party membership.

TABLE 25
Growth in Nazi Party membership, 1924–45

1924	55,287
1928	70,000
1931	130,000
1933	849,009
1935	2,493,890
1939	5,339,567
1942	7,100,000
1945	8,500,000

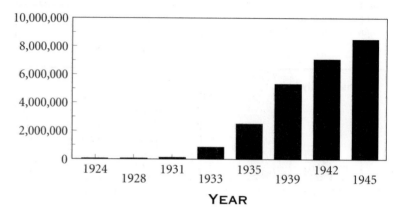

period 1919–45 has been carried out by Michael Kater (*The Nazi Party: A Social Profile of Members and Leaders 1919–1945*, Blackwell, 1983). He shares the general conclusions drawn by other researchers, that membership was predominantly male-dominated and lower middle class with the working class under-represented and the elite groups over-represented. This social structure is summarised in Table 26 and its accompanying graph. Kater argued that there were no major social differences between party officials and the rank and file. Differences developed after 1933 when more women became members and social divisions grew with the over-representation of elite groups.

B *Age structure of Party membership*

Party membership was also youthful. In January 1935 65.5 per cent of Party members were under the age of 41 and 37.6 per cent under 30.

TABLE 26
Social structure of Nazi Party membership, January 1933, compared with percentage in society (excluding unemployed)

	% in Party	% in society
Workers	31.5	46.3
White collar	21.0	12.4
Self-employed	17.6	9.6
Civil servants	6.7	4.8
Peasants	12.6	20.7
Others	3.7	6.2

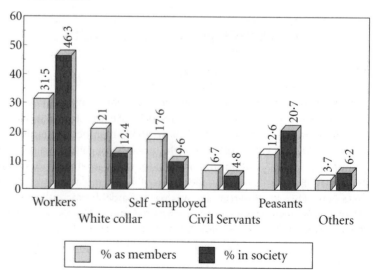

PERCENTAGE

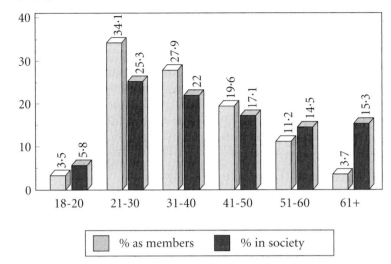

TABLE 27

Age structure of Nazi Party members, January 1935, compared with percentage in society

	% in Party	% in society
18–20	3.5	5.8
21–30	34.1	25.3
31–40	27.9	22.0
41–50	19.6	17.1
51–60	11.2	14.5
Over 61	3.7	15.3

Many of the people who joined the party and/or voted Nazi had spent their formative years during the crises of the Weimar Republic when they had suffered from the periods of high unemployment. Another reason for the predominance of the young was to be found in the purge of the SA in June 1934 which removed many of the older members.

C *Regional studies of Party membership*

A number of regional studies on Nazi Party membership have also been carried out, most notably by G. Pridham who has discussed the social background of Party membership in Bavaria in *Hitler's Rise to Power: The Nazi Movement in Bavaria* (Hart-Davis, MacGibbon 1973). He found that the early members of the Party were the lower middle class, representing an 'extremism of the centre' in a period of industrial change. Between 1930 and 1933, however, the membership changed, attracting more workers during the depression period. The unemployed joined, but did not become leaders. Peasants did not join, possibly because the priests stopped them, though some voted Nazi. Pridham concluded that 'while workers were strong in the Bavarian Party, the lower middle class provided the activist element and the professional middle classes were more prominent at leadership level.' J. Noakes has carried out a similar study on *The Nazi Party in Lower Saxony, 1921–1933* (Oxford UP 1971). Concentrating on the middle-class nature of the Party's appeal, Noakes concluded that before 1929 the Party's attempt to organise the worker had led it into an impasse: between 1928 and 1930 success came through integrating the middle class. Only after 1930 did it make any impact on the workers.

D *Sectional studies of Party membership*

There have also been a number of 'sectional' studies and, among these, studies of the SA by Conan Fischer are the most interesting ('Occupational Background of the SA Rank and File' In P. Stachura (ed.), *The Shaping of the Nazi State*). Fischer concluded that the SA was not a predominantly lower-middle-class group, though the leadership was middle class. Manual workers were in a class majority though not entirely dominant before 1933. After the seizure of power it seems that more workers joined so that 'social polarisation between a largely working-class SA and a lower-middle-class Nazi Party increased'. Most SA men seem to have been trained for a white- or blue-collar job, though about 70 per cent were unemployed and remained so even in 1934. Fischer suggests that those who joined the SA were motivated more by the availability of soup kitchens and hostels than by ideological considerations. While the SA leaders had a good grasp of Nazi ideology, 'the most striking feature of the rank and file is its lack of intellectual consistency or coherence', for even by Nazi standards the ideological intelligence of SA men was 'abysmal'. So why did they join the NSDAP rather than the KPD? Fischer concludes 'The choice of a particular activist organisation lay in their immediate material suffering, they sought the fastest possible escape from their misery'.

7 ↶ HITLER, CHANCELLOR OF GERMANY

The new leader of Germany was a man of extraordinary characteristics.

- He was often unwilling to make decisions; he was also unwilling to settle for a stable consolidation of his power and possessed a central belief in struggle and war.
- Compared with other major European figures, he had no political origins but was an 'outsider', which partly explains why he got away with so much.
- The Party he led had originated as a small right-wing 'fringe' group, made up of cranks who could not integrate themselves into post-war society. He exerted his authority because of the lack of political skills of others in the Party.
- He possessed great organisational and speaking skills; people were personally attracted to him and thousands joined the NSDAP after his rallies, which gave him an advantage over others in the Party. A disunited group were kept together by his leadership. The NSDAP used as its second title, 'Hitler's Party'.

Apart from his strengths as a leader, Hitler benefited from a number of other factors.

He owed his position in the Party to its divisions and to the absence of serious opponents. Nobody who challenged Hitler's authority got anywhere as the Strasser brothers were to discover (see pages 102–3). During the early 1920s the NSDAP was one of several right-wing racist groupings which attracted people dissatisfied by the chaos around them. Hitler benefited from divisions within his rivals. Hitler's superiority was proven while he was in prison, when the NSDAP collapsed under the leadership of Rosenberg (see page 66), an extraordinary incompetent chosen by Hitler. Attempted rebellions by the SA and the Strasser brothers forced members to chose, and the majority were unwilling to break with Hitler who had been the reason for their joining.

He became head of government not because of the strength of the NSDAP, but because of the weakness of the opposition, and the bankruptcy of Weimar's political parties. The DVP (the German Peoples' Party) under Stresemann split over reparations, the economy and questions of taxation and relations with France. The period of the 1920s into the 1930s saw a bankruptcy of the political alternatives to the NSDAP. Weimar's democratic system was wrecked by these parties, but they were not strong enough to find an alternative. They created opportunities for someone from outside to enter and so quickly establish a political dictatorship.

Hitler was the direct beneficiary of this fragmentation. Between 1932 and 1933 the **elites**, who had no love for political democracy, allied with Hitler and let him do their 'dirty' work. The army (the *Reichswehr*) believed Hitler would give them a massive rearmament programme and so were prepared to support Hitler who pursued the policies they wanted. The police, disgusted with the rise in crime, were willing to go along with a government which promised order. Moreover, the conservatives, led by Papen and the DNVP, were unable to generate popular support and looked to Hitler for this, but were too weak to control him. There were no real alternatives to Hitler with the disappearance of the conservative opposition.

Hitler established a remarkably powerful **dictatorship** and was able to remain in power despite the destructive nature of his policies. He had considerable popular support, especially in the 1930s, and an effective police apparatus while his rivals were ineffective. The regime built on order, strength and respect, it reversed the Treaty of Versailles, stabilised the economy and brought about a fall in unemployment.

Hitler also appreciated that in the foreign policy sphere the political situation in Europe favoured his plans. Britain was reluctant to allow France to establish its dominance after the events surrounding its occupation of the Ruhr in 1923–4. France had vague alliances in eastern Europe, while the Soviet Union was kept outside the European security framework. All this left Hitler with great political opportunities and he was willing skilfully to use the divisions of his political opponents at home and abroad. Goebbels' propaganda, aimed at creating a Hitler 'myth' which emphasised his far-seeing political genius, was also effective. This myth generated great support and helped him develop government.

KEY ISSUE

How was Hitler able to become head of government?

elites the collective name for the rich landowning class, the owners of large industries and those who held high administrative posts in the civil service and judiciary

dictatorship absolute rule by one man

8 ❧ BIBLIOGRAPHY

There are a number of collected editions of primary sources which are readily available. For the themes covered in this chapter J. Noakes and G. Pridham (eds), *Nazism 1919–1945, A Documentary Reader, Vol 1 – The Rise to Power 1919–1934* (University of Exeter 1983, Chapters 3 and 4) is probably the most accessible for students. It is as useful for the commentary as for the documents.

Amongst the secondary sources there are a number of general histories which cover the Weimar years and Hitler's accession to power. William Carr, *A History of Germany 1815–1945* (Arnold 1992) and Volker Berghahn, *Modern Germany* (Cambridge UP 1987) contain extensive statistical tables while Gordon Craig, *Germany 1866–1945* (Oxford UP 1981) gives a fuller, narrative treatment. J. Laver, *Imperial and Weimar Germany* (Hodder & Stoughton, History at Source, 1992) contains many written and visual sources as well as a very useful commentary and advice on how to tackle essays and source-based questions. There are now several studies of the Weimar Republic, the most recent publication in English is E.J. Feuchtwanger, *From Weimar to Hitler: Germany 1918–1933* (Macmillan 1995). J.W. Hiden, *The Weimar Republic* (Longman Seminar Studies 1974) contains some documents, although the long introduction is more useful in analysing the issues, as is the collection of essays edited by Ian Kershaw in *Weimar: Why did German democracy fail?* (Weidenfeld & Nicolson 1990). S. Taylor, *Germany 1918–1933* (Duckworth 1986) contains many documents and visual sources and looks at the history of Weimar from the perspective of the workers and middle class along with the rise of Fascism. Parts 1 and 2 of D.G. Williamson, *The Third Reich* (Longman Seminar Series 1982) provide students with a useful introduction to Adolf Hitler and his seizure of power. This can be used as a starting point for a more detailed follow-up. A detailed examination of NSDAP membership is to be found in M. Kater, *The Nazi Party: A Social Profile of Members and Leaders 1919–1945* (Oxford UP 1983). J.C. Fest, *The Face of the Third Reich* (Weidenfeld & Nicolson 1974) provides a series of biographical accounts of leading Nazi personalities and a potted biography of Hitler against the background of the period.

9 ❧ DISCUSSION QUESTIONS

A *This section consists of questions that might be used for discussion or testing your understanding of the main themes covered in this chapter.*

1. Did the Nazis come to power because there was widespread and genuine enthusiasm for their policies?
2. What were the strengths and weaknesses of Hitler as a leader?
3. What weaknesses still remained in the Nazi position by January 1933?
4. Who voted Nazi on March 5th?

10 ～ ESSAY QUESTIONS

A *Two-part questions.*

1. (a) Describe the economic and social composition of the different groups in society who supported Hitler and the Nazi Party in the years 1930–33.
   (b) Why did these groups vote for the NSDAP?

2. (a) In what ways did the economic depression of the years 1929–33 help to increase support for the Nazi Party?
   (b) What other factors help to explain Hitler's success in becoming Chancellor in January 1933?

3. (a) In what ways did the Nazi Party change in the years 1928–33?
   (b) Why was Hitler able to draw on a wide range of support in Germany in the years 1928–33?

B *Essay questions.*

1. 'People voted NSDAP more out of dislike for Weimar's democracy rather than support for Hitler's policies'.
   To what extent do you agree with this view?

2. Among which social groups, and why did, the Nazi Party establish itself most securely in Germany in the years 1928–33?

3. '6 million unemployed'.
   To what extent did the onset of economic depression in the years 1929–33 account for the success of Hitler and the NSDAP?

4. To what extent was Hitler personally responsible for the Nazis gaining power in Germany in 1933?

5. 'The strength of Nazism lay in the Protestant and predominantly rural area of the North German plain rather than in the big cities and in the industrial areas'.
   To what extent do you agree with the view?

11 ～ AN INTERPRETATION OF THE COLLAPSE OF WEIMAR DEMOCRACY

The following is intended to offer one interpretation of whether the Weimar Republic was doomed from the start. It should be used as a discussion document rather than as a definitive interpretation. It is based on the premise that there was much about democracy that was unsatisfactory and fragile and that by 1933 it had failed to secure general acceptance by the people. Readers are encouraged to develop a counter-argument to that presented here.

Historians will probably never cease to wonder how such a grotesquely horrible regime as that of the Nazis could ever have attained power in a relatively civilised and sophisticated social and political system like the Weimar Republic. Clearly resentment against the Versailles Settlement and the hardship brought by the great economic crisis of 1929 had a good deal to do with it. But these reasons can only provide an imperfect and incomplete explanation. There seems to have been a deep-rooted incompatibility between the political system of Weimar and its social structure. Although the Kaiser abdicated in 1918, this event was not followed by the removal of the remaining elites. They continued to dominate the bureaucracy and civil service. Unfortunately, they lacked not only the training to manage a democratic system of government, but also the motivation and commitment.

The timing of the Weimar Republic's introduction was not favourable. It was associated with the Treaty of Versailles which had ignored the 'good' peace promised in the American President's, Woodrow Wilson's, Fourteen Points. The armistice was a 'dictated' peace whose terms were a shattering blow especially to the republican parties. The Social Democrats, who had been responsible for the revolution in Berlin which led to the abdication of the Kaiser, temporarily withdrew from government rather than accept responsibility. The legend grew that Germany had been 'stabbed in the back' and this proved to be a powerful force for Germans inexperienced in the methods of democratic government. One reason for the ultimate failure of the Weimar Republic was the liberty which the constitutional parties allowed the Republic's enemies. An instance of this was that no attempt was made to 'purge' the bureaucracy or judiciary, resulting in a situation where the Republic could not protect its own supporters against reactionary judges. Neither could it secure adequate punishment of violent young nationalists who committed 'patriotic' crimes. The constitutional parties made themselves weak because of their strict adherence to legality, their desire for order and their reliance on 'national' elements, including the army, to suppress internal disorders.

In this situation it is perhaps not surprising that the enemies of the Weimar Republic grew in the face of its failure to tackle its recurring economic problems. The 'revolution' of 1917 was limited in that, apart from the removal of the imperial government and the Kaiser, the remaining elites, landowners and industrialists, were left in possession of their estates and factories. The officer corp reconstituted itself and chose with care the commanders and men of the new army. The army and the civil service had existed long before the parliamentary institutions of either the Empire or the Republic. Their great successes had made them almost universally respected, while their failures during the recent war were covered up in the popular belief of a 'stab in the back' by politicians. During the Weimar period, therefore, the bureaucracy was able to maintain both its reputation and its relative independence of the political parties. Yet these very people, together with the industrialists, were among the most conservative elements in Germany. They were responsible for the success of democratic government, but they lacked the necessary training and were contemptuous of Weimar's experiment in democracy.

The role of the German elites, particularly the leading industrialists, in bringing Hitler to power remains a matter of debate, but there is also a considerable agreement between historians. It is now generally recognised that the army and the large estate-owners, mainly the *Junker* aristocracy in Prussia east of the Elbe, were more immediately involved in bringing Hitler to power than the industrialists. Only a few untypical figures among the captains of German industry actively backed Hitler. The two most prominent industrial supporters of the Nazis were Emil Kirdorf, a major figure in Ruhr heavy industry before the First World War, and Fritz Thyssen, a leading steel magnate. More typical were a group of leading industrialists, mostly coming from west German heavy industry, who were very uncertain in their attitude to the Nazis. The two parties through which they had normally made their political influence felt were the DVP and the DNVP, the main right-wing nationalist party. Both these parties had, by the early 1930s, become virtually ineffective. The DVP lost almost all its vote; the DNVP had also been heavily reduced and was led by Alfred Hugenberg, with whom other industrialists found it very difficult to collaborate. The ability of the Nazis to absorb almost all the voting strength of these parties, as well as the support of Hugenberg, frustrated these industrialists. With some reluctance they came to support the inclusion of the NSDAP in a right-wing government. Hitler's courting of the industrialists was, however, never fully successful before 30 January 1933. But neither did they favour the Republic. Through their influence in the DVP, German industrialists were largely responsible for disintegrating the last fully parliamentary cabinet in March 1930 and opening the way for government by emergency decree under Article 48 of the Constitution. Once Hitler was in power, the major German industrialists, like the other sections of the German elites, quickly switched their support to him. Their acceptance of Hitler can, in part, be seen as their desire to preserve a conservative, authoritarian system of government. They believed that they could 'tame' Hitler to act as their 'puppet'.

Another weakness of the existing political system was proportional representation in the *Reichstag*. This fragmented the political system into a multiplicity of parties and permitted the Nazis to survive as a political entity during their early years. Its presence need not have made the Weimar Constitution unworkable, for it should still have been possible to form effective coalition governments. That this proved so extraordinarily difficult was due to the various parties' commitment to principles and opposition to compromise. This in turn was due to their political immaturity and inexperience of office under the German Empire. At the same time the major parties, the Social Democrats, Communists, and Centre Party, did represent genuine interest groups and they generally enjoyed the loyalty of their traditional supporters. They therefore tended to maintain their electoral strength, though they were unable to use it to exercise effective power.

Seen in this context the various economic crises appear not as causes of the progressive collapse of the Weimar Republic but as occasions for it. So long as conventional party politics remained deadlocked, social disunity prevailed, and effective government was apparently lacking, there was always a great opportunity for some other party to offer a solution. Here the Nazis had enormous advantages in what would otherwise have been great disadvantages – their apparent lack of principle and coherent policy.

As a radical socialist party the National Socialist German Workers' Party was unsuccessful. The industrial workers whom they had hoped to enlist preferred instead to remain loyal to their Social Democratic or Communist leaders. But the left was nonetheless unable significantly to extend its electoral following. The Centre Party, although equally able to rely on the loyalty of its Catholic supporters, also lacked the sort of social and economic consensus necessary to play an effective political role. Really important changes were taking place, however, among the smaller, moderate parties of the 'liberal' centre and right, the German Democratic Party and the German People's Party. These parties lost the basis of their support amongst artisans and peasants. The crucial breakthrough for the Nazis, and the obvious illustration of their essential opportunism and ruthlessness, was their decision to switch the emphasis of their campaign from the working classes, so that by 1932 they had gained the overwhelming support of the Protestant middle class. Indeed, as Noakes points out (in *The Nazi Party in Lower Saxony, 1921–1933*), virtually the entire North German Plain, with the exception of big cities like Hamburg and Berlin, became solidly Nazi.

At the same time, the election returns for 1928–33 show quite clearly that the Nazis were also benefiting from an increased turnout as well as at the expense of the liberals and the minor splinter groups. This was very largely due to their claim to be the party of national unity surmounting sectional differences and saving the country from the Bolshevik menace. They cast the Social Democrats as the 'November Criminals' who had betrayed the German people into the hands of their enemies at home and abroad. In this way the Communists, who never succeeded in undermining the Social Democrats' lead with the working classes, were made a scapegoat for an attack on the only political element that was really loyal to the Weimar Republic. Here the Nazis were greatly helped by the fact that in 1928 the Social Democrats came back into a coalition government for the first time since 1920. This gave the Nazis the opportunity to remind the people of the role they had played in agreeing to the Versailles Treaty and reparations which were seen as the causes of the economic ills.

It should not be overlooked, however, that the Nazis failed to secure a ruling majority. There was, indeed, still a reasonable possibility for a coalition government to survive in the spring of 1930 or for other anti-Nazi combinations to be made. But the left were too divided by internal jealousies and rivalries to work together to exploit their electoral strength. As it was the Nazis had only to contrive the *Reichstag* fire in order to complete the disintegration of the German Communist Party, and heighten their terror tactics to paralyse the opposition of the Social Democrats, in spite of the fact that in the *Reichbanner* the latter had a parliamentary organisation which might have challenged the SA.

On none of these successes, however, could the Nazis have confidently reckoned in advance, and it is fascinating to observe how worried their leaders were. Their electorate, which even by March 1933 had still not given them an overall majority, was clearly unreliable. The tolerance and co-operation of the right-wing establishment, on which their immediate and long-term success depended, might easily have been withdrawn out of fear. The failure of the conservative establishment to reject extreme ideas and methods that were so alien to their class and tradition was as extraordinary as the passiveness of the left. Hitler and Goebbels certainly feared that the right would eventually reject them.

But the right's desire to return to the past, their contempt for the Weimar Republic and their fear of Bolshevism, all combined to deceive them into thinking that they could use and destroy the Nazis. As the leading political general of the period, Kurt von Schleicher, put it in 1932, 'if the Nazis did not exist, it would be necessary to invent them'. In all this Hitler gave the conservative nationalists a great deal of encouragement. Their intrigues and negotiations with him in 1932 and 1933 led them to believe that here was a realistic politician with whom they could make a deal. They believed that he would control his more undisciplined followers. The conservatives got the authoritarian state that they wanted but they never expected to pay for it by surrendering an almost unchallengeable control and use of it to such a nobody as Hitler.

12 ⌒ MAKING NOTES

Using the information contained in this and preceding chapters.

1. Draw up a profile of the main political parties mentioned in Table 24 (page 117): The *Reichstag* election of 5 March 1933. In your answer include an analysis of the reasons why different groups of people voted for the parties mentioned.
2. Compare the performance of the parties identified in Table 24 with that in Table 15 (page 83): The *Reichstag* election of May 1928. Record your findings as follows:

Political party/parties	Performance between 1928 and 1933	Reasons for this performance
NSDAP		
DNVP		
DNP		

3. Why was Hitler successful in attracting a cross section of German society to vote NSDAP? What motives influenced them to vote Nazi?
4. Draw up a profile of a typical non-Nazi voter.

13 ∽ DOCUMENTARY EXERCISE ON THE *REICHSTAG* FIRE

Study the sources below and the questions which follow:

SOURCE A *Joseph Goebbels,* My Part in Hitler's Fight *(1935).*

At nine, the Führer came to supper. We had a little music and talked. Suddenly the telephone rang. The *Reichstag* is burning! I thought the news was pure fantasy and, at first, did not inform the Führer. After a few more calls, I was able to confirm that the terrible news was true... We raced to the scene at top speed... Göring met us and soon von Papen arrived. It had already been established that the fire was due to arson. There could be no doubt that the Communists had made a final attempt to seize power by creating an atmosphere of panic and terror.

SOURCE B *Sefton Delmer, British correspondent to the* London Daily Express, *writing in* The Germans and I *(1936).*

Twenty to thirty minutes after the fire was discovered Hitler said to von Papen: 'This is a God-given signal. If this fire, as I believe, turns out to be the handiwork of the Communists, then there is nothing that shall stop us from crushing out the murderous pest with an iron fist...' That evening Hitler said to me, 'God grant that this be the work of the Communists. You are witnessing the beginning of a new age in German history.'

SOURCE C *Herman Rauschning, a former Nazi who left the party in 1936 to become one of its leading critics in exile,* The Voice of Human Destruction *(1940).*

Göring, Himmler, Frick and a number of *Gauleiter* from the western provinces were talking together. Göring was giving details of the *Reichstag* fire, the secret of which was still being carefully guarded. I myself had unhesitatingly ascribed it to arson on the part of persons under Communist, or at any rate Comintern, influence. It was not until I heard this conversation that I discovered that the National Socialist leadership was solely responsible, and that Hitler knew of the plan and approved it.

The complacency with which this close circle of the initiated discussed the deed was shattering. Gratified laughter, cynical jokes, boasting – these were the sentiments expressed by the 'conspirators'. Göring described how 'his boys' had entered the *Reichstag* building by a subterranean passage from the President's palace, and how they had only a few minutes at their disposal and were nearly discovered... Göring, who had taken a leading part in the conversation, closed with the significant words: 'I have no conscience. My conscience is Adolf Hitler'.

Hitler then began to discuss the *Reichstag* fire...

'Go and look at it,' he said. 'It is the beacon of a new era in the history of the world... I have sown fear and apprehension in the hearts of those old women, Hugenberg and company. They're quite prepared to believe I instigated it. They take me for Old Nick himself.

And it's a good thing they do. I have no choice,' he exclaimed. 'I must do things that cannot be measured with the yardstick of bourgeois squeamishness. This *Reichstag* fire gives me the opportunity to intervene. And I shall intervene.'

He then explained to us further that he must shock the middle class in order to rouse their fears of the designs of the Communists and their dread of his own severity.

'The world can only be ruled by fear.'

SOURCE D *Hitler discusses the fire in a private conversation, from Hermann Rauschning,* The Voice of Human Destruction *(1940).*

I was a member of the Communist Party until 1929... In Holland, I read that the Nazis had come to power in Germany. In my opinion, something had to be done in protest against this system... since the workers would do nothing. I had to do something myself. I thought arson a suitable method. I did not wish to harm ordinary people, but something belonging to the system itself. I decided on the *Reichstag*. As to the question whether I acted alone, I declare emphatically that this was the case. No one at all helped me.

SOURCE E *Marinus Van der Lubbe's statement to the police, 3 March 1933.*

I had nothing to do with it... I can tell you in all honesty, that the *Reichstag* fire proved very inconvenient to us. After the fire, I had to use the Kroll Opera House as the new *Reichstag*. I must repeat that no excuse was needed for taking measures against the Communists. I already had a number of perfectly good reasons in the form of murders...

SOURCE F *Hermann Göring at the Nuremberg Trials in 1946.*

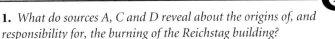

1. *What do sources A, C and D reveal about the origins of, and responsibility for, the burning of the Reichstag building?*

2. *Use your own knowledge to explain how Hitler exploited the Reichstag Fire for his own propaganda and political purposes.*

3. *How valuable are sources C and F to an historian studying the events surrounding the Reichstag Fire?*

4. *Using sources A–F, and your own knowledge, explain why the events surrounding the burning of the Reichstag building remain one of the great 'whodunits' in history?*

6

The Nazi Consolidation of Power

INTRODUCTION

Ignoring disappointment at the failure to secure the desired majority in the 5 March elections, Hitler declared the results to be an overwhelming victory. When the cabinet met on the 7 March Hitler claimed that the election had been a 'glorious and bloodless revolution' in contrast with the bloody Russian revolution of November 1918. Using the powers of the State which he had acquired as Chancellor, he quickly followed this through with actions which stressed the principle of legality. The latter did not always embrace the activities of the SA which at street level could often have been considered illegal. During the spring of 1933 the Nazis manoeuvred to take over the State. Control of the media, press and radio were secured with the appointment on 13 March of Goebbels as Minister of Propaganda and Popular Entertainment. The chapter examines the key events in Hitler's consolidation of power.

1 ～ THE DAY OF POTSDAM

Goebbels set about creating the cult image of Hitler as a national hero who was uniting National Socialism with the forces of old Germany stretching back through Bismarck to the military glory of Frederick the Great. This image was reinforced by the spectacle staged on 21 March, the 'Day of Potsdam'. This event refers to the celebrations surrounding the opening of the newly elected *Reichstag*. Goebbels arranged a ceremony at Potsdam Garrison Church, in the presence of President Hindenburg, the Crown Prince, son of the exiled Kaiser, and many of the army's leading generals, with the aim of reassuring the people that Hitler could be trusted. This event has been described by a number of eyewitness accounts. One such account comes from Erich Ebermeyer, a dramatist, whose father was a former public prosecutor of the Supreme Court at Leipzig. Though his family was liberal and unsympathetic to Nazism, he was won over by the event, for as he wrote, 'no one can escape the emotion of the moment. Father too is deeply impressed. Mother has tears in her eyes', in response to the scene of 'Hindenburg laying wreaths on the graves of the Prussian kings. The old Field Marshal shakes hands with the World War corporal. The corporal

KEY ISSUE

How did Hitler strengthen Nazi control of Germany?

makes a deep bow over the hand of the Field Marshal. Cannons thunder over Potsdam, over Germany'. Douglas Reed, a journalist has also vividly described the events of the day in his account of these years, *Insanity Fair*, which was published in 1938:

I looked about me curiously on this fitfully sunny day, 21 March 1933. The bells of Potsdam were clanging, the flags waving, and an enormous concourse had come out.

Hindenburg came, stepped out of his car, looked slowly round and stiffened as he saw the soldiers. That always galvanised him into life. Here were no perplexing politicians, but ranks of field-greys, entirely immobile save for their heads, which turned like the leaves of a book as he went past...one hand rested on his sword and with the other he raised the field-marshal's baton in salute.

Sinking his head in humility, Hitler met him. Hitler, whose Goebbels had derided Hindenburg's senility by asking, 'Is Hindenburg still alive?'. Now little Goebbels sat in hushed reverence inside the Church with the other members of the Cabinet, waiting to see the marriage of the old and the new Germany.

Göring, too, stood at the door of the Church, monumental in morning clothes. Nearby was a wooden pen, reserved for the Generalhood. Here were the representatives of the spirit of Potsdam, of the doctrine that Germany has the divine right to expand by force of arms. For years these men had been figures of fun in a disillusioned Germany; now they had come into their own right.

What was this all about, this pilgrimage to Potsdam?

Hindenburg was neither quite clear what he had done nor whether he had done right. In the misty recesses of his darkling mind the question still prompted itself whether by making Hitler Chancellor in January and by approving the rape of the Constitution in February he had really honoured his oath 'to do justice to all men'. In March Hitler had found a way to allay his doubts, one of those ceremonies of symbolic patriotism so dear to the German mind.

This was the meaning of the Potsdam ceremony. Before the new *Reichstag*...met, a dedicatory service was to be held in the Garrison Church, the new regime was to be pledged to 'the spirit of Potsdam', and Hindenburg and Hitler were to shake hands over the tomb of Frederick the Great. The torch of German ambitions for world power was being passed on, from Field-Marshal to Bohemian corporal.

As he entered the Church, sixty-seven years after his first visit, tears filled Hindenburg's eyes as he saw around him all the symbols of the old martial Germany. He nodded ponderous approval when Hitler said, thanks to him, 'the marriage has been consummated between the symbols of the old greatness and the new strength'.

Then came the famous handclasp, which meant, to Germans, that the years between 1918 and 1933 had been blotted out of the German history books, that Hindenburg had handed over his command to Hitler.

Q *What, in your view, is the significance of the events described in this eyewitness account?*

TABLE 28

Date chart of chief events in Hitler's consolidation of power

1933	March	Nazis occupy all Socialist, Communist and trade union offices and publishing companies; power is seized in the *Länder*; Goebbels sets up Reich Propaganda Ministry; first concentration camp established at Dachau; 'Day of Potsdam' opening of newly-elected *Reichstag*; Enabling Act is passed; SA attack Jews and Jewish businesses
	April	Official one-day boycott of Jewish shops on 1 April; Jews and non-Germans excluded from public service; *Gestapo*/secret state police established by Göring
	May	Trade unions abolished; German Workers' Front established; books of 'un-German' authors burnt in university cities
	June	SPD banned; other political parties dissolve themselves soon after
	July	All political parties except NSDAP banned; one-party state established; Reich Film Law passed; Concordat concluded with the Papacy
	October	Germany leaves the League of Nations and the Disarmament Conference
	November	First elections for one-party state give NSDAP 92 per cent of vote
1934	January	Law for the Ordering of National Labour weights industrial relations in favour of management against workforce; Rosenberg appointed Party ideological supervisor; German-Polish 10-year non-aggression pact; independent state governments abolished
	April	Himmler becomes chief of Prussian *Gestapo*; People's Court established to deal with treasonable offences
	June	Vice-Chancellor Papen denounces the continuing Nazi revolution; 'Night of the Long Knives' purges Röhm and about 70 other SA leaders
	July	Himmler appointed Reichsführer of the SS, now independent of the SA; Austrian Nazis murder the President, Dollfuß, hoping to gain control of the government; Papen appointed German envoy to Austria
	August	Death of Hindenburg; Hitler declares himself Führer; armed forces take oath of personal loyalty to Hitler; plebiscite records large majority in favour of Hitler's new powers

2 ⌐ THE ENABLING LAW

Two days after the Potsdam ceremony the new *Reichstag* met at Kroll Opera House in Berlin, the *Reichstag* building having been burnt down in the February. It was attended by the 288 Nazi deputies elected on 5 March and 52 Nationalists. The 81 Communist deputies had been outlawed while many of the Socialists were also absent, either out of fear, or because they were in hospital, or had fled the country. The atmosphere in the building has been described by one eyewitness as one of death and destruction. The building was surrounded by members of the SS in their sinister black and silver uniforms, while inside stood long lines of SA troops, a spectacle designed to intimidate representatives of the other political parties as they took their seats. The main purpose of this meeting was to consider the Enabling Law which (as recorded in Noakes and Pridham, *Nazism 1919–1945, A Documentary Reader, Vol 1*) Hitler had already discussed in the 7 March cabinet meeting when he had said:

> what was needed was an Enabling Law passed by a two-thirds major-ity. He, the Reich Chancellor, was firmly convinced that the *Reichstag* would pass such a law. The deputies of the German Communist Party would not appear at the opening of the *Reichstag* because they were in jail... With regard to the internal political situation, the Vice-Chancellor stated that yesterday (6 March) Dr Kaas had been to see him. He had stated that he had come without previously consulting his party and was not prepared to let bygones be bygones. He had, more-over, offered the co-operation of the Centre Party...

Passage of the Enabling Act would give Hitler dictatorial powers for it transferred, for a period of four years, powers from the *Reichstag* to the government. It gave the Chancellor, rather than the President, the right to draft laws and sign treaties with foreign states. Hitler spoke first, his style restrained and moderate, reassuring his audience (quoted in *Hitler* by J.C. Fest):

Q

What was the significance of the Enabling Act for the Reichstag, the remaining political parties and the power of Hitler in 1933?

> The government intends to make use of this Act only to the extent required to carry out vitally necessary measures. The existence of neither the *Reichstag* nor the *Reichsrat* is threatened. The position and rights of the President are not affected... The existence of the states will not be eliminated... The rights of the Churches will not be dimin-ished... The number of cases in which an internal necessity exists for having need of such a law is in itself a limited one. All the more, however, the Government insist upon the passing of the law. They prefer a clear decision.

Hitler sat down to the sounds of loud applause and the deputies stood up and sang *Deutschland über Alles*. After a break, the leader of the Social Democrats, Otto Wels, rose to address the largely hostile assembly. Against a background of chanting by the SA and SS, Wels made a brave and defiant speech, explaining why his party would not support the Bill. Showing unchecked anger, Hitler stood, mocked his opponent and tore his speech to shreds. 'I do not want your votes', he screamed, 'Germany will be free, but not through you... The star of Germany is in the ascendant, yours is about to disappear, your death-knell has sounded'. With the support of his Nazi deputies and the Nationalists, Hitler could depend on gaining 341 of the 432 votes he needed to secure a two-thirds majority. The exclusion of the Commu-nist deputies meant that the outcome lay with the Catholic Centre Party. It had originally been opposed to the Act, but it gave in after

Hitler promised to respect the rights of the Catholic Church. Outside the building a mob of SA chanted, 'Give us the Bill or else fire and murder'. In a situation little removed from farce, the three readings of the Bill took place in only a few minutes before the Enabling Act was passed by 441 to 94, with only the Social Democrats opposing it. When the outcome was announced, the Nazi deputies stood, gave the raised arm salute and sang the party anthem, the *Horst Wessel* song.

As a result of this act, the *Reichstag* ceased to play an active role in politics and Weimar's remaining political parties became out of date. Within three months of becoming Chancellor, Hitler had become independent of his conservative allies and the first phase of his seizure of power was completed. Those who had helped him to power on the 30 January, particularly von Papen, had intended that he should be little more than a figurehead in a cabinet still dominated by conservative nationalists. Von Papen had declared to a Prussian aristocrat, who had warned him of the dangers of allowing Hitler and the Nazis any share of power, that he had 'the confidence of Hindenburg. In two months we will have pushed Hitler into a corner so that he squeaks'. Von Papen and his fellow conservatives had underestimated Hitler's political abilities, viewing him as an ambitious ex-corporal, inexperienced in politics, unlike themselves. They had thought it was their birthright to control the fate of Germany and that they could use Hitler to create the illusion that they enjoyed the support of the masses. They believed that, given his humble birth and inexperience in politics, they would continue to decide policy. The events that followed showed how wrong they were in this belief and gave weight to the warnings of an ex-supporter of Hitler's, General Ludendorff. On 1 February, only two days after Hitler's appointment as Chancellor, Ludendorff had written to President Hindenburg warning him that he had 'delivered the country to one of the greatest demagogues of all time'. This extreme right-wing nationalist, who had supported Hitler in the Beer Hall *Putsch* of 1923, predicted: 'this damnable man will plunge our Reich into the abyss and bring inconceivable misery down upon our nation. Coming generations will curse you in your grave because of this action'. The Enabling Act, which had legally transferred power to Hitler, was extended in 1937, 1941 and 1943.

3 ➵ GLEICHSCHALTUNG

KEY ISSUE

The main features of Hitler's policy of unifying Germany under Nazi rule – Gleichschaltung.

After these events of March, Hitler's next task was to make himself supreme by getting rid of those who would challenge his authority. Armed with his new-found dictatorial powers to govern by decree, he launched a policy of *Gleichschaltung*, the creation of a National Socialist constituency through a policy of co-ordination. This aimed at a complete unity of political, social and economic life with the application of terror as a deterrent to any resistance. The date chart in Table 28 (page 140) shows the progress of this policy.

The *Gestapo* (State secret police) was developed by Göring during

April/November 1933. No one who dared to oppose the regime would be spared. Hitler benefited from the great outburst of genuine national patriotism which flourished during these early months along with a wave of terror. He carried through a degree of unification which would have been considered impossible by his predecessors.

- Independence from the *Reichstag* was followed by the subordination of the state governments (*Länder*) to Berlin through the appointment of governors (*Reichstatthalter*).
- The system of elections was abolished throughout the whole of state provincial and municipal government. The traditional 'federal' Germany with its many competing sovereignties was replaced by a centralised, unified German State.
- Other potential opponents were also removed, despite their attempts to appear to be loyal supporters of the regime.
- On 2 May 1933 the SA and SS occupied trade union offices, union funds were confiscated and their leaders, many of whom were sent to concentration camps, were portrayed by Goebbels' propaganda machine as swindlers of workers' payments. Trade unions were replaced by the German Labour Front (*Deutsche Arbeitsfront*), headed by Robert Ley, the former Reich Organisation Leader, by the Law for the Ordering of National Labour in 1934.

Within two years of takeover of power, the whole life of the German people, with the most important exception of religion, had been co-ordinated under Nazi control. Agriculture, industry, the 'free' professions, lawyers and doctors were organised on Nazi lines. All those involved in influencing public opinion were under the official control of the Propaganda Ministry, which issued directives to newspapers, radio, film and theatre. Goebbels made the Propaganda Ministry a powerful instrument for moulding public opinion to accept Nazi policies which affected all aspects of people's lives.

The surviving political parties had already become redundant and they now offered no resistance to Hitler. He proceeded to complete the process of unification by first of all removing his left-wing opponents. The Communist Party (KPD), whose deputies had already been banned from taking their seats in the new *Reichstag*, had its property confiscated. Some members of the Party fled into the underground movement of resistance, while others deserted to the National Socialists out of a sense of self-preservation. After the co-ordination of trade unions, the Social Democratic Party (SPD) had its headquarters, property and newspapers seized on 10 May 1933, followed by its ban and surrender of seats in the *Reichstag* in June.

The other political parties, without waiting for hostile action, decided to disband themselves voluntarily. The Democratic Party (DDP), the Peoples' Party (DVP), the Catholic Centre and the Nationalist (DNVP) parties liquidated themselves at the end of June/beginning of July. The *Stahlhelm*, the ex-soldiers' organisation of the Right, affiliated mainly to the DNVP and with strong anti-republican tendencies (Hindenburg was a member), was absorbed by the SA on 21 June 1933.

The leader of the *Stahlhelm*, Franz Seldte, had become Minister of Labour in Hitler's cabinet in January 1933.

The process of unification was completed with a government decree of the 14 July 1933 which declared the NSDAP to be the only political party in Germany.

This rapid destruction of all political forces from left to right is one of the most striking features of the Nazi seizure of power. Hitler achieved in less than five months a seizure of power which had taken Mussolini seven years to achieve in Italy. In the pursuit of such power, Hitler achieved a political centralisation which amounted to a revolution. But it would be wrong to suppose, as its socialist and communist critics did, that the Nazi regime was a dictatorship imposed by force on an unwilling people. Hitler carried through his policy of *Gleichschaltung* without serious resistance. He was surprised by the collapse of opposition when it was confronted with the strength and determination of the Nazis, although the ever-present threat of violence also played its part.

4 ↩ REIGN OF TERROR

Intimidation and violence were vital ingredients in Hitler's methods to achieve and maintain power. There has been inadequate study by historians to explain the wave of terror which spread in the spring of 1933. Most historians concentrate on the deliberate use of terror by the leadership, but there is evidence that it was also begun by the rank and file. It was often unplanned and uncontrolled by the Party's leadership, who were forced to act in response to this terror.

Evidence for such an opinion has been drawn from events such as:

	KEY ISSUE

The role played by intimidation and terror in the unification process.

1. The boycott of Jewish shops which was started by the SA. On 1 April, uniformed SA posted themselves at entrances to Jewish businesses and displayed placards to passers-by which warned them against buying from Jews. At first, Hitler was concerned to contain extremist threats against the Jews in the interests of political stability, public order and economic recovery. Subsequently he aimed to control the event by declaring a centrally co-ordinated boycott of Jewish shops. This ban, which Hindenburg and Neurath insisted should only run for a day, was not extended because of public indifference, hostile foreign reaction and the danger to the economy.
2. The abolition of trade unions was a similar response to action taken by gangs of Nazi thugs six weeks before the leadership officially occupied trade union offices and absorbed them into the German Labour Front.
3. Hitler also had to deal with complaints from foreign consuls about the persecution of foreigners living in Germany. Reports came in from many towns of incidents in which storm troopers had attacked anyone speaking a foreign language or having a dark skin.

Use of terror benefited Hitler because it frightened his political opponents and it was useful for 'co-ordinating' the state governments which he did not control. It gave him the opportunity to get rid of the previous governments by pressure from below. The Party marched in to occupy town halls and detain former leaders so that the Nazis captured positions of power at regional and local level by terrorising their opponents. Members of the SA were motivated by a desire for rewards to compensate them for the long, dangerous and exhausting years they had spent helping the leadership before 1933. They had marched, fought off opponents, attended meetings and suffered injuries and were now impatient for results. By mid-February 1933 the SA had got out of hand. They started to work on their own initiative and intimidated governmental authority at regional and local level. There was evidence for this from the pressure which was put on businesses to employ SA as commissars, another name for a 'protection racket'. The SA also had a desire for revenge. They established unofficial concentration camps in cellars and deserted factory buildings to imprison Nazi opponents.

The government was very worried by these developments. Göring, as Minister of the Interior, felt obliged to take action against the SA who were working outside the law. During March/April 1933, when the policy of *Gleichschaltung* was being introduced, the government feared that the accompanying wave of terror would provoke either a civil war or a general strike by those who were exposed to this violence. It was found difficult to control the situation and the Nazi leadership feared that the army would intervene to take control. There were frequent government warnings to the SA about their independent action, but these were ignored. The one below by Wilhelm Frick, Reich Minister of the Interior, was delivered on 6 October 1933 (quoted in Noakes and Pridham, *Nazism 1919–1945, A Documentary Reader, Vol 1*):

> Despite repeated announcements by the Reich Chancellor, and despite my numerous circulars, new infringements by subordinate leaders and by members of the SA have been reported again and again during the past weeks. Above all, SA leaders and SA men have independently carried out police actions for which they had no authority whatever...and [which] cannot be reconciled with the existing laws and regulations of the National Socialist government.
>
> These infringements and excesses must now cease, once and for all. I make it the duty of Reich Governors, State governments and all subordinate institutions to intervene sharply against any attempt at unauthorised interference.

Q

What impression of the attitudes and motives of the SA is given in Frick's warning?

The reaction of the Nazi leadership suggests that the traditional ruling elites had become anxious, particularly when attacks on business and the civil service occurred. They disliked the takeover of the police by the SA and the general disorder. They feared that these attacks would be used against them. They offered to legislate for a number of Nazi goals such as purging the civil service of Nazi opponents. Accordingly on 7 April a law was published which purged the civil service of Jews, except those who had served in the First World War, and politically unreliable persons. Public order was restored by the *Gestapo*. SA members responsible for beating up and murdering opponents were dealt with while their concentration camps in SA cellars were closed.

Between 1933 and 1934 there was an intense struggle for power between those who favoured an authoritarian conservative regime and those ideologically committed National Socialists, led by Röhm and the SA. This struggle caused the first major domestic political crisis in the events which became known as '*Die Nacht der langen Messer*', 'The Night of the Long Knives'.

5 ⌐ 'THE NIGHT OF THE LONG KNIVES' – THE BLOOD PURGE OF JUNE 1934

A *Problems facing Hitler 1933–4*

The challenge to Hitler's dictatorship came from the competing pressures and priorities which faced him between June 1933 and June 1934. He was faced with three interconnected problems.

The first arose from the split in the NSDAP between the conservative, nationalist, capitalist element and that of the socialist left who demanded the 'Second Revolution'. Part of the problem was that Hitler's tactics and goals differed from those of Röhm. There was also the problem of the relationship between the SA and the *Reichswehr*. Finally, faced with the declining health of Hindenburg, Hitler feared that, on the latter's death, the conservative elites would push on him a new conservative President. such a man would block his plans to unite the posts of Chancellor and President which would make him the undisputed political leader of Germany as opposed to Chancellor and head of Party.

Hitler was pushed by the left wing of the Nazi Party, led by Röhm, and his supporters for a second, social, revolution to complete the political seizure. This was a vague idea but was based on the belief that the existing ruling elite would thus be replaced by the Nazis with their different set of values. Röhm and his supporters wanted changes in the relationship between different social classes. In fact, the bloodless seizure of power in January 1933 was followed by many of the old leaders of Weimar – the capitalists, generals, *Junker* and conservative politicians – joining Hitler's 'bandwagon' and taking posts as compromises were made with established institutions. This infuriated Röhm who was also disillusioned by the lack of rewards for the SA, many of whom were unemployed. He also wanted the SA to become Germany's new revolutionary national army. Ill-feeling increased when Hitler demanded the end of SA revolutionary activities because these alarmed the public. For his part, Hitler was aware that he needed the support of the German army (*Reichswehr*) in order to remain in power and succeed to the presidency. He also needed their technical expertise for the rearmament programme which he launched in summer of 1933. Moreover, Hitler did not want to risk losing the support of the two new leaders of the Army, the Defence Minister, Blomberg and the new Chief-of-Staff, Reichenau. These two eventually persuaded Hitler to make a choice between themselves and the SA. The differences between Hitler and Röhm made a showdown inevitable.

KEY ISSUE

Disunity within the Nazi party. The challenge by Röhm and the SA to Hitler's leadership.

B *Röhm's challenge to Hitler*

From May 1933 onwards Röhm was continually criticising the regime for its foreign policy, attacks on the unions and repression of freedom of opinion. He denounced Goebbels, Göring, Himmler and Hess in sharp terms and was personally outraged by what he regarded as Hitler's dishonesty. He issued an order warning the SA against 'false friends' and 'false celebrations' and reminding them of unfulfilled goals. He warned that the SA and SS would not tolerate the German revolution 'going to sleep or being betrayed at the half-way stage by non-combatants'. He followed this up, in June, with a bitter newspaper article attacking Hitler whom he described as 'rotten'. The article (quoted in *Hitler* by J.C. Fest) went on to say:

> He's betraying all of us. He only goes round with reactionaries. His old comrades aren't good enough for him. So he brings in these East Prussian generals. They're the ones he pals around with now... Adolf knows perfectly well what I want. I told him often enough. Not a second pot of the Kaiser's army, made with the same old rounds. Are we a revolution or aren't we?... Something new has to be brought in, understand? The generals are old fogies. They'll never have a new idea...
>
> He wants to inherit a ready-made army all set to go. He wants to have it knocked together by 'experts'. When I hear that word I blow my top. He'll make it National Socialist later on, he says. But first he's turning it over to the Prussian generals. Where the hell is the revolutionary spirit to come from afterwards? From a bunch of old fogies who certainly aren't going to win the new war? Don't try to kid me, the whole lot of you. You're letting the whole heart and soul of our movement go to pot.

Q

What are Röhm's criticisms of Hitler?

Hitler's response to these challenges was to deliver a speech to his *Gauleiter* in Berlin, on 2 February 1934. He warned them against continuing revolution which could only lead to 'a permanent state of chaos' and called for loyal officials who would accept the authority of the leader and not threaten the 'revolution' with internal struggles. 'Only one man could be leader...there must not be any internal struggles...we must not engage in more than a single fight at a time.' He was aware that Röhm represented a permanent threat of a possible *putsch*. But it was not just Hitler whom Röhm challenged. He also antagonised the ambitious other Nazis in power so that all were willing

KEY ISSUE

Hitler's response to Röhm and the SA challenge.

to push Hitler towards destroying the SA. Thus there was the display of simultaneous unification and civil war.

C Events leading to the Blood Purge of 30 June 1934

The prospect of Hindenburg's death led Papen and his conservative allies to make some sort of a stand. On 17 June 1934 at Marburg University, Papen made a very bitter speech, written by Edgar Jung, in which he condemned the National Socialist revolution for its violence and radicalism. Papen also criticised the policy of *Gleichschaltung* and protested against the 'unnatural claim to totality'. He warned against 'a permanent uprising from below', and declared that, 'if there was a second "wave of new life" it must do so not as a social revolution, but as the creative completion of work already begun.' This speech caused a great stir and raised the hopes of many, but words were not followed by action.

Hitler, in a great rage, regarded Papen's re-emergence as a personal challenge. Even so, he tried to reason with Röhm in a five-hour conversation on 4 June. He asked Röhm to forget the idea of a second revolution and not to cause trouble. Although he promised not to disband the SA, he ordered it on leave for August during which time no uniforms were to be worn. By this time Hitler had decided that Röhm and his followers had to be removed, though he was pushed into final action by Göring's and Himmler's reports of a rumoured SA uprising, planned for 31 June, in Berlin and Munich. On 28 June, Hitler visited the Rhineland to attend the wedding of a *Gauleiter* and to inspect some local factories. He ordered Röhm to command senior SA leaders to join him on 30 June at Bad Wiessee, 30 miles south of Munich, where Röhm was staying. The SS and SD (State security service, *Sicherheitsdienst*) were put on an intensive watch of the SA. The support of the army was guaranteed after Hitler promised that it would remain the national source of power and that the SA would be kept subordinate. During the night of 29/30 June Hitler flew to Munich and arrested Röhm in his hotel. Röhm refused to shoot himself and was executed two days later in his cell. Other SA were arrested on their way to the meeting and subsequently executed. Göring in the meantime ordered arrests in Berlin and other cities. No one knows how many were killed, but it is estimated that 77 leading Nazis, along with about 100 others, most of them on the left wing of the Party, were eliminated. Amongst the SA leaders purged were Edmund Heines, Fritz von Krausser, August Schneidhüber, Karl Ernst, Hans Hayn and Peter von Heydebreck. Hitler took the opportunity to purge his enemies, opponents and critics, not only within the NSDAP, but also generally. This included several members of Papen's staff, one of whom was Edgar Jung, together with General von Schleicher, his wife and a friend, General von Bredow, a number of Catholic clergy, including Father Bernard Stempfle, as well as Gregor Strasser and Gustav von Kahr (see pages 58–59), the man who had

> **KEY ISSUE**
>
> *The response of Papen and the elites to Röhm's challenge.*

THEY SALUTE WITH BOTH HANDS NOW.

betrayed his initial promise to support the 1923 Beer Hall *Putsch*. A number of Jews were shot to provide entertainment for the SS.

D *Significance of the event*

By this event, Hitler solved the main problems that faced him. He got rid of Röhm and his rebellious SA, thereby satisfying the demands of the army and ending public dissatisfaction with street violence and terrorism. The SA lost its importance but the SS, led by Himmler, soon took its place as the most powerful and sinister empire within the Nazi state. Hitler had also blocked conservative counter-plans led by Papen and yet remained independent of all. He sacrificed the 'old fighters' to his major objectives: political stability and economic recovery. The 'Röhm Affair', as the purge became known, increased his personal standing, prestige and popularity at the expense of his own movement. In a speech to the *Reichstag* on 13 July, Hitler justified his actions as protecting the German people against the 'bad behaviour' and 'drunken excesses' of men who were 'in the highest degree detestable'. Frick drafted a law that declared all actions by Hitler in the purge to be legal and statesmanlike. It was passed quickly by the *Reichstag*, which by now had become a Nazi assembly.

6 ⌐ DEATH OF HINDENBURG

On 2 August 1934 Hindenburg died at the age of 87. He had served as President of the Weimar Republic for nine years. His popularity had been based on his reputation as an eminent Field Marshal of the 1914–18 war and on the fact that he seemed to represent to the German people a symbol of honour and stability. In a government announcement, he was applauded as 'a monumental memorial of the distant past', whose 'almost incalculable services' culminated in the fact that 'on January 30 1933...he opened the gates of the Reich for the Young National Socialist Movement', that he led the Germany of yesterday to 'profound reconciliation' with the Germany of tomorrow and became in peace what he had been in war, 'the national myth of the German people'. During the last five years of his life he had shown signs of increasing senility, but Hitler, recognising the importance of Hindenburg's reputation and standing both with the German people and the army, was prepared to wait. Within an hour of the news of the old President's death, Hitler announced that the positions of President and Chancellor would be merged and that he would take the titles of *Führer* and *Reichskanzler*. Using presidential powers he became Commander-in-Chief of the Armed Forces. Officers and men took an oath of allegiance to Hitler who was mentioned by name in the oath. The Nazi revolution was complete. However, Hitler still had important restraints on his power: he had not yet gained control of the army and the churches and he was still dependent on an alliance with the elites. Apart from these considerations, the supremacy of the Führer was applied in every sphere of Party and State. He decided policy, made laws and controlled foreign policy. (We will be looking at Hitler's mastery of the Third Reich in the next chapter.)

On 6 August the members of the *Reichstag* assembled at the Kroll Opera House to hear Hitler's funeral address in commemoration of the old Field Marshal. He turned the occasion into a theatrical event and used it to the full for propaganda purposes with the use of Wagnerian music and parades of both the German army and the SS. In his address Hitler told the people the name of Hindenburg would remain immortal 'even when the last trace of his body has vanished'. He ended with, 'Dead warlord, now enter into Valhalla!'

On 19 August the German people were invited to take part in a plebiscite to indicate their approval of Hitler's assumption of the title 'Führer'. Before the vote took place Hindenburg's political testament, which was thought to have been lost, was conveniently discovered. In it the Field Marshal spoke warmly of his friendship with Hitler and of his work in creating national unity. Then, as a final emotive gesture, Hindenburg's son, Colonel Oskar von Hindenburg, broadcast to the nation on the eve of the vote, 'my father had himself seen in Adolf Hitler his own direct successor...I am acting according to my father's wishes when I call on all German men and women to vote for the handing over of my father's office to the Führer'.

As a result of the plebiscite, 95.7 per cent of the 45 million voters went to the polls and of these 89.93 per cent voted 'Yes'. Only 4.5 million had the courage to vote 'No', while a further 870,000 spoiled their papers. On the day following this result, Hitler wrote to the Minister of Defence, General Werner von Blomberg, a Nazi sympathiser, expressing his gratitude for the support and loyalty of the **Wehrmacht**. He promised to 'support the continued existence' and independence of the armed forces and to establish the army as 'the sole bearer of arms in the nation'.

KEY ISSUE

Hitler completes the Nazi revolution.

Plebiscite, page 21

Wehrmacht army of the Third Reich, a term in use from 1935 superseding *Reichswehr*, the name used during the Weimar years

7 ⌐ HITLER SECURES HIS DICTATORSHIP 1934–8

A *Factors influencing Hitler's maintenance of power after 1934*

After 1934 the key institutions of government lost much of their importance. The cabinet was dominated by Hitler and other top Nazis and was used less as the central instrument of government. The *Reichstag* did not disappear, but the political parties did. The *Reichstag* became a Nazi assembly composed of select party men. It did not legislate, but only advised and approved Hitler's policies.

The government, administration and party organisation of Nazi Germany was very complicated. Germany was organised into states, provinces and districts, but these political and administrative areas did not coincide with party areas (*Gaue*). The army had its own geographical areas (*Wehrkreise*), whilst the SA, SS and Hitler Youth had their own separate organisations. Power fell into the hands of a number of competing separate personal empires: Police (Heinrich Himmler), the Second Four Year Plan (Hermann Göring), Propaganda (Joseph Goebbels) and the Labour Front (Robert Ley). Inside their respective spheres, these major Nazi leaders exercised considerable independence, though Hitler was ultimately supreme (we will be returning to Hitler's rule in the Nazi state in the next chapter). The system worked with ruthless efficiency.

Hitler carried out his various functions as Party Leader and Head of State through four chancelleries or offices:

- Presidential under Dr Meissner
- State as Prime Minister and Reichskanzler under Dr Lammers
- Party under Rudolf Hess
- Chancellery of the 'Führer, to deal with his personal activities, under Philipp Bouhler

The unchallenged supremacy of Hitler reduced the importance of government by cabinet whose meetings became infrequent. Ministers were no longer independent or free to argue or discuss. They became agents of Hitler and of party policy.

Hitler succeeded in creating a new sense of self-confidence and a belief that all of Germany's problems would be overcome; order and discipline would be restored and the threat of communism averted. People accepted Hitler and his strong government. Economic recovery was the basis of Nazi success, for Hitler recognised that maximum support of the people was essential. We will be looking at the regime's restoration of the economy in Chapter 13, but it is sufficient to say that recovery was achieved through a fall in unemployment, a rise in profits, control of inflation and a sound currency. It was a State-led revival based on a large amount of state investment in public works and, after 1936, in industries which served the regime's rearmament drive, so that

> **cartel** central selling organisation allowing each member to produce a specific share of total output, fining those who exceeded their share

by 1939 there was a shortage of labour. Industrialists, freed from trade union restrictions, were given vast orders at profitable rates. They were allowed, by a law of July 1933, to develop a **cartel**. The aristocratic landowners, particularly in Prussia, were not totally won over, but they enjoyed some advantages. Prices of products were fixed high above costs. They were given State credit on easy terms and relieved of the fear of loss of their land. Elites in the army were won over by Hitler's expansionist foreign policy. This provided opportunities for sons and reconciled the landowning nobility to the Nazis. Hitler showed supreme skill in handling the army for the latter was the greatest factor in establishing his regime on a firm basis.

A reign of terror underpinned Hitler's rule. He used a combination of persuasion and deception in an organised form for the masses. This was combined with terror through the SA and SS, the concentration camps, *Gestapo*, detention, imprisonment and execution. The SS became an instrument of tremendous power – respected and feared. It was a very active, brutal and ruthless force in carrying out police duties and administering the camps. The camps, such as that built at Dachau in March 1933, became the leading instrument of terror – Jews, communists and socialists were subjected to brutal discipline. The camps were used to quash opposition and prevent criticism and discontent. People were successfully intimidated. (Opposition and resistance is discussed in Chapter 11.)

B *The regime takes a radical turn, 1938*

> The Hossbach Memorandum, pages 388–90

From its establishment in 1933, until the opening months of 1938, the Nazi regime was dependent on the co-operation of the existing power elites in German society, in particular the army (*Reichswehr*) and the business community. The Hitler Cabinet only became possible through the support of the former, personified by the appointment of von Blomberg as Minister of Defence (see page 195). The co-operation of industry and business was required to achieve the economic recovery without which the Nazi regime could not have found general acceptance. The collaboration of industrialists with Hitler was personified by the appointment of Schacht as the effective economic overlord. Since Hitler's installation as Chancellor by President Hindenburg had been carried out in an overtly legal manner, though in effect a revolution, the whole bureaucratic apparatus of Germany was also at the disposal of the new regime. As far as foreign policy was concerned, this meant that Hitler had initially to operate through the German foreign office and the traditional diplomatic corps, a co-operation signalled by the continuance in office of Neurath as foreign minister.

This dependence on the elites came to an end following a meeting Hitler held on 5 November, 1937 with the chiefs of the German armed forces and the German Foreign Minister, von Neurath, in the Chancellery in Berlin. Those present from the armed forces were Field Marshal von Blomberg, the Minister of Defence, Colonel-General von

Fritsch and Admiral Raeder, Commanders-in-Chief of the army and navy, and Göring in his capacity as head of the air force. The meeting was called to discuss the distribution of scarce steel between the armed services, in particular the navy's share. Hitler took the opportunity to outline the next stage of his plan to reverse the territorial settlement made at Versailles. This met with widespread support in Germany, particularly among the conservative elites. Those of their representatives present at the Hossbach meeting made no objection to Hitler's aims concerning Austria and Czechoslovakia. The reservations of Blomberg, Neurath and Fritsch related only to timing, risks and the state of German rearmament. Nevertheless Hitler was sufficiently aware of their ability to put a brake on his policies to welcome the opportunity to get rid of them. In November 1937 he could not have anticipated the circumstances of the Blomberg–Fritsch crisis, but when it came he turned it to his advantage. The marriage, on 12 January 1938, of Blomberg to a lady who was found to have been a prostitute, and false accusations of homosexuality brought against Fritsch, led both men to resign. This triggered a chain of events that enabled Hitler to carry out major changes in the personnel and organisation of the armed forces and the *Auswärtiges Amt* (Foreign Office).

At the beginning of February he personally assumed the supreme command of the armed forces, (*Oberkommando der Wehrmacht* or *OKW*), with Keitel as his chief-of-staff. Brauchitsch, a Nazi sympathiser, replaced Fritsch in the supreme command of the army (*Oberste Heeresleitung, OHL*). Ribbentrop, a man whose sole wish was to please the Führer, became the foreign minister in place of Neurath. There were a large number of lesser military and diplomatic changes. This naturally created the impression that there was something of a crisis in the regime and it was to divert the spotlight from such a charge that Austria was annexed in March 1938 without a shot being fired. This *Anschluss* (Union) was so great a triumph for Hitler that the chances of opposing him from within the top ranks of the German military and civilian establishment were henceforth much reduced. Freed from dependence on the elites, more radical Nazis now became prominent in exerting their influence and an aggressive policy was adopted at home against those individuals labelled racially impure – Jews, gypsies and the mentally and physically handicapped.

> *Anschluss*, pages 390–1

8 ⌐ BIBLIOGRAPHY

Chapter 5 of J. Noakes and G. Pridham (eds), *Nazism 1919–1945, A Documentary Reader, Vol 1 – The Rise to Power 1919–1934* (University of Exeter 1983) covers Hitler's seizure of power 1933–4. It has good commentary and sources which detail the main stages in Hitler's legal revolution.

Most of the general histories include an account of Hitler's seizure and consolidation of power, though these events tend to be covered in very general terms. These include William Carr, *A History of Germany*

1815–1945 (Arnold 1992), Volker Berghahn, *Modern Germany* (Cambridge UP 1987) and E.J. Feuchtwanger, *From Weimar to Hitler: Germany 1918–1933* (Macmillan 1995) and also *Germany 1916–1941* (Sempringham Studies, 1997), John Laver, *Hitler, Germany's Fate or Germany's Misfortune?* (Hodder & Stoughton 1995). Gordon Craig, *Germany 1866–1945* (Oxford UP 1981) gives a full, narrative treatment. Part 2 of D.G. Williamson, *The Third Reich* (Longman Seminar Series 1982) provides students with a useful introduction to Hitler's legal revolution and the consolidation of power including the defeat of the Second Revolution. This can be used as a starting point for a more detailed follow-up such as that to be found in J.C. Fest, *Hitler, Book V: Seizure of Power* (Weidenfeld & Nicolson 1973).

9 ⌐ DISCUSSION QUESTIONS

A *This section consists of questions that might be used for discussion or for testing your understanding of the main themes covered in this chapter.*

1. What part did legality and terror play in the Nazi seizure and consolidation of power 1933–4?

2. Why did Hitler not meet with more opposition to his take-over of power between 1933–4?

3. (a) 'The key to Hitler's power lay in the speed with which he acted to neutralise his potential opponents in the first few months of his Chancellorship'.
   (b) 'Not until 1938 at the earliest was Hitler's dictatorship secure'. Which of these two statements provides the more convincing view of Hitler's consolidation of power after January 1933?

10 ⌐ ESSAY QUESTIONS

A *Two-part questions.*

1. (a) Who were the most important victims of the 'Night of the Long Knives'?
   (b) What did the regime lose and gain as a result of the purge of June 1934?

2. (a) Describe the aims of those who hoped for a 'Second Revolution' in 1933 and 1934?
   (b) Why did they fail to achieve their objectives?

3. (a) Describe the role of Ernst Röhm in the events leading up to the purge of June 1934.
   (b) Why did Hitler carry out the purge of June 1934?

A *Essay questions.*

1. To what extent, and how, did Hitler consolidate his position by the end of 1934?

2. What did the Nazi regime gain, and what did it lose, by the events of 1934, from the crisis of June to the triumphant Nuremberg Party rally of September?

3. 'A period of simultaneous unification and civil war'.
To what extent do you agree with this assessment of the Nazi consolidation of power in 1933 and 1934?

4. 'The events of 1934 proved that the Nazi regime had no intention of carrying out its promises to bring about a Social Revolution in Germany'.
How far do you agree with this view?

5. 'Important restraints remained on Hitler's freedom of action after 1934'
How far do you agree with this view?

6. 'The Nazis consolidated their hold on power so easily in the period January 1933 to June 1934 simply because of the use of terror and intimidation'
To what extent do you agree with this view?

11 ⌐ MAKING NOTES

Read the advice section about making notes on page xx of Preface: How to use this book, and then make your own notes based on the following headings and questions.

1. *Hitler secures his dictatorship*
This section is concerned with the various stages by which Hitler secured his position. In Hitler's own words, 'the Constitution only mapped out the area of battle not the goal'. Note the policies he pursued to consolidate his position within the *Reichstag* and within the country:

(a) Why did he call the election of 5 March 1933? Comment on the part played by each of the following:
  ● 'Appeal to the Nation' speech;
  ● use of Göring, Minister of Prussia, as 'principal instrument';
  ● *Reichstag* Fire, 27 February 1933;
  ● the Emergency Decrees for the Protection of the German People – Hitler's use of them as a 'kind of coup d'état' so that 'by taking advantage of the fire the Nazis made the deed their own';
  ● campaign against the communists.
But the success of these policies was limited as the results of the 5 March elections highlighted.
  ● 5 March elections – role of the SA and Party activists. Compare the result with that of the preceding November elections; where did the extra Nazi vote come from?
  ● 'Day of Potsdam', 21 March – significance of that event?
  ● The Enabling Law, 23 March – what part was played by the Centre Party? What powers did the Act give Hitler and how did he seek to use them?

(b) Note the policies Hitler pursued to achieve the concept of co-ordination known as *Gleichschaltung*. In your analysis refer to the unification of each of the following:
- *Reichstag* – the Enabling Law;
- trade unions;
- political opposition/parties;
- *Länder*/state governments.

2. *What challenge did Röhm and the SA offer to Hitler which gave the appearance of a period of simultaneous unification and civil war and which meant that the SA represented an 'embarrassing legacy of the years of struggle'?*

(a) What were the main differences in the political priorities of Hitler and Röhm at this time which resulted in a challenge to Hitler's leadership?

(b) What part did the *Reichswehr* and Hindenburg play in this Hitler/Röhm crisis?

(c) In what way can it be said that Hitler moved 'erratically and with spells of doubt and indecision towards a showdown with the SA'?

(d) What final agreement did Hitler reach with the Generals?

3. *How did Hitler use a 'reign of terror' to crush opposition?*

12 ◠ PLANNING A TWO-PART QUESTION

Use the following plan to help you to write a two-part AS type essay answering the following questions

(a) In what ways did Hitler and the Nazis dismantle the democratic freedoms of Weimar Germany?

(b) To what extent did Hitler consolidate his Chancellorship by the end of 1933?

Sub-question (a) requires you to identify the different means Hitler adopted to dismantle the democratic freedoms. This involves some understanding of what is meant by the term 'democracy' and the legal and illegal methods adopted by the regime.

Sub-question (b) requires you to analyse the extent to which Hitler had removed restraints on his freedom of action by the end of 1933. It includes some assessment of the restraints that remained after 1933.

Two-part question
(a) In what ways did Hitler and the Nazis dismantle the democratic freedoms of Weimar Germany?
(b) To what extent did Hitler consolidate his Chancellorship by the end of 1933?

Paragraph	(a) In what ways	Evidence
1	Definition of the term 'democratic freedoms' and discussion of how this was secured and preserved under the Weimar Republic	
2	Theme of this paragraph is the legal means Hitler adopted to dismantle the democratic freedoms. Having learnt from the failure of his 1923 Munich Putsch that illegal methods would not succeed, Hitler used democracy to destroy itself.	- Use of the ballot box – speech 31 January – 5 March elections. - Decree for the protection of the people – ban on KPD, which suspended the liberal freedoms, granted by W/R. - Enabling Law – removal of checks and balances built into the W/R constitution - Moulding of public opinion, censorship and control of the media, stage managed rallies – loss of right of free speech - Negotiation, or rather the appearance of such, with political party rivals, trade unions
3	This explores the illegal methods employed – associated with the rule of terror.	- Intimidation/persecution such as that associated with boycott against the Jews or hostility encouraged against intellectuals and the Churches. - Activities of the SA and SS, secret police, *Gestapo* and camps, – Street violence and gang fights, use of thugs to break up meetings of rivals. - Ban on activities of rivals during the election campaign, which deprived people of the freedom to choose their democratic representatives.
Paragraph	(b) To what extent	Evidence
5	This second half of the question analyses the short time it took Hitler to consolidate his Chancellorship – five months from January to June 1933. This paragraph deals with the political arena.	- Events of January to 5 March 1933 election. - *Gleichschaltung* of the political parties/*Reichstag* and *Länder/Gaue* - Laws to persecute and remove the non-German elements in the state and Hitler's opponents. - Control of the Churches
6	Deals with the social and economic control established over the people.	- Reich Labour Front - Compulsory membership of the party for some professions/exclusion of women - Special interest groups set up to represent every possible area. - Control of education and lives of the people.
7	Deals with the constraints on Hitler's power after 1933.	Cover the power of the left, the army, elites, *Reichstag*, Hindenburg, Nationalist allies and the internal opposition offered by the SA, to restrict Hitler's freedom of action, put a brake on his 'revolution'.

7 Adolf Hitler

1 ✏ HITLER'S PERSONALITY

Hitler is possibly one of the most easily recognised figures of the twentieth century. Images of him have ranged from a comic figure with a ridiculous moustache to a firebrand speaker at mass rallies or a dark, sinister, evil figure. You might already have some impression of him from the comments made in the previous chapters.

A *Hitler's strengths*

Historians studying the evidence provided by contemporary sources and film of the period have viewed Hitler's personality and appeal in various ways, and have differed in their assessment of his strengths and weaknesses. On the one hand, he has been seen as a 'boring, squalid, uncouth monster' (C. Fitzgibbon in *Adolf Hitler, Faces of a Dictator*), while others believe that 'it is impossible to judge Adolf Hitler correctly without knowing the true facts concerning his youth' (F. Jetzinger in *Hitler's Youth*). A contemporary of Hitler's, Albert Speer, said that 'the nation was spell-bound by him'. It seems to be generally accepted that Hitler had a magnetic personality and that he was genuinely popular with some sectors of German society. Hitler himself was very aware of the power of propaganda for he believed that 'the broad masses of the people can be moved only by the power of speech' (*Mein Kampf*). His power to influence the feelings of his contemporaries has been frequently commented upon by historians, such as J.C. Fest, who wrote that when 'Hitler gave up speaking in public, his power over men's minds deteriorated' (*The Face of the Third Reich*). He was one of the greatest orators of the twentieth century, with a superb sense of timing and an ability to manipulate an audience to support him. Many ignored the brutal and repulsive aspects of his character, his intolerance and vindictiveness, his lack of generosity, his pursuit of power, and saw him only as their saviour and redeemer. He was sensitive to their mood and atmosphere and could modify his performance accordingly. But this gift was not totally natural. His passionate outbursts were carefully rehearsed for he spent hours practising in front of a mirror before each public meeting.

Hitler was a man with many faces reflecting his complex personality. He possessed strengths which made him an effective dictator.

- he had a gift for grasping the possibilities of a situation more swiftly than his opponents, as shown in the events which brought him to power in 1933.

- He showed strong will-power, energy and determination which allowed him to play many roles within the Nazi party. Apart from being its leader, he determined the Party's organisation after 1926 and was responsible for its ideology and tactics.
- He possessed a vision of Germany's future and a total belief in his own genius to achieve it.

Germany appeared to be a one-party state under the sole rule of Hitler. 'Our constitution is the will of the *Führer*,' wrote Hitler's lawyer, Hans Frank, in the Nazi newspaper *Völkischer Beobachter* on 20 May 1936. Hitler established an extraordinarily powerful dictatorship which had considerable popular support especially in the 1930s. It was supported by an effective police apparatus which made Hitler's rivals ineffective. The word **totalitarian** has been used to describe such a system of government, but this is now recognised by historians as too simple and misleading a description of the actual state of affairs.

The cult of the Führer was projected in various propaganda images which served to emphasise that decisions came down from above instead of being worked out by discussion from below. Führer worship was the most important theme cementing National Socialism. He dominated Europe for ten years, it took six years of war on a vast scale to destroy both him and the Germany he created while his memory still lives with us today.

totalitarian a form of government that does not allow rival political parties and demands total obedience from the people

B *Hitler's weaknesses*

Set against this image of the strong dictator is the picture of a man driven by anxieties. Hitler was a neurotic who showed his faults in a number of ways: a concern to assert his superiority over others, an inability to accept the opinions of others and a belief that he was never wrong. He was suspicious, moody, easily angered and extremely sensitive to the slightest criticism. He was contemptuous of anyone who questioned whether his tactics were wise. Given this personality, only by completely subordinating themselves to his authority could associates in close contact with Hitler survive in the long run, as the Strasser brothers and Röhm discovered (see pages 102–3 and 148). Such behaviour was hardly likely to win for Hitler a wide circle of political friends. He was horrified by the prospect of death, cancer and illness and relied heavily on his personal physician, Doctor Theodor Morell who, by 1942, was prescribing him 30 different drugs. He was afraid of dirt and germs and was very precise about his clothing. He wore gloves, washed his hands, and bathed frequently. He was a vegetarian and did not drink or smoke. He followed routine down to the smallest detail, though this did not stop him from living an unhealthy lifestyle, an insight into which has been provided by Albert Speer (in *Inside the Third Reich*):

> When, I would often ask myself, did he really work? Little was left of the day; he rose late in the morning, conducted one or two official conferences; but from the subsequent dinner on he more or less wasted his time until the early hours of the evening.

The effect of this lifestyle on his health quickly became evident. Good health in 1933 gave way to complaints of stomach pains in 1936, while after 1940 he aged noticeably, reaching a point of collapse by 1943. By the spring of 1945 Hitler was a dreadful and pitiful sight. He suffered regularly from sleeplessness, had poor eyesight which gave him a fixed look; he had a bent frame, his left arm and leg shook and he walked unsteadily and with a limp. He had uncontrollable temper tantrums and rapid changes in mood. He came to distrust all those who questioned his decisions, especially his generals, and eventually lost his sense of reality. This physical and mental decline, as we shall see later in the chapter, eventually undermined the effectiveness of his dictatorship.

2 ⌐ THE NATURE OF HITLER'S LEADERSHIP

A *Hitler's domination of the Nazi Party and the idea of the Führer Principle*

According to Hitler's lawyer, Hans Frank, the Nazi regime was 'Hitler's regime, it was Hitler's policy, Hitler's rule of force, Hitler's victory and defeat – nothing else'. Between 1921 and 1929 the NSDAP had become not a socialist or a workers' party, but Hitler's Party so that, according to J.C. Fest, 'what we call National Socialism is inconceivable without his person'. Hitler mapped out for the Nazi Party not only its organisation and ideology, but also its strategy and tactics for achieving power. As a result of his **charisma**, many surrendered to him for he represented their need for a strong leader. In many respects, especially after the defeat of the second revolution, National Socialist ideology became subservient to Hitler's personal ambitions.

charisma the ability of someone to arouse devotion and enthusiasm in others

National Socialist ideology had never been taken seriously. Seizure of power during the course of 1933 was not achieved so much by the NSDAP or National Socialism as by Hitler himself. His success, together with the people's acceptance of him and willingness to submit themselves to him, transformed National Socialism into Hitlerism. As early as 1920 Hitler called the Twenty-five Point Programme (see pages 52–3) his 'publicity campaign'. The strength of the Nazi Party lay not in ideology, but in the personal commitment of its members to the Führer principle (*Führerprinzip*). The faith of the rank and file in Hitler was the basis of the strength of the Party. Hitler was an aloof figure who did not involve himself in party disputes provided members remained loyal. Only when the leadership principle was challenged as in 1926 was he obliged to intervene. In 1926 the Strassers presented the Hanover programme at Bamberg (see pages 76–7) in which they presented the left-wing demands of the Party (confiscation of property and use of violence) despite the fact that these had been discredited after the 1923 failed Munich (or Beer Hall) *Putsch*. They also criticised Hitler's domination: 'we need no pope who can claim infallibility'. Hitler attacked the programme and opposition crumbled away. Loyalty to the charismatic leader was recognised as a fundamental rule of the movement and Hitler's rulings were accepted without objection. The main ingredients were then clearly established in the 1920s, loyalty and fear rather than friendships.

The cult which developed around his personality enabled him to destroy these attempts to achieve a democratic structure. After 1926 Hitler pursued a policy of centralisation designed to bind the members more closely to the charismatic leader in unquestioning obedience.

KEY ISSUE

How was Hitler able to establish his dominance over the Nazi Party?

1. The Party was structured on military-type lines, and made wholly dependent on him.
2. Elections ended and all local branches of the Party recognised the leadership of Munich, Hitler's base.
3. *Gauleiter* were brought under central control and with them all political and economic activities, civil defence and the mobilisation of labour in the regions. The party programme was declared as fixed.
4. The SA was reformed and made subordinate to the party leader.
5. Special separate associations were also set up for youth, women, teachers and doctors.

Hitler's position was enormously strengthened by these changes. His dominance meant that all party members became subordinate to him and were expected to be loyal. Those who were inspired by the desire to reconstruct society remained a minority. Few of Hitler's chief followers joined the Party because they were influenced by ideological aims. Rather they reflected Hitler, in that they were neurotic and some, like Göring, Goebbels and Himmler, shared his unbalanced nature and were regarded as failures. They were ready to use force and accept authoritarian government. Hitler provided the leadership they required. He possessed superior talents confirmed by his struggle for power in the Party and his ability to influence people's thought processes. He forged the separate forces together so that Hans Frank could state, 'everything came exclusively from Hitler himself'. He was the most effective appeal of a movement devoid of any programme. The Party's power to attract the masses was due to the word 'Hitler', not to its organisers. Hitler's belief that the crisis facing Germany in 1929–33 needed strong action attracted the masses to the NSDAP because they shared this view. As far as Hitler was concerned the men he wanted around him were, 'those who, like myself, see in force the motive element in History and who act accordingly'. His relationship with these other Nazi leaders was influenced by a combination of factors. These ranged from his personality, which worked on distrust, to the *Führerprinzip* with its insistence on dictatorship and emphasis on the charismatic leader, as well as his centralisation of the Party and unchallenged authority under the personal system.

KEY ISSUE

The personal relationships between Hitler and the men around him were based on loyalty and fear rather than friendship.

B *The relationship between Hitler and other leading Nazis*

The Führer circle consisted of about 76 leading Nazis whom Hitler had personally promoted to high office at national level, or to party organisations and associations along with those who held posts at regional party level (*Gauleiter*). They were rewarded for their loyalty to Hitler rather than for their ability. All of these officials had a standing invitation to lunch with Hitler and this is how many of them secured his endorsement of a line of action. Inevitability it was this apparently spontaneous decision making that gave the appearance of confusion of government and contributed to warring factions such as Göring against Röhm, or Göring and Himmler against Goebbels, or Himmler against Bormann. Some historians have claimed that Hitler deliberately encouraged such confusion and uncertainty as a means of maintaining his dominance. By playing off one individual against another he prevented the emergence of serious rivals and established himself as the final arbiter. There is some evidence of such a divide and rule policy at the lowest level in the party in order to increase the dependence of rivals on his Führer's favour. On the other hand more recent commentators on the administrative structure of Nazi Germany claim that, rather than dividing his officials in order to rule, he preferred to let rivals fight it out and only intervened to reward the victor, in accordance with his social Darwinist philosophy.

Within this large Führer circle there was a smaller group of about 12 men, who have been termed by William Carr in his *Hitler: A Study in Personality and Politics,* (Arnold, 1978), a 'kitchen' cabinet. Many had been with Hitler since the early Munich days of the party. Inevitability membership changed over time, but included:

- Göring (see pages 164–5) – he had been of great value to Hitler during the crucial early years when Hitler sought to acquire respectability and entry to aristocratic circles. Hitler rewarded him and he became heir apparent, but he found it difficult to copy Goebbel's extreme idolisation of the Führer. Under Hitler's influence the backbone of Göring's personality gradually disintegrated; he became subservient, feared Hitler and had terrible stormy quarrels which reduced him to tears and submission. He was a powerful figure from 1935 to 1940, but then his influence waned rapidly.
- Himmler (see page 165) – another powerful and sinister figure from 1936 to 1945.
- Goebbels (see page 166) – the most loyal, he was described by Hitler as his 'faithful, unshakeable shield-bearer'. He was rewarded for his loyalty and remained on very friendly terms with the Führer, apart from brief interludes.

Other members of the kitchen cabinet included Rudolf Hess, Hitler's deputy to 1941, Adolf Wagner, Bavarian Minister of Justice and Gauleiter of Bavaria, who was a close personal friend until his death in

1944, Erich Koch, Gauleiter of East Prussia and Reich commissioner for the Ukraine during the war, Fritz Sauckel, Gauleiter of Thuringia who was given powers to direct labour 1942–5, Karl Kaufmann, Gauleiter of Hamburg and Reich commissioner for shipping, Josef Bürckel, Reich commissioner for the Saarland, Austria and Lorraine, Franz Scharz, the Party Treasurer, and Martin Bormann, who after Hess's departure, became the most powerful figure in Germany.

Hitler's promotion of individuals on the basis of an instinctive decision rather than on hard fact increased still further the degree of dependence of those fortunate to win his favour. This is apparent in the careers of all the top Nazis. In the case of Reinhard Heydrich (see page 167), Hitler was prepared to use him despite his Jewish ancestry. Hitler regarded his gifts and value to the movement, despite recognising that he was a very dangerous man. Heydrich was grateful to Hitler and obeyed blindly out of fear and loyalty. Hitler adopted a system of rewards and punishments to achieve unchallenged authority. He demanded, and achieved, until shortly before his death, absolute obedience. He punished opposition by expulsion, as in the case of Gregor Strasser, or death as with Röhm, or indifference or refusal to see him, as with Rosenberg and Ribbentrop. Even the top Nazis of the 'inner guard' were not immune from his system of control, for when they became too powerful or were seen by Hitler as a challenge, he acted accordingly. Thus, Göring was denied access to Hitler's person and ignored in policy discussions after 1941; Goebbels was 'cold-shouldered' in the good years of the Third Reich until Hitler needed him again in 1942; whilst Heydrich was sent to Prague, where he was assassinated. In the last few hours of Hitler's life, when he was dictating his will and political testament to his secretary Bormann, he continued to exercise his control. Both Himmler and Göring were 'punished' for their disloyalty and expelled from the Party, losing all their rights. The succession was given to Admiral Dönitz, who was President of the Reich and Supreme Commander of the Armed Forces. To the very end, Hitler still viewed himself as master and he expected his decisions to be obeyed.

The personal feuding and scrambling for office which was the inevitable consequence of such a personal system did not greatly bother Hitler. At times he seemed to have encouraged it, as in the case of Göring against both Röhm and Goebbels, and Himmler and Bormann against Heydrich. Such rivalries enhanced his own position as the final decision-making power. Hitler was very concerned to prevent the rapid rise of anyone who might try to challenge his leadership as in the case of Heydrich. Hess was appointed 'deputy to the Führer' because he represented no danger to Hitler. He subordinated himself to Hitler and was loyal in that he never desired power unlike the other Nazi bosses. Hitler had a neurotic suspicion of opposition, not surprising given the endless intrigues which went on around his person. He was prepared to act violently to deal with such a threat and demonstrated on many occasions that not even the top Nazi leaders, 'friends' and long-time associates could rely on his faithful and consistent support. In this situation it is perhaps not surprising that the men around him would

Q

To what extent was Hitler's system of 'divide and rule' deliberate or a consequence of his personality?

remain loyal, at least outwardly, and afraid of him whilst few could claim to be his friends. Hitler did not possess the personality to keep friends.

Hitler was also served by a small personal staff which dealt with his private affairs and controlled his appointments. It included Julius Schreck, first leader of the SS and his chauffeur until his death in 1936, and Julius Schaub, a personal bodyguard and a founder member of the SS, who looked after Hitler's houses in Munich and Berchtesgaden and stayed with him to the end. His appointments were controlled by Wilhelm Brückner, who was chief adjutant from 1935 to 1941, and Fritz Wiedemann. Finally, during his leisure hours Hitler chose quite different associates. These were his old Munich friends, Heinrich Hoffman, the party photographer, his doctor, Theodor Morell, Albert Speer whom Hitler regarded as reliable, sympathetic and non-political and finally, and unknown to most contemporaries, Eva Braun, Hitler's unacknowledged mistress and secret companion. Of this inner circle, only Speer exerted any real influence over Hitler but this was in his capacity as Minister of Armaments, rather than as a member of this private circle which existed to provide Hitler with the adoring audience he needed.

C Key roles played by leading Nazis in Hitler's personal system

Imperial War Museum MH6041
PICTURE 26
Herman Göring

HERMANN GÖRING (1893–1946)

He was the number two Nazi, Hitler's named successor and high military and economic leader of the Third Reich. Son of a colonial officer and a much decorated air ace, he joined the Nazi Party in 1923. He took part in the failed Nazi attempt to seize power in 1923 and was injured in the groin. He took morphine for the pain and became an addict, which later accounted for his personal and professional decline. He married a wealthy woman and used his connections with the elites and Hindenburg on behalf of the Nazis. In 1932 he was elected Speaker of the *Reichstag* having convinced Hitler of his value as a 'high society Nazi'. He was very popular but resented for his ambition and greed for power. A man of great personal vanity, he loved to show off. He acquired wealth and works of art, much of which was plundered from Nazi victims. He was one of the richest men in Germany.

Some historians see him as the most evil of the Nazis since he was brutal and ruthlessly exploited others. He was concerned with his own pursuit of power rather than with any allegiance to Hitler or the Nazi Party. Göring's contributions to the State can be summed up in the various offices he amassed. He expanded his 'circle of duties' 1933–5 to include Reichstag President, Reich Minister of Aviation, Prussian Minister of the Interior, Head of the

Gestapo, President of the Prussian State Council, Commander-in-Chief of the Luftwaffe, and in 1936 Commissioner of the Four Year Plan. 1936 marked the peak of his career when he was second man and Hitler's heir apparent, but thereafter he was physically in decline. In 1937 he was denied the office of minister in charge of the army, despite being a part of the intrigue to topple the previous holder. He was at the peak of his popularity in 1939, but failures during the early years of the war cost him Hitler's approval; between 1939 and 1942 he was excluded by Hitler though he still remained in control of his high offices. By 1943 he ceased to be a part of the top leadership. He was arrested, and sentenced to death at Nuremberg but committed suicide.

HEINRICH HIMMLER (1900–1945)

He was the most colourless personality of the inner circle. An agricultural graduate, he had been a poultry farmer in Bavaria before joining the NSDAP in 1923. He had a weak and timid appearance, himself, yet he dreamt of a master race of tall, blond, blue-eyed supermen personified by the early recruits for Hitler's personal bodyguard, the SS. He stressed a code of honour and of family pedigree and marriage. He believed in a master race – an Aryan *Herrenvolk*. Though he had taken part in the failed attempt to seize power in Munich in 1923, his career did not develop until after 1934. He became Reichsführer of the SS in 1935, the chief paramilitary elite group and Hitler's bodyguard. Under Himmler its membership grew from 500 to 50,000 and it created its own network of administration. In 1933 he became President of Police in Munich and established a model camp at Dachau. Under Himmler a system of terror was carried out with great efficiency by his deputies such as Eichmann and Hoess. From its base in Bavaria the SS extended its control as the political police of Germany. He controlled a substantial portion of the real power through the police state and as a result of the terror he achieved even greater psychological power. Real power visibly shifted towards him and the SS, which determined the future face and history of the Third Reich. Subsequent offices acquired by Himmler included Reich Minister of the Interior. Even in his lifetime there was a 'Himmler myth'. The basis of this evil reputation was his association with the SS state, the extermination camps and system of terror. Behind the myth was a man who was mediocre, undistinguished by any special character trait, a man described by Albert Speer as a 'half crank, half schoolmaster'.

Imperial War Museum MU7315
PICTURE 27
Heinrich Himmler

PICTURE 28
Joseph Goebbels

JOSEPH GOEBBELS (1897–1945)

Goebbels was born into a working class Roman Catholic family at Rheydt in Westphalia. Physically handicapped from birth, he walked with a limp. In 1920 he graduated from Heidelburg University with a doctorate in literature and in 1922 joined the Nazi Party. It soon became clear that Hitler had gained the services of a brilliant orator and propagandist. In 1926 Goebbels was appointed Gauleiter of Berlin-Brandenburg and, a year later, founded the Nazi newspaper, *Der Angriff* (The Attack). Truth was of no significance to him; in the interests of the Party he was prepared to distort facts and lie. After being elected to the *Reichstag* in 1928, he became closely associated with the left-wing views of Röhm and Strasser. He was fortunate to have had a change of heart in time to avoid being a victim of the Night of the Long Knives in 1934. He was probably spared because of his value to the Party as their skilled Minister of Public Enlightenment and Propaganda. He was one of the most gifted propagandists of modern times and one of the few real powers complementing Hitler. Preaching National Socialism as if it were a religion, his oratorical skills exceeded those of his leader and he was chiefly responsible for promoting Hitler as a cult-type figure. Goebbels also played a major role in exploiting the *Reichstag* fire in 1933 and in organising both the burning of the books in May 1933 (see pages 334–5) and the events of *Kristallnacht* in November 1938 (see page 276). He was a skilled broadcaster and played a major role in the development of the German film industry. His marriage to a rich divorcee, Magda Quant, by whom he had six children, did not prevent him from being a womaniser. At one stage Hitler had to warn him about his behaviour and, at least in public, he had to settle to being a dedicated husband and father. Short, dapper and always well-dressed, he was disliked by other Nazis who nicknamed him the 'Black Dwarf' or 'our little doctor'. Goebbels' loyalty to Hitler was absolute and persisted until the end of his life. A keen diarist, his work later proved invaluable to historians. Hugh Trevor-Roper described him as 'the only really interesting man in the Third Reich besides Hitler'. Goebbels and his family committed suicide with Hitler in the bunker in April 1945.

Imperial War Museum MH7430
PICTURE 29
Rudolf Hess

RUDOLF HESS (1894–1987)

Egyptian-born Hess served in the same regiment as Hitler during the First World War. After the war he joined a *Freikorps* unit and was at Hitler's side during the Beer Hall *Putsch*. As a consequence he served a prison sentence with Hitler, during which Hess wrote down part of *Mein Kampf* as Hitler dictated. He had the title of deputy to the Führer from 1933 to 1941, but this did not bring him real power. Hess was unknown to the people; an idealist and as such represented no danger to Hitler, which was the reason for his selection as Vice-Führer. He subordinated himself to Hitler and acted as his secretary. His most important contribution to National Socialism was that he gave Hitler the concept of *Lebensraum* (living space). He never craved power like the other Nazi bosses, but existed solely to serve Hitler whom he regarded as saviour. Hess was very sincere in his worship of Hitler. He was sentenced to life imprisonment at Nuremberg and died in mysterious circumstances as the last prisoner at Spandau Prison in 1987.

REINHARD HEYDRICH (1904–1942)

He was Deputy Chief of the Gestapo. He looked typically German, but was of Jewish blood. He has been described as 'a young evil god of death'; 'the blond beast' and *'der Henker'* (the hangman). More so than Himmler, he was very intelligent, brilliant in many fields – music, sport and languages. Heydrich aimed at nothing less than the actual leadership of the Third Reich, and was utterly selfish in this aim. He was superior to Himmler, and was more dangerous and indispensable. Heydrich was the originator of the plan to develop the police force of the Third Reich from the SS with himself in control of the party security police. He realised that state security offered unrestricted power. He accumulated offices rapidly. In 1934 he became head of the political police, in 1936 of the criminal police and by 1936, at the age of 32, was one of the most powerful men in Germany. In 1939, he organised the Reich Central Security Office nominally subordinate to Himmler, but it became independent and a part of his offices and activities. He developed a system of surveillance throughout Germany and Europe. He was given responsibility for destroying opposition from the churches and from the Jews. He never shrank from any task, including herding the Jews out of Europe and sending them to their deaths. He devised the plan to make vast areas of the East available as an 'experimental field' for breeding. He devised the idea of forcing the Jewish communities to organise the **Final Solution** at its lowest levels, by causing the Jewish councils to choose the quota of Jews to be sent to the camps. In 1941 Heydrich was sent to Prague, after Himmler and Bormann had joined forces to remove him from the centre of power and curtail his rapid rise which they regarded as threatening. In January 1942 he chaired the meeting at Wannsee (see pages 437–8) at which plans were made for the Final Solution of the Jewish question. Heydrich was assassinated in Prague on 27 May 1942 by agents sent from London. Hitler was outraged and ordered savage retribution. The entire male population of the Czech village of Lidice was shot and every house burned to the ground. In Prague a further 860 were executed, as well as 360 at Brno. Himmler was very relieved at Heydrich's death, but called him a 'master by birth and by behaviour'.

Imperial War Museum STT773
PICTURE 30
Reinhard Heydrich

Final Solution Nazi policy of exterminating European Jews, resulting in the murder of six million Jews in concentration camps between 1941 and 1945

PICTURE 31
Martin Bormann

MARTIN BORMANN (1900–?1945)

A protégé of Rudolf Hess, Bormann's rise through the Party's ranks was more steady than spectacular. In 1933 he was elected to the Reichstag and, in 1938, became Gauleiter of Thuringia. His real opportunity for advancement came in 1941 after Hess's flight to Britain when Bormann was appointed head of the Party Chancellery. Two years later he became the Führer's official secretary. Described by William Shirer as 'a mole-like man who preferred to burrow in the dark recesses of Party life to further his intrigues', he was a bureaucrat and workaholic. Known to his Party colleagues as 'the man of the shadows', he was a power seeker prepared to use his position to win maximum influence. He kept detailed records on each of the Nazi hierarchy and prevented others from having easy access to the Führer. He constantly schemed to manipulate and outmanoeuvre his rivals. Although he worked reasonably well with Goebbels, Göring loathed him and Himmler had little respect for him. Always available to do Hitler's bidding, who referred to him as 'my most loyal Party comrade', Bormann was responsible for reorganising the Party. This involved him in conflict with Himmler as the leader of the SS, which became the Party's rival for supreme power in the State. Mystery surrounds Bormann's fate after he disappeared during the final days of the war. Did he flee to South America, or was he blown up by a bomb during his escape?

PICTURE 32
Albert Speer

ALBERT SPEER (1905–1983)

He joined the Nazi party in 1931. He was regarded by Hitler as sympathetic and reliable. In 1933 Hitler appointed him as 'master-builder' of the Third Reich designing the monumental buildings of Nuremberg and Berlin. He was the inventor of the 'forest of flags' and lighted vaults which gave a solemn setting to the mass meetings. He refused to associate himself with the horrors of the regime and rejected an honorary rank in the SS. In 1941 he was appointed Minister of Armaments and Munitions. He reshaped his ministry and under his direction armament production increased impressively even though he had to accept the necessity to employ slave labour from the camps. He was sentenced to 20 years imprisonment at Nuremberg.

3 ∼ HITLER – MASTER OF THE THIRD REICH OR WEAK DICTATOR?

Historians, writing soon after the end of the Second World War, focused on Hitler and the nature of his dictatorship. They were influenced both by the evidence of the experiences of victims and opponents of the regime and by the public trials of Nazi war criminals at Nuremberg. Hitler was portrayed as a leader who dictated events and who established an ascendancy over all who came into contact with him, even though they might disagree with his decisions. He was seen as master in the Third Reich. As a result of the legislative changes carried out between 1933 and 1934, Hitler appeared to exercise a unique degree of power. He could decide policy, issue orders, and initiate legislation. His all-powerful position as Führer was made explicit on a number of occasions, such as in a speech by Hans Frank, head of the Nazi Association of Lawyers and of the Academy of German Law in 1938 (quoted in Noakes and Pridham, *Nazism 1919–1945, A Documentary Reader, Vol 2*):

KEY ISSUE

How effective was Hitler as ruler of Germany?

> **1.** At the head of the Reich stands the leader of the NSDAP as leader of the German Reich for life.
>
> **2.** He is, on the strength of being the leader of the NSDAP, leader and Chancellor of the Reich. As such he embodies simultaneously, as Head of State, supreme State power, and, as chief of the government, the central functions of the whole Reich administration. He is Head of State, and chief of the Government in one person. He is Commander in Chief of all the armed forces of the Reich.
>
> **3.** The Führer and Reich Chancellor is the...delegate of the German people, who...decides the outward form of the Reich, its structure and general policy.
>
> **4.** The Führer is supreme judge of the nation...There is no position in the area of constitutional law in the Third Reich independent of the...will of the Führer.

Q *What is meant by 'Führer' in relation to the leadership of Nazi Germany?*

By the 1960s a new generation of historians, who had grown up since the Second World War, had started to take a different view of the regime. While accepting the image of Hitler's all powerful personality and his integrating role as a leader, they claimed that a different picture was presented by the multiplicity of overlapping bureaucracies and authorities in the Nazi state. They concentrated on the administrative inefficiency and impulsiveness of the Führer which appeared to lead to chaos and improvisation in government. Historians, such as Hans Mommsen, writing in *Civil Servants in the Third Reich*, 1961, wrote of a Hitler 'reluctant to take decisions, often uncertain, concerned only to maintain his own prestige and personal authority and strongly subject to the influence of his environment for the time being – in fact, in many ways a weak dictator'. These revisionist historians now recognised the limits of Hitler's power, for, they claimed, he did not enjoy absolute authority in internal affairs and, to some extent, in foreign affairs as well. They concentrated on the authoritarian anarchy of the regime brought about by individuals who, while claiming to be Nazi, were really concerned with the personal pursuit of their own power and ambition. The term 'structuralist' has been coined to describe this new generation of historians. They now emphasised the weakness of Hitler as a dictator in contrast to the Nuremberg view of a master who had a blueprint of intention to plan and wage an aggressive war of conquest accompanied by crimes against humanity, specifically the Jews. The Master versus Weak arguments of these two conflicting 'schools' of historians can be summarised as follows:

HISTORIANS' DEBATE

Differing views of Hitler's power as Führer

Weak Dictator	Master of the Third Reich
Hans Mommsen, *Civil Servants in the Third Reich*, 1961	Hugh Trevor-Roper, *The Last Days of Hitler* (Macmillan 1947)
Martin Broszat, *The Hitler State* (Longman 1981)	Alan Bullock, *Hitler, A Study in Tyranny* (Odhams 1952)
They argue that Hitler was weak because he was a prisoner of various forces operating within the State which he could not, or would not, control. These forces limited his freedom of action so that, under Hitler, Nazi Germany suffered from a a leadership crisis. From the mid-1930s Hitler abandoned the normal business of government. He resorted to extreme working methods and lifestyles, a development which was commented upon by contemporaries.	They stress that the essential political decisions were taken by Hitler. His ideas and strengths meant that he was the prime mover in domestic and foreign policy. So important was the leadership principle that they claim that National Socialism can be called Hitlerism.

As mentioned in the previous chapter, Hitler governed through the cabinet, but this was used less as the central instrument of government and did not meet after 1938. The *Reichstag* did not disappear; it became a Nazi assembly composed of key party men which did not legislate, but only advised and approved Hitler's policies. Reference has already been made to Albert Speer's comment on Hitler's unhealthy lifestyle which was characterised by lethargy. Hitler also disliked the routine work of government, according to Speer (in *Inside the Third Reich*):

In the eyes of the people Hitler was the Leader who watched over the nation day and night. This was hardly so… According to my observations, he often allowed a problem to mature during the weeks when he seemed to be entirely taken up with trivial matters. Then after the 'sudden insight' came, he would spend a few days of intensive work giving final shape to his solution… Once he had come to a decision, he lapsed again into his idleness.

Another member of government, Ernst von Weizsäcker, State Secretary in the Foreign Office, complained that ministerial skill in the Third Reich 'consisted in making the most of a favourable hour or minute when Hitler made a decision, this often taking the form of a remark thrown out casually, which then went its way as an "Order of the Führer".' (quoted in *Hitler, A Study in Tyrrany* by Alan Bullock).

Hitler preferred to spend his time at his mountain retreat in Berchtesgaden, renamed the Berghof, 130 kilometres southeast of Munich, where only those whom he chose to see were invited. He did not actively intervene in government, and his withdrawal made the machinery of government more chaotic because important decisions were not taken. He did not issue written orders and the absence of such evidence has further contributed to the debate on Hitler's role in decision-making. In this situation there appeared to be administrative inefficiency combined with impulsive decision-making. Government disintegrated and real power seemed to rest with individuals concerned with a personal pursuit of power. This was exercised by a number of competing separate personal empires headed by major Nazi leaders who had secured considerable independence: police (Himmler), the Second Four Year Plan (Göring), propaganda (Goebbels) and the Labour Front (Ley). Hitler, though ultimately supreme, was content to leave the detailed work of administration to these key men because he expected, and achieved, their complete loyalty. In his name, they carried out most of the radical policies of the regime, such as the **euthanasia** campaign to kill the mentally and physically handicapped, and the extermination of the Jews and gypsies. The system worked with ruthless efficiency despite the fact that Hitler increasingly retreated from regular contact with the machinery of government. Hitler became more dispensable in this very personal system.

The debate amongst historians about the role of Hitler can be summarised on the following pages.

> **Q**
> *What different views of Hitler's Führership are given by Frank, Speer and Weizsäcker?*

euthanasia the 'mercy' killing of the terminally ill, usually with their consent, illegal in most countries. For the Nazis, the deliberate killing, without their consent, of those handicapped or mentally ill, they considered of no value

HISTORIANS' DEBATE

Was Hitler master in the Third Reich or a weak Dictator?

Weak Dictator | *Master of the Third Reich*

1. Hitler was a prisoner of his own personality

Hitler's lazy and apathetic nature meant that he regularly avoided making unpopular decisions which would harm his prestige and image. It is possible to cite a number of examples of Hitler yielding to pressure to override unpopular decrees, e.g. in 1934 Ley was stopped from increasing the authority of his Labour Front at the expense of employers and the Trustees of Labour and in 1935 he was defeated over proposals to unify wages because Hitler did not want to antagonise his economics minister, Schacht, or the industrialists. In the early years of Nazi rule Hitler had to bow to economic pressures and unpleasant decisions were forced on him, e.g. in 1933 financial support for Jewish department stores to stop staff cuts at a time of high unemployment. He failed to give clear planning and consistent direction. This led to disorganised and fragmented government. Mommsen wrote that Hitler was a propagandist, aware of presenting an image and exploiting the opportune moment. Statements about ideology were seen as propaganda rather than firm statements of intent.

1. Hitler was in total command of key decisions

Intentionalists argue that it would be unwise to see Hitler's concessions as examples of a weak dictator. There is no convincing example of a directive held by Hitler to be of central importance that was ignored, or blocked, by his subordinates or others, though he produced very few for domestic politics. An example of his determination to push through an unpopular policy is his Sterilisation Law, which was passed despite Catholic protest. His aims were to eliminate the enemies of the State, mobilise the economy and prepare the people for war, wage a war of conquest to acquire living space (*Lebensraum*), and create a racially pure State through the elimination of Jews, gypsies, the mentally and physically handicapped. He pursued these policies regardless of opinion.

2. Hitler was a prisoner of others

Historians emphasise Hitler's dependence on obscure people of the 1920s who had helped him to power. Some were rewarded with the office of Gauleiter which gave them control of the regions. Those historians who argue that Hitler was weak, claim that he never ran counter to the opinions of his Gauleiter, which meant that he lost his freedom of decision though he retained his supremacy. Hitler's policies were not his own. Gauleiter, writing after the war, seemed to confirm this.

2. Hitler adopted a divide and rule policy to secure mastery

Intentionalists argue that Hitler remained supreme by deliberately blurring the lines of command and creating a duplication, even a triplication, of offices e.g. he broke up unified control over the Party organisation set up by the Strassers and established himself as leader of the Party's political organisation dividing power between Hess and Ley. Likewise Hitler refused to support Frick, the Minister of the Interior, who attempted to establish under his command central control over the Reich governors and *Gauleiter*. Hitler continued to control his power of patronage and deal directly with his *Gauleiter*. He was not in their power, rather he removed those whose loyalty he doubted. He was slow to move against party feuds, but when he did he was ruthless as his destruction of opposition in the Night of the Long Knives 30 June 1934 testifies. He governed on the principle of personal loyalty, particularly in his relations with his *Gauleiter* whose interests he protected, thereby securing a powerful body of support to him alone.

3. Hitler was a prisoner of different forces operating within the State which he could not control

Hitler was Head of State, of the Armed Forces, and of the Party, but he was not a bureaucrat and wrote very little. It was impossible for one man to govern all, so he allowed a polycratic system to develop, where power was decentralised. This led to administrative chaos. Hitler was weak because decision-making was split resulting in the absence of clear rational policies. His personal scope for action was limited by the presence of real fluctuating centres of power and rivalry. Given the absence of Hitler's intervention, Lammers, Head of the Reich Chancellery, could have misled Hitler because he gave verbal accounts of what needed to be done. Hitler would give a verbal response which could subsequently be watered down. Göring, Himmler, Speer and Bormann also packaged requests in such a way as to get the desired response. Hitler tended to listen to the last person who had spoken to him.

Hitler was aware of the need to conciliate the elites, especially the army, which was one major institution that was not Nazified. It retained its independence, it was very powerful, controlled weapons and could plot against Hitler.

3. Hitler's distance from the bureaucracy meant that he could take key decisions without any interference or control

It is now accepted that Hitler promoted the setting up of huge power bases by men such as Himmler, Ley, Göring and Bormann whom he trusted above others because they gave him personal loyalty. He was suspicious of attempts to impose restrictions on his power. He overstretched himself in terms of his grip on government so that it was impossible not to fragment. But this should not be taken too far, because all acted in the interests of the Führer. Hitler consciously protected his authority against any potential attempts to limit it institutionally, so that the chaos of government must not be seen as weakness. His willingness to allow rivals to fight it out and the practice of resolving disputes before meetings with him, combined with his distant leadership, helped further the Führer myth cult, his popularity and his mastery. He was never frustrated in the exercise of power, but deliberately chose to keep out of wrangles among his subordinates. He had little interest in the legislative process, but he was central to foreign and race policy.

Hitler was not a prisoner of the army because its generals were in agreement with his foreign policies. They tied themselves to Hitler and after 1938 the armed forces became a functional vehicle of Nazi rule.

4. Hitler was a prisoner of tensions operating within the State and economy which he could not control

Hitler was weak between 1936 and 1941 because of tensions in the State and economy which did not respond to his will and which threatened working-class unrest. Hitler was in a weak position and developed no consistent social policy, but showed increasing apathy and inaction. Such tensions influenced the timing of the Second World War and provoked a major crisis for the regime. During the war German people were not asked to make a total sacrifice and mobilisation was only half-hearted and incomplete. This crisis also explains why Hitler did not push through the full mobilisation of women.

4. Hitler's decisions were not motivated by a state of crisis

Hitler and the Nazi leadership, supported by the military and economic elites, intended to wage a war which would solve Germany's problems. However, that war only gradually took shape and not in the way that Hitler had intended. By 1937–9 he was less interested in domestic matters compared with strategic questions and foreign affairs. By 1939 Hitler got the war he intended but against the 'wrong enemy'. Mobilisation was only half-hearted and incomplete which explains why Hitler did not push through the full mobilisation of women. He showed no consciousness of a general political crisis 1937–9 forcing an imminent war. Structuralist historians, such as Tim Mason and Alan Milward, have exaggerated the scale of the unrest and its political significance. The timing of the war was due to the international balance of power and the comparative armament positions of Germany's rivals and not to fears of internal unrest reinforced by Hitler's weakness. Little that happened in domestic politics before the middle of the war ran counter to, or contradicted, Hitler's 'will'. This supports the conclusion that he was not a weak dictator, though neither was he master in the Third Reich in the implied meaning of unlimited infinite power.

4 ⁓ RECONCILIATION OF DIFFERENT INTERPRETATIONS

Historians now recognise that a rational method of systematic decision-making and rule did not exist in the Third Reich. Hitler was a dictator who did not appear to dictate, but instead produced the biggest confusion in government. He removed all clarity of leadership so that a shambles of government existed which belied the propaganda image of efficiency. The elaborate, well-trained state organisation which had survived both the 1918 revolution which had swept away the Kaiser and the Nazi seizure of power 1933–4, continued to function even though a parallel system of Nazi-controlled ministries was developed alongside.

The term **'polycratic'** has been applied to describe such a system of overlapping but rival centres of power. However, there was no coherent body at the head of it. Hitler did not like the routine business of government so he did not intervene but hoped that things would sort themselves out. The administration had links with Hitler but there ceased to be a framework for centralised government and decision making, unlike Mussolini's Italy or Franco's Spain. His authority was never undermined, although he allowed subordinates to fight it out, he remained in overall control as the top Nazis who plotted to become his successor discovered. By early 1943 Goebbels was writing of a leadership crisis because Hitler had detached himself from government, but Goebbels was not allowed to take control. Despite this picture of chaos, however, parts of the system worked efficiently and showed remarkable dynamism. This was true of the army which was highly technical and modern and worked with efficiency, while Albert Speer reorganised the armaments industry so that production was higher in 1944 than in 1942. This helps to explain why it still took five years of war to defeat the regime. There are no examples of major policy decisions by Hitler being successfully opposed by subordinates or by the Party until the later stages of the war when Speer and the generals questioned his orders. He was determined not to be restricted in any way, or to have a rival, both of which might have undermined his authority. Nothing was done which he did not approve and his orders were not ignored. He was not prevented from doing what he wanted to do in Germany, but was only constrained by foreign powers and war. His power was real and he was only a prisoner of forces of his own making. This is not the sign of a weak dictator.

> **polycratic** a decentralised system of government. It describes the complex power structure in Nazi Germany in which Hitler's personal authority was only one element

5 ⌐ HITLER'S ROLE IN POLICY-MAKING

What if there had been no Hitler? It is now recognised that between 1933 and 1941 Hitler was central, but the linkage was less direct than was once believed to be the case. Hitler had a vision of a future utopia based on racial regeneration and purification from within. It was in order to achieve this vision that he allowed certain developments to happen which would not have otherwise occurred. This is certainly true of the growth in the ideologically pure SS-police empire until it became a 'state within a state'. Racial genocide associated with the elimination of Jews and other racially impure peoples would not have happened if Hitler had not made the final decision, though the presence of hot head radicals within the SA and Party would have led to some spontaneous persecution from below as evidenced by the events associated with the boycott of Jewish premises in 1933, the Nuremberg laws of 1935 and the Night of broken Glass *(Kristallnacht)*. Finally the outbreak of war in 1939 was Hitler's sole decision taken despite its unpopularity with, not just the army and people, but also high-ranking Nazis such as Göring.

> **KEY ISSUE**
>
> *To what extent was the role of Hitler all-important in the government of Germany?*

How was this possible given the reality of a dictator who absented himself from the routine business of government? Professor Ian Kershaw, one of the most recent historians of the Third Reich, has suggested that the answer is to be found in the ferocious contest among Nazi subordinates for Hitler's favour so that people did what they thought Hitler wanted. This 'working towards the Führer along the lines he would wish' was commented upon by Werner Willikens, State Secretary in the Ministry of Food as early as 1934, (quoted in Ian Kershaw, *Working Towards the Führer*, Contemporary European History, Vol. 2, Issue 2, Cambridge University Press, 1993).

> Everyone who has the opportunity to observe it knows that the Führer can hardly dictate from above everything he intends to realise sooner or later. On the contrary, up till now everyone with a post in the new Germany has worked best when he has, so to speak, worked towards the Führer ... in fact it is the duty of everybody to try to work towards the Führer along the lines he would wish. Anyone who makes mistakes will notice it soon enough. But anyone who really works towards the Führer along his lines and his goals will certainly both now and in the future one day have the finest reward in the form of the sudden legal confirmation of his work.

Professor Ian Kershaw believes that 'working towards the Führer' provides the key insight not only into Hitler's role in policy-making but also into how the Nazi state functioned throughout the twelve years of its life. Hitler's obsessions with the conquest of living space, removal of the Jews and achievement of a racially pure national community mobilised officials into making their own orders as they interpreted what they believed was required of them. Far from acting under orders many of their administrative decisions were retrospectively legitimised. The system could not have functioned without Hitler, for he acted as the final source of authority and integrated the many different and often warring, factions and individuals who acted in his name.

Kershaw argues that there were four important areas where Hitler's personal intervention was central. Firstly, in pursuit of his territorial ambitions, he swept aside guarantees and promises and was responsible for the collapse of the international order which had been built on the foundations of the Treaty of Versailles. The first blow to this order came with the march into the Rhineland, March 1937, a decision which was taken by Hitler alone. He made no reference to the army or his cabinet but sounded out individuals. He believed the time was ripe as a result of the weakness shown by the European powers over Mussolini's invasion of Abyssinia. After the Munich Conference in 1938, Hitler was taken up with events as he seized the opportunities which were presented to him by appeasement and achieved his pan-German goals of absorbing Austria, then Czechoslovakia before turning to Poland.

Secondly, Hitler's ideology became the embodiment of social ideas, a symbol. It was interpreted and aggressively policed by the SS under

Treaty of Versailles, see pages 20–1
Appeasement, see page 387
Munich Conference, see page 394

Himmler. Germany became a police state, opposition was ruthlessly crushed and after 1937, when Himmler acquired the exclusive right to handle Jewish affairs, Jews were encouraged to emigrate. This policy of purging racial outcasts was subsequently extended as new territories were absorbed – reaching a climax with the setting up of the New Order in the east when SS units embarked on a terrible and casual brutality which culminated in the death camps.

Death camps, see page 439

Thirdly, Hitler's style of decision-making encouraged the disappearance of ordered government. By the late 1930s it often took prominent cabinet ministers two to three years before they could see Hitler. This disintegration of a system was accelerated during the war years when he was either 'on the road' or conducting war operations from his 'wolf's lair' in Eastern Prussia. Eventually, it was the system which went out of control not Hitler. Responsibility for this state of affairs must be attributed to Hitler. Reference has already been made to his apparent reluctance to dictate from above so that those at the lower administrative levels initiated policies themselves within what they considered to be the spirit of the regime. His non-interventionist style was commented upon by Fritz Wiedemann, one of his adjutants, who wrote of Hitler's dislike of studying documents and his willingness to take important decisions even though he had not studied the relevant papers. However, this casual style was not the sole explanation, it also fitted in with his ideas of **social Darwinism**. Hitler's personal philosophy, his *Weltanschauung*, was based on the idea that struggle was a permanent feature of life and only the strong survived. He believed that the modern state, instead of devoting itself to protecting the weak, should reject its inferior population in favour of the strong and healthy. This idea became the theme of most of his speeches: victory goes to the strong and the weak must be eliminated. It was the ideology behind his subsequent policies to kill the mentally and physically handicapped and the Jews. He was hostile to any religion or ideology which put emphasis on the rights of the weak or the poor, such as Christianity or socialism, since this would distort the natural processes through which the stronger and healthier race would always triumph.

social Darwinism a social and political philosophy derived from Charles Darwin's views of natural selection through survival of the fittest

Finally, Hitler must bear the responsibility for the regime's descent into ever increasing barbarity, a consequence of the actions of those who 'worked towards the Führer'. This gave an enormous licence to experiment by different social groups in the areas of racial policies, eugenics and euthanasia. There was a clear link between the disintegration of an ordered system and the dropping of civilised restraints.

● It was competition between the heads of the five offices that made up the Führer's chancellery which led to the introduction of one of the most repulsive policies of the regime – the Children's Euthanasia Programme 1938–9. This involved the compulsory killing of handicapped children in institutional homes. As early as 1929, at a Nuremberg party rally, Hitler had expressed the view that Germany's future would only be secured if the birth rate rose and the sick and weak were eliminated. Despite the fact that he rejected the suggestion of euthanasia in 1935, he had agreed to a compulsory sterilisation programme of the mentally and physically handicapped in July 1933. By 1945, this had affected some 320,000–350,000 people. The background to the introduction of the euthanasia programme reveals not only the regime's racist ideology but also the chaotic way in which the system worked. In 1938, a casual letter, one of hundreds, arrived at the Führer's chancellery from the parents of a child born brain damaged, deaf, missing a leg and part of an arm, requesting that the child be 'put down'. Career-motivated officials under Phillip Bouhler, seeing an opportunity to expand their role, decided that this petition should be given to Hitler. They were fully aware of his views on racial purity and believed that bringing the petition to his attention involved 'working towards the Führer'. After the child had been examined by his own doctor, Hitler gave a verbal agreement to the petition. He also let it be known to Bouhler that subsequent requests to repeat the process would meet with his approval. The policy got out of control so that very quickly doctors and other medical officials drew up their own criteria for selecting children who would be referred for treatment. The outbreak of war was followed by an extension of the policy to sick adults. Public protest led to the programme being abandoned in 1941, but not before 72,000 people had been killed. It continued secretly in concentration camps between 1941 and 1943 when possibly a further 30,000–50,000 died. The euthanasia programme showed how civilised restraint could be abandoned by those who sought to please a leader who spoke in visions.

● It was this desire to please which also lay behind the escalating policies of increasing radicalism against the Jews. Here again it was groups like the SA and individuals such as Goebbels 'working towards the Führer' who took the initiatives (this theme is considered in greater detail in Chapter 10). During the 1930s, Hitler had distanced himself from the violent anti-Semitism of Julius Streicher's paper *'Der Stürmer'* and had said very little despite the most violent anti-Jewish measures. The policy was unattractive even in Nazi circles, so Goebbels said the Jewish question was not to be mentioned in Hitler's speeches. Hitler spoke only in the broadest terms. From 1940 onwards Himmler and his deputy, Heydrich, rather than Hitler, took the initiative to extend the policy first to Poland and then, in the summer of 1941, to Russia. Few historians support the controversial claim, made in 1983 by David Irving (*The War Path: Hitler's Germany 1933–1939*, Papermac), that the absence of Führer-signed decrees meant that he was not responsible and that Himmler kept Hitler uninformed until 1943. Hitler sanctioned their actions. Thus the 'final solution' came into being as a build-up of local actions.

Final Solution, pages 438–40

Hitler's role was to legalise different groups' attempts to fulfil his wishes. His role was as a 'figurehead'; without him the regime would have collapsed because he was the integrating force.

6 ∽ HITLER'S AIMS

Did Hitler have a blueprint of aggression or just intent?

Historians have taken contradictory and conflicting views on Hitler's aims in foreign policy. Writing in the aftermath of the Second World War and the liberation of the death camps, historians such as Hugh Trevor-Roper, *The Last Days of Hitler*, and Alan Bullock, *Hitler, A Study in Tyranny*, argued that it was Hitler's war – while it was successful he took the credit for it. Historians who take this intentionalist view that Hitler planned the Second World War, refer to Hitler's writings and speeches, particularly to *Mein Kampf* and the Hossbach Memorandum of 1937 (see pages 207 and 388–90). The latter document (named after Hitler's adjutant who compiled it) represented the minutes of a meeting Hitler had with the chiefs of the German armed forces and the German Foreign Minister, von Neurath, in the Chancellery in Berlin. It became a principal prosecution document at the Nuremberg Trials after the war. The substance of the Memorandum coincided with what Hitler said on other occasions around this time. It also reflected his long-term beliefs and plans which can be gathered from his writings and sayings from *Mein Kampf* onwards. Bullock therefore argued that the Memorandum represented a blueprint for war and conquest, which was remarkably followed in practice. Such would be the strongly intentionalist interpretation of the events leading to the outbreak of the Second World War, an interpretation which lasted until 1961 when A.J.P. Taylor published *The Origins of the Second World War* (Hamish Hamilton).

A.J.P. Taylor made the highly controversial claim that there was nothing distinctive about Hitler, apart from being a 'German'. He pointed to policy continuities between Nazi Germany and the politicians of Imperial Germany. He argued that Hitler did not have a clear plan – he was not a planner, but a vague romantic who had ideas but did not know how to achieve them. He was an opportunist making maximum use of the occasion. According to Taylor, Hitler's general aim was to restore Germany to its former place in Europe and end the inferiority imposed by Versailles. Taylor argued that it was impossible to stop such a powerful economic force as Germany from recovery especially as the Treaty of Versailles actually strengthened Germany by stripping her of her divergent parts. Germany, unlike France and Austria–Hungary, experienced no devastation of home territory while the disintegration of Austria–Hungary benefited Germany. Taylor concluded that the Second World

War was not solely Hitler's war, that other countries and statesmen shared this responsibility.

Taylor preferred to base his interpretation on the diplomatic record of these years. He presented a different picture of a Hitler not knowing where he was going in the 1930s and getting into a war by mistake, having been misled by British and French politicians. Taylor caused a tremendous stir. He was attacked for whitewashing Hitler and claiming that the Second World War was unnecessary. Taylor's views produced a storm of protest and a debate over how typical Hitler was. Friends described Hitler as fanatical with a streak of craziness. An Austrian, he was not of the political elite, and in fact came to power not because he was typical but because of his personal magnetism. Hitler was seen as a man of destiny. He pursued his goals fanatically and by 1938 he was regarded as dangerous by the conservative elites. Taylor was correct, there were some continuities between Hitler and his predecessors, but there were also crucial differences because of his obsessions.

Q

To what extent did Hitler have a 'blueprint' of intent?

By 1925, the time that *Mein Kampf* was published, Hitler's ideology was coherent and centred on two core themes.

The first was anti-Semitism and the removal of the Jews and the influence of Jewry. According to Hitler, racial conflict was the key to history in contrast with the views of Karl Marx who stressed class conflict. According to Hitler, the State was a means to an end to establish a racial new order in Germany and subsequently beyond. The dating of these ideas is not clear, possible dates suggested are 1917 during Hitler's down-and-out days in Vienna, or the defeat in 1918, or the 1919 Treaty of Versailles or later. Preference appears to be for the earlier date, the Vienna years, while the effect of war and the 'stab-in-the-back' reaction cemented these ideas from September 1919 onwards. A letter written by Hitler in September 1919 was precisely on anti-Semitism in the form of a racial onslaught while the early 1920s speeches were full of anti-Semitism. Hitler's ideas, however, were not out of the ordinary, but reflected the *völkisch* or nationalistic tradition of Germany in the nineteenth and early twentieth centuries.

Hitler's second obsession was with the conquest of 'living space' (*Lebensraum*) in the east largely at the expense of Russia. In a confidential memo at the end of 1922 *Lebensraum* is mentioned and, by 1924, under the influence of Rosenberg, the conquest of territory in the east is firmly in evidence. Hitler also had a hatred of Bolshevism and Marxism. As a preliminary to his territorial ambitions, he wanted to reverse Versailles and the restraints on rearmament. He also wanted to bring all Germans together in a 'greater Germany' which represented a continuity with the pan-German tradition and policies of the nineteenth century.

Hitler took control of foreign policy and his influence was decisive.

Taylor's dismissal of Hitler's plans outlined in *Mein Kampf* as 'fantasies behind bars' is now discredited. Historians acknowledge that there was a clear continuity between *Mein Kampf* and Hitler's policies of the 1930s, though his timetable to achieve this was flexible. In 1933 there was a decisive shift away from collaboration with Russia, to agreement with Poland, while the reintroduction of rearmament in 1935 was followed by the 1936 remilitarisation of the Rhineland and union with Austria in 1938. The latter event was followed by the expulsion of Jews from Vienna. This process was continued as other countries were absorbed. Hitler is now seen as having possessed a blueprint of intent, based on a strong and coherent ideology which inspired his policies (Hitler's ideology and philosophy are discussed in Chapter 9), accompanied by a complete opportunism in method and tactics.

7 ⌐ HITLER – REVOLUTIONARY OR COUNTER-REVOLUTIONARY?

Questions such as: did Hitler have clear and consistent social beliefs? did Hitler aim to change Germany's social structure? was Hitler forward-looking?, reflect the fundamental disagreements among historians on the character of Nazism, its social aims and intentions. Hence Nazism has been interpreted by some leading historians as genuinely revolutionary in content and by others as counter-revolutionary. Hitler's attitude and policy towards revolution changed over time as circumstances and his political priorities changed, as suggested in his own comments on this issue. Before becoming Chancellor, he had frequently said that 'Germany will have to be recast by revolution from the ground upwards' (28 July 1922), but this gave way, after January 1933, to 'Revolution is not a permanent state' (6 July 1933).

A *Hitler the revolutionary*

In some respects Hitler could be termed a revolutionary, for he had the skill to combine an idea of drastic change with the power to mobilise the necessary forces. The basis of Hitler's political beliefs, as already explained, was a harsh social Darwinism. A recurring theme in Hitler's speeches from 1922 onwards was the *weltanschaulich* or ideological element in Nazism: 'the victory of a party is a change of government. The victory of a *Weltanschauung* is a revolution' (Hitler at Munich, 19 March 1934).

It was in terms of a *Weltanschauung* or world-view that Hitler always described the Nazi Party, and also their coming to power in 1933. At the heart of the *Weltanschauung* was the concept of a 'struggle', a word which appeared most frequently in his speeches, 'man has become great through struggle' and 'the first fundamental of any rational *Weltanschauung* is the fact that. . .force alone is decisive'. He regarded struggle as the basis of all achievement, 'only through struggle has man raised himself above the animal world' (Kulmbach, 5 February 1928). 'The concept of struggle was one of the three fundamental principles which controlled the existence of every nation, the other two were purity of blood and the ingenuity of the individual' (Chemnitz, 2 April 1928). These principles also provide the key to Hitler's dislike of other people's beliefs. He criticised those who ignored the interests of race and the rule of a great leader, and who valued peace above conflict. Hitler showed a shrewd understanding of the state of mind of many Germans who had experienced war, the Treaty of Versailles, inflation, reparations and the economic depression. He preached independence as the source of power, 'a people must understand that its future lies only in its own ability, its own energy and its own courage. The world gives no help, a people must help itself' (Königsberg, 4 March 1933).

These various elements in Hitler's political beliefs were summed up in his address to the party rally at Nuremberg in 1937: 'The main plank in the National Socialist programme is to abolish the democratic idea of the individual...and to substitute for [it] the *"Volk"* community, rooted in the soil and bound together by the bond of its common blood'. Hitler believed that 'it was only by the creation of a real national community, rising above the interests and differences of rank and class, that class conflict could be avoided, for the object of National Socialist policy was to create a truly classless society where national interest could best be served by an **absolutist state**'.

> *Volk*, page 244

> **absolutist state**
> government with
> unrestricted power

The events surrounding Hitler becoming Chancellor, and subsequently establishing his dictatorship, represented a political revolution. Society was moulded in the image of Hitler, but his impact on the social order was complex and difficult to express. Not all of Hitler's ideas were clearly understood by all in the Party. Many argued, both before they came to power and for the first two years afterwards, for a social revolution such as occurred in Russia. This could only have been achieved if Hitler had been prepared to carry out a bloodbath in terms of purging society of those who had governed by virtue of their birth, wealth and power. This demand, as we saw in the last chapter, threatened the security of his regime and led to his purge of the left-wing revolutionaries in his party. This event illustrates the revolutionary character of National Socialism. Despite his defeat of the 'Second Revolution' on 30 June 1934, both publicly and privately for the remainder of the Third Reich Hitler continued to refer to the establishment of the Nazi regime as one of the greatest transformations in world history. Major changes in society followed on from his ideas, though the regime's life was too short for long-term changes, associated with the impact on youth of education and the change in social ideas and values, to take effect. Nevertheless, German society, which had been no different in 1933 compared with 1918 or even 1914, had changed by 1945. The strongest argument for Hitler achieving a social revolution is based on the regime's social destruction. The elimination of so many people, the mentally and physically handicapped in the euthanasia programme, Jews and gypsies in the racial purge, and people as a result of war, produced a different society in 1945 compared with 1933 or even 1939 (we will be returning to the social impact of Hitler and his regime in Chapter 10). Historians describe this as a revolution of **nihilism**.

B *Conclusion – Hitler's concept of revolution*

The word 'revolution' implies sudden, dramatic changes in the ruling elite, and in the relationship between different social groups often accompanied by violence. All revolutions need not necessarily fit such a pattern, but they nevertheless base change on a system of values and ideas opposed to the previous regime's.

Hitler certainly regarded his accession to power as a 'revolution' though he was aware that his 'revolutionary process in Germany had a particular character of its own'. He often stated, as in his address to the *Reichstag* on 30 January 1937, that his revolution possessed 'unique characteristics which made it difficult for contemporaries to understand the profound nature of the transformation that took place'. He made frequent references to his 'model revolution' which had been carried out in an ordered and planned fashion and with remarkably little bloodshed. He had carried out a political revolution where organisation and values changed, but this had not been accompanied by a social revolution in terms of the removal of the socially dominant elites. Hitler's purge of the left who had pressed for theses changes conciliated the leaders of the army, economy, and civil service who had viewed the attempts to continue the Nazi revolution with ever-increasing concern.

Hitler was a superb tactician who was prepared to accept the limitations to Nazi seizure of power imposed by the conservative forces in the *Reichswehr* and bureaucracy which survived. Failure to establish a clear position of power over the Establishment, such as occurred in the USSR, meant that he made no attempt to create a political vacuum. Instead he created a new and hostile division of power roles between State and Party, where neither possessed sole or independent power but had to rely on that conceded by the Führer.

> **nihilism** a total rejection of current beliefs by someone who finds nothing to approve of in the established order

8 ⌐ IMPACT OF THE WAR ON THE CHARACTER OF HITLER AND THE NATURE OF HIS REGIME

The historian, Hugh Trevor-Roper, in his *The Last Days of Hitler* (Macmillan 1947), regarded Hitler's final days in the Bunker in Berlin as a carefully produced theatrical piece reflecting his previous history. It was stage-managed by Goebbels, while those who surrounded him represented a court 'as negligible in its power of ruling, as incalculable in its capacity for intrigue, as any oriental sultanate'. Hitler's death was a 'spectacular annihilation' which was accompanied by the collapse, defeat and death of Germany also.

Hitler's anxieties became more exaggerated and the long-term consequences of his unhealthy lifestyle were highlighted. By April 1945 he was a physical wreck, the consequences both of the manner of his

> **KEY ISSUE**
>
> *Did Hitler lose his mastery and become a weak Führer during the closing years of the Nazi regime?*

lifestyle and of the medications provided by his doctor, Morell, which 'poisoned' his system. In the last days in the Bunker, 16 January to 28 April, his anxieties multiplied and he had 'an emaciated face, grey complexion, stooping body, shaking hands and feet, a hoarse and quivering voice, a film of exhaustion over his eyes'. His eccentricity became more pronounced. He frequently washed his hands and changed his clothes. The image of a concentrated will-power and intelligence, which had existed in earlier days, ended. He still manipulated his behaviour and temper for an audience as he had done in the past, but his outbursts became increasingly out of control as witnessed by his hysterical reaction to the failures of the *Luftwaffe*, and the news of Himmler's 'betrayal', when Himmler, believing Hitler to be dead, opened negotiations with the Allies. He showed an increasing tendency to lose touch with reality and spent hours studying architectural plans for the rebuilding of Germany at a time when Germany was being defeated on all fronts.

These insights into the decline in Hitler's character are highlighted by events in April in the Bunker, particularly the conference which was held on 22 April. It was called to discuss strategy for the defence of Berlin, including all all-out attack by troops under the SS general, Steiner. Hitler was informed at the meeting that his orders had not been carried out. He 'flew into a rage, shrieked that he had been deserted, denounced the army as traitors, spoke of universal treason, corruption, failure and lies' (*The Last Days of Hitler*). This type of behaviour and language represented Hitler's reaction to opposition, or criticism, particularly in his relationship with the army High Command. The conference was very significant in providing a new insight into Hitler's character. For the first time he despaired of his mission. 22 April was the day that he recognised his failure and the defeat of the Third Reich, events which, given his Darwinist views, signalled his acceptance of his failings. It is probable that this was the day when Hitler decided to commit suicide. However, he still looked for a scapegoat and he continued to blame the Jews.

Behind this increasingly frequent and violent temper lay Hitler's essential distrust of people. His retreat to the Bunker represented the final isolation of a leader who had always been remote; now he was totally cut off from human contact. He believed that the generals were intriguing against him, reflecting his fear of treachery which had always been present in his character. His personality traits of hatred, resentment and insensitive contempt of people were reflected in the spiteful orders to destroy people and property which he gave in these last days. On the 28 April, infuriated by the support of his own brother-in-law, Hermann Fegelein, for Himmler, Hitler ordered his execution as well as that of any German officer who had 'failed' in his duty to carry out Hitler's orders, and all prisoners and hostages. Finally he issued the scorched-earth order, covering all of Germany, to burn crops and destroy anything that might be of use to the Allies. In other words Hitler intended his suicide to be accompanied by an orgy of deliberate destruction. He would go to his grave surrounded by human sacrifices to accompany the ritual burning of his body. As early as February 1942 Hitler had declared, 'if one had not a family to bequeath one's house to, the best thing would be to be burnt in it with all its contents. . .a magnificent funeral pyre'. Once again he relied on Goebbels to stage-manage this final scene as he had the Nuremberg rallies which were an obvious comparison.

Hitler's decision, probably made on 22 April, to remain in Berlin despite the allied advance and to take his own life, came after a year of harsh and strained behaviour. During this last year he had clung to his obstinate belief, against all advice and evidence, that Germany would win the war. His surrender of this belief emphasised the decline which had occurred in his self-assessment of his genius. He lost his sense of mission and of being superior. Whereas in the past he had shown resentment and hatred against his critics, he was now, in April, ready to admit that he had made mistakes. However, he still retained a personal presence which explained the remarkable obedience he continued to command in the last week of his life. He retained control until the end, though he disliked coming to decisions as even his hesitation and then sudden resolve over his suicide showed. He decided war strategy and ignored the advice of the Chief of Army General Staff, General Guderian, reflecting the distrust, suspicion and hostility he felt towards the army. He sent them angry strategic lectures and withdrew from the company of competent military advisers, preferring to rely on SS amateurs who continued to underpin the Hitler State. Hitler's final orders of April regarding the conduct of war strategy bore no relation to reality. He would defend Berlin, but at the same time he ordered its final destruction. Hitler's decisions reflected the essential nihilism of Nazi philosophy, 'the authentic voice of Nazism: world power or ruin' (*The Last Days of Hitler*).

In the view of Trevor-Roper, Hitler's group of advisers in the Bunker became less a war cabinet, more an 'oriental court of flatterers and toadies'. Goebbels, Speer and Himmler remained loyal and devoted to Hitler though they continued to intrigue amongst themselves. During these Bunker days relations were dominated by the succession question as Hitler's physical decline was evident to all. Hitler continued to use the policy of 'divide and rule' to ensure his dominance, but also reflecting his social Darwinism philosophy, as in the case of the growing rivalry between Himmler and Bormann, representing the SS versus the Party for ultimate domination of Germany. Hitler's support was vital to maintain individuals in power, especially in the case of Martin Bormann, and this restrained his enemies. The only new development in the regime during these days in the Bunker was that Hitler came to rely on Bormann who exercised power as Hitler's secretary. Göring and, after 20 July, Himmler, were in decline due to the corrupting influence of absolute power which led to a marked deterioration in the characters of all the Nazi leaders, and they shared Hitler's increasing unreality. By April defeat was obvious, but the inner circle competed for the decreasing remnants of power apart from the succession. Goebbels intrigued for the post of Foreign Minister in place of Ribbentrop. Trevor-Roper described these personalities as 'a set of flatulent clowns swayed by purely random influences'. Hitler's support was vital for their survival but in the last decisive moment few remained loyal to him, apart from Goebbels and some members of his household.

The last days in the Bunker reflected the contradictions of Nazism which had always been present at various periods. Slogans of victory were proclaimed from the Bunker, but privately everyone prepared for defeat and this encouraged a total breakdown of discipline and organisation. Almost everyone was individually engaged in secret negotiations for surrender or desertion. In a regime which was based on the existence of personal empires rather than a totalitarian government, such activities were bound to lead to disintegration as individual leaders were well served within their own realms. Himmler's subordinates, for instance, remained totally loyal to him and followed his lead, while Speer used the loyalty of his men to defeat Hitler's order to destroy the country's infrastructure e.g. roads, bridges and factories.

9 ⌇ BIBLIOGRAPHY

There are a number of collected editions of primary sources which are readily available. For the themes covered in this chapter J. Noakes and G. Pridham (eds), *Nazism 1919–1945, A Documentary Reader* (University of Exeter 1984), *Vol 2 – State, Economy and Society 1933–1939*, is probably the most accessible for students. It is as useful for the commentary as for the documents. Other collections of primary sources relevant to the themes covered in this chapter are N. Baynes (ed.), *The Speeches of Adolf Hitler* (Oxford UP 1942); A. Hitler, *Mein Kampf*, with introduction by D.C. Watt (Hutchinson 1969); A. Hitler, *Table Talk, 1941–1944*, ed. Martin Bormann, introduced by Hugh Trevor-Roper (Oxford UP 1988) and A. Speer, *Inside the Third Reich* (Weidenfeld & Nicolson 1970).

Amongst the secondary sources there are a number of general histories which examine the Hitler state: for a revisionist interpretation of Hitler's role in Germany read the structuralist argument presented by M. Broszat, *The Hitler State* (Longman 1981); Two interpretative accounts are to be found in K. Hildebrand, *The Third Reich* (Allen & Unwin 1984) and J. Hiden and J. Farquharson, *Explaining Hitler's Germany* (Batsford 1989).

For a study of Hitler, the pioneering work was written by A. Bullock, *Hitler: A Study in Tyranny* (Odhams 1952). Writing soon after the Second World War Bullock presented the intentionalist perspective of Hitler. Bullock has also written a general history on *The Third Reich* (Weidenfeld & Nicolson 1955) and a later study, *Hitler and Stalin: Parallel Lives* (HarperCollins 1991). Other histories include J.C. Fest, *Hitler* (Weidenfeld & Nicolson 1974), and *The Face of the Third Reich* (Weidenfeld & Nicolson, 1970), H.R. Trevor-Roper, *The Last Days of Hitler*

(Macmillan 1947), N. Stone, *Hitler: The Führer and the People* (Hodder & Stoughton 1980), J.P. Stern, *Hitler, The Führer and the People* (Fontana 1975) and W. Carr, *Hitler, A Study in Personality and Politics* (Arnold 1978).

More recent publications on Hitler include I. Kershaw, *The 'Hitler Myth', Image and Reality in the Third Reich* (Oxford UP 1987) and *Hitler* (Profiles in Power Series, Longman 1991). For A level: D. Geary, *Hitler and Nazism* (Routledge, Lancaster Pamphlets, 1993) and John Laver, *Hitler, Germany's Fate or Germany's Misfortune?* (Personalities and Powers Series, Hodder & Stoughton 1995).

Finally there are several studies of the different interpretations of Hitler: these include H.W. Koch, *Aspects of the Third Reich* (Macmillan 1985); W. Laqueur, *Fascism: A Reader's Guide* (Penguin 1979) and I. Kershaw, *The Nazi Dictatorship, Problems and Perspectives of Interpretation* (Edward Arnold 1989). A controversial view of Hitler is found in D. Irving, *The War Path: Hitler's Germany 1933–1939* (Papermac 1983).

10 ⌒ DISCUSSION QUESTIONS

A *This section consists of questions that might be used for discussion or for testing your understanding of the main themes covered in this chapter.*

1. What skills did Hitler display as a leader?
2. (a) What was the Hitler myth?
   (b) Why was it important?
3. What do historians mean when they write that Hitler had a policy of divide and rule?
4. To what extent was the Third Reich well-organised?
5. What were Hitler's aims in foreign policy?
6. To what extent did Hitler's aims differ from those of the leaders of Imperial Germany before 1914?

11 ⌒ ESSAY QUESTIONS

A *Two-Part Questions.*

1. (a) What were the main strengths and weaknesses of Hitler as a dictator?
   (b) Describe the ways in which Hitler secured his domination of the Party and the State.
2. (a) What were Hitler's main aims as Führer?
   (b) Why is Hitler regarded as a revolutionary?

B *Essay Questions.*

1. 'Hitler was master of the Third Reich'.
   How far do you agree with this view?
2. Examine the view that Hitler's role was important in the government of Germany'.
3. 'Hitler's role and power in the government of Germany changed over the course of the period 1933–45'.
   How far do you agree with this view?

4. 'Hitler was a weak dictator who oversaw a mass of private and conflicting empires headed by independent Nazi barons'.
To what extent do you agree with this view?

12 ⌁ MAKING NOTES

Read the advice section about making notes on page xx of Preface: How to use this book, and then make your own notes based on the following headings and questions.

1. *Hitler's control of the NSDAP*
(a) In what ways and with what success did Hitler exert his control over the NSDAP?
(b) Who made up Hitler's inner guard of advisers, friends and companions?
(c) What was the basis of the relationship between Hitler and other high ranking Nazi officials?

2. *Hitler's role as Führer*
(a) What were Hitler's strengths and weaknesses as a dictator?
(b) What is meant by the phrase 'working towards the Führer'? What effect did this have on the government of Germany?
(c) To what extent can Hitler be held responsible for the crimes against humanity associated with the regime?
(d) What were Hitler's main aims as dictator and how consistent were his ideas?
(e) To what extent can Hitler be regarded as a revolutionary?

3. *Impact of war on the regime*
(a) To what extent had Hitler deteriorated by April 1945 and how was this revealed by the conference held on 22 April?
(b) Why did Trevor-Roper describe Hitler's 'inner guard' as 'an oriental court of flatterers and toadies'?
(c) To what extent did Hitler remain in control during the last days of the regime?

13 ⌁ MULTI SOURCE DOCUMENTARY EXERCISE ON HITLER AND HIS REGIME 1943–5

Study the sources below and answer the questions which follow:

Observers who had watched the rise of these twin engines of power wondered what would happen when Himmler and Bormann at last began to conflict. In 1943, when Himmler was made Minister of the Interior, that moment had come. Till then, relations between the two men had been excellent...now, the slightest attempts by Himmler to exercise authority outside the SS were openly resented by Bormann.

'Bormann immediately reported such cases to Hitler and exploited them. To our surprise (it is Speer who is speaking), it did not take long for Bormann to stalemate Himmler.'

Such are the advantages of a central position.

In the same way, after the Plot of 20 July 1944 [a failed bomb attempt by a group of army generals to assassinate Hitler], Bormann was quick to exploit the errors and omissions of his rival. While Himmler naively believed (with Göring out of favour) that he was the obvious heir apparent to the throne, Bormann was seeing to it that Himmler was not moving upwards and towards the centre of power but outwards and away from it. In the dark days of the last winter of the war, Bormann secured the appointment of Himmler as Commander-in-Chief of Army Group Vistula east of Berlin.

SOURCE A *A British observer writing after the German surrender, Hugh Trevor-Roper in* The Last Days of Hitler *(1947).*

Bormann has turned the Party Chancellery into a paper factory. Every day he sends out a mountain of letters and files which the *Gauleiter*, now involved in battle, no longer even have time to read...totally useless stuff of no practical value in our struggle...The situation is such that only a word from the Führer can relieve the crisis of morale in which the people have been plunged. I regard it as a grave mistake that the Führer does not speak...It is not only in victory that we should speak but in misfortune as well. It is at present very difficult to get decisions from the Führer. He is occupied exclusively with the situation in the west and barely finds time for other problems... The *Luftwaffe* comes in for the sharpest criticism from Hitler. Day after day, Göring has to listen, without being in a position to argue back.

SOURCE B *Goebbels, in complaining mood, from a diary entry for 3 April 1945.*

Meanwhile, a telegram had arrived from Göring, which Bormann hastily brought to Hitler... In the telegram, Göring merely asked Hitler whether, in keeping with the decree on the succession, he should assume the leadership if Hitler remained in Fortress Berlin... but Bormann claimed that Göring was launching a *coup d'état*... At first, Hitler responded with the same apathy he had shown all day. But Bormann's theory gained support when another radio message arrived...it read:

'To Reichsminister von Ribbentrop,

If, by 10 pm 23 April, it is clear that the Führer is no longer free to conduct the affairs of the Reich, his decree of June 1941 becomes effective, by which I am heir to all his offices. If, by midnight 23 April, you receive no other word, you are to come to me at once by air.'

Göring, Reichsmarshal

SOURCE C *Göring and the succession – the events of 22 April 1945 described by Albert Speer,* Inside the Third Reich *(1970).*

Here was fresh material for Bormann. 'Göring is engaged in treason, my Führer!' he exclaimed excitedly. Although Hitler had remained calm over the first telegram, Bormann now won his game. Hitler immediately stripped Göring of his rights of succession – Bormann himself drafted the radio message – and accused him of treason and betrayal of National Socialism... An outburst of wild fury followed, with bitterness, self-pity, and despair mingled... Then, with startling abruptness, Hitler lapsed back into his apathy. 'All right. Let Göring negotiate the surrender. If the war is lost, it does not matter who does it.'

Admiral:
Since all divisions have failed to arrive and our position seems hopeless the Führer dictated last night the attached Political Testament. Heil Hitler!
Bormann

...Before my death, I expel former Reichsmarshal, Hermann Göring from the Party and withdraw all rights conferred on him by the decree of 20 June, 1941... In his place I appoint Admiral Dönitz as President of the Reich and Supreme Commander. Before my death, I expel the former Reichsführer and Minister of the Interior, Heinrich Himmler from the Party and from all state offices... Apart altogether from their disloyalty to me, Göring and Himmler have brought irreparable shame upon the whole nation by secretly negotiating with the enemy against my will and also by illegally attempting to seize control of the State...

SOURCE D *Hitler's Political Testament, 29 April 1945.*

Witnessed and signed by: Joseph Goebbels, Martin Bormann, General Krebs, General Burgdorf

Q

1 *What does source A reveal about the reasons why the previously 'excellent' relations between Bormann and Himmler had declined by 1943?*
2 *Use the evidence of the sources and your own knowledge to explain the importance of Martin Bormann.*
3 *In what ways does the view of Hitler's personality and leadership shown in source B contradict the opinions expressed in source C?*
4 *How useful are sources A and C to an historian studying the nature of Nazi leadership in 1944–5?*
5 *Study the sources A-D inclusive and use your own knowledge. Explain how far you agree with the view that 'Hitler's position at this time was that of a Weak dictator'.*

The Nazi State

1 ✐ HISTORIANS' ASSESSMENTS OF THE GOVERNMENT OF THE THIRD REICH

Early commentators on the Nazi State who used the evidence of the experiences of victims and opponents described the Third Reich as 'a rationally organised and highly perfected system of terrorist rule'. Gradually historical research showed this idea to be in need of revision. While it is in many respects true of Hitler's powerful personality and his integrating role as a leader, a different picture was presented by the presence of many rival departments and authorities with shared responsibilities in the Nazi State (a *polycratic* system of government). This complex state of affairs was also the basis of the continuing importance of the various organisations, such as the SS, which supervised and policed the one party state. As we have seen in Chapter 7, there is general agreement that Hitler was master. He, rather than the **Reichsleitung**, controlled the *Gauleiter*, but historians have also written of an administrative inefficiency and inconsistency which existed alongside an apparent dictatorship.

Commenting on Hitler's role in the State in *The Hitler State*, Martin Broszat wrote that:

> The unrestrained will of the Führer and the personal loyalty (not primarily dependent on office) demanded by him increasingly caused in the State, as it had already done so in the Party, the collapse of normal codes of conduct and of the institutional, corporate unity and coherence of the government. . .

In state matters, Hitler's use of the Party and the SS bypassed the power of the civil service. His appointment of individuals and agencies for particular roles conflicted with government departments and ministries. The Four Year Plan, for instance, conflicted with the Ministry of Economics, the Reich Labour Service, and the Hitler Youth. The cabinet did not operate so the Reich Chancellery under Dr Hans Heinrich Lammers became a co-ordinating agency. Hitler tended to let conflicts work themselves out, and only took decisions when absolutely necessary. Dr Lammers, probably one of the best qualified to comment on Hitler's style of leadership, in a discussion about the Reich Ministry of Economics (quoted in Noakes and Pridham, *Nazism 1919–1945, A Documentary Reader, Vol 2*), is reported to have said to the Lord Mayor of Hamburg that:

Reichsleitung a term applied collectively to several officials high in Nazi affairs

Q

What links do you think existed between Hitler's system of personal loyalty and the regime's descent into barbarism?

He (the Führer) found it difficult to make decisions about personnel. He always hoped that things would sort themselves out on their own. A decision had not yet been made because the Führer was not satisfied with the nomination of only one state secretary and would prefer to appoint a minister. He kept hoping that the question of personnel would solve itself. He, Lammers, had proposed the appointment of super ministers to whom some of the ministers would be subordinated as far as particular issues were concerned. The reason was that he found it extremely difficult to work with this large cabinet...

Q

Did Hitler's style of leadership reflect his social Darwinism?

Hitler allowed this confusion to flourish because the only unifying force was obedience to his person. In the words of one commentator, 'new institutions grew, flourished or died, spawned mutations, struggled for survival and thrust their offshoots under the very doors of the established ministries' (D. Schoenbaum, *Hitler's Social Revolution*). Hans Mommsen also commented upon the element of chaos and on-the-spot decision-making when he wrote of an 'unparalleled institutional anarchy and increasing divorce from practical reality in the process of decision-making at all levels, the system being held together externally by the Führer myth'. Karl Bracher wrote of the contradiction between the claim to rule by one man on the one hand and on the other, the presence of competing and overlapping power groups creating confusion and organised chaos. The propaganda empire is a useful example of this state of affairs. Rivalry flourished between Goebbels as Reich Minister of Propaganda, Rosenberg as the agent supervising the Nazi *Weltanschauung* (see page 256), Otto Dietrich as the Nazi press chief and Philipp Bouhler as head of a censorship office. Each of the major power blocs sought to protect its interests; this was true of the army (now renamed the *Wehrmacht*), big business, the SS, the senior members of the civil service, the office of the Führer's deputy, Hess, and the Party's organisation. In this situation, historians now concentrate on the 'authoritarian anarchy' of the regime. Central to this revised understanding is a recognition that the State was not ruled by the Party, especially between 1933 and 1939, but by individuals who, while claiming to be Nazi, were really concerned with personal pursuit of ambition.

KEY ISSUE

Recent research about the way Germany was governed.

This complex and chaotic structure did not replace, but was superimposed on the traditional civil service which had governed Germany under the Weimar Constitution. Hitler's acquisition of the highest functions of the State by August 1934 was not accompanied by a bloodbath such as had happened in Russia, so that the aristocratic elite who had dominated German society continued to enjoy their privileges of wealth and political power. Explanations of Hitler's reasons for allowing this confusion of conflicting power groups and personal connections to exist have ranged from a reflection of his social Darwinist beliefs to one that enabled him to hold his key position. Otto Dietrich, Hitler's press chief, wrote in his memoirs (quoted in Noakes and Pridham, *Nazism 1919–1945, A Documentary Reader*, Vol 2):

> In the twelve years of his rule in Germany Hitler produced the biggest confusion in government that has ever existed in a civilised state. During his period of government, he removed from the organisation of the State all clarity of leadership and produced a completely **opaque** network of competencies. It was not laziness or an excessive degree of tolerance which led the otherwise so energetic and forceful Hitler to tolerate this real witch's cauldron of struggles for position and conflicts over competence. It was intentional. With this technique he systematically disorganised the upper echelons of the Reich leadership in order to develop and further the authority of his own will until it became a despotic tyranny.

opaque a confused /unclear division of responsibilities

The success of the regime, in spite of this break-up of organisation, can partly be explained by Hitler's political skill, but also by the willingness of the conservative elites who controlled the army, industry and the civil service, to work with the Nazis. The alliance was partly based on a recognition of common interests, but also on the fear of a communist alternative. This relationship between the elites and the regime is explored in further detail below.

2 ∽ POLITICAL REALITIES IN 1933

A *The conservative elites*

German political life in 1933, despite the political revolution which had led to the abdication of Kaiser Wilhelm II in 1917, and his replacement by a parliamentary democracy, continued to be dominated by the aristocracy. The Kaiser went into exile in Holland, but a social revolution did not follow so that in many respects the changes of 1917 constituted a 'pseudo' revolution for many of the old imperial attitudes and privileges continued to be enjoyed by an autocratic elite. The elite included the *Junker*, a rich landowning class who dominated the rural plain of Northern Germany. They were descended from the former militaristic Prussian nobility and controlled over one-sixth of Germany's total arable area. Their interests were represented in the *Reichslandbund*, a conservative and nationalist organisation which was bitterly opposed to communism. They had received financial help and protection from successive Weimar governments but the Brüning government in its closing moments decided to sponsor a scheme for the resettlement of the unemployed on some of the *Junkers'* estates. The landowners complained loudly about 'agrarian Bolshevism' and used their influence with the president to induce him to dismiss Brüning. The *Reichslandbund*, heavily infiltrated by Nazis, again contributed, through their influence with Hindenburg, to the fall of Schleicher and to the appointment of a cabinet headed by Hitler. By having the ear of the president, the agrarian elite had a more direct influence than the industrialists on key events in the collapse of the republic and the advent of Hitler. Also to be found amongst the elites were the capitalist barons based in the Ruhr basin, North-Rhine, Westphalia and the Saar. They were dominated by the Krupp, Loewe, Wolf, Kirdorf, Flick and Mercedes-Benz families who, between them, controlled the iron, coal, steel, armaments, chemicals and car industries.

Finally there was the group which composed the 'old bureaucracy', who held high administrative posts in the civil service, judiciary and services. The continuing presence of these elites after 1933 meant that Hitler still had some important restraints on his power. They expected him to continue with the system of rule by presidential decree. There was no suggestion that a new system of government, the Third Reich, would be introduced. They were quickly disillusioned as the events of 1933–4 highlighted the revolutionary nature of Nazism and as the supremacy of the Führer was applied in every sphere of Party and State.

B *Civil service*

The civil service, along with the *Reichswehr*, symbolised the old imperial order especially in inner government circles and in the ministries. It strengthened its position and influence during the years when government was conducted under the presidential emergency decrees allowed by Article 48 of the Constitution (see page 19). It represented the tradition of government by people who were the servants of the State rather than being identified with a particular party. However, the men who staffed the ministries had no experience of, or liking for democracy. Higher civil servants, especially in Berlin, favoured the conservative right in politics, but this meant the DNVP, rather than the NSDAP. However, in Hitler's favour it should be noted that younger civil servants did not represent this link with the past and here the NSDAP won numerous supporters from 1930–1 onwards. Also, as parliamentary democracy declined with increased use of emergency decrees, the Republic came to be run by civil servants, and Hitler continued with this practice which made possible his seizure of power.

C *The* Reichswehr

The Treaty of Versailles had reduced the Army to about 100,000 in 1933, but it remained in a very strong position. It was dominated by the *Junker* families especially in the highest military positions. Three out of five generals were aristocrats, 20 per cent of all *Reichswehr* commissions were held by the aristocracy with some middle class represented, and most of its officers came from military families. Under Weimar this aristocratic dominance had increased. The army symbolised a high regard for honour and for its own interests and the German tradition. Respected by the conservative elites, under the Weimar Republic the army had remained neutral though it sought to dominate the life of the Republic. Up to 1938 the army continued to believe that it was the final judge of the political fate of the Reich. Its failure to act in 1933 made a major contribution to Hitler coming to power. When Hitler took office,

Generals Gröner and Schleicher were succeeded by General Werner von Blomberg (1878–1946) (see page 205) upon whose ability to handle the *Reichswehr* Hitler's regime depended. His appointment as Minister of Defence on 30 January 1933, in succession to Schleicher, was a key element in the formation of Hitler's cabinet. He was a professional officer with a brilliant war record, but little judgement. From 1930, he commanded the East Prussian Military District. Here, he came under the influence of Reichenau, his chief of staff, who believed the *Reichswehr* could work with the Nazi movement; and of Müller, an army chaplain, who was a fanatical Nazi and later as Reich bishop of the Lutheran churches promoted the German Faith Movement, a form of Christianity from which the Jewish elements were removed (see page 231). Blomberg's appointment removed the remaining doubts of Hindenburg concerning a Hitler cabinet. Blomberg was determined to maintain the *Reichswehr*'s neutrality towards the new government and to keep it separate from the Nazi State and Party. In the Third Reich Hitler wanted its support because this would give him the appearance of respectability and legality, but the *Reichswehr* was determined to obstruct the influence of the NSDAP more effectively than all other branches of the executive.

KEY ISSUE

The restraints on Hitler's freedom of action inherited from the Weimar regime.

3 ⌐ DEVELOPMENTS IN THE CIVIL SERVICE AND LEGAL SYSTEM 1933–45

A *The legal system*

Hitler's need to reconcile these traditional power groups to his regime if he was to achieve his long-term goals in foreign policy led to the emergence of two overlapping and often conflicting centres of authority within the State. The civil service and the legal system, while ultimately subordinate to the Führer, were allowed to function as they had done under Weimar. This represented an element of continuity though inevitably intervention in the name of the Führer overrode their authority and undermined the law. This is especially apparent in the area of the judiciary where the regime intervened to deal with those considered to be the enemies of the State. As early as 21 March 1933 the Malicious Practices Law (*Heimtückegesetz*) was introduced which banned outspoken criticisms of the regime. Special courts were set up to deal with offenders. Many of those considered to be enemies of the regime were sent to concentration camps without being tried in court. The *Gestapo* was active in dealing with those who resisted or opposed and on 10 February 1936 their actions were placed above the law. Any form of protest was seen as a political crime and the regime reacted promptly with very public acts of punishment. Numbers are difficult to assess, but about 1,200,000 Germans were sent to concentration camps of which 500,000–600,000 were political prisoners. Death sentences, possibly 12,000, were imposed for political reasons. The outbreak of war in 1939 led to demands by Hitler and other party leaders for stiff

KEY ISSUE

The extent to which the law was used to serve the regime's purposes.

wartime penal laws, which led to the passing of a mass of new laws, covering listening to enemy radio broadcasts, economic sabotage of the war effort, disrupting the armed forces and crimes of violence, with the death penalty for infringement. Before 1933 there were three categories of offence carrying the death penalty, by 1943–4 there were 46 such categories. The Ministry of Justice records a rise in death sentences passed from 23 in 1938 to 4,438 in 1943. Between 1938 and the latter part of 1944, 11,733 were executed.

Hitler was not content with this ruthless increase in the severity of legal sentences. In the autumn of 1939 he ordered Himmler to use the security police to carry out the immediate execution, without a court trial, of anyone suspected of committing acts against the State as well as sabotage. The executions were mostly carried out in concentration camps by members of the SS and security police who were protected from legal enquiries by the State prosecutors by the introduction, in October 1939, of special SS and police tribunals. Between 1943 and 1945 it took 40,000 of the *Gestapo* to 'neutralise' opponents. The rise in numbers detained in camps in Germany was part of Hitler's measures to remove 'internal enemies' along with 'inferior' national elements. These developments led to the decline of legal order.

B *The civil service*

The civil service saw a decline in official government institutions as the authority of the Party and the SS increased. Hitler's unwillingness to intervene actively in day-to-day government should have increased the powers of civil servants, but this did not happen. Although he retained the existing administrative ministries he undermined them by a growing tendency to bypass them in important areas of policy. He allowed new agencies to be created which took over responsibilities from existing government departments so that their sources of information and power were reduced. By 1942, there were 11 new agencies at Reich level established in special areas covered by existing ministries, but not under ministerial control. As new laws were passed and policing intensified, so new posts were created for Göring, Speer, Himmler and Bormann.

In the case of the economy, while the non-Nazi, Hjalmar Schacht, was Minister of Economics, after the introduction of the Second Four Year Plan in 1936 a separate but parallel ministry developed under Göring, who was given far-reaching powers as **Minister Plenipotentiary** to set up an organisation to gear the economy for war. The resulting Office of the Director of the Four Year Plan developed 17 subordinate agencies, none of which was co-ordinated with comparable agencies in the ministerial system (see page 348 for diagram of structure of the Four Year Plan). A similar duplicating of functions occurred with the growth of the SS which eventually became almost a state within a state for, as its powers and authority increased, so it undermined and dissolved existing State institutions (we will be looking at the SS's organisation and role in greater detail later in this chapter). The Party's

Minister Plenipotentiary a person who is given full power of independent action

power and influence grew at central and local level. Commissioners for
the Defence of the Reich were appointed on 1 September 1939 in each
of the 18 **Wehrkreis** of the Reich. The Reich governors and *Oberpräsi-
denten*, that is the most important *Gauleiter*, were selected for this role.
They became more important in 1942 when the Reich became involved
in total war and the Party *Gaue* became Reich defence zones. There was
a 'jungle' of overlapping responsibilities, with the Party in a strong position, so that the existing civil service was increasingly bypassed. Similarly, the Party gained a strong position in the civil services in newly
annexed areas, where party authorities were generally very strong
anyway. These wartime developments helped to increase Bormann's
power greatly, first through his office as the Führer's deputy for party
affairs, and later as the Führer's secretary.

> **Wehrkreis** an army
> district containing the
> headquarters of one
> infantry corps whose
> commander was also
> the *Wehrkreis*
> commander

4 ⌐ DEVELOPMENTS IN STATE–PARTY RELATIONS 1933–45

A *Position of the Party at the time of the seizure of power* (Machtergreifung)

It might be assumed that, since Nazi Germany was a one-party state, the
Nazi party would have become the effective and exclusive government
of Germany after the seizure of power in 1933. A comparison with the
Soviet Union is useful. In the USSR the party ruled the State: the
General Secretary of the party was the head of government, though in
some cases he may also have the title of President, and the Politburo
was the cabinet, while the Party Congress functioned as the major governmental body and party members played a leading role at lower
levels. On the surface it might appear as if the NSDAP played a similar
role; certainly it is an impression conveyed by popular commentators,
such as W. Shirer who wrote that, 'Hitler's immediate task, after gaining
power, was to make his party the exclusive master of the state'.

> **KEY ISSUE**
>
> *Did the Party ever rule
> Germany?*

The Nazi victory in 1933 seemed inevitable; its organisation was
superior to that of the other parties, party membership was rapidly
increasing, and the massive propaganda effort made it all look unstop-
pable. Historians of the Nazi Party, such as D. Orlow in his *A History of
the Nazi Party 1933–1945* (David & Charles 1973), have concentrated
attention on the progressive development of party organisation during
the 1920s, the perfecting of the central party organisation in the late
1920s under Gregor Strasser, and the development of affiliated and
front organisations through which the Party infiltrated other political,
professional and social organisations in order to take them over when
the opportunity presented itself. Without this organisation, it is argued,
the Nazis would have been unable to cope with the large inflow of party
members once the movement took off.

All was not what it seemed, though, and the Nazi Party faced major
problems in the early 1930s, stemming largely from the character of its

earlier development. These problems are examined in J. Noakes, *Government, Party and People in Nazi Germany* (University of Exeter 1984). He discussed the tensions between the charismatic leadership of Hitler and central party apparatus (the PO), with the *Gauleiter* as the key individuals in the development of the Party in the provinces. After 1928 the central party apparatus and the *Gauleiter* were both undermined. They suffered from the growth of separate interest sections affiliated to the Party, such as for Nazi teachers, doctors and lawyers, and by the increasing specialisation of roles as the Party grew, as in the case of Goebbels' propaganda department. With Strasser's failure to establish a tightly centralised party organisation and his consequent resignation, the Nazi Party, on the eve of the seizure of power, was a loose organisation held together by the hope of power. In a sense there was not one but 43 Nazi parties in 1933. This meant that the Party had severe limitations: it was too divided and too lacking in genuine administrative ability to create a proper Nazi State. The Party was not a tight, well-integrated group, but a movement which was often paralysed by quarrels and mutual distrust. Nazi leaders were more concerned with building up their own power rather than developing agreement for future action.

Q

What problems faced the Party, affecting its ability to rule?

Organisation of the Nazi party	
Der Führer Adolf Hitler	He was the undisputed leader of the party
Reichsleitung der NSDAP (Reich leadership)	There were several Reich leaders with specific responsibilities, such as the party treasurer, and the Führer's deputy in charge of party affairs
Landesinspekteur (regional inspector)	Originally there were nine regional inspectors, each with responsibility for a *Gau*, but they were eventually replaced by the *Gauleiter*
Gauleiter (district leader)	There were 36 leaders of *Gaue* or districts, such as Saxony or Swabia. The number grew with the inclusion of Austria, Sudetenland and Danzig
Kreisleiter (circuit leader)	This was the next lower administrative unit, equivalent to a rural council
Ortsgruppenleiter (local group leader)	These were leaders responsible for a town section
Zellenleiter (cell leader)	Based on a neighbourhood (4–5 blocks of households) or employment unit
Blockwart (block warden)	These were the lowest officials just above the ordinary member
Pg. – Parteigenosse (Party comrade)	These were the ordinary members

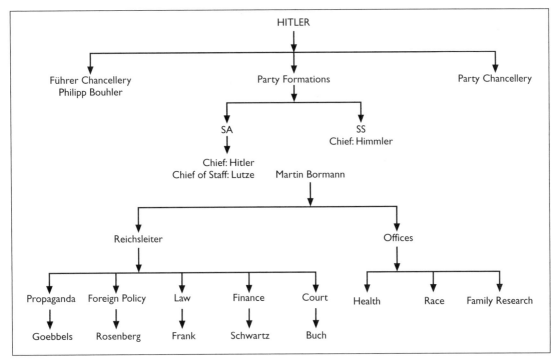

DIAGRAM 3
The structure of the Nazi Party

B *The attack on the State during* Gleichschaltung

As we have seen in Chapter 6, the attack on the Weimar State took a variety of forms:

- Starting with an attack on political freedoms, following the Reichstag fire, in the Emergency Decrees for the Protection of the German People of 28 February 1933, it led on to the destruction of parliament through the Enabling Law of 23 March 1933.
- This was followed by the destruction of individual state governments during 1933 by the appointment of Reich commissioners who were Nazis or sympathisers.
- This process was finally concluded by two laws, one of which purged the judiciary and civil service of Jews in April 1933, the other being the Law to Ensure the Unity of the Party and State of 1 December 1933.

This did not mean that the Party had taken over the State, even though Hitler claimed that the Party had become the State and that all power now rested with the Reich government. In fact, once in power the Party began to disintegrate. According to J. Noakes, some specialist sections sought independence. Propaganda, for instance, became a ministry. Many party leaders took state offices so that there seemed to be a danger that the Party would be absorbed into the state apparatus. In January 1933 of 827 Nazi *Gauleiter* 69 had become district officers, 150 lord mayors and 37 mayors, while 3,963 local branch leaders had become parish council chairmen. There were just enough Nazis of sufficient expertise to occupy all the state jobs. The *Gauleiter* became very independent of the central party organisation in Munich. All but nine of 43 *Gauleiter* had senior state offices. It was just not clear what the role of the Party was to be. With the exception of the *Gauleiter*, the tendency was for Nazi officials to become separated from the Party once they had a state office.

C *Party developments in the 1930s*

Initially, the Party was given the task of reducing unemployment. Hitler planned to give the Party the role of preparing the German nation psychologically for war through indoctrination with Nazi ideology. Rudolf Hess, the Führer's deputy for party affairs and Martin Bormann, his chief of staff, planned to build up this party office, so that it would monopolise the Party's relations with the State, and bypass the central party organisation under Robert Ley. Such clearly defined lines of authority from the top, which would have dominated the State through the party apparatus, did not meet with Hitler's approval. He wanted a 'Hitler' party instead. Even so, Bormann persisted in trying to outmanoeuvre the *Gauleiter*, all of whom were appointed by Hitler, so that a party apparatus could be developed. This would be responsible for the German people right down to street and apartment-block level. It did not work as planned, though, as there was a lot of apathy. The quality of Nazi Party membership, now flooded by newcomers, was poor. From 5 March to 1 May 1933 over 1.5 million applied to join the Party. The party files were closed on 1 May 1933 and were not reopened until 1 May 1937. In 1939, however, the bar to further membership was lifted completely. Hitler said that about one in ten of the population should be in the Party. By 1945 there were about six million members.

D *Party–State relations during the 1930s*

There was no consistency in the policy pursued regarding the relations between Party and State. In general there was a Nazification of state appointments since promotion often depended on party membership. By 1937, 86 per cent of civil servants in Prussia and 63 per cent in the rest of Germany were party members, but of these only 48 per cent in Prussia and 11 per cent elsewhere were old party members, those who had formed the Party in its early days of struggle before 1928. Before 1933 civil servants were 6.7 per cent of party membership; this figure went up to 29 per cent by 1935. The excesses of SA members led Hitler to emphasise the State as opposed to the Party, both in his Law to Ensure the Unity of the Party and State of 1 December 1933, and in his speech to the *Gauleiter* conference on 2 February 1934. Hitler's critics within the SA were finally eliminated on 30 June 1934 (see pages

148–9). Hess's and Bormann's attempts to increase the party's powers throughout the country continued and Hess's office controlled the appointment and promotion of civil servants. At regional level, party appointees, the *Gauleiter*, established independent control in their regions and were prepared to answer only to Hitler. They increasingly came to resent party interference in their areas and argued that the role of the Party should be confined to propaganda activities. The problem was made worse by the fact that of the 32 *Gauleiter*, 23 had also acquired senior state office either as **Reichstatthalter**, or as **Oberpräsident**, or, as in Bavaria, as Minister or **Regierungspräsident**.

There was a danger that the Party would be absorbed into state and local governments with party leaders being attracted by the status and salary of government posts. Such concentrations of power led to rivalries in the regions and Hitler left them to fight it out. For instance, Fritz Sauckel, Reich Governor and Gauleiter of Thuringia, in 1936 complained about the growing centralisation of state authorities which was reducing his powers. Hitler agreed with him but did nothing. There was similar conflict in Bavaria. In the Law for the Reconstruction of the Reich of 30 January 1934, Frick tried to put Reich governors under the Ministry of the Interior, but it did not work. At local level, conflict occurred too between mayors and local NSDAP leaders.

Reichstatthalter
governor of a state or *Land*

Oberpräsident
governor of a Prussian province

Regierungspräsident
governor of a county, such as Bavaria

E *The Party 1939–45 and the impact of war*

During the Second World War a number of developments led to an increase in the power of the Party. Among these, as discussed in the last section, were the appointment of the most important *Gauleiter* as Commissioners for the Defence of the Reich in September 1939, and the way the Party was able to capitalise on its strength in the civil services of the newly annexed areas.

Another factor was the increase in Bormann's power, (see page 168), first as the Führer's deputy for party affairs, and later as the Führer's secretary. Bormann was an unknown in 1939, but he assumed the direction of the Party Chancellery in May 1941 after Rudolf Hess's flight to Britain. Even more important for Bormann's rise to prominence was his position as Hitler's personal attendant and secretary. He became the vital intermediary between Hitler and the outside world. He matched Hitler's eccentric hours and controlled the issuing of the Führer's orders. This gave him a central position and, as Hitler became more isolated, it was soon realised that Bormann was the main person to lobby. He had the power to interpret and carry out Hitler's orders.

During the war every development strengthened Bormann's authority. The *Gauleiter* became subordinate to him and old party members were replaced by new, younger fanatics who owed everything to Bormann. Under Bormann, the party machine grew and encroached on the work of the armed forces, especially in matters of administration and supply, fortification and evacuation. Like Himmler with the SS, he took advantage of every army defeat to make the Party stronger and more indispensable. This brought the SS and the Party into conflict.

Prior to 1943 the relations between Himmler and Bormann had been excellent, but in that year Himmler became Minister of the Interior and thereafter sharp conflicts broke out. The slightest attempts by Himmler to exercise authority outside the SS were openly resented by Bormann. The latter reported to Hitler any attempts by the SS to encroach on the authority of the *Gauleiter*. It did not take Bormann long to limit Himmler's powers as Minister of the Interior. In the same way after the 1944 July Plot by the army to assassinate Hitler, Bormann was quick to exploit his rival's errors. In the last days of the war he secured Himmler's appointment as Commander-in-Chief of Army Group Vistula, a new formation fighting a last-ditch battle against the Russians east of Berlin. Thus Bormann secured Himmler's removal from Berlin and Hitler's presence. Bormann made a point of drawing Hitler's attention to Himmler's failure to stop the advance of the Red Army. The war also gave increased opportunities for advancement for Goebbels, Speer and, most importantly, the SS (see pages 219–21).

F *Reasons for the failure of the Party to govern the State*

A number of factors, some outside its control, ensured that the Party failed in its attempts to rule Germany.

The first factor was the political circumstances in which the Nazis came to power. The absence of a political vacuum, such as had existed in Russia, meant that the Party was confronted with a powerful State machine, and with a personnel who had a reputation for service in German politics and society.

Secondly, the Party lacked the organisation and personnel which would have allowed it to adapt to changing conditions after 1933 and find a role in the new Reich. From 1926 onwards, after his release from prison, Hitler had concentrated on reorganising party machinery on the basis of decentralisation, so that all power rested with him. He controlled all appointments even down to village level.

Thirdly, the regional leaders, the *Gauleiter*, dealt directly with him rather than with party headquarters in Munich. The latter was responsible only for membership lists and party dues. Many of these *Gauleiter*, who were extremists in terms of their anti-Semitism, were ambitious and recognised that their first loyalty was to Hitler. Outside of Munich they established independent control of the Party and were hostile to any attempt to extend central party bureaucracy into their territories. They needed Hitler's official recognition of their position as *Gauleiter* so that they could establish their dominance over local party activists. Hitler achieved complete control over his *Gauleiter* by 1926 and henceforward regarded them as his key agents in the field, making them directly responsible to him for all political activities in their *Gaue*. In theory, this could have led to divided loyalties though in practice they looked to Hitler first. Up until 1928 they were successful in asserting their authority without too much interference from party headquarters.

After 1928 the position of the *Gauleiter* and of the Central Party Office was undermined by the growth of membership which gave the Party a much broader basis of support and one which was less fanatic in its anti-Semitism.

Fourthly, the Party was further splintered by the growth of separate sections and interest groups, such as the paramilitary wing of the NSDAP, the SA and SS. They referred directly to Hitler and acted independently of party organisation. Interest groups representing specific social and/or economic groups also developed, which further encouraged a decentralisation of the Party into many separate organisations. The latter owed their formation not to party initiative but to that of individuals, such as Hans Schemm, who organised teachers, Jakob Sprenger, civil servants, Hans Frank, lawyers and R.W. Darre, agricultural workers. These men waited until they had received official recognition from party headquarters and then developed centralised bureaucracies of their own which, in some cases, became private empires to further their ambitions and power. Thus in the case of propaganda, separate departments were developed at *Gau*, *Kreis* (circuit) and *Ortsgruppen* (local branch) level which were most effective in co-ordinating propaganda campaigns. The presence of these departments removed from the political leaders, *Gauleiter*, *Kreisleiter* and local branch leaders, control over propaganda which had been their main function.

Finally, the Party was also undermined by Hitler's refusal to carry out a major purge of the civil service. He did not want to endanger his compromise with the traditional German elites on which his regime was based initially. They were prepared to co-operate to achieve goals which they considered coincided with their own. Neither was he prepared to risk disrupting his main priorities of a return to full employment and the introduction of a major rearmament programme.

In conclusion it should be noted that the Party's failure to govern Germany resulted from Hitler's determination not to be restricted in any way or to have a rival. Both of these developments might have undermined his authority. He had always regarded the Party as a Hitler party and his leadership was so strong that he imposed this view on the Party.

5 ↩ THE RELATIONSHIP BETWEEN THE REGIME AND THE ARMY 1933–45

In any political system the role of the armed forces is essential for political stability. A failure to gain the support of the military could mean that a regime would be undermined in both its domestic and foreign policies and, under some conditions, could be challenged by a military coup.

A Relationship between the army and the regime 1933–8 – years of consolidation

KEY ISSUE

Was there a common interest between Hitler and the German Army?

Reference has already been made to the reputation, prestige and role played by the army under Weimar and in Hitler becoming Chancellor (see pages 96–7). For his part, Hitler realised that he needed to proceed cautiously for the leading generals exerted considerable influence, as was shown in the intrigues of 1932–3.

1 He made the defence machinery stronger by setting up in April 1933 an imperial defence council under his chairmanship on which the defence minister sat with the foreign, interior, finance and propaganda ministers to strengthen Germany for war. This tied the Ministry of Defence to Party control while the armed forces' concerns about the challenge of the Party's private army, the SA, which outnumbered them three to one, were resolved on the night of 30 June 1934 (see pages 148–9).

2 Thereafter, Hitler adopted a policy of gradual infiltration, recognising that the influence of Nazi ideas was bound to increase amongst officers and men especially as members of the Hitler Youth came forward for military service.

He was also aware that his determination to break the restrictions imposed at Versailles and to recreate the German *Reichswehr* to its full strength was sufficient to win him the sympathy and support of the officer corps. His views that lost lands could only be recovered through armed force agreed with the views of the *Reichswehr*. United by a common set of interests, Blomberg became increasingly sympathetic to Nazi ideas while Hitler could be assured of gradual influence in the *Reichswehr* without the effort of direct propaganda. The only criticism of Hitler's strategy for dealing with the army came from Röhm, but this was silenced with Röhm's execution in June 1934. The *Reichswehr* was guilty of scheming for this 'blood purge', though it was carried out by the SS led by Göring. It is debatable whether Hitler actually concluded a secret pact with the generals, as suggested by Alan Bullock in his *Hitler, A Study in Tyranny* (Odhams 1952), whereby in exchange for the elimination of Röhm they would support him as Hindenburg's successor, but it is obvious that both parties had strong reasons for co-operation. In the view of G.A. Craig in *Germany 1866–1945* (Oxford UP 1981), there is indisputable evidence that the *Reichswehr* supplied weapons and lorries to the SS units. In the aftermath, it accepted Hitler as Chief of State and pledged its loyalty to him with the belief that, if it so willed, it could unmake the 'Caesar' it had made.

After June 1934 the *Reichswehr* was left in a position of considerable strength:

● It was essential to Hitler's major rearmament programme and reintroduction of conscription.
● Unlike the other institutions, the *Reichswehr* was not co-ordinated during the process of *Gleichschaltung* (see pages 142–4) and its

leaders were confident that they had gained a certain mastery as Hitler had agreed to the destruction of his own SA.

It was even believed by many *Reichswehr* officers that the extremist element within Nazism had been removed and that they could make the Nazi State work according to their interests and wishes. Events after 1934 were to prove to the army that it could not preserve its original position of being a 'state within a state'. In the aftermath of the Röhm purge, and on the same night that Hindenburg died, 2 August, the army was committed to a personal oath of loyalty to Hitler. This new oath, demanded by Hitler of all his soldiers and accepted by Field Marshal von Blomberg, the War Minister, and General von Fritsch, the Commander-in-Chief of the Army, declared:

> I swear by God this sacred oath: that I will render unconditional obedience to the Führer of the German Reich and people, Adolf Hitler, the Supreme Commander of the Armed Forces, and will be ready as a brave soldier to risk my life at any time for this oath.

Thereafter the *Reichswehr* concentrated on rearmament, conscription and the reoccupation of territories taken from Germany in 1919.

Committed to a sense of duty and honour, such an oath, sworn on the regiment's colours at a ceremonial parade in accordance with tradition, meant that future resistance was seen as an act of treachery. In the years which followed, many might have been disgusted by Hitler's policies, but they felt they had bound themselves by oath to his regime. This did not make them his submissive instrument, but it did partly explain why it was not until the bomb plot against Hitler on 20 July 1944 that some in the army showed resistance.

The July Plot, pages 313–18

In the years 1934–7 the relationship between the Nazi State and the army remained co-operative. Encouraged by the rearmament programme and the reintroduction of conscription in March 1935, which increased the Army to 550,000, the High Command fooled itself into believing that its privileged position was being preserved. In fact, the power of the SS was growing fast, while Hitler himself had little respect for the conservative attitudes held by many officers. It was merely political necessity which prevented him from interfering in army affairs until 1938. During these years the social gulf between officer and man began to close, instruction was given in Nazi theory, while Blomberg encouraged army and Party to work together. The army appeared to become more open and democratic. At the same time Hitler had proceeded with his aim of recovering Germany's losses in the Treaty of Versailles, notably the Saar and the Rhineland. By the end of 1937 Germany's diplomatic position had improved; it was no longer isolated and Hitler had made considerable progress in preparing his armed forces for war.

B *The Hossbach Meeting, November 1937*

Historians are divided on Hitler's actions following his successes in 1935 and 1936. A.J.P. Taylor has argued that, after dismantling

Versailles and Locarno (see page 74) Hitler was 'at a loss what to do next even if he had the power to do it'. It was claimed by the Allies at the Nuremberg Trials and by historians in the aftermath of 1945 that Hitler produced a blueprint of aims at a secret meeting, at the Reich Chancellery on 5 November 1937, with the chiefs of the German armed forces and the German Foreign Minister, von Neurath. Those present from the armed forces were Field Marshal von Blomberg, the Minister of Defence, Colonel-General von Fritsch and Admiral Raeder, Commanders in Chief of the Army and Navy, and Göring in his capacity as head of the Air Force.

WERNER VON FRITSCH (1880–1939)

He was Commander-in-Chief of the German army until February 1938. Originally appointed by Hindenburg, he was an orthodox Prussian officer who believed in keeping the army out of politics. He accepted the Nazi regime but wanted to limit its influence in the army. He voiced doubts about Hitler's plans, as unveiled at the conference held on 5 November 1937 and recorded in the Hossbach Memorandum. Göring and Himmler prepared the charges of homosexuality against him, which enabled Hitler to remove him from his post on 4 February 1938. It was one of the most important of the personnel changes which allowed the Führer to get control of German foreign and military policy. Although Fritsch was soon reinstated, he could not bring himself to turn his case into a general protest by the German officer corps against the Nazi regime. His attitude to National Socialism was in fact mixed. He was given a regimental command and it is widely believed that he deliberately sought death when his regiment was attacking Warsaw in September 1939.

CONSTANTIN VON NEURATH (1873–1956)

He was a professional diplomat who became Foreign Minister in Papen's June 1932 cabinet. He retained the post under Schleicher and Hitler, thus lending the appearance of continuity to German foreign policy. He was removed from the Foreign Ministry in February 1938 and succeeded by Ribbentrop. From 1939 to 1943 he held the post of Reich Protector of Bohemia and Moravia, in which his power was largely ceremonial, while real control was exercised by men like Heydrich, Himmler's deputy. Neurath was sentenced to 15 years imprisonment at Nuremberg.

WALTER VON REICHENAU (1884–1942)

He was a professional soldier who, as adviser to Blomberg in the rank of colonel, played a crucial role in 1933 and 1934 in promoting the acceptance by the *Reichswehr* of the Nazi regime. He was chiefly responsible for the role played by the army in support of the SS during the Night of Long Knives, 30 June 1934, and he devised the oath to Hitler as Supreme Commander, when he succeeded Hindenburg as Head of State in August 1934. He failed, however, in his attempt to succeed Fritsch as Commander-in-Chief of the Army in February 1938 and the post went to Brauchitsch. He held important field commands on the Western and Eastern Fronts, but died prematurely of a stroke following a forced landing of his plane.

Mention has already been made of the Hossbach meeting in Chapter 6, in terms of its significance as a turning point in Hitler's fortunes as Chancellor, and of the resulting Hossbach Memorandum. The conservative elites present at the Hossbach meeting accepted his pan-German aims to recover German land and people lost in Central Europe, but Blomberg, Fritsch and Neurath, given Germany's state of military unpreparedness, were seriously concerned by Hitler's talk of war and conquest. Their reservations related only to timing, risks and the state of German rearmament, but Hitler may well have concluded that these and other representatives of the old elites in high places would block his plans.

The Hossbach Memorandum, pages 388–90

These doubts convinced Hitler that the army leadership was weak but he was also sufficiently aware that they could oppose his policies. He looked for any opportunity to get rid of them, though in November 1937 he could not have anticipated the circumstances of the Blomberg–Fritsch crisis. When it came he turned it to his advantage to establish his control over the army. Blomberg's marriage, on 12 January 1938, to a woman who was found to have been a prostitute, followed by allegations of Fritsch's homosexuality, triggered a chain of events that led Hitler to carry out major changes in the personnel and organisation of the armed forces and the *Auswärtiges Amt* (Foreign Office). These events, in February 1938, damaged the army's independence.

The first was that Hitler abolished the post of War Minster and became Commander-in-Chief of all armed forces with a personal high command, the *Oberkommando der Wehrmacht* (OKW), headed by a loyal follower, General Keitel, Blomberg's son-in-law. Keitel was completely subservient to Hitler, for whom he had shown enthusiasm at least as early as 1933. This earned him the nickname *Lakeitel* (lackey). He used his position to authorise many of Hitler's criminal orders during the war, for example the order of June 1941 to liquidate all political commissars in the Soviet Union. Chief of the OKW 1938–45, he was condemned to death at Nuremberg and executed.

General Brauchitsch was appointed as the new Commander-in-Chief of the army to replace Fritsch. He did not oppose Hitler's takeover of the work of the Ministry of Defence. Brauchitsch accepted Hitler's authority although he had doubts about Hitler's war plans and knew of the military plotting against Hitler. He had personal reasons for his loyalty to Hitler, who had in 1938 funded Brauchitsch's divorce proceedings against his first wife. His second wife was a fanatical Nazi and had much influence on him.

Hitler also took the opportunity created by the events of February 1938 to retire 16 generals and transfer 44 high-ranking officers, who represented a threat to him. Hossbach was sacked. He later rose to the rank of general and commanded an army on the Eastern Front.

These changes greatly increased Hitler's control over foreign and defence policy and made it possible for him to complete the process of securing his power. More radical Nazis were now in command, but these changes also created a sense of crisis in his regime. Hitler attempted to divert the spotlight from events at home by embarking on a sensational move in foreign policy – the *Anschluss* or union with Austria (see pages 390–1). Göring, in particular, supported this foreign policy move to cover up the role he had played in promoting the false accusations of homosexuality that led to the fall of Fritsch. The Blomberg–Fritsch crisis made many in the army realise their true position, though few were prepared to act to defend their independence. The majority in the army continued to support the Führer and his policies, whether out of fear or a sense of loyalty to their oath as soldiers. The relationship between the army leadership and the Nazi regime in these years 1934–8 were described by General von Frisch in 1938 (recorded in Noakes and Pridham, *Nazism 1919–1945, A Documentary Reader, Vol 3*):

Q

Why, according to General Fritsch, was he removed from office?

On 3 January 1934, I was appointed Commander-in-Chief against the Führer's wishes, against Blomberg's wishes, but under the strongest pressure from Field Marshal von Hindenburg.

I found a heap of ruins, in particular a severe crisis of confidence within the High Command.

Reichenau's and the Party's struggle against me began on the day of my appointment in so far as it had not already begun. Reichenau's opposition is understandable, for he wanted to take over command of the Army and still does. The Party sees in me not only the man who opposed the ambitions of the SA, but also the man who tried to block the influx of party-political maxims into the Army. Apart from the fact that the basis of our present Army is National Socialist and must be so, the infiltration of party-political influences into the Army cannot be tolerated since such influences can lead only to fragmentation and dissolution. The task given me by the Führer was: 'Create an Army as strong and united as possible and with the best conceivable training'. I have followed these instructions ever since.

As Blomberg's Chief of Staff, Reichenau's scheming meant that my relationship with Blomberg was continually troubled. Throughout these years I have never succeeded in establishing a relationship with Blomberg based on trust as should have been the case...

In the autumn of 1934, there was great agitation as a result of the machinations of the SS. The SS maintained the Army was preparing a *putsch*, and reports came in from all military districts that the SS was planning a big coup. Then the Führer decided to order the leading figures in the Party and many senior officers to a meeting. The Führer made a speech which was a clear statement of loyalty to the Army and to myself as its leader. After the Führer's speech, the SS agitation decreased somewhat. But from the summer of 1935 it increased again. While we managed to establish a good relationship with all Party agencies, this was not true of the SS. As far as our side was concerned, this may have derived from the fact that there was hardly a single senior officer who did not feel the SS was spying on him. It is continually coming to light that, contrary to express instructions from the Führer's deputy, SS people serving in the Army have received orders to provide reports on their superiors.

Finally the SS **Verfügungstruppe**, which is being continually expanded, must create conflict with the Army through its very existence. It is the living proof of mistrust towards the Army and its leadership.

Although the Army has a certain right to supervise the training of the SS *Verfügungstruppe*, this SS troop is developing completely separately and, as I see it, in conscious opposition to the Army. One cannot avoid the impression that the negative attitude towards the Army in the SS *Verfügungstruppe* is positively encouraged.

> *Verfügungstruppe* formations of the SS, absorbed by the *Waffen-SS* in 1939

C *Relationship between the army and the regime 1938–40 – years of dominance but not subjection*

There is little doubt that from 1938 the army's ability to shape political developments within Germany was drastically reduced. Whereas in the early years of the Nazi regime Hitler had correctly recognised the need to work with the army leadership, by early 1938 he was strong enough to mould it more closely to his requirements. It could still not be called Hitler's submissive instrument, but it had been forced to accept his dominance. Thus, it was still recognised by Hitler's opponents that the army remained the one institution with the technical means of striking successfully at the regime. In the summer of 1938 a plan was drawn up by a number of disillusioned generals to arrest Hitler in the event of a European war breaking out over the Sudeten crisis, but it was abandoned with Hitler's success at Munich. From 1938 there was a definite movement within certain military circles, with the support of some civilian critics of the regime, to avoid a war. Once war broke out the plan changed to one which sought to limit the extent of a war which, it was felt, Hitler could not win. Hitler's sensational successes leading to allied defeat in June 1940 caused all opposition to collapse for a while.

> The Munich Agreement, pages 394–6

Moreover, once Germany found itself at war, resistance was seen as treasonable and unpatriotic.

D *Relationship between the army and the regime 1942–4 – years of challenge*

By 1943 Germany's military situation had changed dramatically (Germany at war will be examined in detail in Chapter 15). Hitler's defeats in Russia together with allied landings in North Africa increased resistance. Many generals believed that the war could not be won yet found themselves fighting for a regime which was involved in the atrocities of the concentration camps. It was in this situation that a number of civilian resistance figures contacted generals hostile to Hitler, such as Ludwig Beck, in order to plan the assassination of Hitler and his replacement with a civilian government.

Beck was chief of the general staff of the German army from 1935 to 1938. He opposed, with increasing determination, Hitler's plans to attack Czechoslovakia in 1938, which he felt would lead to a general war which Germany could not win, and resigned on 21 August 1938. He was increasingly motivated by moral opposition to the criminal aspects of the Nazi regime and became a principal figure in the military plot against Hitler. He succeeded in winning over some of the other generals: General Henning von Tresckow, chief of staff in Army Group Centre on the Russian front, Olbricht, head of the supply section of the reserve army, Stuelpnagel, military governor in France, Oster, chief of staff of the *Abwehr* (counter-intelligence) and Field Marshal von Witzleben, retired since 1942, together with more junior officers: Claus von Stauffenberg, chief of staff to General Fromm, commander of the reserve army, who was in and out of the conspiracy, and Schlabrendorff, staff officer under Tresckow on the Eastern Front. They were joined by members of a civilian resistance group called the Kreisau Circle (see pages 310–11) including Moltke, legal adviser to the *Abwehr*, who advised non-violence, and the political leader Goerdeler, former lord mayor of Leipzig. Others who knew of the conspiracy, but did not take an active part, included Field Marshals Rommel and Kluge, the latter Army Group Commander in France. They were, however, important for the plotters relied upon them to conclude the war and negotiate an armistice with the Allies before Germany was totally defeated. They were all united by the belief that, 'we must prove to the world and to future generations that the men of the German Resistance movement dared to take the decisive step and wager their lives on it'. Details of the failed July 1944 Plot will be covered in Chapter 11.

Hitler's punishment was extreme; all the conspirators were hunted down, handed over to the tortures of the *Gestapo* and brought before the dreaded People's Court (*Volksgericht*). Beck committed suicide. The fate of the leading conspirators was meant to act as a warning to others. The number of those killed as a direct result is estimated at 180–200, but many more were killed (some estimates, thought to be exaggerated, have put the figure at 5,000 of whom 2,000 were reckoned to be officers), in a massive blood purge greater than that of 1934. Whole families were eliminated, an event which significantly reduced the numbers of the aristocracy, contributing unintentionally to the achievement of Hitler's social revolution.

The failure of the July Plot marked the end of the powerful and privileged position of the army in German society. In 1924 Hitler had written in *Mein Kampf* that he looked upon the army General Staff as 'the mightiest thing the world has ever seen', but, once he had achieved power, he discovered that it was not prepared to be a powerful instrument of his policy. It had a policy of its own. It believed that it could dictate terms to the Führer as it had done to the Kaiser. The army had not been won over, but Hitler's dependence on it to achieve his territorial ambitions meant that he had to tolerate it. Unable to achieve its submission directly, he had set out to undermine it from within by making pro-Nazi appointments, but by 1938, this policy had met with only partial success. The General Staff, under Halder, plotted to depose the regime in 1938 at the time of the Munich crisis, but the plan was withdrawn after Hitler's success at Munich (see pages 394–6). Without foreign support, Hitler's opponents in the army found themselves powerless against a dictator who appeared to be so spectacularly successful. For a time the opposition of the General Staff became insignificant, especially as, up until 1942, the policy of the regime was similar to their own. Both had wanted Germany to be a great power, capable of supporting an efficient, well-paid and privileged army, which could be achieved by a return of its Empire, and recognition from the other powers.

Where they had differed was over the scale and extent of conquests. The leaders of the General Staff believed in a policy of limited conquest and were opposed to Hitler's plans for war with Russia, the traditional ally of the *Junker*. Their interests separated after the conquests of Poland and France. In 1941 Hitler accused the generals of a loss of nerve, and a refusal to recognise his ('the corporal's'), strategic genius. He took over the High Command of the German army and the most able of the generals, Halder, was dismissed. In the view of some historians, such as Hugh Trevor-Roper, opposition to Hitler in the army grew between 1941 and 1944. Its leaders had planned the assassination of Hitler from January 1942 onwards, though it could not become a reality until the Hitler myth had been undermined through defeat. By 1944 these conditions had been achieved.

> **Q**
>
> *What was the significance for the army of the failure of the July Plot?*

E *Relationship between the army and the regime 1944–5 – a year of submission*

Many officers were among those arrested or executed in the brutal *Gestapo* enquiry which followed the failure of the July Plot. However, possibly even more significant than the blood purge were the orders subsequently issued:

1 The Nazi salute became compulsory throughout the army.

KEY ISSUE

To what extent did the Army become Hitler's submissive instrument after the failure of the 1944 July Plot?

2 Political officers were appointed to oversee the indoctrination of the army.

3 Himmler, who had personally scored a notable success, was appointed Commander-in-Chief of the Home Army and this brought the Army under SS control.

4 Fifty members of the General Staff and hundreds of lesser officers were purged, whilst others killed themselves.

5 Himmler took over from the armed forces the control of all prisoner-of-war camps. The last traces of the army's independence had been suppressed.

However, though Himmler had never seemed more powerful, the plot also indicated that he was in decline. It was not due to him that the plot had failed, but chance. In fact, there is some doubt as to whether Himmler knew of the plot, though Schellenberg, who was a member of his staff, knew about it in general terms. Apart from Keitel and General Wilhelm Burgdorff (who was to remain with Hitler throughout the last days in Berlin), Hitler regarded all officers as traitors and increasingly surrounded himself with officers from the navy and the *Luftwaffe*. This rejection of the army and its High Command had a disastrous effect on the character of his headquarters. According to Hugh Trevor-Roper, in *The Last Days of Hitler*, it hastened its conversion from a war cabinet into 'an oriental court of flatterers and toadies'. Hitler's destruction of the High Command was accompanied by a demoralisation of the remaining members. Those who survived the bloodbath competed with one another in reassuring Hitler of their loyalty and allegiance. Hitler had finally achieved the unquestioning obedience of his generals, but by 1945 there were no more armies left with which to fight. With surrender the entire army became the prisoners of war of the allied powers who had pledged themselves to the destruction of Prussian militarism.

F *Significance of Hitler's policies on the army*

The willingness of the army to work with Hitler gave his regime the appearance of respectability and acceptance so that in 1938 when Blomberg was replaced by General Keitel there was no real disturbance in the officer corps. However, although Hitler changed the top military personnel, the relations between the Party and the *Wehrmacht* continued to conform to Blomberg's scheme of non-infiltration.

● The army insisted that none of its members would be allowed to join the Party and there are examples of the bureaucrats of the army weapons department overruling the Führer.

● The army did not experience any major social changes, although the vast post-1933 expansion eventually began to affect quality. The High Command continued to be drawn from the ranks of the aristocracy; 20 per cent of all *Reichswehr* posts were held by the aristocracy. Pro-Nazis were not promoted beyond the rank of major until the outbreak of war when they then swamped the highest ranks. The rapid growth in size led to fears being expressed by the High Command that the army's technical efficiency and sense of identity would be undermined. In fact, these developments led to an improvement in the relations between officers and men while drill ground procedures became more reasonable. Rank and file members of the *Wehrmacht* benefited not only from more social services, and greater prestige and status, but also from the handout of money, lands, promotions and medals.

- The army found that its unity and opposition to the regime were undermined by this bribery so that Hitler's anti-monarchist policies, such as purging the army of members of the ex-royal families were accepted. Despite this, the army appeared to be shielded against political control so that opponents of the regime looked for protection and hiding within it.
- Compared with the Party or their great rivals, the SS, the army appeared to be more humane as occupiers of conquered territories. However, we should beware of exaggerating this because in the East there was very little difference between the SS and the army in terms of executions and deaths (see below).

> **Q**
>
> *Did association with the Nazi regime have any impact on the Army?*

In other respects association with the regime did serve to undermine the character of the army:

- It was corrupted by the influence of the regime; men intrigued for promotions, while amongst the rank and file volunteers could easily be found to man the execution squads to shoot deserters.
- Military law was harshly applied to punish offenders so that the German army had 10,000 executions for desertion compared with one on the Allied side. There was very little to separate the army from the SS in its behaviour in the East in terms of looting, killing and destroying Jewish communities who were seen by the *Reichswehr* as the 'spiritual carriers of the Bolshevik terror'. There were 55,000 executions in the Ukraine of Jewish prisoners of war held by the *Wehrmacht*.

Finally, it was Hitler's distrust of the army which he had failed to make his submissive instrument which accounts for his willingness to allow the SS to develop its military role to rival the army.

6 ⌐ THE SS EMPIRE – A 'STATE WITHIN A STATE' 1933–45

A *The problem of a balanced perspective*

Historians' study of the *Schutzstaffel* (SS) has been complicated by the difficulty of achieving a balanced perspective. It has been very difficult to ignore the Black Order's monstrous cruelty in running the concentration camps and the terror apparatus which it developed to police the National Socialist State. Moreover, the SS, though it left deep traces on

Europe, nevertheless was in historical terms very short-lived. It 'lived' for only 20 years, of which the first seven were spent in the background as Hitler's bodyguard before it went on to become the party police of the National Socialist movement. The SS's unique expansion of power meant that it never had a period of stability in its short history. It had an enormously varied character; it was a loose collection of offices and branches where each carried out different duties (see Diagram 4, page 218, on the SS Organisation). Judgement is, therefore, shaped by whatever branch or aspect of the 'SS State' is studied: whether as an army through its *Waffen-SS* and as the authority in German-occupied countries, or as the Death's Head squads responsible for the extermination camps, or as a security force through the SD (*Sicherheitsdienst*) and secret service or finally as an economic empire. Each section of the SS was distinct so that it is difficult to draw any general conclusion on the Black Order. The whole was held together by Himmler and by a united view of themselves as 'political soldiers'. They regarded themselves as responsible for eliminating the enemies of National Socialism – Marxism, Freemasonry and Christianity. Despite the problems of arriving at a balanced judgement historians, such as Bucheim, Reitlinger and Steiner, have recognised the importance of the SS within the Hitler State. As D.G. Williamson writes in *The Third Reich*:

> KEY ISSUE
>
> *The difficulty in arriving at a balanced assessment of the SS Empire.*

It is quite probable that without the steadying effect of Himmler, Hitler's divided state might well have collapsed as a result of its own internal contradictions. Himmler underpinned the Third Reich with his Gestapo and the SS.

B *Origins of the SS*

The origins of the SS go back to the early days of the Nazi Party. The unit was formed in 1925 when 120 men of absolute reliability were selected to look after Hitler and given the official title, *Leibstandarte SS Adolf Hitler*. The Party needed a dedicated group of men prepared to carry out 'special tasks' relating to security. Such a unit needed to be far more reliable and disciplined than the large, working-class based stormtroopers of the SA. Recruits were completely dominated by Nazi ideals and blind obedience to Hitler's orders, but it remained a relatively minor section of the SA with only 300 members until 1929 when it was taken over by Himmler. He has been variously described as a 'shrewd practitioner of power with an eye to the main chance' and a man 'more sinister than Hitler himself'. J.C. Fest has described him as 'the most colourless personality in the Nazi inner circle', a 'half crank, half schoolmaster' and as a 'man who combined crankiness with normality'. Whatever has been said of him, the new leader, a strange if ambitious man who was totally dedicated to Hitler, saw to it that membership of the movement was limited to an elite of fanatical Nazis. Himmler's personality undoubtedly had an influence on the development of the SS (see page 165). He was a master at amassing power in

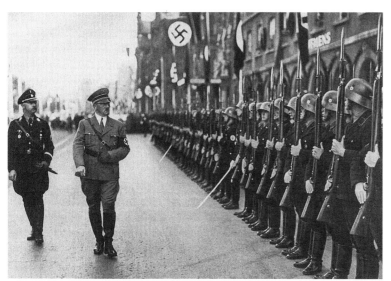

Imperial War Museum

the administrative chaos of the Third Reich. The SS were the most extreme supporters of Nazi ideology sharing Himmler's belief in **'blood and soil'**.

Himmler also believed that if Germany were to achieve the position in the world to which its racial superiority entitled it, it would have to expand its agricultural area through a policy of peasant settlement in the east (western Russia) and the Baltic states. This belief was subsequently introduced in the conquered eastern territories where land was seized and redistributed amongst the hierarchy of the SS and every soldier also had a portion.

Himmler took as his model for the SS the Jesuit order. The latter regarded themselves as the spiritual police of the Roman Catholic Church and members gave total dedication in the service of the order and of the Pope. He also used the Teutonic Order, an order of knights, who had used their role as Christian missionaries to carve out an empire in Eastern Europe. Himmler intended his 'order' to be a racial elite. To this end he issued an SS Marriage Order of 31 December 1931 in which he insisted that the wives of SS men should be racially pure (strictly Nordic origin) and hereditarily sound. A Clan Book of the SS recorded successful applicants though between 1932 and 1940 most failed to meet all the requirements. Himmler wanted to create a new Nazi elite measured by race and personal qualities though he also recognised the propaganda value of recruitment from the traditional aristocracy. By 1933 the SS numbered 52,000; selection procedures were systematised, loyalty and absolute obedience to the Führer were the sole determinants, and cults and rituals were developed to replace those which were Christian-based.

Himmler had also created in 1931 a special security service, *Sicherheitsdienst* (SD) to act as the Party's own internal police force. By 1933, he had used his influence with Hitler to bring all Germany's police

'blood and soil' the Nazi belief that a strong and healthy peasantry was the key to the biological and moral health of the German people

forces under his control – these included the infamous state secret police, the *Geheime Staatspolizei* (*Gestapo*). In the course of 1933–4 he assumed control of all the political police in the *Länder* (states), including the *Gestapo* in Prussia. Despite these developments, the SS remained a force within a force, nominally subordinate to the general organisation of the SA. Its absolute loyalty to Hitler made it the natural choice to carry out the purge of the SA on 30 June 1934 (see pages 148–9). Himmler said later, quoted in 'The SS: Wardens of Hitler's Europe' by P. Masson in *20th Century*, Vol 13, eds. A.J.P. Taylor, J.M. Roberts, Alan Bullock:

> On 30 June 1934 we did not hesitate to do the duty laid down for us and put guilty friends up against the wall and shoot them... We didn't talk about it among ourselves... Each of us found it appalling, yet we are all sure that if such orders were ever necessary again, we would carry them out as we did then.

In reward for its loyalty and brutal efficiency, the SS became an independent organisation within the Party. In 1936 all police powers were unified under Himmler's control as Chief of the German Police. As Reichsführer SS, Himmler had a massive police apparatus which was answerable to Hitler himself. In the years to come the SS–police–SD system grew into one of the key power blocs in the Third Reich and supported the Nazi Party, another key power bloc.

C *Organisation of the SS*

By 1939 the SS, with its 250,000 members, comprised the elite of the Party and of the Third Reich. It was composed of three main branches:

1 Intelligence or SD which towards the end of the war absorbed the armed forces' intelligence services.
2 The military section of the SS composed of four regiments known collectively as the *Vertfügungstruppe*, who were troops at Hitler's disposal. These were enlarged and reorganised in 1940 to become the *Waffen-SS*, or armed SS.
3 The police who, under SS control, were split in two: the regular police (*Orpo*) and the security police (*Sipo*), itself composed of the state criminal police (*Kripo*), and the state secret police (*Gestapo*) along with the secret service (the Reich Security Office or *RHSA*) and the courts. In their search for enemies of the state, the *Gestapo* were allowed to operate outside the law and take suspects into custody. Such victims were liable to be tortured and sent to the concentration camps. These camps were run by special units of SS men, the indescribably barbaric *Totenkopf Sturmbanne* or Death's Head units.

The interests of the SS were not limited to running a police state; the movement rapidly grew into a vast, sprawling empire with interests in every aspect of German life:

- It dealt with all race issues, authorised marriages, produced genealogical certificates and ran some educational establishments.
- It issued passports and sanctioned overseas travel.
- The SS also ran a massive business empire, including 296 brickworks and china factories, controlled 75 per cent of all non-alcoholic beverage consumption and possessed considerable financial resources.

By 1940 the SS organisation was independent as far as administration and recruitment were concerned. It established its own army, the *Waffen-SS*, the 'fighting SS', which only recruited volunteers who conformed to Himmler's strict physical and moral conditions (though both of these criteria changed after 1942): 'We never took on anyone with the least physical defect, even if it were a filled tooth. We were able to bring together in the SS the most superb elements of our race' (P. Masson, 'The SS: Warders of Hitler's Europe'). During the war, the SS produced some of the most feared units within the German fighting services. Made up of men who were fanatics, they were prepared to fight to the death for Hitler and the Nazi cause. These included *SS Panzer* units and infantry units such as the *SS Hitler Jugend* division and *SS Adolf Hitler* division. After the war started, the SS recruited units from men in the occupied countries to form a reserve. Units consisting of French, Dutch, Belgians, Danes and Russians, particularly Ukrainians, were formed and even a volunteer unit recruited from British prisoners of war, the so-called British *Freikorps* or the Legion of St George led by John Amery. For racial reasons, these units were affiliated to, but never became an integral part of, the SS. Up to 1942, membership of the *Waffen-SS* had been based on voluntary enlistment but after that date men were drafted to serve with SS units.

D *The power and role of the SS*

The role of the SS in Nazi Germany was most important. Some historians, such as D. Schoenbaum, have argued that Himmler created an organisation which 'potentially superseded the State and perhaps even the Party as well'. As the 'aristocracy' of National Socialism, the SS had a certain ethos. Its members were totally dedicated to what they regarded as the supreme virtues of Nazi ideology, loyalty and honour. They saw themselves as the protectors of the German/Aryan way of life and the defenders of the people against agitators, the criminal classes and those they saw as being responsible for the Jewish-Bolshevik threat. They also saw it as their duty to supervise the process of gaining *Lebensraum* or living space and the successful German colonisation of the newly acquired territories. It is true that the power of the SS lay in the fact that it was a symbol of terror and beyond its organisation only the German armed forces retained any real independence although even that was limited by the accepted seniority of the SS.

By 1941 the 'SS State' was a reality. Schoenbaum said of it, 'In one form or another the SS made foreign policy, military policy and agricultural policy. It administered occupied territories as a kind of self-

KEY ISSUE

The SS: a 'state within a state'.

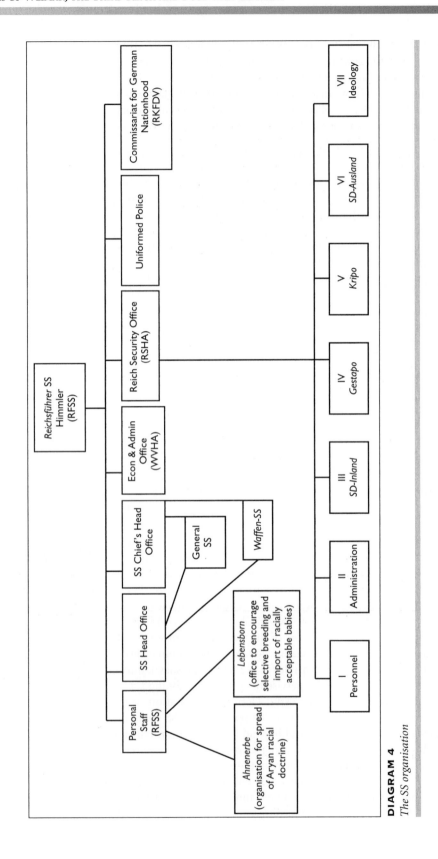

DIAGRAM 4

The SS organisation

contained Ministry of the Interior and maintained itself economically with autonomous enterprises.'

Neither the foreign office nor the army were able to defend themselves against such an 'invasion'. The army was unable to preserve its original position of being a 'state within a state' after 1938 when, as we have seen, its independence was irreversibly damaged after the Blomberg–Fritsch affair which gave Hitler the opportunity to abolish the post of war minister and take over command of the army himself.

THE WIDE-RANGING POWERS OF THE SS

Himmler organised, in the face of opposition from the army high command, a 'second army', the SS reserve troops, the core of the later *Waffen-SS* which challenged the delicate balance of power between the political (the Party) and military (the *Wehrmacht*) forces in Germany. In the early years of its growth Himmler deceived the army generals with its small size and this deceit was not realised by them until 1938 when the SS reserve troops numbered 14,000 and were about to expand even further. The High Command lost control of this recruitment while the Blomberg–Fritsch scandals resulted in a general loss of political influence. The SS exploited this situation to its own advantage when in 1938 a Führer order drafted by Himmler gave the SS reserve troops a 'mobile role as part of the wartime army' and later it developed into a full-time division. These developments gave the SS an advantage in its quarrel with the army and decided that the SS would share with the army in the military conquests to come. The only dispute arose over their assignment, size and organisation. Himmler had finally succeeded in securing a foothold on army territory. The *Waffen-SS* rapidly developed into a separate army, though it did not challenge the power of the *Wehrmacht* until 1943. In 1939 it was composed of three divisions which rose to 35 by 1945, so that it eventually rivalled the power of the army.

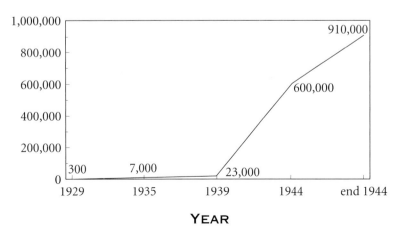

NUMBER OF RECRUITS

YEAR

TABLE 29

Growth in number of SS recruits, 1929–44

1929	300
1935	7,000
1939	23,000
1944	600,000
end 1944	910,000

The SS achieved this increase by recruiting men outside the Reich frontiers so that Germans in south eastern Europe and the Baltic states, as well as non-Germans in western and northern Europe were allowed to enlist. This development, dictated by the pressures of war, led the *Waffen-SS* to become a multinational force. This was consistent with the ideological and power-political aim of the SS which was to become the elite of a 'Greater Germanic Empire'. The demands of war also threatened the SS principle of voluntary enlistment. Opportunities for forcing large numbers of young people to enlist meant that by 1942 this had become the main method for recruitment. The *Waffen-SS* acquired a legendary military reputation, but they had extremely high losses especially among officers which threatened its political and ideological identity and unity. The elite *Panzer* divisions became a small part and by 1943, with its growth in numbers, the *Waffen-SS* ceased to be a military elite. The SS leadership accepted this only because it hoped to use this structural change towards a mass army for its long-term political aims. These consisted of a massive resettlement programme which Himmler planned in his capacity as Reich Commissar for the Consolidation of German Nationhood. Its military planning for the post-war period involved reorganisation of the *Waffen-SS* as the military spearhead of the SS order with the wartime elite divisions as its core. This would lead to a Germanic-European army which would not be a part of the SS, but would be controlled by it. This army would consist of the other formations with their mainly foreign troops. Its grip on such a European army would have made the SS the key power in a National Socialist dominated Europe.

The SS were put in charge of Jewish affairs and encouraged emigration, to be followed in 1939–40 by transfer to Poland and after 1941 extermination. The Death's Head units of the SS administered the concentration camps (see page 222) and were charged with carrying out the Final Solution after 1941.

It was given responsibility for German minorities living outside the frontiers of the Reich in eastern, southern and central Europe which would become allies or victims of expansionist policies. The policing of future German colonies also came within its orbit and it formed the core of a future police force against Bolshevism. The SS administered newly acquired territories, such as Austria and the Sudetenland, a role which rapidly expanded the SS State. The basis of SS power in the occupied territories was laid in 1939, when Himmler was appointed Minister Plenipotentiary with special, far-reaching powers to deal with resettlement questions in occupied Europe. The SS tried, but failed, to influence Hitler's foreign policy decisions though it did play a role in carrying out general political guidelines. Its foreign policy role was undermined by the opposition of the foreign office. Despite the appointment of Ribbentrop, a friend of Himmler and the SS, as Foreign Secretary in 1938, division soon appeared between Ribbentrop and Himmler.

This was increased still further when Himmler was later appointed

Reich Commisar for the Consolidation of German Nationhood. The Commissariat was responsible for creating the 'New Order' in eastern Europe – the resettlement and extermination of the various 'inferior' races. Such a scheme provided opportunities for plunder and power on a massive scale, which members of the SS exploited to the full.

THE ECONOMIC BASE OF THE SS

Himmler also sought to make the SS economically independent by forming companies to exploit the labour in the concentration camps. By 1938 it had begun systematic economic expansion and by 1945 had created a vast commercial empire built on slave labour. The SS owned 40 different enterprises covering 150 works; quarrying, earthworks, food, drink, agriculture and forestry, timber and iron processing, leathers, textiles and publishing. Himmler had regular meetings with industrialists and businessmen through his friendship circles which supported the work of the SS with large sums of money and cheap loans. (See Map 14, page 439.)

TABLE 30
Primary SS enterprises, spring 1944

Area	Location	Enterprise
Greater Germany	Flossenbürg, Groß-Rosen, Mauthausen, Stutthof	Area of gravel and stone workings, and concentration camps
	Buchenwald, Neuengamme, Sachsenhausen	As above but also armaments
	Ravensbrück, Dachau	Concentration camps and armaments
Occupied Territories	Natzweiler (Alsace-Lorraine)	Gravel and stone workings, concentration camp
	Poland, e.g. area around Lublin	Area of gravel and stone workings, armaments
	Treblinka, Chelmno, Sobibor, Maidenek, Auschwitz-Birkenau, Belzec	Six extermination camps

THE INTERNAL POLICY OF THE SS

The elitist attitude of the SS influenced the character of its development. Himmler, who in 1933 took over ideology and propaganda, saw the restoration of a pre-Christian Germanic culture and lifestyle as the main task of the SS. This would be achieved by sponsorship of different cultural and scientific activities, articles, books and films and the setting up of institutional homes for children who conformed to the Aryan blond, blue-eyed ideal. This was the *Lebensborn* programme which identified as 'pure Aryans' those children who had been seized from the conquered lands in the east, especially Poland, and sent to Germany for adoption. Himmler's ideal man was a fair-haired, blue-eyed superman-athlete who despised most developments in modern culture. He was a man who left all political and social judgement to his leaders and gave them unquestioning obedience. He was essentially a destructive man, ready to act on whatever order no matter how sickening.

Internal security was achieved by three means:

1   The secret service (SD) which set out to monopolise all intelligence activities under Heydrich, though this was not complete until 1944 when it took over the *Wehrmacht*'s counter-intelligence agency, the *Abwehr*.

2   The concentration camps, introduced as early as 1934 at Dachau and developed as a centralised, repressive machine, strictly policed by the SS Death's Head units which by 1939 numbered 9,000 men. The existence of these camps gave the SS freedom of action independent of the existing system of justice. Anyone could be arrested and sent to the camps without legal procedure even when freed by the courts. This lack of legal security helped to intimidate the people and cripple the forces of opposition.

3   The police force was absorbed in several stages, starting in 1933–4 when Himmler was given control of the secret police in the *Länder*. This was extended in 1936 when he was made Reichsführer-SS and Chief of German Police which made it possible to integrate the police force into the administrative structure of the SS. The plan was for an eventual amalgamation of both organisations into a gigantic 'state protection corps'. This ended the federal structure in the police and changed it to an instrument of the Führer's will.

By 1939 the SS–police–SD system was more than a 'state within a state'. It was a huge vested interest which had begun to obscure other interest groups in terms of power and influence. As German troops gained control over more parts of Europe the power of the SS inevitably grew. The task of internal security became greater. By 1945 the *Gestapo* had grown to 40,000 and SS officers were granted all-embracing powers to viciously crush opposition. However, it is only now being realised that a vital element in accounting for the success of the SS–police–SD role was the co-operation of the people who showed a willingness to report on those whom the SS considered to be the enemies of the regime.

This growth in organisation and influence shows that the SS aimed at a reform of society, but Himmler was aware, especially during the war, of the danger of the SS breaking down into its separate parts. He attempted to link the individual activities of the SS as closely as possible. Loyalty to Himmler would be the main means of keeping the SS together, along with commitment to a common ethnic ideal. Other unifying forces consisted of education for a wide range of activities along with the constant transfer of young SS leaders to new and different posts and the integration of SS and police personnel.

THE LIMITS ON THE POWER OF THE SS

By the end of the 1930s the influence of the SS was extensive and varied, but it had its limits. The old elites remained, apart from the police force, and this meant that the SS reached the limits of its power when it had to compete with old or new leadership groups without having Hitler's backing. The SS was also hampered in achieving its goal of becoming the new aristocracy of a National Socialist society as a result of competition from other political groups.

Development of the SS up to 1938 had resulted from the initial period of domestic infighting. After 1938, expansion would result from foreign conquests and war which gave the SS a unique opportunity to maintain its momentum and extend beyond German frontiers. Himmler had been aware of the necessity for a war as early as 1938 if the SS was to become the dominant power in a new 'Germanic Europe'. However, Himmler did not realise this ambition because the course of the war from 1942 prevented the SS from achieving its aims. Even though the *Waffen-SS* was to experience its most rapid rise after Stalingrad, so that by 1944 it numbered 900,000, there were at the same time decisive changes both in scope and structure of the concentration camp organisation.

The SS used the camps as a means of repression which served a number of different purposes, though the outcome was usually the same – death. The camps were used by the SS to execute the Final Solution and to amass large numbers of prisoners whose labour became valuable to the war effort. The SS Economy and Administration Board was set up in 1942 as part of Himmler's plan to develop a vast SS armaments industry which would make the SS independent of the state budget. This changed their basic role, but despite the increasingly large numbers who were sent to the camps to provide cheap labour, the SS did not care for them and the death rate was high in the face or repression, de-humanisation and physical extermination as suggested by the following quote from *Inside the Third Reich* by Albert Speer:

> After Hitler had become excited by the V-2 project, Himmler entered the picture. He came to Hitler to propose the simplest way to ensure secrecy for this vital programme. If the entire work force were concentration camp prisoners, all contact with the outside world would be eliminated.
>
> Hitler agreed to this plan and we had no choice... The result was that we had to work out a joint undertaking with the SS leadership – what was called the Central Works. ...we remained in charge of the manufacturing but in cases of doubt we had to yield...to the SS leadership. Thus Himmler had put a foot in our door.

> In a lonely valley in the Harz mountains, a widely ramified system of caves had been established before the war... Here in December 1943, I inspected the extensive underground installations where...prisoners were busy setting up machinery... The conditions for these prisoners were barbarous and a sense of profound involvement and personal guilt seizes me whenever I think of them... Sanitary conditions were inadequate, disease rampant: in the damp caves the mortality among them was extraordinarily high. That same day I allocated the necessary materials to build a barracks camp on an adjacent hill. I pressed the SS command to improve conditions and upgrade the food... (but a month later) my Ministry described the hygienic conditions at the Central Works in the blackest colours.

This inhuman approach is borne out by a report by Otto Brautigam, Head of the Reich Political Department in the Eastern Territories, October 1942 (quoted in G. Pridham and J. Noakes, *Nazism 1919–1945, A Documentary Reader, Vol 3*):

> It is no longer a secret that hundreds of thousands of prisoners have died of cold and starvation in our camps... It is true that we have, by unceasing efforts, achieved a substantial improvement in the lot of prisoners of war. But this improvement cannot be put down to political wisdom, but to the sudden realisation that our labour market urgently needs replacements. We now see the grotesque spectacle that after the tremendous starvation of prisoners of war, millions of labourers must hurriedly be recruited from the occupied Eastern territories in order to fill the gaps.
>
> ...With the usual unlimited abuse of Slav people...and without regard for health or age, people were shipped to Germany, where it soon turned out that well over 100,000 had to be sent back because of illness and other disabilities.

Q

To what extent do both these extracts highlight the problems affecting the supply of labour in wartime Germany?

E *Conclusion*

It was particularly during the war that the various components of the SS became clear. These were the camps, armaments, *Waffen-SS*, resettlement–extermination and SS interests in home affairs. This network of interlocking interests tightened as Himmler took over more and more offices and functions in the regime. From Reichsführer SS, he became Reich Commissar in 1939, in 1943 Minister of the Interior and in 1944 he was given command of the prisoner of war camps which remained in *Wehrmacht* hands. In 1944 he was also made Commander-in-Chief of the Reserve Army and head of army armaments after the 20 July Plot. Himmler's empire resulted from an exceptional historical situation arising from the revolutionary character of Hitler's National Socialism. The SS profited from the events of 1933, followed by the restructuring of Germany after the National Socialist seizure of power, and then from the military reorganisation of Europe in the war. Between 1933 and 1938 the SS succeeded in establishing its power only after strong competition both with older elites and with rival Nazi groups. Between 1938 and 1945 the SS helped continue the National Socialist revolution which speeded up as the regime's chances of survival declined. Himmler reached the peak of his power at a time when Germany's defeat was no longer in doubt.

7 ↪ THE RELATIONSHIP BETWEEN THE REGIME AND THE CHURCHES 1933–45

In this examination of the complex structure and shifting power groups which composed the Nazi State, an examination of the role of the churches is also relevant to our understanding of the extent to which Hitler carried through his National Socialist revolution.

The Nazi Party's basic attitude to religion was expressed by Alfred Rosenberg who was appointed to supervise Nazi ideology. The racial ideas he developed in his work *The Myth of the Twentieth Century*, show that Nazism was based on a fundamentally anti-Christian philosophy and was hostile to, and irreconcilable with, Christian ethics. Nazism worshipped strength, violence and war, Christianity taught love, respect and forgiveness for each other. Moreover, Christianity was associated with the Jews, regarded by the Nazis as an 'inferior' race which meant that the Jews could not play a part in Nazi plans for a people's community (*Volksgemeinschaft*) composed of 'pure' Germans.

A *Position of the churches in 1933*

Some leading Nazis, such as Himmler and his deputy, Heydrich, openly showed their disgust of the two churches, Protestant and Catholic. Himmler described Christianity as 'the greatest of all plagues'. Hitler himself was more guarded though he probably revealed his true feelings in a private conversation in 1933 in which he claimed that neither of the denominations 'had any future left' that would prevent him 'stamping out Christianity in Germany root and branch'. According to Hitler, 'one was either a Christian or a German', but not both. Even so, in the early years of the regime when he was securing his position, Hitler was not prepared to show openly his hostility and generally avoided direct attacks upon the churches.

Moreover, the relationship was not as clear-cut as the rival ideologies suggested. Christianity should have represented a total contradiction to the ideology of Nazism, but this did not occur in practice. Both churches had been adversely affected by the 1919 peace.

> **KEY ISSUE**
>
> *The common interest between the churches and the Nazi regime.*

1 Protestantism (which had a ratio of one minister to 2,500), had been undermined as a result of its status as the state religion of imperial Germany. Within the Protestant Church there were those who not only shared Hitler's hostility to Versailles and Weimar

democracy, but also the general anti-Semitism of the day. They viewed the Weimar Republic as un-German and ungodly, a charge reinforced by Weimar's separation of Church and State.

2 Catholicism (which had a ratio of one priest to 1,000), was equally hostile to the Weimar Republic and challenged its legality, seeing the events of November 1918 as high treason. However, despite this hostility, the Catholic Church made some advances under Weimar when it was given the right to create new bishoprics, abbeys and over 1000 new religious settlements. Catholics, who had been excluded from political power in imperial Germany, found themselves supporting democracy through the Centre Party's membership of successive coalition governments. Hitler was well aware of the strength of support for the Catholic Church shown in states such as Bavaria (see Map 6), the birthplace of Nazism. Bavaria showed a marked hatred of the political left, Weimar democracy and the Jews, and this explains its violent swing to the right after 1919.

Both churches found that a common ideological ground existed not only between themselves but also with the Nazi regime. The Catholic Church shared with Protestantism the anti-Semitism of many Germans and hostility towards Jewish influence, particularly in the Press, theatre and literature. Despite these similarities, there was no such thing as a

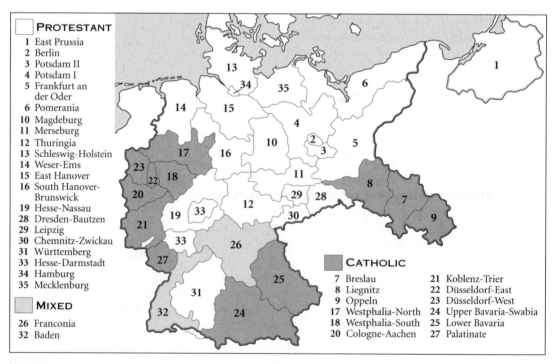

PROTESTANT

1 East Prussia
2 Berlin
3 Potsdam II
4 Potsdam I
5 Frankfurt an der Oder
6 Pomerania
10 Magdeburg
11 Merseburg
12 Thuringia
13 Schleswig-Holstein
14 Weser-Ems
15 East Hanover
16 South Hanover-Brunswick
19 Hesse-Nassau
28 Dresden-Bautzen
29 Leipzig
30 Chemnitz-Zwickau
31 Württemberg
33 Hesse-Darmstadt
34 Hamburg
35 Mecklenburg

MIXED

26 Franconia
32 Baden

CATHOLIC

7 Breslau
8 Liegnitz
9 Oppeln
17 Westphalia-North
18 Westphalia-South
20 Cologne-Aachen
21 Koblenz-Trier
22 Düsseldorf-East
23 Düsseldorf-West
24 Upper Bavaria-Swabia
25 Lower Bavaria
27 Palatinate

MAP 6
Religious divide of Germany

political agreement between the two churches. As we have seen in Chapter 5, Protestants voted and/or belonged to the conservative, right-wing DNVP and DVP, both parties losing to NSDAP between 1928 and 1933. Catholics voted for the Centre Party which was prepared to ally with the Social Democrats.

B *Reaction of the churches to Hitler's appointment as Chancellor*

The Nazi seizure of power placed both churches in an unusual and difficult position. Both churches reacted adversely to the Nazi propaganda campaign which presented Hitler as the saviour and redeemer of Germany and in his claim that the State had unlimited power. Hitler wanted to control and undermine the churches both from within and by external means, though these policies were not apparent at the beginning. Initially the regime adopted a friendly attitude towards the churches and in his first speech as Chancellor Hitler identified them as central to the preservation of the nation. Members of the SA were encouraged to attend church services in order to convey the impression that Nazism coincided with nationalist Protestantism. The 'Day of Potsdam', 21 March (see pages 138–9) which saw the opening of the new *Reichstag*, further gave the impression of unity between the Protestant Church and the State. For its part the Catholic Church, frightened by the threat of a culture conflict (***Kulturkampf***) was concerned to safeguard its position.

> ***Kulturkampf*** a state of tension/hostility between State and Church

The churches found themselves in different situations which affected their attempts to resist Nazi 'co-ordination' of Church and State. Hitler, in his attempts to control the churches from within, had a greater chance of success with the Protestant Church. It was organised into councils and divided into various regional churches which were more open to Nazi infiltration than the more independent and compactly-organised Catholics. Individual Catholics, despite being part of a universal church which looked to Rome and the Pope, nevertheless showed support for Hitler's brand of German nationalism.

C *Hitler's initial reaction to the churches*

The National Socialist regime looked for a compromise with a section of Protestantism leading to the establishment of a German Christian State Church, but this was impossible with Catholicism. The Catholic leadership at all levels, during the early years of the regime, looked for a working relationship with Berlin by means of the Concordat of June 1933. As early as April 1933 discussions took place in Rome between Göring, Papen (who made a 'good impression in the Vatican') and members of the Catholic hierarchy. These discussions, which were regarded as a 'political event of the first importance', were commented upon at a subsequent Catholic Conference in Berlin (25–26 April 1933) where it was expressed that 'nothing should be done to make the relationship between Church and State more difficult' and the Nazi

> **KEY ISSUE**
>
> *Hitler's early moves to establish a good relationship with the Churches.*

movement was 'especially valued because of the struggle against Bolshevism and immorality'. The minutes of the Conference (quoted in Peter Matheson, *The Third Reich and the Christian Churches*) reported that:

> Herr von Papen has come to an understanding with Hitler that the freedom of the Catholic Church should not be infringed, since a *'Kulturkampf'* would be fateful for the young state. It is expected, on the other hand...the clergy should exercise discretion in their political activities... The lower levels of the NSDAP will certainly be brought to order if they attempt to launch actions against Catholic organisations...

This Concordat, made between the Papacy and the Third Reich on 20 July 1933, agreed that in return for the Vatican's diplomatic recognition of the National Socialist regime the Catholic church would be allowed to retain a closely defined control over education, though its leaders were expected to submit politically, as the following documents indicate (quoted in Peter Matheson, *The Third Reich and the Christian Churches*):

> **Article 1**
> The German Reich guarantees freedom of belief and of public worship to the Catholic faith. It recognises the right of the Catholic Church, within the limits of the law of the land, to order and administer its own affairs and to make laws and regulations upon its members in matters within its competence.
>
> **Article 16**
> Before bishops enter upon the government of their dioceses they are to take an oath of fealty either to the representatives of the Reich government in the provinces or to the president of the Reich in the following words: 'Before God and on the Holy Gospels I swear and promise – as becomes a bishop – loyalty to the German Reich and to the...state.
>
> **Article 21**
> Instruction in the Catholic faith is a regular part of the curriculum in the elementary, technical, intermediate and high schools and is taught in accordance with the principles of the Catholic Church. It will be a special concern of religious instruction, as is the case with all other subjects, to inculcate a sense of patriotic, civic and social duty in the spirit of Christian faith and morality.
>
> **Article 31**
> The property and activities of those Catholic organisations whose aims are purely religious, cultural or charitable and which, therefore, are under the authority of the hierarchy, will be protected.

Q *What important concessions were made by the Catholic Church in its Concordat with the Nazi regime?*

The National Socialist regime made a number of minor concessions to reassure anxious conservatives in both churches.

- It recognised seven Roman Catholic feast days as legal holidays.
- The Prussian government ended interdenominational schools and made religious instruction compulsory.

SA membership showed mass support for various church sacraments particularly weddings and baptisms. However, the regime's agreement was totally insincere, the concessions were intended to be temporary while the dictatorship was being established. By the end of 1933 Nazi interference in religious affairs was causing resentment and disillusionment in both churches. The Catholic leadership soon discovered that the privileges promised in the Concordat were being disregarded:

- 44 priests were harassed and arrested;
- Catholic schools were interfered with and organisations, such as youth clubs, were undermined.

That the Church had doubts about the honesty of the Concordat is shown in the following extract from a letter from Cardinal Bertram to the Vatican dated 10 September 1933 (quoted in Matheson, *The Third Reich and the Christian Churches*). It warned:

> Delay of the ratification of the Reich Concordat is not recommended. On the contrary it is desirable that the ratification should take place very soon. . .
>
> It is being said quite widely that the government has gone too far in its concessions; that a move in the opposite direction would be desirable. Such voices will only become louder if ratification is delayed.
>
> We will only be able to take more decisive action against countless anti-Catholic actions after ratification. . .and it is highly desirable that an end to the grievances should be demanded at the same time as ratification is effected. . . Reference can be made here to the following current grievances:
>
> On all sides, Catholic associations are publicly slandered, being accused of political unreliability, of lack of patriotism, of enmity against the state. . .
>
> Parents no longer want to let their children belong to Catholic organisations. . .because of pressure from the subordinate organisations of the NSDAP which are not effectively restrained by the higher authorities. . .and everywhere teachers are under pressure to direct children to the Hitler Youth. . . Thus the living reservoirs for the Catholic associations are being cut off. . . Catholic newspapers are forbidden to describe themselves as 'Catholic'. . . There should, it is said, no longer be a Catholic press, but only a German press.

Q *What hopes and fears are expressed by Cardinal Bertram? On this basis, might the Concordat have seemed disappointing to Catholic leaders?*

This anxiety that the Concordat would not lead to peace in Church–State affairs was well founded. As this extract from a secret SS report on the activities of Catholic clergy in May 1934 observes, Catholic clergy were guilty of subversive actions which threatened the agreement (from Matheson, *The Third Reich and the Christian Churches*):

Munich: Cardinal Faulhaber is generally regarded as the intellectual leader of the Catholic resistance to the National Socialist state, especially in the foreign Press... His occasional exhortations to the clergy that they should 'co-operate with the state'...are eclipsed by the disruptive effects of his sermons on Judaism and...about Germanism.

...the statements made about Germanism...can only be characterised as a political misuse of the pulpit, especially when they were taken as the theme for a New Year's Eve service. The sermons attracted huge attendances and in book form they sold like hot cakes...

The most dangerous activity of countless Catholic clergy is the way in which they 'mope about', spreading despondency. Favourite topics are 'the dangers of a new time', 'the present emergency', 'the gloomy future'. Prophecies are made about the speedy downfall of national Socialism or at the very least mention is made of the transience of all political phenomena, compared with the Catholic Church which will outlive them all. National Socialist achievements and successes are passed over in silence.

Q *What were the main complaints made in this secret report? What were likely to be the consequences?*

Despite these reservations expressed by the Catholic Church, Hitler appeared to have success with the churches, especially the Protestants. Church spokesmen joined the growing number of those who expressed support for the National Socialist regime in its work of national reconstruction. The aims of the Reich government had long been those of the Catholic Church, such as hostility to communism, liberalism and permissiveness; and the government received support from both Catholic and Protestant churches for Nazi racism such as the April 1933 boycott campaign (see page 275).

However, the real intention of the National Socialist regime, as far as the churches were concerned, was to establish state, that is, National Socialist, control. It sought to undermine people's loyalty to religion and Christianity because that was believed to rival their loyalty to the State and to the Führer. The regime directed its attacks against institutions, traditions and values which were resisted by both the Protestant and Catholic churches.

D *Hitler's relationship with the Protestant Church*

In the Protestant Church *Gleichschaltung* (see pages 142–4) was put into effect by the *Deutsche Christen* (German Christians), who managed to combine their evangelical devotion with Nazi ideas of the recovery of Germany. Hitler wanted control through the Nazi-dominated German Christian State Church which aimed to restructure the whole of the German Protestant Church in its theology and organisation. In 1933 the opportunity came with the Church elections. With the support of the SA, the German Christians gained three-quarters of the votes which gave them the majority in most provinces. A new Church constitution was drafted in 1933 with the Nazi sympathiser, Ludwig Müller, as first Reich Bishop.

LUDWIG MÜLLER (1883–1945)

Müller spent the mid 1920s as a Protestant army chaplain in Königsberg, East Prussia where he established a reputation for his strong patriotic and anti-Semitic sermons. In 1926 he was brought to the attention of Hitler by General Blomberg, who was then commander of the East Prussian military district. The similarity of their views meant that Hitler, on becoming Chancellor, quickly promoted Müller. On 4 April 1933 he was put in charge of all matters relating to the Evangelical Church. From then on he became the central figure in the struggle between the German Faith Movement (*Deutsche Glaubensbewegung*), which was supported by Hitler, and the Confessional Church (*Bekenntniskirche*) which was led by Martin Niemöller. On 23 July 1933, Müller was appointed Reich Bishop by a national synod in Wittenberg and he implemented Hitler's policies against the Confessional Church. Though he was a fanatical supporter of the Nazi regime and Hitler's doctrines on race and leadership, he never enjoyed Hitler's complete confidence. Dismissed by Hitler as a 'man of no stature', his influence declined from 1935 onwards as Hitler put church problems in the hands of a Reich Church Commission. He died in Berlin on 31 July 1945.

Hitler's policies were supported by some Protestant extremists at the Berlin Sports Palace in November 1933. They called for a purge of the Gospels of all un-German traces such as 'the scapegoat and inferiority theology of Rabbi Paul'. This led to a counter-reaction among many Protestant pastors and there soon developed an opposition group, the Confessing Church which held orthodox German Lutheran Protestantism and rejected Nazi infiltration. This was open opposition to the National Socialist regime. In 1934 Protestant-rural Franconia, which had been loyal to Nazism in 1933, was alienated when the regime removed the head of the Lutheran church. But on this occasion protest was limited to a demand to restore the bishop and end the challenge to the Church. Hitler intervened and the Party lost face, but there was no general disapproval of the regime. Hitler continued to force the Protestant leadership into co-operating with Müller though opposition came from a breakaway group called the Confessional Church.

The Confessional Church was determined to defend the Church against State interference and to challenge Müller. Although 7,000 clergy joined, its effectiveness was weakened by splits between moderates and extremists led by Pastor Martin Niemöller. But in spite of internal disagreements, the presence of the Confessional Church undermined Müller's leadership. It embarked on a protest campaign conducted in the press. As a result, the regime changed its tactics and in 1935 created a new Department of State for Church Affairs under Reichsminister Kerrl, who replaced Müller. This appointment indicated a change in Nazi policy from intervention to manipulation of the splits within the Protestant groups from the outside.

MARTIN NIEMÖLLER (1892–1964)

Niemöller served in the First World War as a U-boat commander, for which he was awarded with the highest decoration, Pour le Mérite, for his services. He studied theology after the war and was ordained in 1924, serving as pastor of the wealthy Berlin-Dahlem Church 1931–7. As a committed nationalist and opponent of communism he initially joined the Nazi Party but became disillusioned when Hitler insisted on state supremacy over religion. He took over leadership of the Confessional Church which remained loyal to traditional Lutheran Protestantism and set up the Pastors' Emergency League. In 1934, 7,000 pastors joined this opposition group but many subsequently left in the face of Nazi persecution. He was regarded by people of all denominations as a folk hero and his opposition aroused Hitler's anger. Niemöller's last sermon in 1937 in which he said 'we must obey God rather than man' was followed by his arrest. Instead of detaining him indefinitely, Hitler decided to have him tried for 'underhanded attacks against the state', by a special court with the responsibility for trying such cases. To Hitler's fury, the court sentenced him only to seven months imprisonment in a fortress (an honourable prison for officers) and a fine of 2,000 marks. On his release from his detention, Niemöller was arrested again by the *Gestapo* and kept in custody in various concentration camps until he was freed by the Allies in 1945 when they liberated Dachau. In 1946 he admitted Germany's war guilt in a speech in Geneva and in 1947 became first bishop of the Evangelical Church of Hesse-Nassau, a post he held until his death in 1964.

E *Hitler's relationship with the Catholic Church*

The Catholic Church's official relationship with the regime was largely governed by a sense of fear that, despite the Concordat of 1933, they were not protected against attacks. As the extract from the letter from Cardinal Bertram to the Vatican on page 229 showed there was a widespread belief that the regime was failing to honour the promises of non-interference which it had made with the Papacy.

These fears were reinforced by a detailed campaign against political Catholicism, which took a number of forms. Members of the Hitler Youth were required to reject the influence of priests, followed by an order in 1936 that membership of the Hitler Youth was compulsory for all over the age of 10. This undermined the Catholic-run youth clubs. In Bavaria the Nazis succeeded in their campaign to end Catholic schools by persuading most parents to send their children to mixed schools. Finally between 1936 and 1937 monasteries and convents, which represented a key area of the Catholic Church, were accused of scandalous behaviour, resulting in hundreds being brought before the law courts on charges of sexual wrongs and illegal currency deals which Goebbels insisted should be widely published in the newspapers. Despite these extreme measures, the regime failed to destroy people's respect for priests, especially in the villages.

By 1935 it was clear that the Nazi *Gleichschaltung* of the churches had achieved only limited success. Even so, the Nazi leadership was divided between a policy of suppression, which could antagonise large numbers of Germans, and a policy of limited persecution, which could allow the churches an unacceptable degree of independence outside state control. Ultimately aiming at total submission, from 1935 the regime embarked on a series of measures to wear away the churches' hold over people. A Ministry of Church Affairs was set up and introduced a wide range of anti-religious measures to weaken the reputation of both churches, including the abolition of religious schools and campaigns to disgrace the clergy. Those individual priests who resisted were arrested and sent to Dachau, the most famous being Martin Niemöller. The Papacy attacked the Nazi regime in its encyclical of 1937, 'With Burning Concern'. Within Germany, Catholic priests used the pulpit to read out papal circulars condemning these charges and calling upon Catholics to remain loyal and resist such pressures. However, the Church could not prevent loss of its influence on youth. Warnings were issued by the leadership that in the event of a break between Church and State, 'the loyalty of many Catholics towards the Church might fail the test'. The Catholic Church feared this development and this influenced individual members to vary in their attitudes, from the anti-Nazi stand by the Bishop of Berlin to those who preached loyalty and obedience even when visiting the concentration camps. However, the effectiveness of the Catholic Church's opposition was undermined by the common interests, anti-Marxism, anti-Semitism and nationalism, it shared with the regime. Thus it supported the Nuremberg Laws of 1935 which banned inter-racial marriages and gave a blessing for the successful reoccupation of the Rhineland and subsequently other lands.

Apart from the policies described above, Hitler also tried to undermine the churches by external means. In place of Christianity the Nazis tried to encourage a racial Teutonic paganism, whereby the anti-Christian element in National Socialism was expressed through the growth of the German Faith Movement. Its followers were called 'God-believers' and they represented Nazism in a spiritual form. Although never fully clarified, the Movement centred around four main themes representing complete rejection of Christian ethics and the replacement of Christian ceremonies, marriage and baptism, by pagan equivalents. Hitler's personality was praised as was the policy of blood and soil (see page 245). The German Faith Movement did not achieve any large-scale support, only 5 per cent of the population were recorded as members in the 1939 census, but it represented another example of how the regime tried to undermine the churches.

F *Incidence of Church–State conflict 1933–45*

The German Faith Movement led a number of campaigns.

The 'Church Secession Campaign' encouraged individuals to withdraw from Church membership. It was successful among the professions, such as the civil service and teachers, who depended on the regime for their jobs. They were forced to become full-time Party workers. The movement de-christianised the rituals surrounding birth, marriage and death, and altered religious feast days, such as Christmas, into pagan festivals. A number of practices were tried in their place, particularly by the SS who made use of carved runes though these did not succeed in replacing the star and the cross in the public's mind.

In the Catholic regions of Germany, which accounted for a third of the population – Bavaria, the Rhineland, the Mosel valley, Baden, the Palatinate, substantial parts of Silesia and Westphalia and the Catholic districts of Oldenburg – there was a campaign to remove the cross, and in 1937 the crucifix, from classrooms in an attempt to undermine the influence of the churches. The removal of the symbols of Christianity from the schools brought the church struggle into an open, widespread resistance to the introduction of government decrees, and created hostility which threatened to burst into a mass revolt. The wave of civil disobedience, involving petitions, protest letters, mass meetings and school strikes presented the Nazi authorities with a situation which could not be controlled by intimidation. Both in Oldenburg and in Bavaria the authorities eventually gave in and popular opinion had scored a significant, if limited victory. The campaign was not abandoned, however, and the Second World War saw the gradual removal of the cross and the crucifix from hospitals and schools.

The defeat over christian symbols in classrooms did not prevent the regime from making prayers optional in schools in 1935 and arresting 700 Protestant ministers. Only licensed ministers and priests could give religious instruction while in schools teachers were encouraged to drop religious teaching gradually from the school curriculum by 1941 for children over 14.

Despite these efforts the regime had more success with suppressing Protestant youth organisations in the early years whereas the Catholic Young Men's association lasted till 1939 in spite of piecemeal suppression. During the war some recovery of their youth groups was made by both churches until the age of conscription was lowered to 16.

Apart from the campaigns aimed at the churches, hostile public opinion was also roused on two moral issues which were not directly linked with a particular religious belief – the sterilisation measures, and the euthanasia programme, both elements in Hitler's policy of

KEY ISSUE

The extent of the churches' success in opposing the Nazi regime.

eugenics. The euthanasia programme of 1939, whereby mentally and physically handicapped people were killed, was a policy which provoked widespread protest. Sermons, such as that preached by the bishop of Münster, Cardinal Count von Galen, on 3 August 1941, played a key role in mobilising the campaign which eventually influenced Hitler to intervene personally. Thousands of copies of the sermon were printed and distributed and were followed by other protest letters from Church leaders along with hostile demonstrations. Under the pressure of these events Hitler abandoned the programme on 24 August 1941, though it continued unofficially in the camps (this topic is considered further in the study of Hitler's *Volksgemeinschaft* in Chapter 10).

The secrecy surrounding these policies indicates both the regime's doubts about the response of public opinion, and an awareness of the limited extent to which the racial element of Nazi ideology had been accepted by the people. Party leaders became increasingly aware of the need to reassure the people. Protest letters poured into party and government offices so that leading Nazis began to question the wisdom of proceeding unofficially instead of within a published law. However, even in these controversial areas opposition was limited. Some protested at the illegal, rather than the ethical, issues involved in the euthanasia action. Outside of Catholic ranks, opinion seemed to be divided on the issue and even among Church leaders the euthanasia issue did not bring about a united attack on the Nazi state.

The outbreak of war initially brought about a more cautious policy, as the regime wanted to avoid unnecessary tensions. However, following the easy victories against Poland and France, and then the invasion of Russia, the persecution intensified even though pro-Nazi priests persuaded Catholics to take up arms and support the invasion of Russia. This persecution was more the result of pressure from anti-Christian fanatics, such as Bormann and Heydrich, rather than the work of the weak and ineffective Minister of Church Affairs. The regime continued with its anti-Catholic policies:

- monasteries were closed;
- church property was attacked and church activities were severely restricted;
- in 1941 the Catholic press was closed down;
- church bells were melted down;
- charges of cowardice were made against individual priests.

Even so, Hitler did not allow subordination of the churches to give way to wholesale suppression within Germany. It was only in the recently absorbed regions in Poland, the area selected as an experimental example of the 'New Order', that events were allowed to run their logical course. Here the area was declared 'free of churches', many of the clergy were executed, churches were closed down and the influence of the Holy See was excluded. In the end the Nazi persecution of the churches failed, but only because the war itself was lost.

eugenics controlling human breeding, thus altering the population to achieve a 'super race' with desirable inherited characteristics

G *Conclusion*

The Nazi regime achieved only limited success in its religious policy; the churches were severely handicapped, but not destroyed. Equally, the churches failed as well, for in their concern to defend Christianity itself they failed to offer a moral lead to oppose such a monstrous regime. Their conservatism meant that they distrusted the politics of the left, which seemed to threaten the existing order of society and which in its extreme form of communism rejected the existence of religion itself. Equally though, there was a nationalist sympathy for Nazism, especially after the problems of 1918–33. The Protestant Church particularly was compromised by its alliance with the State. Finally both churches rightly feared the power of the Nazi State so that resistance was offered only by individual priests.

German Catholicism succeeded in maintaining its unity and the allegiance of a substantial hard core of believers by a policy which swung from resistance to acceptance, for example no spiritual sanctions were taken against Catholics who made up a fifth of the SS. People remained loyal and shunned those who left the Church though those who returned during the war were accepted.

The Protestant Church was more divided and this produced a more varied response, such as that on the Jewish question, the supreme moral issue. The churches did not come out in open defence of the Jews either in fear of government revenge or of alienating public opinion or because they regarded persecution of the Jews as proof of God's curse.

> **KEY ISSUE**
>
> *The extent of the Nazi regime's success in making the churches its submissive instrument.*

8 ⌁ BIBLIOGRAPHY

There are a number of collected editions of primary sources which are readily available. For the themes covered in this chapter J. Noakes and G. Pridham (eds), *Nazism 1919–1945, A Documentary Reader, Vol 2 – State, Economy and Society 1933–1939* (University of Exeter 1984), have chapters (9 and 10) that examine Party/State Relations at central and regional level, Chapters 21 and 22 look at Law and Order and the SS–Police State respectively.

A number of specialist texts exist on the aspects of the Nazi State covered in this chapter. M. Broszat, *The Hitler State* (Longman 1981) looks at the structuralist arguments concerning Hitler's role; the growth in the organisation of the Nazi Party is covered by D. Orlow, *A History of the Nazi Party 1933–1945* (David & Charles 1973); while the problems stemming from the character of its early development are examined in J. Noakes, *Government, Party and People in Nazi Germany* (University of Exeter 1984). The history of the SS has been written by Gerald Reitlinger, *The SS: Alibi of a Nation 1922–1945* (Heinemann 1957) and Helmut Krausnick and Martin Broszat, *Anatomy of the SS State* (Paladin 1968); and that of the churches by Peter Matheson, *The Third Reich and the Christian Churches* (T. & T. Clark 1981); J.S. Conway, *The Nazi Persecution of the Churches* (Weidenfeld & Nicolson

1968); and G. Lewy has written on *The Catholic Church and Nazi Germany* (Weidenfeld & Nicolson 1964). For an account of the German Army refer to R.J. O'Neill, *The German Army and the Nazi Party, 1933–1939* (Cassell 1966) and J.W. Wheeler-Bennett, *The Nemesis of Power: The German Army in Politics 1918–1945* (Macmillan 1961).

9 ⁓ DISCUSSION QUESTIONS

A *This section consists of questions that might be used for discussion or for testing your understanding of the main themes covered in this chapter.*
1. What were the main weaknesses of the Nazi Party?
2. What role did the Party play in the Nazi State?
3. What was the significance of the Hossbach Memorandum of November 1937 in Hitler's relations with the Army?
4. What were the main changes which occurred in the relationship between Hitler and his generals from 1938 to 1945?
5. What part did Generals Blomberg and Fritsch play in their management of the Army on behalf of Hitler.
6. What decisive changes were brought about in the relationship between Hitler and the German Army by the Blomberg-Fritsch affair?
7. Why did Hitler not succeed in making the Army his submissive instrument?
8. What was the origin and role of the SS?
9. What different organisations did the SS develop which made it a state within a state?

10 ⁓ ESSAY QUESTIONS

A *Two-Part Questions.*
1. (a) What restraints did Hitler face on his freedom of action in 1933?
   (b) Why did the Nazi Party fail to govern Germany?
2. (a) Why was there common interest between Hitler and the German Army?
   (b) What measures did Hitler take to establish his control of the Army between 1933–45?
3. (a) In what ways did the SS extend its powers and influence in Germany between 1933–45?
   (b) Why did the SS fail to establish complete control of the State by 1945?
4. (a) In what ways did Hitler and his regime attempt to control the Churches in Germany?
   (b) Why was the regime unable to secure complete control of the Churches by 1945?

B *Essay Questions.*
1. 'The Nazi dictatorship was more apparent than real'.
   How far do you agree with this assessment?
2. To what extent had the SS become 'a state within a state' by 1945?
3. To what extent were the Churches successful in their resistance to the Nazi regime?

11 ∽ MAKING NOTES

Read the advice section about making notes on page xx of Preface: How to use this book, and then make your own notes based on the following headings and questions.

1. *The army*
Read Section 5 on pages 203–213 and revise previous work on the role of the *Reichswehr* in bringing Hitler to power.
(a) What unity of interests and aims existed between the Third Reich and the army which made possible Hitler's success in 1933?
(b) What forms did Hitler's cautious policy of gradual infiltration of the army take?
(c) What role did the High Command of the army play in Hitler's quarrel with Röhm and subsequent events of 30 June 1934?
(d) Why was there a divergence of aims and interests between Hitler and the army from 1938 and 1944?
(e) Why was the army the one instrument which Hitler could not destroy or force to submit?
(f) What impact did the July Plot have on Hitler's relationship with the army and its High Command and on the character of his HQ?
(g) What was the significance of Hitler's policies on the army?
(h) How did the army show the impact of the corrupting influence of the Third Reich?

2. *The SS*
(a) Trace the origins and development of the role of the SS from 1925 to Himmler's appointment as its Reichsführer in 1936. Include in your answer an analysis of its evolution through its various stages:
   (i)   protection squads (such as in the events of 1934);
   (ii) custodian of Party values;
   (iii) personal bodyguards to Hitler;
   (iv) representatives of the elitism of the Party/Reich;
   (v)   the *Waffen-SS* as a model of the ideals which were to be instilled into the army;
   (vi) political role of the SS – include reference to the suppression of internal subversion or a military *putsch* by the army.
(b) What were the main factors behind the growth of the SS in the two periods:
   (i) 1933–8;
   (ii) 1941 onwards?

(c) What were the main features of the three branches which composed the organisation of the SS:
   (i)   intelligence – the work of the SD;
   (ii) police – regular and security (criminal/*Kripo*) and (secret/*Gestapo*);
   (iii) military – stages of growth 1933–6, 1936, 1938, 1940–1?
(d) What were the main powers of the SS by 1941 which amounted to its being a 'state within a state'? In your answer assess the SS's contribution in each of the following areas in the Nazi state:
   (i)   domestic security;
   (ii) *Waffen-SS*;
   (iii) administration of conquered territories;
   (iv) administration of Jewish affairs;
   (v)   administration of the camps;
   (vi) administration of its economic empire.
(e) What was the basis of the relationship between the SS and the Party and the army?

3. *The churches*
(a) Position of the churches in 1933:
   (i)   What were the main developments in both the churches under the Weimar Republic?
   (ii) In what ways did the Nazi seizure of power place both churches in a difficult situation?
(b) The regime's relationship with the Protestant Church:
   (i)   How did Hitler seek to control the Protestant Church from within? Refer to his attempts to restructure the whole of German Protestant Church in its theology and organisation and to the activities of Müller as Reich Bishop.
   (ii) What degree of success did the policy of co-ordination achieve? Include reference to the activities of the Confessional Church.
   (iii) What was the background to the regime's decision to replace Müller in 1935 with a new Ministry of Church Affairs under Reichsminister Kerrl? What change in policy followed?
(c) The regime's relationship with the Catholic Church:
   (i)   How did the regime attempt to reduce the power of Catholicism?
   (ii) How did the Catholic Church respond to these activities and with what success?
   (iii) What anti-Catholic policies were introduced during the war years?
   (iv) What part was played by the churches in resisting the regime's eugenic policy and euthanasia programme?
(d) Hitler's attempts to 'co-ordinate' the churches by external means:
   (i)   What were the main themes of the German Faith Movement and how much support did it enjoy?
   (ii) How did the German Faith Movement seek to undermine Christianity and the churches? In your answer refer to the

- Church Secession Campaign;
- de-Christianising of rituals;
- campaigns to displace the cross and the crucifix, to ban prayers in schools, against priests and against Church youth organisations.

12 ⌐ PLANNING AN ESSAY

Read the advice section about writing essays given on pages xviii–xx in Preface: How to use this book. The following is a suggested plan for an A2 type question shown in the title: 'The Nazi dictatorship in the 1930s was more apparent than real? How far do you agree with this judgement?

   This is a difficult question which requires you to agree, or disagree with the statement. You have to review the arguments on both sides and give a verdict. You will need to show not only an understanding of the nature of the dictatorship, the structures of power at work, but also its limitations. Balance is important in so far that you should not concentrate exclusively on one of the claims – either apparent or real though you might decide more in favour of one claim, eg that the dictatorship was more real than apparent. Remember that planning your answer is crucial to achieve balance. The following structure is a guideline to help you practise writing this type of question.

Essay Planning Sheet: A2 type essay

Title: 'The Nazi dictatorship in the 1930s was more apparent than real.' How far do you agree with this judgement?

Paragraph 1 Introduction:
Reassessment by historians of the validity of the claim to 'totalitarianism'.

Para.	Main theme of paragraph	Evidence
A 'Yes' argument – Way in which the dictatorship was more apparent		
2	There were limits to Hitler's power	• Lifestyle, lack of clear lines of authority, overworked civil service. • Independence of lower levels of the apparatus: men did things in the name of the leadership. • Limitations on the power of the Party: did not govern Germany.
3	The apparatus of terror such as the dreaded *Gestapo* was not very large	• Nature of the police oppression: the *Gestapo*, remarkably small, developed out of secret police organisation in Prussia. Beginning of 1934: 1,700, spread throughout the Reich, 3,000 in 1935, rising to 7,000 in 1937 (out of a population of 65/70 million). At the beginning of 1944 there were 31,000 to police the whole of Europe. So how did they achieve their ends?

Para.	Main theme of paragraph	Evidence
B 'No' argument – Way in which the dictatorship was real		
4	The way in which Hitler took power is important in understanding how the dictatorship developed	● Destruction of opposition, of trade unions, of political parties, achieved through the exercise of state power and extra-legal violence and intimidation of opponents. ● Pressure exerted by the SA: police and stormtroopers marched through working-class areas, no attempt to stop this by the regime. ● Creation of concentration camps (disused abandoned factories) to get rid of opponents.
5	It was not just a repressed regime by the police or crime against humanity	● Key element: absence of political pluralism, no legitimate politics outside of the political establishment, destruction of initiatives from elsewhere. ● Destruction of the power to speak: no ideas broadcast other than those of the ruling group. ● Lack of meaningful political participation. ● Destruction of the rule of law: ability of the leadership to do what it wanted, crimes against humanity, nothing to stop the regime, absence of a risk of a *coup d'état*. ● These conditions existed in spite of the fact that the Weimar Constitution was not formally abolished until 1945.
6	Policy of co-ordination of institutions reinforced the Nazi regime	● Restrictions on press freedom, powers of the police, radio and film. ● Destruction of autonomous public sphere 1933–4 taken further with purges of regime's enemies, opponents, the start of a profound breakdown of the rule of law. ● All civil servants took oath of allegiance personally to Hitler, as Führer not to the State. By August 1934 there was no source of authority independent of the Nazis. ● Progressive centralisation of the police achieved by 1936 when Himmler became chief of police.
7	Dictatorship not just due to coercion – also stemmed from consent of the people	● Political triumphs of the 1930s: fall in unemployment, gains in foreign policy, people benefited. ● Support for repression of 'asocial' elements: workshy, homosexuals, juvenile delinquents.
8	The Nazi dictatorship governed and policed by consent	● People willing to denounce friends, enemies and neighbours: Hamburg in 1940s – 100,000 participated in the auction of Jewish property. ● Co-operation was achieved within the framework of severe repression: camps were outside the legal framework as became brutally apparent in the last stages of the war. ● Participation distinguishes democracy from dictatorship but the Germans participated through means of violence and crime not political democracy.
C What else was significant?		
Conclusion: Despite its limitations, the Nazi dictatorship was real. Hitler benefited from the wide range of responses to his regime from committed followers to those who gave an unwilling acquiescence, but few were prepared to resist and there was only one attempt to depose him – in 1944.		

9

National Socialist philosophy and ideology

Political parties usually present their programme of policies in terms which are likely to be vote-catching. This was particularly true of the Nazis, who were influenced by Hitler's views expressed in *Mein Kampf* that 'all propaganda must be presented in a popular form and must fix its intellectual level so as not to be above the heads of the least intellectual of those to whom it is directed'. Add to this the Nazi belief that support for the Party should be based more on faith in, and loyalty to, the leader than on logical thought and it is easy to see how a Nazi leader, Hans Frank, could write as early as 1924 that 'our programme, in two words, reads "Adolf Hitler" ', or how Göring could state in 1934, 'the programme reads "Germany" '.

In fact the leading writer of National Socialist ideology was not Hitler, but Alfred Rosenberg (see page 66). He was one of the early members of the Party and the editor of its newspaper, *Völkischer Beobachter*. He wrote a number of anti-Semitic pamphlets, and reissued a nineteenth century pamphlet of uncertain authorship called *The Protocols of the Elders of Zion*. This claimed to describe a Jewish plot to achieve world domination, was later identified as a forgery, but was accepted by Hitler. In 1925 Rosenberg published his great work, *The Myth of the Twentieth Century*, which was regarded as a National Socialist bible for its racial theories. In it he restated the racial doctrines developed in *Mein Kampf* with reference to the superiority of the Nordic race. He equated the latter with the German people while at the same time he denounced the Jews as parasites. He also attacked Freemasonry, Christianity and communism. Hitler's endorsement of the views expressed in *The Myth* made them the official philosophy of the Third Reich. In 1934 Rosenberg was made responsible for training all Nazi Party members in National Socialist ideology.

In these circumstances it is not surprising that people at the time, and many historians and commentators since, doubted whether Hitler really had a consistent ideology. The traditional view of National Socialist ideology was first put forward by Hermann Rauschning, the ex-Nazi leader of the Danzig Senate, who quarrelled with Hitler and subsequently settled in America. In *Hitler Speaks* he attacked Hitler for showing 'an unscrupulous opportunism which discards with perfect ease everything that a moment before has passed as a fixed principle', while Melita Maschmann, looking back in 1970 on her years in the Hitler Youth Movement, questioned 'where were they, then, those great, deep ideas and certain truths which had been the foundations for the new world we had sought to build. A barely audible voice within me said: "nowhere, they never existed" '. Another commentator of the Third Reich, William Shirer, has gone so far as to describe Hitler's ideology as 'a grotesque hodge-podge concocted by a half-baked, uneducated neurotic'. National Socialist ideology was seen as inconsistent, confused and contradictory. However, this view was not shared by all historians. Alan Bullock, a foremost expert on Hitler, believes that Hitler showed considerable consistency in adhering to certain ideas and conceptions throughout 25 years of political activity. Another biographer, William Carr, described Hitler's skilful marriage of his philosophy of life with tactics to exploit people and situations to achieve absolute power as, 'an unprincipled opportunism'.

The debate about whether Hitler showed a consistency of aim partly stems from the few available sources, which makes it very difficult to trace the development of his ideas. The German archives were partly destroyed during the war but, as has already been noted in Chapter 7, of even more importance was the nature of Hitler's personal rule. He left few written records and did not keep a diary; even *Mein Kampf* was dictated to Emil Maurice and Rudolf Hess. He made no marginal comments on official documents, preferring to discuss problems unofficially with close subordinates at his mountain retreat, the Berghof. Thus the historian is left with the two general works dating from the early period of the 1920s: *Mein Kampf* and his *Zweites Buch* (Secret Book) written in 1928 but not published in Hitler's lifetime. The latter book represents the final stage in the clarification of Hitler's ideas since his early beginnings as a nationalist agitator in 1919. The question in dispute is whether Hitler revealed his true intentions in these works. Certainly Hitler always spoke of possessing a basic philosophy which had evolved over the years in the light of his experiences as a down-and-out in Vienna, in the First World War and in the difficult times which harassed Germany under Weimar. During his Vienna years he developed his ideals (*Weltanschauung*) which became the driving forces in his life. These forces consisted of a fanatical nationalism and his concepts of race and blood, struggle and domination, the Aryan versus the Jew, the master race versus inferior peoples, hatred for Jews and Marxism and a conviction that Fate had chosen him to do great things. Although historians differ about the importance of *Mein Kampf* to an understanding of Hitler's subsequent policies, it is still a vital source for understanding his basic mind and beliefs. Commenting on its significance, E. Jäckel has said, 'seldom or perhaps never in history has a ruler before coming to power sketched so accurately in writing that which he subsequently carried out than Adolf Hitler'. (See pages 62–6 for details of the background to the writing of, and main themes explored in, *Mein Kampf*.)

KEY ISSUE

The Nazi Party ideology and philosophy.

ideology means a set of ideas and values; philosophy is the theory behind those ideas

Volk a people purified of the material and spiritual influences of other peoples; a term representing race, mysticism and anti-Semitism.
gemeinschaft a tightly bound, organic rural community

1 ⌐ MAIN THEMES IN HITLER'S IDEOLOGY AND PHILOSOPHY

A *The German Volk and the need for racial purity*

At the core of Nazi ideology lay Hitler's obsession with achieving a racially pure national community (*Volksgemeinschaft*) based on the principle of *Gemeinnutz geht vor Eigennutz* ('Common good before the good of the individual'). It was a recurring theme from the earliest days of the party's 25 Point Programme to his Germanisation of the east under the SS during the 1940s. Hitler's vision, representing the most radical form of ethnic nationalism, was to create a racial state where membership would be open only to pure Germans in an *ein Volk, ein Reich,* (one people, one empire). This meant the exclusion not only of biological outsiders, such as the Jews and gypsies, but also of the sick and infirm. It also meant a recovery of the Reich's territories (Alsace, Lorraine, and parts of Poland) and people lost to Germany in the Treaty of Versailles. He extended his criteria of *ein Volk* to take in all ethnic Germans including those of Austria, Czechoslovakia and Poland. In *Mein Kampf* he wrote that 'people of the same blood should be in the same Reich'. It was an attractive policy for many Germans, especially the army, for there was a strong sense of resentment against the Treaty of Versailles. Hitler owed much of his success to the desire of many to restore German greatness and empire. He remained constant to this aspect of his ideology even though the creation of such a single Reich of ethnic Germans threatened the stability of central and central-eastern Europe (see Map 10 page 395) and eventually engulfed Europe in a Second World War. People were to be made aware of their ethnic and political unity. In *Mein Kampf,* Hitler set out the need to educate young people to understand the meaning of racial purity and the importance of maintaining the racial blood uncontaminated to ensure the preservation of the German race. According to him:

Q

What was Hitler's main argument for stressing the purity of blood?

What we must fight for is to safeguard the existence and reproduction of our race and our people, the sustenance of our children and the purity of our blood, the freedom and independence of the fatherland, so that our people may mature for the fulfilment of the mission allotted it by the creator of the universe ...Those who are physically and mentally unhealthy and unworthy must not perpetuate their suffering in the body of their children.

Hitler had a romanticised view of his national community which would be based on the peasantry whom he regarded to be racially the purest element of the *Volk*. He was critical of modern industrial society which had destroyed traditional values. The Nazi regime stressed that the future Germany, 'can only be a peasant state' and Hitler talked in *Mein Kampf* of establishing a *völkisch* state south of the Ukraine, 'The Crimea especially we will resettle exclusively with Germans. It will cause us no trouble to push the existing population to some other place. The German settler will be the military farmer.' Within such a peasant state a new social order would emerge consisting of four classes: a National Socialist aristocracy (named a *Herren* class) hardened by battle; a hierarchy of Party members who would form the new middle class; the great mass of the anonymous with no power who would accept the leadership of the Führer; and, a class of subject alien races which would represent a modern slave class. Existing divisions caused by class, occupation, religion or region were to be overcome by the stronger ties of blood and race. Achievement of this unity of interest and commitment implied a social revolution, for membership of the national community would become more important than belonging to a particular sector of society. Hitler's vision of a classless society featured prominently in Nazi propaganda which aimed to create the illusion of a 'brave new world', a utopia. Various images were adopted to mould public opinion to abandon the class divisions and conflicts of previous years and achieve a change in attitudes. Slogans proclaimed that *Arbeit adelt* ('work ennobles') and *Arbeit macht frei* ('labour liberates'). Idealised images of the worker and the peasant featured prominently in propaganda while Hitler was referred to as 'the first worker of the nation'. May Day was turned into a 'National Day of Labour'. Social conformity was symbolised by a new series of public rituals, parades and speeches which the *Volksgenossen* (national comrades) were expected to attend and show their enthusiasm for by hanging out flags. Positive images of a national community at work would be provided through an extended system of public welfare available to all who qualified for membership. (We will be looking at the social policies of the regime in Chapter 10.)

Hitler's concept of a 'people's community', a *Volksgemeinschaft*, has been dismissed by some historians as, 'nothing more than a rag-bag of anti-urbanism, blood and soil racism and pseudo-socialism'. There is some truth to this charge. Although Nazi support for the peasantry has been described as one of the few consistent principles of Nazi life, it failed because of the contradictions in Hitler's goals.

His plans to recover lost German lands and people required rearmament and this conflicted with the preservation of a pre-industrial, peasant class. Before their seizure of power the Nazis had made much in their propaganda campaigns of reversing the trend towards urban living to one of creating a new nobility of the peasantry through a policy of *Blut und Boden* (blood and soil). For their part the farming community had been attracted to the Nazi cause by the promise of economic aid and by the apparent sympathy of National Socialism for its role in society. However, there were serious inconsistencies in his claims, for Hitler failed to stop the growing urbanisation and industrialisation of Germany. Schemes of rural resettlement did not fit in with Hitler's determination to reverse the Treaty of Versailles while his expansionist plans required rearmament which in its turn was dependent on indus-

> **KEY ISSUE**
>
> *Criticisms of Hitler's belief in a people's community.*

trialisation and urbanisation. His aims were also incompatible with the trend of a rural drift to the towns. Furthermore, as a political realist, Hitler recognised that he needed to maintain the support of the elites, whose landowning interests were threatened by Nazi support of the peasantry as the backbone of society.

Hitler's *Volksgemeinschaft* ideology was drawn from various roots: from nineteenth-century intellectual thought associated with the writings of Johann Fichte who was concerned with expansion to include all Germans outside her frontiers, and from the *völkisch* philosophy of late-eighteenth-century Romanticism. During his Munich years in the early 1920s, Hitler had also been deeply impressed by the *Thule Gesellschaft*, one of about 75 *völkisch* groups under Weimar, which was founded during the First World War. Taking its name from the Nordic legendary homeland of the ancient German race that had come down from the north, the Thule society was committed to extreme nationalism, race mysticism, occultism and anti-Semitism. Many Thulists joined the German Workers Party and eventually the Nazi Party, including Rudolf Hess and Alfred Rosenberg. They supported the Pan-German dream of a new, powerful German Reich, used the swastika symbol and had the motto *Gedenke, dass Du ein Deutscher bist. Halte dein Blut rein!* (Remember that you are a German. Keep your blood pure!) In *Mein Kampf* Hitler wrote 'the basic ideas of the National Socialist movement are *völkisch* and the *völkisch* ideas are National Socialist'. Despite these roots, he dissociated his movement from the typical *völkisch* clubs.

Hitler remained consistent to his *Volksgemeinschaft* ideology (see Chapter 10). By the end of 1938, he had succeeded in incorporating people of the same blood into the same Reich or *Volk* with his annexation of Austria and Czechoslovakia. Once war broke out in 1939, the successes of the German army in the east, were followed by the appointment of Himmler as Reich Commissar for the Consolidation of German Nationhood. He set about achieving racial purity through an organised policy of mass extermination. Those considered to be 'racial degenerates', such as Poles, Russians and Czechs, as well as Jews, were killed, either through mass gassings or executions, or as a consequence of overwork or medical experiments. In 1941 Alfred Rosenberg was appointed Reich Minister for the Eastern Occupied Territories. In this post he promoted the Germanisation of Eastern peoples under brutal conditions, supervised camp labour, rounded up quotas of workers sending them to work in Germany and arranged for the extermination of the Jews.

> ## KEY ISSUE
>
> *Hitler's views: the debt to his predecessors.*

B *Racial superiority of the Aryans*

It follows from what has been said about Hitler's *Volksgemeinschaft* vision that racial doctrine played an important part in the history of the Third Reich. Here, as in so many other aspects of his philosophy, Hitler drew upon the ideas of nineteenth-century thinkers such as Arthur Gobineau and, particularly, Houston Stewart Chamberlain, though he did not acknowledge this. Not content with proclaiming the superiority of the white over the coloured races, these philosophers identified a hierarchy within the white race itself. They developed the myth of Aryan superiority which became identified with the Nordic peoples of Scandinavia. Gobineau claimed that true civilisation had existed in Europe only where the Aryans were dominant because they were superior in intellect and energy. Chamberlain developed two themes in his *The Foundations of the Nineteenth Century*: that the Teutons (Germans) were the creators and bearers of civilisation, while the Jews were a negative racial force and a disruptive, degenerating influence in history. Chamberlain idealised the pure-blooded Teuton, claiming that they were totally responsible for world progress. He described them as men with golden hair, tall, well-built with a high and long forehead, blue eyes, fair skin and an ever-active brain. In contrast, he warned that the Jews, who had obtained a disproportionately important place in German life in the nineteenth century, should be viewed as a social and political danger. Chamberlain's views were adopted by Hitler's hero, Richard Wagner, who claimed that the Germans, by reason of greater racial purity, surpassed other peoples in the greatness of their leaders.

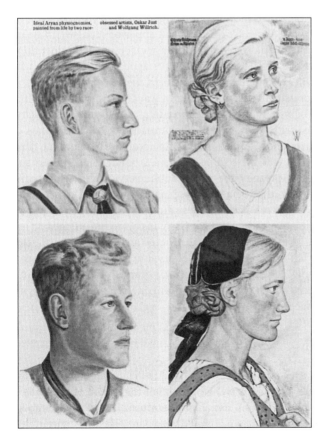

PICTURE 34

Examples of 'ideal Aryan features' painted by Oskar Just and Wolfgang Willrich, two race-obsessed artists

Wagner feared that the Jews were a disintegrating force amongst the Germans. These racist views became popular in Germany where they were identified with nationalism.

Hitler's obsessive racial beliefs and prejudices were developed in his chapter 'People and Race' in *Mein Kampf.* He identified three racial groups: the creators of culture who were Aryan; the bearers of culture, by whom he meant those people who were not capable of creating culture themselves but could copy the example of the superior race and inferior peoples; and, the Jews, whom he saw as the destroyers of culture. History, he wrote, had proved with terrible accuracy how each time Aryan blood became mixed with that of inferior peoples, the result was the end of the 'culture-sustaining race'. In *Mein Kampf* he warned that:

> Blood mixture and the resultant drop in the racial level is the sole cause of the dying out of old cultures; for men do not perish as a result of lost wars, but by the loss of that force of resistance which is contained only in pure blood.

Germans should not be allowed to mix with other races so that the main task of the State was to preserve the ancient racial elements to ensure its survival. But he was equally concerned to preserve the perfection of the Aryan race by removing all those who were weak or handicapped. The Aryan Nordic German superior race, whom he called the *Herrenvolk,* would be involved in a racial struggle against the parasitic Jew. Hitler's racial views might have appeared confused but they were consistent. His attempts to transform the German nation into a super race expressed itself in a number of ways. There was Himmler's *Lebensborn* programme of selective breeding and seizure of 'racially acceptable' children from occupied countries of Poland, France, Norway, Yugoslavia and Czechoslovakia for adoption by German families. Set against this was the regime's eugenics policy. Since Aryan superiority rested in a capacity for work, public service and self-sacrifice, those who, by virtue of being homosexual or physically or mentally handicapped, could not perform these duties were to be sterilised or compulsorily put to death. Healthy Germans were encouraged to engage in physical training and were instructed in heredity, racial science and family. Hitler's racialism was legalised in the 1935 Nuremberg Laws on citizenship and race. Citizenship was granted to 'all subjects of German or kindred blood' but denied to anyone classified as belonging to the Jewish race and gypsies.

C *Anti-Semitism*

For Hitler, the Jew was the opposite of the Aryan. Hitler's hatred of the Jewish race was not new. Anti-Semitism, which had been prevalent throughout Europe since the Middle Ages, became concentrated in the later nineteenth century in Hungary and Russia which had large Jewish minorities. Hostility was not based solely on religion, but also stemmed from Jews' economic wealth and power. Hitler's hatred probably dated from his years in Vienna where Jews were more numerous than in Germany and were more conspicuous as a result of their dress and loyalty to tradition. He regarded the Jews as lacking a homeland and incapable of sacrificing for a greater communal good. They were described as parasites who, through international finance and communism, corrupted nations and were responsible for all the ills which had plagued Germany since its defeat in 1917. They were blamed for the ills of modern life, they were corrupters of moral values, and they were responsible for Germany's defeat in the First World War, for the revolution of 1918 which swept away the Kaiser and for the introduction of the ill-fated Weimar government. Hitler saw a vast Jewish conspiracy to corrupt the Aryan race. He was not alone in his radical vision of wanting to get rid of them but in the early days of the regime he was restrained from putting his theories into practice as a result of the opposition of the elites, fear of unfavourable foreign opinion, the requirements of economic recovery and the indifference of the people to any suggestion of persecution. This explains why anti-Semitism did not feature prominently in pre-1933 election propaganda and why Goebbels said that the Jewish question was not to be mentioned in Hitler's speeches. The latter only spoke in the broadest terms and distanced himself from the frenzied anti-Semitism of Julius Streicher's *Der Stürmer*. Despite this apparent inconsistency, there was no change in Hitler's anti-Semitism. There was always a general aim to get rid of the Jews, though how this could be achieved changed over time. The regime moved cautiously and slowly against them. Policies were largely dictated by circumstances and evolved from depriving Jews of their civil liberties and economic livelihood to increased persecution and violence, symbolised by the **pogrom** of 1938, and reached a climax in their forced removal to the death camps of the east from 1942 onwards.

pogrom organised destruction and massacre

D *Conquest of 'living space', (Lebensraum) in the east and hostility to Russia*

Hitler's pan-German plans were not sufficient to satisfy him. In *Mein Kampf*, he considered the problems which had faced the Kaiser's government in 1914: an increase in population resulting in increased pressure on land and available resources which meant that Germany was a *Volk ohne Raum* (a people without space). These problems could be solved by policies of birth control. Hitler rejected such control not only because it weakened the race, but also because he was concerned with Germany's small size compared with the other European powers. He believed that Germany was not a world power. The Kaiser had tried to solve the problem by increasing exports, but this had proved inadequate and had brought Germany into conflict with England. Hitler wanted to encourage Germany's population growth, but that would

KEY ISSUE

The role of territorial expansion in Hitler's ideology.

lead to overcrowding and a risk of moral and political decay. He believed that the solution lay in *Lebensraum*, the acquisition of living space at the expense of others. One possible answer was to take possession of colonies but these could not be easily defended and could be cut off by naval action as had happened between 1914 and 1918. Furthermore, any attempt to seize colonies would arouse the hostility of Britain. Hitler decided that the solution lay in an acquisition of territory for settlement in eastern Europe and Russia which had a good supply of food and raw materials. As Hitler expressed in *Mein Kampf*:

> Germany has an annual increase in population of nearly nine hundred thousand souls. The difficulty of feeding this army of new citizens must grow greater from year to year and ultimately end in catastrophe, unless ways and means are found to forestall the danger of starvation and misery in time... The acquisition of new soil for the settlement of the excess population possesses an infinite number of advantages, particularly if we turn from the present to the future...it must be said that such a territorial policy cannot be fulfilled in the Cameroons, but almost exclusively in Europe...
>
> The foreign policy of the folkish state must safeguard the existence on this planet of the race embodied in the State, by creating a healthy, viable natural relation between the nation's population and growth on the one hand and the quantity and quality of its soil on the other hand. As a healthy relation we may regard only that condition which assures the sustenance of people on its own soil... Only an adequately large space on this earth assures a nation of freedom of existence...in addition to its importance as a direct source of a people's food, another significance, that is, a military and political one, must be attributed to the area of a state... Hence, the German nation can defend its future only as a world power.

Q

What were Hitler's main arguments to defend his policy of expansionism?

This policy ran the risk of war which was welcomed by Hitler for a number of reasons.

● War fitted in with his social Darwinist view which saw struggle and war between peoples as a natural part of history. Here he was influenced by such nineteenth-century philosophers as Georg Hegel, Heinrich von Treitschke and Friedrich Nietzsche, who were obsessed with violence and glorified war since it was 'both justifiable and moral' whereas 'perpetual peace was impossible'.

● War against Russia was seen as a crusade against Marxism and communism. This had the support of the elites and the middle class who had seen Hitler in 1933 as the best alternative to a Marxist government.

● War against Russia would be a war of the superior Aryans against inferior Slavs whom Hitler intended to be the slave class in his New Order. It would also be a blow against an international Jewish conspiracy which was to be found in international Marxism and finance.

MAP 7
Germany's territorial ambitions and acquisitions

Hitler saw the relationship with Russia as 'the most decisive point in determining Germany's foreign policy'. If he was to achieve his German Reich stretching from the North Sea to the Urals he would have to safeguard its rear. This meant that peace had to be made with France. Hitler always believed that 'France is and will remain the implacable enemy of Germany' and was becoming a 'threatening menace to the existence of the white race in Europe'. To safeguard its security, an alliance should be made with Britain, even though this would require Germany to surrender its colonial and naval ambitions. Conquest of land in the east and Russia would be followed by a policy of *Germanisation* whereby the native population would be replaced by German farmers. Hitler's racialism and anti-Semitism were combined in his plans to protect the Aryan race/German people through territorial expansion at the expense of weaker and inferior peoples. Hitler had been influenced by a contemporary academic, Professor Karl Haushofer, (one of whose students had been Rudolf Hess), who popularised the **geopolitics** current amongst a group of academics at Munich University.

As with so many other aspects of his beliefs, Hitler's hostility to Russia and expansionist plans at its expense did not appear to be consistent. Very little reference was made to *Lebensraum* between 1930 and 1933 probably because he was more concerned with attacking the Weimar republic for its failure to deal with unemployment and revise the terms of the Treaty of Versailles. No mention was made of Russia in

geopolitics a social science drawing on geography, politics, strategy and related disciplines. Concepts such as *Lebensraum* could be said to be geopolitical in nature

his meeting with his chiefs-of-staff in November 1937 when he outlined his plans for territorial expansion at Austrian and Czechoslovakian expense. The non-aggression pact which the regime signed with Russia in 1939 appeared to be a further contradiction. But there was no change in his long-term strategy as his invasion of Russia in 1941 indicated. At the end of 1944, and in the spring of 1945, Hitler was still fixed on his world philosophy of defeat of Russia, conquest of territory and elimination of the Jews. These ideas never left him as shown in his last will and political testament where he refers to his consistent personal philosophy. Hitler adapted to circumstances so that while remaining consistent in aim, he was opportunist in tactic.

It is curious that foreign statesmen did not read *Mein Kampf* more closely, though there was, to some extent, a feeling that circumstances had changed. Hitler, as head of the German state, would not do what Hitler, the agitator, had written in the early days of the Nazi revolution, even though in the second part of *Mein Kampf* he clearly advocated the future conquest of territory at the expense of Russia. This apparent blindness was not shared by all. One academic, Stephen Roberts from Sydney University who was visiting Berlin in 1936, warned of the direction in which Germany was moving (quoted in *The House that Hitler Built*):

> there is hardly a boy in Germany who does not view the preparation for ultimate war as the most important aspect of Hitler's life... Hitlerism cannot achieve its aims without war; its ideology is that of war... Hitler has worked up Germany to such a state that the people are ready to accept war at any moment.

HISTORIANS' DEBATE

Did Hitler plan the Second World War?

Linked with the debate on how consistent and clear was Hitler's aim to establish a vast empire based on a 'pure' German race, is the secondary question as to whether he really planned for Germany to fight another war. The classic statement of the causes of the Second World War was made as early as 1940 by Michael Foot and Michael Howard in *Guilty Men* and it presented what became the 'popular stereotype of a wicked Hitler plotting a war of conquest, opposed at the eleventh hour by the timorous democracies who had whetted his appetite by shameful surrenders' (A.P. Adamthwaite, *The Makings of the Second World War*, Allen & Unwin, 1977).

This interpretation persisted as late as 1963 with *The Appeasers* by M. Gilbert and R. Gott, because it seemed to fit the facts. It was felt that a war which was fought on such an enormous scale and with such destruction had to be deliberately planned by a man whose ultimate aim, according to Hermann Rauschning was 'power and dominion'. It was not until 1961 that an attempt was made to revise this view with the publication of A.J.P. Taylor's *The Origins of the Second World War* (Hamish Hamilton), which challenged the accepted view of the great majority of historians that Hitler intended war. Taylor dismissed the possibility that Hitler was a system-maker, 'deliberately preparing. . .a great war which would destroy existing civilisation and make him master of the world'. He argued that Hitler's foreign policy was 'that of his predecessors, of the professional diplomats at the Foreign Ministry and virtually all Germans'. It was aimed at making Germany the 'greatest power in Europe from her natural weight'. Taylor's interpretation provoked a fierce and bitter debate which to many of his critics seemed to confirm what they thought – his book was an academic exercise to show that using the same evidence one could reach a radically different conclusion from previously accepted versions.

His most radical critics have been among the German historians of the 'Programme School' led by Andreas Hillgruber, *Hitlers Strategie, Politik und Kriegsführung, 1940–1941* (Bernard & Graefe, 1965) and K. Hildebrand, *The Foreign Policy of the Third Reich*, (Batsford, 1973), who argue that Hitler's foreign policy was devised in the 1920s and 'remained remarkably consistent. . .in spite of his flexible approach to details'. The Programme thesis depends primarily on a close reading of Hitler's *Mein Kampf* and *Zweites Buch* (Secret Book) and whether Hitler revealed his true intentions in these works. Over the years opinions have been sharply divided. Trevor-Roper in his 1953 introduction to *Hitler's Table Talk* wrote that *Mein Kampf* was 'a complete blueprint of his intended achievements and in no significant point different from its ultimate actual form'. However, only in a very general sense is that true since it contained no detailed timetable for aggression, nor could there be such a one since the history of the 1930s shows quite clearly that Hitler could not ignore the interaction between his plans and events. Alan Milward writes that 'the military strategy of Germany, her economic organisation and her pre-war diplomacy are all of a piece, they went together' and they were all influenced by the ideology of National Socialism. Even in *Mein Kampf* Hitler revealed his complete cynicism about detailed programmes which he saw as a means to an end of power and expendable once the end was achieved. It is the evidence of such a sense of opportunism that led A.J.P. Taylor to conclude that Hitler was an empty-headed power seeker and opportunist whose commentaries in *Mein Kampf* and the *Zweites Buch* had little influence on his subsequent conduct. In making this claim Taylor took no account of Hitler's will-power and single-mindedness of purposes in his pursuit of Germany's destiny. Hitler was a skilful manipulator of men and situations and even historians of the Programme School such as Hillgruber warn that it is unwise to accept what Hitler said on any occasion as a precise indication of his immediate intentions.

In the absence of documents other than the two discussed, *Mein Kampf* and *Zweites Buch*, historians have fallen back on the few records which exist of his confidential addresses in the 1930s to members of his entourage, high-ranking party officials and army

Nazi policies against Jews, see Chapter 10

Hitler's territorial expansion, see page 407
The non-aggression pact, see page 397

commanders. These reveal a surprising consistency in respect of the objectives of Nazi foreign policy. The ultimate basis of Hitler's whole policy was always eastward expansion. It united the supporters of National Socialism and exemplified the imperialist content of Nazi foreign policy. The views of Taylor and the supporters of the Programme thesis have provoked considerable criticism. Taylor's contribution to the debate was that he forced many historians to revise their views on the causes of the Second World War. Nevertheless, he has been criticised, by T.W. Mason amongst others, that he underestimated the revolutionary content of National Socialist ideas.

The apparent contradiction between Hitler's long-term goals and short-term tactics has been reconciled to some extent by more recent commentators. It is now recognised that he was neither the crazy fanatic of the traditional view nor Taylor's cynical opportunist; he was each in turn. He did not show consistent planning, but he had a vision of what he wanted to achieve. Central to this ideological vision was purifying the German nation and conquering living space, but he did not know how to achieve this. Hitler did not have a timetable or blueprint for aggression. In that respect, his foreign policy, 'combined consistency of aim with complete opportunism in method and tactics'.

E Power of the State and the Führer principle

In *Mein Kampf* Hitler condemned democracy as foolish and made it clear that the coming Third Reich would replace irresponsible parliamentarianism by the absolute responsibility of a leader and an elite of assistant leaders. In this respect he shared the strong anti-parliamentary and anti-democratic sentiments of many of his contemporaries who regarded Weimar democracy as un-German and divorced from Germany's imperial past. It had been imposed as part of the hated peace settlement and was equated with war guilt, reparations and humiliation. He attacked it for its weakness and failure to protect the people against the 1923 and 1929 economic crises. He wrote in *Mein Kampf*:

Q

What were Hitler's main criticisms of parliamentary democracy?

Mustn't our principle of parliamentary majorities lead to the demolition of the idea of leadership? Does anyone believe that the progress of this world springs from the minds of majorities and not from the brains of individuals? By rejecting the authority of the individual and replacing it by the numbers of some momentary mob, the parliamentary principle of majority rule sins against the basic aristocratic principle of Nature, though it must be said that this view is not necessarily embodied in the present-day decadence of our upper ten thousand...

This invention of democracy is most intimately related to a quality

> which in recent times has grown to be a real disgrace, to wit, the cowardice of a great part of our so-called 'leadership'. What luck to be able to hide behind the skirts of a so-called majority in all decisions of any real importance!

Although National Socialism was supposed to be a mass movement, Hitler had little trust in the masses. He attacked democracy's reliance on elections, negotiation, and compromise and in its place advocated command, discipline and obedience to an all powerful leader. He believed that democracy encouraged division, not unity, and would not be sufficiently strong to defeat communism. Drawing upon the ideas of Hegel and Treitschke he believed that the State should be supreme and that individuals should sacrifice themselves in its service.

A strong leader was necessary who would express the will of the people and unite them in a national community. In *völkisch* thought this was symbolised by the Führer. He was a mystical figure who personified the nation's destiny. What this meant in practice was that decisions were made without discussion or reference to the people. The two nineteenth-century roots to this concept of leadership were Friedrich Nietzsche's elite of ruthless leaders under a superman and views current in conservative right-wing groups in Kaiser Wilhelm's day. The Nazis interpreted the *Führerprinzip* to mean a man of destiny – determined, forceful and radical – who would destroy the old privileged and class-ridden society and replace it with an ethnically 'pure' and socially unified national community. This cult of the leader was central to understanding the appeal of National Socialism and Hitler. As early as July 1921 he had insisted that the *Führerprinzip* (Führer principle) should be the law of the Nazi Party. The principle was applied to all National Socialist organisations so that there were many Führers of different grades who formed the new elite and who were independent of the will of mass followers. As we have already noted, the image of Hitler as saviour and redeemer of the people was one of the factors which led people, after 1930, to desert the weak Weimar parties and support National Socialism. The elites chose him because they wanted a return to an authoritarian, conservative nationalist government. They believed they could 'tame' Hitler so that they remained the effective rulers of Germany. They were to be proved wrong in making this assumption, but they retained their privileged economic and social position in society. Though in theory the Weimar Constitution was never rejected, Hitler quickly implemented the legal basis of his position as Führer and sole representative of the nation's will. Nazi propaganda presented him as a *Volkskaiser* who demanded unconditional loyalty and obedience in order to achieve the *Volksgemeinschaft*. His acceptance by the masses persuaded the non-Nazi elites to accept his authority in the crucial period between 1933 and 1937, when he was securing his dictatorship against all challenges within the country and the Party. Ernst Huber, the Nazi political theorist, defined Hitler's position as Führer as 'free, independent, exclusive and unlimited'.

Hitler's legal position as Führer, see pages 140–2

F *A Philosophy of life*

Weltanschauung (world view) was the word used to describe National Socialists' philosophy of life. The drive behind Hitler's personal world view consisted of a belief in history as racial struggle, fanatical anti-Semitism and a belief that Germany's future could be secured only through the conquest of *Lebensraum* (living space) at the expense of Russia. Though his ideology was deeply rooted in Germany's past, the intensity with which he pursued his goals made it revolutionary. He did not regard liberalism as the enemy for it had become discredited under the failure of Weimar democracy, whereas Marxism was a rival *Weltanschauung* able to exert a powerful attraction over the masses. It represented mass democracy and equality which was in opposition to Hitler's beliefs in the value of an authoritarian state and the aristocratic rule of an elite: its belief in equality between peoples challenged Nazi racial inequality and the domination of the strong, its class solidarity opposed Hitler's call for national unity founded on the *Volk*, whilst its internationalism countered his nationalism. There could be no compromise with Marxism, rather Germany would be involved in a fight to the death to destroy the Marxism and the 'Jewish Bolshevism' of the Soviet Union.

It is possible to identify a number of roots for Hitler's *Weltanschauung*. His obsession with violence, struggle and war can be traced back to the writings of Treitschke, who saw war as both justifiable and moral, and to a misapplied social Darwinism. The latter ideology provided the basis for Hitler's policy of genocide. He interpreted social Darwinism to mean that nature is governed by selection, victory goes to the strong and the weak must be eliminated. War and struggle were at the heart of man's existence. The term 'struggle' was used frequently by Hitler in speeches and writings from 1922 onwards and to describe the Nazis coming to power in 1933. It was at the core of his philosophy, for according to him, 'man has become great through struggle' and 'the first fundamental of any rational *Weltanschauung* is the fact that ... force alone is decisive'. He regarded struggle as the basis of all achievement, for 'only through struggle has man raised himself above the animal world' (Hitler's speeches at Kulmbach on 5 February 1928 and at Chemnitz on 2 April 1928). Along with the concept of struggle, he believed that there were two other main principles which controlled the vitality of every nation; these were purity of blood and the creativity of the individual (Hitler's speech at Chemnitz 2 April 1928). These three principles provided the basis to Hitler's hostility to international communism, democracy and the rights of the individual and a peace policy (Hitler's speech on 22 November 1926 at Essen). Three months after becoming Chancellor, he warned the people that they '... must understand that its future lies only in its own capacity, its own industry and its own courage. The world gives no help, a people must help itself ...' (Hitler's speech at Königsberg 4 March 1933). These various elements in Hitler's *Weltanschauung* were summed up in his address to the party rally at Nuremberg in 1937, when he told his audience: 'The main plank in the National Socialist programme is to abolish the liberalistic concept of the individual and the Marxist concept of humanity and to substitute for them the *Volk* community, rooted in the soil and bound together by the bond of its common blood.'

Hitler's *Weltanschauung*, with its stress on struggle, had a mixed reception:

- It was not well received by the people. They looked for an end to the violence associated with the street fighting of the SA which challenged the rule of law. His euthanasia policy to eliminate the weak and inferior eventually provoked a public reaction which led to its withdrawal in 1941 though it was carried on unofficially during the war years. While Hitler's peaceful unravelling of the Treaty of Versailles was well received, they were also opposed to the prospect of a second world war.
- The German foreign office, the diplomatic corps and the military leaders supported many of the aims Hitler was trying to achieve, but they were disturbed by his willingness to gamble with high risks. Decisions suddenly taken for apparently ideological reasons alarmed them. Their opposition, if it can be called that, to some of Hitler's decisions was, however, progressively undermined by the success of the Dictator's policy and by the popularity among the German people he enjoyed as a result.

Hitler was well aware of this mixed reception but he relied on propaganda to mould the people to accept his *Weltanschauung*. In this he was not completely successful but this did not influence him to abandon his central beliefs.

2 ↪ CONCLUSION

In looking at Hitler's *Weltanschauung* historians have debated whether Hitler was simply mad or whether he had a programme or plan that was systematically set in motion. Despite the noticeable decline in Hitler's physical condition after 1940, and his various phobias and temper tantrums, it is generally agreed that Hitler was not insane in a clinical sense. There has been far more debate over the historical and ideological roots to Hitler's *Weltanschauung*. He was reluctant to commit himself on paper and most of his written documents were the result of verbal communication dating from the early phases of his career. The main exception was his table talk, recorded by Martin Bormann, at the headquarters during the Russian campaign, when he was talking relatively frankly. Nevertheless, those historians, who have studied his ideology have always been struck by the astonishing similarity between views recorded when he was a failed provincial politician in the 1920s, and the course of events as they actually unfolded a decade or more later. Never, it has been claimed, had a major historical figure revealed his intentions so clearly. It became a common criticism of the policy of appeasement that its advocates were blamed for not having taken enough notice of Hitler's *Mein Kampf*. If only they had read it, so the argument went, they would not have fallen so easily for Hitler's declarations of peaceful intent.

A closer analysis of *Mein Kampf* and *Zweites Buch* shows, however, that these writings were very much influenced by the circumstances in which they were produced. *Mein Kampf*, as we have noted, was an unoriginal rehash of ideas current among *völkisch* (racialist) circles. Its more detailed solutions for German policy were heavily influenced by the continued French occupation of the Ruhr in 1925. At that time Britain, and to a lesser extent Italy, were seen, almost universally, by Germans as possible allies in the struggle to get the French out of the Ruhr. Britain and the USA were in fact crucial in securing a French change of policy. An aggressive anti-Bolshevism was popular amongst all radical right-wing groups in Germany at a time when memories of the revolutions and upheavals of the post-war period were still fresh. The idea that Germany might form a great continental block drawing on the resources of Eastern Europe and Russia was widely held during the First World War and to some extent realised in the brief interval in 1918 between the defeat of Russia and Germany's own collapse. *Mein Kampf* is, therefore, more of a clue to Hitler's mentality rather than a detailed blue-print for expansion.

Hossbach Memorandum, see pages 388–90

It is evident from later documents of the regime, such as the Hossbach Memorandum, that Hitler could not even then predict with any accuracy the sequence of events. It is, however, also clear from the Hossbach Memorandum that Hitler's mentality, as regards the role of conquest and domination, had changed little from the days of *Mein Kampf*. He was determined to seize the initiative and embark upon a dangerous course of expansion. In his book *The Origins of the Second World War* A.J.P.Taylor portrays him as a mere opportunist, who was no different than almost any other German nationalist. This theory has been generally rejected. From 1938 the initiative was almost entirely with Hitler and all the other major powers could do little but react to his moves. As these were seemingly more and more successful, Hitler's opportunism was replaced by planned action to achieve his social-Darwinist ideology of conquest and domination. This is the conclusion reached by Professor Ian Kershaw who has written in his book *Profiles in Power: Hitler* (Longman, 1991) that Hitler's ideology should not be seen as a 'programme' consistently followed but rather 'a loose framework for action which only gradually stumbled into the shape of realisable objectives'.

3 ⌒ BIBLIOGRAPHY

The most obvious source to read for an account of Nazi ideology is Hitler's, *Mein Kampf*, translated by Ralph Mannheim (Hutchinson 1969). However, ideology is more than *Mein Kampf*. Other primary sources which could be consulted are Hitler's, *Table Talk, 1941–1944*, ed. Martin Bormann, introduced by Hugh Trevor-Roper (Oxford UP 1988) and Hermann Rauschning's *Hitler Speaks* (Butterworth 1939).

Amongst the secondary sources which include some general analysis of ideology and philosophy are A. Bullock's *The Third Reich* (Weidenfeld & Nicolson 1955), and *Hitler, A Study in Tyranny* (Odhams 1952); D. Geary, *Hitler and Nazism* (Routledge Lancaster Pamphlets 1993); R.G.L. Waite, *Hitler and Nazi Germany* (Holt, Rinehart & Winston 1969) has a chapter by Alan Bullock and another by A.J.P. Taylor; W. Shirer, *The Rise and Fall of the Third Reich* (Secker & Warburg 1960) looks in some detail at the intellectual and historical roots of National Socialism from the perspective that Nazism was deeply rooted in German history. For a more specialised examination of Hitler's ideas look at E. Jäckel, *Hitler's Weltanschauung: A Blueprint for Power* (Middleton, Conn. 1972); G. Stoakes, *Hitler and the Quest for World Dominion* (Berg 1986) examines the ideological origins of Hitler's Foreign Policy, while Norman Rich, *Hitler's War Aims: Ideology, the Nazi State and the Course of Expansion*, 2 vols (Deutsch 1974), concentrates on the relationship between ideology and Hitler's war aims.

4 ⌐ DISCUSSION QUESTIONS

A *This section consists of questions that might be used for discussion and/or testing your understanding of the main themes covered in this chapter.*

1. Did Hitler have consistent ideas?
2. To what extent was Nazi ideology rooted in Germany's past?
3. What were the main features of Nazi ideology at the time that Hitler came to power?
4. Why were different sections of German society attracted by Nazi ideology and philosophy?

5 ⌐ ESSAY QUESTIONS

A *Two-Part Questions.*
1. (a) What were the main features of Nazi ideology?
   (b) Describe the ways in which Nazi ideology conformed to the ideas of Imperial Germany.

B *Essay Questions.*
1. 'Nazi ideology was confused and contradictory'
   How far do you agree with this view?
2. 'Coherent and consistent'
   How far do you agree with this judgement on Nazi ideology and philosophy?

6 ⌒ MAKING NOTES

Read the advice section about making notes on page xx of Preface: How to use this book, and then make your own notes based on the following headings and questions.

1. *Summarise Hitler's six consistent ideas under the following headings:*
- The *Volk*
- Aryanism and racial purity
- Anti-Semitism
- Power of the State, the Führer principle and submission of the individual
- Expansionism/living space
- Social Darwinism

2. *Which aspects of his Nazi ideology did Hitler compromise in order to retain the support of the elites?*

3. *Which aspects of National Socialist ideology appeared 'confused and contradictory'? In your analysis consider the following contradictions, especially between theory and practice:*
- Aryan policy
- Anti-Semitism
- Social ideology
- Social revolution
- Support of the peasant v. economic policy and rearmament

4. *What was the image of the* Volksgemeinschaft *which Hitler sought to cultivate as the basis of his new social order?*

7 ⌒ MULTI SOURCE DOCUMENTARY EXERCISE ON NAZI IDEOLOGY AND PHILOSOPHY

Study the sources below and answer the questions which follow:

During Hitler's struggle for power a large percentage of his followers were young people. Many young Germans had been disappointed by the revolution of 1918 and the events that followed. They believed that a thorough change in economic conditions was necessary, but German democracy, even in its Social-Democratic branch, was essentially conservative. In particular, lower middle-class idealists who regarded Versailles as a national humiliation were prone to dream about a strong Reich...and Hitler seemed to offer this.

Another section of German youth followed Hitler because he promised a social revolution which would at the same time be 'national'. They believed communism was 'Russian', 'cruel', 'un-individual' and 'anti-national'; they wanted a German revolution, a German socialism. Hitler promised a future, jobs, recovery, a new national honour. And to those who supported him actively by fighting in the SA, he offered three marks a day, food, uniforms, and an adventurous life.

SOURCE A *An American view of the positive attractions of Nazism for young German voters reported in the newspaper, 'The Nation' 27 June 1936.*

When the territory of the Reich embraces all the Germans and finds itself unable to ensure them a livelihood, only then can the moral right arise, from the need of the people, to acquire foreign territory. The plough is then the sword; and the tears of war will produce the daily bread for centuries to come.

SOURCE B *Hitler's views on Germany's territorial expansion, recorded in* Mein Kampf, *1925.*

Should the Jew, with the aid of his Marxist creed, triumph over the people of this world, his Crown will be the funeral wreath of mankind, and this planet will once again follow its orbit through ether, without any human life on its surface, as it did millions of years ago.

And so I believe today that my conduct is in accordance with the will of the Almighty creator, in standing guard against the Jew I am defending the handiwork of the Lord.

SOURCE C *Hitler reveals his hostility to the Jews, recorded in* Mein Kampf, *1925.*

SOURCE D *Nazi propaganda poster messages against Jews, March 1933.*

The Jews of the world are trying to destroy Germany.
German people, defend yourselves! Don't buy from the Jews!

Among the events which are fundamentally constant, which remain the same in all ages and only vary with regard to the form of the means employed is war. Nature teaches us at every glance at its doings that it is dominated by the principle of selection, that the strong is victorious and the weak is defeated ... Above all Nature is unfamiliar with the concept of humanity which says that the weak must in all circumstances be preserved and assisted ... What appears cruel to man is self-evidently wise from the point of view of Nature. A nation that cannot maintain itself vanishes and another takes its place ... Nature distributes living beings all over the world and lets them fight for their fodder, their daily bread; the strong keeps or gains his place and the weak loses it or fails to gain it. In other words war is inevitable. The fact that a state, a nation or a people is small does not fill Nature with pity, on the contrary, it will mercilessly do away with whatever is not strong enough and this apparently merciless cruelty in the last resort contains cold common sense.

SOURCE E *Hitler explains his social Darwinist views to German generals at the end of 1944.*

Q

1. What does source A reveal about the reasons for young people voting for the NSDAP?

2. Use your own knowledge to explain the reasons for Hitler's hostility to the Jews.

3. How far does a study of sources B and E support the view that Hitler had changed his views between the time of writing *Mein Kampf in* 1925 and the final year of the regime in 1944?

4. How reliable are sources A and C to an historian studying the nature and appeal of Hitler's ideology?

5. How useful are sources A to D inclusive to an understanding of Nazi ideology and philosophy?

Hitler's Volksgemeinschaft

10

TABLE 31

Date chart of chief events in Hitler's People's Community

1933	February	First restrictions on homosexual rights groups
	March	Racial Hygiene department set up in Interior Ministry
	April	One-day national boycott of Jewish shops and businesses on 1 April; literature by Jehovah's Witnesses banned; Jews and non-Germans barred from civil service
	May	Trade unions abolished; German Workers' Front established
	June	Marriage loan scheme for racially eligible applicants; law to reduce unemployment
	July	Sterilisation Law for Prevention of Hereditarily Diseased Offspring
	September	Work begins on autobahns; Reich Entailed Farm Law
	December	Reich Food Estate set up
1934	January	Law for the Ordering of National Labour weights industrial relations in favour of management against workforce
	September	New Plan to control imports
	October	Winter Relief Scheme; special government department on abortion and homosexuality set up; start of nationwide arrests of homosexuals
1935	April	Ban on Jehovah's Witnesses in civil service followed by nationwide arrests
	June	Law for compulsory labour service
	September	Reich Citizenship Act (Nuremberg Laws) and beginning of discriminatory measures against Jews; Jews not allowed to marry German nationals
1936	June	Women banned from legal profession
	July	First group of gypsies sent to Dachau
	August	Masonic lodges closed
	September	Second Four Year Plan
	December	Hitler Youth becomes a state youth organisation; Spring of Life (*Lebensborn*) organisation set up
1937	March	Mass arrests of 'habitual criminals'
1938	January	Faith and Beauty organisation set up for women 17–21
	April	Employment of Jews in business concerns is terminated
	July	Ban on Jewish doctors
	August	Synagogue in Nuremberg demolished; Jews compelled to take additional forenames Sarah or Israel
	September	Jewish lawyers banned; Jews have to carry identity cards
	October	Jewish passports to be stamped with 'J'

1938	November	*Kristallnacht* (Night of Broken Glass); expulsion of Jewish students from schools and universities; Jews banned from cinemas, theatres and sports facilities
	December	Compulsory closure and sale of all Jewish businesses to Aryans; all gypsies ordered to register with police
1939	August	War-time economy measures begin in Germany; start of euthanasia programme
	September	Curfew introduced for Jews
	October	Himmler appointed Reich Commissar for the Consolidation of German Nationhood; Jews placed in the hands of the SS; Jews expelled from Vienna
	December	Deportation of Jews starts – to German-occupied Poland
1940	February	Clothing coupons for Jews in Germany stopped
	August	'Madagascar Plan' devised (transport of Jews from Western Europe to Madagascar) but dropped owing to British supremacy at sea
1941	March	Employment of Jews for compulsory labour inside Germany
	July	Göring orders Heydrich to prepare for the 'Final Solution' of the Jewish question
	September	All Jews over the age of 6 forced to wear a yellow Star of David; transport of Jews to concentration camps begins; tests on gassing Jews begins at Auschwitz
	October	Jews require special permission to leave their homes or travel by public transport; Himmler bans emigration
	November	Confiscation of possessions of Jews who have left country; first extermination camp established
1942	January	Final details of the Holocaust agreed at Wannsee Conference
	March	Mass killings of Jews from ghettoes in southern Poland; Sauckel becomes Chief of Manpower to oversee slave labour
	April	Jews must display Star of David on their houses
	June	Jews forced to surrender all available clothing; well-known Jews deported to the east
	July	Education of Jewish children forbidden in Jewish schools
	September	Jews, persons in custody, gypsies, Russians and Ukrainians are handed over to Himmler for 'destruction by work'
1943	June	Reich Union of Jews, last Jewish organisation, dissolved
1944	July	Goebbels starts to mobilise remaining resources for total war; compulsory labour service introduced to women up to 50
	September	All able-bodied men between 16 and 60 called up to serve in the *Volkssturm*
	Autumn	Liquidation of Jews suspended in order to use them for the total war effort
1945	January	Last broadcast speech by Hitler
	March	Hitler's 'Nero Order' to destroy all industrial plant to prevent it falling into enemy hands, blocked by Speer
	April 16	Start of Battle for Berlin
	28	Himmler offers to surrender to the Allies

1945	29	Hitler's last will and testament recognises Admiral Dönitz as his successor as head of state; Hitler presses the German people to continue their 'merciless opposition' to 'international Jewry'
	30	Hitler commits suicide in the Berlin bunker
May	1	Radio news tells of Hitler's 'heroic death' and of Goebbels' suicide

1 ↶ THE NATURE OF GERMAN SOCIETY IN 1933

Germany in 1933 was still a socially conservative country where the majority of people continued to live in villages. There had been no dramatic transfer of property and wealth, no major social upheaval following the Kaiser's abdication in 1918 so that conservative and authoritarian attitudes continued to prevail. The economic and social changes of the Weimar years which saw the continuing growth of a modern industrial structure served to emphasise the social and structural contrasts in the economy and society. The peasantry disliked the modern age of trade unions and industry, they became a radicalised force and wanted government to protect their interests. They were joined by small businessmen and inefficient craftsmen (making toys and clocks) who found their demand shrinking and were alienated by democracy. The industrial recession which hit Germany in 1929 was the worst business catastrophe in its history which came on top of the 1924 inflation. By 1932 two in every five of the workforce were unemployed. The number of registered unemployed was five to six million though the actual figure was nearer nine million. This catastrophe affected not only the new economic order but also the peasantry and craftsmen. The outcome was a sense of profound anxiety and disillusion with democracy and many questioned whether Capitalism was doomed. Amongst the intellectual elite influenced by the *völkisch* tradition of the later nineteenth and early twentieth centuries, there was a call for Germany to be reborn. Some commentators have sought to explain Hitler's success against the background of a collective trauma produced by the double stress of political and economic experiences so that in the early 1930s the Reich seemed to be on the point of total collapse. In this situation many chose Hitler because he promised moral renewal, a social harmony and a reborn Germany in which all class rifts and bitter conflicts would be healed. As W. Shirer states in his book, *The Rise and Fall of the Third Reich* (Pan, 1960): he appeared to be 'a truly charismatic leader' whom they were prepared 'to follow blindly, as if Hitler possessed a divine judgement, for the next twelve tempestuous years'.

A *The elites*

The elites, as a group, have already been discussed in Chapter 8. Besides the great *Junker* landowners, the group also included managers, higher civil servants, academic professionals and business men. The elites,

KEY ISSUE

The Nazi regime and the main social groups.

representing 2.78% of the total population, looked for economic policies to protect their interests against peasants and workers, which meant that they looked for wage reductions, a fall in social welfare payments and for a fall in state interference in the economy. Their membership of the Nazi Party in 1930–2 was disproportionate to their total percentage in society.

B *Farmers/Peasants*

In 1933 the farming population, despite a steady decline since 1850, still accounted for 35 per cent of the employed population and were to be found mainly along the North German plain and east of the Elbe. They owned about one-sixth of the total land though the size of their farms varied. At the top of the social ladder in the village were those who were known as the 'horse farmers' owning a lot of land, some 10 to 30 hectares. They were commercial farmers producing for the market, and employing full-time and casual labourers. During the 1920s, the prices for their farm products only rose by 30 per cent, whereas the prices of manufactured goods rose by 57 per cent. In addition, there was no significant growth in agricultural productivity because mechanisation was spreading so slowly. Below the horse farmers were those with one to nine hectares. They were called 'cow farmers' because they used cows, rather than horses, to work the land. Their land holding was too small to support them totally, so they were forced to look for supplementary work. The lowest level in the village were the worker-peasants, called 'goat farmers'. They owned either a 'small strip of land' (about one-tenth to one hectare) or rented an allotment. They grew their own food but otherwise relied solely on employment either as casual farm labour or in industry. They did not identify with their working-class counterparts in the towns but tried to keep their traditional village lifestyle. Very small holdings were found in the cottage-industry areas of Thuringia and the wine growing area of the Rhineland. There were local variations whilst the average income, in 1932, of peasants was 600 to 650 marks a year, whereas the average income of working-class people in towns was around 1,000 to 2,000 marks depending on level of skill for workers. By 1933 the strong community spirit, which expressed itself in membership of societies such as choral societies, book reading and local cooperatives, was already beginning to break down in the face of a growth in socialism amongst some of the worker-peasants. Consequently the recreational clubs split into nationalist and socialist ones. It was this growth of a working-class culture in the village which accounts for the failure of the Nazis to gain an absolute majority in a free local election.

C *The Industrial Workers*

The industrial workers accounted for 46 per cent of the population but they were not a unified social group. They ranged from those who were

Economic activity	Percentage
Agriculture and forestry	24.5
Industry and handicrafts	34.2
Commerce and trade	15.6
Public service and the free professions	7.1
Domestic service	3.3
Self-employed without a profession	15.3

TABLE 32
Distribution of the population by economic activity, based on the census of 16 June 1933

employed in large factories or mines to those in small workshops or self-employed. Workers tended to be craft, not factory workers and thought of themselves as 'masters' or 'apprentices'. Around 30 per cent of the total manufacturing working class were handcraft workers of four to a workshop. As a group they were under-represented in Nazi Party membership between 1930–2.

D *The middle class (the* Mittelstand*)*

By 1933, despite the growth of a modern capitalist system of large industries, Germany, like France, was a country of small businesses and light manufacturing with large numbers of traditional craftsmen, retail shops and cafés. During the 1920s they were not as well placed as the semi-skilled workers because they suffered from competition from cheap American goods. They, like the peasantry and lower middle-class clerical workers, suffered from the widespread poverty arising from the difficulties of the economy of 1920s. The onset of the 1929 depression affected them in a variety of ways. Those who remained in employment found that there was a widespread reduction in the number of hours worked, in some cases by as much as eight hours in a five-day week, so that even those who remained at work found that their wages declined. In the case of some small businesses, income was cut by up to 50 per cent between 1929–32. This represented a catastrophe for middle-class business owners who had nothing on which to fall back. Denied access to public welfare payments which favoured the factory worker, they had no alternative but to rely on soup kitchens.

Apart from the small businessmen, the middle-class group also included those who were employed in providing services such as doctors, lawyers, school teachers and those intellectuals who contributed to the cultural and artistic life of Germany. The latter group included such famous literary names as Bertolt Brecht, Thomas Mann, Jacob Wassermann, Hermann Hesse, Franz Kafka and the artist Max Lieberman as well as the sculptors Ernst Barlach and Käthe Kollwitz. Other famous people of the period were the composer Arnold Schoenberg and the eminent scientist and exponent of the 'Theory of

DIAGRAM 5

Analysis of Nazi Party membership by social grouping, 1930–2

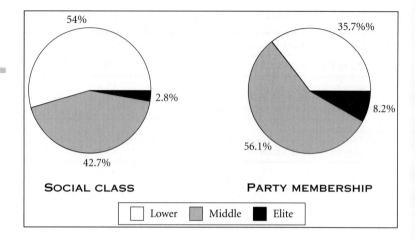

54%

2.8%

42.7%

SOCIAL CLASS

35.7%%

8.2%

56.1%

PARTY MEMBERSHIP

☐ Lower ▨ Middle ■ Elite

Relativity', Albert Einstein. Many of those mentioned were German Jews destined to leave their homeland and seek refuge abroad.

By 1933 those who comprised the middle class had became increasingly disillusioned and politically extreme. They felt that they had been the victims of the economic crises which beset Weimar. They were disenchanted with the democratic parties of the right, the DNVP, the DVP and the DDP, which, they felt, had not preserved their interests. After 1930, they deserted these weak and ineffectual democratic parties in favour of the more aggressive NSDAP which promised salvation with the result that the middle class were over-represented in the NSDAP in terms of their percentage share within society.

2 ⤳ THE ROLE OF 'THE NATIONAL COMMUNITY' IN IDEOLOGY AND PROPAGANDA

A *Ideology*

As discussed in Chapter 9, Hitler's ideology of a new social order, a *Volksgemeinschaft*, implied a classless society where the national comrades (*Volksgenossen*), were expected not only to be submissive and loyal, but also to be active in the various organisations of the regime. Various propaganda images and campaigns were adopted to achieve this sense of national unity and equality irrespective of social class and occupation.

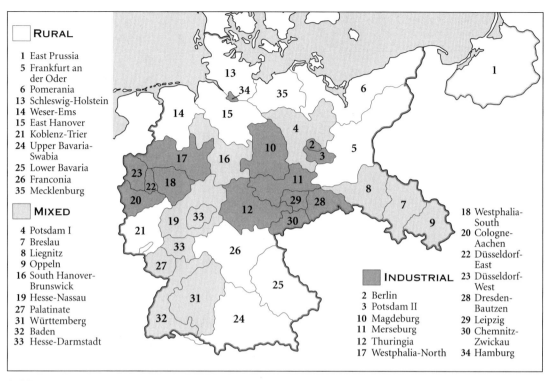

RURAL

  1 East Prussia
  5 Frankfurt an
    der Oder
  6 Pomerania
 13 Schleswig-Holstein
 14 Weser-Ems
 15 East Hanover
 21 Koblenz-Trier
 24 Upper Bavaria-
    Swabia
 25 Lower Bavaria
 26 Franconia
 35 Mecklenburg

MIXED

  4 Potsdam I
  7 Breslau
  8 Liegnitz
  9 Oppeln
 16 South Hanover-
    Brunswick
 19 Hesse-Nassau
 27 Palatinate
 31 Württemberg
 32 Baden
 33 Hesse-Darmstadt

18 Westphalia-
   South
20 Cologne-
   Aachen
22 Düsseldorf-
   East
23 Düsseldorf-
   West
28 Dresden-
   Bautzen
29 Leipzig
30 Chemnitz-
   Zwickau
34 Hamburg

INDUSTRIAL

  2 Berlin
  3 Potsdam II
 10 Magdeburg
 11 Merseburg
 12 Thuringia
 17 Westphalia-North

MAP 8
Economic activity in Germany by electoral district in the 1920s

B *Propaganda*

KEY ISSUE

The role of propaganda.

The community was based on '*ein Volk, ein Reich, ein Führer*', (binding together one nation under one people, one Empire and one Leader). Propaganda was used to cement the national community together and convey the message of a community working together where each member would accept his/her assigned role. Social policy, the basis of the *Volk*, was made attractive to all social groups though, in practice, emphasis was put on the peasant farmer, whom Hitler declared to be 'the most important participant at this historic turning point in our fortunes', the worker, youth and the Jews.

Racial propaganda to promote the ideal Aryan type led to a concentration on the themes of *Volk und Heimat* (people without a homeland) and *Blut und Boden* (blood and soil) which emphasised peasant virtues and the sacredness of the German soil. Artists idealised peasant features and pastoral scenes which showed a rural community in tune with nature. Men ploughed the fields using horses rather than tractors protected by a square-jawed storm trooper in the background. There was a preoccupation with the naked female form to symbolise fruitfulness and fertility. The picture of a peasant family with blond-haired children and the message, 'If you need counsel or aid, turn to your local Party

PICTURES 35–36

Propaganda images of Hitler's Volksgemeinschaft

organisation,' projected the model family. Pictures were issued showing a family sitting around the table listening to the *Volksempfänger* (people's receiver) which was used by Goebbels to promote Germany's cultural heritage.

The loyalty of the working class was sought through a number of propaganda campaigns associated with the activities of the '*Kraft durch Freude*' (Strength through Joy) and '*Schönheit der Arbeit*' (Beauty of Work) organisations, set up by the German Labour Front. Both aimed to convince workers that they were experiencing an improvement in their status and working conditions. Much was made of campaigns with slogans invented to publicise good working practices such as 'Fight against noise', 'Good ventilation in the workplace' and 'Clean people in a clean plant'. The 'Strength through Joy' organisation introduced sporting activities and provided workers with the opportunity to share in luxury pursuits such as sea cruises to Madeira and Scandinavia. Whereas few could afford such luxury holidays, many did take advantage of the cheap package tours in campaigns which promised 'You too can now travel'. Posters urged workers to 'save five marks a week for your own KdF-car' (the *Volkswagen*). Workers responded enthusiastically and paid in millions of marks to the saving scheme though none had received a car by the time war broke out in 1939.

Young people were particularly open to the propaganda directed at them. They responded to the new comradeship of belonging to the Hitler Youth, while messages such as, 'this hand [Hitler's] guides: German youth, follow it in the ranks of the Hitler Youth' and 'Youth serves the Führer. All ten-year-olds join the Hitler Youth', convinced many that they were directly involved in the rebirth of Germany. Slogans like 'Youth must be led by youth' appealed to a longing to be independent and to challenge traditional authority figures, such as parents. For many, however, there was a more practical attraction and that was the promise of work and social advancement which had been denied during the depression years between 1929 and 1933.

People's sense of national unity was encouraged through the branding of Jews as scapegoats for all the ills which had affected society prior to the arrival of Hitler. A Jewish stereotype based on the message, 'The Jews are our misfortune', developed which depicted the Jew as an evil money-grabbing communist. A constant comparison was made with rats and parasites, suggesting that the Jew differed from the Aryan not only in body but also in soul, so that it was necessary to get rid of them. The message was always the same, if the Jews left Germany all would be 'sweetness and light'. Propaganda did not, however, show how this would be achieved.

3 ⌐ SUCCESS OF THE REGIME IN CREATING A 'PURE' *VOLKSGEMEINSCHAFT*

Hitler's drive to achieve a *Volksgemeinschaft* of Aryans of a healthy physical and mental condition proved to be the most consistent, coherent and revolutionary aspect of Nazism. Nazism has been defined as 'national regeneration through racial purification and a racial Empire'. Hermann Rauschning in *Hitler Speaks* (1939) recounted the views of the Minister of Agriculture, Walter Darré.

'The new aristocracy will arise in this way. We shall gather in the best blood only', said Darré, pointing to his iron filing-cabinets. 'Just as we have again produced the old Hanover type of horse from sires and dams who had little of the old purity left, so we shall again, in the course of generations, breed the pure type of the Nordic German by means of recessive crossing. Perhaps we shall not be able to purify the whole German nation again. But the new German aristocracy will be a pure breed in the literal sense of the term.'

Q

Why was the regime so concerned with racial purity?

Hitler wanted to avoid a decline in the quality of the race even if this meant that Germany would have to 'lose the weak so that the final result would be strength'. The regime embarked on a campaign against a variety of groups who were considered to be 'alien to the community' and who were often defined in biological terms. Nazism had grown in the years following defeat and revolution in 1918. In the view of Hitler one of the main causes of Germany's collapse had been the decline of the German people as a result of neglect of the principles of race and eugenics (see page 235). The main goal of the Nazis was to create out of the German people, previously divided by race, religion and ideology, a new and unified 'national community' based on ties of blood and race. They believed that this united national community would then possess the necessary morale to enable Germany to aim for world domination.

KEY ISSUE

*'One nation, one
people, one Empire, one
Leader'.*

The members of this national community, the *Volksgenossen* were
expected to be of Aryan race, genetically healthy, socially efficient and
politically and ideologically loyal to Nazism. On coming to power the
Nazis were determined to discriminate against or persecute all those
who failed to fulfil their racial criteria. In its determination to achieve
racial purity, the regime directed its hostility at all those who were considered to be a threat. The desire to achieve a pure community was at
the heart of Nazi social policy which was speeded up during the Second
World War. Following the success of the German army in conquering
large parts of eastern Europe, Himmler was made Reichskommissar for
racial matters with responsibility for strengthening the German race.
The New Order, which aimed to achieve Hitler's *völkisch* state 'south of
the Ukraine', led to the resettlement and extermination of those races
considered to be 'impure'. In so doing it produced a different society
both in Germany and in its conquered territories, but one based on
social destruction.

A *Treatment of 'asocials'*

Asocials were those defined as the socially inefficient whose behaviour
went against the social standards of the national community. This
group included the workshy, prostitutes, criminals, homosexuals, alco-
holics and juvenile delinquents. The socially inefficient were subjected
to harsh controls. Tramps and beggars, some 300,000 to 500,000, many
of whom were young, homeless unemployed, were rounded up in September 1933 because they were regarded as a threat to public order.
They were organised into a mobile labour force to do compulsory work
in return for their keep. Disorderly persons, many of whom were
tramps, were sent to preventive detention and sterilised. With an
increasing shortage of labour after 1936, the regime sent some 10,000
workshy to concentration camps where experiments were carried out,
often on the young. This policy appeared to be popular with many
Germans and was welcomed by local authorities as a means of getting
rid of problem people. It was only defeat in 1945 that ended plans to
extend this policy of compulsory sterilisation and probable eventual
death through hard labour in concentration camp conditions.

B *The fate of the gypsies as biological outsiders*

Racial outsiders were non-Aryans, such as gypsies and Jews, as well as
the mentally and physically handicapped who were regarded as posing a
threat to the future strength of the German race. Many textbooks have
tended to ignore the plight of Germany's 30,000 gypsy population
under the regime. In contrast to the asocials, gypsies were more harshly
treated because they were regarded as both biological outsiders and asocials. They had a history of persecution and had long been treated as
social outcasts. Their dark Romany looks, dialect and customs, along
with their life as travellers with no regular employment, meant that they
were frowned upon by society. They were branded as thieves and

beggars. During the 1920s the police, first in Bavaria, and then in Prussia, organised special offices to regulate the gypsies, who were photographed and fingerprinted. When the Nazis came to power the gypsies were persecuted both for their distinctive lifestyle and their inferior racial character.

Nazi policy against the gypsies, as in the case of the Jews, was confused and changed over time. They did not attract attention during the early years of the regime because their small number and minor role in the economy meant that they were not seen as such a serious racial threat as the Jews. They were, however, included in the Nuremberg Law for the Protection of German Blood and Honour of 15 September 1935 which banned marriage and sexual relations between Aryan and non-Aryans. From then on they were the subject of intensive research by racial experts of the Research Centre for Racial Hygiene and Biological Population Studies. The aim was to catalogue pure gypsies and part gypsies, with persecution being directed against the latter who came within the terms of the Nuremberg Law's ban on intermarriage. Part gypsies were regarded as asocials to be rounded up into detention camps and made to work as well as being sterilised as part of the policy of ethnic cleansing.

In December 1938 Himmler issued a Decree for the Struggle against the Gypsy Plague which introduced a more organised registration of gypsies based on the research of the racial experts. Colour-coded papers were given to gypsies depending on their racial status, so pure gypsies received brown papers, part gypsies blue and nomadic non-gypsies grey ones. The aim was 'once and for all to ensure the racial separation of gypsies from our own people to prevent the mixing of the two races' and to regulate their living conditions. After the capture of Poland, gypsies were rounded up into labour camps and, starting in May 1940, 2,800 were deported to the east. This programme was then stopped because of the problems of organisation in the ghetto areas. Within the Nazi leadership, Himmler pressed for a different policy to be applied to the pure gypsies. He admired them for their racial purity and wanted to put them into villages to live their traditional life and be 'museum' pieces. His plan was overruled by Hitler and Bormann, and from December 1942 gypsies were sent to Auschwitz. Here families were allowed to live together, but medical experiments were carried out by Dr Mengele. Of the 20,000 transported, 11,000 were murdered, while the others were transferred elsewhere. Within eastern Europe, especially in Russia, thousands more (some estimates put the figure at 500,000) were murdered by the extermination units of the SS. Within Germany only 5,000 of the 30,000 survived the war.

C *The fate of the Jews as biological outsiders*

Hitler's policy against the Jews, who numbered about 500,000 in Germany, also proceeded by stages. Orthodox Jews were an easily identified group and they became a focus of envy because they were seen as being privileged. By 1933 Jews accounted for less than 1 per cent of the

KEY ISSUE

The position of the Jews in German society in 1933.

total population and many had become assimilated into German society. Their influence in cultural life and in aspects of business, commerce and some of the professions was well above their numerical strength, a matter which disturbed anti-Semites. Jews composed, as a percentage of the total employed in 1933, 16 per cent of lawyers, 15 per cent of brokers/commission agents, 10 per cent of doctors, 8 per cent of dentists, and in the media 5 per cent were employed as film and theatre directors and as editors/writers. In fact far more were employed in more low paid/low status jobs, in industry and handicrafts, agriculture and forestry, while 15 per cent of the Jewish community were self-employed without a profession. Only 7 per cent were employed in public service and the professions.

In Weimar Germany any formal discrimination against Jews had ceased. It was a commonly held view in the late 1920s that anti-Semitism was no longer of major importance. When the Nazis made rapid headway among German voters in the late 1920s, anti-Semitism was never absent from their message, but it was not as prominent as it had been when the Party was appealing to a narrower group of voters. The conclusion must be that it was not of crucial importance to an electorate panicked by economic collapse. Even Hitler himself said nothing about Jews when it suited him so that anti-Semitism as a factor in making Nazism into a mass movement was seemingly of minor importance. However, in Hitler's eyes, according to Richard Grünberger (*A Social History of the Third Reich*) the Jews were blamed for all the ills of the Weimar years:

Q

What specific evils did Hitler blame on the Jews?

A few prominent Jews had helped to found the Republic, or had been active in the press, in literature and the theatre – the arenas in which battle had been joined between order and freedom, between outdated and permissive attitudes.... They were blamed for the twenties cult of the new and the sensational that saddled Germany with twice its pre-war cosmetics bill, fostered the smoking habit among women, riveted public attention on six-day bicycle races and puriently reported murder trials. Yet the main charge against the Jews was that they dominated such spheres as banking, business, real estate, brokerage, money lending and cattle trading.

Hitler's hatred of them was the dominant and consistent theme of his political career. Lucy Dawidowicz, in *The War against the Jews 1933–45* (Weidenfeld & Nicolson 1975), argued that anti-Semitism was 'the core of Hitler's system of beliefs and the central motivation of his policies', a view not shared by A.J.P. Taylor who saw it as 'a showy substitute for social change', while R.A. Brady, regarded it as a 'scapegoat for the popularly recognised abuses of capitalism'. The translation of Hitler's racial ideas into practice was to lead to economic boycotts, racial laws, government-inspired violence and pogroms and finally, with the acquisition of millions of Jews in eastern Europe, to the mass shootings and gas chambers associated with the Final Solution from

1941 onwards. German historians give 5.29 to 6 million as the total number of Jews killed. Hitler made use of the anti-Semitic traditions in Germany, though no German could have conceived of the extent to which he would go to achieve racial purity.

THE REGIME'S POLICIES AGAINST THE JEWS 1933–8

The fate of the Jews during the **Holocaust** (we will be returning to this in a later chapter, pages 438–43) was not foreshadowed in the regime's policies prior to 1941. Initially Hitler was aware that he did not have the support of the population whose attitude towards the Jews ranged from indifference to sympathy. However, this was to change as the regime tightened its repressive grip, and people saw that the position of the Jews was hopeless. Then, some reacted out of fear and self-preservation so that increasingly Jews found themselves subjected to persecution and intimidation by ordinary German people who often willingly connived with the regime.

the **Holocaust** the mass murder of Jews under the Nazi regime

In looking at the chronology of Nazi policy against the Jews (see Table 31, page 263) some observations can be made:

Between 1933 and 1935 the Jews, on the whole, experienced a period of relative freedom from persecution as Hitler and the regime directed its efforts to consolidate its position and bring down unemployment. Thus, after the initial burst of hostility against Jewish businesses by the SA which led to the national boycott, the regime confined its anti-Semitic policies to prohibiting Jews from the professions.

This policy changed during the course of 1935, when Hitler was in a stronger position. Although the SA had been brought under control after the purge of Röhm, there was a fresh outburst of anti-Semitism among the rank and file who demanded a 'Jew-free economy'. This Hitler resisted because Jewish firms were still important for economic recovery. He did, however, surrender to the propaganda contained in Julius Streicher's *Der Stürmer*, which demanded restrictions on sexual contact between Jews and non-Jews, when he passed the Nuremberg Laws on 15 September 1935. These laws declared that a citizen of the Reich had to be of German blood, and banned marriage between Jews and German citizens. Jews were deprived of all voting rights besides public office and pension. Hitler met with no resistance from his civil servants who viewed the legalising of anti-Semitism as a defence against further disorder on the streets. Placards displayed 'Jews not Wanted' in resorts, public buildings, cafés, restaurants and businesses.

Despite this increase in hostility, the Jews, up to the end of 1937, succeeded in keeping control of their businesses and could still use most of the amenities open to other Germans.

Signs of a more radical policy appeared in the winter of 1937–8 following the powers given to Göring in the Second Four Year Plan to seize the assets of Jewish businesses 'in the interests of the German economy'. As the German economy moved into rapid expansion, the big industrial concerns, eager to get rid of their Jewish competitors, pressed the regime to proceed with the 'Aryanisation' of the economy. Göring, plenipotentiary for the Four Year Plan reduced the amount of raw materials allocated to Jewish businesses and they ceased to receive public contracts after the spring of 1938. Following the *Anschluss* with Austria in March 1938 (see pages 390–1) Göring ordered Jews to register all property over 5,000 marks in value and they were prohibited from selling without permission. The employment of Jews in business concerns was terminated by the law against 'camouflage of Jewish business undertakings' while Jewish doctors, dentists and lawyers were forbidden to offer their services to Aryans. Names given to Jewish children were specified to include Israel or Sarah. The climax to these increasingly hostile anti-Semitic policies came on 9 November in the event known as *Kristallnacht* (Night of Broken Glass), so named in reference to the huge amount of broken glass caused by the widespread destruction. The assassination of Ernst von Rath, a diplomat at the German embassy in Paris, by a Jew two days earlier had given the regime the opportunity to launch its first state-led persecution of its Jewish community. Jewish shops, homes and synagogues were destroyed, 100 Jews were killed and 20,000 sent to concentration camps, though some Jews were subsequently released after a few months of detention. The flow of Jewish emigrants grew after the events of 1938. *Kristallnacht* shocked the world and led to a trade boycott on German goods, but this did not stop the persecution.

The position of Jews deteriorated more rapidly after 1938 as a number of discriminatory decrees followed. Jewish pupils were expelled from schools, and universities, and Jews barred from cinemas, theatres and sports facilities. In many cities, where the bulk of the Jewish population lived, Jews were banned from entering designated Aryan areas. This law was carried out with great zeal by local fanatics, so that by the time of the outbreak of the Second World War Jews had been isolated within German society.

REASONS FOR INCREASING ANTI-SEMITISM

This increase in the severity of the regime's anti-Semitic policy on the eve of war was not due solely to Hitler's influence, but can also be explained by political developments, which might seem to give weight to the arguments of those who incline to a structuralist interpretation of decision-making (see page 279).

1   During the course of 1937–8, as we have already noted (see page 152), power shifted to the more extreme elements in the Nazi Party as the regime became more aggressive in foreign policy. Hitler's meeting with his Chiefs of Staff on 5 November 1937 (see page 153), at which he announced a new stage in foreign policy, led to a significant change in the balance of power. Those members of the elites whom he had been forced to accept in 1933 were replaced. The Economics Minister, Schacht, who had always been aware of the international repercussions of a policy of Aryanisation, resigned leaving Göring in supreme command of the economy. Göring was determined to create a 'Jew-free' economy as quickly as possible. The resignations of Generals Blomberg and Fritsch were followed by Hitler's assumption of control of the

Wehrmacht, while the Foreign Office came under the control of another Hitler admirer, Ribbentrop, who replaced Neurath. These changes removed those who might have tried to curb an increasing persecution of the Jews. This policy of increasing persecution also helped unify the Nazi leadership which had been divided by *Kristallnacht*. It had been started by Goebbels, who was concerned to heal relations with Hitler who was critical of his affair with a Czech actress. Göring, Himmler and Heydrich, enemies of Goebbels, were kept ignorant of the plan and bitterly complained to Hitler of the adverse effects the event might have on their voluntary emigration policy. Hitler sided with Goebbels but he agreed to Göring's suggestion that the time had come for a properly co-ordinated and centrally directed policy. All finally agreed with an intensified policy of persecution and Göring was put in charge, to the benefit of the large industrialists.

2 As the threat of war grew, Hitler, revealing his distrust and hatred of the Jews, warned the *Reichstag* that the Jewish race in Europe would vanish in the event of a war caused by international financial Jewish interests. About the same time, he told the Czech foreign minister that 'we are going to destroy the Jews. They are not going to get away with what they did on 9 November 1918', when they 'betrayed' Germany by masterminding the German 'Revolution'. These, and other comments in the spring of 1939, are interpreted by 'intentionalist' historians as evidence that the extinction of the Jews was still Hitler's aim in 1939, as it had been in 1919. Against this interpretation it can be argued that just because the Holocaust happened, not every statement by Hitler can be seen as leading up to the gas chambers. He often talked wildly. The Nazis had no clear idea where their anti-Semitism was leading them and Hitler often tended to support the dominant power group at any one time. This explains his support of the emigration policy endorsed by Himmler and the SS, who had favoured such a solution of the German 'Jewish question' since 1934 when it was realised that the activities of the SA damaged Germany's reputation. Emigration was not really successful, only 120,000 of Germany's 503,000 Jews had left by 1937 and many had subsequently returned, lulled into a false sense of security that the worst was over by the regime's cautious policies.

3 The annexation in March 1937 of Austria, which had 190,000 Jews, had alarmed many of the extreme anti-Semites who did not want to see any increase in numbers. From his base in Vienna, Adolf Eichmann of the security service of the SS (the SD), persuaded 45,000 Jews to leave Austria within six months and used the confiscated property of Jews to finance the emigration policy. Göring, who still had overall responsibility for anti-Semitic policies, supported the plan. In January 1939 he gave his approval and recognised Heydrich, chief of the Reich security head office, as responsible for its implementation. During 1939 78,000 Jews were forced out of Germany and 30,000 out of Bohemia and Moravia. It became increasingly difficult to find countries which were prepared to take Jewish refugees so that the SD worked with Zionist organisations to ship Jews illegally to Palestine, a policy which was opposed not only by Britain but also by other Nazi organisations who favoured dispersal of Jews throughout Europe. Hitler watched these power struggles but rarely interfered directly, though when he did it was to support the SS against their rivals.

THE OUTBREAK OF WAR

The outbreak of war in September 1939 opened up a new and more shocking extension in the policy against the Jews. This is associated with the activities of the *Einsatzgruppen*, or Death's Head squads, who followed the German armies into Poland. They murdered thousands of officials, priests and intellectuals, in an attempt to rob the Poles of their ruling class. It was at this stage that the outline of a new 'solution' of the 'Jewish question' began to emerge. Hitler informed close associates of his plans to remodel eastern Europe on racial lines, turning their peoples into slaves serving a master race of German settlers. As a first step, three million Polish Jews were rounded up into ghettos in specified towns in eastern Poland and finally re-settled in a huge reserve south of Lublin. Himmler, as Reich commissioner for the strengthening of Germanism in the east, a crucial appointment, was given special powers which placed the Jews at the mercy of the SS.

Over half a million Jews from Danzig–West Prussia and certain other provinces were deported to German-occupied Poland and came under the administration of Hans Frank. They joined an existing 1,400,000 Jews, placing a great strain on food supplies so that Frank protested to Göring who was still technically in charge. Frank was given the power to refuse to accept further transports so that the deportations ended. Within the occupied territories in Poland Jews were subjected to a curfew, had to wear the yellow star on their clothing and had to do forced labour. Frank's refusal to continue with the resettlement plan could not have been decisive on its own. It is probable that Hitler wanted to focus his attention on the western campaigns. However, during the summer of 1940 a new plan was devised, the 'Madagascar Plan', the existence of which challenges the intentionalist view of an unwavering commitment to Jewish extermination for, had the plan succeeded, four million Jews would have been transported from western Europe to this disease-infested island. Eastern Jews were to be left in Poland as a deterrent to American intervention in the war. Himmler supported the resettlement plan, which had been popular in the 1920s, and some early exploration was made of its feasibility. Hitler approved a draft plan, but it was defeated by British refusal to allow free access by sea.

A NEW DIRECTION 1941–5

After 1941 Nazi policy against the Jews changed when Hitler decided to attack Russia. He warned his staff that the campaign would be fought on racial lines. In June 1941 he signed the Commissar Order for the assassination of all captured Jews in the service of the Communist Party and state. To carry out these instructions four new action squads composed of SS, criminal police and security police moved in behind advancing armies. It would appear that the action squads went beyond their orders and rounded up and killed all Jews, amounting to half a million during the winter of 1941–2 alone. It is at this point in the chronology of Nazi anti-Semitic policies that historians diverge in their interpretations. The arguments of the two opposing schools of historians are summarised below:

HISTORIANS' DEBATE

When did Hitler make the decision to launch the Final Solution?

Structuralists

Historians, such as Martin Broszat and Hans Mommsen, argue that the decision was made only in late autumn of 1941. The 'structuralists', while accepting that Hitler exercised considerable influence on the course of events, do not believe that he was always the initiator of events. They argue that the Holocaust was not planned by Hitler but developed out of a deteriorating situation not expected by the Nazis though probably made inevitable by the increased extremism of their anti-Semitism. On what many might consider rather weak evidence, they argue that the Final Solution was pre-dated by a policy to resettle European Jewry east of the Urals and that failure to defeat Russia wrecked the plan. Even so Hitler in October 1941 ordered the transportation of Jews to the eastern territories to begin and because there was no way over the Urals they collected in the ghettoes of eastern Poland until resources were strained to breaking point and epidemics started to break out. The response of local SS was to begin, on their own initiative, to murder Jews either by gassing or shooting, but there was the problem of getting rid of the bodies. Some time in October or November Himmler was supposed to have informed Hitler of these events and he approved the extension of these practices to include the whole of European Jewry. It is even possible that the initiative was taken, not by Hitler, but by Himmler.

Intentionalists

Historians, such as Eberhard Jäckel and Andreas Hillgruber, argue that Hitler decided on the Final Solution some time in the summer of 1941. They argue that Hitler made his decision in the summer of 1941 in the belief that a Russian collapse was approaching and that the opportunity had arrived to achieve his life-time ambition. It is not known whether he gave a specific order, or merely a 'prompting initiative'. No written order has been found but, as we have already seen, that was typical of Hitler's method of working. A number of factors were present to achieve the change in policy. On the one hand, expansion had brought under Nazi control far more Jews whose condition in Poland was far worse than in Germany. Forced expulsion from the countryside into ghettoes created difficulties of no food or accommodation. Such problems encouraged the decision that led to the Final Solution. On the other hand, 'Operation Barbarossa', launched in 1941 as a plan to conquer Russia, killed tens of thousands of Jews. Hitler decided, under pressure, in December 1941 to deport Jews from Germany to the east. The decision to establish extermination camps on Polish soil stemmed from failure to defeat Russia. Hitler agreed but he left others to implement it.

The timing of the decision, whether it was made in the summer or autumn, is crucial for behind it lies the question of Hitler's role and control over decision-making, particularly regarding the Holocaust. Neither the intentionalist nor structuralist analysis was totally adequate and there has been much research on this question. There is now a general view that the decision was made in the summer of 1941 and that details were worked out by the spring of 1942. The chaos in eastern Poland in the autumn and the local shootings and gassings were not because a resettlement plan, which the structuralists argue existed, had failed. The orders given to the *Einsatzgruppen* in the spring of 1941 represented Hitler's decision to embark on an outright genocide of the Jews.

Hitler wanted extermination rather than resettlement but he expected others to achieve this objective. This explains why his precise role is so unclear. It is known that Göring gave orders to Heydrich on 31 July 1939 to complete the task he had given him in January 'to bring about a complete solution of the Jewish question within the German sphere of influence in Europe' and thus draw up a plan for the Final Solution of the Jewish question. Himmler referred to this order at a meeting of top Party and SS officials, under the leadership of Heydrich, in January 1942 at a Conference at Wannsee, when the final details for that extermination were worked out. The word 'extermination' was not mentioned but the intention was clear, Jews were to be worked to death or gassed. At the start, there was a process of trial and error as the SS worked out the best methods to round up and exterminate the proposed 11 million Jews. During the spring, extermination camps were set up at Auschwitz, Chelmno, Maidanek and Treblinka. For two years the transports moved vast numbers eastward from all parts of Europe, some five to six and a half million. During the autumn of 1944 Himmler ordered the suspension of the execution of Jews and those under arrest were to be used for the total war effort. Himmler hoped to escape from some personal responsibility. The evacuation of prisoners continued as the Allies advanced, but many died from hunger and exhaustion. Finally on 26 January 1945, Auschwitz was liberated by Soviet troops.

KEY ISSUE

Public indifference to the fate of the Jews.

PUBLIC REACTION TO THE REGIME'S ANTI-SEMITIC POLICIES

Public reaction to the persecution of the Jews was chiefly indifference. Between 1933 and 1935 there was sporadic violence linked to attempts to force the Jews out of the economy. However, the regime found it very difficult to convince people of the necessity of the 'boycott movement' and the order to break economic ties with the Jews. The reasons for this reluctance were obvious. Material self-interest was mixed with sympathy for the Jews suffering such violence, along with middle-class dislike of disorder and the methods used by the Nazi Party. Such hostility was particularly strong in the Catholic regions. But eventually the volume of anti-Jewish propaganda had its effect and people came to approve of the aims of the Nazis' anti-Jewish policy. The basic lack of interest of the population in the Jewish Question showed itself in the quiet reactions to the publication of the Nuremberg Laws in September 1935. Many reports did not even mention the laws; others suggest that people viewed the laws as a satisfactory and legal framework which ended the violent, 'wild' anti-Semitism of the summer of 1935, while others took the laws for granted.

Between the publication of the Nuremberg Laws and the summer of 1938 the Jewish Question was not important in influencing the opinion of the majority of people. This is evident in public reaction to the murder of a Nazi official by a young Jew in Switzerland in February 1936. The event aroused very little interest amongst the population as a whole. Goebbels, recognising the lack of anger in 1936, manipulated hostility in November 1938 at the time of *Kristallnacht*. Then Goebbels approved the destruction of all Jewish synagogues and violence against the Jewish communities in retaliation for the murder of Ernst von Rath, a secretary in the German Embassy in Paris, by a young Jew. Extensive evidence of reactions to the November pogrom suggest that the event further alienated popular opinion rather than won it over to support the regime's anti-Jewish measures. Rejection of the pogrom was most evident in the relatively urbanised, more densely settled Catholic south and west, and among the intellectuals and the liberal and conservative bourgeoisie. The reports of the secret police, the SD, state, 'the actions against the Jews in November were very badly received'. Many Germans believed that they had openly to support the Jews. The destruction of the synagogues was declared to be reckless. Many people gave their sympathy to the 'poor repressed Jews'. Despite this, the pogrom had no lasting effect on popular opinion. It was the only occasion in the Third Reich that the Jewish Question, which was at the centre of Nazi ideology, appeared to be foremost in people's minds and at the centre of popular opinion. Within only a few weeks memory of the event had retreated. The regime found it difficult to convert an underlying prejudice against the Jew into an open and active hatred by the majority, yet it was sufficient to ensure that there would be no opposition to the regime's attempts to purify the German race.

During the years of the Second World War, interest in the fate of the Jews declined still further, though there were individual acts of resistance in support of individual families. The deportations continued without attracting open public attention. Most people seemed detached about the fate of the Jews, a fact which can partly be explained by the relative number and concentration of Jews in specific areas, but also the war dominated attention to the exclusion of other considerations. People chose to ignore the stories about the atrocities in the occupied countries; there were rumours about extermination, but the systematic gassing programme in the camps appears, according to Professor Ian Kershaw, to have been largely unknown. The last two years of the war saw even less interest despite an increase in hostile propaganda, perhaps because the Jew had become a 'museum piece'.

Nazi propaganda failed to incite hatred against the Jew, apart from special occasions as in November 1938. Otherwise opinion ranged from those who feared the Jews, to a minority who rejected the Nazi doctrine of racial hatred either out of their sense of Christianity, or of humanity, or just because it was morally wrong. The constant propaganda against the Jews did not succeed in making people hate them but merely showed that there was a widespread lack of interest. However, it was this very fact of widespread indifference which allowed the few to pursue their policy of racial hatred and extermination.

SOME CONCLUDING THOUGHTS ON THE REGIME'S POLICIES TO ACHIEVE A PURE RACE

KEY ISSUE

Sharing the blame.

In conclusion, it is a great mistake to focus attention only on Hitler, but neither can he be left out. Though no written order from Hitler for the killing of the Jews has ever been found that does not prove, as historians such as David Irving have suggested, that there was no such order. Hitler was the 'activator' and 'enabler'. His constant encouragement ensured that the work continued even when Germany's military position had deteriorated and scarce resources could not really be spared to continue with the mass executions. However, the German people cannot escape from blame. In the fierce contest for Hitler's favour people did what they thought Hitler wanted. This gave enormous licence to experiment which was not confined to racial policies. The law was corrupted, as is evident in the case of the sterilisation programme. The start of euthanasia was not found in ordered government, but in Hitler's use of discretionary powers; he was pressed and gave in, using private paper. With the breakdown of an organised system of government, the regime descended into a barbarism. The Nazis also made use of society's prejudices against minorities, such as gypsies and homosexuals. People were intimidated and were too afraid of their own lives to ask questions. The regime's policy of extermination was also made possible by the actions of a criminal minority. Some of the party fanatics, Himmler, Heydrich and Eichmann, genuinely believed in the righteousness of the Final Solution but there were also some real psychopaths and sadists. Many of the SS who ran the camps were ordinary men while the battalions who carried out the Final Solution in Poland were not even SS. This is true of Reserve Police Battalion 101, which was made up of 500 men who were not SS and were too old to be drafted into the army. They were ordinary, middle-aged family men of working and lower-middle class from Hamburg, which was one of the least Nazified cities in Germany. Few were members of the Nazi Party and they had been called up because of the manpower shortage. They had spent only a few weeks in German-occupied Poland, but 80 per cent of them carried out their orders to round up and kill 38,000 Jews while another 42,000 Jews were herded like cattle into trucks for deportation to the gas chambers at Treblinka. The willingness of ordinary Germans to carry out the regime's genocide policies has been put down to wartime brutalisation, to racism, to obedience to orders, but for many it was simply a matter of conforming and not breaking ranks. Many found it easier to shoot than to 'stand up and be counted'. The Nazi regime set a standard which came to be regarded as the moral standard. It was the willingness of many thousands of such helpers amongst ordinary Germans which made the Holocaust possible. In that respect the German people must bear a collective guilt.

D *Treatment of the mentally and physically handicapped as biological outsiders*

The mentally and physically handicapped suffered as well, as a result of the regime's acceptance of the theory of eugenics. Eugenics was a belief that the 'race' could be improved through the encouragement of selective breeding. Such ideas had had wide support in the late nineteenth century, especially amongst the German people and medical profession. Many people accepted the idea of genetic breeding, not just in Germany, but also in the USA and Europe. In 1900 a group of large industrialists, including Krupps, awarded 50,000 marks in prize money for the best essay on the principles of evolution, which was won by a doctor. Such theories became widely accepted during the 1920s and 1930s against a background of:

KEY ISSUE

What were the historical origins of, and the part played by, the Sterilisation Law and euthanasia in Hitler's policies of racial cleansing.

- declining birth rates and the destruction of a generation of healthy members as a result of the First World War;
- economic depression which added to the debate about the feeding of useless mouths;
- fears of the race deteriorating in the next generation, which was increased by progress in medical science – more people with hereditary defects were surviving into reproductive adulthood.

During the 1920s a number of doctors and psychiatrists in Germany began to propose a policy of sterilisation of those with hereditary defects, such as had already been carried out on a limited scale in the USA since 1899. From 1929 onwards the proposal gained increasing support and draft legislation for a sterilisation bill existed from the end of 1932 when the Prussian authorities sought voluntary sterilisation of those with hereditary defects. The only difference with the Nazi Sterilisation Law of 14 July 1933, the pressures for which did not come solely from Hitler, was that the voluntary element was removed. Courts were set up to define hereditary illness but they did not confine their criteria to simple-mindedness. Those suffering from depressive illness, diseases such as Parkinson's, and persistent alcoholism were also included. In these instances sterilisation was a very questionable practice, but it had become fashionable to blame many social ills, alcoholism, poverty, prostitution and crime, on heredity.

Eugenics was seen as a way of getting rid of the dregs of society, including the 'asocials' (see page 272). From 1934 to 1945 between 320,000 and 350,000 were sterilised. The regime claimed that once sterilised an individual would be restored to full status as a 'national comrade' though given the emphasis on fertility this was not true. The regime also embarked on a *Lebensborn* (Fountain of Life) programme, which initially started as institutional care for unmarried mothers of good racial credentials. It subsequently led to 'stud' farms run by the SS and to the 'captives' programme whereby children from occupied territories were seized from their families and sent to German orphanages for adoption by German families. If these children failed to meet the inspection required to establish their 'Aryan' credentials they were sent to labour or concentration camps. Few ever returned to their rightful parents.

Euthanasia was directed against those who had incurable and/or severely crippled handicaps and injuries. The idea had first been aired in 1920 with the publication of a book by Karl Binding and Alfred Hoche, *The Granting of Permission for the Destruction of Worthless Life, its Extent and Form*. Hitler was prepared to accept the measure in principle and after 1933 a propaganda campaign was waged to get rid of those who were a burden on society, but the time was not yet ready. The initiative had to come from the medical profession who pressed for the law which was granted in 1939. The euthanasia programme was preceded in 1938 by a petition from the parents of a severely handicapped baby requesting a mercy killing. It went to the Chancellery of the Führer where Philipp Bouhler seized on the request, Hitler agreed and the child was killed (see pages 177–8). The Chancellery then asked for an extension of the practice and Hitler agreed to the Child Euthanasia Programme of 1938–9. Midwives were required to report cases of babies born with birth defects. These defects were defined in a 'Highly Confidential' circular, issued to the state governments by the Reich Interior Ministry on 18 August 1939 (quoted in Noakes and Pridham, *Nazism 1919–1945, A Documentary Reader, Vol 3*):

> (i) Idiocy and Mongolism (particularly cases which involve blindness and deafness)
> (ii) Microcephaly (an abnormally small skull)
> (iii) Hydrocephalus (abnormally large skull caused by excessive fluid)
> (iv) Deformities of every kind, in particular the absence of limbs, spina bifida
> (v) Paralysis...(including Spastics)

It should be noted that in 1939 people began to question the practice and the Chancellery requested a written authorisation, which was given by Hitler in October 1939. It was not a decree or a law but five lines on Hitler's personal private notepaper, which indicates the extent to which the Nazi State had descended into barbarity. A secret organisation was set up to carry out the programme initially for 3-year-olds, then up to 12- to 16-year-olds, and about 5,000 children were killed either by injection or through malnutrition. The death certificate always reported death from an insignificant disease, such as measles.

In August 1939 Hitler ordered that the euthanasia programme should be extended to adults and another secret organisation was set up. Individuals were given no choice, they were selected and gassed. The criteria for selection ranged from mental illness, such as schizophrenia and epilepsy, to senile illness or feeble-mindedness, or simply not possessing German nationality or related blood. The Catholic Church felt growing unease as news came out; in August 1941 it made a brave condemnation and Hitler gave the order to stop it though it continued secretly in the concentration camps. By the time the programme was abandoned, under the impact of public protest, the Nazis calculated (based on reports from doctors in asylums) that 72,000 had died. However, between 1941 and 1943, another 30,000–50,000 people were sent off to concentration camps and gassed on grounds of mental illness, physical incapacity or simply racial origin, either Jew or gypsy. Those who had acquired expertise in gassing techniques were subsequently sent to Poland to advise the SS who were setting up their death camps between 1941–2 to destroy the other biological outcasts of Nazi Germany, the Jews and gypsies.

4 ⮑ SUCCESS IN CREATING A 'UNITED' *VOLKSGEMEINSCHAFT* BASED ON SOCIAL CONFORMITY

Many Germans, and foreign observers, were impressed by what appeared to be a change in people's attitudes. After 1933 the image of German society conveyed by Nazi propaganda in newsreels and the press was of mass enthusiasm and commitment. The regime introduced a number of policies to strengthen people's belief that they belonged to a new national community. As part of the drive to achieve social conformity, the term *Volksgenossen* (national comrades) was adopted. Everyone was expected to attend the numerous parades and speeches which became a feature of the new public rituals which celebrated important events in the Nazi calendar. Germans were required to show the national community at work and at its heart lay the propaganda image of the family.

A *Cult of the family as the focus of the community – the role of women in Nazi ideology and propaganda*

Women formed a crucial focus for Nazi social policy through their central roles within the community as mothers and wives, and the Nazi belief that men and women had separate roles in life based on their biological function. The position of women in Hitler's Germany was summed up in a speech which Hitler delivered at the Nuremberg party rally on 8 September 1934 (quoted in *The Speeches of Adolf Hitler, April 1922 – August 1939, Vol 1* by N.H. Baynes):

> If one says that man's world is the State, his struggle, his readiness to devote his powers to the service of the community, one might be tempted to say that the world of woman is a smaller world. For her world is her husband, her family, her children, and her house... Providence has entrusted to woman the cares of that world which is peculiarly her own, and only on the basis of this smaller world can the man's world be formed and built up. These two worlds are never in conflict. They are complementary to each other, they belong together as man and woman belong together... Every child that a woman brings into the world is a battle, a battle waged for the existence of her people. Man and woman must therefore mutually value and respect each other when they see that each performs the task which Nature and Providence have ordained. And from this separation of the functions of each there will necessarily result this mutual respect.

Q *In what ways, and with what success, did Hitler change the status and role of women?*

This separate spheres' ideology was based on the theory that a woman's place was in the home looking after her husband and children and was summed up in the propaganda slogan, *'Kinder, Kirche, Küche'* ('Children, Church, Kitchen'). It was extended to include young girls, who were taught the traditional female domestic skills through their membership of *Jungmädel* and the German Girls' League. It had the support of traditional groups, such as the rural population and the Churches. However, it was reactionary because it ran counter to the ideas of female emancipation which had characterised the later nineteenth and early twentieth centuries. By 1933, when Hitler became Chancellor, women had gained the vote and had increased their employment in industry, the professions and commerce, especially in the non-manual and unskilled sectors, though they still did not have equal rights with men. Their liberation was personified in the image of the *Berlinerin* of the Weimar period who was seen as a wild and immoral woman, though it was mainly the middle-class professional women who would be hardest hit by Nazi measures to take them out of the labour market. On coming to power, Hitler sought to control the dress and behaviour of women by discouraging the wearing of cosmetics and trousers, and smoking, and encouraging the wearing of simple peasant-style clothes. This campaign met with a certain success among the German Girls' League, but it roused a counter-reaction amongst the fashion conscious, including Goebbels' wife. Women were excluded from key positions in Nazi politics; there was not a single female Nazi deputy in the *Reichstag* and a party regulation of 1921 excluded women from all senior positions within its structure, apart from their special interest groups.

The regime attempted to make 'motherhood' an attractive financial proposition. It introduced a series of grants and interest-free loans to newly married couples and tax relief schemes, provided the wives withdrew from the labour market. It was also concerned to increase population and this was encouraged in a number of ways:

- Anti-abortion laws were enforced and contraceptive advice and facilities were restricted.
- Family allowances were improved, 10 marks a month were given for the third as well as the fourth child and 20 marks for the fifth.
- Couples who had larger families were given additional rewards such as a child subsidy given to those on limited incomes. It was a lump sum to be spent on furniture and clothing. A quarter of the marriage loan was converted to an outright gift on the birth of each of the first four children.
- Fertile mothers were awarded the Honour Cross on 12 August each year (Hitler's mother's birthday) – bronze for four and more children, silver for more than six and gold for eight.
- Mothers received preferential rations and safer air raid shelters during the Second World War when mother-worship was at its peak and the boast was 'I have donated a child to the Führer'.
- Mothers were given domestic help by means of the compulsory year of labour service that all young people were expected to perform during the war while foreign labour was allocated to agriculture.
- Marriages were arranged between single people and divorce encouraged amongst childless couples to facilitate remarriage and the possibility of children.
- Medical inspections discouraged 'racially inferior stock' along with a programme of compulsory sterilisation.

Statistics on marriage and birth rates suggest that these policies were not successful (Table 33). The statistics show that from a low point in 1933 the birth rate increased, reaching a peak in 1935, but thereafter it slowly declined again. The problem for historians is to decide whether Nazi population policy produced this rise or whether other social, economic and even personal psychological reasons were responsible. In the main historians have argued that the policies, representing Hitler's

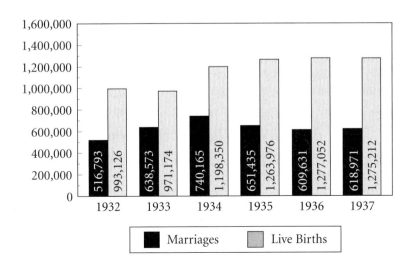

TABLE 33

Numbers of marriages and live births in Germany, 1932–7

Year	Marriages	Live births
1932	516,793	993,126
1933	638,573	971,174
1934	740,165	1,198,350
1935	651,435	1,263,976
1936	609,631	1,277,052
1937	618,971	1,275,212

social engineering on behalf of the people's community, were not responsible for the rise in the birth rate. It was more likely to be the result of the end to the Depression and a younger age of marriage, such as occurred in other countries. Nazi views on women conflicted with the realities of twentieth century trends, which saw the emancipation of women, and were also contrary to Nazi objectives of rearmament.

The Nazi Women's League sought to indoctrinate women to accept their role and it embarked on a wide-ranging programme of voluntary work, though it also pushed for the emancipation of women. Many professional women saw their jobs taken away from them, women were dismissed from the medical and civil service and excluded from the judicial system. They were not allowed to stand as jurors and the number of female students fell at the universities. Hitler's attempts to confine women to the home won some acceptance amongst German women who found that, on balance, economic security and the mother-hood cult more than compensated for sex discrimination. Attempts to exclude them from the workplace was only an issue with academic and professional women.

However, as with other aspects of its ideology, Nazi policy towards women and the family was contradictory and confused and ultimately a failure. Women were not consistently excluded from the workplace. This was certainly the experience of women teachers; the number employed fell at the beginning of the regime, levelled off by 1938, and revived again during the war years. Nor were women ever entirely displaced from the civil service; by 1938 every tenth post was held by a woman and many more were employed in the Party's own civil service, the Nazi Women's League, the National Socialist People's Welfare and the women's section of the German Labour Front. The regime could not stop the growing trend of young adult women employed in the consumer goods industry and the necessity to employ women because of the growing labour shortage (we will be returning to this theme of women in the labour market in Chapter 15). Despite its efforts to encourage marriage, the divorce rate rose steadily, and incidences of juvenile delinquency increased from 16,000 in 1933 to 21,000 in 1940. Family relationships were undermined as a result of quarrels over the treatment of barren wives or cast-off wives, and conflicts increased between generations, especially between mothers and sons over such issues as premarital sex and maternity cases. By 1945, 23 per cent of all young Germans had venereal disease, and prostitution had quadrupled.

B *Policies to benefit the people*

Other aspects of the regime's policies to achieve a *Volksgemeinscahft* based on social conformity were more successful.

● Many people came to feel a sense of pride in Germany's future and accepted Hitler for his strong government. Economic recovery was at the basis of Nazi success, for Hitler recognised that maximum support of the people was essential. This was achieved through a fall in unemployment, a rise in profits, control of inflation and a sound currency. Hitler's economic policies 1933–7 successfully achieved a fall in unemployment from the six million of January 1933 to one million in January 1935. It was a state-led revival based on construction of roads, land drainage and public works which aimed to give the people 'bread and work'. He introduced military conscription in 1935 and an official rearmament in the Four Year Plan of 1936. By 1939 there was a shortage of labour.

- Safeguarded from attack by Hitler's purge of the left wing of his Party in June 1934, the elites continued to prosper and be dominant.
- Industrialists, freed of trade union restrictions, were given vast orders at profitable rates.
- The great landed estates of the Prussian *Junker* were not carved up, while the High Command of the army remained in the hands of the aristocracy. The regime's rearmament programme restored the army, and with it its *Junker* officer corps, to its prestigious pre-war position in society. The humiliating terms of the Treaty of Versailles were reversed and expansion was achieved without war. This provided opportunities for sons and reconciled the landowning nobility to the Nazis. Hitler showed supreme skill in handling the army for the latter was the greatest factor in establishing his regime on a firm basis. Hitler's policies also brought the owners of large estates economic benefits. Selling prices of products were fixed well above costs. They were given state credit on easy terms and relieved of the fear of loss of their land. Land values rose as a result of heavy government spending on the construction of roads, airfields and barracks. In addition the *Wehrmacht* bought its horses from the *Junker*. The regime passed a law fixing mortgage interest rate at 4.5 per cent in June 1933 and gave generous credits for improving silos, drainage and labourers' houses on large estates. The re-employment of millions led to rising market demand which benefited farmers and enabled them to increase their investments. But, despite this increased financial security, the *Junker* were not totally won over. Though on the surface the Nazis displayed a scrupulous regard for titles to land, and resettlement plans were rarely implemented, many *Junker* were aware that increased wealth concealed a decline in their status and that they became administrators rather than owners of their own estates.
- Small town rural Germany welcomed the destruction of decadent culture and art associated with Berlin nightlife.
- The young people of Germany enjoyed the freedom and activities associated with membership of the Hitler Youth.
- A number of welfare measures were introduced to give people an opportunity to present a vivid expression of the *Volksgemeinschaft* at work and proof of their loyalty to the regime. Hitler emphasised the importance of the individual and collective responsibility of the people as opposed to that of the State. A fundamental expression of

PICTURE 37

Girls of the Bund Deutscher Mädel *(League of German Girls) exercising on the Baltic coast*

Imperial War Museum HU7126

this responsibility was the door-to-door collection of money (and sometimes bedding, clothing and other household items; and food) to help fund the regime's public welfare and 'Winter Help' programmes providing food, shelter and support for the needy.

However, not all sections of society shared this positive response. Many of the middle classes were disillusioned and felt that their interests had been 'betrayed' as a result of rearmament. Election promises to

TABLE 34

Welfare policies and their aims

Policy	Features
Winter Relief (*Winterhilfe*) Scheme	An annual charity collection (October to March) to help finance relief for the unemployed or poor. Once a year on a Sunday all Nazi organisations were expected to make their personnel available for extensive street collections. Party workers and celebrities from media appeared at centrally located spots in the cities to help with the collection. For the dedicated Nazis it became a test of political faith for the masses. Even after full employment had been achieved by 1937–8 (after 8.9 million had received relief) the system continued, becoming a massive ritual aimed at raising popular feeling and encouraging self-sacrifice. Failure to give or to give not enough Winter Help was condemned so that what was presented as a voluntary charity became a compulsory tax which reduced workers' wages, making some of them in turn eligible to receive relief.
The 'One-Pot' Meal Scheme (*Eintopfgericht*)	This was a propaganda exercise, called 'the meal of sacrifice for the Reich', imposed by the Nazis during the war years 1939–45. The idea was to eat a frugal single-dish meal six times a year between September and March, with the money thus saved going to the Winter Relief scheme. As well as raising money, the scheme was intended to foster a community spirit.

Imperial War Museum MH11093

PICTURE 38
Hitler and Goebbels at table eating the Eintopfgericht *or one-pot meal*

protect small businesses against the large department stores were ignored. Moreover, between 1942 and 1943 shops and workshops were closed down because they were not necessary to the war effort.

C *Popular support for the regime?*

The reaction of people to life in the people's community is difficult to assess. In trying to understand how the people really felt during these years the historian is faced with serious problems for an independent public opinion did not exist:

- Freedom of speech and assembly were suppressed and there were no opinion polls.
- Terror was always in the background and was ruthlessly applied when necessary.
- Elections and plebiscites were rigged and the media was strictly controlled. Newspapers are of limited value as a source to the historian because they were censored and controlled by Goebbels' Propaganda Ministry.

There were difficulties, too, for the regime in gauging what the German people were thinking and feeling. A number of agencies were responsible for finding out the state of popular opinion. The security service of the SS (the SD), the *Gestapo*, the Party, regional government offices and the judicial authorities all prepared regular reports on public morale and the popular response to such issues as food shortages, price increases, fears of war and the employment situation. Such reports were concerned about active resistance and/or opposition and were gathered from informers scattered throughout the population who recounted conversations with 'national comrades' or what they had overheard. Despite obvious problems of interpretation, the reports of these agencies provide valuable information for the historian.

Another important source on popular opinion is the monthly

KEY ISSUE

How people reacted to the regime.

reports prepared by the Sopade, the exiled SPD in Switzerland, based on information on life in the Third Reich regularly supplied by former SPD members in Germany. Again, despite problems of interpretation, they provide a remarkable source for attitudes to the regime among various sections of the population. Although the regime had institutionalised terror it is equally clear that it operated on a remarkable degree of consent from the people. Central to this was the positive image of Hitler as the Führer who was above Party and political conflicts. He presented himself as a man of the people who had saved Germany from decline. The problems faced by the Weimar Republic between 1929 and 1933 left people feeling that Germany needed a strong leader. Hitler was portrayed as the leader who dedicated himself to the service of the people and provided them with the leadership they had sought since 1918. This positive image endured beyond 1939, even though popular support did not extend to Nazi Party officials who were seen as over-zealous. However, positive leadership had also to be accompanied by concrete successes, such as full employment and the restoration of Germany's position as a world power. This extract is from one of the Sopade reports for 1936 (quoted in Noakes and Pridham, *Nazism 1919–1945, A Documentary Reader, Vol 2*):

> In general, one can say that almost everybody blames the previous system for failing to get the unemployed, and particularly youth, off the streets. The reduction in unemployment, rearmament, and the drive it shows in its foreign policy are the big points in favour of Hitler's policy and, on the basis of his own observations, he personally believes that only a tenth of the population does not recognise these facts. People feel that the previous governments were weak-willed and the parties as well. He assured me that was not his own view because he knew the great feats of the Republic very well, but it was the almost unanimous view of public opinion. Hitler knew how to handle the popular mood and continually to win over the masses. No previous Reich Chancellor has understood anything of that.

Q

What factors, in the opinion of his left-wing opponents, account for Hitler's success with the people?

By the spring of 1939 Hitler's position appeared secure and was even reported upon by Sopade. His successes at home and abroad convinced even his enemies that 'as a politician Hitler is greater than all his opponents'. There are a number of reasons to explain this apparent success.

Hitler's policies were popular, his process of *Gleichschaltung* (see pages 142–4) was seen as dynamic while his *Volksgemeinschaft* would become the platform to rebuild Germany as a strong European power. To a certain extent everyone, apart from those considered to be racially impure, benefited from the regime, especially in terms of the economic revival.

Moreover, a very large section of the German people shared the basic attitudes of Nazism, such as nationalism and militarism as well as hostility to unpopular minorities. They also supported the firm line taken to overcome unemployment and discourage deviant groups such as homosexuals, tramps, criminals and the workshy. Although Germany was a police state where opposition was punished ruthlessly, recent studies have emphasised the degree of support given by ordinary people. A network of spies and informers kept the system of terror going as neighbour denounced neighbour. People, aware of the danger of criticising the regime, sought escape by becoming inward-looking and retreating into the home and family, as this Sopade report from the exiled SPD leadership comments in the case of Saxony in 1938 (quoted in Noakes and Pridham, *Nazism 1919–1945, A Documentary Reader, Vol 2*):

> . . .never has participation in day-to-day political events been so limited as it is now. It seems to us that the indifference which has gripped large sections of the population has become the second pillar supporting the system. For these indifferent groups simply want to get by and to know nothing about what is going on around them. And that suits the Nazis fine. Only the continual collections for the Winterhelp campaign and the periodic shortages of various foodstuffs give these groups cause for slight grumbling. It is extremely rare to hear a critical word from workers who are laid off because of raw material shortages. On the other hand, one cannot speak of popular enthusiasm for National Socialism. Only the school children and the majority of those young men who have not yet done their military service are definitely enthusiastic about Hitler.

The regime also understood the importance of organising the people and of controlling not only their work lives through the German Labour Front, but also leisure. Clubs and private associations which had been characteristics of German life, were put under the control of reliable party members as part of the policy of national co-ordination (*Gleichschaltung*). The effect of this Nazi technique of organisation was that people withdrew from political involvement. They were persuaded that politics should be left to Hitler, their rewards were a radio, the promise of a car, holidays and leisure activities. They were not encouraged to ask questions and many did not question the regime until the 1939–45 war.

Even so, dissent and unrest existed amongst both the peasantry and the industrial workers, although this did not express itself in open opposition. The regime's opponents were weak due to ignorance, lack of political will and the fear produced by its coercive powers (opposition and resistance to the regime are discussed in the next chapter). However, great reserves of support remained, especially among the young, so that it would be a mistake to overemphasise the extent of adverse opinion in 1934. Middle-class disappointment had no political significance for fear of communism and a lack of political power guaranteed approval of the Nazi government. Sopade, commentated on the division of opinion among those hostile to the regime in 1934 (quoted in Noakes and Pridham, *Nazism 1919–1945, A Documentary Reader, Vol 2*):

The weakness of its opponents is the strength of the regime. Its opponents are ideologically and organisationally weak. They are ideologically weak because the great mass are only discontents, grumblers whose dissatisfaction arises solely from economic reasons. That is especially so among the *Mittelstand* and the peasantry. These groups are the least prepared to fight seriously against the regime because they know least of all what they should fight for... The fear of Bolshevism, of the chaos which, in the opinion of the great mass, in particular of the *Mittelstand* and the peasantry, would follow on the fall of Hitler, is still the negative mass base of the regime as far as the masses are concerned.

Its opponents are organisationally weak because it is of the essence of a fascist system that it does not allow its opponents to organise collectively...the labour movement is still split into Socialist and Communist and within the two movements, there are numerous factions... However, if the terror was reduced...it would become apparent that these factions would soon merge into a great mass movement... The attitude of the Church opponents of the regime is not uniform. Their struggle is evidently not least directed towards improving the position of the Churches within the regime...

> *Mittelstand, page 267.*

> **Q**
>
> *What main weaknesses of the regime's opponents are highlighted in this report?*

5 ⟿ SUCCESS IN CREATING A PEASANT-BASED *VOLKSGEMEINSCHAFT*

In part the farming community had been attracted to the Nazi cause by the promise of economic aid and by the apparent sympathy of National Socialism for its role in society. Peasant hopes were based on a number of pronouncements in which Hitler emphasised the importance of agriculture and the German peasant as the 'essential pillar on which all political life must rest'. This led them to expect a return to material prosperity and social prestige as part of Hitler's attempts to achieve a 'sound peasant stock', whom he regarded as the backbone of society, and 'the best protection in all times against social and political evils' (*Mein Kampf*). The Official Party Manifesto of March 1930 expressed Hitler's concern to achieve self-sufficiency in food production so that Germany could be freed from dependence on foreign food imports which represented a drain on scarce foreign exchange.

Initially the peasants were won over to Hitler's promises. These were to create a stable class of peasants with adequate sized farms and secure tenancies. In contrast with his predecessors, Hitler sought to help them overcome an increasing indebtedness which had meant that 'the farmers are unable to acquire the necessary stock' to provide the 'stimulus to increased production', which had been lacking, 'since farming no longer pays'. A number of policies were introduced designed to protect peasants' and farmers' markets.

1   Tariffs were imposed on imported foodstuffs while home demand for dairy produce was stimulated.

2 Cheap loans were offered to encourage production and farmers were exempted from tax and from unemployment and health insurance payments.

3 Other benefits included family allowances, improved housing and some protection against the unreasonable demands of estate owners.

In addition a Reich Food Estate (*Reichsnahrstand*) was set up in December 1933 to regulate market prices and control the distribution of agricultural produce. It was an independent organisation with responsibility for all aspects of food production. All farmers, farm workers and agricultural wholesale dealers were compelled to join it. Through a series of marketing and supervisory boards it controlled crop prices and the distribution of food as well as being responsible for the future planning of German agriculture. A Reich Entailed Farm Law was passed on the 29 September 1933 to guarantee the future of smaller peasant farmers and smallholders. Its aim was to 'retain the peasantry as the blood stock of the German nation', and it was one of the few pieces of Nazi legislation inspired by ideology. It aimed to give the peasantry (of German blood), security of ownership by ruling that farms between 7.5 and 10 hectares could not be split up in the course of inheritance. The farms were to remain the permanent possession of the original peasant owners and consequently could not even be offered as security against a loan. Although the law only applied to about 35 per cent of agricultural land in Germany (37 per cent including forestry), it was an extremely conservative measure which fixed the German peasantry in their condition at the time of the act. It curbed the development of large-scale modern farming units and contradicted the regime's attempts at self-sufficiency. Although some farm ownerships were created between 1933 and 1936, and peasants were also settled in eastern Europe, Poland and Posen, the overall effect was that land could not be sold and younger children were dispossessed.

Historians have differed in their interpretation of these policies.

Some have seen in these tentative policies indications of a social revolution because they defied social trends elsewhere, but there is no agreement on this. However, the 1933 inheritance laws and resettlement had occurred before the time of the Nazis and resettlement did not proceed far under the Nazis.	Others have seen the policy towards the peasantry as a front to get them to work harder and provide more food in line with a policy of **autarky**.

autarky economic self-sufficiency, reducing reliance on imports of raw materials, foodstuffs etc.

Despite these promises and expectations, the regime failed in its aim to create a community based on a stable class of landholding peasants. Schemes of rural resettlement were bound to fail because they conflicted both with Hitler's expansionist plans and with the long-term trend of a rural drift to the towns. The realities of the politics of the

Third Reich – Hitler's need to retain the support of the elites, whose interests were threatened by Nazi support of the peasantry – led Hitler to choose the *Junker*. Not only were their vast estates not carved up, the number of estates was increased by the inclusion of former Polish territory. The *Junker* continued with their traditional way of life and the peasantry were sacrificed, so that not only was there no substantial change in their position, it was in fact worse in 1939 than it had been in 1932.

Peasant disappointment with the regime's broken promises led to growing unrest between 1936 and 1939. A number of factors account for growing peasant disillusionment resulting in a swing in opinion away from the regime among a group who had otherwise been a backbone of Nazi support before 1933.

First, the shortage of rural labour owing to the attraction of better-paid jobs in armaments demoralised those peasants who remained on the land and as early as 1934 economic-based social unrest had appeared.

Secondly, the provisions of the Reich Entailed Farm Law of September 1933 resulted in many peasants feeling a lack of freedom to dispose of their property or to provide for their children as they had been accustomed to do. The removal of farm property from the market had the practical consequence that the supply of rural credit virtually dried up. The mixed response to the law is amply illustrated by the following Sopade report for 1934 recounting its impact on north-west Germany (quoted in Noakes and Pridham, *Nazism 1919–1945, A Documentary Reader, Vol 2*):

The medium sized and big peasants of Oldenburg and East Friesland, who were once enthusiastic Nazis, are now virtually unanimous in rejecting the Nazis and in reaffirming their old Conservative traditions. Among the East Frisian animal breeders and rich peasants the Entailed Farm Law bears the main responsibility for this. Among the medium-sized farmers it is mainly the controls on the sale of milk and eggs which are responsible. The farms near towns previously delivered their milk direct to the consumer and received 16 pf. per litre. Now the consumer pays 20 pf. per litre for delivery via the central co-operative, while the peasant only receives 10–12 pf. There is a similar situation with the sale of eggs. The ensuing losses for the peasant farms are in proportion to their size, very large, the hostility to the Nazis goes so far that East Frisian farmers kicked out representatives of the local party who were demanding the re-employment of dismissed workers. When the Nazis threatened to come back and bring the SA with them, the peasants replied that then there would be deaths. A peasant who was arrested after an incident with Nazis received support from his colleagues in the form of them doing his work for him, thereby demonstrating to the system their solidarity with the arrested man.

Q

In the opinion of the regime's socialist opponents, what factors account for its loss of peasant support in north-west Germany?

Thirdly, there was also growing resentment among wide sections of the peasantry at the increasing intervention of the Reich Food Estate in the running of their farms and in the control of marketing of agricultural produce. It was over-regulated and worked to the disadvantage of livestock farmers who relied on imported fodder.

These various factors account for the serious loss of confidence among the peasantry reported by some commentators who even claimed that the mood was as bad as it had been in 1917 and 1918. Though this was an exaggeration, there was once again growing peasant unrest between 1936 and 1939. This was because of the pressures of rearmament, a labour shortage crisis, demoralisation and discontent and farmers were reported to be 'close to despair'. The drain of rural labour to the better-paid jobs in the armaments industry 'gave the peasantry the feeling of being crushed and produced a mood which turned partly into resignation and partly into an attitude of downright revolt against the peasant leadership'. The Reich governor of Bavaria added, in a long report compiled in the spring of 1939, that 'the lack of labour has reached indescribable limits...the mood of the peasantry has reached boiling point'. Peasant reaction to the regime fluctuated between an open expression of great discontent by older farmers, to a serious division of opinion among the peasantry, with the result that the discontent failed to develop into a serious political challenge to the regime.

Though the regime had more success with the peasants than with the industrial workers (see page 301) in Hitler's *Volksgemeinschaft*, by 1939 the peasants found that, far from becoming the backbone of society, there had been no change in their class position and their economic status had deteriorated compared with 1933. There was a flight from the land, possibly as much as 10 per cent by 1939, a disastrous labour shortage despite Nazi efforts to stop this, and they had to work harder and longer hours. They had a lower standard of living and suffered from disease and a 20 per cent drop in productivity. Public opinion reports showed the negative reaction to the regime. In status terms the peasants recognised that they were still seen as peasants with no concept of Fatherland or *Volksgemeinschaft*.

6 ⌐ SUCCESS IN CREATING A CLASSLESS *VOLKSGEMEINSCHAFT*

Hitler claimed, in a speech in Berlin on 1 May 1937, that he had succeeded in breaking down the old class system with all its prejudices and achieved a genuine people's community. This extract is quoted from *The Speeches of Adolf Hitler* edited by N. Baynes:

> We in Germany have really broken with a world of prejudices...I too am a child of the people; I do not trace my line from any castle: I come from the workshop. Neither was I a general: I was simply a soldier, as were millions of others. It is something wonderful that

> amongst us an unknown from the army of the millions of German people – of workers and of soldiers – could rise to be head of the Reich and of the nation. By my side stand Germans from all walks of life who today are amongst the leaders of the nation: men who were once workers on the land are now governing German states in the name of the Reich. It is true that men who came from the middle class and former aristocrats have their place in this Movement. But to us it matters nothing whence they come if only they can work to the profit of our people. That is the decisive test. We have not broken down classes in order to set new ones in their place: we have broken down classes to make way for the German people as a whole.

KEY ISSUE

Assessing the social impact of the regime.

A *A problem of interpretation*

Hitler's claim 'to have broken down classes' has been hotly debated by historians who disagree on the extent to which German society had changed by 1945 under the impact of the National Socialist regime. Since war is its own powerful engine of change, historians have tended to concentrate their debate on the extent of change and continuity in the 'normal' peacetime period of 1933–9. Part of the historical debate stems from the nature and limitation of the evidence. Historians have to use the research methods of the sociologist to arrive at an understanding of social hierarchy with its elements of class, status, social mobility and social revolution. This raises the problem of definition, for such terms and concepts can be vague and are influenced by an individual's perspective and politics. Social science disappeared in Germany after 1933 and this makes historical reconstruction difficult though not impossible. Statistics continued to be published, newspapers and periodicals were informative and many problems affecting agriculture and industrial labour were discussed in public.

Central to the debate is an analysis of people's attitudes and patterns of response to the regime and this requires a different kind of source base, one which includes 'history from below'. Major advances in the availability of such evidence on the experience of different social groups only occurred in the 1960s and 1970s when there was a growth of interest in the 'history of everyday life'. One such source, a 'Life History and Social Culture in the Ruhr 1930–1960', edited by Lutz Niethammer, was published in *History Today* in February 1986. It was based on the findings of a very large oral history project carried out by the universities of Essen and Hagen.

The findings of Niethammer's survey, carried out on blue and white-collar workers in the Ruhr, indicate that people had very good memories of the 1930s and their time within the national community. The period up to the mid-1930s is described at length, very little is said about the 1930s until they are directly affected by war, conscription and bombing in the 1940s and then they again have a lot to say. Words such as 'quiet', 'good' and 'normal' occur frequently to describe the 1930s, which were seen as an economic miracle, rather than 'terror' and 'mass murder' which subsequent commentators have tended to associate with these years. Those questioned were obviously more concerned with issues of employment, economic boom, order and peace after the hard times of the 1920s, which had been characterised by uncertainty and periodic unemployment. The 1930s under National Socialism were recalled as a time of work, promotion in the workplace, a well-ordered family life, a loosening of ties with old friends and colleagues, and free time spent in the church choir with scarcely any reference to the 'whole political business'. These were the years when they had a guaranteed pay packet and leisure pursuits – visits to the theatre, holidays abroad or distant parts of Germany organised through 'Strength through Joy' – adequate food and a stable political system.

Obviously there are major difficulties in interpreting such sources given the image of terror, mass murder and war associated with National Socialism.

B *Differing perspectives*

Historians' perspectives on the impact of Nazism on German society have often been influenced both by their political perspective and by their point in time and place. The debate is also affected by fundamental disagreements on the nature of Nazism, its social aims and intentions and about the terms used to define social change. Part of the problem stems from the contradictions within the Nazi Party itself and its ideology.

In spite of these problems of interpretation, the most recent writings on the Third Reich reject the view that the existing class structure was altered. Those historians who are critical of the view that society was restructured have described the changes between 1933 and 1939 as a 'revolution of form not substance', stemming from Hitler's concern to 'deceive' the people. Historians have argued against the previously held view of the 1960s that class consciousness changed in the sense of coming to an end. They argue that, if anything, peasants and workers were more aware of their class status and position in society in 1939 than they had been in 1933. They believe that subjective attitudes towards the regime continued to be influenced by people who did not feel themselves to be part of the German 'people's community'. Hitler's new social order contained in *Volksgemeinschaft* was, in many respects, merely a propaganda gimmick. Its social effects were in fact contradictory – some modernising, others reactionary. In reality deep social divisions and serious discontent existed beneath the propaganda image and were dealt with by severe repression. If a social revolution was achieved it came as a result of the elimination of people: Jews, those elites implicated in the plot to assassinate Hitler in July 1944, priests, and the mentally or physically handicapped in the euthanasia programme. The strongest argument for a revolution is based on the regime's social destruction. Social change was provoked by war but this was not intentional. The Third Reich had important consequences for post-war society, as a result of its total collapse and the new starts that were necessary in the various zones which composed defeated Germany.

HISTORIANS' DEBATE

Did Hitler achieve a social revolution?

Interpretation	Main characteristics of interpretation
Favoured by those historians who are inclined to a Marxist/Socialist view: R. Brady, *The Spirit and Structure of German Fascism* (Gollancz 1937). F. Neumann, *Behemoth: The Structure and Practice of National Socialism* (Cass 1967). T. Mason, 'Labour in the Third Reich, 1933–39' (*Past and Present*, 33, 1966).	*Historians of this school stress the class character of the Third Reich, 'the essence of National Socialist policy consists in the acceptance and strengthening of the prevailing class character of German society' (Neumann, p.298). They argue that, whatever superficial changes were made in social forms and institutional appearances in the Third Reich, the fundamental substance of society remained unchanged, since the position of capitalism was strengthened and the existing class structure survived. According to T. Mason, 'Hitler failed to overcome the stubborn despairing refusal of the working classes to become the selfless servant of the regime.'*
Favoured by those historians who take a 'liberal' pro-western democratic view: R. Grünberger, *A Social History of the Third Reich* (Weidenfeld & Nicolson 1971). Ralf Dahrendorf, *Society and Democracy in Germany* (Weidenfeld & Nicolson 1968). David Schoenbaum, *Hitler's Social Revolution* (Weidenfeld & Nicolson 1967).	These historians suggest that the changes in the structures of society and in social values brought about directly or indirectly by Nazism were so profound that they can be called a 'social revolution'. Grünberger (p.34) claims that, 'Hitler dragged Germany, half-heartedly kicking and screaming, into the 20th century of the common man', while Dahrendorf, a German sociologist, argued that, 'National Socialism completed for Germany the social revolution that was lost in the faultings of Imperial Germany and again held up by the contradictions of the Weimar Republic'. He argued that the Nazis were radical innovators, compelled to revolutionise society in order to stay in power, 'through the destruction of traditional norms, loyalties and values Nazism finally absorbed the German past as it was embodied in Imperial Germany. What came after it was free of the mortgage that had burdened the Weimar Republic at its beginning. There could be no return from the revolution of National Socialist times' (chapter 25, p.402). Unwittingly, according to Dahrendorf, Nazism had paved the way for a democratic society in post-war Germany. Similar claims were made by David Schoenbaum, an influential American historian, who believed that Hitler's social revolution amounted to a destruction of the traditional relationships between class and status. He wrote that, 'in the Third Reich, relative approximation of class and status came to an end, since nobody knew "what was up and what was down"' (pp.280–1). He based his conclusions on three arguments: the destruction of the old elites as a result of the political events of the Third Reich; their replacement by 'new' men who would not have occupied such positions in the past; there were no reliable indicators of class or status and this classlessness was reflcted by those who joined the resistance.

C *Impact of the regime on the workers*

The success of Hitler's *Volksgemeinschaft* is usually measured by how far it succeeded in winning over the working class, who were a key group accounting for 46 per cent of the population. Hitler's attitude towards them was that all they needed was 'bread and circuses', by which he meant that they should be kept happy, though he also recognised their social importance. To this end, the regime provided an impressive programme of work creation, increased leisure activities and improved living and working conditions. Hitler's success in achieving an economic recovery and full employment was not accompanied by a change in workers' actual inequality. They continued to play a traditional role as workers. Propaganda campaigns such as 'Strength through Joy' and 'Beauty of Work' did not win them over to National Socialism for many saw the destruction of the trade union organisation as hostile to the aims and interests of the working class. They failed to overcome their 'stubborn and despairing refusal to become the selfless servants of the regime' and resented being controlled.

1. They lost their trade union protection and were forced to join the Labour Front, while their wages were fixed by the Reich Trustees of Labour.
2. The shortage of labour after 1937 meant that many worked long hours and for low wages.
3. They had limited opportunities to voice their resentment but many, particularly in mining, building and metal-working industries showed passive resistance in the form of sickness, breaches of contract, refusal to work overtime due to tiredness and more openly, sabotage and bodily harm against Nazi officials.
4. Bitter criticism was directed against working conditions, the Labour Front and the Nazi party, the lack of social justice shown in the contrast between the low wages of the workers and the large salaries and dividends of business men and the waste of money on Nazi prestige buildings at a time of a housing shortage.

Nazi reports referred to a 'growing ill-feeling against government and Party' amongst the workers. Sopade reports from big industrial districts, the Ruhr, Saxony and Berlin, recorded, 'feverish unrest in all sections of the population' and a growing militancy leading to work stoppages, short strikes, absenteeism, indiscipline and a rapid turnover of the labour force, many of whom left without notice. However, none of this stopped them taking advantage of the various schemes and benefits and to give the regime some credit for introducing them. In conclusion, to the question 'Did the regime succeed in persuading the workers to give their first loyalty to the 'people's community?', the answer must be that it failed, but it did secure their passive support. This was equally true of other social groups.

7 ⌐ BIBLIOGRAPHY

There are a number of collected editions of primary sources which are readily available covering the themes discussed in this chapter, such as J. Noakes and G. Pridham (eds), *Nazism 1919–1945, A Documentary Reader, Vol 2 – State, Economy and Society 1933–1939* (University of Exeter 1984); N. Baynes (ed), *The Speeches of Adolf Hitler* (Oxford UP 1942); and A. Speer, *Inside the Third Reich* (Weidenfeld & Nicolson, 1970).

Amongst the secondary sources there are a number of general histories which provide an outline of Hitler's *Volksgemeinschaft* as a useful starting point. These include William Carr, *A History of Germany 1815–1945* (Arnold 1992) and Volker Berghahn, *Modern Germany* (Cambridge UP 1987). Gordon Craig, *Germany 1866–1945* (Oxford UP 1981) gives a fuller, narrative treatment. John Laver, *Nazi Germany 1933–1945* (Hodder & Stoughton, History at Source, 1991) contains many written and visual sources as well as a very useful commentary. A similar collection of documents and commentary is to be found in William Simpson, *Hitler and Germany* (Cambridge UP, Topics in History, 1991). A recent publication in English is E.J. Feuchtwanger, *From Weimar to Hitler: Germany 1918–1933* (Macmillan 1995). Geoff Layton, *Germany: The Third Reich 1933–1945* (Hodder & Stoughton, Access to History, 1992) and D.G. Williamson, *The Third Reich* (Longman Seminar Series 1982) both have chapters on the social impact of the Third Reich. R. Grünberger, *A Social History of the Third Reich* (Penguin 1974), F. Grunfeld, *The Hitler File: A Social History of Germany and the Nazis* (Random House 1974) and D.J.K. Peukert, *Inside the Third Reich, Conformity and Opposition in Everyday Life* (New Haven 1987) both provide a more detailed follow-up, while R. Bessell, *Life in the Third Reich* (Oxford UP 1987) has a number of perceptive essays. For a detailed analysis of the social revolution thesis read Ralf Dahrendorf, *Society and Democracy in Germany* (1968); David Schoenbaum, *Hitler's Social Revolution* (Weidenfeld & Nicolson 1967) and J. Noakes (ed.), *Government, Party and People in Nazi Germany* (University of Exeter 1981). For specific indepth analysis of the peasantry there is J.E. Farqharson, *The Plough and the Swastika* (Sage 1976) and for anti-Semitism, M. Gilbert, *The Holocaust* (Fontana/Collins 1986) and Lucy Dawidowicz, *The War against the Jews, 1933–45* (Weidenfeld & Nicolson 1975).

8 ⌐ DISCUSSION QUESTIONS

A *This section consists of questions that might be used for discussion and testing your understanding of the main themes covered in this chapter.*

1. What methods were used by the regime to control the people?

2. What were the main policies upon which the regime achieved the support of the people?

3. What different themes were projected in Goebbels' poster campaigns after 1933?
4. Was propaganda effective?

9 ➳ ESSAY QUESTIONS

A *Two-Part Essays.*
1. (a) What was the status and role of women in Nazi ideology?
   (b) How far did the regime succeed in persuading women to accept their role as wives and mothers?
2. (a) What were the hopes and expectations of the peasantry?
   (b) Why did the regime fail to satisfy the peasantry?
3. (a) In what ways did German society change under Nazi government from 1933–45?
   (b) Why was the regime successful in implementing its racial and social policies in the years 1933–45?
4. (a) What role did the peasantry play in Nazi ideology and philosophy?
   (b) Why was there an increase in peasant discontent in the years 1933–45?
5. (a) Why did Hitler attempt to win over the workers to his regime?
   (b) Describe the methods used by the Third Reich to improve the position of the workers.
6. (a) Describe the key features of the racial policies of the Third Reich 1933–45.
   (b) Why did the regime's policies towards the Jews change between 1941–5 compared with 1933–41?

C *Essay Questions.*
1. 'Hitler secured the support of most of the German people for most of his social policies'.
   How far would you agree with this view?
2. 'The Nazis gave the German people everything they wanted in the period 1933–45'.
   To what extent would you agree with this judgement?
3. 'The Second World War made the Final Solution inevitable'.
   How far would you agree with this view?
4. To what extent were Nazi policies towards Jews and other 'social undesirables' clear and consistent?
5. How successfully did the regime's propaganda persuade women to accept their role of 'Kinder, Kirche, Küche'?
6. How far did the Nazi regime succeed in creating its propaganda image of a *Volksgemeinschaft*?

10 ➳ MAKING NOTES

Read the advice section about making notes on page xx of Preface: How to use this book, and then make your own notes based on the following headings and questions.

1. *Nazi policies towards the peasantry and the workers*
(a) What role did (i) the peasant, and (ii) the worker play in Nazi ideology and propaganda?
(b) What conclusions can you draw on the attractiveness of National Socialism to (i) the peasantry, and (ii) the worker?
(c) What compromises was Hitler forced to make to his policies to win over (i) the peasant, and (ii) the worker in the context of political realities?
(d) How far did Nazi policies lead to an improvement in the position of (i) the peasant, and (ii) the worker?
(e) How did (i) the peasantry, and (ii) the workers react to the regime?
(f) In what ways were (i) the peasants and (ii) the workers worse off in 1939 compared with 1933?
(g) What conclusions can be drawn on the effectiveness or otherwise of Nazi propaganda and policies towards the peasants and workers to persuade them to accept their role and to become loyal servants of the regime?

2. *The regime's policies to achieve a 'pure' community*
(a) What were the historical origins of and the part played by (i) the sterilisation law of July 1933, and (ii) euthanasia in Hitler's eugenics policy of ethnic cleansing?
(b) Who were the 'asocials' in Hitler's Germany and how were they dealt with?
(c) Why were gypsies more harshly treated than asocials? In what ways was Nazi policy against the gypsies 'uncertain and confused'?
(d) What role did the Jews play in Nazi ideology and propaganda?
(e) Why and in what ways did the regime's policies towards the Jews change 1941–5 compared with 1933–41?
(f) How far do historians agree about the chronology of anti-Semitic policies and at what point do they diverge in their interpretation?
(g) How did public opinion react to the persecution of the Jews?

3. *The status and role of women in Nazi society*
(a) What official party image of women's role in society did Hitler present in his speech at the Nuremberg Party rally on 8 September 1934?
(b) What were the main influences on Nazi attitudes towards women and how did Hitler make this apparent on coming to power?
(c) What policies did the regime introduce to achieve 'Kinder, Kirche, Küche' and what effect did they have on marriage and birth rates?
(d) Why did the regime's policy towards women and the family prove to be confused and contradictory, and ultimately a failure?

Opposition to the Nazis

11

INTRODUCTION

In the election of March 1933 (see pages 116–17) 43.9 per cent of the German electorate voted for Hitler's National Socialist German Workers' Party (NSDAP). Even then, at this high water mark of support for the Nazis, well over half the electorate voted for other parties. The Socialists and outlawed Communists together managed to attract 30.4 per cent of the vote and the Centre Party a further 14.1 per cent. After the passing of the Enabling Act in March 1933 (see page 140) all non-Nazi political parties were banned and trade unions declared illegal. In much changed circumstances, would those Germans who had not voted for the NSDAP and those who had been outspoken critics of the Nazis in the *Reichstag* and across the country generally dare to continue their opposition?

1 ∽ *WIDERSTAND* – RESISTANCE

Denied civil rights and individual liberties, the German people were subjected to the most rigorous form of indoctrination as Joseph Goebbels used his propaganda machine to encourage support for Nazi ideology and policies (see pages 269–71). However, it would be wrong to believe that the great mass of German people were bullied and cajoled into accepting Nazi rule. As unemployment fell and the living standards of many improved, so more German workers began to enjoy the security of regular work and a weekly pay packet. In addition, many welcomed moves to restore national prestige as Hitler refused to continue reparations payments, began a programme of rearmament and made known his plans to correct the injustices imposed on Germany 15 years earlier at Versailles. The majority, pleased with the trend of events, were willing to go along with Nazi policies. There were also those naive enough to believe that if things didn't work out, they would be able to oust the Nazis at the next election. Some, many more than would admit it today, even began to associate with the Nazi slogan, '*Deutschland erwache, Jude verrecke!*' – 'Germany awake, Judaism is damned.' It would also be wrong to assume that all Germans were swept along in a wave of pro-Nazi **euphoria**. Some clearly disliked what was happening to their country but would-be dissenters had to contend with the SS and *Gestapo*, the watchdogs of the Nazi police state, and also beware of informers. Those who persisted were liable to the most severe penalties

Why did the majority of Germans accept Nazi rule?

Q

euphoria a feeling of well-being which is often groundless

TABLE 35
Date chart: opposition to the Nazis

1933	March	First concentration camp opened at Dachau; Reichstag passes Enabling Act
	May	Trade unions abolished
	June	SPD banned; other political parties dissolved soon afterwards
	July	Law for the Protection of Hereditary Health; Concordat with Roman Catholic Church agreed; establishment of German Faith Movement under Ludwig Müller; Confessional Church set up to counter German Faith Movement
	November	Popitz, Finance Minister of Prussia, resigns over Nazi treatment of Jews; Kreisau Circle formed
1934	April	Establishment of People's Court to deal with treasonable offences
1935		Pacifist Carl von Ossietzky prevented from receiving Nobel Peace Prize
1937	July	Martin Niemöller arrested
1938	February	Crisis over Blomberg and Fritsch
	May	Ludwig Beck issues statement critical of Hitler
	September	Plan to remove Hitler at time of Munich crisis
1939	September	Hammerstein-Equord's plan to assassinate Hitler
1941	August	Hitler orders end to euthanasia programme
1942		Spy ring run by *Rote Kapelle* discovered
1943	February	Rosenstraße protest in Berlin; Hans and Sophie Scholl executed
	April	Dietrich Bonhoeffer arrested
1944	July	July Plot – Stauffenberg attempts to assassinate Hitler as a prelude to an anti-Nazi coup; subsequent round-up and execution of those involved
	November	Leaders of the Edelweiß Pirates hanged in Cologne-Ehrenfeld
1945	January	Socialist leader, Julius Leber executed; Helmuth von Moltke executed
	February	Alfred Delp and Carl Goerdeler executed

including detention in the new concentration camps. The stated aim of the camps was to 'reform political opponents and turn anti-social members of society into useful citizens.'

2 ↞ THE NATURE OF RESISTANCE TO THE NAZI REGIME

For reasons of either contentment or apathy, ordinary and erstwhile decent Germans seemed content to place economic well-being before concern at the erosion of their rights and liberties. Even so, there were those who refused to acclimatise to Nazi rule. Opposition took several forms.

A *Passive resistance*

The majority of those who had previously supported non-Nazi parties took an ambivalent line and were prepared to co-exist with Hitler's regime. It was simply easier and safer. Some engaged in passive resistance. Passive resistance can take many forms ranging from non-cooperation to peaceful demonstration of public opinion. Hitler paid scant regard to the barometer of public opinion and preferred to mould it rather than yield to it. The Nazis were expert at diverting public opinion by reviving deep-seated prejudices against Jews, gypsies, homosexuals and other minority groups.

Even so, there were occasions when the Nazi leader did react to public unease. As we have seen, once the German people became aware of the reality of the Law for the Protection of Hereditary Health (1933), which involved the use of sterilisation and the systematic murder of the mentally and physically handicapped, there was sufficient disquiet for him to insist that the euthanasia programme be restricted and continued in greater secrecy. Similarly, the Nazi policy to remove the crucifix from the classroom was reversed. There were also other examples of adverse public opinion. Motivated by the quest for racial and bodily purity, the Nazis launched a massive anti-smoking campaign to safeguard the people against 'racial poisons'. In spite of the campaign, during the 1930s tobacco consumption actually increased. Some have suggested that smoking became an act of defiance, a kind of cultural resistance.

Although the penalties involved meant that few dared risk any open condemnation of the Nazi regime's treatment of the Jewish community, there were those prepared to offer shelter to Jewish families. In 1945, at the end of the war and in spite of the extensive measures taken against them, 40,000 German Jews, some 20 per cent of the original number, survived. In his book, *Resistance of the Heart: Intermarriage and the Rosenstraße Protest in Nazi Germany* (W.W. Norton, 1996), the American historian, Nathan Stoltzfus, tells of German women married to Jews who stood by their husbands. In 1943, at a demonstration in the Rosenstraße in Berlin, they protested sufficiently vigorously to win their husbands' release from the concentration camps. At that time, Nazi propagandists were mobilising the German people for **total war** and wanted to avoid antagonising Berlin's female population.

B *Opposition from the political left*

Once banned, left-wing political parties formed cells and went underground. They met in secret, operated **clandestine** presses and distributed anti-Nazi literature and posters. Even in such dire circumstances, the socialists refused to co-operate with the communists. Even though half their membership had been arrested and their leaders were living in exile in Russia, the communists were still the most active. With their activities directed from abroad, organised opposition was difficult. After his arrest, the bravery of Robert Stamm, a former KPD *Reichstag* deputy, impressed both his fellow-prisoners and captors. Charged with treason, he was beheaded at Plotzensee Prison in Berlin in 1937. Julius Leber was amongst the thousands of socialists arrested. From prison, he wrote, 'One can terrorise the people by every means possible but love

> **KEY ISSUE**
>
> *Hitler's reaction to public opinion.*

total war a war which involves the whole country – the civilian population as well as the military

clandestine concealed or hidden

can only grow out of humanity and justice'. Indignant at the suppression of their movement, some trade unionists formed active resistance groups. One, Wilhelm Leuschner, travelled the country to make contact with other like-minded people until he too was arrested and executed. Carl von Ossietzky, a dedicated pacifist and outspoken critic of the military, had earlier been arrested by the Weimar authorities on charges of treason. Re-arrested in 1933, he was held in a concentration camp and, in 1935, prevented from accepting the Nobel Peace Prize award.

C *Conservative opposition*

The conservative wing of the anti-Nazi movement was made up of politicians, diplomats, civil servants and senior army officers. They favoured a monarchist alternative to National Socialism and the restoration of the old imperial social order. They included such men as Ulrich von Hassell, the former German ambassador to Italy. When he openly declared his opposition to the Nazis, he was dismissed. Afterwards, he used his many contacts in the service of the resistance until his arrest and execution in 1944. Another career diplomat involved was Adam von Trott zu Soiz, a former Rhodes scholar at Oxford and considered one of the most brilliant minds in the German foreign office. Carl Goerdeler, the mayor of Leipzig, was actively involved in the opposition to Hitler until, betrayed by an informer, he was arrested and executed. Johannes Popitz, former Prussian Minister of Finance, had first welcomed National Socialism but, in 1938, resigned in protest at the treatment of the Jews. He was executed just before the war ended in 1945.

D *Opposition in the military*

Military opposition to the Nazis was closely linked with the conservative wing of the movement. There had never been any love lost between the *Junker* aristocrats who formed the bulk of the German High Command and Hitler, an upstart whose highest military rank had been that of corporal. As we have seen, President Hindenburg, himself a *Junker* ex-field marshal, tried to use his position to hinder Hitler's progress to the chancellorship. Although self-interest had encouraged the army to stand aside and allow the SS to murder the leadership of the SA on the night of 30 June 1934 (see pages 146–9) animosity and distrust remained. In 1938 Hitler tried to gain greater control over the army when he dismissed von Blomberg and von Fritsch and replaced them with the more reliable von Keitel. Even so, within the German High Command there remained those concerned by Nazi lawlessness and alarmed that Hitler's policies brought closer the prospect of another major European war. Eminent amongst these was Chief of Staff, Ludwig Beck. In July 1938, he went as far as to prepare a statement intended for Hitler:

> The Commander-in-Chief of the army, together with the most senior generals, regret that they cannot assume responsibility for the conduct of a war of this nature without carrying a share of the guilt for it in face of the people and of history. Should the Führer, therefore, insist on the prosecution of this war, they will resign from their posts.

Beck resigned to be replaced by General Fritz Halder, a man no more supportive of Hitler than his predecessor. The best chance of a successful anti-Nazi coup came in 1938 when a number of generals planned to take advantage of the Czech crisis (see pages 391–6) and remove the Führer. They assumed that Britain and France would force Hitler to climb down and that the consequent loss of face would give them the opportunity to remove him from power. The surrender of Chamberlain and Daladier at the infamous Munich Conference put an end to their plans. At the Nuremberg Trials in 1945–6, Halder stated that had the Western powers stood their ground in 1938 a coup would have been most certainly attempted.

KEY ISSUE

The response of the German military to the events of 1938.

E *Resistance of the German churches*

Hitler attempted to come to a working arrangement with the Roman Catholic Church when he undertook to safeguard the rights of Catholics by a Concordat agreed in 1933 (see page 228). He had less success in reaching an understanding with German Protestants and set up a rival church, the *Deutsche Glaubensbewegung*. This German Faith Movement was neo-pagan and supportive of Nazi racial policy. Neither Catholics nor Protestants were well placed to resist the Nazis although the Protestants did establish the *Bekenntniskirche*, the Confessional Church, as a counter to the German Faith Movement. Even so, it is the view of many historians that the Christian leaders in Germany sought more to protect the interests of their own members than challenge the Nazis. Any truth in these allegations should not detract from the bravery of individual churchmen who did have the courage to speak out.

Martin Niemöller was one such person (see page 232). After defying Hitler, he was banned from preaching and then arrested. He spent a total of eight years in solitary confinement at Sachsenhausen and Dachau concentration camps. Although his execution was ordered by Hitler, he was freed by American troops before the order could be carried out. After the war, Neimöller insisted on taking a share of the guilt. As he put it in *Here Stand I*:

> First they came for the Jews. I was silent, I was not a Jew. Then they came for the communists. I was silent, I was not a communist. Then they came for the trade unionists. I was silent, I was not a trade unionist. Then they came for me. There was no one left to speak for me.

Q

Were the churches sufficiently outspoken in their opposition to the Nazi regime?

The scholar and evangelical theologian, Dietrich Bonhoeffer refused to be used by the Nazis. Instead, he gave his support to the Confessional Church which declared Christianity incompatible with National Socialism. Later, he became an active member of the resistance, assisted with intelligence activities and helped Jews to escape to Switzerland. In 1943 he was arrested and spent the rest of the war in a concentration camp. He was executed in 1945. Alfred Delp, a Jesuit priest, became a leading member of the Kreisau Circle (see below) and allowed his home to be used for some of their meetings. He produced outline plans for a new Christian social order which he hoped, one day, would replace the Nazi regime in Germany. Arrested in 1944 and sentenced to death, before his execution he wrote, 'Bread is important, freedom is more important but most important of all is loyalty to your faith and steadfastness in worship'. Professor of theology, Karl Barth, was arrested for refusing to begin his lectures by raising his arm and saying 'Heil Hitler'. Clemens von Galen, the Catholic Archbishop of Münster, issued a pastoral letter in which he criticised Nazi racial theory and publicly denounced the euthanasia programme. In 1941, he said in a sermon (quoted in the *Guide to the Plotzensee Memorial, 1975*):

> Justice is the State's foundation. We lament, we regard with great concern, the evidence of how this foundation is being shaken today, how justice...is plainly not being implemented and maintained for all... Since none of us know of a way that might give us impartial control over the measures of the *Gestapo*...large number of Germans feel they are without rights, and what is worse, harbour feelings of cowardly fear...

Both Barth and Galen survived their ordeals.

3 ⌐ RESISTANCE ORGANISATIONS

A *The Kreisau Circle*

Though not strictly speaking a resistance group, one of the most famous of the anti-Nazi movements was based on a group known as the Kreisau Circle. Led by Helmuth von Moltke and Yorck von Wartenburg, it usually met at the Moltke family home on their estate at Kreisau in Silesia. Moltke, himself a Christian Scientist with an English mother, was the great-grandnephew of the eminent Prussian general of the same name. For some time he served as a legal adviser to the German army but, after 1933, became a leading opponent of the Nazis. Other members of the Kreisau Circle included eminent churchmen, scholars and politicians. Christian socialist in outlook, the movement was morally opposed to political assassination or any other violent means of overthrowing the regime. Something akin to an anti-Nazi think-tank, they engaged more in making plans for their country in a post-Nazi period than becoming involved in active resistance. In 1944 many of the group, including Moltke, were arrested and executed. They died 'not for what they had done but for what they had thought'.

B *The Freiburg Circle*

The Freiburg Circle was led by the historian Gerhard Ritter and was made up of academics at Freiburg University. They were opposed to the Nazis and accused them of misleading the German people. Strongly nationalistic, they were prepared to bring about the downfall of Hitler but were not willing to contribute to Germany's defeat in the Second World War. They were critical of the *Rote Kapelle* (see below) and accused them of being involved in treacherous activities. Ritter, a close friend of Goerdeler, was arrested in 1944 but survived his imprisonment.

C **Rote Kapelle**

Rote Kapelle, the Red Orchestra, was made up of pro-Soviet Germans dedicated to replacing the Nazis with a communist regime. Its leaders included Arndt von Harnack, son of a noted religious historian, and Harro Schulze-Boysen, grandson of the famous admiral, Alfred von Tirpitz. Directed from Moscow, it operated a spy network and carried out acts of sabotage in Germany. In 1942 it was finally tracked down by Nazi counter-intelligence agents and its leaders executed.

D *Student and youth organisations*

It is not unusual for students to be politically active and, in spite of the risks, this was true of Nazi Germany. Between 1939 and 1941, former pupils of Rütli School in Neukölln, Berlin, duplicated and distributed anti-Nazi pamphlets. More famously, students and their lecturers at the University of Munich formed the *Weiße Rose* (White Rose) organisation to oppose the Nazis. One of their leaders, Kurt Huber, a professor of philosophy, drafted a leaflet which was widely circulated. It read: 'In the name of German youth, we demand of Adolf Hitler that he return to us the personal freedom which is the most valuable possession of each German and of which he has cheated us in the lowest possible manner.'

Other members of the *Weiße Rose* included the brother and sister Hans and Sophie Scholl. Helped by other students, in 1943 they organised the first public demonstration against the Nazis in Germany when they took to the streets of Munich and handed out leaflets. The leaflets read: 'Germany's name will remain disgraced forever unless German youth finally rises up immediately, takes revenge, stones, smashes its torturers and builds a new spiritual Europe.'

Hans and Sophie Scholl were arrested by the *Gestapo* and brutally treated. At the time of her execution Sophie, her leg broken, limped to the scaffold. There were also many other individual acts of defiance. In

PICTURE 39
Brother and sister Hans and Sophie Scholl, student members of the Weiße Rose *who were executed for distributing leaflets and taking part in anti-Nazi demonstrations*

1942, a 17-year-old Jehovah's Witness, Helmuth Hubener, was hanged for listening to the BBC and informing his friends of the contents of news bulletins. Adolescent cult groups collectively known as the *Edelweißpiraten*, the Edelweiß Pirates, first appeared in Germany during the later 1930s. Individual groups adopted exotic names such as the Roving Dudes and Navajos and their antics became a matter of concern. Considered anti-social delinquents, to start with the *Edelweißpiraten* were not politically motivated although they did engage in street fights with members of the Hitler Youth. During the 1940s their activities became more political as they distributed anti-Nazi leaflets and provided sanctuary for army deserters and escaped forced labourers. In 1944, the SS took action against them and their leaders were publicly hanged. The *Swing-Jugend*, Swing Youth, rejected the narrowness of Nazi culture in favour of popular American music and dance. Easily identified by their way-out dress and hairstyles, Swing clubs existed in most German towns and cities. Their liking for jazz and American-style dancing was considered degenerate and, even though they were more anti-establishment than anti-Nazi, they were repressed and their leaders sent to concentration camps.

KEY ISSUE

The involvement of teenage cult groups.

---

4 ⌁ ATTEMPTS ON HITLER'S LIFE

As mentioned, a plot to remove Hitler which involved Ludwig Beck, Franz Halder and other high-ranking army officers was planned at the time of the escalating crisis over Czechoslovakia in September 1938. Anglo-French appeasement of the Führer ensured the plan came to nothing (see page 394). Afterwards, a series of attempts on Hitler's life failed either because of technical failure or the Nazi leader's uncanny sense of **premonition**. In September 1939, shortly after the outbreak of war, General Kurt von Hammerstein-Equord acted alone when he tried unsuccessfully to lure Hitler to army headquarters and 'render him harmless once and for all'. The following month, General Franz Halder and another young officer, Henning von Tresckow, intended to use a bomb to assassinate Hitler but the device failed to detonate. Far more imaginative was the plan of Field Marshal von Witzleben. He intended to shoot Hitler as he took the salute at a parade in the Champs Elysees. Sadly, Hitler declined his invitation to visit Paris. In 1943, Tresckow, now serving on the Eastern Front, and Lieutenant Fabian Schlabrendorff invited Hitler to army headquarters at Smolensk with the intention of shooting him whilst he was at lunch. Unfortunately, Field Marshal von Kluge, who was senior to Tresckow, turned down the plan stating that it was unseemly for German officers 'to shoot a man at lunch'. Tresckow did not give up easily! Two months later, he and Schlabrendorff plotted to assassinate Hitler as he returned to his aircraft after visiting army headquarters. This time the plan failed because the Führer took an alternative route. Likewise, Tresckow's plan to blow up Hitler whilst in flight using a bomb concealed in a bottle of brandy came to nothing because of a faulty fuse. His next attempt depended on the self-sacrifice of a friend, Colonel von Gersdorff. The colonel agreed to pack his uniform with explosives and blow up both himself and Hitler when the two men shook hands. When the time came, Gersdorff failed to get close enough to the Führer and had to dash away to disarm himself! Papers recently released by the Public Record Office reveal that during the war, the SOE (the Special Operations Executive) also made plans to assassinate Hitler. The aim of Operation Foxley was to send agents, volunteer German prisoners-of-war with a hatred of Hitler, to Berchestgaden and shoot him as he strolled in the grounds of his mountain retreat. Other plans included infecting the water supply in the Nazi leader's private train or blowing it up in a tunnel. At a time when Hitler was unavailable, an even more outrageous plan was to hypnotise Rudolf Hess and send him back to Germany to assassinate Himmler. They remained highly imaginative but unfulfilled wartime plots.

> **premonition** a feeling that something is going to happen

5 ∽ OPERATION VALKYRIE – THE JULY PLOT

The most celebrated attempt on Hitler's life was made by Claus von Stauffenberg on 20 July 1944. It came closer to success than any other and was intended to be the prelude to a nationwide coup. The plot was code-named Operation Valkyrie. In Scandinavian mythology, the Valkyries were maidens who rode into battle to select from those killed the heroes who were to journey to Valhalla.

A *Background*

By 1944 Hitler's Third Reich had become a nightmare catastrophe. In addition to hardships on the home front, it had become clear that the tide of war had turned in favour of the Allies. By the end of April, the Russians had virtually driven the German invaders from their homeland whilst, in Italy, the Allies were in striking distance of Rome. On 6 June Allied armies landed in France to begin the liberation of Europe from the west. Various attempts were made through intermediaries to bring about a negotiated peace but they failed. With victory in sight, the Allies demanded nothing less than Germany's unconditional surrender. Amongst the German High Command there were men who thought it essential that the war was brought to an end immediately.

B *The plan*

To have any chance of success, an anti-Nazi coup would require detailed planning and be based on a carefully synchronised timetable. It would need the backing of sympathetic units of the *Wehrmacht* as well as eminent politicians and other men of influence. It would also need the support of a substantial section of the German people. Put simply, the plan was to assassinate Hitler, neutralise the SS and the remainder of the Nazi leadership and take over the government. With Berlin as the focal point, it was to be a military operation with the politicians subordinate to the army commanders. Once Hitler's death was confirmed, loyal units of the *Wehrmacht* would occupy major towns and cities, declare martial law and take Nazi officials and SS leaders into custody. When the time was suitable a provisional government would be set up with powers to negotiate an end to the war. The intended President was to be the old soldier Ludwig Beck and the Chancellor either Carl Goerdeler, the former mayor of Leipzig, or the Socialist, Julius Leber. There were many imponderables. Which local *Wehrmacht* commanders could be trusted and enlisted? What would be the attitude of younger *Wehrmacht* officers, many of whom had been promoted through the ranks of the Hitler Youth? What would be the reaction of the German people to what many would regard as an act of treason? Might the whole episode lead to the horror of a civil war? Most immediately, after so many failures, could the murder of Adolf Hitler be achieved with certainty?

> **KEY ISSUE**
>
> *The shortcomings of the plan.*

C *The conspirators*

The leaders of the centre of the plot were a group of high-ranking *Wehrmacht* officers serving on the Russian Front. These included Generals Henning von Tresckow, Erich Hoepner, Friedrich Olbricht and Hans Oster. General Karl von Stuelpnagel, the German military commander in France, had also agreed to co-operate. Others who knew of the plot but declined to take an active part in it included Field Marshals Günther von Kluge and Erwin Rommel, former highly regarded commander of the *Afrika Korps*. Although numerous politicians and other public figures promised their support, members of the Kreisau Circle would have no part of it. Von Moltke explained: 'We're not conspirators, we're not capable of being, we've not learned how to do it, we shouldn't try to make a start now, we would make an amateur job of it. . .'. Members of the Circle were, however, willing to take part in the political reorganisation of Germany if the coup proved successful.

CLAUS VON STAUFFENBERG (1907–44)

The Stauffenberg family were amongst the most aristocratic in Germany. A descendant of the Prussian field marshal, von Gneisenau, Count Claus von Stauffenberg had served with distinction in the early stages of the war but, in 1943, was badly wounded. After showing some early admiration of Hitler, the excesses of Nazi racial policies caused him to change his mind and he came to regard Hitler and the Nazis with utter contempt. He became closely associated with, though not a member of, the Kreisau Circle. Stauffenberg joined the resistance early in 1944 and immediately his energy and enthusiasm gave the movement a new sense of direction. He was 'the **catalyst**, the solidifying agent' that held the movement together. Promoted Chief of Staff of the Reserve Army, Stauffenberg frequently attended the Führer's headquarters, the *Wolfsschanze* (Wolf's Lair) at Rastenburg. Once it became clear that Hitler's death was the key to the success of the whole plot, he offered to carry out the assassination himself. He had no illusions about the task he had set himself and was well aware that the plot had only a limited chance of success.

PICTURE 40
Claus von Stauffenberg

catalyst something which helps to bring about a change

Tresckow summed up the feelings of the conspirators:

> The assassination must be attempted at all costs. Even if it should not succeed, an attempt to seize power in Berlin must be undertaken. What matters now is no longer the practical purpose of the coup, but to prove to the world and for the records of history that men of the resistance movement dared to take this decisive step. Compared to this objective, nothing else is of consequence.

D *The Events of 20 July 1944*

Hitler called a conference of his military advisers at the *Wolfsschanze* at Rastenburg on 20 July 1944. The meeting was to be held in the *Gästebaracke*, a wooden hut. Stauffenberg arrived shortly after 10 am with a bomb hidden in his briefcase. After greeting the Führer, he placed his briefcase beneath the conference table and then made an excuse to leave the room to make a telephone call. There was an explosion and Stauffenberg, convinced that Hitler was dead, bluffed his way through the guard posts and caught a plane to Berlin. He did not realise that an officer had moved his briefcase and, although the explosion had severely shaken Hitler, the Nazi leader had survived. When Stauffenberg arrived in Berlin, he was still firmly convinced that Hitler was dead. Immediately, the conspirators sealed off the government offices and began to put into operation their plans for a coup. The enormity of what they were attempting soon became obvious. Their plans had not been adequately thought through and there was chaos. Chaos turned to panic once they realised that Hitler was still alive and that the SS were moving in to restore order. Beck committed suicide whilst Olbricht and Stauffenberg were shot by firing squad. Tresckow took his own life the following day and Kluge shortly afterwards. In a radio broadcast, Hitler announced his survival to the nation (quoted in Joachim Fest's *Hitler*):

> My German racial comrades!
> I speak to you today…first in order that you should hear my voice and should know that I am unhurt and well and secondly that you should know that there has been a crime unparalleled in German history. A small clique of ambitious, irresponsible and at the same time, senseless and stupid officers have plotted to eliminate me… The bomb planted by Colonel Count Stauffenberg…wounded some of my true and loyal collaborators but myself I am entirely unhurt apart from some minor bruises, scratches and burns. I regard this as a confirmation of the task imposed upon me by Providence… The circle of these traitors is very small and has nothing in common with the spirit of the German *Wehrmacht* and, above all, none with the German people. It is a gang of criminals which will be destroyed without mercy.

In *Account Rendered*, Melita Maschmann, formerly a member of the League of German Maidens, recalled her feelings at the time:

> On July 20th, I left the office for home… As usual, the first thing I did was switch on the radio. The first sentence swept my feet from under me. An attempt had been made on Hitler's life… I cried out loud and felt sick; although the second sentence did give the reassuring news that, as if by a miracle, the Führer was almost unharmed… A friend who lived next door arrived… I think we were both in tears. To us Hitler's death would have meant the complete breakdown of our world… The perpetrators of such a deed could only be criminals or madmen.

Unaware of events taking place in Berlin, conspirators in Paris, Vienna and Prague began to put their plans into operation. In Paris, General Karl von Stuelpnagel, who was far better organised than those elsewhere, managed to arrest 1,200 members of the SS and *Gestapo* without any opposition. Following the collapse of the plot, Stuelpnagel was ordered to Berlin. During the journey, he failed in a suicide attempt and was later hanged.

E *The aftermath*

By midnight on 20 July, Nazi authority had been restored in Berlin. During the weeks which followed, Hitler took his terrible vengeance on those directly and indirectly involved in the plot. Tracked down by the SS and *Gestapo*, they were dragged before the *Volksgericht*, the dreaded People's Court, which sat under the presidency of Roland Freisler. They were humiliated before being found guilty and executed at Plotzensee. Some were hanged with piano wire, some garrotted and some beheaded. Hitler saw to it that the whole nauseating episode was filmed. Among the estimated 200 victims were other *Wehrmacht* officers, numerous members of the Kreisau Circle, including Moltke, and other eminent figures such as Goerdeler and Leber. The whole of Stauffenberg's family was arrested and his brother, Berthold, executed. In order to avoid public disquiet Rommel, a close friend of Steulpnagel, was allowed to commit suicide. Such ruthlessness ensured that there would be no further challenge to Nazi rule in Germany.

6 ∽ THE SIGNIFICANCE OF THE JULY PLOT

With inadequate planning, no realistic assessment of the likely support to be expected from the *Wehrmacht* and the German people, and with

KEY ISSUE

Hitler removes those whose loyalty he doubted.

PICTURE 41
The interior of the execution chamber at Plotzensee shows the hooks on which the condemned men were hanged. A guillotine can also be seen in the room

so many other obstacles to overcome, the failure of the July Plot was predictable. The leadership pressed ahead with their plans even though some anticipated failure. It was a pipe dream to imagine that the death of Hitler would bring about the immediate collapse of the Nazi regime and, when direction was needed, no one seemed to have any idea what was going on. Some of the coup's military leaders were half-hearted since they had reservations about being involved in an act of treason and a loss of honour. Others put forward moral reasons for not taking part in an event which might lead to civil war and a blood-bath. The conspirators had insufficient popular support and badly underestimated the extent of the loyalty that Hitler was still able to command. At the time, General Heinz Guderian, a leading tank expert, described the conspirators as 'cowards and weaklings who had preferred the road of disgrace to the only road open to an honest soldier, the road of duty and honour'. After the war, he pointed out the flaws in the plot (taken from his book, *Panzer Leader*):

> Even if Hitler had been killed and the conspirators had succeeded in seizing power, they would have still required an adequate body of reliable troops. They had not a single company at their disposal... The officers and men assembled for Operation Valkyrie had not the slightest idea what was going on... Links between the conspiracy and the enemy countries were very slender. If the assassination had succeeded, Germany's condition would not have been one jot better off than it is today. Our enemies were not solely interested in destroying Hitler and Nazism.

The views of Albert Speer, Hitler's armaments Minister, were more generous (quoted in Gitta Sereny, *Albert Speer: His Battle with Truth*):

> Today, fifty years later as I write, the Twentieth of July remains a subject of controversy in Germany and elsewhere. How was it possible, people ask, that the cream of Germany's General Staff...had so misjudged the situation that the coup was almost bound to fail? How could they not know the extent of the loyalty Hitler still commanded? ... But certainly, these were desperate and courageous men and their purpose was honourable.

7 ⌒ AN EVALUATION OF GERMAN RESISTANCE TO THE NAZI REGIME

Whatever its form, dissent, non-cooperation or active resistance, German opposition to the Nazis did not exist as one unified movement. Fragmented, often along class lines, it lacked organisation and had no acknowledged leadership. To make matters worse, the wartime Allies seemed unwilling to recognise that there was any opposition to the Nazis. For the military, there was the issue of conscience versus loyalty. Each soldier had taken an oath of loyalty to 'render unconditional obedience to the Führer of the German Reich and people, Adolf Hitler' and promised 'at all times to stake my life for this oath'. Unlike the majority, General Ludwig Beck was sure of the point at which the dictates of conscience overrode an oath of loyalty:

> History will indict those commanders of blood guilt if, in the light of their professional and political knowledge, they do not obey the dictates of their conscience. The soldier's duty to obey ends when his knowledge, his conscience and his sense of responsibility forbid him to carry out a certain order.

Q

Did German resistance to the Nazi regime really amount to anything?

Whether soldiers or civilians, at the time those engaged in resistance to the Nazi regime would have been considered enemies of the people by most Germans and incurred the stigma, traitor! Even today, some find it hard to forgive what they still regard as treason. On the other hand, post-war Germany rewarded some of those involved in resistance. In 1949, Konrad Adenauer, a former anti-Nazi mayor of Cologne, became the first elected Chancellor of the German Federal Republic. Willy Brandt, a member of the socialist underground, finally fled abroad and took Norwegian citizenship. After the war he returned home and again became active in German politics. After serving as mayor of West Berlin he was appointed West German Chancellor in 1969.

Today, historians hold differing views regarding both the extent and the effectiveness of German opposition to the Nazis, as the following Historians' Debate shows. But, in making any final assessment, it should be remembered that between 1933 and 1944 the Reich Ministry of Justice sentenced 13,405 Germans to death for political offences. During 1945 a further 800 were executed. In addition, during the war 9,413 German officers and men were shot. Many were executed for their political and religious views and some for refusing to carry out atrocities.

German opposition to the Nazis

There are some historians who see accounts of resistance as a convenient post-war invention aimed at redeeming the nation's conscience. It has been used, they say, to help restore some degree of national respectability in the face of worldwide revulsion at the extent of Nazi excesses. Alan Bullock, writing in 1952, warns of this danger. Others see German opposition to the Nazis as a noble and too little publicised sacrifice made by a number of brave and honourable men. The speech made by Theodor Heuss in 1960 reflects this view. The German historian, Klaus Hildebrand, writing in 1979, is perhaps more accurate.

HISTORIANS' DEBATE

Alan Bullock, *Hitler, A Study in Tyranny:*
There is some danger, in talking of the German opposition, of giving too sharp a picture of what was essentially a number of small, loosely connected groups, fluctuating in membership and with no common organisation and no common purpose other than their hostility to the existing regime. To diversity of motives must be added considerable divergence of aims.

Theodor Heuss, President of the German Federal Republic:
...the failure of their undertaking does not rob...their sacrifice of any of its dignity. Here, at a time when infamy and the petty, cowardly and therefore brutal concept of power had defiled and besmirched the name of Germany, was the pure determination, fully aware of the danger to life, to rescue the State from this murderous, evil regime and, if possible, save the Fatherland from utter destruction... The shame into which we Germans were forced by Hitler was washed from the sullied name of Germany by their blood.

Klaus Hildebrand, *The Third Reich:*
There is still no comprehensive account of German resistance covering all groups and avoiding condemnation on the one hand and special pleading on the other. We shall certainly not come near to understanding it until it is treated not only as...opposition to Hitler's dictatorship but also as part of the story of the Third Reich and of its place in modern German history.

8 ↪ BIBLIOGRAPHY

Although there are a number of accounts of German resistance to the Nazi regime, the majority of books deal only with aspects of the resistance or with the personalities involved. General surveys include *The German Resistance* by G. Ritter (Allen & Unwin 1958), and T. Prittie's *Germans Against Hitler* (Hutchinson 1964) and *German Resistance to Hitler* by Peter Hoffman (1988). An interesting insight is also provided in *The von Hassell Diaries: The Story of the Forces Against Hitler Inside Germany, 1938–1944* by Ulrich von Hassell (Doubleday 1947).

Other works include *Stauffenberg: The Architect of the Famous July 20th Conspiracy to Assassinate Hitler* by Joachim Kramarz (Macmillan 1967), J.S. Conway's *The Nazi Persecution of the Churches* (Weidenfeld & Nicolson 1968), *The German Churches Under Hitler* by E.C. Helmreich (1979), *Count von Moltke and the Kreisau Circle* by Peter Ludlow (1971) and the more recent *Plotting Hitler's Death: The German Resistance to Hitler 1933–45* by Joachim Fest (Weidenfeld & Nicolson 1996). A great deal of useful detail is also provided in a booklet available from the Plotzensee Memorial in Berlin.

9 ↶ DISCUSSION TOPICS AND TWO-PART ESSAY QUESTIONS

A *This section consists of questions that might be used for discussion (or written answers) as a way of expanding on the chapter and testing understanding of it.*

1. Why did so many Germans accept Nazi rule without protest?
2. Would it be accurate to say that Hitler paid no regard whatsoever to German public opinion?
3. Of those actively involved in resistance, which group presented the greatest threat to the Nazis?
4. What do you think might have been the likely consequences of a successful attempt on Hitler's life during the early 1940s?
5. With what justification might some contemporary Germans have considered the perpetrators of the July Plot to have been traitors?

B *Two-part essay questions.*

1. (a) Describe the extent and nature of the resistance of the German churches to the Nazi regime.
   (b) To what extent might it be claimed that the military represented the only real threat to Hitler's regime?
2. (a) 'More a debating society than an active resistance group.' Is this a fair assessment of the Kreisau Circle?
   (b) To what extent might it be claimed that the July plotters had no real chance of success?

10 ↶ MAKING NOTES

Read the advice section about making notes on page xx of Preface: How to use this book, then read this chapter again and provide the detail needed to complete the following chart:

Opposition	Made up of	Nature of opposition and its effectiveness
Former left-wing political parties		
The conservatives and elites		
The churches and other religious groups		
Resistance organisations		
Student and youth organisations		
The military		

11 ⌐ SINGLE-SOURCE DOCUMENTARY EXERCISE ON THE NATURE OF GERMAN RESISTANCE TO THE NAZI REGIME

Study the following source carefully and then answer the questions based on it.

> The kinds of resistance were as varied as the motives, ranging from quiet disapproval and withdrawal to efforts on behalf of the persecuted and finally to active opposition to the Nazi regime... Easiest to understand are those people who strongly disapproved of the Nazis from beginning to end, particularly political opponents... Somewhat more complicated are those...whose early enthusiasm for the Nazis turned to disappointment, anger and finally bitter rejection. Yet another strand is represented by Ernst von Weizsäcker, the state secretary in the Foreign Office, who travelled a <u>slippery path between conformity on the one hand and resistance on the other</u>. Other cases are stranger, like Count Wolf-Heinrich von Helldorf, a coarse, boorish man who, for good reason, rose within the ranks of the SA. More unfathomable still was the transformation of SS Gruppenführer Arthur Nebe, one of the architects of the <u>totalitarian police state</u>...who found his way into resistance circles... No case is the same as others... These brief examples show that conspirators, though frequently bound together by personal ties...had no real common denominator or unifying idea, not even a collective name. Far from representing a tightly knit <u>social elite</u>, the opposition to Hitler consisted of a motley collection of individuals who differed greatly in their social origins, habits of thought, political attitudes and methods of action. Even the term resistance was not used until after the war...

SOURCE *From* Plotting Hitler's Death: The German Resistance to Hitler *by Joachim Fest.*

(a) Explain what is meant by (i) *totalitarian police state* and (ii) *social elite.*

(b) To what extent did the groups involved in resistance to the Nazis share the same motives?

(c) How valuable is the source to the understanding of the extent and nature of German resistance to Hitler's Nazi regime? (In your answer use your own relevant background knowledge as well as information derived from the source.)

Education and Culture in Nazi Germany

12

1 ⌐ NAZI CONTROL OF EDUCATION

A *Introduction*

Not surprisingly, Adolf Hitler, a man with unhappy memories of his own school days and embittered by his failure to advance in further education, had a strong dislike of intellectualism. Nevertheless, he had very defined views on the role that education was to play in making future Reich citizens aware of their race, their country and the demands of National Socialism. In *Mein Kampf* he observes, 'the general rule is that a strong and healthy mind is found only in a strong and healthy body'. He then continues:

> ...the educational system ought to foster the spirit of readiness to accept responsibilities gladly. Formal instruction in the sciences must be considered last in importance... It is nonsense to burden young brains with a load of material of which...they retain only a small part... Not a single day should be allowed to pass in which a young pupil does not have one hour of physical training in the morning and one in the afternoon... In the education of the girl the final goal always has to be kept in mind that she is one day to be a mother.

In order to submit the young to Nationalist Socialist-style schooling, the Nazis had to control the education system – the teachers, the pupils and the curriculum.

B *Teachers and pupils*

In spite of Hitler's aversion to academics, the hierarchy of the Nazi Party included three former teachers and lecturers, Rust, Speer and Streicher, and a goodly number of university educated men, Frank, Frick, Goebbels, Hess, Kaltenbrunner, Neurath and Ribbentrop. In fact, the Nazis started with the advantage that many German teachers and academics were already sympathetic to National Socialism. A law of April 1933 made membership of the NSDAP compulsory for civil servants. By 1936, 36 per cent of teachers were party members, a considerably higher percentage than was to be found in most other professions.

TABLE 36

Date chart: education and culture in Nazi Germany

1926		Hitler Youth Movement founded
1927		League of German Maidens formed
1929		League of Struggle for German Culture set up by Rosenberg; Thomas Mann awarded Nobel Prize for Literature
1932	March	Goebbels appointed Minister for Popular Enlightenment and Propaganda
	April	First National Political Training Institutes established
	May	Burning of books in Berlin and elsewhere in Germany
	June	Von Schirach appointed Youth Leader of the German Reich
	September	Creation of Reich Chamber of Culture
		During the year Brecht, Einstein, Heinrich, Thomas Mann, Reinhardt, Schoenberg and other artists and intellectuals flee Germany
1934	February	Education in Germany made the responsibility of Rust
	April	Rust promoted to Reich Minister for Science, Education and Culture; Riefenstahl's film, *The Triumph of Will*; Gropius flees to Britain; Speer appointed Reich Architect
1935		National Socialist Teachers' Alliance formed
1936		Riefenstahl's film on the Berlin Olympics; all non-Nazi youth organisations banned
1937		Degenerate Art Exhibition in Munich
1938		Law passed allowing confiscation of degenerate art
1939		Completion of new Reich Chancellery by Speer
1945	January	Premier of *Kolberg* in Berlin

With the removal of undesirable teachers such as Jews and those who held left-wing views, the dominance of pro-Nazi teachers was near complete. In 1935, the *NS-Lehrerbund*, the Nationalist Socialist Teachers' Alliance, replaced all existing teachers' groups. By 1937 virtually all teachers belonged to the NSLB and were rigorously controlled. Although there was some disquiet, the majority of teachers accepted that the needs of *Gleichschaltung* required the ideological indoctrination of their pupils. Responsibility for education, formerly that of the *Länder*, became centralised under the Reich Ministry for Science, Education and Culture. The Reich Minister responsible was Bernhard Rust.

Some German universities, already well-established nationalist strongholds, fell quite easily under Nazi control. After some 12,000 unsuitable lecturers were removed, control of the universities passed to reliable, pro-Nazi rectors. Professors and lecturers had to adjust to the teaching requirements of the new regime and those that refused were replaced. Their positions were often taken by men who lacked the qualifications and experience expected of university teachers. From 1933 all schools and universities had to limit the proportion of Jewish entrants to 1.5 per cent of the total. During the following year Jewish students were banned from medical, dental and legal courses. In 1936 Jewish teachers were forbidden to even give private tuition to Aryan children and, in November 1938, Jewish children were finally excluded from all German schools. By this time, many eminent Jewish scholars had fled abroad.

KEY ISSUE

Teachers and membership of the Nazi Party.

KEY ISSUE

The education of Jewish children.

BERNHARD RUST (1883–1945)

Rust, who came from a farming background, was born in Hanover in 1883. He attended universities at Munich, Berlin and Halle where he studied classics. In 1908 he qualified as a secondary schoolteacher. During the war, he served in the army with distinction. In 1922 he joined the Nazi Party and was appointed Gauleiter of Hanover and Braunschwing. He continued to work as a teacher until 1930, when he was dismissed for molesting a schoolgirl. In the same year he was elected as a Nazi deputy to the *Reichstag*. In 1933 Rust was made Prussian Minister of Culture and, the next year, was appointed to Hitler's Cabinet. He was responsible for education in Germany throughout the years of the Third Reich.

C *The school curriculum*

As part of the process of indoctrination, pupils greeted their teachers with the Nazi salute and chorused '*Sieg Heil*'. Classrooms were adorned with swastika flags, propaganda and racist material and photographs of Hitler. Guidelines were issued to regulate the content of textbooks and although *Mein Kampf* was not read from cover to cover, extracts from the book were discussed and sometimes put to memory. The additional emphasis on physical education was intended to develop fitness, discipline and **esprit de corps**. In senior schools, five hours a week were devoted to physical education and boxing was made compulsory. Pupils who failed to reach an adequate standard were barred from higher education. Although all subjects were affected by syllabus changes, the most significant came in the teaching of German culture, history and biology. Young Germans were made aware of their racial identity and lessons emphasised the idea of the *Volk*. History lessons were concerned mainly with the story of the Nazi revolution and Hitler's part in it. They were also taught German mythology and the achievements of the Aryan race. In biology, pupils were instructed in the issues of race, how to distinguish between racial types, of the need for racial purity, the laws of heredity and the doctrine of Aryan superiority. Geography was also important since it explained and justified the need for *Lebensraum*.

> **esprit de corps** loyalty to the group to which one belongs

In an article in *History Today* in 1985, Gerhard Wilke quotes a German pupil recalling memories of his schooldays:

No one in our class ever read *Mein Kampf*. I myself only took quotations from the book. On the whole we didn't know much about Nazi ideology. Even anti-Semitism was brought in rather marginally at school... Nevertheless, we were politically programmed to obey orders, to cultivate the soldierly virtue of standing to attention...and to stop thinking when the magic word 'Fatherland' was uttered and Germany's honour and greatness were mentioned.

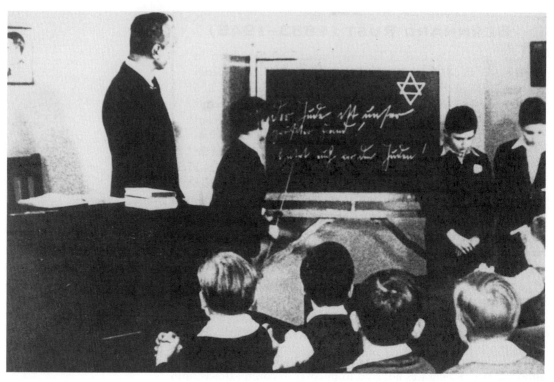

PICTURE 42
Education, Nazi style – Jewish boys are ridiculed during a lesson on race

Another German remembered things differently (quoted in *Nazi Culture* by G. Mosse):

> Every subject was now presented from a National Socialist point of view. Most of the old books were replaced by new ones which had been written and censored by government officials. Adolf Hitler's *Mein Kampf* became the textbook for our history lessons. We read and discussed it chapter by chapter...when we had finished we started again from the beginning... A new subject, the Science of Races, was introduced and religious instruction became optional...

D *The Nazi schools*

In addition to their control of state schools, the Nazis created a range of schools specially designed to educate those destined to become the elite of the Third Reich.

Nazi schools

The *Nationalpolitsche Erziehungsanstalten (Napolas)* or National Political Training Institutes
With the motto 'Believe, Obey, Fight', these schools, known as *Napolas*, admitted boys aged 10–18. Under the control of August Heissmeyer, they attracted sons of reliable Nazi families. By 1933, there were 23 such schools with 5,000 students. On completion of

their studies, the young men went directly into the German armed forces, usually the *Waffen-SS*

The *Adolf Hitler Schule* or Adolf Hitler Schools

The Adolf Hitler Schools were set up in 1937 by Robert Ley. They were intended to be the 'finishing schools' for the future governing elite of Nazi Germany. Children aged 12–18 were admitted. Largely selected from high-achieving members of the Hitler Youth, their training followed military lines and, like those attending the *Napolas*, they were subject to constant political indoctrination. On graduation, students looked for places at the universities or at the *Ordensburgen*.

The *Ordensburgen* or Order Castles

The *Ordensburgen* took their name from the fortresses built by the Teutonic Knights and represented the pinnacle of excellence in the training of the future Nazi elite. Students qualified for entry after six years at an Adolf Hitler School, two and a half years in the *Reichsarbeitsdienst* (the State Labour Service) and a period of full-time involvement in party work. Entrants were usually in their mid-twenties and acceptance by the *Ordensburgen* was considered a distinct honour. Hitler's aim, writes the American historian Louis L. Snyder, was 'to create a violently active, dominating brutal youth. It was to be indifferent to pain, without weakness and tenderness'. Graduates passed into the higher ranks of the Nazi Party with some going straight into the armed services.

2 ⌒ THE HITLER YOUTH

The *Hitler Jugend*, Hitler Youth, was founded in 1926 with Kurt Gruber as its leader. At that time, it had to compete with a wide range of other youth organisations. In 1931, Hitler appointed the more dynamic Baldur von Schirach to lead the movement. Something of a romantic with a liking for poetry, Schirach joined the Nazi Party in 1925. Referred to by some as the Party's poet laureate, he knew how to flatter Hitler. The Nazi leader was sufficiently impressed to consider him 'a true follower and dependable young man'. In 1929 Schirach was appointed to run the *Nationalsozialistischer Deutscher Studentenbund*, the National Socialist German Students' League. Two years later, he became the leader of the *Hitler Jugend* and worked hard to instil in the movement the 'true spirit of National Socialism'. Although some made fun of his effeminate behaviour, he rose to the top ranks in the Party.

Within the Nazi youth organisations, the youngest group was the *Pimpfen* or Little Fellows. Aged 6–10, they wore short-trousered versions of SA uniforms with swastika armbands. Even at this tender age they were taught rudimentary military skills and subjected to indoctrination. In 1933, Schirach divided the *Hitler Jugend* into two groups

TABLE 37

Membership of Nazi youth organisations, 1932–8

1932	107,956
1933	2,292,041
1936	5,437,601
1938	7,031,226

based on age. The *Deutsches Jungvolk*, the German Young People, was intended for those aged 10–14. Beyond that age, boys transferred to the *Hitler Jugend*. For girls, the *Bund Deutscher Mädel*, the League of German Maidens, had existed since 1927. Similarly divided into the *Jungmädel* and the *Mädelschaft*, they enjoyed activities similar to those of boys' groups but with additional emphasis given to domestic subjects.

Across Germany, the *Hitler Jugend* were organised into districts and then sub-divided into smaller units. A *Bann* consisted of 3,000 boys and then came the *Unterbann, Gefolgschaft, Schar* and finally the *Kameradschaft* with only 15 boys. At the end of 1932, the total membership of all the Nazi youth organisations was only 107,956 but, under Schirach's leadership, numbers rapidly increased. In 1936, all non-Nazi youth organisations were banned and, three years later, membership of the Hitler Youth was made compulsory. Members of the *Jungvolk* were required to take an oath:

> In the presence of this blood banner, which represents our Führer, I swear to devote all my energies and my strength to the saviour of our own country, Adolf Hitler. I am willing and ready to give up my life for him, so help me God. One People, one Nation, one Führer!

The motto of the movement was 'Führer command – follow'. In retrospect, many Germans today regard their former membership of the Hitler Youth as being based upon the appeal of uniform, learning arts and crafts, hiking, sports activities and the comradeship of singing around a camp fire. They recall the spirit of competition and achievement and the fact that members had to undertake charitable work and perform public service. It is also true that there were Hitler Youth orchestras, choirs and theatrical groups and that the movement offered opportunities to underprivileged children. Nevertheless, the basic aim of the movement was to indoctrinate the young into unquestioning acceptance of Nazi ideology and to be part of the spirit of *Volksgemeinschaft*. As Melita Maschmann says in *Account Rendered*, 'they learned to obey too often and too unhesitatingly; they learned too little about thinking for themselves and acting on their own initiative.'

In *The House that Hitler Built*, Stephen Roberts recalls his impression of the Hitler Youth:

> In every case the children wanted to join the *Hitler Jugend*... To be outside Hitler's organisation was the worst form of punishment... I have seen groups of boys in their teens gaping almost with idolatry at one of their fellows who had been singled out for a salute from Baldur von Schirach... Their attitude of mind was absolutely uncritical. They did not see Hitler as a statesman with good and bad points; to them he is more a demi-god... It was this utter lack of any objective or critical attitude on the part of youth, even with university students, that made me fear most for the future of Germany.

3 ⤳ AN ASSESSMENT OF NAZI EDUCATION AND YOUTH POLICIES

Nazi teachers tried to undo the natural influence of parents over their children and this led to contradictions between what was taught at school and the views expressed at home. In a speech made at Erfurt in 1933, Hitler said, 'We will educate our youths to that which we later wish to see in them, and if there are people...who think they cannot change their outlook, then we will take their children away from them.' Later, more aggressively, he warned parents, 'What are you? You will pass on. Your children stand in a new camp. In a short time, they will know nothing else...' There were instances when children were removed from parents who, so it was claimed, had influenced them in a way 'hostile to the State'.

The Nazis abandoned the old German concept of a broad-based liberal education for all and replaced it with a curriculum of the type needed to instil Nazi ideology. With the emphasis changed from the teaching of knowledge to producing strong and healthy bodies steeped in the spirit of National Socialism, some subjects were affected more than others. The teaching of religious education was curtailed though not banned. The result was that the education standards of the country, which in imperial and Weimar years had been noted for its scholastic excellence, began to fall. As the quality of academic learning suffered, fewer entered the universities. Between 1932 and 1941, the number of students in higher education fell from 127,580 to only 40,986. Within the universities, too, there was increased opposition to the Nazis. At the University of Munich, students formed the *Weiße Rose* organisation 'to knock down the iron wall of fear and terror' (see pages 311–12).

The Nazis also had to revise their policy regarding the education of women. After 1940, as German manpower was increasingly directed into the war effort, there came an urgent need for women with technical training. In 1939 the number of women in higher education had fallen to 11.1 per cent of all students but, by 1943, this had risen sharply to 44.5 per cent! The decision to dismiss Jewish teachers and lecturers led to the departure of such as Albert Einstein, the 1921 winner of the Nobel Prize for physics, and 19 other future Nobel Prize winners. Most importantly, it robbed Germany of the pre-eminence it had once held in the field of science.

Just how successful was Hitler's attempt to indoctrinate German youth? Did he, as was his aim, produce a generation that was 'slim and slender, swift as a greyhound, tough as leather and hard as Krupp steel'? Brought up in the belief that they were racially superior and that the Führer was their conscience, they were left without the need for independent thought. They rejected old-fashioned ideas of courtesy and chivalry, showed scant regard for their elders and became brash and undisciplined. Whilst it is impossible to calculate with any accuracy the overall influence of Nazi education and youth policies, it can certainly be claimed that they produced a hard core of Nazi fanatics blindly

KEY ISSUE

Declining standards of education during the Nazi period.

obedient to the will of the Führer. There is no better evidence than the conduct of those who later served in the *Leibstandarte Adolf Hitler*, *Totenkopf*, *Hitler Jugend* and other divisions of the *Waffen-SS*. They fought with a ferocity and loyalty seldom matched elsewhere and unquestioningly carried out the most barbaric atrocities against prisoners-of-war and civilians. Such men were also responsible for the management of the death camps. On the other hand, compulsory membership of the *Hitler Jugend* led to a small but significant backlash. Whilst 10 per cent of German youth managed to avoid membership, some opted to join teenage cult groups such as the *Edelweißpiraten* and *Swing-Jugend* (see page 312) and embarrassed the authorities by baiting members of the Hitler Youth.

> **Q**
>
> *How successful were Nazi attempts to indoctrinate German youth?*

4 ⟿ NAZI CULTURE

A *Introduction*

Bearing in mind that Hermann Göring is supposed to have said, 'Whenever I hear the word culture, I reach for my gun', some might be tempted to consider the term 'Nazi culture' a contradiction in terms. Yet in *Mein Kampf* Hitler saw the Aryan race as 'the standard bearer of human progress' and claimed that its robust muscular power and first-class intellect had 'created the monuments of human civilisation'.

The Nazi approach to culture was anti-intellectual. Dogmatic and narrow in approach, they saw modernism and all forms of non-German culture as decadent and sought to rid Germany of all non-Aryan influences. This led to the destruction of the work of unacceptable artists and writers and the loss of artistic and literary treasures. Consequently, many of Germany's leading artists, writers, musicians and actors were obliged to leave their homeland. Under the Nazi regime, all forms of culture were subject to institutional controls. The guardians of Nazi culture were Alfred Rosenberg and Joseph Goebbels. In 1929, Rosenberg set up the *Kampfbund für Deutsche Kultur*, the League of Struggle for German Culture. Its aim was to remove Jewish influence in German cultural life and promote the alternative views of the Nazis. In 1937 Hitler referred to this as 'cultural cleansing' and he promised 'a cultural renaissance in Germany'. As in all aspects of German life, cultural activities were to be co-ordinated so that they conformed to the needs of *Gleichschaltung*. The approach of Goebbels, who was no admirer of Rosenberg, was different. In 1933 he was put in charge of the *Reichskulturkammer*, the Reich Chamber of Culture. Divided into seven sections for literature, music, films, theatre, radio, fine arts and the press, the aim of the Chamber was to make sure that the regime controlled all forms of cultural expression. Authors, musicians, actors and others denied membership of the Chamber were as good as barred from their professions. The activities of the Chamber were closely linked with Goebbels's other responsibilities as head of the Ministry for Public Enlightenment and Propaganda.

B *The role of propaganda*

The dictionary definition of propaganda is 'any activity or plan which aims to spread an opinion'. In Nazi Germany, indoctrination, as an aspect of propaganda, extended into every aspect of life, particularly education and culture. As a master of mass psychology and with the ability to exploit the media, Joseph Goebbels proved himself a master propagandist.

Successful propaganda has two **prerequisites**. Firstly it must control the media in order to press home its own message; secondly, it must have the means to prevent the expression of opposed views. Goebbels achieved both. He exercised absolute control over the media and all forms of expression and enforced strict censorship laws.

prerequisites
conditions that must be satisfied

5 ⌐ THE MEDIA

A *The press*

With over 4,700 national and regional newspapers and a great many magazines to consider, control of the German press was not easily achieved. Immediately the Nazis came to power in 1933 they banned all opposition newspapers. The Reich Press Law of October 1933 called for 'racially pure journalism' and consequently newspapers were purged of all Jewish, left-wing and liberal editors and reporters. The existing Reich Association of German Newspapers was placed under the control of Max Amann, director of the Nazi publishers, *Eher Verlag*. Since membership of the Association was compulsory, all publications which were considered ideologically incorrect disappeared. Amann, who had been Hitler's company sergeant during the First World War, was among his earliest followers. He had also been responsible for the publication of *Mein Kampf*. He next reorganised German newspapers and placed the majority under his own *Eher Verlag*. By the end of 1942, less than a thousand German newspapers remained and Amann controlled 70 per cent of them. The Nazi Party's own daily paper was the *Völkischer Beobachter* (Racial Observer). Edited by Rosenberg, it was the best seller with a daily circulation of over a million. Other Nazi papers included Goebbels's *Der Angriff* and Julius Streicher's semi-pornographic, *Der Stürmer* (The Stormer). The Propaganda Ministry organised daily press conferences to instruct editors what could be published and issue directives about the use of photographs. All foreign news had to be obtained from one source, the Nazi controlled German Press Agency. Newspapers had no choice but to comply and follow the party line. The result was drab, repetitive newspapers and as people tired of a diet of propaganda so readership declined.

KEY ISSUE

The censorship of the press.

B *Radio*

Joseph Goebbels showed his appreciation of the propaganda value of broadcasting when he commented, 'What the press was in the nineteenth century, radio will be for the twentieth century'. After 1933 he moved quickly to place broadcasting under the control of Eugen Hadamovsky's Reich Radio Company. With radios, People's Receivers, available cheaply or paid for by instalments and the licence fee only 2 marks a month (about £4 a year), radios were available to all Germans. By 1939 70 per cent of households possessed radios. Throughout the day, sets installed in homes, schools, offices, factories and even in the streets, broadcast propaganda extolling the virtues of Hitler and Nazi ideology. In addition, there would be news bulletins, speeches by eminent Nazis and the classical, folk and military music of German composers. Much was made of Nazi successes and wartime military victories whilst failures and reversals went unmentioned. Goebbels also used the radio to broadcast Nazi propaganda to the rest of the world. During the Second World War, he acquired the services of an Irish-American, William Joyce. Joyce, who became known as 'Lord Haw-Haw', was in Germany at the outbreak of war and agreed to work for the Nazis. Listening to overseas broadcasts was considered a treasonable offence and, during the first year of the war alone, some 1,500 Germans were punished for tuning in to the BBC.

C *Cinema*

Convinced that films worked powerfully on the subconscious and could be used successfully to influence the masses, one of Goebbels' greatest achievements was his contribution to the German film industry. He was no novice. He had studied film technology as a hobby and had always been fascinated by motion pictures. At home he enjoyed watching Hollywood-made epics and musicals. His favourite films were *Gone with the Wind* and *Snow White and the Seven Dwarfs*. He considered the latter an 'artistic delight'. Once in charge of the cinema industry, Goebbels removed all Jewish film producers, directors and actors. These included Fritz Lang and Ernest Lubitsch as well as Kurt Weill, who had composed the music for *The Threepenny Opera*. Among the actors and actresses who left were Fritz Kortner and Conrad Veidt. Although it was untrue, Veidt declared himself a Jew in a racial questionnaire and then left Germany. Marlene Dietrich, of *Blue Angel* fame, left Germany in 1933 to make her home in Hollywood. Some German film stars, such as the beautiful Renate Müller, committed suicide. The family of the popular actor Joachim Gottschalk died together in a suicide pact. Gottschalk had a Jewish wife.

Other film directors were eager to work for Goebbels. It was his view that they needed to produce what the public wanted, escapism rather than propaganda. One of the most outstanding film producers was Leni Riefenstahl. The quality of the camera work used in the making of *Triumph des Willens* (Triumph of Wills), a documentary about the sixth Nazi Party Conference held at Nuremberg in 1934, greatly impressed Hitler. Later, she made an equally fine film about the 1936 Berlin Olympics. Allowed considerable freedom, her friendship with Hitler placed her outside the Propaganda Minister's control and this con-

cerned him. Elegant, charming and protective of his stars, Goebbels had affairs with several actresses and those who rejected his advances found themselves out of work. Between 1936 and 1938 he became infatuated with a 22-year-old Czech actress, Lida Baarova. This caused a stir when the long-suffering Magda Goebbels, who had long endured her husband's infidelities, asked for a divorce. The Führer, who sent Albert Speer to mediate, ordered the affair to end. Against Goebbels' wishes, Hitler insisted on making anti-Semitic films. The most famous, *Der Ewige Jude* (The Eternal Jew), included scenes so horrific that they upset German film-goers who stayed away. Far more subtle was *Jud Süß* (The Jew Süss) whilst *Ich Klage* (I Accuse), a film about the Nazi euthanasia programme, attracted only moderate audiences. After 1940 an effort was made to boost morale by providing the escapism wartime audiences needed. *Die Abenteuer des Baron Münchhausen* (The Adventures of Baron Münchhausen), a lavish comedy about a man given immortality by a magician, proved popular but did not match the even more extravagant *Kolberg*. This technicolour epic was seen by Goebbels as his legacy to the German film industry. Produced during the latter stages of the war, thousands of soldiers were withdrawn from the front to act as extras. The film was premiered on 30 January 1945. Between 1933 and 1945, Goebbels' film studios, which were the most advanced in Europe, produced 1,361 films.

6 ⌁ ART AND ARCHITECTURE

Hitler, who considered himself something of an authority on art and architecture, took a close interest in both. The Nazis considered impressionism, expressionism, cubism, Dadaism and all other forms of modern art to be degenerate and examples of 'cultural Bolshevism'. They preferred genre painting, pictures which portrayed things realistically such as landscapes and scenes of everyday life, and showed the true Aryan spirit. Nudes were encouraged as long as they showed examples of a healthy and pure Aryan race.

In the so-called 'battle for art', the Reich Chamber of Visual Arts, which included painters and architects, regulated all forms of art. Artists had to be licensed to teach and exhibit and studios and galleries were liable to be raided by the *Gestapo*. Suppliers were forbidden to provide banned artists with paints. In 1936 the Nazis set up a tribunal to visit galleries, assess paintings and remove all decadent art. Altogether, some 13,000 paintings, including those of Cézanne, Gauguin, Picasso and Van Gogh were confiscated. Some were used as evidence of degenerate art at specially arranged displays. Among the many artists who fled abroad were Walter Gropius, founder of the Bauhaus, and George Grosz. Artists who remained in favour with the Nazis included Adolf Ziegler and Hermann Hoyer, famous for his portrait of Hitler and his supporters at the time of the Munich *Putsch*. During the Second World War, art treasures were looted from the occupied countries and sent to Germany. Many ended up as part of the art collections of such as Hermann Göring.

The Führer looked upon architecture as the best way of expressing racial superiority and national greatness. To start with, Hitler's favourite architect was Paul Troost. Troost, who designed the new party headquarters in Munich, favoured a somewhat austere, classical style with little or no ornamentation. In 1934, Albert Speer became the new Reich architect. Speer had first come to Hitler's attention in 1933 when he was entrusted with the technical arrangements for the party rally. Afterwards, he was commissioned to build the arena for the Nuremberg rally, the stadium for the 1936 Berlin Olympics and the rebuilding of the Reich Chancellery. Speer worked tirelessly to realise Hitler's architectural dreams, of which the most ambitious was a plan to rebuild Berlin. Although grandiose designs were made for great avenues, buildings, colonnades and domes, the plan was first delayed and then abandoned due to the coming of war.

7 ⌐ LITERATURE, MUSIC AND THE THEATRE

As in other areas of German culture, Nazi ideologists denounced hundreds of writers as degenerates and banned their works. The stage was set when, on the night of 10 May 1933, a torchlight procession of students and young Nazis marched the length of the Unter den Linden to ransack private and public libraries and burn thousands of books in large bonfires. The German and foreign authors targeted were Jews, pacifists and socialists and included Karl Marx, Maxim Gorky, Thomas and Heinrich Mann, Erich Maria Remarque, Emile Zola, H.G. Wells and Jack London. L.P. Lochner, a reporter working for Associated Press, witnessed the event:

> Here the heap grew higher and higher, and every few minutes another howling mob arrived adding more books to the impressive pyre. Then as night fell, students mobilised by the little doctor performed Indian dances...as the flames began to soar skyward. When the orgy was at its height, a cavalcade of cars drove into sight. It was the Propaganda Minister himself, accompanied by his bodyguard and a number of torchbearers of the new Nazi Kultur. 'Fellow students, German men and women!' he cried... 'The age of extreme Jewish intellectualism has now ended, and the success of the German revolution has again given the right of way to the German spirit... You are doing the right thing in committing the evil spirit of the past to the flames. It is a great symbolic act, an act that is to bear witness before the world to the fact that the spiritual foundation of the November Republic has disappeared. From the ashes there will rise the phoenix of a new spirit.'

The Reich Chamber of Literature, which controlled authors, publishers and bookshops, had the ultimate say in what was acceptable. Every book was thoroughly vetted before it was published. The most popular authors approved by the Nazis were Gottfried Bean and Hans Grimm. Many of the 2,500 writers who fled Germany settled abroad and wrote damaging anti-Nazi books and articles. Nevertheless, the Nazi period did produce one best-seller. By 1939 *Mein Kampf* had sold over 5.2 million copies!

Home of the composers Beethoven, Brahms, Mendelssohn, Schumann and Wagner, no country is richer in musical tradition than Germany. The Nazis particularly encouraged the music of Beethoven and Wagner but banned that of the Jewish composer, Mendelssohn, and foreign composers they thought too modern, Mahler, Schoenberg and Stravinsky. American jazz was considered Negro-inspired and therefore decadent. Nazi anti-Semitism and anti-modernism meant that many highly talented composers, musicians and singers were driven into exile and settled abroad, mainly in the United States. Otto Klemperer, an outstanding Jewish conductor, the composer Arnold Schoenberg and Bruno Walter, who had been director of both the Munich and Vienna opera houses, all went to America. The great Polish-born pianist, Artur Rubinstein, left his place of exile in France and in 1940 moved to the United States. The Austrian tenor, Richard Tauber, took British nationality. Some remained to continue their careers in Germany. Norbert Schultze, a friend of Goebbels, achieved fame through the song *Lili Marlene* which became enormously popular with both German and British soldiers. Schultze also wrote other morale-boosting songs such as *Bombs on England*.

During the years of the Weimar Republic, the German theatre won a high reputation for the excellence of its productions (see page 79). As with the film industry, the Nazi regime saw to it that all plays had to conform to the new ideology. Jewish playwrights, producers, directors and actors were all banned. Among those to move abroad were Max Reinhardt and Bertolt Brecht. Reinhardt, born Max Goldmann, was the talented director of the *Deutsches Theater* in Berlin; Brecht, a Marxist dramatist, reached the United States by way of Denmark. In exile, he directed his attacks on Hitler's regime and wrote *The Private life of the Master Race*. Leading German playwrights who co-operated with the Nazis included Hanns Johst, who was head of the Reich Theatre Chamber, and the very highly-regarded Gerhart Hauptmann who had won the Nobel Prize for Literature in 1912. The authorities did allow plays by some foreign dramatists including William Shakespeare and George Bernard Shaw.

KEY ISSUE

The flight of intellectuals and leading figures in the art world from Germany.

Who were acceptable to the Nazis?

On the chart below, identify the aspect of German culture to which each of the following contributed and indicate whether or not they were acceptable to the Nazi regime:

Erich Maria Remarque	Joachim Gottschalk	Hans Grimm
Marlene Dietrich	Paul Troost	Albert Speer
Kurt Weill	George Grosz	Otto Klemperer
Bertolt Brecht	Norbert Schultze	Gerhart Hauptmann
Conrad Veidt	Leni Riefenstahl	Thomas Mann

	Acceptable	Unacceptable
Cinema		
Art		
Architecture		
Literature		
Music		
Theatre		

---

8 ⌐ ON MATTERS OF MORALS

The Nazis had long been critical of what they regarded as the laxity and freedom of the Weimar Republic. They blamed the Republic for the moral decline and cultural disintegration of the period and claimed that Berlin had become 'the sinful **Gomorrah** of a degenerate civilisation'. They came to office as advocates of law and order and promised to create a new, higher morality based on ideas of national pride and racial purity. According to Hitler, Aryans had to display the highest moral standards based on restraint and self-control. Unfortunately, there was a major divergence between the ideological standards preached by the

Gomorrah a biblical town known for its wickedness

Party and the morals practised by many of the Nazi hierarchy. Hitler, on the face of it a paragon of virtue, was a non-smoker, teetotal and vegetarian who disliked crude humour and saw no reason for women to wear cosmetics. Yet, in the late 1920s he had a torrid affair with his teenage niece and, after her suicide, began a relationship with Eva Braun who was his mistress for 12 years and his wife for a day. Of the other bizarre eccentrics associated with the Führer, Goebbels' affairs with various actresses were well known; the corpulent, luxury-loving Göring was a morphine addict capable of behaviour which bordered on the infantile; Robert Ley was an alcoholic; Julius Streicher, a sadistic rapist and pornographer, and Ernst Röhm, a flagrant homosexual.

In issues of morals, there were many contradictions. Officially, sex was regarded as a means of procreation and not pleasure. Professor Max von Gruper of Munich University, a Nazi spokesman on sexual matters and the author of *Hygiene des Geschlechtslebens* (Sexual Hygiene), went as far as to specify the acceptable frequency of sexual intercourse and stated that no woman should be expected to undergo more than seven or eight pregnancies.

The Nazis considered homosexuality degenerate and contrary to the concept of a healthy racial community. Yet Röhm and other leaders of the SA were homosexual and unconcerned about their reputations. Even though Hitler knew that Röhm flaunted his homosexuality and attended gay meeting places, the SA leader was too valuable to him for him to take action. However, once Röhm had been murdered in 1934, homosexuals were increasingly victimised and sent to concentration camps to be rehabilitated. Himmler even suggested a return to the Roman custom of drowning such offenders in peat-bogs! Members of the SS found to be homosexual were executed. Prostitution was condemned as evidence of sexual permissiveness and because it led to the spread of venereal disease. Syphilis, formerly known as the 'French disease', now became the 'Jewish disease'. The Nazis banned brothels, sent pimps to concentration camps and sought to curb street prostitution by encouraging early marriage. Later, medically supervised brothels reappeared mainly for use by German soldiers and foreign workers. The Salon Kitty, in the Giesebrechstraße in Berlin, was used by high-ranking Nazis and foreign dignitaries. Reinhard Heydrich, chief of the security police, had the brothel bugged in order to eavesdrop on pillow-talk conversations.

Although abortion was frowned upon and illegitimacy was condemned, the children born to Aryan unmarried mothers were well cared for. It was another contradiction that Himmler's programme of *Lebensborn* (Fountain of Life), encouraged racially sound German girls to become pregnant, preferably by SS men. They were sent to special maternity centres and well cared for. During the war, acceptable children with Aryan features living in the occupied countries were kidnapped to add to the German racial stock.

The Nazis pleased decent, family-orientated Germans by organising campaigns to suppress pornography, dissuade homosexuality, clear prostitutes from the streets, deal severely with criminals and juvenile offenders and round up tramps, beggars and those thought to be work-shy. The Nazis, who contended that criminal behaviour was biologically determined, were of the view that there should be no crime without punishment. The German legal system, controlled by the Reich Ministry of Justice, allowed the courts to reach and pass arbitrary judgements and sentences. The most extreme measures were taken against those who opposed or conspired against the State and, by 1945, there were 43 crimes which merited capital punishment. The death sentence could be passed on criminals aged as young as 14. Apart from imprisonment and internment in camps, the use of chastisement and the stocks was also approved. Sex offenders were liable to be castrated. During the war, juvenile delinquency increased to such an extent that a special youth concentration camp was set up at Moringen near Hanover. The authorities also had to deal with an increase in alcoholism as well as problems created by army deserters, escaped foreign labourers, black-marketeers and looters.

9 ⌐ BIBLIOGRAPHY

Virtually all the standard texts about the Third Reich contain sections on education and culture in Nazi Germany. Specialised books on Nazi education and youth policy include *Education in the Third Reich* by G.W. Blackburn (1985), Detlev Peukert's *Youth in the Third Reich* (Penguin 1987) and *Hitler Youth and Catholic Youth* by D. Walker (1970). In *Account Rendered* (1963), Melita Maschmann recalls her own experiences at school and in the Hitler Youth. As far as culture is concerned, a collection of primary sources can be found in *Nazi Culture* by George L. Mosse (Grosset & Dunlap 1966) whilst various aspects are covered in *Hitler and the Artists* by Henry Grosshans (1983), *German Literature Under National Socialism* by J.M. Ritchie (1983), *Captive Press in the Third Reich* by O.J. Hale (Princeton UP 1964) and *Propaganda and the German Cinema, 1933–1945* by D. Welch (1983). Sex and morals are considered in *Strength Through Joy: Sex and Society in Nazi Germany* by H.P. Bleuel (Lippincott 1970).

10 ⌐ DISCUSSION TOPICS AND ESSAY QUESTIONS

A *This section consists of questions that might be used for discussion (or written answers) as a way of expanding on the chapter and testing understanding of it.*

1. To what extent were school syllabuses changed to accommodate the teaching of Nazi ideology?
2. What provision was made to prepare selected young men for leadership roles in Nazi Germany?

3. Why did the quality of academic learning decline in schools and universities during the Nazi period?
4. What did the Nazis mean by 'cultural cleansing'?
5. Just how successful were the Nazis in their attempts to deny freedom of expression in Germany?
6. How valid would it be to describe the Nazis as a law and order party?

B *Essay questions.*
1. To what extent were the Nazis successful in their attempt to indoctrinate German youth. Explain your answer fully.
2. 'A cultural wilderness.' How valid is this assessment of Nazi Germany?

11 ⌁ SINGLE SOURCE DOCUMENTARY EXERCISE ON THE HITLER YOUTH

Study the following source carefully and then answer the questions based on it.

> There was no pressure put on me by my father or anyone else to join the Hitler Youth – I decided to join it simply because I wanted to be in a boys' club where I could strive towards a nationalistic idea. The Hitler Youth had camping, hikes and group meetings… I joined in 1930… There were many boys from all classes of families though mainly middle class and workers. There were no social or class distinctions, which I approved very much. There was no direct or obvious political indoctrination until later. I think most of the boys joined for the same reason as I did. They were looking for a place where they could get together with others in exciting activities. It was also a depressing time and there were many evil influences abroad from which decent boys wished to escape.
> (From *The Nazi Seizure of Power* by W.S. Allen, 1966.)

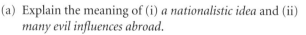

(a) Explain the meaning of (i) *a nationalistic idea* and (ii) *many evil influences abroad.*
(b) To judge from the source, what were main reasons why German boys joined the Hitler Youth?
(c) How valuable is the source to an understanding of the aims and nature of the Hitler Youth Movement? (In your answer use your own relevant background knowledge as well as information derived from the source.)

13

The German Economy Under the Third Reich

INTRODUCTION

As with so many other aspects of the Third Reich there has been much debate over the German economy – did Hitler achieve an economic miracle? Was big business the pawn of the regime? At what stage did the regime embark on rearmament? Did Hitler plan for total mobilisation in 1939? Part of the debate stems from controversy over the reliability of statistics on the Third Reich, especially those relating to the scope and scale of rearmament. The statistics used in this chapter reflect the different interpretations.

1 ⌐ GERMANY'S ECONOMIC CONDITION IN 1933

In January 1933 Germany had all the features of a depressed economy:

● foreign trade had declined;
● industrial production, and with it national income, had fallen by 40 per cent;
● there was mass unemployment, with a third of the working population unemployed;
● wages and real income had fallen with inevitable consequences for those who produced consumer goods.

This depressed economy had all the makings of a major social and business catastrophe. Many felt that there was little prospect of restoring employment and that the end of capitalism was imminent. There was widespread poverty and the effects of the economic difficulties faced in the 1920s with post-war inflation emphasised this. People had been affected unevenly by these problems: big business and trade unionists did well, but peasants, the intelligentsia and white-collar workers did less so, compared with the experience of pre-1914 when they had fared better. The average income of peasants was 600 marks a year compared with 1,000 marks for workers. Germany, like France in the 1920s, was a country of small businesses and light manufacturing, with large numbers of traditional craftsmen, retail shops and cafés. Their standard

1933	March	Hjalmar Schacht becomes President of the *Reichsbank*; SA attack Jewish businesses
	April	Nationwide one-day boycott of Jewish businesses
	May	Trade unions abolished; German Workers' Front established; employment contracts to be regulated by the Reich Trustees of Labour
	June	Law for the reduction of unemployment; German firms begin to contribute 0.5 per cent of wage costs to NSDAP
	September	Reich Food Estate established; work begins on autobahns; Reich Entailed Farm Law
	November	Beauty of Labour and Strength through Joy organisations established
1934	January	Law for the Ordering of National Labour weights industrial relations in favour of management against workforce; Law for the Reconstruction of the Reich
	March	'Battle for Work' begins
	August	Schacht appointed Minister of Economics
	September	Schacht introduces New Plan to reinvigorate economy
	October	Winter Relief Scheme introduced
1935	March	Compulsory military service introduced
	June	Compulsory labour service introduced
1936	April	Göring appointed Commissioner for Raw Materials
	September	Second Four Year Plan aiming to make German economy self-sufficient and laying preparations for a war economy
	October	Göring placed in control of the Second Four Year Plan
1937	February	*Reichsbank* and *Reichsbahn* (railway system) placed under government control
	July	Founding of Göring's steel production works
	November	Schacht resigns as Economics Minister
1938	April	Employment of Jews in business concerns terminated
	December	Compulsory closure and sale of all Jewish businesses to Aryan competitors
1939	January	Schacht dismissed as President of *Reichsbank*
	August	Food rationing introduced
	September	War Economy Decrees
	October	Clothing coupons introduced

TABLE 38

Date chart of chief events in the economy, 1933–9

of living was below the level of semi-skilled workers. Small businesses were disadvantaged by the competition of cheap American goods and had to pay more in welfare payments. Their situation had a detrimental effect in small towns and villages through their role as a credit source. This group was **marginalised** economically in the 1920s. It was hit by widespread poverty across society and shared with the peasantry and impoverished clerks the difficulties of the economy of the 1920s.

The Wall Street Crash of 1929 had not been the cause of collapse of the German economy. It was already in recession by the spring of 1929 so that the crash sent it into a further downswing. There was a shortage of gold and foreign exchange reserves, preventing the purchase of overseas technology, raw materials and foodstuffs, but we need to be clear about the impact of the withdrawal of American cash. There was a net inflow of money until 1931, but German investors moved their money

marginalised pushed to the limit, especially in the sense of having or making no further profit

to safer havens in Switzerland, Holland and England so that there was an outflow of German-based investment. Thus the recession in Germany was not a by-product of the international economy though it was affected by it.

The downturn of the weak domestic economy between 1929 and 1931 is more important. Textbooks have stated that at the height of the depression the number of registered unemployed reached six million, but recent research has shown the figure to be much closer to eight and a half million. The difference represents the number of unemployed who were removed from the register by the government through its programme of voluntary labour service, different kinds of welfare funding or because they were female. The unemployed were not the only ones to suffer; those who were in work found that they were on a short-day week amounting to four days' work with the corresponding reduction in earnings. Small businesses and shops suffered a decline in income by as much as 50 per cent between 1929 and 1932 as consumer demand fell. This was a catastrophe for their owners because they had no reserves. It particularly affected small businessmen, including bankers. As many as 10,000 businesses a year were ruined between 1929 and 1933. This business failure inevitably affected the middle classes and because, as owners of businesses, they did not qualify for welfare payments, they had no recourse but to rely on private charity, such as that offered by soup kitchens. It follows, from what has been said, that the economic crisis of 1929 to 1933 affected all social groups and this goes a long way to explaining the success of the NSDAP and its ability to attract nationwide support.

2 ⌐ HITLER'S RESPONSE TO THE ECONOMIC CATASTROPHE

Even though a recurring promise made during the various *Reichstag* election campaigns of 1928–33 had been *Arbeit und Brot*, (bread and work), Hitler had no preconceived strategy or programme for dealing with the crisis in business. In 1933, he believed that it was a 'matter of will', though he had economic aims based on his election promises to provide workers with work and bread, to rescue the middle class, to carry out land reform in the peasants' favour and to revive business fortunes. Not all of these promises were capable of being achieved because they were in competition with his determination to re-arm Germany rapidly and develop a self-sufficient economy. He was prepared to spend public money to stimulate the economy, but he was also keen to control inflation. Equally, he was aware that he could not politically afford to introduce rationing or sacrifice the working classes' standard of living.

However, earlier interpretations of the economy of the Third Reich that concentrated on Hitler or Göring, and that suggested that economic planning was confused and a victim of competing arguments by various groups, have given way to a belief that a clear economic programme was followed. This does not mean that it could not also be opportunist. In the early years of the regime policies tended to evolve out of the demands of the situation rather than being the result of careful planning. No single unified economic system prevailed and Hitler adopted a political, rather than an economic, view of problems. Despite the anti-capitalist tone of early Nazi manifestos, political realities meant that he frequently had to compromise between a number of competing and often conflicting forces, to meet his election promises and satisfy the different economic interest groups. Hitler wanted to unite the people in a 'people's community' under Nazi leadership. Germans would have to abandon class, economic and religious differences and become one people totally dedicated to the needs of the State. Industrialists, landowners, the middle class and the urban and rural working classes were all to submit to the common interest (see Chapter 10). Every one had to accept the necessity to work hard and to make sacrifices to restore Germany's greatness. Hitler was willing to work with the leaders of big business because he needed their expertise and support to restore confidence and prosperity (we shall be looking at this relationship in greater detail in section 6, page 360). It was not until the end of 1937, when the economy had been revived, that control passed to more radical Nazis. Hitler was opposed to reckless experiments and preferred to continue with pre-1932 modest attempts at the control of inflation and expansion of government spending and employment. He also set out to restore the health of Reich finances with the appointment in March 1933 of Hjalmar Schacht as President of the *Reichsbank* and in August 1934 as Minister of Economics.

> ## KEY ISSUE
>
> *Hitler's role in solving the economic problems.*

> ## HJALMAR SCHACHT (1877–1970)
>
> Schacht was born in Schleswig in January 1877 to a family with Danish origins. His parents had spent the early 1870s in the United States before returning to Germany. Schacht studied medicine, then political science and finally took a doctorate in economics at Berlin.
>
> Ambitious and very able, Schacht quickly made his career in banking and established a reputation as a financial wizard. In 1923, as special currency commissioner in the Finance Ministry, he was mainly responsible for ending the disastrous inflation of that year and setting up a new currency, the *Rentenmark*. At the end of 1923 he was appointed president of the *Reichsbank*, Germany's leading financial institution, a post he held until he resigned in 1930 in protest against the Young Plan (see page 85). A fervent nationalist, he was hostile to the amount of money Germany was expected to

pay the Allies as reparations for war damage and to the growing foreign debt of the Weimar government.

In 1930, having read *Mein Kampf,* he decided that Hitler was a political genius who, unlike the incapable Weimar politicians, might save Germany by supporting a sound economy in a strong state. Schacht left the DDP (which he had helped found in 1919) and became a supporter, though never a member, of the Nazi Party. He helped Hitler secure financial support from the rich Rhineland industrialists from 1930 onwards. He supported Hitler's cause in the prolonged negotiations which preceded the Nazi rise to political power in 1932–3. Hitler rewarded him for his loyalty in March 1933 by making him again president of the *Reichsbank.* This was followed by his appointment as Reich Minister of Economics, from August 1934 to November 1937 when he resigned in protest at Göring's policies under the second Four Year Plan. He was dismissed from the *Reichsbank* in 1939 after a disagreement with Hitler, charged with treason and interned by the Nazis. At the Nuremberg Trials after the war he was acquitted of crimes against humanity.

3 ⌐ THE ROLE OF SCHACHT IN GERMANY'S ECONOMIC RECOVERY 1933–7

Schacht's appointment as Economics Minister reflected the need of the Nazi leadership to work with the powerful forces of big business, for Hitler relied on Schacht's reputation as a respected international banker and a man of great ability. By a law of 3 July 1934 Schacht was given dictatorial powers over the economy and he contributed as much as Hitler to the reconstruction of the Third Reich. Schacht recalls his relationship with the Nazi leadership in his book, *Account Settled,* published in 1949:

> As long as I remained in office, whether at the *Reichsbank* or the Ministry of Economics, Hitler never interfered with my work. He never attempted to give me any instructions, but let me carry out my own ideas in my own way and without criticism… However, when he realised that the moderation of my financial policy was a stumbling block in his reckless plans (in foreign policy), he began, with Göring's connivance, to go behind my back and counter my arrangements.

His approach to the problems of high unemployment and depression in the German economy was influenced by the contemporary British economist, John Maynard Keynes. Keynes urged a policy of state intervention in the economy through public works' schemes which would encourage employment and consumer demand. This was known as the concept of the multiplier.

Initially, the regime under Schacht embarked on a policy of **deficit financing**. In this respect the regime continued with the policies of its predecessors, Brüning and Schleicher, which were already beginning to have an effect. By the time Hitler became Chancellor, the economy was beginning to come out of depression and unemployment was past its peak (see Table 43 on page 351). Schacht was also the economic expert behind German rearmament and he used the financial facilities of the *Reichsbank* to their fullest extent. He enjoyed the full confidence of most of the industrial interest groups who felt he was coping successfully. Profits in key industries increased, wages were kept low and employers were freed of trade union interference. Germany appeared to be regaining her position as a major economic power.

Assessments of Schacht's contribution have varied between those who claim that he 'contributed as much as Hitler to the construction of the Third Reich', to those who criticise him for 'only papering over the cracks'. It is true that he played a vital role in laying down the economic foundations of the Nazi state. By the end of 1935 Germany actually had a trade surplus, unemployment had fallen and industrial production had increased by 49.5 per cent since 1933. However, such successes hid fundamental structural weaknesses for, although he had hidden the balance of payments problem by a series of clever financial schemes, he could not settle the competing demands for scarce resources. Agriculture and industry competed for foreign exchange, while between 1936 and 1937 there was an 80 per cent increase in armament spending. In 1936 matters came to a head with a balance of payments crisis. Schacht believed that a budget deficit and a balance of payments could not be maintained indefinitely. In early 1936 it became clear to him that as the demands of rearmament and consumption increased, the German balance of payments would go deeply into debt. He therefore suggested a reduction in arms expenditure, in order to increase the production of industrial exports to earn foreign exchange. Such a solution was not acceptable to the army or Nazi leadership and Schacht's influence declined, as he described in *Account Settled*:

> **deficit financing**
> spending money on public works to create jobs as an artificial stimulus to demand within the economy, while vigorously controlling prices and wages

> Göring set out, with all the folly and incompetence of the amateur, to carry out a programme of economic self-sufficiency, or autarky, envisaged in the Four Year Plan. Hitler had given him as chief of the Four Year Plan operations in order to extend his own influence over economic policy, which he did not find difficult, since he was now, of course, in a position to place really large contracts... On December 17th 1936, Göring informed a meeting of big industrialists that it was no longer a question of producing economically, but simply of producing. And as far as getting hold of foreign exchange was concerned it was quite immaterial whether the provisions of the law were complied with or not... Göring's policy of recklessly exploiting Germany's economic substance necessarily brought me into more and more

Autarky, page 295

What reasons does Schacht give for the decline in his influence?

Q

acute conflict with him, and for his part he exploited his powers, with Hitler and the Party behind him, to counter my activity as Minister of Economics to an ever-increasing extent. . .

Schacht failed to convince Hitler of the necessity for scaling down rearmament and found his responsibility for the economy reduced in 1936 with the introduction of the second Four Year Plan and the appointment of Göring as its minister. He resigned in 1937 after the November 1937 Hossbach Conference, to be replaced by Walter Funk. From 1936 onwards a more vigorous policy of self-sufficiency or autarky was pursued based on the creation of a trading community in Central Europe under the dominating influence of Germany. Along with this went a defence economy, *Wehrwirtschaft*, whereby the peace-time economy was 'geared to war'.

4 ⤳ THE ROLE OF GÖRING IN GERMANY'S ECONOMIC RECOVERY 1936–9

With Göring's appointment as Minister Plenipotentiary for the second Four Year Plan, he became effectively the economic overlord of Germany and the man in charge of rearmament. He acquired vast powers for amassing property and directing industry. From 1937 onwards, he amassed a vast fortune through the Reichswerke-Hermann-Göring, a state-owned mining and industrial enterprise which was used to keep big industry under control. It became the largest industrial enterprise in Europe, controlling iron ore and coal mining, smelting and refining iron and steel, and manufacturing the finished iron as armaments or heavy machinery. It produced synthetic petrol and ran transport businesses. Göring, through his Hermann Göring Ore and Foundry Company, played an active role in planning the development of Germany's iron ore fields at Salzgitter in Hanover and in Franconia in the south to relieve dependence on imported superior Swedish iron ores. He also planned a similar development of iron and steel plants using coking coal from the Ruhr. The scheme was uneconomic and met with little success. Production at Salzgitter fell below the target while the Franconian iron and steel plants were not built. Territorial expansion brought under German control more lucrative sites which were incorporated into Göring's industrial empire. By the late 1930s Germany was second only to the United States as the largest producer of iron and steel.

Göring also developed a close relationship with the massive chemicals firm, I.G. Farben, Germany's largest private business. The company was committed to developing synthetic chemicals, rubber, petrol, oil and textiles and it persuaded the regime to increase its investment on the promise that it could help Germany achieve economic self-

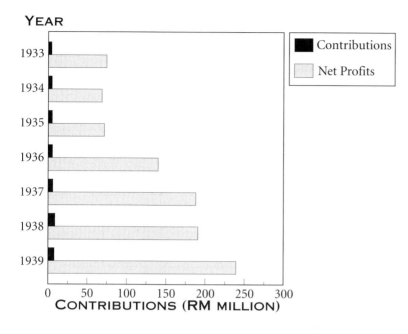

YEAR

CONTRIBUTIONS (RM MILLION)

■ Contributions
□ Net Profits

TABLE 39

*Contributions to the NSDAP and net profits of I.G. Farben, 1933–9 (**RM** million)*

Year	Contribution	Net profits
1933	3.6	74
1934	4.0	68
1935	4.5	71
1936	4.9	140
1937	5.5	188
1938	8.2	191
1939	7.5	240

RM *Rentenmark* or revalued mark. In 1923 after hyperinflation associated with French occupation of the Ruhr, a new currency, the *Rentenmark*, replaced the old mark which had lost all significance as money (see also pages 46–7).

sufficiency. In return the company made increasing financial contributions to the Party, though not on the scale of its profits, and accepted top Nazis on its Board of Directors (Table 39).

Göring developed an administrative structure based on a General Council with its own personnel to administer the Four Year Plan which eventually rivalled and replaced the Ministry of Economics (see Diagram 6). He made all the decisions and also became involved in questions to do with foreign exchange and raw materials as well as taking responsibility for labour allocation, agriculture, price control, industrial investment and foreign trade. From late 1936 onwards Göring floated loans and made large-scale investments in the name of the State. He also increased government regulation so that by late 1938 he was considering a complete nationalisation of heavy industry in order to achieve the Nazi economic and military programme. The impact of Göring's influence in the economy can be seen from the changes in the pattern of industrial investment. In 1937–8, the State accounted for 66 per cent of the total fixed capital investment in industry through the Four Year Plan, which was concentrated in iron, steel, chemicals and machine engineering at the expense of consumer production and house-building. Göring appointed his own commissioners to supervise key industries to ensure that targets set in the Four Year Plan were achieved. He was also given special powers to take over Jewish businesses which would be used for 'national' purposes and which became absorbed into his drive for rearmament. Big business found increasingly that it now had to work within the framework laid down by the Nazi leadership (see section 6 on page 360).

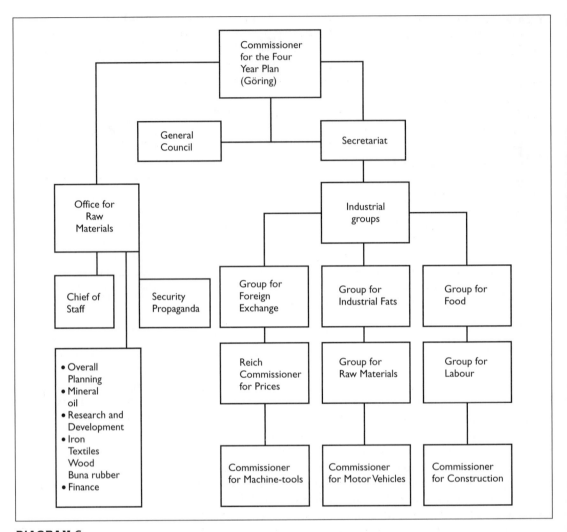

DIAGRAM 6
The organisation of the Second Four Year Plan

5 ⌁ POLICIES TO ACHIEVE ECONOMIC RECOVERY 1933–9

A *Government controls*

A foreign exchange crisis in September 1934 led Schacht to make use of the economic powers he had been given in July 1934. He refused to pay reparations and bargained with Germany's creditors, such as Britain, for a reduced settlement of its debts.

He introduced the New Plan in September which extended the existing system of government control over foreign exchange and import regulation. Importers had to obtain foreign exchange approval before, rather than after, importing goods. Permits had to be obtained for each deal from one of the special supervisory offices which were set up to regulate and control specific commodities. This arrangement allowed the government not only to set the priorities on those goods and raw materials that should be imported but also to prioritise its trading partners. The New Plan gave Schacht the power to pursue a vigorous protectionist policy against Western European countries and the United States with whom it traded at a loss. Pursuing a policy of self-sufficiency or autarky, the regime signed bilateral trade treaties with economically weak countries, such as South America, the Balkans and eastern Europe (Yugoslavia, Romania and Hungary), who could provide the materials vital to Germany's economic recovery. Trade was on a barter basis, Germany exported manufactured goods to its Balkan trading partners in return for raw materials such as chrome, bauxite and oil. Under this barter system the value of the mark was negotiated and varied. Schacht also introduced large-scale export subsidies to bring down prices to a competitive level on the world market. Despite following an autarkic policy, the increasing demands of the armaments industries led to an expansion in the import of industrial raw materials (from 27 per cent in 1932 to 37 per cent in 1937), especially Swedish iron ore, while food imports fell (from 46 per cent in 1932 to 35 per cent in 1937).

Autarky, page 295

B *State-led investment*

As part of the drive to reduce unemployment, Hitler was prepared to rely on the experience of the business community. He wanted to avoid appearing to control the economy too closely, preferring to rely on providing a suitable environment for growth. He hoped that private business would create the economic revival. However, this did not happen so that the regime became permanently involved in the economy, which became state-led. State policies after 1933 led on to a complete system of controls, what Franz Neumann called the 'capitalist command economy'. Without such intervention, the economy might not have recovered to the extent that it did or in the way that Hitler's future war plans dictated. The period 1933–8 saw a considerable economic revival, which to many contemporaries had the appearance of a miracle, which could not have been achieved by the private sector in such a short time. A high level of government spending was embarked upon, increasing from 17.9 per cent in 1932 to 33.5 per cent in 1938 and accelerating after 1936 when the second Four Year Plan and a policy of rearmament

	1928	1932	1934	1936	1938
Total expenditure (current prices) (RM bn)	11.7	8.6	12.8	15.8	29.3
Government expenditure as a percentage of GNP	14.8	17.9	22.9	22.5	35.5

TABLE 40
Government expenditure, 1928–38

TABLE 41
Public expenditure by category, 1928–38 (RM bn)

	1928	1932	1934	1936	1938
Total expenditure including	23.2	17.1	21.6	23.6	37.1
Construction	2.7	0.9	3.5	5.4	7.9
Rearmament	0.7	0.7	3.0	10.2	17.2
Transport	2.6	0.8	1.8	2.4	3.8
Work creation	–	0.2	2.5	–	–

Gross National Product (GNP) an economist's term for the measurement of the total 'value' of the economy

infrastructure services essential for the creation of a modern economy (and the waging of war): power, transport, housing, education, health services, etc.

Q

For what reasons might it be claimed that 'not all businessmen benefited from recovery of the economy'?

were launched. **Gross National Product (GNP)** grew at a remarkably fast rate in Germany during the 1930s, overtaking the level achieved before the years of depression.

Government investment in construction and transport (superseded by rearmament after 1936) played a key role in producing the initial growth which achieved the economic recovery. Hitler sought to solve the unemployment problem by embarking on a vast new building programme to create an **infrastructure** which people would associate with the Thousand Year Reich. The recurring propaganda image of him opening the latest stretch of autobahn was symbolic of this vision. He hoped that a higher standard of living for all Germans would also follow.

However, after 1936 the amount spent on rearmament was particularly high for a peacetime economy, accounting for two-thirds of spending. The economy was restructured to gear it for waging war. Restraints were put on consumer expenditure so that scarce resources could be moved from consumer to capital goods and industrial raw materials (refer to Table 42). Heavy industry benefited, iron, steel and chemicals in particular showed massive growth. The undistributed profits of big business grew from 1.3 to 5 billion RM. By 1939 Germany had a capitalist command economy with 40–50 per cent of the workforce employed on war-related projects.

TABLE 42
Relative growth of producer and consumer goods in Germany, 1929–38 (base year 1928 = 100 for comparison)

	1929	1932	1938
Total production	10.9	58.7	124.7
Capital goods	103.2	45.7	135.9
Consumer goods	98.5	78.1	107.8
Pig iron	113.8	33.4	157.3
Machinery	103.8	40.7	147.7
Chemicals	91.8	50.9	127.0
Textiles	92.4	79.2	107.5
Household furniture	104.2	69.6	113.6

C *Battle for work*

This was one of several propaganda campaigns launched in the first years. It aimed to restore confidence and create the impression of 'something being done'.

- It included a bookkeeping manoeuvre which removed from the unemployment records the names of all those involved in Labour Service and Emergency Relief Schemes, which absorbed 1 million young people.
- This was followed by a number of work creation schemes, starting in June 1933 with the Law to Reduce Unemployment. This aimed to make government-led recovery more effective, but there was a limit to such schemes which only absorbed about 600,000 at their peak.
- The real boost to employment came as the State provided the money for private institutions to engage in work creation schemes and government contracts for railways, roads, bridges and canals. This dragged the heavy industry branch of the economy out of depression more rapidly than the consumer goods industry. Money was poured into public works, such as construction, and subsidies were given for private construction or renovating old buildings.
- A separate law initiated a large-scale plan for building 7,000 kilometres of motorway, which encouraged both employment and subsidiary industries.

But there was no consumer boom. Consumer industries were discriminated against over investment and contracts, so that their performance by late 1938 was lower than in the 1920s. Income tax rebates and loans were issued to increase industrial activity in the private sector. There was also an attempt by the German Labour Front to improve working conditions through its promotion of various organisations, such as *Kraft durche Freude* (Strength through Joy) and *Schönheit der Arbeit* (Beauty of Work).

The 'battle for work' policies were very successful and, combined with an upturn in the **trade cycle**, brought the 1929 depression to an end. Unemployment fell rapidly from the 1932 registered figure of 5.6 million to 2.7 million by 1934 and had been eliminated by the spring of 1939 when there was even a labour shortage and great pressure was put on labour. This decline in unemployment was an impressive achievement and one which won admiration at home and abroad.

Trade cycle alternating periods of trade boom and depression

Q

How successful were these policies?

	1928	1932	1934	1936	1938
Gross national product (1928 prices) (RM bn)	89.5	57.6	66.5	82.6	104.5
Industrial production 1928 = 100	100	58	83	107	122
Unemployed (in millions)	1.4	5.6	2.7	1.6	0.4

TABLE 43
Economic recovery and its impact on unemployment, 1928–38

D *Protection of farming*

We have already looked at the role of the peasantry in Nazi propaganda, ideology and the people's community in previous chapters. This section is concerned with the regime's policies towards agriculture as an industry. The problems confronting the agricultural industry in 1933 partly stemmed from Germany's shortage of foreign currency along with the collapse of world trade which meant that foreign food imports fell. Added to this there were problems arising from poor weather conditions; it was a harvest failure in 1928 which had flung the economy into a depression even before the Wall Street Crash. National Socialist policy towards agriculture was to achieve self-sufficiency, particularly in fats, partly to relieve continuing pressure on scarce foreign currency but also for defence in the event of future war. A 'battle of production' to increase grain production was introduced but this policy was hampered by poor harvests in 1934 and again 1935. New measures for agricultural production were introduced in 1936 under Göring's Four Year Plan organisation, but these favoured arable rather than livestock farmers. These measures included reduction in fertiliser prices, mechanisation subsidies and grants for bringing new land into cultivation, and, combined with good harvests in 1938–9, led to a rise of 20 per cent in production compared with 1928–9. Livestock farmers, however, still had to rely on imports of feed and were given fewer subsidies. The regime's support of agriculture met with some success. By 1938–9 self-sufficiency had been achieved in bread grains, potatoes, and sugar, closely followed by vegetables and meat, but there was a crucial shortfall in animal fats. Attempts to grow substitute oil seed plants were uneconomic and of marginal significance. However, the main obstacle to agricultural expansion was the shortage of labour, which had become

TABLE 44

Revenue and costs of agriculture 1928–39 (base year 1932/33 = 100 for comparison)

Year	Revenue	Costs
1928/29	163	145
1932/33	100	100
1933/34	117	102
1934/35	132	103
1935/36	141	111
1936/37	145	116
1937/38	157	124
1938/39	172	133

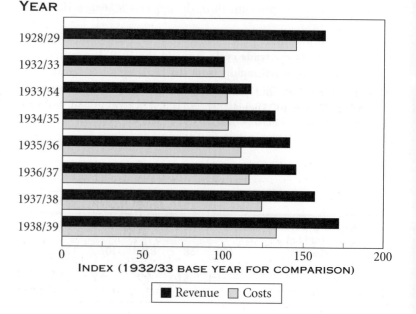

serious by 1939 and which was only partly met by the drafting in of foreign labour. Food consumption per head of the population increased by about 4–5 per cent but only 57 per cent of the demand for fats was met. The price of foodstuffs was strictly controlled after 1935, but was allowed to rise more than farm costs. Price increases varied, but all remained below those for 1928–9. Even so, with the increase in production after 1935, farmers' incomes went up by 41 per cent between 1933 and 1938; this was small compared with trade and industry's 116 per cent, but significant when compared with the 25 per cent gain enjoyed by industrial workers.

E *The second Four Year Plan 1936*

By 1936 the regime had gone a long way to achieving Hitler's primary goal of redeeming his election promises of 'bread and work', a success which secured his position. In 1936 he issued his Secret Memo in which he discussed the 'programme for a final provision of our vital needs'. This is one of the central documents of the Third Reich and it represents Hitler's response to his critics, such as Schacht, Reich Minister for Economics, and the opposition of German business to all large-scale plans to achieve economic self-sufficiency (autarky) in the interests of rearmament.

The Secret Memo is valuable to historians:

- as an insight into Hitler's war aims;
- as evidence that he was planning for war from 1936;
- as evidence of Hitler's views on the economy and its relationship to political and rearmament objectives;
- as an account of Nazi rearmament objectives in 1936.

In other words, its *value* is as a serious statement of intent to wage a war. Its *limitation* is that it is not possible to say what kind of war Hitler was planning, or the extent of Germany's preparedness in 1939.

The Memo, and the second Four Year Plan which it launched, outlined his plans for completely converting the economy and the armed forces for war within four years. This extract, from the Memorandum on the Four Year Plan, August 1936, is quoted in Noakes and Pridham, *Nazism 1919–1945, A Documentary Reader, Vol 2*:

> **KEY ISSUE**
>
> *The economy is geared for war 1936–9.*

The world has been moving with ever-increasing speed towards a new conflict, the most extreme solution of which is Bolshevism... I therefore draw up the following programme for a final provision of our vital needs:
i. Parallel with the military and political rearmament and mobilisation of our nation must go its economic rearmament and mobilisation... In future the interests of individual gentlemen can no longer play any part in these matters. There is only one interest, the interest of the nation; only one view, the bringing of Germany to the point of political and economic self-sufficiency.

ii. ...foreign exchange must be saved in all those areas where our needs can be satisfied by German production...

iii. ...German fuel production must now be stepped up with the utmost speed and brought to final completion within eighteen months.

iv. The mass production of synthetic rubber must also be organised and achieved with the same urgency. From now on there must be no talk of processes not being fully determined and other such excuses... This has nothing whatever to do with the Ministry of Economics. Either we possess today a private industry, in which case its job is to rack its brains about methods of production; or we believe that it is the Government's job to determine methods of production, and in that case we have no further need of private industry.

v. ...If we really are obliged to build up our domestic economy on autarkic lines, which we are...then the price of raw materials individually considered no longer plays a decisive part.

It is further necessary to increase German iron production to the utmost limits... The job of the Ministry of Economics is simply to set the national economic tasks; private industry has to fulfil them. But if private industry thinks itself incapable of doing this, then the National Socialist State will know how to resolve the problem on its own... Nearly four precious years have now gone by... There has been time enough in four years to find out what we cannot do. Now we have to carry out what we can do.

I thus set the following tasks:

i.   The German armed forces must be operational within four years.

ii. The German economy must be fit for war within four years.

Q *Why was autarky such an important priority for Hitler in 1936?*

The Memo highlighted four priorities: to achieve an increase in agricultural production, to retrain key sectors of the labour force, to impose government regulation of imports and exports, and to achieve self-sufficiency in raw materials. Official production goals were set for the production of raw materials vital to the rearmament drive – oil, rubber and metals.

The emphasis of the Four Year Plan, and a recurring theme in all Hitler's speeches, was Germany's scarcity of foodstuffs and raw materials in relation to the competing demands of the population and rearmament. Scarce resources created a conflict between 'guns before butter' and people were unwilling 'to tighten their belts'. It was recognised from the beginning that there was a direct relationship between rearmament and the people's standard of living for Germany's foreign exchange reserves could not cover unlimited quantities of both. The Four Year Plan was designed to re-orientate the economy for war, by achieving self-sufficiency in essential war materials of oil, rubber, and steel. This would relieve pressure on scarce foreign exchange which would enable Germany to continue with its food imports until the long-term solution of living space had been secured. As would appear from the concluding comments to the Memo, Hitler's concern was to

TABLE 45

German production increases in the sphere of the Second Four Year Plan

Commodity	1936 output (000 tons)	Output in 1936 as a percentage of 1940 Plan target	1938 output (000 tons)	Output in 1938 as a percentage of 1940 Plan target	Plan target (000 tons)
Mineral oil, including synthetic petrol	1,790	12.9	2,340	16.9	13,830
Aluminium	98	35.9	166	60.8	273
Buna rubber	0.6	0.6	5	4.2	120
Nitrogen	770	74.0	914	87.9	1,040
Explosives	18	8.1	45	20.2	223
Steel	19,216	80.1	22,656	94.4	24,000
Iron ore	2,255	40.6	3,360	60.5	5,549
Brown coal	161,382	67.1	194,985	81.1	240,500
Hard coal	158,400	74.4	186,186	87.4	213,000

ensure that 'the German armed forces must be operational within four years' and 'the economy must be fit for war'.

By 1936 the regime had come to a turning point.

1 Having achieved a dramatic fall in unemployment, a rise in investment and a secure foreign trade, which did not leave Germany a debtor, Hitler then expected the revitalised economy to be geared to rearmament. He had recognised that a strong economy was required if he was going to achieve the massive military machine which would enable him to achieve his long-term foreign policy goals of *Lebensraum* with its attendant threat of war with Russia.

2 Massive rearmament was not well received by either Schacht or important businessmen, including the armaments baron, Gustav Krupp, who believed that the regime should continue with its drive to raise people's standards of living and levels of consumption and expand foreign trade. They were not opposed to some limited rearmament but not at the cost of consumers.

This divergence of views regarding the future direction of the economy led to an intense debate between ministers, the army and business leaders. Hitler's Secret Memo, and the Four Year Plan which it launched, marked a significant new stage in the regime's economic strategy. Control of the economy increasingly passed to the ambitious Göring who was made Minister Plenipotentiary for the Second Four Year Plan while Schacht's influence was reduced (see sections 3 and 4, pages 344–8). State control and the direction of industry was tightened in the interests of preparing the economy for war. Hitler completed his control at the beginning of 1938 when he made himself supreme commander of the armed forces. Delivered from his dependence on the elites which had acted as a restraint on his freedom of action, Hitler proceeded with his massive rearmament programme.

KEY ISSUE

What type of war was Hitler planning?

F *The role of rearmament 1936–9 – early research on Germany's war effort*

What was the level of German rearmament in the 1930s? Was the economy fully mobilised for war? Historians' answers to these two questions have changed over time as the availability of sources has grown and the technique of statistical sampling has become more sophisticated. A further complication is added by misconceptions about the size of the armed forces. The Nazis always exaggerated their size, especially the number of aircraft, for propaganda purposes. This meant that some contemporaries, such as Churchill, and later the Allies in the Second World War, thought that the Nazis must have been preparing for war as fast as they could. Also, in spite of the mass of material about Nazism, there are gaps in information about the 1930s and, in any case, it is difficult to isolate armament expenditure from other investment. Hitler's autobahns were part of his 'battle for work' campaign, but they also had a military significance in their capacity to move large numbers of men and materials quickly by road. Consequently historians have not been able to agree whether the building of the autobahns should be included in rearmament. Another area of doubt is the issue of **MEFO bills** which were a means of raising money to finance the recovery of heavy industry. It is difficult to say what proportion of the MEFO bill issue was for financing arms, though one source claims it was as much as 50 per cent in the mid 1930s.

MEFO bills a form of deficit financing, named after the Metallurgische Forschung GmbH (Metallurgical Research Inc) used to camouflage their secret purpose in financing rearmament

Given the limitations of the sources, historians until the mid 1980s tended to agree that:

Blitzkrieg lightning war

- Hitler was planning a series of short sharp lightning wars or **Blitzkrieg** which did not require the tremendous rearmament associated with total war. He was concerned that there should not be a repeat of the hardships suffered by the German people in the First World War which had cost the Kaiser his throne.
- The economy did not become fully mobilised until at least 1942, when Albert Speer became Minister of Armaments, while a full-scale commitment was not achieved until 1944.
- Hitler's ambitions were out of phase with economic and military planning.

HISTORIANS' DEBATE

The nature of Germany's war effort

A.J.P. Taylor: 'Hitler and the Origins of the Second World War', in **E.M. Robertson (ed.),** *The Origins of the Second World War* **(Macmillan, 1971).**

He took the most extreme view that 'Hitler was not really planning for war in 1939 and the proof of this lay in the level of German rearmament which by 1939 was by no means great enough to sustain a European, let alone a world, war'. Few of the statistics available since the 1960s support Taylor's interpretation. The limited character of German rear-

mament which, according to Taylor, proves that he did not want a war, is only really supported by the early figures published in 1959 by B.H. Klein (Germany's Economic Preparations for War*) when the study of the German economy under the Third Reich was still in its infancy and source material was unsatisfactory and incomplete.*

Since the publication of Taylor's view there has been much debate about German levels of armaments in the 1930s and the question whether Hitler planned to go to war. The fierceness of the debate led to the critical testing of his interpretation using revised statistics on the German economy. The figures compiled by Klein were superseded by those of B.E. Carroll in 1968.

T.W. Mason: 'Some Origins of the Second World War' in E.M. Robertson (ed.), *The Origins of the Second World War* (Macmillan, 1971).

He criticised A.J.P. Taylor for ignoring the effects of rearmament on the German economy which saw a change in its structure in the 1930s: an increase in public spending which put greater importance on heavy industry, the trend towards autarky, and the suppression of consumer spending. By 1939 a long-term crisis had appeared associated with a huge labour shortage, inadequate exports and a generally overheated economy. This put important restraints on Germany's ability to rearm which could only be overcome if new sources of raw materials, food and labour were found. Hitler was forced to go to war to divert attention away from these structural strains which had first appeared in 1937 and were inherent in the economy. According to Mason, German armaments were not sufficient in 1939 to sustain a long war, so that 'Hitler was planning to employ *Blitzkrieg* or 'lightning war' tactics rather than preparing for long campaigns of trench warfare'.

A.S. Milward: *The German Economy at War* (Athlone Press, 1965)

He argues that there was an ultimate connection between economy, strategy and Nazi ideology. The lack of raw materials meant that short wars were the preferred method. This avoided mobilising the whole German economy for war which would have placed enormous strains on the economy and led to civilian unrest. Hitler did not trust the German people, so he had to offer them victories at least cost because he could not expect them to agree to sacrifices. Hitler did not mobilise totally for war so that 'at no time was anything like the full capacity of the German economy devoted to war production'.

B.E. Carroll: *Design for Total War: Arms and Economics in the Third Reich* (Mouton, 1968)

The title is misleading in so far as she does not agree with the view that the Nazis planned a total war. Her conclusions are that from 1934 onwards Germany moved towards a war-orientated economy. In 1936 armaments dominated government expenditure for goods and services as well as investments. In 1938 the economy was on a

TABLE 46
Klein's estimates of armament expenditure, 1933–9 (RM million)

1933–5	5
1935–6	6
1936–7	10
1937–8	14
1938–9	16
April–Sept 1939	4

war footing but military expenditure did not dominate the economy until 1942 when 50 per cent or more of economic resources were devoted to war purposes. By 1939 Britain was spending a similar percentage of gross national expenditure which would suggest that Germany was not more prepared for war than Britain – except of course that it was growing from a wider armament base as a result of stockpiling from 1934.

TABLE 47

Comparison of German and British military expenditure as a percentage of GNP/National Income (taken as Equivalent), 1933–9

Year	Germany (RM billion) GNP	%	Britain (£ billion) National Income	%
1933	59	3	3.7	3
1934	67	6	3.9	3
1935	74	8	4.1	2
1936	83	13	4.4	5
1937	93	13	4.6	7
1938	105	17	4.8	8
1939	130	23	5.0	22

GNP exceeds National Income, but for the purpose of this table the two may be taken as the same.

Q

Who was more prepared for war in 1939?

G Recent research on Germany's war effort

R. J. Overy in 'Hitler's War and the German Economy – a Re-interpretation' (*Economic History Review*, May 1982), has rejected the prevailing interpretation that Hitler planned for a limited war with limited resources. He argues that historians have ignored the detailed figures. Hitler planned for a total war and when war broke out Germany mobilised as fast as it could. Overy supports this argument by citing:

- The revolution in politics and the economy from the mid-1930s, particularly after 1938 when Hitler appointed people who agreed with his idea of a large-scale war effort.
- Economic planning which aimed to transform the economy in readiness for war. It would occur in two stages: expansion in central and eastern Europe to provide a big resource base for raw materials and gold for the war effort. This stage was not completely achieved until the absorption of Austria and Czechoslovakia in 1938, followed by Poland in 1939. The second stage, introduced in 1936, was a policy of autarky in preparation for the big war effort.
- Göring's references in 1938 to what he called a 'war of great proportions' which could last a long time (15 years), and which would begin in around 1943 or 1944, and to Speer's 'victory buildings' which would be completed by about 1951.
- Hitler's speeches which saw Russia as the enemy whose super-economic power potential Germany would have to equal.

● The dominant role of rearmament in the economy between 1936 and 1939, when two-thirds of industrial investment was devoted to war preparation including expansion of the chemical, aluminium, aviation and engineering industries. By 1939, over a quarter of the industrial workforce was working on orders for the armed forces. This commitment was much bigger than was needed for *Blitzkrieg*.

Germany was to 'leapfrog' Britain and France to face the USA and the USSR. Plans for the American Bomber, an intercontinental bomber, were authorised in 1938, the German airforce was to be expanded five-fold, a vast battle fleet would be built and the army would be motorised. These plans were not to be completed until the mid-1940s. 'This will not be like 1914', Hitler told his generals in 1939. It was a high-risk policy because there were many among the elites, army and business owners who did not agree with Hitler's strategy and its risks to the economy. However, these plans failed to materialise. Hitler did not think the Polish war would spread because he did not believe the British would do anything since they were pressing Poland to give up Danzig. Hitler, badly advised by German intelligence that Britain was ill-prepared, believed that any war with Poland would be small and localised. Germany was not really ready for war in 1939, and, according to Overy, the limited mobilisation was not planned but resulted from the great inefficiency of German economic planning.

TABLE 48

Percentage of German industrial labour forces working on orders for the armed forces by 1939

	1939
All industry, including	21.9
Raw materials	21.0
Metal manufacture	28.6
Construction	31.5
Consumer goods	12.2

KEY ISSUE

How successful were these plans?

TABLE 49

Select statistics comparing German and British war effort by 1939

Comparison	Germany	Britain
Index of consumer expenditure (per head) 1938 = 100	95.0	97.2
Employment in war industries % of all employed	21.9	18.6
% of women in the total of civilian employment	37.3	26.4
% of war expenditure in total national income	32.2	15.0

The production goals were never achieved (see Table 45 on page 355) because of the problem of finance. There was an attempt to solve this by increased government control as part of a 'capitalist command economy'. Taxes were increased, **promissory notes** were issued and prices were controlled (1936–7).

There was some success with the second Four Year Plan, for war in 1939 could not have happened but for the Plan, despite Schacht's doubts. His successor, Walter Funk, believed that the Four Year Plan should divert resources away from other sectors, especially consumer to meet armament and war needs. This meant discrimination against consumer goods and workers, which had been demanded by industry, the

promissory notes signed documents containing a written promise to pay a stated sum to the named person or the bearer at a specified date or on demand

army and civil service who wanted priority to go to armaments. This demand was rejected by the Nazi leadership who 'feared' the people and doubted their loyalty in a crisis, as had occurred in 1918. The policy of terror and propaganda had a limited success and this led the leadership to provide material concessions. Workers were provided with housing estates through the 'Strength through Joy' initiative and with leisure activities especially for the low paid (see Chapter 10). There was the promise of car ownership, whilst labour shortages meant that workers demanded and won higher wages though these were absorbed by the rising cost of living.

Labour mobilisation was a major indicator of the level of economic mobilisation as a whole. Heavy industry and metalworking, the latter suffered from a labour shortage, expanded their labour supply whereas building and consumer industries contracted up to 1941, but then numbers in the consumer industry went up again in 1943. In the metal manufacturing industry, which included most arms production, the increase in numbers working on orders for the army was most marked, rising from 28.6 per cent in 1939 to 68.8 per cent by 1941, but only to 72 per cent by 1943. The proportion in the consumer sector working on military orders rose from 12.2 per cent in 1939 to 27.8 per cent in 1941, at a time when there was a fall in total numbers working in this sector from 3.58 million in 1939 to 2.56 million by 1942. In 1941 the services took 40 per cent of textiles output and 44 per cent of all clothing, which left much less capacity for civilian needs than output figures suggest.

Overy also rejects, as a statistical illusion, the claim that Germany, unlike Britain, failed to mobilise women for war work. His most recent statistics show that by 1939 women already constituted a much larger part of the workforce in Germany than in Britain, 37.3 per cent compared with 26.4 per cent, and this lead was maintained overall.

6 ⌐ RELATIONSHIP BETWEEN THE REGIME AND BIG BUSINESS

The position of big business under the Third Reich has been the subject of some debate amongst historians. Was the relationship based on subservience, co-operation or opposition? Equality or subservience? The debate highlights that this is an area where research is still in its infancy. The relationship is important for it is relevant to the question – how did Hitler come to power?

A *Was Hitler the 'pawn' who was submissive to the interests of big business?*

The question central to the Marxist analysis of the whole phenomenon of Nazism is the 'agent' theory – was Hitler merely the pawn of German monopoly capitalism in its imperialistic ambitions? This was certainly the view taken by the Comintern, the Soviet-controlled international federation of Communist parties in 1935 when it described German fascism as 'the openly terroristic dictatorship of the most reactionary, the most chauvinistic and most imperialist elements in finance Capitalism'. Even the propaganda of Social Democratic parties in the 1930s was often not very different, and portrayed Hitler simply as an agent of big business. According to those historians who take a determinist view of history, the Third Reich was the creation of powerful economic forces. They claim that big business interests sought to use Hitler's ability to attract and control the masses to stave off a challenge from the rising socialist/communist forces in Germany. Through financial assistance and pressure-group manoeuvring, they handed him the chancellorship though real power would remain in their hands. They expected Hitler to crush the political left, suppress the labour movement and thus allow their businesses to function freely.

KEY ISSUE

Was Hitler the pawn of big business?

The best discussion of big business in control of the Nazis is A. Merson's 'Nazis and Monopoly Capital' in H.A. Turner (ed.), *Nazism and the Third Reich*. His argument is that the Nazis soon lost their anti-capitalist stance because setting up the Labour Front put employers in control. According to his interpretation, Nazi Germany in the 1930s saw a rapid development in monopoly capitalism where priority was given to rearmament. Monopoly capitalism is a Marxist term to describe big business. It means the concentration of the means of production/industry in one or a few hands. Industry was concentrated in the Ruhr Basin, North-Rhine, Westphalia and the Saar, and it included such families as the Krupps (armaments), Farben, Flick and Mercedes-Benz. One example already mentioned in the preceding pages is the massive chemicals firm, I.G. Farben, which was Germany's largest private business. The company controlled the production of synthetic chemicals, rubber, petrol, oil and textiles.

In Merson's view, the power of the great monopolies expanded not only during the armament boom of the 1930s but also during the period of conquests, 1938–42. Göring became the economic chief, not as the Nazi spokesman against big business but, on the contrary, because he enjoyed the confidence of the monopolies concerned. Some of the great monopoly firms, such as I.G. Farben, Krupp and Flick exploited the defeated countries. Friedrich Flick used slave labour in his Ruhr industries, the majority of whom died, while Alfred Krupp's armament company, Krupp von Böhlen und Halbach, plundered the industrial plant of occupied Europe and exploited concentration camp labour. After 1942 the interests of monopoly capital found expression through Speer, and Göring's influence declined. Merson commented on what he regarded as a significant absence of important representatives of monopoly capitalism in the bomb plot of July 1944. According to him, the leading sections of monopoly capital backed Hitler to the end – 'until Anglo-American armies began to take over'.

Such views have not found a great deal of favour or support among western writers on Nazism. Writers, such as Karl Bracher in his influential *The German Dictatorship* (Weidenfeld & Nicolson 1971), and H.A. Turner, 'German Big Business and the Rise of Hitler' (*American*

Historical Review, LXXV, 1969), have denied any real connections between Nazism and capitalism. Turner's argument is that although big business did not like Weimar and parliamentary democracy, neither did they support the Nazis. Most recent research suggests that substantial amounts of money were not paid by the big families; the one million marks contribution by Fritz Thyssen, heir to one of the great steel enterprises of the Ruhr, was an exception. Most of the big business money went to the conservative opponents of the Nazis, especially to Papen. Many hoped that the NSDAP would not come into power except as an alternative to a communist takeover of the State. Hitler only got money once he had become Chancellor and this helped in his consolidation of power. Most of the financial support came from small and medium-sized businessmen who were the real victims of the depression. They cannot be described as 'monopoly capitalists'. The giant businesses of the country knew from past experience that their importance to the national economy was so great that no government could afford to let them go bankrupt. Anyway, big business was too divided and too uncertain to play a crucial role in bringing Hitler to power and they believed Papen, not Hitler, would be the key figure in the new government of January 1933. If there was any link between Nazism and capitalism, it was the benefit that Hitler gained from the long-term economic and social problems which affected the economy 1928–33. In that respect 'National Socialism was thus undeniably a child of the capitalist order'.

B *Was big business submissive to National Socialism 1933–45?*

The best discussion of the Nazis in control of big business is T. Mason's 'The Primacy of Politics – Politics and Economics in National Socialist Germany' in H.A. Turner (ed.), *Nazism and the Third Reich* (1972). Mason's argument is that the Nazis always claimed to set up the 'primacy of politics'. The Nazis came to power pledged to solve the economic crisis and set up a new social harmony. In this process of reconstruction, there is little evidence that economic pressure groups had any say in the formulation of the economic policy of the Third Reich. According to Mason's argument, the 1930s was a difficult period for the industrial power block as a result of the lack of foreign exchange, of new materials and labour. Heavy industry lost its old political supremacy and the chemical industry rose to influence. Other firms squabbled amongst each other for new materials and labour. The rapid success of the army in extending Germany's sphere of influence made plunder possible, but also necessary, because of Germany's lack of raw materials and labour.

In his attempts to create a new Germany economically, socially and morally, Hitler had to re-inflate the domestic economy to achieve full employment and growth. This required policies which purposefully broke the links between the German capitalist economy and that of the rest of the world, especially with Europe and America. This is evident in the introduction of extreme controls on trade, on exchange, and on the granting of import/export licences. Scarcity of foreign exchange meant that exports could not pay for the imports required and currency speculation was organised on a large scale. By 1935 international economic controls against German trade also became more extreme and by 1936 it was evident that there was no way that the Nazi economy could blend with the rest of Europe. The regime's aggressive foreign policy further contributed to its isolation. At the same time, in 1936 domestic economic planning began to take second place to rearmament. The proportion of domestic expenditure devoted to work-creation schemes was reduced as the second Four Year Plan sought to create new industries – synthetic rubber and oil – and to develop to a larger extent old industries such as steel.

Introduction of a capitalist command economy was not necessarily in the best interests of all industrialists and businessmen. Bilateral trading agreements discriminated against some export-based industries. The regime was not interested in helping private businesses to foster economic ties with other countries. As part of the massive rearmament programme Hermann Göring's industrial empire was allowed to develop steel works which were hostile to private business interests. Hitler was furious at criticisms in business circles about production costs and he threatened, if the private sector could not comply with the demands of autarky, to resort to state intervention to achieve his purpose. The setting up of the state-run Hermann Göring-Werke to process low grade steel ore was just such a response to opposition from steel magnates to the high production costs of such ores.

In his chapter entitled 'Fascism and the Economy' in W. Laquer (ed.), *Fascism, A Reader's Guide* (Penguin 1979) Alan Milward argues that the anti-capitalist nature of Nazi policies became more evident during the war. War benefited the munitions-based industries as production expanded on a vast scale. The directors of I.G. Farben became public officials directing the second Four Year Plan, whereas many industries, particularly those which relied on consumer demand, found their interests were increasingly squeezed out. Government control of research, development and production in a war economy increased against the interests of some businesses. Labour was difficult to recruit because work permits ensured that it would be diverted to war industries to the disadvantage of consumer industries. But even more serious for industry was that from 1941, despite the clear need for more workers, Hitler embarked on the extermination of the Jews and the brutal treatment in the camps of peoples of the east who died from starvation or diseases. Moreover, transport of Jews to the camps was given priority on railway lines instead of raw materials for war production.

Milward acknowledges that his interpretation is not based on objective statistical analysis, but on his belief that capitalism and Nazism had different visions of society. Confirmation of this interpretation is impossible because it requires an answer to one of the great 'ifs' in history – what would have happened if Germany had won the war?

KEY ISSUE

Was big business the pawn of National Socialism?

C *Did big business co-operate with Hitler?*

The present state of statistical evidence gives greater weight to a relationship based on co-operation rather than antagonism. In recent years historians, such as Ian Kershaw, have emphasised the importance of ideology in determining policy. He argues that leading capitalists, recognising that the Weimar Republic could not solve Germany's economic problems, were prepared to accept Nazism because it could further their interests. They believed that Hitler's government would solve the economic crisis by political measures starting with the crushing of the left. The holding down of wages by the regime in the years which followed, coupled with the massive increases in government investment, profits and dividends, showed clearly that they could benefit from the Nazi dictatorship. Businessmen during these mid-years of the 1930s concentrated on rebuilding their firms and increasing their profits, with great success in some cases.

Even though the Four Year Plan did not benefit those industries that were geared to the export or the consumer market, it showed how closely state and industrial leadership were tied together. The directors of I.G. Farben, who administered the Plan, found that their interests and profits became so closely identified with its success that it came to be known as the 'I.G. Farben plan'. Kershaw believes that the industrial leaders did not realise that the regime's policies would end in destruction not reconstruction until the end phase of the war in 1944 when defeat was obvious. He sees no conflict between war-orientated elements of industry and the National Socialistic leadership as evidenced by the absence of representatives of big business, or specific sections of it, among the 1944 July conspirators. The war economy brought profits to considerable sections of capitalist enterprise while the racialist policies of the regime, especially from 1941 onwards, did not conflict with the interests of big business. There were no protests from the latter against the extermination of the Jews, major camps such as Auschwitz had workshops employing slave labour and capitalists, like the Krupps, were prepared to run slave camps/factories 'employing' eastern peoples.

This further knitting together of the interests of the regime with that of some industry was symbolised by the close co-operation of the SS and industrial leadership through Himmler's 'friendship circles' (*Freun-*

TABLE 50

Profits in German firms, 1933–7 (figures in RM millions)

Firm	1933	1934	1935	1936	1937
United Steel	8.87	21.24	22.85	27.01	27.60
Krupp	6.65	11.40	16.60	17.61	17.80
Mannesmann	2.09	3.39	5.84	7.30	8.35
Daimler-Benz	2.47	4.12	4.10	6.23	2.51
Ford, Cologne	–	–	0.06	0.36	0.41
Total for the 1400 largest companies	36,000	45,000	50,000	59,000	–

deskreis). These met regularly, once a month, to discuss policies to serve their mutual interests and help the SS make decisions in running its expanding economic empire. The future SS State was one, therefore, in which capitalist enterprise still had a major role to play. Kershaw regards such developments as producing a capitalist society of a 'peculiar' kind which would, once war ended, produce a 'New Order' in the east.

7 ⌐ LIMITATIONS TO THE REGIME'S ACHIEVEMENTS

By 1939 the economy had been revived under the regime's control, but economic self-sufficiency was not achieved as the shortfalls in the targets of the Second Four Year Plan indicate.

Weak spots remained: in finance; in shortage of labour, of raw materials and of foreign exchange. The strains produced by competing demands on scarce resources and the difficulties these represented for the regime were perceptively assessed in the following report by an SPD analyst in July 1938 (quoted in Noakes and Pridham, *Nazism 1919–1945, A Documentary Reader, Vol 2*):

> Under the lash of the dictatorship, the level of economic activity has been greatly increased. The exploitation of labour has been increased; female employment has been increased despite the totally contradictory Nazi ideal of womanhood; and a large number of the *Mittelständlern* [self-employed people] have been transformed into wage-labourers despite the totally contradictory Nazi ideal of their status... But even Nazi trees cannot grow up to the sky. It is true...each year 12–13 billion RM are squeezed from the national income for rearmament... But one cannot do everything at once with the extorted billions...to increase armaments for the land and air forces ad infinitum, to build up a massive battle fleet, to fortify new extended borders, to build gigantic installations for the production of ersatz [synthetic] materials, to construct megalomaniacal grandiose buildings...one can do either one or the other or a bit of everything, but not everything at the same time and in unlimited dimensions...

KEY ISSUE

Were the regime's successes short lived?

Q

How does this source help to explain the relative failure of the Four Year Plan? (Look also at Table 43.)

However, these strains were not sufficient to create, as some historians have argued, an economic crisis in 1939 which persuaded Hitler to go to war. They did mean that there were limitations to the regime's achievements for several of the different economic interest groups which Hitler had promised to protect and reward.

A *For the worker*

The regime's success in reducing unemployment, to the extent that there was even a labour shortage by 1938, and stabilising the economy, was achieved at a cost to some workers. These economic achievements, however, require qualification. Improvements in German standards of living fell behind those of other western economies and did not return to the pre-1914 levels. The reward of a radio, car, holidays and leisure activities, sports fields and swimming baths was accompanied by long hours, primitive conditions and a fall in the purchasing power of wages. Amongst low-paid civil servants and salaried workers, there was a decline in the consumption of important foodstuffs – beer, tropical fruit, meat, bacon, milk and eggs – and a rise in the consumption of cheaper substitutes such as potatoes and rye bread. Private consumption as a percentage of national income fell from 64 per cent in 1936 to 59 per cent by 1938. This was a third below that of Britain and a half below that of the USA. There were two main reasons to explain this. Firstly, Hitler's concern to control inflation meant that any significant improvement in workers' standards of living was sacrificed. Secondly, the idea of a planned economy in which the material situation of all social groups was subordinated to the over-riding aim of rearmament ('guns before butter') demanded the cutback of the consumer sector. This meant that not all workers suffered a similar deterioration in living standards and so the response of the working class was varied and complex. Those employed in consumer-based industries, such as the cotton industry, suffered from short-time working and reduced wages in contrast to those employed in the capital goods sector. Boom conditions produced a fierce competition for scarce labour and led to the 'poaching' of workers and offers of wage increases in defiance of the regime's wage controls. Miners, metalworkers and construction workers experienced a rise in real incomes by 1939 but at the expense of increased tiredness with the introduction of a longer work day, night shifts and overtime. The regime failed to win the support of workers who resented being regimented and directed. They could articulate their discontent only to a limited extent, but as the reports of the Reich Trustees of Labour indicate, sections of demoralised workers, particularly in the mining, building and metalworking industries showed passive resistance in the form of sickness, breaches of contract, refusal

TABLE 51

Real wages and private consumption in Germany, 1932–8 compared with 1928

Q

Can it be claimed that 'economic recovery was achieved at a cost to the workers'? (Use Table 43 on page 351 with Table 51)

	1928	1932	1934	1936	1938
Real wages (1913/14) = 100)	110	120	116	112	112
Real earnings (1925/29 = 100)	106	91	88	93	101
Wages as a percentage of National Income	62	64	62	59	57
Private consumption as a percentage of National Income	71	83	76	64	59

Real wages – the value of money wages in terms of the amount of goods and services that can be bought.
Real earnings – the value of all earned income, as above, taking account of overtime, short-time and absenteeism.

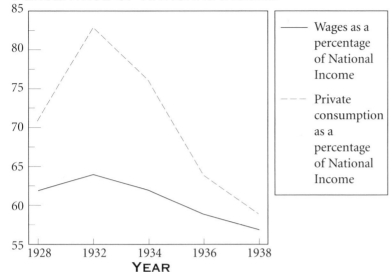

PERCENTAGE OF NATIONAL INCOME

—— Wages as a percentage of National Income

- - - Private consumption as a percentage of National Income

YEAR

DIAGRAM 7
A graph showing real wages and private consumption in Germany, 1932–8 compared with 1928 (see Table 51)

to work overtime due to tiredness and, more openly, sabotage and bodily harm. Despite these negative features, many workers did nothing more than grumble and for many Hitler's *Volksgemeinschaft*, which had provided them with work, was a stabilising and integrating force.

B *For the farmer*

Some short-term gains were experienced in the early years of the regime by some sections of the farming industry. Large and medium-sized farmers were helped to offset the burden of their debt by providing low interest rates and part cancellation of debts but smaller farmers did not see this money until 1935. Arable farmers were helped with subsidies but livestock farmers had to rely on expensive imported fodder. Restrictions on the rise in people's wage levels and price controls on foodstuffs meant that food consumption and hence farmers' markets by 1938 showed only a marginal rise from the crisis-year of 1932. All farmers suffered from a shortage of labour because of the flight from the land. Under these conditions farmers' incomes, which rose by 41 per cent, lagged behind that of industry's 116 per cent. The effect of the regime's policy to achieve autarky was over-regulation and control which strangled commercialised initiative and encouraged black barter and trade in black market goods. As with industry, many complained of overwork and disease and a feeling that their interests had been sacrificed to the rearmament drive.

Flight from the land, see page 297

C *For businessmen*

There was a general benefit to all businessmen stemming from the regime's regulations to reduce its foreign debt, stabilise the credit structure and take over control of banking. After 1933 many businessmen found it possible to borrow from state-managed banks to finance their operations, but increasingly those in the consumer-based goods industries were discriminated against. The regime introduced a whole range of controls – on imports, the distribution of raw materials, prices, wages and deployment of labour – which determined production levels, market prices and profit levels. Business remained in private hands but the performance of the consumer-based industries was lower than in the 1920s, forcing business owners either to sell up or move into the armaments sector. Resentment was blunted by the general prosperity of the later 1930s but those businessmen who were not prepared to work with the regime left the country.

8 ∽ BIBLIOGRAPHY

There is no comprehensive history of the Nazi economy although a number of collected editions of primary sources are readily available. For the themes covered in this chapter J. Noakes and G. Pridham (eds), *Nazism 1919–1945, A Documentary Reader, Vol 2 – State, Economy and Society 1933–1939* (University of Exeter Press 1984) is probably the most accessible for students. It is as useful for the commentary as for the documents. Amongst the numerous secondary sources are general histories covering economy in general terms such as D.G. Williamson, *The Third Reich* (Longman Seminar Series 1982). There are a number of specialist texts on specific themes explored in this chapter. For an analysis of the relationship between big business, industry and the regime consult H.A. Turner, *German Big Business and the Rise of Hitler* (Oxford UP 1985); and *Nazism and The Third Reich* (1972). The historiography of the relationship between the regime and big business is covered in T.W. Mason, 'The Primacy of Politics – Politics and Economics in National Socialist Germany' in H.A. Turner (ed.), *Nazism and the Third Reich*; Alan Milward, 'Fascism and the Economy', in W. Laqueur (ed.), *Fascism. A Reader's Guide* (Penguin 1979). The most recent research on the economy and Göring is by R.J. Overy, *The Nazi Economic Recovery 1932–1938* (Macmillan 1982) and *Göring The Iron Man* (Routledge, Kegan & Paul 1984). He has also written several articles for A Level students, 'Hitler and the Third Reich', *Modern History Review*, November 1989; 'German Domestic Crisis and War in 1939', *Past and Present*, August 1987; 'Hitler's War and the German Economy, A Re-Interpretation', *Economic History Review*, May 1982; 'Business and the Third Reich', *History Review*, 13, 1992. For a detailed account of the peasantry and agriculture read J.E. Farqharson, *The Plough and the Swastika* (Sage 1976). On the Nazi economy are B.E. Carroll, *Design for Total War: Aims and Economics in the Third Reich* (Mouton 1968). For the German economy at war, see A. Milward, *War, Economy and Society, 1939–1945* (University of California Press 1977).

9 ⌐ DISCUSSION QUESTIONS

A *This section consists of questions that might be used for discussion and/or testing your understanding of the main themes explored in this chapter.*

1. (a) Did the Nazi government embark on a state-led economic revival that was not assured till after 1936?
   (b) Was the revival achieved at a cost to the worker?
2. Was Germany facing an economic crisis from 1936 onwards?
3. To what extent did Hitler go to war to escape an economic crisis?
4. To what extent was the economy geared for war during the years 1933–9?

10 ⌐ ESSAY QUESTIONS

A *Two-Part Questions.*

1. (a) Describe the main ways in which the Nazi regime embarked on a programme of economic revival in 1933.
   (b) Explain why these policies threatened an economic crisis from 1936 onwards.

B *Essay Questions.*

1. How successful did the Nazi regime reinflate the economy?
2. To what extent was the German economy ready for war in 1939?
3. 'Full employment was Hitler's sole gift to the masses.'
   How far do you agree with this view?
4. To what extent did the Nazi regime achieve an economic miracle by 1939?
5. 'Germany's economic miracle was short-lived and achieved at tremendous cost'.
   How far do you agree with this judgement?

11 ⌐ MAKING NOTES

Read the advice section about making notes on page xx of Preface: How to use this book, and then make your own notes based on the following headings and questions.

1. *Recovery of the economy 1933–9*
(a) What were the main economic problems facing Germany in 1933?
(b) Identify the five main strategies of Nazi economic policies for recovery represented by each of the following:
   i   propaganda campaigns;
   ii   appointment of Schacht;
   iii a planned economy/four year plans;

iv discrimination against the consumer goods industries and workers;

v favour shown to big business.

(c) What was the effect of war preparations on economic growth in the periods:

i 1933–6;

ii 1936–9.

(d) What problems face historians in assessing the role of rearmament expenditure compared with other investment of the 1930s?

(e) Identify the adverse effects caused by the rearmament programme on:
- finance;
- consumer demand;
- balance of payments;
- the regime's relationship with:
  - i industrial workers;
  - ii big business;
  - iii *Mittelstand*.

(f) Conclusion – state of the economy by 1939:
- What weaknesses still existed?
- To what extent was the economy ready for war?
- What differing conclusions have historians drawn from Hitler's war plans?

12 ↪ MULTI SOURCE DOCUMENTARY EXERCISE ON THE REGIME'S ECONOMIC RECOVERY TO 1939

Study the sources below and answer the questions which follow:

SOURCE A *An American foreign correspondent in Germany describes Germany's economic recovery (W.L. Shirer,* The Rise and Fall of the Third Reich*).*

The foundation of Hitler's success in the first years rested...on Germany's economic recovery which in party circles and even among the economists abroad was hailed as a miracle... Unemployment, the curse of the Twenties and early Thirties was reduced from 6 million in 1932 to less than a million... National production rose 102% from 1932 to 1937 and the national income was doubled. To an observer, Germany in the mid-Thirties seemed like one vast beehive. The wheels of industry were humming and everyone was busy as a bee.

Superficially it seemed that by the end of 1937 the Nazi regime had produced a considerable degree of economic recovery. This was caused mostly by the spur to industry of war preparations. Unemployment had fallen to 1,870,000 – only about 600,000 more than in 1929, the best year since the War: and the volume of industrial production was back almost to the 1929–30 level. But this not very substantial boom was only achieved at frightful cost. The economic fabric of the country stretched and sagged.

In 1929 German exports amounted to approximately 13,000,000,000 Reichsmarks. By 1933 they had fallen to a value of scarcely 5,000,000,000 Reichsmarks and in 1934 to only 4,187,000,000... German industry, normally, lives by its foreign trade. This began to disappear on account of the high gold value of the Reichsmark, the increase of import restrictions abroad, and the international boycott.

Yet Germany had to continue to pay for imports. It needed silk, rubber, nickel, manganese, chromium, tungsten, raw textiles, tin, copper, gasolene. Using every available facility of cash and credit, Germany bought immense stores of these goods. Purchase of Swedish iron ore by the German Steel Trust doubled by...August 1934. German imports of raw nickel – an essential war material – tripled between 1932 and 1935. And every effort was made to produce agricultural self-sufficiency, so that the Reich could feed itself despite blockade... Wages were mercilessly deflated by means of forced payments to relief, the labour front, the air defence league, and so on... Hitler has no interest in economics...but economics may be his ruin. The permanent realities of the economic situation in Germany wait upon no Hitlers, no Schachts, no Thyssens. If Schacht fails, Hitler will find another Schacht...

But Germany must feed sixty-five million people; it must borrow or export enough to pay for imports: it lives by the manufacture of raw materials, and no financial hocus-pocus can alter the inflexible law that goods, somehow, must be paid for.

The day of reckoning will come for Hitler – in gold as well as guns.

SOURCE B *An American journalist comments on policies to restore the economy (John Gunther, Inside Europe).*

SOURCE C (TABLE 43)
Economic recovery and its impact on (un)employment, 1928–38 (adapted from R.J. Overy, The Nazi Economic Recovery 1932–1938).

	1928	1932	1934	1936	1938
Gross national product (1928 prices) (RM bn)	89.5	57.6	66.5	82.6	104.5
Industrial production 1928 = 100	100	58	83	107	122
Unemployed (in millions)	1.4	5.6	2.7	1.6	0.4

	1928	1932	1934	1936	1938
Real wages (1913/14 = 100)	110	120	116	112	112
Real earnings (1925/29 = 100)	106	91	88	93	101
Wages as a percentage of National Income	62	64	62	59	57
Private consumption as a percentage of National Income	71	83	76	64	59

Real wages – the value of money wages in terms of the amount of goods and services that can be bought.
Real earnings – the value of all earned income, as above, taking account of overtime, short-time and absenteeism.

SOURCE D (TABLE 51)
Real wages in Germany, 1932–8 (adapted from R.J. Overy, The Nazi Economic Recovery 1932–1938).

Q

1. *What does source B reveal about the extent of German economic recovery up to 1938?*

2. *How far does a study of sources A and C give support for the claims made in source B about the success of Nazi economic policies?*

3. *How reliable are sources B and D as evidence to an historian of the extent of economic recovery in Germany in the 1930s?*

4. *Using the evidence of all the sources and your own knowledge, explain how far you agree with the view that 'full employment was Hitler's sole gift to the masses'?*

Nazi Foreign Policy

14

INTRODUCTION

Hitler's main political interests lay in the field of foreign affairs and much of his domestic policy was designed to help him achieve the aims of his foreign policy. It is certainly true that it was an area of policy-making over which he ruled supreme and in which he seldom sought the advice of others. At his trial at Nuremberg in 1945–6, Hermann Göring told the court, 'Foreign policy above all was the Führer's own realm. By that, I mean to say that foreign policy, on the one hand, and leadership, on the other, enlisted the Führer's greatest interest'. The view of the German historian, Klaus Hildebrand, is that Hitler 'treated foreign affairs almost entirely as his private preserve', whilst Ian Kershaw concludes that 'There seems little disagreement. . .that Hitler did take the 'big' decisions in foreign policy. . .'. Much of *Mein Kampf* is devoted to foreign policy issues and in it Hitler detailed his plans with surprising frankness. On the first page, he wrote:

> It has turned out fortunate for me that Destiny appointed Braunau-am-Inn to be my birthplace. . .that little town is situated on the frontier between those two states the reunion of which seems a task. . .to which we should devote our lives. German-Austria must be restored to a great German Motherland. . . When the territory of the Reich embraces all the Germans and finds itself unable to assure them a livelihood, only then can the moral right arise, from the need of the people, to acquire foreign territory. The plough is then the sword; and the tears of war will produce the daily bread for the generations to come.

It is a theme to which he returns time and time again:

> . . .our task today is to make our nation powerful. . .in order that we may put into practice a foreign policy which will serve to guarantee the existence of our people in the future, fulfilling their needs and furnishing them with those necessities of life which they lack. . .
>
> If the German people are imprisoned within an impossible territorial area and for that reason are face to face with a miserable future. . . So also in the future our people will not obtain territory. . .as a favour from other people, but will have to win it by the power of the triumphant sword.

TABLE 52

Date chart: Nazi foreign policy

1933	July	Concordat agreed between Nazi Germany and the Papacy
	October	Germany leaves the Disarmament Conferences and the League of Nations
1934	January	Ten-Year non-aggression pact agreed between Germany and Poland
	March	Rome Protocols
	July	Attempted Nazi *Putsch* in Vienna; murder of Chancellor Dollfuß of Austria; Britain and France guarantee independence of Austria
1935	January	Saar plebiscite
	March	Hitler repudiates disarmament clauses of Treaty of Versailles; introduction of military conscription in Germany
	April	Stresa Conference opens
	June	Anglo-German Naval Conference
	October	Italian invasion of Abyssinia
1936	January	Mussolini withdraws guarantee of Austrian independence and leaves Stresa Front
	February	Mussolini agrees not to oppose German occupation of the Rhineland
	March	Hitler denounces Locarno Treaty; German troops march into the Rhineland
	June	Start of Spanish Civil War
	August	Berlin Olympics
	September	Four Year Plan proclaimed
	November	Rome–Berlin Axis announced; Germany and Japan agree Anti-Comintern Pact
1937	April	Guernica destroyed by German Condor Legion
	November	Hitler's conference with his military leaders (recorded in Hossbach Memorandum)
1938	February	Ribbentrop appointed German Foreign Minister; meeting between Hitler and Austrian Chancellor, Schuschnigg, at Berchtesgaden; Seyss-Inquart appointed Austrian Minister of the Interior
	March	Schuschnigg calls for referendum on Austrian independence; German invasion of Austria; *Anschluss* completed
	April	Sudeten Germans demand autonomy
	August	Runciman's mission to Czechoslovakia
	September	Chamberlain meets Hitler at Berchtesgaden; second meeting between Chamberlain and Hitler at Bad Godesberg; Munich Conference; Munich Agreement
1939	March	German troops occupy the remainder of Czechoslovakia; Hitler demands return of Danzig and Polish Corridor; Memel occupied by German forces; Hitler announces non-aggression pact with Poland; Britain and France guarantee Polish independence.
	April	US President, Roosevelt, appeals to Hitler to respect independence of European nations; Britain, France and Russia fail to agree a defensive alliance
	May	Hitler and Mussolini agree Pact of Steel
	August	Nazi-Soviet Pact; appeals for peace from Pope Pius XII and President Roosevelt
	September	German invasion of Poland; Britain and France declare war on Germany.

He was also prepared to indicate where *Lebensraum* or living space would be found: 'History proves that the German people owes its existence solely to its determination to fight in the east and obtain land by military conquest. Land in Europe is only to be obtained at the expense of Russia.'

KEY ISSUE

The German need for Lebensraum.

1 ✎ HITLER'S FOREIGN POLICY

In *Europe 1919–1938: Prelude to Disaster*, the American historian J.H. Huizinga writes:

> ...on January 30, 1933, the nations of Europe awoke to find themselves confronted with a Germany now wholly different from the one with which they had dealt in the twenties – a Germany wholly in the grip of that lunatic fringe, openly vowed to the most barbaric cults, the most outspoken expansionism, the most murderous racism.

A *Aims and origins*

In considering Hitler's foreign policy, historical opinion broadly falls into two categories, the intentionalist and the structuralist.

Historians' views on the aims of Hitler's foreign policy

HISTORIANS' DEBATE

Intentionalist view	Structuralist view
Intentionalists place greatest emphasis on Hitler's personal determination to carry through a pre-planned foreign policy programme. They see Hitler as a man of great will-power and vision whose character and drive are the key factors in shaping German foreign policy. Further, they see his policy as based on a clearly defined programme of objectives. Some consider that his aim was to progress towards his ultimate goal on a stage-by-stage basis, according to a **Stufenplan**.	*Structuralists see German foreign policy as being determined collectively by a whole range of different factors, some determined by the Nazi Party and some not. They reject the idea that German foreign policy was set to follow a rigidly defined course. Instead they claim that it was unclear and without specific aims and that Hitler was a man of improvisation and experiment.*

Stufenplan a plan carried out in stages

It is clear that Hitler's overriding foreign policy aim was to create adequate living space, *Lebensraum*, through the conquest of land for the future settlement of the Germanic people. Ideally, he would have liked to restore the boundaries agreed with Russia at Brest-Litovsk in 1917 and then lost in 1919. To achieve this, it would be necessary to relocate or eliminate the inferior Slav races then in possession of that territory, namely Poles and Russians. The Nazi leader saw the Jews as the main challenge to his plans since they, in league with the Marxists, were in his view intent on world domination. Part of his strategy was to cultivate the friendship of Britain. He hoped that if Germany was supportive of the British Empire, Britain would allow him a free hand in Eastern Europe. He also planned to isolate France and destroy the Little Entente, the system of alliances organised by France in the hope that it would maintain the status quo in central Europe, and help guarantee its own security. In effect, it placed a ***cordon sanitaire*** around Germany.

cordon sanitaire a safe area

Hitler's other foreign policy aims were largely revisionist, based on the need to revise the terms imposed on Germany after the war. He sought to overturn the Treaty of Versailles and reclaim the territories lost in 1919. He wanted to embrace into a *Großdeutschland*, a Greater Reich, all people of German origin currently living beyond Germany's frontiers. He had in mind Austrians, Germans living in the Sudetenland region of Czechoslovakia and those who remained in land surrendered to Poland in 1919. There were also sizeable German minorities in Hungary and the Baltic States. In addition, he promised to refuse to pay further reparations and rearm Germany. Revisionist policies aimed at reversing the injustices of Versailles and restoring the prestige of the nation were universally popular amongst the German people.

B *Some historical interpretations*

As we have seen, historians have differing views about the origins and intentions of Hitler's foreign policy. The German historian, Fritz Fischer, was of the view that Hitler's policy was simply a continuation of that followed earlier by Bismarck and Wilhelm II. The expression *Lebensraum* was not invented by Hitler and had long been in use. Prior to 1914 it was used to describe the growth of Germany's already sizeable overseas empire. In 1896, the Kaiser boasted, 'The German Empire has become a world empire' and five years later, 'We have fought for our place in the sun and won it'. After 1918, it was used to express Germany's demand for the return of her colonies forfeited at Versailles. Hitler's usage gave the term a new dimension – the conquest of territories in eastern Europe for future German settlement and the enslavement of those peoples already living there. It has also been argued that some of Hitler's aims differed little from those of Stresemann. Whereas, at Locarno in 1925, the former German foreign minister refused to accept his country's eastern frontiers and sought adjustments through negotiation, Hitler was more direct and spoke quite openly about Germany's need for 'fresh *Lebensraum* in the east' and his intention to ensure that the area was 'ruthlessly Germanised'. The British historian,

A.J.P. Taylor, caused controversy when he claimed that Hitler, like all German politicians, simply wanted to restore Germany's position in Europe. In his view, the Führer's policies were determined by the course of events and he merely took advantage of the opportunities offered him. In the end, war was not his intention, it just came about. In *The Origins of the Second World War*, Taylor wrote:

> *Lebensraum*, in its crudest sense, meant a demand for empty space where Germans could settle. Germany was not overpopulated compared with most European countries; and there was no empty space anywhere in Europe... *Lebensraum*, in short, did not drive Germany to war. Rather war, or warlike policy, produced a demand for *Lebensraum*. Hitler and Mussolini were not driven on by economic motives. Like most statesmen, they had an appetite for success. They differed from others only in that their appetite was greater...

The majority of historians disagree and some are scathingly critical of Taylor's views. They emphasise what they saw as the overwhelming evidence of *Mein Kampf*, of Hitler's policy statements made at the Hossbach Conference in 1937 (see page 388), the fact that Hitler geared the Germany economy to the needs of his rearmament programme and his aggressive expansionist policies. Hugh Trevor-Roper's view is that *Mein Kampf* was a 'complete blueprint of his intended achievements' and that Hitler was a systematic thinker whose views should have been taken more seriously. Further, his overriding aim was to secure adequate *Lebensraum*. To a large extent, Hildebrand agrees. In his opinion, Hitler's foreign policy was formulated in the 1920s and remained remarkably consistent. Even intentionalists disagree about the extent of Hitler's expansionist ambitions. Some, the continentalists, regard his foreign policy ambitions as limited to German supremacy in Europe. Globalists, on the other hand, see his lust for territorial conquest as extending beyond Europe into Africa and Asia and, eventually, the Americas. His ultimate aim, they claim, was world domination.

2 ⌐ A CAUTIOUS START

During the period immediately after he came to power in 1933, Hitler had to move cautiously. Germany was in a difficult and vulnerable position. Officially its army was still limited to 100,000 men, conscription was forbidden and, although secret arrangements had been made to evade the restrictions placed on its armaments, it remained militarily weak. Surrounded by nations suspicious of its intentions, Germany was isolated. During the 1920s, Czechoslovakia, Romania and Yugoslavia had formed a so-called Little Entente with the purpose of maintaining the existing state of affairs in central Europe. The French closely watched Hitler's every move whilst Mussolini was concerned about German intentions in Austria. Communist Russia, a country with a much-loathed ideology, seemed an unlikely ally. At home, Hitler had to play his hand carefully since he still needed to retain the support of conservative, non-Nazi members of his government.

A *German withdrawal from the Disarmament Conferences and the League of Nations*

Since 1932, the representatives of six major nations had met regularly under the auspices of the League of Nations to consider progress towards world disarmament. The meetings were held at Geneva in Switzerland. Little progress was made mainly due to the fact that France persisted with the demand that a scheme to guarantee international security should be put in place before agreement about disarmament. Hitler cunningly supported British plans for a general reduction in armaments knowing full well that the French would disagree. In October 1933, when the anticipated French refusal came, it provided the Nazi leader with the excuse he needed to withdraw German delegates from the conference. With some justification, he pointed out that Germany had already disarmed and that, in the interests of peace, other major powers should follow her example. As they were not prepared to do so, Germany was being treated unfairly.

Four days later, on 17 October, Hitler went a step further and withdrew Germany from membership of the League of Nations. The move, which was backed in Germany by a plebiscite, was not without risk. It increased misgivings about Germany's future intentions and might have led to the imposition of sanctions by the League. As it was, no action was taken. As Bullock says, 'It was the first of Hitler's gambles in foreign policy and it succeeded'.

Hitler backed these moves with a propaganda offensive which aimed to convince others that Germany's intention was to live in peace. In a widely reported speech to the *Reichstag* he said, 'For a decade and a half, the German people have hoped and waited for a time when at least the end of the war should also become the end of hate and enmity.' He told a *Daily Mail* correspondent, 'Nobody here desires. . .war. Almost all the leaders of the National Socialist Movement were actual combatants. I have yet to meet a combatant who desires a renewal of the horrors of those years.'

B *Pacts and alliances*

To indicate to the world Germany's peaceful intentions, Hitler appeared to settle down to a pattern of normal international relations. Central to his immediate foreign policy aims was a need to isolate France and establish closer ties with other nations, particularly Britain and Italy. There were hopeful signs. Britain had been against the occupation of the Ruhr in 1923 and had appeared to be more understanding of the German position regarding reparations. Italy had shared German disappointment with the terms of the post-war treaties and, since 1922, had been ruled by the Fascist dictator, Mussolini. To start with, Hitler showed admiration for the Italian leader and even copied him. Mussolini, however, was suspicious of Germany's intentions in Austria. In July 1933, the Nazi government agreed a Concordat with the Papacy (see page 228). Following meetings between German officials and Cardinal Eugenio Pacelli, the future Pope Pius XII, an agreement was signed at the Vatican which, on the face of it, settled differences between the Nazis and the Holy See. The Concordat was a diplomatic victory for Hitler since it was universally welcomed by Catholics and, at home, ensured that the Catholic Church would be less likely to meddle in German politics. In January 1934, Hitler agreed a ten year non-aggression pact with Poland. In view of the Weimar Republic's former antagonism towards her eastern neighbour and the views previously expressed by the Führer, this came as a surprise. Hitler knew full well the damage the pact would do to the French system of alliances and so weaken the united front it presented against Germany. Up to that time, Poland had been an ally of France and had played an important part in the French plan to achieve a system of collective security. He was also aware that the Polish army had been involved in military manoeuvres and the pact would forestall any possible Polish attack on Germany. In fact the pact proved disappointingly counter-productive since it had the effect of driving France and Russia closer together. The following month, they too signed a non-aggression pact. At the same time, Mussolini indicated his unease at events in Germany by strengthening his ties with Austria and Hungary by the Rome Protocols.

> **KEY ISSUE**
>
> *Hitler's need to undermine and isolate France.*

3 ⌐ JULY 1934, FIRST MOVES TOWARDS *ANSCHLUSS*

Hitler's ambition to bring about *Anschluss*, the political union of Germany and Austria, was well known. Before the Nazis came to power, a proposal to form an Austro-German customs union was declared illegal in 1931 by the International Court of Justice at The Hague. After 1933, Hitler revived demands for the union of the country of his birth and his adopted country. The Austrian Chancellor, Engelbert Dollfuß, was opposed to such a union. In order to forestall Nazi designs on his country he set up a dictatorship of his own and dealt ruthlessly with political opponents on both the left and the right. Within Austria, groups of Austrian Nazis were responsible for a campaign of terror which reached a climax on the 25 July 1934 when a number of Austrian Nazis entered the Chancellery building and murdered Dollfuß. The intended coup was foiled by Kurt von Schuschnigg who rallied loyal government forces and regained control. In Italy, Mussolini mobilised four divisions and sent them to the Austrian frontier. Hitler, who denied any involvement in the coup, was forced to abandon his plans to annex Austria, at least for the time being. In August, Britain and France guaranteed Austrian independence.

> **KEY ISSUE**
>
> *The role of the Austrian Nazis.*

DIAGRAM 8
Military expenditure in Germany, 1932–8 (amount in billions of marks)

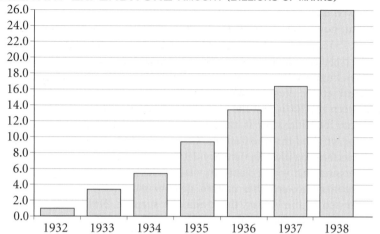

MILITARY EXPENDITURE AMOUNT (BILLIONS OF MARKS)

DIAGRAM 9
Size of the German army, 1933–8 (in battalions)

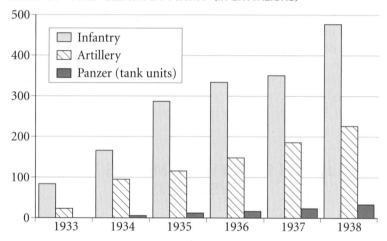

SIZE OF THE GERMAN ARMY (IN BATTALIONS)

- Infantry
- Artillery
- Panzer (tank units)

DIAGRAM 10
German aircraft production 1933–9 (in 1000s)

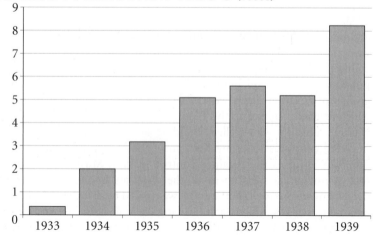

AIRCRAFT PRODUCTION 1933–9 (1000s)

4 ꝏ VERSAILLES CHALLENGED

As we have seen, Germany had been secretly increasing her armed strength beyond the limits set at Versailles for some time. After walking out of the Disarmament Conferences and the League of Nations, it was clearly only a matter of time before Hitler would openly announce his intention to begin the rearming of Germany. During April 1934 50,000 men were recruited into the German armed forces and, in October, a further 70,000. This more than doubled the strength of the German army. By the end of 1934, Germany already had an airforce of 2,000 planes. Yet in a speech to the *Reichstag* in May 1933, Hitler was still able to claim that Germany was the only country to have disarmed and demand that other European powers should follow her example.

A *The Saar Plebiscite, 1935*

1935 began spectacularly well for Hitler. In 1919, control of the Saar, a German district on the left bank of the River Rhine, had passed to the League of Nations with the output of its coalfield going to France. After 15 years, the future of the region was to be decided by a plebiscite. On 13 January 1935, over 90 per cent of the people of the Saar voted to return to Germany. The Führer was delighted. The significance of the Saar vote lay in the fact that it gave the Nazi leader confidence to press ahead with other contentious issues.

On 16 March he publicly declared Germany's **repudiation** of the disarmament clauses of the Treaty of Versailles and the introduction of conscription. It was his aim to increase the size of the army to 550,000 and, to the delight of the military and big business interests, he announced his intention of rearming Germany. Rearmament went hand-in-hand with massive increases in German military expenditure. In 1935 it represented only 14.1 per cent of the national net domestic product but, by the start of the Second World War in 1939, it had risen to 38.1 per cent. Britain, France and Italy protested at Hitler's decisions but took no action.

> **repudiation** refusal to accept

B *The Stresa Conference, April 1935*

During April 1935 the prime ministers of Britain, France and Italy, Ramsay Macdonald, Pierre Flandin and Benito Mussolini, met at Stresa on Lake Maggiore in Italy to discuss forming a common front against Germany. The Stresa Front, as it became known, lodged a further protest which Hitler ignored. Commenting on this last joint action taken by the former war-time Allies against their former common enemy, A.J.P. Taylor wrote (*The Origins of the Second World War*):

> It was the last display of Allied solidarity, a mocking echo from the days of victory... This was an impressive display of words, though rather late in the day... Did any of the three mean what they said?

> ...in truth each of the three powers hoped to receive help from the others without providing anything in return; and each rejoiced to see the others in difficulty.

In spite of everything, in May, Hitler restated Germany's wish for peace and willingness to abide by the Locarno Treaty but this did not prevent a further diplomatic scramble in search of security. France and Russia signed a pact promising to support each other if attacked by an unprovoked aggressor. Russia also signed a pact with Czechoslovakia by which it promised to help defend the young republic, providing France honoured its pledge to Czechoslovakia first. Hitler was not put off by these developments. He was confident that there was sufficient distrust between the countries involved to ensure the pacts were meaningless and was convinced that Britain and France wanted to maintain peace in Europe at any price. Nevertheless, he still thought an understanding with Britain important to his foreign policy.

C *The Anglo-German Naval Treaty of June 1935*

As a result of discussions held in London, Britain and Germany signed an agreement which allowed the German navy to be 35 per cent of the size of the navies of Britain and its Commonwealth. The negotiations ended abruptly with an ultimatum from the leading German delegate, Joachim von Ribbentrop, that the terms on offer were 'fixed and unalterable' and that a British response was required by the weekend. Acceptance came without any consultation with its Allies. Consequently France and Italy regarded the British move as high-handed and an act of bad faith. Britain also gave the impression that it approved of Germany's right to ignore the disarmament clauses of the Treaty of Versailles. Paul Schmidt, the German interpreter present, was surprised at the outcome and later commented, 'The British must have been extraordinarily anxious to come to an agreement to give in so completely in a few days. . .'. From the British viewpoint, it could be claimed that the Germans had agreed to restrict the future size of their navy but, without doubt, the episode was a diplomatic triumph for Hitler. The **unilateral** British action put an end to the unity of the Stresa Front and appeared to be the first stage of an Anglo-German alliance. The limit agreed presented no real problem for Germany. It would take them ages to construct a navy even 35 per cent the size of the British. Michael Bloch's *Ribbentrop* records German reaction to these events:

unilateral involving one party only

> Ribbentrop left England. . .and flew to join Hitler at Hamburg, where he received an ecstatic reception. The Führer declared that the conclusion of the agreement marked the happiest day of his life. . . In Germany, Ribbentrop was the hero of the hour, and showered with praise and honours. Ribbentrop confirmed the belief of the Nazi leaders that he possessed extraordinary influence in England and special skill as a negotiator. . . Ribbentrop, who during previous two years had hardly been visible as a party figure, was a celebrity everyone wanted to meet.

Finally, Ribbentrop was appointed German ambassador to London in the hope that he might be able to further improve Anglo-German relations.

JOACHIM VON RIBBENTROP (1893–1946)

The son of a retired army officer, Joachim Ribbentrop was born in 1893 at Wesel on the River Rhine. After leaving school, he travelled widely and, for some time, worked in London as a shipping clerk before moving on to Switzerland and finally the United States. In New York he found work as a journalist. At the outbreak of war in 1914 he returned home and briefly served in the German army. A gifted linguist who spoke English fluently, in 1915 he was attached to the German embassy in New York. After the war, he was appointed secretary to the German delegation which went to Versailles. He socialised with the monied aristocracy and, in 1920, married the daughter of Otto Henkell, a man who had made a fortune out of manufacturing sparkling wine. His wealthy but ambitious wife dominated every aspect of his life. They lived well and included amongst their friends leading Jewish bankers. Lacking the noble title 'von', Ribbentrop paid an aunt, who had the title, to adopt him. He first met Hitler in 1929 and, in the early 1930s, used his influence to find financial backers for the Nazi Party. It was a favour that Hitler did not forget. He became the Nazi leader's foreign policy adviser and, in 1934, a German delegate at the Disarmament Conferences. A year later, he was sent to London to negotiate the Anglo-German Naval Treaty and then returned to Britain as the German ambassador. A regular party-goer and with excellent manners, *Punch* magazine nicknamed him the 'Wandering Aryan'. With an inflated idea of his own importance, he was arrogant and domineering and became thoroughly disliked. He was refused membership of London clubs and his son was turned down by Eton. Capable of the most outrageous blunders, his period as ambassador proved a disaster. Disillusioned, Ribbentrop returned to Germany, taking with him a hatred of Britain. Other leading Nazis thought him a buffoon. Goebbels said of him that 'he bought his name, married his money and swindled his way into office', and Schacht's opinion was that 'he wasn't good enough to be a bootblack'. Even so, in 1938 Hitler appointed him German Foreign Minister.

Imperial War Musem MH6081

PICTURE 44

Joachim von Ribbentrop, the German Foreign Minister

5 ⌒ GERMANY AND ITALY: A REALIGNMENT IN THE BALANCE OF POWER IN EUROPE

A *The tragedy of Abyssinia*

On 2 October 1935 Italian forces invaded the independent African state of Abyssinia, present-day Ethiopia. From the start, Britain and France were highly critical of Mussolini's action and supported the League's decision to impose economic sanctions on Italy. The Fascist leader was offended that his former allies, themselves two of the world's greatest colonial powers, should deny Italy's right to a corner of Africa. His immediate reaction was to withdraw the Italian guarantee of Austrian independence and formally leave the Stresa Front. In February 1936 he also let it be known that he would not oppose any German attempt to reoccupy and militarise the Rhineland. In a spirited speech to the League of Nations made in May, the Emperor of Abyssinia, Haile Selassie, reminded the world of what was at stake:

> I...am here today to claim that justice which is due to my people... I assert that the problem...is not merely the settlement of Italian aggression. It is the very existence of the League of Nations. It is the value of promises made to small states that their independence be respected. God and history will remember your judgements.

On the sidelines, Hitler bided his time. Officially, Germany remained neutral in the dispute but Hitler refused the League's instruction to impose economic sanctions and continued to trade with Italy. Whilst the Soviet Union pressed for even tighter sanctions including oil, Britain and France did nothing. In an attempt to repair relations with Italy, Sir Samuel Hoare, the British Foreign Secretary, and the French Prime Minister, Pierre Laval, put forward a compromise plan intended to placate Mussolini. Such was the opposition to the proposed Hoare–Laval Pact that both men were forced to resign. The situation was clear for all to see. The League of Nations was unable to prevent aggression and, when it occurred, Britain and France were not prepared to stand against the aggressor. With Fascist Italy moving closer to Nazi Germany, Hitler was aware that new opportunities were opening for him.

B *The re-occupation of the Rhineland*

In February 1936 Hitler protested bitterly that the recent agreed Franco-Soviet Pact broke the Locarno agreements. Using this as an excuse, on 7 March 1936 he violated both the Versailles and Locarno Treaties and ordered German troops into the Rhineland. His generals were against the move since they anticipated possible French military intervention and even the involvement of Poland. Germany was not yet strong enough to face such a challenge and Hitler ordered his troops to make a fighting withdrawal if challenged by the French. Although the British government protested, there was some sympathy for the German position. As Lord Lothian said, 'After all they are only moving back into their own back garden'. Without British support, the French were not prepared to take military action. As the Rhinelanders welcomed the German troops, Hitler had proved his judgement to be superior to that of his generals. In retrospect, it might be claimed that Britain and France had thrown away the opportunity to challenge Hitler's expansionist policies before they got out of hand.

The reoccupation of the Rhineland completed, Hitler returned to a more conciliatory line by offering to agree a non-aggression pact with France and Belgium which would be guaranteed by Britain and Italy. He even hinted that Germany might rejoin the League of Nations. Encouraged by Hitler's recognition of the Italian right to Abyssinia and to Mussolini's acceptance of Germany's reoccupation of the Rhineland, the two nations grew closer. Another significant move was the appointment of Count Ciano as Italian Foreign Minister. Married to Mussolini's favourite daughter, Edda, Ciano was strongly pro-German. In July 1936 relations between the two countries were further improved when, as the result of an Austro-German Convention, Hitler promised not to interfere in Austrian affairs and the Austrian Nazis were allowed a greater say in the country's political affairs.

In the midst of these upheavals, the Nazis gained a major propaganda success when they received universal praise for their superb management of the Olympic Games held in Berlin in the summer of 1936, as recorded in this extract from 'Berlin Olympics, 1936' by Brian Glanville (*Purnell's History of the Twentieth Century*, Part 54):

> Preparations were meticulous. Party directives went out to clean up the countryside and ensure that people were friendly and helpful to tourists. Anti-Semitism was played down... The opening ceremony was a triumph of stage management. Fanfares sounded, there was a roar from the crowd and Hitler appeared... The crowd sang **Deutschland über Alles** and the Horst Wessel Song, and the march-past started. Most teams complied with the official wish to give the Fascist salute. The French won a roar of approval when they hailed Hitler. But the British were greeted by an ominous silence when they gave a conventional eyes right. Hitler took it as a personal affront. When the athletics got under way, Hitler received a severe blow for the results were a decisive contradiction of the Nazi creed of Nordic supremacy. He had to witness one triumph after another by 'inferior' negro athletes...

Q *To what extent was Hitler's decision to occupy the Rhineland a gamble?*

KEY ISSUE

The propaganda value of the Berlin Olympics.

Deutschland über Alles Germany Above All, the German national anthem

C *Foreign intervention in the Spanish Civil War*

In July 1936 a civil war broke out in Spain when the army, led by a Fascist general, Francisco Franco, attempted to overthrow the country's elected left-wing Popular Front government. The civil war was not to remain a domestic affair but soon became the battleground of the conflicting ideologies, communism and fascism. The government side, the Republicans, received financial and material aid from the Soviet Union and the support of foreign volunteers who formed an International Brigade. Franco's Nationalists had the full backing of both Hitler and Mussolini. Italy sent 50,000 men as well as tanks and aircraft whilst Germany contributed only 16,000 men. More significantly, they supplied eleven squadrons of aircraft which formed the Condor Legion. In 1937, these aircraft were used to test the effectiveness of terror bombing on civilian targets. On 26 April over 1,600 people were killed when the Basque town of Guernica was destroyed by a new form of aerial bombardment, *Blitzkrieg*. The civil war continued until 1939 when, following a Nationalist victory, Franco became the Fascist dictator of Spain.

D *The significance of the Spanish Civil War*

Hitler hoped to gain several advantages from his involvement in the war. A pro-German government in Spain would be an additional embarrassment to France, it would give Germany access to essential raw materials, namely Spanish iron-ore, and it would ensure Franco's support of his foreign policy strategy. Hitler and Mussolini also gained the prestige of seeming to be the only national leaders prepared to take a stand against the advance of communism. After a series of diplomatic comings and going between Berlin and Rome, in October 1936 Hitler and Ciano signed the secret October Protocols by which Germany and Italy agreed to co-operate on a wide range of issues. So close had the two powers now become that, speaking in Milan on 1 November, Mussolini boasted that 'This Berlin–Rome connection is not so much a **diaphragm** but rather an axis, around which can revolve all those states of Europe with a will towards collaboration and peace'. Afterwards the close collaboration between Nazi Germany and Fascist Italy became referred to as the Rome–Berlin Axis although no formal agreement linked the two countries until the Pact of Steel in 1939 (see page 397).

diaphragm a thin partition which separates

Even though Italy had replaced Britain as Germany's best hope for an alliance, Hitler still wanted closer ties with Britain. It was for this reason that, in 1936, he appointed Ribbentrop as German ambassador to London. His mission was to secure British agreement for a German free hand in eastern Europe in return for German support of the British Empire. Ribbentrop failed and returned home a bitter man determined to find other potential allies for Germany.

E *The Anti-Comintern Pact, 1936*

In 1919 the Russian revolutionary leader, Lenin, set up a Third International. This became known as the Communist International or Comintern. Based in Moscow, Comintern aimed to support revolutionary activity across the world. Its agents looked for opportunities to cause unrest and create conditions favourable to revolution. Comintern had been active in Germany during the years of the Weimar Republic and Hitler still regarded their influence as a threat. In November 1936 Ribbentrop gained another diplomatic success when he managed to negotiate an agreement between Germany and Japan by which they agreed to co-operate to oppose Comintern and stem the advance of international communism. The following year, Italy also joined the Pact.

By the end of 1936, the political situation in Europe had undergone a considerable change. Hitler had won a series of notable diplomatic successes – the return of the Rhineland, alliances with Italy and Japan, the collapse and disintegration of the Stresa Front and the French-backed system of collective security. He had also succeeded in strengthening Germany's position relative to France. Plagued by serious domestic problems, the French seemed to have lost heart. Although still security conscious, they had come to put great faith in the Maginot Line, a magnificent defensive system of fortifications which stretched along their common frontier with Germany from Luxembourg to the Swiss border. Belgian objections prevented them continuing the line northwards to the Channel coast. The Nazi leader, who had already proved himself willing to take advantage of the Anglo-French fears of another European war, spoke continually of his peaceful intentions. In speeches to the *Reichstag* and at meetings with foreign correspondents, Hitler persisted that his aim was peace in Europe. Most Europeans were sufficiently gullible to accept his statements and, although the word was not yet generally used to describe the Anglo-French approach to Germany, **appeasement** had begun to sharpen Hitler's appetite for further conquest. In 1936, Göring, responsible for the Four Year Plan which was the basis of Germany's rearmament programme, spoke bluntly when he told the German people, 'Guns will make us powerful; butter will only make us fat'. The following year, Hitler removed his Economics Minister, Schacht, when he protested at the damage being done to the German economy by the high expenditure on armaments.

> **Q**
> *To what extent had Germany's position in Europe strengthened by the end of 1936?*

> **appeasement** making concessions in order to pacify a potential aggressor

6 ↷ FROM CAUTION TO NAKED AGGRESSION

In retrospect it is possible to look upon 1937 as a year of preparation, the quiet before the storm. It was a time during which German rearmament went on apace and when Hitler made plans to abandon caution and move towards more adventurous policies. As we shall see, his acts of naked aggression involved risks which, in the end, led to the outbreak of the Second World War.

A *The Hossbach Memorandum*

On 5 November 1937, at a secret conference held at the Reich Chan-cellery in Berlin, Hitler outlined the aims and strategy of his future foreign policy. Present were Foreign Minister Constantin von Neurath, Defence Minister Werner von Blomberg and the chiefs of the German armed forces, Werner von Fritsch (army/*Wehrmacht*), Erich Raeder (navy/*Kriegsflotte*) and Hermann Göring (airforce/*Luftwaffe*). Also present was Colonel Friedrich Hossbach, Hitler's military adjutant who, against instructions, made notes of much of what was said. Afterwards, using his notes and recall from memory, he produced a document based on Hitler's two-hour monologue which later became known as the *Hossbach Niederschrift*, the Hossbach Memorandum. This docu-ment covers three main issues. Firstly, Hitler outlined the future aims of German foreign policy (quoted from *Documents on German Foreign Policy*):

> The aim of German foreign policy was to make secure and to preserve the racial community [*Volksmasse*] and to enlarge it. It was therefore a question of space. The German racial community comprised over 85 million people and, because of their number and the narrow limits of the habitable space in Europe, constituted a tightly-packed racial core such as was not to be met in any other country and such as implied the right to a greater living space... Germany's future was therefore wholly conditional upon the solving of the need for space.

He next concluded that these problems would not be solved by either striving to achieve self-sufficiency, autarky, or through the acqui-sition of overseas colonies. He asked 'where could she [Germany] achieve the greatest gain at the lowest cost?' For the first time he identi-fies Britain as a hostile power when he says that 'German policy had to reckon with two hate-inspired antagonists, Britain and France, to whom a German colossus in the centre of Europe was a thorn in the flesh, and both countries were opposed to any strengthening of Germany's position either in Europe or overseas...'. He held the view that Britain could not effectively oppose German expansion because of troubles within her Empire, particularly in India and Ireland; France, too, was badly placed to interfere because of her domestic difficulties. He stated that his first priorities were to annex Austria and destroy Czechoslovakia and concluded that 'Germany's problem could only be solved by means of force and this was never without attendant risk'. It is, he says, a matter of 'when' and 'how'. Finally, Hitler detailed three possible scenarios which might allow him to achieve his aims (recorded in *Documents on German Foreign Policy*):

KEY ISSUE

Hitler considers three possible scenarios.

Case 1. To take action during the period 1943–5; after this date, from our point of view, the situation could only change for the worse. The preparation of our army, navy and *Luftwaffe* was nearly complete.

Equipment and armament were modern... If we did not act by 1943–5, any year could be regarded as a 'waning point'. Besides, by then the world would be expecting our attack... The opportunity for action before 1943–5 would arise if two other options came about.

Case 2. If internal problems in France should turn into such a crisis that it involved the French Army completely and render it incapable of use for war against Germany; then it would be possible to take action against the Czechs.

Case 3. If France became involved in a war with another country so that she could not take action against Germany.

Four days after the conference, Fritsch called on Hitler to express his concern at the prospect of the German army having to face joint Anglo-French opposition to his plans. Blomberg and Neurath voiced similar misgivings. Afterwards, Hitler found excuses to dismiss all three (see page 206). The more compliant Alfred Jodl and Walter von Brauchitsch became the new commanders of the *Wehrmacht* whilst Ribbentrop was appointed Foreign Minister. Fourteen other generals were retired as part of a clear-out of the old conservative influence in the army.

B *A consideration of the Hossbach Memorandum*

Was the Hossbach Memorandum genuine? If so, was it truly a blueprint of Hitler's plans for future aggression in Europe? True, the document which survived was not the original but a copy of a copy. Nevertheless, it was used to provide the most condemning evidence of Nazi war intentions at the Nuremberg Trials (1945–6) (Chapter 16). Today, the majority accept the Hossbach Memorandum as genuine although there is some disagreement about its significance. Although when Hitler began to implement his policy, there were differences in the timetable and details of strategy, in broadest terms, the Memorandum correctly revealed the events that were to come. The historian, A.J.P. Taylor, was one who disagreed (*The Origins of the Second World War*):

Hitler's exposition was in large part day-dreaming, unrelated to what followed in real life. Even if seriously meant, it was not a call to action, at any rate not to the action of a great war; it was a demonstration that a great war would not be necessary... Why then did Hitler hold this conference?...it was a curious gathering. Only Göring was a Nazi. The others were old-style conservatives who had remained in office to keep Hitler under control; all of them except Raeder were dismissed from their posts within three months... Why did he reveal his innermost thoughts to people he distrusted? The question has an easy answer; he did not reveal his innermost thoughts... The conference was a manoeuvre in domestic affairs...

...the Hossbach Memorandum contains no plans of any kind... The Memorandum tells us what we knew already, that Hitler (like

> every other German statesman) intended Germany to become the dominant power in Europe. It tells us how he speculated this might happen. His speculations were mistaken... A racing tipster who only reached Hitler's level of accuracy would not do well for his clients.

And what became of the document's author, Colonel Hossbach? In 1938, he was dismissed from his post as Hitler's military adjutant for forewarning General von Fritsch that he was about to face charges of homosexuality (see page 206). The following year, he made a comeback and was restored to the General Staff. During the war, he rose to the rank of general and commanded the German Fourth Army on the Russian Front. In January 1945, he was again dismissed for disobeying Hitler's orders.

C *The* Anschluss *completed*

Although forbidden by the Treaty of Versailles, Hitler's initial plan was to avoid aggression and, by various means, gradually absorb Austria into the Reich. In July 1934 the Austrian Nazis were responsible for riots which led to the murder of Chancellor Dollfuß and the movement of Italian troops to the Austrian frontier (see page 379). Hitler denied any involvement in these events and calmed the situation by promising to respect Austrian neutrality. For his part, the new Austrian Chancellor, Kurt von Schuschnigg, allowed the Austrian Nazis to become more involved in political affairs and a leading Austrian Nazi, Arthur Seyss-Inquart, entered the government. During 1937, Nazi pressure on the Austrian government increased. Schuschnigg was in a difficult position. Within Austria, his predecessor, Dollfuß, had eliminated the Socialists and so robbed him of their support. Internationally, Mussolini, who had stood by Austria in 1934, now stated that he had no objection to the German annexation of the country. Britain and France appeared to recognise the inevitability of a Nazi take-over. Even worse, on a visit to Berlin, Lord Halifax, the British Foreign Secretary, had said that his government 'desired a peaceful correction of German grievances'.

In January 1938, the Austrian police raided Nazi Party headquarters in Vienna and found evidence of a plan for a Nazi takeover. The Austrian Nazis aimed to stir up unrest and then invite German troops into the country to restore order. On 12 February, Schuschnigg met Hitler at his mountain retreat at Berchtesgaden. The Führer raged at the Austrian Chancellor and warned him that his patience was at an end. Schuschnigg gave way under the torrent of abuse and promised to take measures to ensure that Austrian foreign and economic policy were speedily integrated with those of Germany. He also agreed to allow the Austrian Nazis complete freedom and to appoint Seyss-Inquart as Minister of the Interior and Edmund von Glaise-Horstenau as War Minister. This effectively handed control of the police and the army to the Austrian Nazis.

On his return to Austria, Schuschnigg at first complied. Then his courage returned and, before Hitler could make further demands, he called a plebiscite to allow the Austrian people a say in their future. The act of defiance outraged Hitler. He could not allow the plebiscite to take place since a vote against union with Germany would be an embarrassment and make it difficult for him to justify his plans. Events moved quickly. Under enormous pressure, Schuschnigg was forced to abandon his plans for a plebiscite and resign. On 12 March 1938 German troops marched into Austria. Immediately Hitler decided that the two countries would not form a union but, instead, Austria would become a province of the Reich. For the most part, the German troops received a rapturous welcome. The European powers stood by as these events unfolded. Italy refused to contemplate any action; France, in the middle of a political crisis, was without a government. Britain did protest but then claimed that Schuschnigg was himself partly to blame for the crisis.

As a result of the annexation of Austria, Germany had common borders with Italy, Hungary and Yugoslavia and was strategically better placed to threaten Czechoslovakia. Germany also gained valuable additional resources of manpower, raw materials and foreign exchange. In April 1938 Hitler ordered his own plebiscite on the issue of Austrian independence. In a speech on the eve of the poll, he said 'Tomorrow may every German recognise the hour and measure its importance and bow in humility before the Almighty, who in a few weeks has wrought a miracle upon us'. The result of the plebiscite showed that 99.75 per cent of Austrians favoured the union of their country with Germany! The historian Mary Fulbrook comments in *The Fontana History of Germany, 1918–1990*:

> Later myths of 'the rape of Austria' and being 'Hitler's first victim' notwithstanding, the entry of German troops was greeted by many Austrians with considerable enthusiasm. Whilst those Austrians of left-wing and liberal opinions viewed the *Anschluss* with foreboding, others gave a rapturous welcome to the triumphant return of Adolf Hitler to his native land, in which, a quarter of a century earlier, he had collected his ideas and fomented his rag-bag of prejudices. Austrian Jews had good reason to be worried, a virulent anti-Semitism was unleashed, soon making their situation even more demoralising and unpleasant than that of the Jews in Germany.

Q *To what extent were Hitler's reasons for the annexation of Austria justified?*

7 ⤳ THE CZECH CRISIS, 1938

Czechoslovakia, a republic created after the First World War, consisted of the former Austrian provinces of Bohemia and Moravia, parts of Austrian Silesia and the former Hungarian lands of Slovakia and Ruthenia. The country had a democratic system of government, was prosperous and militarily strong. Although steps had been taken to safeguard the interests of the various nationalities, there was friction between the Czechs and Slovaks. Even more troublesome were the three million

German-speaking Czechs living in the Sudetenland, a region bordering Hitler's Reich. In spite of the measures taken by the Czech government to remedy their grievances, they still claimed, with some justification, to be discriminated against.

A *Henlein and the Sudeten Nazis*

KEY ISSUE

The Karlsbad demands.

In 1933 Konrad Henlein, a former bank clerk and schoolmaster, formed the *Sudeten Deutsche Partei*, a Nazi-type political party which agitated for greater freedom for the Sudeten Germans and their eventual inclusion within Germany. From the start, Henlein's party received substantial support from Nazi Germany and, in the elections of 1935, won 44 seats in the Czech parliament. The elimination of the Czech Republic was essential to Hitler's foreign policy aims and the completion of the *Anchluss* made the prospect more viable. In April 1938, in a speech at Karlsbad, Henlein made a series of demands on the Czech government which included greater autonomy for the Sudeten Germans, changes in foreign policy and closer ties with Germany. Although under threat, the Czech President, Eduard Beneš, felt secure in the knowledge that his country could depend on the support pledged by France and the Soviet Union and that, at least nominally, Czechoslovakia was allied with Romania and Yugoslavia. His country also had a formidable army, a first-rate armaments industry based on the Skoda works at Pilsen and a well-established line of fortifications ready to repel any German invasion. In truth, the support he could expect was only impressive on paper. Britain had made no commitment to Czechoslovakia, and France made it clear that it would only become involved with British support. Similarly, the Soviet Union would only act with French backing. Anyway, the Poles, with their historic dislike of the Czechs, would never allow the passage of Russian troops across their country. Hungary was worried about the fate of the Hungarian minority in Slovakia and, when the time came, both Poland and Hungary hoped to have some small share of the spoils. Meanwhile, a Soviet suggestion that a common front be formed against Nazi aggression met with little enthusiasm. In fact, Britain and France were already pressing Beneš to take a more conciliatory line with the Sudeten Germans.

B *The crisis of 1938*

In May 1938 the crisis worsened when two Sudeten German motorcyclists were shot by the Czech police and the German press denounced Czech atrocities in the Sudetenland. When France and the Soviet Union hinted that they could honour their pledge to Czechoslovakia, the immediate threat of a German invasion faded. Hitler was annoyed that the British press saw this as a climb down. In Berlin, Ribbentrop warned the British ambassador that if the situation in the Sudetenland 'was allowed to drift. . .and there was bloodshed, Hitler would be compelled to take immediate action, at whatever cost to Germany and the world'.

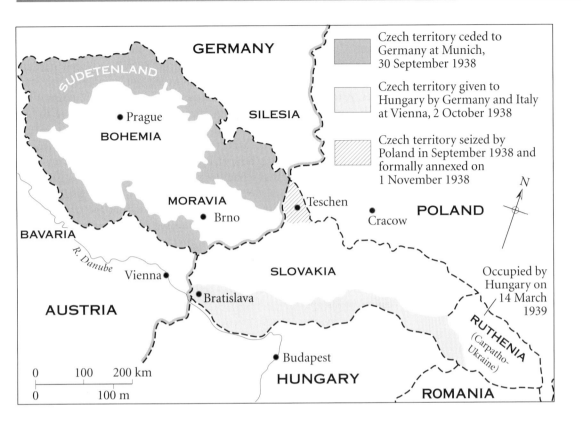

MAP 9

The German occupation of Czechoslovakia

In conversation with the French ambassador, the German Foreign Minister also criticised the Franco-Czech alliance and commented 'how grotesque to think that two lions might come to blows over a Czech mouse'. The war of words intensified when, in the same month, Hitler spoke of his 'intention to smash Czechoslovakia by force in the near future'. At the same time he ordered preparations for Operation Green, the annexation of the Czech provinces of Bohemia and Moravia. During the remainder of the summer, relations between Germany and Czechoslovakia worsened even though Beneš made a genuine effort to grant some of the Karlsbad demands. In August, the British government sent Lord Runciman to Prague to try and arrange a settlement. This high-handed move offended the Czechs since the envoy appeared to side with the Sudeten Germans. By the beginning of September, the situation had become critical. Once again Hitler warned that the Sudeten Germans were 'neither defenceless nor deserted'. Following a period of rioting largely stirred up by German propaganda, the Czech government declared martial law. As a result, Henlein and hundreds of Austrian Nazis fled to Germany to escape arrest. It was in such a climate that Neville Chamberlain, the British Prime Minister, decided to play peacemaker and, on 15 September, made the first of his three journeys to Germany to negotiate with Hitler. Their first meeting was at Berchtesgaden. Although not impressed with Chamberlain who he thought feeble, Hitler treated him courteously. The German leader told him bluntly that if the Sudetenland was not passed to Germany there would be war. Chamberlain offered to negotiate the transfer of those regions which contained a majority of Germans. Hitler agreed largely because he believed the British Prime Minister would not be able to convince Beneš. After consulting his own colleagues and the French, but not the Czech government, Chamberlain pressed the Czechs to agree to the compromise. Without the backing of France and Britain, they had no choice. The British Prime Minister returned to Germany for a second meeting with Hitler, this time at Bad Godesberg. The Führer was surprised and annoyed that Chamberlain had won concessions from the Czechs since this meant he had been robbed of an excuse to go to war. Far from placated, Hitler's response was to state that the terms earlier agreed would no longer suffice and increased his demands. Further, he threatened that if his terms were not met by 1 October there would be war. In the midst of the crisis, Mussolini called for a four-power conference to discuss the issue. Hitler agreed and in a conciliatory move said that once the Sudeten issue was settled, he had no further territorial claims in Europe.

C *The Munich Agreement, 29 September 1938*

As Europe prepared for war, Chamberlain flew to Germany for a third time. In Berlin Ribbentrop, seemingly determined on war, used his position to prevent those leaders and diplomats who favoured a peaceful solution to the crisis from gaining access to Hitler. The final conference, held in Munich, was also attended by Hitler, Mussolini and his son-in-law, Count Ciano, and Daladier, the French Prime Minister. Whilst Soviet representatives were not invited, the Czech delegation was forced to wait, uncalled, at a nearby hotel. Hitler's victory was complete when Chamberlain and Daladier finally accepted his demands. The Sudetenland was to be occupied by German troops on the 10 October to a line to be agreed by an international commission. Then, after the additional claims of Hungary and Poland had been met, the four powers were to guarantee the frontiers of what was left of Czechoslovakia. Afterwards Beneš, who had tried so desperately to defend his homeland and begged for the views of Czechoslovakia to be heard, resigned. On his return to London, Chamberlain told the British people, 'I believe it is peace for our time'. In Berlin, Hitler joked, 'He seemed a nice old gentleman, I thought I would give him my autograph as a souvenir'. A week later, in the House of Commons, Winston Churchill said, 'All is over. Silent, mournful, abandoned, broken Czechoslovakia recedes into darkness... We have sustained a defeat without a war'.

Q

Were the Czechs betrayed by Britain and France?

D *The significance of the Munich Agreement*

From the Czech viewpoint, the consequences of the Munich Agreement were far-reaching. Not only did it lose nearly 2,850,000 hectares of land, including 70 per cent of its iron and steel production, but it also had to abandon its strategic defensive positions in the Sudeten mountains.

This meant that what was left of Czechoslovakia could be easily overrun at any time. The agreement led to the total disillusionment of the Czechs and the name, Munich, became synonymous with betrayal. Those associated with the agreement, later branded the 'men of Munich', were held responsible for an act of cowardly appeasement. In reality, it was not that simple. Few historians today regard Chamberlain's motives as cowardly but more those of a man so dedicated to peace that he was easily duped by Hitler's false promises. Some see him, too, as a man who bought time for a nation ill prepared for a war. As with the Rhineland and Austria, Hitler gambled – correctly – that Britain and France would not interfere with his plans for Czechoslovakia. In spite of the reservations of his generals and diplomats, he had once again been proved right. The outcome was his greatest foreign policy triumph to date and many Germans began to believe in his infallibility. As William Shirer wrote in *The Rise and Fall of the Third Reich*:

> Hitler had got what he wanted, had achieved another great conquest without firing a shot. His prestige soared to new heights. No one who was in Germany in the days after Munich, as the writer was, can forget the rapture of the German people. They were relieved that war had been averted; they were elated and swollen with pride at Hitler's bloodless victory, not only over Czechoslovakia, but over Great Britain and France.

MAP 10

Germany's expansion, 1933–9

As his prestige rose, even those who had once thought Hitler a reckless adventurer became increasingly impressed, and those who had plotted an anti-Hitler coup despaired of Anglo-French appeasement and gave up (see page 309). To all but the naive, Munich showed that Hitler's territorial ambitions were far from satisfied. His basic aim remained the same – the creation of a Greater Reich with adequate *Lebensraum* gained at the expense of Poland and the Soviet Union.

8 ↩ 1939 – THE PRELUDE TO WAR

Those who had put their faith in Hitler's promises were soon to have their illusions shattered. In January 1939, in yet another effort to moderate Hitler's aggressive intentions, Chamberlain went to Rome in an attempt to win the support of Mussolini. His mission was in vain.

A *The end of Czechoslovakia*

autonomy the right of self-government

With the Slovaks demanding greater **autonomy** from the Czechs, what was left of Czechoslovakia remained torn by internal strife. In an act of crass folly the Slovak leaders sought Hitler's help. In a rapidly worsening situation, on 15 March the Czech President, Emil Hacha left for Berlin to appeal to Hitler. The Führer subjected the 67-year-old President to verbal abuse and when he threatened to bomb Prague, Hacha fainted. Afterwards, Hacha signed an agreement which allowed German troops into Czechoslovakia to restore order and so provided Hitler with the legal justification of occupying his country. As German forces crossed the border, Hitler boasted, 'I shall go down in history as the greatest German'.

In late March, in yet another act of aggression, German troops annexed Memel. The Lithuanian town, which lay in the north-east corner of East Prussia, had a predominantly German population.

B *The origins of the Polish crisis*

To all Germans, the most resented of the territorial losses imposed on Germany at Versailles was that of a part of Silesia, Danzig and the Polish corridor to Poland. To Hitler, the existence of Poland was intolerable. In a speech in 1939 (quoted in *The Speeches of Adolf Hitler* by N.H. Baynes) he said:

> We demand the return to us of the Polish Corridor which is like a strip of flesh cut form our body. It cuts Germany in two. It is a national wound that bleeds continuously, and will continue to bleed until the land is returned to us.

Pressure on Poland began in October 1938 when the Germans wanted to build road and rail links across the Polish Corridor to more easily connect Germany with East Prussia. They also made no secret of the fact that they wanted the return of Danzig. The Poles were prepared to consider the transport links but refused to even discuss the transfer of the port or any rearrangement of their frontiers. The situation became more tense following the German occupation of Memel. Then, following the policy used against the Czechs over the Sudetenland, they began to accuse the Poles of ill-treating Germans living under their rule. On 31 March 1939 the British government signed a defence pact with Poland. Although the pact infuriated Hitler, British reaction to his earlier aggression led him to believe it was a bluff. Anyway, in the event of war, it would be impossible for Britain to send any worthwhile help to Poland. In April, Hitler mocked an appeal by the American President, Franklin D. Roosevelt, when he asked the German leader to respect the independence of European nations, but he was perturbed by Anglo-French efforts to reach an agreement with Russia over Poland having thought the British and French half-hearted and lacking in urgency. However, the negotiations finally broke down when the Poles refused to allow Russian forces into Poland in the event of a German invasion. Encouraged by the failure, Hitler ordered preparations to be made for Operation White, the invasion of Poland. The date was fixed for 1 September 1939.

C *The Pact of Steel, May 1939*

On 22 May, the Rome–Berlin Axis (see page 386) became an offensive military alliance when Germany and Italy agreed a Pact of Steel. Under the terms of the Pact, the two nations would support each other if one was involved in a war with another power. Count Ciano was concerned that such a formal alliance could lead Italy into war but Ribbentrop promised that would never be the case. Hitler even went as far as to say 'I am unshakeably convinced that neither England nor France will embark upon a general war'.

D *The Nazi-Soviet Pact, August 1939*

To the amazement of the rest of the world, on 23 August 1939 a pact was signed in Moscow by Ribbentrop and the Russian Foreign Secretary, Vyacheslav Molotov. The Pact (sometimes called the Ribbentrop–Molotov Pact) agreed between representatives of two such hostile ideologies was as unexpected as it was complicated. The two countries agreed not to support any third power, if that power attacked the other of them. In addition, they promised to consult with each other on matters of common interest and undertook not to join any alliance aimed at the other. Not made public was the secret agreement to invade and then divide Poland between them and allow the Soviet Union to occupy the Baltic States – Latvia, Lithuania and Estonia. The Pact was a cynical arrangement between two arch-enemies aimed at bringing

Q

Why did the Pact surprise the rest of the world?

WONDER HOW LONG THE HONEYMOON WILL LAST?

short-term advantages to both countries. Stalin drove a hard bargain
and made the greater gains whilst, for Hitler, the Pact was a matter of
expediency. From the Russian leader's viewpoint, it was some recompense for being left out in the cold by Britain and France and it
removed the threat of a capitalist alliance against Russian communism.
It also gave Russia time to continue its military build-up and the partition of Poland would create a buffer state between the Soviet Union and
Germany. For Hitler, it removed the fear of the prospect of having to
wage war on two fronts simultaneously. It also gave him an opportunity
to eliminate Poland and secure Danzig without a war whilst the partition of Poland meant that he was ideally placed to plan the future invasion of Russia. On his return from Moscow, Ribbentrop was welcomed
personally by Hitler who hailed him as 'a second Bismarck'. The Pact
caused concern in Europe and across the world. If nothing else, the fact
that Hitler was prepared to agree a pact with a country he planned to
attack provided further evidence of his lack of scruple. In effect, it was
this act of appeasement by Russia which sealed the fate of Poland and
made the coming of war more inevitable.

E *3 September 1939: the declaration of war*

In spite of the undertakings by Britain and France to assist Poland if she
were attacked and Mussolini's warning that Italy was not sufficiently
prepared to enter a war, Hitler pressed ahead with his plans. Even
though he claimed that Polish provocations had become intolerable and
accused them of numerous frontier incidents, as late as 29 August he
still indicated a willingness to negotiate a solution to the problem. The
Poles refused his offer and began to mobilise their forces. Last-minute
appeals for peace made by Pope Pius XII, Roosevelt, the American President, and Daladier were ignored. Following a further series of rigged
frontier violations, Hitler issued orders for war. Walter Shirer, in *Berlin
Diary: The Journal of a Foreign Correspondent*, recorded the orders:

> Now that all the political possibilities of disposing by peaceful means of a situation on the Eastern Frontier which is intolerable for Germany are exhausted, I have determined on a solution by force. Date of attack: September 1, 1939. Time of attack: 4.45 a.m.

Accordingly German troops began the invasion of Poland on the morning of 1 September 1939. The British and French governments immediately sent an ultimatum demanding the withdrawal of all German forces from Poland. On the 3 September, when no reply had been received, the two powers declared war on Germany. On the following day, in a broadcast to the German people, Neville Chamberlain gave his own assessment of Hitler's foreign policy (recorded in *Documents on German–Polish Relations*):

> He gave his word that he would respect the Locarno Treaty; he broke it. He gave his word that he neither wished nor intended to annex Austria; he broke it. He declared that he would not incorporate the Czechs in the Reich; he did so. He gave his word after Munich that he had no further territorial demands in Europe; he broke it. He gave his word that he wanted no Polish provinces; he broke it. He has sworn to you for years that he was the mortal enemy of Bolshevism; he is now its ally. Can you wonder his word is, for us, not worth the paper it is written on?

9 ⤳ BIBLIOGRAPHY

Hitler's foreign policy is well covered in K. Hildebrand's *The Foreign Policy of the Third Reich* (Batsford 1973), *Arms, Autarky and Aggression* by William Carr (Edward Arnold 1972) and *Germany and Europe* by J. Hiden (Longman 1977). Some texts consider Nazi foreign policy as a background to the coming of the Second World War. These include 'Hitler and the Origins of the Second World War' by Alan Bullock in *The Origins of the Second World War*, E.M. Robertson, ed. (Macmillan 1971), *The Approach of War* by C. Thorne (Macmillan 1967), *Hitler's War Aims* by N. Rich (Andre Deutsch, 1974) and more recently, *The Origins of the Second World War* by R. Overy (Longman 1987). A.J.P. Taylor's *The Origins of the Second World War* (Hamish Hamilton 1961) and *The War Path: Hitler's Germany 1933–1939* by David Irving (Papermac 1983) cover the same ground but are more controversial.

10 ⌁ DISCUSSION TOPICS AND AN INTERPRETATIVE ESSAY QUESTION

A *This section consists of questions that might be used for discussion (or written answers) as a way of expanding on the chapter and testing understanding of it.*

1. In considering German foreign policy, in what ways do the views of intentionalists differ from those of structuralists?
2. To what extent was Hitler justified in withdrawing German delegates from the Disarmament Conferences in 1933?
3. In your view, was the Anglo-German Naval Treaty (1935) a diplomatic triumph for Germany?
4. Why did the Italian invasion of Abyssinia bring about a realignment of the balance of power in Europe?
5. To what extent did the Spanish Civil War develop into a trial of strength between fascism and communism?
6. What did Mussolini mean when he spoke of a Rome–Berlin axis?
7. Explain the significance of the Hossbach Memorandum.
8. To what extent did the Austrians themselves contribute to the annexation of their country by Germany in 1938?
9. Did Germany or the Soviet Union gain most from the Nazi-Soviet Pact of 1939?

B *Interpretative essay questions.*

1. The aims of Hitler's foreign policy.

Study the two interpretations below and answer the question that follows.

The main objective of Hitler's foreign policy was to remove the limitations that had been imposed by the Versailles settlement. Reparations had already been abandoned, but the restrictions on Germany's armed forces still applied, and the Rhineland was still a demilitarised zone.
(M.L.R Isaac, a British historian, in *A History of Europe since 1870*, 1960.)

He wished to bring under German rule all German speakers… His long-term plans were more ambitious. Because the Germans were a master Aryan race, Hitler thought that he was entitled to conquer extra 'living space' or Lebensraum… No less importantly, the conquest of the Soviet Union would bring about the destruction of 'Jewish Bolshevism'.
(Neil De Marco, a British historian, in *The World This Century*, 1987.)

Analyse and evaluate these two interpretations of the aims of Hitler's foreign policy.

11 ⌁ DOCUMENTARY EXERCISE ON GERMAN FOREIGN POLICY DURING THE 1930S

Study the following sources carefully and then answer the questions based on them.

It is, however, in the interests of all that present-day problems should be solved in a reasonable and final manner. No new European war could improve the unsatisfactory conditions of the present day... Nevertheless, Germany is at all times willing to undertake obligations in regard to international security, if all the other nations are ready on their side to do the same, and if this security is to benefit Germany.

SOURCE A *Hitler in a speech to the* Reichstag *on 17 May 1933.*

In this historic hour, when German troops are taking possession of their future peacetime garrisons in Germany's western provinces, we unite to testify to two holy articles of faith. First, to the oath to yield to no power or force in the re-establishment of the honour of our nation. Secondly, to the affirmation that we shall now all the more work for European understanding and particularly for an understanding with the Western powers and our Western neighbours.

SOURCE B *Hitler's statement on 7 March 1936 as German troops marched into the Rhineland, reported in* The Times.

WHAT NEXT?

State Historical Society of Missouri, Colombia

SOURCE C (PICTURE 46)
'What next?' A cartoon in the St Louis Post-Dispatch *of 25 September 1938 shows Hitler on top of a Nazi steamroller with Czechoslovakia crushed beneath it.*

SOURCE D *Extract from the agreement signed by Hitler and Neville Chamberlain at Munich on 30 September 1938.*

We regard the Agreement signed last night, and the Anglo-Naval Agreement, as symbolic of the desire of our two peoples never to go to war with one another again. We are resolved that the method of consultation shall be the method adopted to deal with any other questions that may concern our two countries. . .and thus to contribute to assure the peace of Europe.

SOURCE E *Hitler in a secret speech made to the representatives of the German press in November 1938.*

It has been pressure of circumstances that has made me talk of peace for decades on end. For only by repeatedly emphasising the German wish for peace. . .could I hope gradually to secure for the German people. . .the right kind of armament which has always been the indispensible requirement for any further move. Such peace propaganda lasting over a decade has had its questionable side-effects. For many people may think that the existing [Nazi] regime agrees with the proposition and the wish to keep peace at any cost.

SOURCE F *From a broadcast made by Neville Chamberlain on 4 September 1939.*

He gave his word after Munich that he had no further territorial demands in Europe; he broke it. He gave his word that he wanted no Polish provinces; he broke it. He has sworn to you for years that he was the mortal enemy of Bolshevism; he is now its ally. Can you wonder his word is, for us, not worth the paper it is written on?

(a) Comment on the reliability of Sources B and C.
(b) Compare Sources A and D. How far do they agree that Hitler wanted to maintain peace in Europe?
(c) To what extent do Sources B and E support the view expressed in Source F?
(d) How valuable are the sources to an understanding of German foreign policy in the 1930s? (In your answer use your own relevant background knowledge as well as information derived from the sources.)

Hitler's War

15

INTRODUCTION

The term 'Hitler's war' may not seem entirely appropriate since there were other factors which contributed to the outbreak of a major European conflict in September 1939. Even though the failure of the League of Nations, the example set elsewhere by the expansionist policies of Japan and Italy, and the appeasement of Germany by Britain and France all played their part, there is no doubt that Hitler's foreign policy ambitions were the major cause of war. The war, which at the start was largely confined to Europe, was to become a world war involving nations in all five continents. It is possible to consider the war in three phases. The period 1939 to late-1942 was a time of near uninterrupted German successes during which Hitler's armies overran much of Europe. The twelve months from November 1942 marked the turning of the tide in favour of the Allies. The remainder of the war was a period of setbacks and reversals for the Axis powers and their allies and culminated in the final defeat of Germany in May 1945. The war against Japan continued for a further four months and ended in September of that year.

1 ⌐ THE WAR IN OUTLINE

A *Early successes and the Nazi conquest of Europe*

1939

The use of *Blitzkrieg*, fast moving *Panzer* divisions backed by the terror bombing of the *Luftwaffe*, allowed the German armies to race across the plains of western Poland. As previously agreed, on 17 September Russian forces invaded from the east and, by the end of the month, Warsaw had fallen and Polish resistance came to an end. Afterwards, the Soviets annexed the Baltic states, Estonia, Latvia and Lithuania and, in October, invaded Finland.

1940

A period of inactivity, usually referred to as the 'Phoney War', ended in April 1940 when Hitler ordered the invasion of Denmark and Norway. Since 51 per cent of Germany's imported iron-ore came from Sweden and passed through Norwegian ports, control of the country's coastal waters was essential to her war effort. In addition, Norway's fjords would provide safe anchorage for German shipping. The Norwegian forces were ill-prepared and the Nazi success was partly achieved through the betrayal of a traitor in their government, Vidkun Quisling. Denmark survived only a few hours and, in spite of British help, Norway was in German hands by the end of April. In Britain, the Norway episode was seen as a fiasco and as evidence of government incompetence. Chamberlain was forced to resign and Winston Churchill became the country's new wartime leader.

On 10 May, the Germans simultaneously invaded Holland, Belgium and Luxembourg. As part of the offensive, German *Panzer* divisions thrust through the wooded Ardennes and reached the Channel coast at Abbeville. This meant that the BEF, the British Expeditionary Force, and large numbers of French troops were encircled in a pocket close to the Belgian port of Dunkirk. Hitler was reluctant to call for an all-out assault on the beleaguered men since the speed of the German advance had made their flank vulnerable to a possible counter-attack. He was also confident that the encircled armies could be dealt with by the *Luftwaffe*. His caution allowed an armada of small ships to cross the North Sea and bring off an amazing rescue operation, the so-called 'miracle of Dunkirk'. Although some 330,000 British and French soldiers were taken from the beaches to fight another day, most of their equipment fell into German hands. In *The Ordeal of Total War*, Gordon Wright comments, 'Hitler's error (at Dunkirk) allowed a salvage operation of inestimable military and psychological importance to be carried out which revitalised the flagging morale of the British people.' With the Maginot Line now outflanked, French resistance crumbled. When German troops entered Paris on 14 June 1940, the French government moved to Bordeaux. As Rommel commented, 'The war had turned into a lightning tour of France.' Eight days later, France asked for an armistice. A jubilant Hitler arranged for the French surrender to be signed at Compiègne in the same railway carriage as that used by the Allies to accept the German surrender in 1918. He went to Paris to attend a victory parade and beneath the Arc de Triumph did his famous jig as he literally danced for joy. In the meantime, Mussolini, now confident that he was backing a winning side, joined Germany in the war. Hitler decided to occupy only the north and west of France and allowed the remainder, some 60 per cent of the country, to be administered from the town of Vichy by a puppet government led by Marshal Philippe Pétain, a former hero of the First World War.

Why were the Germans so successful? A.J.P. Taylor is of the opinion that much of the credit for the achievements of the German army in the early stages of the war must go to Hitler. Acting against the advice of his generals, he played his hunch that the low state of French morale would make his *Blitzkrieg* tactics irresistible. In Heinz Guderian and Erwin Rommel, he possessed *Panzer* commanders of exceptional ability who completely outwitted the Allied generals. It is certainly not true that the Germans had overwhelming numerical superiority since in terms of

KEY ISSUE

An opportunity lost – the Dunkirk evacuation.

Q

Why were the Germans able to overrun France so easily in June 1940?

divisions the Anglo-French allies and the Germans were just about evenly matched. The difference lay in the quality of the weapons available. The allied line was strung out and, Maginot Line apart, had no depth. This meant that fast, *Luftwaffe*-supported armoured columns were able to strike deep into France. The allied generals, lacking adequate reserves and means of rapid movement, could not cope with German mobility. In addition, France had been defensively-minded for too long and the morale of both its politicians and the military was easily shattered.

Hitler assumed that, alone and in a seemingly hopeless situation, Britain would sue for peace. He still had no quarrel with Britain, providing he was allowed a free hand in Europe, and even had hopes of arranging an Anglo-German crusade against communism. A defiant Churchill saw things differently and warned 'We shall never surrender'. When all failed, Hitler issued orders for preparations to be made for Operation Sea Lion, the invasion of Britain. He said, 'Since England, despite its hopeless military position, still shows no sign of willingness to come to terms, I have decided to prepare a landing operation against England and if necessary carry it out.' He told his military leaders, 'England's hope is in Russia and the United States...if Russia is destroyed, England's last hope is shattered. Germany will then be master of Europe and the Balkans... The sooner Russia is crushed the better.'

Before the invasion of Britain could be put into effect, the Germans had to win command of the skies by destroying the RAF. At the beginning of August 1940 Göring's *Luftwaffe* lost 1,733 aircraft (the RAF claimed 2,698). With far fewer aircraft to start with, the RAF lost 915 planes and, for Fighter Command, the situation was critical. As a result of their failure, and in retaliation for an RAF raid on Berlin, the *Luftwaffe* switched tactics and Göring ordered daylight terror raids on London. Again heavy losses forced him to alter his plans and turn to night attacks on British towns and cities. Göring failed to appreciate that by diverting air attacks to populated areas he was giving the RAF a desperately needed breathing space. By mid-September, Hitler accepted that the Battle of Britain could not be won and decided to postpone his invasion plans indefinitely. Instead, he began to make plans for what all along had been his major objective, the invasion of the Soviet Union. In October, Mussolini followed the example of the Führer and began the invasion of Greece. Franco, on the other hand, resisted pressure and refused to let Spain join the war.

1941

At the start of the year Germany began to pay the penalty for being harnessed to a weak ally, Italy. In February, the *Afrika Korps* under Rommel had to be sent to bolster the Italian armies fighting against the British in North Africa; in April, Hitler had to order the invasion of Yugoslavia in order to help Italian forces failing badly in their attempt to invade Greece. One of the most extraordinary events of the war came on 10 May when Rudolf Hess, Hitler's deputy, flew from Germany and parachuted into Scotland. His purpose was to convince Churchill that the British and Germans, 'Aryan blood brothers', should not fight each other but join in a war against Bolshevik Russia. Hitler was horrified and Goebbels told the German people that Hess had been the victim of hallucination. The self-styled envoy was imprisoned by the British. On 22 June the Germans began Operation Barbarossa, the invasion of the Soviet Union. Once again, Hitler acted against the advice of his generals, who encouraged greater support for Rommel's campaign in North Africa and an all-out effort to take the Suez Canal. The Führer, however, was determined to attack Russia and considered North Africa as a less important side-show.

Why did Hitler order the invasion of Russia in June 1941?

- He was obsessed with the need to gain *Lebensraum*, living space for the German people.
- He regarded Bolshevism/communism as being directly opposed to National Socialism and, as such, it represented a political creed that had to be destroyed.
- He believed that the defeat of Russia would inevitably force Britain out of the war.
- He had no long-term confidence in Stalin's good faith.
- He needed the grain and oil resources of the Ukraine and the Caucasus.

Operation Barbarossa began as a three-pronged offensive towards Leningrad in the north, Moscow in the centre and through the Ukraine in the south. In spite of warnings given by both the Allies and his own intelligence network, Stalin was taken by surprise. The speed of the *Blitzkrieg* advance, spearheaded again by *Panzer* units, was impressive and by early October Leningrad was under siege and the German armies were at the gates of Moscow. Russian losses were massive with millions of men being killed or taken prisoner. Reserves were brought from the east and the Russian capital city was saved by a counter-offensive ordered by Marshal Zhukov, considered by many to have been the finest general of the war. The speed and success of the German advance into Russia extended their lines of communication and made the maintenance of supplies difficult. In addition, Stalin had ordered the retreating Red Army to carry out a 'scorched-earth' policy of burning all crops and habitation left behind. The onset of winter increased these difficulties but Hitler ordered his forces to hold firm regardless of casualties. The decision was not as ill-conceived as some suggest; to have risked a withdrawal in such appalling winter conditions might have turned a retreat into a rout.

The German U-boat campaign against Britain was enormously suc-

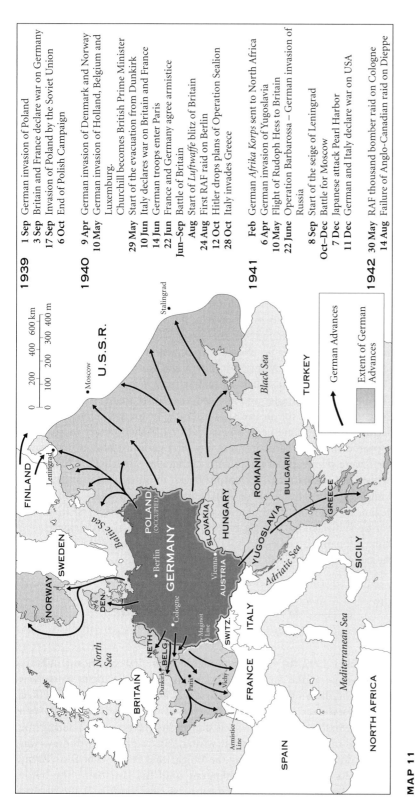

1939	**1 Sep**	German invasion of Poland
	3 Sep	Britain and France declare war on Germany
	17 Sep	Invasion of Poland by the Soviet Union
	6 Oct	End of Polish Campaign
1940	**9 Apr**	German invasion of Denmark and Norway
	10 May	German invasion of Holland, Belgium and Luxemburg.
		Churchill becomes British Prime Minister
	29 May	Start of the evacuation from Dunkirk
	10 Jun	Italy declares war on Britain and France
	14 Jun	German troops enter Paris
	22 Jun	France and Germany agree armistice
	Jun–Sep	Battle of Britain
	Aug	Start of *Luftwaffe* blitz of Britain
	24 Aug	First RAF raid on Berlin
	12 Oct	Hitler drops plans of Operation Sealion
	28 Oct	Italy invades Greece
1941	**Feb**	German *Afrika Korps* sent to North Africa
	6 Apr	German invasion of Yugoslavia
	10 May	Flight of Rudoph Hess to Britain
	22 June	Operation Barbarossa – German invasion of Russia
	8 Sep	Start of the siege of Leningrad
	Oct–Dec	Battle for Moscow
	7 Dec	Japanese attack Pearl Harbor
	11 Dec	German and Italy declare war on USA
1942	**30 May**	RAF thousand bomber raid on Cologne
	14 Aug	Failure of Anglo-Canadian raid on Dieppe

MAP 11

Hitler's war: early successes and the conquest of Europe

cessful. Hunting in packs, during 1941 they were responsible for sinking 30 per cent of all British merchant shipping. In the Battle of the Atlantic, surface raiders such as the *Graf Spee*, *Bismarck*, *Scharnhorst* and *Tirpitz* also took their toll. Always under threat from the Royal Navy, all four had been sunk by the end of 1944.

On 7 December the Japanese attacked the US naval base at Pearl Harbor. Without hesitation, Hitler declared war on the United States and turned what had largely been a European war into a global conflict. Taking on the economic and military might of America has been regarded by many historians as a major error of judgement. On the other hand, he was only anticipating what would have been inevitable and it did give his naval commanders a chance to strike at American shipping before the country was properly prepared. Error or not, the entry of the United States was to contribute largely to Germany's defeat.

KEY ISSUE

The significance of American entry into the war in December 1941.

1942

With the coming of spring, German successes in Russia continued. In June, Hitler ordered an offensive in the Ukraine; *Panzer* columns advanced into the Caucasus towards the Baku oilfields and German troops entered Stalingrad on the River Volga. Such successes were matched by Rommel in North Africa where the *Afrika Korps* had advanced as far as El Alamein in Egypt and were threatening the Suez Canal. In August, an Anglo-Canadian raid on the French port of Dieppe ended in disaster and allowed the Führer to claim that German forces had beaten off an invasion attempt. In the same month, Hitler decided that the time had come to occupy Vichy France. Although it appeared that the Germans were enjoying good fortune on all fronts, there were significant developments taking place. During the year, both British and Russian military output began to outstrip that of Germany whilst a gradual build-up of American troops and weapons had also begun. In 1939 the head of the *Luftwaffe* had boasted, 'The Ruhr will not be subjected to a single bomb. If any enemy bomber reaches the Ruhr my name is not Hermann Göring!' On 30 May 1942 Cologne was the target of the RAF's first thousand-bomber raid.

B The turning of the tide

Late 1942

In October 1942 the Germans suffered their first significant military defeat when, at the Battle of El Alamein, Rommel's *Afrika Korps* was routed and driven from Egypt. Worse was to follow. Because of the Red Army's stubborn defence of the city of Stalingrad, Freidrich von Paulus's Sixth Army found itself dangerously exposed and facing the onset of another severe Russian winter. His request to withdraw was turned down. 'I am not leaving the Volga,' said Hitler. 'The Sixth Army will do its historic duty at Stalingrad until the last man.' The battle which followed, sometimes referred to as 'the Verdun of the Second

World War' was fought with the utmost ferocity and lasted until 2 February 1943. A Russian commander, General Chuikov, wrote (quoted in *Purnell's History of the Second World War*):

> …imagine Stalingrad, eighty days and eighty nights of hand-to-hand struggles. The street is no longer measured by metres but by corpses… Stalingrad is no longer a town. By day it is an enormous cloud of burning, blinding smoke; it is a vast furnace lit by the reflection of the flames. And when night arrives, one of those scorching, howling, bleeding nights, the dogs plunge into the Volga and swim desperately to gain the other bank. The nights of Stalingrad are a terror for them. Animals flee this hell; the hardest stones cannot bear it; only men endure.

1943

With no reasonable alternative, Paulus surrendered on 31 January 1943 and two days later the fighting in the city came to an end. In captivity Paulus, who had only just been promoted field-marshal by Hitler, agreed to work for the Russians and broadcast appeals asking German soldiers to surrender. The battle, which cost the Germans 200,000 casualties with a further 91,000 men taken prisoner, was a disaster for Hitler and a major turning point of the war. Afterwards, as far as German soldiers were concerned, being sent to the Eastern Front was a move best avoided! By the spring of 1943 German armies were in retreat in Russia. In July, the Germans made an attempt to regain the initiative when General von Kluge's Army Group Centre launched a major counter-offensive, Operation Citadel. In the greatest tank battle ever fought, the Germans used nearly 3,000 tanks supported by aircraft to try and eliminate a **salient** around the town of Kursk. The battle ended in another resounding defeat with the loss of 2,900 tanks, 1,392 aircraft and 70,000 men. It was the last German offensive on the Eastern Front.

salient land held by one side projecting outwards into that held by the other

The war was also going badly for the Germans in North Africa. The *Afrika Korps*, forced into headlong retreat across Libya and into Tunisia, found itself trapped between the British Eighth Army and Anglo-American forces which had landed in French North Africa. On 12 May, after three years of desert warfare, the German and Italian forces in North Africa surrendered. In July Allied forces landed in Sicily. On the 26th of that month Mussolini was overthrown and a secret armistice agreed between the Allies and Italy. On 3 September, the day the Allies crossed to the mainland, Italy surrendered. Mussolini's successor, Marshal Badoglio, then brought his country into the war on the side of the Allies. The removal of Mussolini, and what he regarded as Italy's treachery, came as a blow to Hitler.

The heavy bombing of Germany by the RAF had started in 1942. During 1943 this increasingly took the form of thousand-bomber raids on Hamburg, Bremen, Cologne and the major industrial towns of the Ruhr. In May, the famous 'bouncing-bomb' raid on the Mohne and the

Eder dams resulted in widespread flooding and claimed the lives of 1,000 civilians. Both dams were repaired with amazing speed and the raid had barely any effect on German war production. On the night of 24 July, a massive raid on Hamburg created firestorms which killed 30,000 civilians and made a million homeless. As in Britain, the bombing did not break the morale of the German people but, if anything, reinforced it. In addition, the *Luftwaffe* and German anti-aircraft defences made both British night bombing and American daylight raids very expensive. During the raid on the ball-bearing plant at Schweinfurt, 60 American bombers were lost in one night.

During 1943 Admiral Dönitz intensified the U-boat campaign. Although 50,000,000 tonnes of allied shipping were sunk, a record number of U-boats were lost. The losses were too heavy to take and Dönitz called in his submarines to rest and refit.

C *Retreat and the collapse of the Third Reich*

1944

During the early months of 1944 the Allies overcame strong German resistance to make steady progress northwards along the Italian peninsula. After costly landings at Salerno (September 1943) the Anzio (January 1944), stoutly defended Monte Cassino fell on 15 February.

PICTURE 47

A Punch *cartoon of 1944 shows Hitler suffering sleepless nights as he anticipates the Allied invasion*

NO CURE FOR INSOMNIA

Prior to May 1940, RAF raids on Germany had been limited to coastal targets, military installations and the dropping of leaflets.

1940	15 May	99 RAF bombers attacked oil plants and marshalling yards in the Ruhr. The first major bombing raid on Germany.
	25 August	First RAF raid on Berlin. Göring had assured Hitler that this could never happen.
	16 December	First RAF night raid on a German city centre when 134 planes bombed Mannheim.
1942	28 March	RAF night raid on Lübeck. 234 aircraft bombed the city centre in the first large-scale incendiary raid.
	17 April	RAF raid on MAN diesel engine works at Augsburg. 7 of the 12 aircraft involved were shot down. Raid showed the danger of bomber raids without fighter protection.
	30 May	First thousand-bomber raid on a German city. Cologne was devastated with 474 civilians killed and over 40,000 left homeless. RAF lost 40 aircraft.
1943	5 March	RAF night raid on Krupp works at Essen. Of 442 bombers involved, 14 were shot down.
	16 May	RAF 'bouncing bomb' raid on Mohne and Eder dams. Led to flooding with 1,000 people drowned. No appreciable effect on German war economy.
	24 July	RAF raid on Hamburg followed by three further raids. City left in ruins with over 42,000 people killed. German radar confused by strips of tinfoil. Of the 791 bombers used only 12 were lost.
	14 October	American daylight raid on Schweinfurt ball-bearing works. 60 of the 291 planes used were lost. Americans end daylight bombing offensive.
	13 November	RAF night raid on Berlin – the first of 16 mass raids on the German capital involving over 9,000 bombers.
1944	8 March	American raid on Berlin. Bombers escorted by long-range P51 Mustang escort fighters with drop fuel tanks.
	30 March	RAF raid on Nuremberg. Of the 705 planes used, 95 were shot down. Greatest success by German air defences of the war.
	23 September	RAF raid on Dortmund Ems Canal. 'Tallboy' (5430 kilo) bombs used. 10 kilometres of the canal drained.
1945	13 February	The old and historic city of Dresden, at the time full of refugees, was devastated by 805 RAF bombers. Although the total number of deaths was never accurately calculated, it has been estimated at 130,000 – a number higher than those who later perished at Hiroshima on 6 August. It was the most controversial raid of the war.

(Based on statistics compiled by the Imperial War Museum)

TABLE 53
The bombing of Germany: raids of strategic importance

On 2 June, American forces entered Rome. On the Russian Front, the long siege of Leningrad finally ended in January whilst the Red Army made major advances in the south to liberate the Ukraine and cross the Romanian frontier.

Seemingly unappreciative that his allies were already heavily committed on the Italian Front and in the Far East against Japan, Stalin had long pressed the Anglo-Americans to open a 'second front' in western Europe. This finally came on D-Day, 6 June 1944 when, as part of Operation Overlord, British, Canadian and American troops landed on the Normandy coast. Within a week, 440,000 men were ashore. From a German viewpoint, the move had long been expected and it had been a matter of where and when. In anticipation of an allied invasion in the west, Hitler had ordered the building of coastline defences of massive proportions to create *Festung Europa*, Fortress Europe. Built by Fritz Todt using slave labour, the Atlantic Wall stretched from the Bay of Biscay to the east of the Pas de Calais. Overall responsibility for the defence of *Festung Europa* was entrusted to Field Marshal Karl von Rundstedt. Field Marshal Rommel was to command *Armeegruppe B* deployed across Brittany and Normandy. In the event of an invasion, it was Rundstedt's plan to hold his *Panzer* divisions in reserve until the invaders were well ashore. They would then be used to force them back into the sea. Rommel vigorously disagreed. He wanted the *Panzer* to be used immediately the enemy landed. Hitler, whose intelligence reports led him to believe that the invasion would take place along the Pas de Calais, settled the issue by placing the *Panzer* under his own command. Once the invasion started, Hitler still persisted with the belief that the Normandy landings were a diversion and that the real invasion was still to come further to the east. Two days passed before he realised his error and allowed Rundstedt to redeploy his units. The allied break-out from Normandy did not come easily. After a savage battle, Caen was taken by the British and Canadians whilst the Americans fought their way to St Lo. A German counter-attack ended in disaster when their armies were trapped in a pincer movement near Falaise. Once the Falaise gap was closed, the greater part of eight infantry divisions and two *Panzer* divisions surrendered. As a result, Kluge, who was deprived of his command, committed suicide. In a letter to Hitler, Kluge wrote: 'I do not know whether Model [his replacement] can restore the position...but if not, and if your new weapons, in which such burning faith is placed, do not bring success then, *mein Führer*, take the decision to end the war.' Hitler had long claimed that he possessed secret weapons, *Wunderwaffen* or wonder weapons, capable of winning the war. Allied intelligence knew that German scientists were carrying out research into the possibility of making atomic weapons. In 1943 British commandos destroyed a **heavy-water** installation in Norway and also bombed Peenemünde on the Baltic where reconnaissance photographs had provided evidence of rocket-launching sites. A week after D-Day, the first V-1 flying bombs fell on Britain. These small, jet-propelled rockets, known as 'Doodlebugs' were Hitler's *Vergeltungswaffen*, revenge weapons. With a range of 450 kilometres, they were used

---

KEY ISSUE

June 1944 – the opening of a 'second front' in Europe.

---

heavy water water subject to chemical changes needed to produce nuclear weapons

against London and the Home Counties. In September 1944 came the V-2 rockets. Far more menacing, these rockets travelled at supersonic speeds, came without warning and did considerable damage. Rocket attacks on England continued until their launching sites along the French coast had been captured. By that time, they had claimed 8,000 lives. From the allied viewpoint, they now held virtually unchallenged control of the skies. With their bombers protected by the new long-range P51 Mustang escort fighters, any target was safely within their range. The *Luftwaffe* was no longer an effective fighting force.

The late summer of 1944 was a particularly bleak time for Germany. In July came the July Plot (see pages 313–18), an attempt to assassinate Hitler, and the appointment of Goebbels to oversee Germany's commitment to total war. On 11 August, Operation Anvil saw the landing of allied forces in the south of France whilst, in the north, Anglo-American armies liberated Paris on 25 August. Ten days later, British units entered Brussels. In mid-September, the Allies attempted Operation Market Garden, a speedy advance of 90 kilometres to secure a bridge over the River Rhine. To achieve this, airborne forces were dropped in stages at Eindhoven, Grave, Lek and Arnhem. The fourth stepping stone proved to be famously 'a bridge too far'. On 21 October, Aachen became the first German town to fall to the Allies. In a final effort to summon together sufficient reserves to defend Germany, Hitler formed the *Volkssturm*, a People's Army. Made up of old men and young boys, some aged less than 16, it was the German equivalent of the Home Guard. They were supposed to be used in their own localities but some units ended up fighting at the front.

On the Eastern Front, the advance of the Red Army into Poland caused resistance fighters in Warsaw to anticipate their liberation and rise up against the Germans. Inexplicably, the Russian advance came to a halt on the River Vistula. During a period of 60 days of ferocious fighting, the Nazis were able to crush the uprising. Elsewhere, the situation was critical. The Balkan Front was in ruins, Romania had surrendered, Bulgaria had been occupied by the Russians, Belgrade was in the hands of Tito's partisans and the British were in Athens.

Hitler suddenly lost interest in events in the east and turned instead to the war in the west. In December came an unexpected German fightback when Hitler ordered a counter-offensive in the Ardennes. Some historians consider it to have been Hitler's greatest military blunder. John Strawson in *Hitler as Military Commander* outlines this view:

> In deciding to make such a reckless use of the resources he had scraped together, Hitler was about to make the blunder to end all blunders and, in flinging away the last ounce of offensive strength, to ensure that the Reich itself could not be defended. No reason could move him. No appeal could prevail. The Allies would never be defeated by fighting defensively. Only an offensive would serve his purpose. The gambler was resolved to have one more throw.

Hitler's plan was to drive a wedge between the British and American armies, retake Antwerp and then drive the Allies back to the sea – in fact, a repeat of the German success in the Ardennes in 1940. To start with, it appeared that Hitler's desperate plan might work as 250,000 men and 1,100 tanks attacked along a 75 kilometre front. With their airforce grounded by fog, the Americans were forced to retreat in disarray.

1945

Fortunes in the Battle of the Bulge changed early in the New Year when the skies cleared and the Allied counter-attack began. Out of petrol, convoys of German vehicles stretched bumper-to-bumper provided easy targets for the 5,000 Allied aircraft used to smash the offensive. Although it succeeded in delaying the Allied offensive across the Rhine for some six weeks, it was a final fling which cost the Germans dearly. With no reserves, the German generals now had to face the prospect of spring offensives in both east and west. On 17 January the Russians finally liberated Warsaw and ten days later reached Auschwitz to witness the horrors of the most notorious of the Nazi death camps. By early February, the Red Army was on the banks of the River Oder.

Although, it can be claimed with justification that the German blitzing of Warsaw, Rotterdam, London, Coventry and other British towns and cities was the start of terror bombing, as we have seen the Anglo-American air offensive against Germany gave the war a new and awesome dimension. On 13 February, the RAF attacked Dresden in what was one of the most devastating raids of the war. The city, full of refugees and of no strategic importance, suffered a firestorm. Further raids by the Americans followed immediately afterwards. Altogether, the total number of civilians killed may have been as many as 130,000, the Nazi estimate was considerably higher. In the post-war years, the decision to bomb Dresden was to become a controversial issue. In the west, the Germans regarded the River Rhine as their last line of defence. They blew up bridges as they prepared to make their last stand along the river. On 7 March, the Americans reached a bridge at Remagen near Koblenz which was not ready for demolition and, within 24 hours, 8,000 men had secured a position on the other side. To the north the British, who had liberated Holland, crossed the Rhine on 23 March. Shortly afterwards they reached the notorious concentration camp at Belsen. Although pockets of resistance remained in the Ruhr and elsewhere, the Allies continued their advance and, on 25 April, Russian and American patrols met at Torgau on the River Elbe, 40 kilometres to the south of Berlin. Although the Russians were in the outskirts of the city, Berlin still had to be taken. Within the city, secure for the moment in his bunker, was Hitler and what remained of the Nazi hierarchy still loyal to his cause.

Q

Is it possible to justify the bombing of Dresden in 1945?

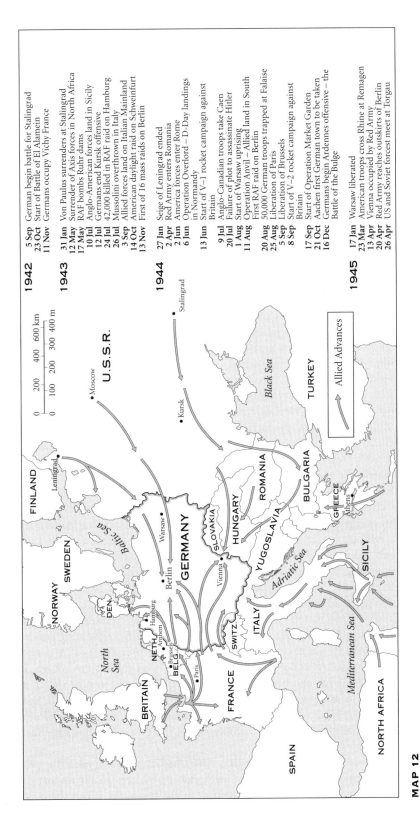

1942
5 Sep   German begin battle for Stalingrad
23 Oct   Start of Battle of El Alamein
11 Nov   Germans occupy Vichy France

1943
31 Jan   Von Paulus surrenders at Stalingrad
12 May   Surrender of Axis forces in North Africa
17 May   RAF bombs Ruhr dams
10 Jul   Anglo-American forces land in Sicily
12 Jul   Germans end Kursk offensive
24 Jul   42,000 killed in RAF raid on Hamburg
26 Jul   Mussolini overthrown in Italy
3 Sep   Allied forces land on Italian Mainland
14 Oct   American daylight raid on Schweinfurt
13 Nov   First of 16 mass raids on Berlin

1944
27 Jan   Seige of Leningrad ended
2 Apr   Red Army enters Romania
2 Jun   America forces enter Rome
6 Jun   Operation Overlord – D-Day landings in Normandy
13 Jun   Start of V–1 rocket campaign against Britain
9 Jul   Anglo-Canadian troops take Caen
20 Jul   Failure of plot to assassinate Hitler
1 Aug   Start of Warsaw uprising
11 Aug   Operation Anvil – Allied land in South
        First RAF raid on Berlin
20 Aug   50,000 German troops trapped at Falaise
25 Aug   Liberation of Paris
5 Sep   Liberation of Brussels
8 Sep   Start of V–2 rocket campaign against Britain
17 Sep   Start of Operation Market Garden
21 Oct   Aachen first German town to be taken
16 Dec   Germans begin Ardennes offensive – the Battle of the Bulge

1945
17 Jan   Warsaw liberated
23 Mar   American troops cross Rhine at Remagen
13 Apr   Vienna occupied by Red Army
20 Apr   Red Army reaches outskirts of Berlin
26 Apr   US and Soviet forcest meet at Torgau

MAP 12
The turning of the tide: retreat and collapse of the Third Reich

2 ⌐ HITLER AS A MILITARY COMMANDER

Although some in the German military hierarchy persisted in regarding Hitler as nothing more than a 'jumped-up corporal' and Allied wartime propagandists dismissed him as a 'strategic dunderhead' and 'facile amateur', the successes of the German army suggest that these views are far from the truth. Hitler, who regarded success in war as the summit of human achievement, was a self-taught strategist. In his early years he had been an avid reader of military histories and, although he had never held high rank or enjoyed military responsibilities, he had served in the front-line as a soldier. This he claimed gave him an understanding of warfare which generals did not possess. He was undoubtedly a brave and self-confident man with a fanatical belief in himself and his cause. It seemed natural to him that as Führer he should command the armed forces of the Reich. Hitler officially became Commander-in-Chief when he took over from Walter von Brauchitsch in December 1941. Brauchitsch, who had replaced the disgraced Fritsch in 1938 (see page 206), was blamed for the German army's failure to capture Moscow. At the start of the war, Hitler treated his military commanders as near equals and was prepared to let them make decisions and decide tactics. With every success, he grew in confidence to a point where he came to regard himself as infallible and would tolerate no opposed views whatsoever. Field Marshals Keital, the Führer's yes-man and mouthpiece, and Alfred Jodl, his chief military adviser, both regarded Hitler as a military genius but this was not a view shared by all Germany's military leaders.

One of the few prepared to challenge Hitler's decisions was Heinz Guderian, the master exponent of the use of the tank and *Blitzkrieg*. Hitler's command organisation was based on the OKW, the *Oberkommando der Wehrmacht*, and decisions were made at regularly held conferences. He enjoyed being referred to as *GröFaz*, an **acronym** for the German for 'the greatest commander of all time'. Even though this was an exaggeration, he tried to live up to it! Hitler's major shortcoming as a military leader was that he would never regard retreat as an option and was quick to dismiss generals he considered unenterprising. He was unwilling to withdraw armies from impossible situations and seemed 'prepared to let his armies bleed to death to redeem a pledge'. He was also guilty of poor judgement and major blunders. As we have seen, he badly miscalculated the situation at the time of Dunkirk, neglected his armies in North Africa, sacrificed the German armies defending Stalingrad (1943), was slow to move armoured units after D-Day (1944) and wasted resources in a final offensive in the west during the winter of 1944–5. He has also been criticised for invading Russia in June 1941 but since this was part of his grand strategy to gain *Lebensraum* it was inevitable. Again it has been argued that he had no need to declare war on the United States in December of the same year but this too must surely have come about.

It has to be remembered that Hitler had at his command the best drilled and equipped army in Europe backed by strategically important *Panzer* units and the modern aircraft of the *Luftwaffe*. When the need

acronym a word made up of the initial letters of other words

arose for the resolve of the *Wehrmacht* to be stiffened, he could depend on the *Waffen-SS* officered by dedicated young Nazis. Although it may be argued that Germany was not herself fully prepared for a lengthy war, Hitler's early successes were gained largely against militarily weak and ill-prepared nations. By the end of 1942, at a time when 'the magic of *Blitzkrieg* was no longer working efficiently', came the German disasters at El Alamein and Stalingrad. The end of Hitler's glory days was fast approaching. In 1945, with the Third Reich crumbling about him, he used fear as motivation when he warned, in a directive issued on 15 April:

> Our deadly enemies the Jewish Bolsheviks have launched their massive attack. Their aim is to reduce Germany to ruins and exterminate our people. Many of you soldiers in the east already know the fate which threatens... While the old men and children will be murdered, the women and girls will be reduced to barrack-room whores. The remainder will be marched off to Siberia... If every soldier on the Eastern Front does his duty...the last assault of Asia will crumble.

At the bitter end, Hitler finally turned upon his military leaders (quoted in *The Last Days of Hitler* by Hugh Trevor-Roper):

> ...my trust has been misused by many people. Disloyalty and betrayal have undermined resistance throughout the war. It was therefore not granted to me to lead the people to victory. The Army General Staff cannot be compared with the General Staff of the First World War. Its achievements were far behind those of the fighting men.

3 ⌐ INSIDE NAZI GERMANY — THE WAR YEARS

At the start of the Second World War, Hitler virtually abandoned public life and left the management of German domestic affairs to Göring, Goebbels, Himmler and Bormann. In 1939 a Reich Defence Council was established under Göring but it failed to co-ordinate the various interests of the ministries and agencies into anything like a centralised organisation. In fact, with so many party officials trying to promote their own self-interest and achieve prominence, it is surprising that such a chaotic system of government was able to sustain the war effort for the best part of six years. The historian, Louis L. Snyder, described wartime Nazi Germany as 'a swampland of intrigue and struggles for power'.

To Goebbels fell the responsibility for motivating the nation and maintaining morale. It was the Minister for National Enlightenment and Propaganda, rather than Hitler, who made the patriotic speeches and toured the bombed towns and cities. At the start of the war, maintaining morale was not difficult since even earlier doubters were won over by Hitler's successes in 1939, 1940 and 1941. Disillusionment was to come later following defeats at El Alamein and Stalingrad. This increased as the allied air offensive intensified and the Allies began to close in on Germany from both east and west. To Himmler fell the responsibility for enforcing obedience and discipline. He had at his disposal the SS, the *Gestapo*, the *Sicherheitsdienst* or SD (the security branch of the SS) and the police. During the course of the war, the authority of the SS extended into every aspect of national life (see Chapter 8). Using the *Gestapo* as well as a network of spies and informers, Himmler was able to root out those who were anti-war or showed any sign of dissent. He held a wide range of appointments. Appointed Reich Minister of the Interior in 1943, this was later extended to include Commander-in-Chief of the Rhine Army Group (1944) and Vistula Army Group (1945). His power was almost limitless and only matched by that of Hitler's confidante and secretary, Martin Bormann.

Behind the scenes, Bormann reinforced Hitler's anti-Semitic policies, raged against Christianity, encouraged the lynching of captured Allied bomber crews, and suggested that war heroes should be rewarded with the right to enjoy polygamy. To the bitter end he remained totally loyal but what finally became of him remains one of the unsolved mysteries of the post-war period.

Lesser party functionaries behaved no better than their seniors. They competed with and spied on each other as they sought to gain the most prestigious positions. They openly flaunted the privileges they enjoyed which were denied to ordinary Germans. Some tried to avoid military service and instead looked for lucrative administrative positions in the occupied countries where they could embezzle and accumulate booty. The Public Record Office has recently released details of a wartime scheme by the OAS to discredit leading Nazis by revealing lurid accounts of their sex lives and their involvement in orgies and hard-core pornography. It is also claimed that, in 1942, a plot was hatched to forge German postage stamps so that they showed the head of Himmler instead of Hitler. This, they hoped, would lead the Führer to believe that the SS leader was planning to replace him. As the war progressed the shortcomings of many Nazi administrators became increasingly obvious. Even so, Hitler tended to stand by them. Incompetence he could stand, cowardice and disloyalty he could not!

Owing to the alarming fall in recruitment, in 1939 party membership previously limited to only 10 per cent of the population, was again made available to all Aryan Germans. In 1942 membership was once again closed, although it remained open to the young. In 1944, the minimum age requirement was lowered from 18 to 17. In limiting recruitment in this way, Hitler hoped to ensure the dynamism and ideological purity of the Party. The pillars of support of the Party – industrialists and manufacturers, the white-collar workers and artisans of the lower middle class, the working class still enjoying regular work

KEY ISSUE

The influence of Martin Bormann.

and good wages, the agricultural community – remained steady. If there was some disenchantment, it was among sections of the elite and upper middle-class professionals such as doctors, teachers and lawyers. Many had tired of Hitler's anti-intellectualism, the erosion of civil liberties and the severity of his racial theories. There was also a marked increase in the number of women who joined the Party (see page 285). This was brought about by the fact that labour shortages made it necessary to reverse Nazi policy relating to the employment of women and this gave them a new importance. Between 1939 and 1944, female membership of the Party increased from 16.5 per cent to 34.7 per cent of the total.

Although there had been no wild celebrations to mark the outbreak of war in 1939, German military successes were sufficient to ensure that patriotic fervour remained high until the beginning of 1943. Even when things began to go wrong and the realities of total war became apparent through constant heavy bombing, people were more inclined to blame the Party than the Führer. There were instances when people denied their membership and hid their party insignia. Goebbels pressed all Germans to make a greater contribution to the war effort. Collecting for winter relief, joining the civil defence and, after 1944, enrolling in the *Volkssturm* were encouraged. The war also provided Himmler with the opportunity to extend party influence over the civil service and legal system. Top civil servants and members of the judiciary who would not comply with his wishes were replaced. Justice was dispensed by the *Volksgerichtshof*, the People's Court, under Roland Freisler. The penal code was extended so that people could be executed for spreading rumours or defeatism, making critical remarks, black marketeering, listening to foreign broadcasts and any crimes committed at night when a blackout was in force.

Day and night bombing by the RAF and American air force took a heavy toll (see Table 53 on page 411). During the course of the war, allied aircraft flew 1,442,280 missions and dropped 2,700,000 tonnes of bombs on Germany killing an estimated 650,000 civilians. The raids did not shatter German morale or reduce industrial production to the level predicted. If anything, seeing their homes destroyed, being forced to live in cellars and shelters and endure shortages and hardships made Germans apathetic. The wounded and those on leave from the front were often more appalled by the destruction they witnessed than the civilian population. Food rationing had been introduced at the start of the war and this provided the German people with a reasonable diet until mid-1944. Although home-grown food was supplemented with that taken from the occupied countries, in 1944 rations were severely cut. Even so, every effort was made to make special provision for those involved in war production. It was not always the scarcity of food which caused a problem; there were also major difficulties in distribution. What was left of Ukrainian harvests was used to feed those serving on the Eastern Front. In Germany, rural areas fared better than urban centres where black marketeering, though punishable, still flourished. The authorities did not consider the evacuation of civilians until late in the war.

4 ✍ IMPACT OF HITLER'S WAR PLANS ON THE GERMAN ECONOMY

A *Was there total mobilisation in 1939?*

Historians have disputed the extent to which the economy was fully mobilised for war in 1939. Some, such as A.S. Milward (*The End of Blitzkrieg*, 1963), have argued that the economy operated on a 'peace-like' war basis until as late as 1942–3, whilst a full-scale commitment was not fully realised until 1944. They believe that there was a clear gap between Hitler's ambitions and economic and military policy. Recent research, such as that carried out by R.J. Overy, has challenged this interpretation and there is now a growing consensus amongst historians that Hitler geared the economy to full-scale total war with the circulation of the Secret Memo (see page 353) in 1936 which launched the second Four Year Plan. According to the evidence of General Thomas, head of the armed forces' economic staff, and in constant touch with the war machine, Germany was totally mobilised for a total war by July 1941.

KEY ISSUE

At what stage did Germany totally mobilise for war?

The foundation of this full economic mobilisation was laid before 1939, in the 'disguised' rearmament of 1933–6 prior to the directive to Göring to 'gear the economy for total war' associated with the Four Year Plan 1936–9. These arrangements provided for rearmament in depth (factory capacity, machinery, raw materials, labour) as well as width (stockpile of armaments) and for the fullest possible use of civilian resources in wartime. Before war broke out the Four Year Plan authorised the Economics Ministry to begin a complete conversion plan for wartime and set up registers of labour to ensure a speedy recruitment of men and women for the war industries. Female labour service was recognised as of decisive significance, as was the psychological preparation of the people to persuade them to accept the cuts in living standards and shortages which would occur with total war. In 1939, these preparations were incomplete and the economy was still in a transitional stage of building the substructure for major industrialised warfare. Hitler expected that war to last for at least five or seven years and so plans were put into place to achieve a phased transition to total war which depended on finance, labour use and expansion of armaments capacity. By 1939 Germany was devoting 32.2 per cent of its national income to war, compared with Britain's 15 per cent – a differential which continued throughout the war, as Table 54(a) shows. The structuralists' claim that Hitler was thinking in terms of a series of *Blitzkrieg* campaigns to broaden his economic base and escape from the limitations of the economy in preparation for general war cannot be supported by the most recent statistics on the German economy.

Neither the statistical evidence nor what Hitler said on various occasions show that *Blitzkrieg* was visualised as an alternative to the broadest possible rearmament programme. Hitler was obsessed with the possibility that, as in 1918, Germany might be defeated by the limitations of her

		1939	1940	1941	1942	1943	1944
(a)	**Percentage of war expenditure in total National Income**						
	Germany	32.2	48.8	56.0	65.6	71.3	–
	Britain	15.0	43.0	52.0	52.0	55.0	54.0
(b)	**Index of consumer expenditure (per head) (1938 = 100)**						
	Germany	95.0	88.4	81.9	75.3	75.3	70.0
	Britain	97.2	89.7	87.1	86.6	85.5	88.2
(c)	**Employment in war industries (percentage of all employed)**						
	Germany	21.9	50.2	54.4	56.1	61.0	–
	Britain	18.6	–	50.9	–	–	–
(d)	**Percentage of women in total of civil employment**						
	Germany	37.3	41.4	42.6	46.0	48.8	51.0
	Britain	26.4	29.8	33.2	34.8	36.4	36.2

TABLE 54

Select statistics on the German and British war effort, 1939–44

Q *Was Germany or Britain more prepared for war?*

resource base. Rearmament in depth was therefore his aim, as his Four Year Plan Memorandum of 1936 shows. The greatest possible commitment to rearmament was limited only by the fact that too great a burden on the population might damage morale, as it had done in the First World War. As a result of the most recent research on the economy, it is now claimed that there were no major changes in economic policy in the middle of the war. Indeed, 'the German economy had converted the great bulk of its labour and capacity to war by the end of 1941' (R.J. Overy, 'Mobilisation for Total War in Germany 1939–1941', *English Historical Review*, 103, July 1988). Overy rejects the view that the German economy made only a limited commitment to war before 1942 at the earliest. He argues that all the evidence on war preparations and military production plans confirms that the general expectation in Germany before 1939 was that any future war would be a total war from the start. The Four Year Plan is seen as a strategy of total economic mobilisation in terms of armament in depth whilst Goebbels' propaganda machine was mobilised to prepare the people psychologically for the expected cuts in their living standards and to accept a 'total war'. Table 54(d) above shows that Britain's war expenditure as a percentage of total income in 1939 was half the amount spent by Germany, though there was less of a difference in terms of workers employed in war industries as a percentage of the total number in employment.

B *Was the war economy effectively managed?*

Problems of supplying essential war materials to the armed forces, as a result of premature involvement in a European, rather than a local war over Poland, became obvious by 1941. The production levels for weapons, submarines, aircraft and bombs which Hitler had laid down in December 1939, had not been achieved. A number of reasons account for this failure:

- By the standards of the 1914–18 war the armaments programme was very ambitious and excessive so that even at the time industry doubted whether it could be achieved. This was despite the fact that there had already been a dramatic increase in the percentage of the industrial workforce working on military contracts. By the summer of 1941, 54.5 per cent of the workforce were working on military contracts compared with only 21.9 per cent in 1939. As resources were redirected to the war effort, civilian consumption fell by more than 20 per cent in the same period. This state of affairs might suggest that the economy was over-stretched.

- More importantly, there was a lack of co-ordination and central planning. The chaotic structure of government, which Hitler had allowed to develop, led to a situation where there were a number of overlapping ministries – the Ministry of Economics, the Ministry of the Four Year Plan, the Ministry of Finance, the Ministry of the armed forces – which competed rather than coordinated activities and decisions. With so many people in charge, confusion prevailed resulting in bottlenecks due to serious problems in transport provision.

- Control of war production was in the hands of the armed forces rather than heads of industry, which led to a stultifying supervision whereby every stage of the production process, from design to inspection of the finished product, was carried out by military engineers. The latter set unreasonable standards which often led to waste as evidenced by the aircraft industry where, despite a doubling of resource allocation, there was only a 20 per cent increase in output between 1939 and 1941. Factories were not modernised in the interests of improving efficiency and output, and the workforce were inadequately trained. This wasteful use of resources was increased by a failure to exploit the resources of its captured territories. Early researchers, such as Klein, took this failure as evidence that Germany was not really preparing for total war. Industrialists found it impossible to plan production in this situation.

C Hitler's response to the failure to achieve total mobilisation 1939–41

The impetus to resolve the weaknesses that had emerged by 1941 was eventually provided by the planned invasion of the Soviet Union. Hitler had always been aware of the threat from Stalin's industrialisation programme of the 1930s which had been increasingly dominated by war preparations. War with Russia was the logical outcome of Hitler's racial and territorial fantasies and its imminence had been discussed in the Secret Memo which launched the Four Year Plan when Hitler had warned that: 'a victory of Bolshevism over Germany would lead not to a Versailles' Treaty but to the final destruction, indeed to the annhiliation, of the German people'. The failure of industry to achieve the production targets he had set in December 1939 led to Hitler's decision, in

May 1941, to set up an inquiry to identify the reasons for this. Lack of central planning and unreasonable interference by the armed forces, which were targeted as the main problems, were dealt with in Hitler's December Rationalisation Decree. Control of the war economy was concentrated in the hands of a Minister of Armaments who was given the authority to carry out the changes he considered necessary to achieve an increase in the quantity of weapons produced from the same sources. Hitler chose someone from his own staff, a civilian, to indicate that he, rather than the chiefs of the armed forces, would exercise a general supervision of the economy in the future. The death, in February 1942, of his first Minister of Armaments, Fritz Todt, gave him the opportunity to appoint his architect, Albert Speer, who was to show brilliant technical and organisational ability.

5 ⤳ THE ROLE OF ALBERT SPEER AS MINISTER OF ARMAMENTS 1942–5

Armed with the Führer's authorisation and support, Speer, in March 1942, set up a Central Planning Board comprising a number of committees each with responsibility for an important sector of the economy. Its members were experts drawn from the world of industry and business. As its director, he reorganised industry to achieve efficiency at all stages of the production and distribution process. He had the authority to control the distribution and allocation of raw materials and to insist on the introduction of modern methods of mass production in order to achieve a rise in productivity. He ended the interference of the chiefs of the armed forces and their personnel and gave industrialists the freedom to meet production targets. From 1942 the building of the essential industries for the war effort was complete with the result that more resources could be released for the production of arms. The effect of this reorganisation on armament production was very quickly apparent.

Production expanded from 1942 until it was interrupted by the bombing of 1943. The availability of additional resources from 1942 to 1944, along with the employment of foreign labour also contributed to the expansion in output. By 1944 weapons production had trebled, an increase which had been achieved through greater efficiency of production techniques rather than any increase in raw materials. By 1944 100,000 tonnes of steel produced 40,000 tonnes of weapons compared with only 10,000 tonnes of weapons in 1941. Such successes were vital given that Speer had a different war to fight from that of his predecessors in terms of scope, scale and intensity.

There were however, limits to Speer's successes. Some of his policies were undermined by a division of responsibility. Labour was put under the command of Gauleiter Fritz Sauckel who was made Minister Plenipotentiary for Labour while Himmler was in charge of the concentration camps. Speer quarrelled with both of these high-ranking Nazis

KEY ISSUE

Speer's success in achieving total mobilisation.

on the issue of the source of the labour required to continue with production and the war effort. Ideological considerations meant that Speer lost his attempts, both to employ more women and to treat camp labour more humanely. About a quarter of the 30,000 employed on building the underground V-2 weapon production plant in the Harz mountains died of exhaustion. As Sauckel commented on the labour conscription programme issued on 20 April 1942, (quoted in Noakes and Pridham, *Documents on Nazism 1919 to 1945*):

> Our armed forces of Greater Germany have surpassed themselves in heroism and endurance on the Eastern front, in Africa, in the air and on the sea. To ensure their victory under all circumstances, it is now necessary to produce more and better weapons, equipment and ammunition...The aim of this gigantic new labour mobilisation is to use the rich and tremendous resources, conquered and secured for us by our armed forces under the leadership of Adolf Hitler, for the armament of the armed forces and also to provide food for the homeland. The raw materials as well as the fertility of the conquered territories and their manpower are to be exploited completely and conscientiously for the benefit of Germany and her allies...All prisoners of war...from the territories of the west as well as of the east, must be completely incorporated into the German armament and nutrition industries. Their productivity must be raised to the highest possible level...a tremendous additional quantity of foreign labour must be found for the Reich. The occupied territories in the east will provide the greatest pool for this purpose...we must requisition skilled or unskilled male and female labour from the Soviet territories...all the men must be fed, housed and treated in such a way as to exploit them to the greatest possible extent at the absolute minimum of expenditure...

Q

Was Sauckel influenced by ideological considerations in recruiting labour for the war effort?

Speer suggested the employment of German women (recorded in his book *Inside the Third Reich*):

> ...Sauckel did not meet his commitments. Hitler's fine talk about drawing labour out of a population of 250 million came to nought, partly because of the ineffectiveness of the German administration in the occupied territories, partly because of the preference of the men involved for taking to the forests and joining the partisans sooner than be dragged off for labour service in Germany... It seemed far more practicable to employ German women rather than assorted foreign labour. Businessmen came to me with statistics showing that the employment of German women during the First World War had been significantly higher than it was now...
>
> I went to Sauckel with the proposition that we recruit our labour from the ranks of German women. He replied brusquely that the

question of where to obtain which workers and how to distribute them was his business. Moreover, he said, as a Gauleiter he was Hitler's subordinate and responsible to the Führer alone. But before the discussion was over, he offered to put the question to Göring, who as Commissioner of the Four-Year Plan should have the final say... I was scarcely allowed to advance my arguments; Sauckel and Göring continually interrupted me. Sauckel laid great weight on the danger that factory work might inflict moral harm upon German womanhood; not only might their 'psychic and emotional life' be affected but also their ability to bear. Göring totally concurred. But to be absolutely sure, Sauckel went to Hitler immediately after the conference and had him confirm the decision. All my good arguments were thereby blown to the winds...

Q

Why did Speer fail to overcome opposition to the employment of German women?

However, the most important setback came from 1943 onwards with the onset of intensive allied bombing and, in late 1944, the advance of their forces from both east and west. It is now acknowledged that this had a far more detrimental effect on Germany's production of armaments which probably declined by 50 per cent. Over this period, Speer reported a 31 per cent decline in aircraft production, a 40 per cent decline in transport production and a 35 per cent decline in tank production. Bombing on such a scale did not halt production but it did set significant limits. Time and manpower was wasted in moving vital factories underground while men, guns and radar were diverted to meeting the threat to German cities. These various resources had to be drawn away from the war effort which also contributed to a decline in productivity. Germany could not match the output of the Allies, particularly Russia and America, which meant that the German economy could not sustain total war indefinitely.

In the view of R.J. Overy, 'If war had been postponed until 1943–5, as Hitler had hoped, then Germany would have been much better prepared and would also have had rockets, jet aircraft, inter-continental bombers even possibly atomic bombs. Though Britain and France did not realise it, declaring war in 1939, prevented Germany from becoming the super-power Hitler wanted. The commitment to full mobilisation had been there from the start, but, as Hitler complained, 'mismanaged'. The drive for total war became *Blitzkrieg* by default.' Yet, to the very end German industry continued to work with the Nazi regime, especially those involved in armaments production, where the material benefits were very attractive. Profits continued to increase, and this encouraged collaboration, though policy, particularly from 1936, was clearly determined by the Nazi leadership.

6 ⟿ IMPACT OF WAR ON THE SUPPLY OF LABOUR

A *Changes in employment patterns for labour*

Waging total war put serious strains on Germany's supply of men who were needed in both the armed forces and expanding factories. The regime tried to resolve these competing demands by drawing up a register of labour and directing labour to where it was most needed. Men were drafted into the armed forces, some 13 million by the autumn of 1944, which led to a fall in the number employed in the labour force from 39.1 million in May 1939 to 30.4 million by September 1944. It was to meet the shortfalls in the war-related industries that labour and investment was redirected from building and the consumer sector into heavy industry such as chemical, iron and steel, synthetic oil and metal-working. The latter industry showed the greatest increase: the labour force rose from 28.6 per cent in 1939 to 68.8 per cent in 1941 and 72.1 per cent in 1943. The armaments industries tried to protect and retain their skilled labour by giving them a special priority rating which disqualified men from conscription. Most of the change in the pattern of labour distribution occurred in the first two years compared with that 1941 to 1943 which gives weight to the views of those historians who argue that Hitler planned for total war from the start. Factories previously devoted to clothing, car and furniture production began to manufacture aircraft, armaments and uniforms. In 1941 the services took 40 per cent of textiles output and 44 per cent of all clothing which left much less capacity for civilian needs than output figures suggest (see Tables 55 and 56). All of these labour changes created problems of training to acquire the new skills of a changing technology.

These strategies were not enough to make up for the labour shortage, which had been a problem since 1937. The Ministry of Labour tried to overcome the problem by publishing regular checklists of labour shortages so that their agents could work out what kind of labourers were required. The workforce was also forced to work multiple shifts as part of the strategy to increase industrial capacity, but this was unpopular and inefficient. The regime was more effective in adding to its labour force by drafting in foreign workers from occupied or allied countries and by using prisoners of war. The latter became merged with the massive slave labour programme associated with the concentration camps and the economic empire of the SS.

Slave labour and concentration camps, see page 439

TABLE 55

Select statistics on the German labour force, May 1939 – May 1943 (in millions)

	1939	1940	1941	1942	1943
All industry, including	10.9	10.1	10.3	9.6	10.6
Heavy manufacturing	3.75	3.87	4.21	4.36	4.81
Consumer goods	3.58	2.94	2.84	2.54	2.59

	1939	1940	1941	1942	1943
All industry, including	21.9	50.2	54.5	56.1	61.0
Raw materials	21.0	58.2	63.2	59.9	67.9
Metal manufacture	28.6	62.3	68.8	70.4	72.1
Construction	30.2	57.5	52.2	45.2	46.7
Consumer goods	12.2	26.2	27.8	31.7	37.0
Base year 1939 = 100 for comparison	100	229	248	256	278

TABLE 56

Percentage of German industrial labour forces working on orders for the armed forces, 1939–43

B *The employment of foreign labour*

The employment of foreign labour in the economy was not new. The crisis of a labour shortage, which had first appeared in 1937, was partly met by the recruitment of skilled labour from France and Belgium. By 1939 they amounted to only 0.8 per cent of the total of employees (see Table 57 on page 429), but the process gained momentum in September 1940 because of heavy unemployment and wage controls within their own country. They were recruited by agencies set up by the Reich Labour Front and were employed on the same terms as German workers. The regime failed to make effective use of their trade skills. Many found that they were drafted into unskilled jobs, such as working on the land, though there was a significant minority who were employed as skilled factory workers. Few, however, were employed in white-collar jobs. They were allowed to work regularly and, unlike the Poles and the Russians, could look for their own lodgings. By the spring of 1941, there were 1.75 million foreign workers from occupied or allied countries representing 8.5 per cent of the total workforce. This was more than the labour supplied by prisoners of war. After 1942, with the reorganisation of the war effort by Speer, pressure was put on the French government to encourage industrial workers to move to Germany. In February 1943, France introduced the Labour Laws which conscripted young skilled workers for compulsory labour so that around 400,000 left France in early 1943, followed by another one million in 1944. For long periods after 1942 there were large numbers of French male workers in Germany and although they had a reputation for careless work and sabotage, their skills made them vital. Since they were well clothed and healthy when they arrived they were sought after by employers. By November 1943, French workers accounted for 1.7 per cent of the total German population. A similar policy of coercion was imposed on other occupied countries of western Europe. By 1943, Dutch workers, for example, accounted for 3.4 per cent of the total German population and were considered to be the best workers whereas the Italian workers, who were employed later on, were considered to be the worst.

These foreign workers were joined, from 1940 onwards, by Poles most of whom were seized under the orders of Hans Frank, the Nazi governor-general of Poland. Somewhere between 1.3 and 1.5 million, of whom around a half were women, were deported to Germany for work as unskilled labour on the land. They were joined by about 400,000 to

480,000 prisoners of war who were either used as workers or sent to concentration camps. Unlike the French and Dutch, the Poles and later on the Russian labourers had no legal status, but they were treated as slaves and abused in terms of their living conditions.

After March 1942, the character, composition and legal status of Germany's foreign labour force changed. Invasion of the Soviet Union led to the seizure of vast numbers of Russians, 1.2 million within the first year. In contrast to the gender of other foreign workers, many of the deported were young girls and women. By the autumn of 1943 the Russian workforce accounted for 1.2 per cent of the total German population. Hitler had originally intended that Russian women would be employed as domestic servants to relieve German women. However, their strength for industrial work soon led to their employment in the aircraft, coal, steel and machine tools industries where they gained the reputation of being the hardest working and most easily disciplined work force. The Russians were despised as 'inferior' slavs, but also feared as Bolsheviks, a fear which was fuelled in Goebbels propaganda campaign based on 'strength through fear' and that the war was an ideological fight to the death. German law insisted that workers from eastern Europe should be marked out from other workers by wearing a badge, paying a special tax, being excluded from security benefits and by being confined to one of the special camps built to house foreign workers. The sanitary arrangements were appalling, and there was little medical attention. They received poor rations and death rate was high. Otto Bräutigam, Head of the Reich Political Department in the Eastern Territories, complained of the ill-treatment of prisoners in October, 1942 (quoted in Noakes and Pridham, *Nazism 1919-1945, A Documentary Reader,* vol 3):

> It is no longer a secret. . .that hundreds of thousands of prisoners have literally died of starvation and cold in our camps. It is alleged that there were not enough supplies of food on hand for them. But it is strange that food supplies are lacking only for prisoners of war from the Soviet Union, while complaints about the treatment of other prisoners – Poles, Serbs, French and English – have not been voiced. It is obvious that nothing was more calculated to strengthen the resistance of the Red Army than the knowledge that in German captivity they were faced with a slow and painful death. . .
>
> We now experience the grotesque spectacle that after the tremendous starvation of prisoners of war, millions of labourers must hurriedly be recruited from the occupied Eastern Territories in order to fill the gaps which have appeared in Germany. Now the question of food was no longer important. With the usual unlimited abuse of Slav people, 'recruiting' methods were used which can only be compared with the blackest periods of the slave trade. . . Without regard for health or age people were shipped to Germany, where it soon turned out that well over 100,000 had to be sent back because of serious illness and other disabilities.

Q To what extent did ideology influence the way in which foreign workers were treated?

	1939	1940	1941	1942	1943	1944
			(millions)			
Germans	39.1	35.2	34.5	33.0	31.7	30.4
Foreign civilians	0.30	0.85	1.75	2.6	4.85	5.3
Prisoners of war	–	0.35	1.35	1.5	1.65	1.8
Total foreigners	0.30	1.2	3.1	4.1	6.5	7.1
Foreigners as a percentage of all employees	0.8	3.2	8.5	11.6	17.7	19.9

TABLE 57
The employment of foreign labour in the economy as a whole, 1939–44

Speer shared Otto Bräutigam's concerns over the inefficiency and wastage of the potential of foreign labour. He argued for keeping industrial workers in occupied areas to work on arms contracts as the most effective means of maximising armaments output. His attempts to implement this policy from June 1943 failed as a result of opposition from Sauckel and Hitler, who both disagreed on ideological grounds (see section 5, page 424). Sauckel continued with his disorganised and inefficient exploitation of foreign labour so that the regime found it increasingly difficult to replace its high losses. Recruitment of foreign labour slowed down noticeably between 1943 and 1944 (when it rose by 12.4 per cent) compared with 1942 to 1943 (when it rose by 52.6 per cent); despite the fact that Sauckel had secured approximately one million additional workers (see Table 57).

C *Changes in the employment of women*

Recent research has now rejected as myth the Nazi propaganda claim that Germany would not mobilize women for war work. Despite the large numbers of foreign and prisoner-of-war workers employed in the German economy, this was not sufficient to make up for the large numbers of Germans drafted into the armed forces. This shortfall was made good by women, especially in the case of work on the land. In fact, the proportion of women in Germany, who worked was exceptionally high. In 1939, 37.3 per cent of the workforce was women, compared with 26.4 per cent in Britain, and this differential continued throughout the war (see Table 54 (d) on page 421). German women shared the same treatment as men; they were subjected to a forced redistribution from the consumer-based industries to war-related industries – metalwork, machinery and chemicals – and were expected to work harder and for longer hours, including night shifts which left them exhausted and demoralised. There was some relief for those women who worked in agriculture with the arrival of Russian women from summer 1942. The increased mobilisation of women was acknowledged in Goebbels' weekly newsreels which showed them contributing enthusiastically to the war effort. Many amongst the working classes became discontented because they believed, with some truth, that middle-class women were not expected to work so hard or in industry. Many working-class

DIAGRAM 11

A comparison of the percentage of German and British women in employment, 1939–44

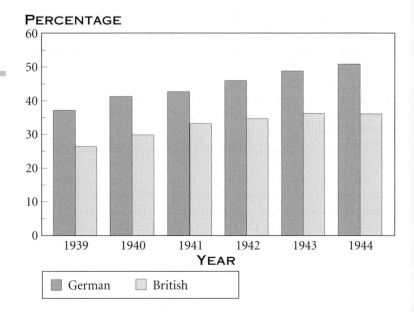

PERCENTAGE

YEAR

■ German   □ British

women found that life became more demanding and hard especially as they had to cope with wartime rationing and shortages. In the eyes of many, Germany remained a class society to the very end.

7 ↬ IMPACT OF WAR ON THE PEOPLE

Hitler's concern not to deprive the people of a basic minimum of food consumption, or to impose rationing, failed. Increased wartime taxation, a shortage of goods and rationing, combined with state control of wages, led to a fall in consumer spending by a quarter between 1939 and 1944 compared with Britain's tenth (see Table 54 (b)). Rationing affected people far more than in Britain particularly as German living standards were below that of Britain and America even before war broke out. Goods were rationed throughout the war which were never rationed in Britain. Ration coupons were sent out to all Germans, restricting them to a boring diet of black rye bread, potatoes and vegetables which replaced fish, eggs, cheese, milk and fats. The decline in consumption rapidly created shortages of essential clothing for labourers, such as boots and overalls, and of other essential civilian equipment which were diverted to meet the demands of the armed forces. Clothes and shoes became virtually unobtainable for many Germans. New shoes had to be exchanged for old, work shoes could only be worn at work, and Nazi officials made regular checks on suspect households and any extra shoes were confiscated.

Civilian hardship intensified after 1943, as Allied bombing started to wreck many cities and the death toll amongst soldiers grew, leaving few German families unaffected. By the summer of 1944 the regime was forced to introduce a total mobilisation of German society with the creation of the *Volkssturm*. Allied bombing initially gave a boost to people's moral and a will to fight, but this did not last long. It is estimated that 400,000 civilians were killed along with the destruction of industrial plants, including synthetic oil. Communications were seriously disrupted. People's confidence in the regime collapsed despite Goebbels' calls for a 'battle for the home front' and his praise for the 'heroic fortitude of the population of the bombed cities'. The regime was criticised for its failure to protect German cities or its inhabitants, a resentment made worse by the experience of many evacuees who were denied shelter and food by other members of the national community. Large numbers of people were moved out of the bombed areas which caused serious labour shortage problems in the affected areas. Absenteeism from work increased and the regime increased its reign of terror. By 1945 half a million Germans were held in 20 main and 165 subsidiary camps compared with 100,000 in 1942. Propaganda made much of the Bolshevik menace so that at the end it was a reluctant loyalty based on fear that motivated people's resistance.

8 ⌒ EUROPE UNDER THE NAZIS

Across Germany and its newly acquired empire of annexed and conquered countries, Hitler intended to establish *Neuordnung*, a New Order, which, he boasted, would last for a thousand years. By a New Order he meant the political and economic integration of Europe under German domination and based on Nazi racial laws. In 1934, as recorded by Ed Lochner in *The Goebbels Diaries*, Hitler said:

> The aim of our struggle must be to create a unified Europe. The Germans alone can really organise Europe... Today we are practically the only power on the European mainland with a capacity for leadership. The Reich will be the master of all Europe... Whoever dominates Europe will thereby assume the leadership of the world.

The Nazis used the term *Weltanschauung* to indicate their idea of a completely new philosophy of life (see page 256). They sought not merely to alter the system of government but to bring about revolutionary changes in attitude and lifestyle.

A *Hitler's European empire*

Within Europe, boundaries were redrawn. Countries considered to be largely Aryan in race and of particular importance to Germany were immediately incorporated within the *Großdeutsches Reich*, Greater Germany. These included Austria, the Czech provinces of Bohemia and Moravia, Alsace and Lorraine, Luxembourg, a large area of western Poland which formed two new German provinces, and territory in northern Yugoslavia. In western Europe, northern France, Belgium, the

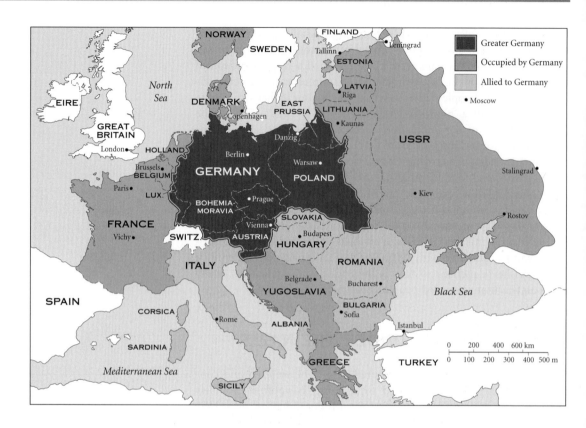

MAP 13

Greater Germany and territories occupied by the Nazis

Netherlands, Denmark and Norway were all subject to armies of occupation. Each had its own government supervised by a Nazi commissioner, *Gauleiter* or Reich protector. Regulated from Berlin, the civil and military administrations sought the assistance of collaborators to govern and exploit the territories under their control. The occupied countries were to be systematically plundered for raw materials, manufactured goods, food and labour. In eastern Europe, the region earmarked for the *Lebensraum*, the people were to be Germanised, moved elsewhere or exterminated.

In Norway, the traitor Quisling was head of government but real power lay with Reich commissioner Joseph Terboven, a man to become infamous for the severity of his rule. Belgium was placed directly under the control of a military commandant whilst the Netherlands were ruled by Seyss-Inquart, the former Austrian Nazi. His aim was to Germanise the Dutch people. The provinces of Bohemia and Moravia were governed by Reinhard Heydrich. In the east, the *Reichskommissariat Ostland* was responsible for the occupied Russian territories. Under Alfred Rosenberg, it was to rule the country with the utmost savagery. Hans Frank was made Gauleiter of Poland. He boasted, 'Poland will be treated like a colony: the Poles will become the slaves of the Greater German Empire.' The Baltic states were run by Heinrich Lohse and the Ukraine by Erich Koch. The warders of Hitler's Europe were the SS. The German administration of the occupied countries was confused and inefficient, with the military and civilian authorities usually working independently. In some areas local administrators acted on their own initiative whilst in others they did nothing without reference to a higher authority. As was often the case, there was conflict between the *Wehrmacht* and the SS.

B *The collaborators*

Even before the war, virtually every European country had its own fascist-type party. Such were the parties of Franco and Salazar in Spain and Portugal, and Degrelle in Belgium. In France, there were several parties of the extreme right, *Action Française*, *Croix de Feu* and *Solidarité Française*, and in Britain, the British Union of Fascists led by Sir Oswald Mosley. In the occupied countries, members of these parties rejoiced at Hitler's successes and looked forward to having a prominent role in the governments of their countries. At a meeting between Hitler and Pétain at Montaire in October 1940, the leader of Vichy France proclaimed, 'To protect the unity of France within the New Order in Europe, I enter today upon a path of collaboration'. In a climate of defeatism, most believed that Britain would soon fall and the rest of Europe would be overrun by the Nazis. Communist parties were in something of a dilemma. Normally they would have been in the vanguard of those opposed to fascism but Communist Russia and Nazi Germany were bound by an alliance. To most, there seemed little point other than to accept the inevitable, make the best of the situation and work with the occupying power.

Collaboration took many forms. Some, hopeful of some political or financial advancement, collaborated fully and worked for the Germans. Some traded with or entertained the Germans and some agreed to collaborate because they were afraid to do otherwise. Some women associated with German soldiers and bore them children. Tempted by the promise of good wages and working conditions and the promise of the early release of prisoners of war, workers from some of the occupied countries, mainly France, Belgium and the Netherlands, were tempted to Germany. Collaborationist governments made their own arrangements to list and round up Jews and formed their own secret police to intimidate the civilian population. None were more feared and hated than the *Malice* of Vichy France. As the war progressed, the SS revised its recruiting programme to include volunteers form the occupied countries. *Volksdeutsche*, foreign nationals accepted as members of the German race, were accepted into the SS from across Europe. They were told that they would be used to help usher in a new era in European history and that they would only be required to fight on the Russian Front. Altogether, some 300,000 volunteered to serve in the German army. Prepared to join in the fight against Stalinist communism, 100,000 Ukrainians came forward to join General Andrei Vlasov's Liberation Army together with a large number of Caucasians, Cossacks, Georgians and White Russians. A Russian prisoner of war explained why he joined (quoted in *Victims of Yalta* by Nikolai Tolstoy):

> You think...that we sold ourselves to the Germans for a piece of bread? Tell me, why did the Soviet Government forsake us? Why did it forsake millions of prisoners? We saw prisoners of all nationalities and they were taken care of. Through the Red Cross, they received parcels and letters from home; the Russians received nothing... Hadn't we fought? Hadn't we defended the Government? ... If Stalin refused to have anything to do with us, we didn't want anything to do with Stalin!

It is interesting that Ukrainians who formed part of the army of occupation in France were considered more brutal than the Germans. Fifty thousand Dutchmen volunteered, whilst Frenchmen joined the Charlemagne SS Division and Scandinavians, the Viking Division. There was a 2,000 strong Indian Legion as well as volunteers from neutral Sweden and Switzerland. A League of St George was recruited from British prisoners of war to serve under John Amery, son of an eminent British politician. Although recruitment into the SS met with undeniable success, it was not without problems. Many of the recruits did not go along with Hitler's idea of a racial elite but joined because they were strongly anti-communist. The German *Waffen*-SS considered the new units to be substandard and Himmler was unhappy at the dilution of his own organisation.

9 ↝ THE RESISTANCE

KEY ISSUE

The Russo-German alliance – a dilemma for European Communists.

As time passed and it seemed less certain that Germany was going to win an easy victory, so national consciousness began to revive and with it the will to resist. Many sovereigns and politicians who had fled abroad to set up governments-in-exile became figureheads of the resistance. Polish, Czech, French and Belgian airmen flew with the RAF during the Battle of Britain and their soldiers fought in campaigns on several fronts. In 1941, the German invasion of the Soviet Union freed communists from their dilemma and in many countries they soon became the backbone of the resistance.

In France, it was the decision to begin the compulsory deportation of workers to Germany which incensed the people. Many young Frenchmen disappeared into the countryside to form resistance groups known as the *Maquis*. The deeds of the 50,000 *Maquisards* would become legendary. From Britain, General Charles de Gaulle, leader of the Free French, called upon his countrymen to join the Resistance. Similarly elsewhere across Europe, resistance grew and secret underground armies came into being. In Belgium, the *Armée Secrète* recruited 50,000 members. In the Netherlands, home of the schoolgirl diarist Anne Frank, German racial propaganda failed hopelessly as the Dutch people reacted with horror at the Nazi treatment of the Jews. The Danes took advantage of their close proximity to Sweden and so saved 7,000 of the 8,000 Jews threatened with extermination. Resistance took many forms, ranging from non-cooperation, anti-Nazi graffiti, operating clandestine printing presses, helping shot-down allied airmen to return home and gathering information, to carrying out ambushes, assassination and other acts of sabotage such as blowing up railway lines and bridges. In eastern Europe, resistance groups were able to take advantage of the forests and mountainous terrain to engage in guerrilla warfare and control vast areas of land. In Yugoslavia, Marshall Tito's Communist **Partisans** were at one stage involved in operations against as many Axis troops as the Allies were fighting in Italy. Polish resistance reached its climax with the Warsaw uprising in August 1944 (see Table 58 below). In the Soviet Union, Partisans operated across the vast areas behind the German lines and used the severe winter conditions to harass the retreating Germans. The most important aspect of resistance was that it occupied so many German troops and prevented them being deployed to the front line. General Eisenhower claimed that the value of the French Resistance to the Normandy landings on D-Day had been equal to ten divisions of regular troops.

Partisans irregular soldiers fighting behind enemy lines

Of course, the SS, *Gestapo* and other German security services fought back. In a situation when normal standards of conduct did not apply and the Geneva Convention was ignored, the Nazis committed the most appalling atrocities against civilian populations. In these, the SS were the worst but they were not the only offenders. It was normally their

April 1942	Norway	Televaag. The village was completely destroyed because local people sheltered Allied agents.
May 1942	Czechoslovakia	Lidice. 1,255 people were executed and the village destroyed in retaliation for the assassination of Heydrich.
March 1944	Italy	Rome. 335 civilians shot in retaliation for a bomb attack on German soldiers.
June 1944	France	Oradour-sur-Glane. 662 people murdered and the town burned to the ground for an attack on an SS *Panzer* unit. The Germans chose the wrong town for their retaliation.
July 1944	France	Vercors plateau. Germans took a month to crush an uprising in mountainous Vercors region. More than a thousand killed or executed.
August 1944	Poland	Warsaw. An estimated 200,000 civilians were killed when the Germans took a month to put down an uprising in the city.
September 1944	Denmark	All Danish police and frontier guards arrested after an uprising in Copenhagen during which 97 people were killed.

TABLE 58
Major Nazi atrocities against civilians

Q

How successful were the Germans in dealing with resistance in the occupied countries?

practice to retaliate by taking and executing hostages and, sometimes obliterating whole towns and villages.

Horrific as these atrocities were, nothing matched the stark brutality of the Nazis when they began the wholesale slaughter of Russian Jews and attempted to destroy Jewish life throughout Europe – the *Endlösung* or the 'Final Solution'.

10 ∽ THE CLIMAX OF THE HOLOCAUST – THE FINAL SOLUTION

The dictionary definition of the term 'holocaust' is 'a sacrifice in which the whole of the victim is burnt'. The Third Reich gave the expression a grotesque new meaning – a merciless act of genocide involving the wholesale slaughter of European Jews and the destruction of their way of life. You will find that historians use the term differently. The majority use it to describe Nazi policy towards the Jews throughout the period 1933–45; some use it more selectively to refer to the years 1942–5, the years of 'the final solution'. In early chapters of this book (see pages 275–278) you will have read of Nazi anti-Semitic policies. At what stage Hitler finally decided to physically exterminate the Jews is impossible to say. In *Mein Kampf* and in his speeches he frequently threatened 'the annihilation of the Jews in Europe'. Other Nazi leaders were equally forthright. Himmler spoke of the need to 'eliminate the Jews and cleanse the Aryan race' whilst in *Der Stürmer*, Streicher wrote, 'If Jewish blood must come to an end, then there is only one way – the extermination of that people whose father is the devil'. Heydrich told his SS officers, 'Jewry is the intellectual reservoir of Bolshevism and must be annihilated'.

A *The* Einsatzgruppen *and* Ordnungspolizei

The first step towards the mass murder of the Jews was taken in 1938 when special mobile units were formed to carry out the liquidation of the Jews in recently annexed Austria and Czechoslovakia. At this stage, the units, known as *Einsatzgruppen*, operated in a relatively small way. They came into their own following the start of the war in 1939 and, even more so, after the summer of 1941. As the all-conquering German armies advanced across Europe, they occupied areas inhabited by millions of Jews. At its greatest, Hitler's new European empire embraced over eight million Jews, with the majority located in Poland (3,300,000) and the Soviet Union (2,100,000). Following the surrender of Poland, Heydrich ordered that all Jews living in the countryside must join those in the towns and be concentrated in areas set aside for Jews, areas known as ghettos. The first Jewish ghetto was set up in Lodz in April 1940. Six months later, the Jews in Warsaw were similarly confined whilst ghettoes were set up in Lublin, Cracow and elsewhere. Surrounded by walls or barbed wire, the Jews were not intended to survive. As Daniel Goldhagen says in *Hitler's Willing Executioners* (1996), they were 'placed in hermetically sealed economically unviable leper colonies that would not receive adequate food supplies...'. Within the ghettoes the Jews continued to live as normal a life as possible. Their children went to school and the people attended the synagogues. Supervised by *Einsatzgruppen*, each ghetto was administered by a Jewish council, *Judenrat*, backed up by Jewish auxiliary police. With little or no food, the people were reduced by famine, cold and epidemics and gradually eliminated. As Mary Fulbrook writes in *The Fontana History of Germany, 1918–1990*:

> By the summer of 1941, the situation [in the Warsaw ghetto] of over-crowding, malnutrition and disease was dreadful. Formerly civilised, cultured human beings were reduced to shivering, starving, ailing bundles of rags, a living caricature of the way in which the Nazis attempted to portray and dehumanise the objects of their persecution.

In the Soviet Union, the *Einsatzgruppen* and special units of police, the *Ordnungspolizei* or Order Police, followed immediately behind the invading armies to begin what we would refer to today as the process of ethnic cleansing. The inhumane mass killing of thousands of Jews, irrespective of their age or sex, occurred widely across the country. Up to 33,000 perished at Babi Yar in the outskirts of Kiev in September 1941, 20,000 at Kharkov in January 1942 and 30,000 at Bialystak in August 1943. They were usually shot and buried in mass graves which they had earlier dug themselves, and there were instances of people being gassed in specially equipped vans, allowed to die of exposure and even beaten to death by the local non-Jewish population. Goldhagen's controversial book claims there was no shortage of volunteers from among ordinary Germans to join the murder squads and that an order existed which allowed men in the *Einsatzgruppen* who found taking part in the killing repulsive to move to other work. He comments, 'Evidence that no German was ever killed or incarcerated for having refused to kill Jews is conclusive'.

B *The Wannsee Conference, 1942*

On 31 July 1941, Göring gave Heydrich (see page 167) a written order to take steps towards a general solution to the Jewish problem in the areas of German influence in Europe.

In January 1942, six months after the invasion of Russia, a high level meeting of leading Nazis took place at Großen-Wannsee, a suburb of Berlin. Discussions centred around the urgent need to agree and plan the *Endlösung*, a final solution to the Jewish question. Heydrich told the assembly that the Madagascar Plan (see page 278) was no longer feasible since the Jews could no longer be transported to Africa. Instead, the Führer had agreed that all Jews would be evacuated to the east and made to work. Only the hardiest would survive the harsh conditions and these, 'the hard core of Jewry and the most dangerous because they

Q

Explain the significance of the Wannsee Conference.

could rebuild Jewish life', would be treated accordingly. By that, he meant they would be sent to extermination camps. He estimated that the planned solution would apply to about 11 million people. Adolf Eichman was made responsible for the mechanics of the programme of genocide and German manufacturers competed to produce the most effective means of mass murder and then disposing of tens of thousands of corpses.

C *The 'Final Solution' in practice*

The extermination or death camps were to be built in Poland because that was the main centre of European Jewry. Jews were to be rounded up all over occupied Europe and transported by train to the camps. Using Zyklon B gas, crystallised hydrogen cyanide or prussic acid, the gassing of the Jews began at Auschwitz-Birkenau in March 1942. Other similar but smaller camps were built at Belzec, Chelmno, Maidanek, Sobibor, Treblinka and Stutthof. The established concentration camps such as those at Bergen-Belsen, Buchenwald, Dachau and Ravensbrück were also expected to contribute their quota. The suffering of those in transit to the camps is described by a Channel Island doctor – one of the relatively few British people to suffer – Madeleine Bunting, in *The Model Occupation – The Channel Islands Under German Rule*:

> We were loaded into cattle wagons, sixty-five or eighty people to a wagon, and the windows and doors were hermetically sealed. In the course of the journey, crammed against each other we suffered terribly from thirst and we were forced to sacrifice the corner of the wagon for the necessities of nature. [Three days later] when the train stopped, the SS made us understand that everyone should leave the wagon and unload the baggage. They ordered us to form up into five ranks. It was raining. . .anyone who tried to put on a waterproof learnt from blows to the head that it was forbidden.

A great many books have been written about the appalling suffering experienced by those sent to the camps. *The Scourge of the Swastika* by Lord Russell of Liverpool (Cassell 1954), provides the cold, factual details of the deprivation, torture, medical experimentation as well as the gassing and cremation of the victims. The film *Schindler's List*, also provides an insight into these events. On arrival at the camps, newcomers had their clothes and personal possessions confiscated. Then they had their hair cropped short, were sprayed with disinfectant and photographed. Finally the prisoners were tattooed on their wrists with their numbers. Inmates were issued with blue-striped grey uniforms, each of which carried a coloured symbol to indicate the reason for their detention. Jews were denoted by the yellow Star of David, political prisoners by red triangles, gypsies by black, criminals by green and homosexuals by pink triangles. Jehovah's Witnesses with violet triangles, only had to renounce their religion to gain their release. Very few did! There were frequent roll-calls during which inmates were harassed and bullied.

MAP 14

Distribution of Nazi concentration camps and SS enterprises based on slave labour from the camps

With a daily ration of food limited to 1,300 calories, prisoners were expected to work from dawn to dusk on a diet of soup made from rotten vegetables and black bread. Housed 40 or 50 to a hut, they slept on three-tier bunks made out of boards covered by threadbare blankets. With little or no provision made for personal hygiene or medical treatment, there were outbreaks of cholera, typhus and typhoid fever. Once their bodies were sufficiently weakened to make them unsuitable for work, they were sent to the gas chambers.

In *Life in the Third Reich*, the German historian, Hannah Vogt writes:

> ...incoming transports were led to 'selection'. Men were separated from women, children torn from their parents. The sick, the aged, the weak and the children were sent to the left: their destiny was death. Those still thought capable of work were sent into the barracks to work as slaves for their miserable food until they died of hunger, or epidemics or were themselves selected for extermination. The threat of death hung ever-present over all; the smell of the crematoria lay like a cloud over the camps... The SS guards held daily roll-calls and forced the emaciated prisoners, in their garb of rags, to stand in the rain, snow and sun... Those who fell down were kicked or beaten... Nobody will ever fully appreciate the suffering...the humiliations, the shame, the agony. We cannot escape by saying we did not know...

TABLE 59
Death toll of the camps

Camp	Approximate number murdered
Auschwitz	2,000,000
Maidanek	1,380,000
Treblinka	731,800
Belzec	600,000
Chelmno	600,000
Sobibor	250,000
Mauthausen	138,500
Sachsenhausen	100,000
Ravensbrück	92,000
Flossenbürg	74,000
Dachau	70,000
Stuffhof	67,500
Buchenwald	63,500
Belsen	50,000

It is estimated that something approaching six million European Jews died in the Holocaust, 72 per cent of the total. Whilst 85 per cent of Polish Jews perished, other countries were more successful in protecting their Jewish citizens. In Bulgaria, 86 per cent survived, in Italy 74 per cent and in France 70 per cent. Only 19 per cent of German Jews, some 40,000, were still alive at the end of the war.

D *Is it possible to explain the Holocaust?*

As Daniel Goldhagen writes in *Hitler's Willing Executioners:*

> Explaining the Holocaust is the central intellectual problem for understanding Germany during the Nazi period... How the Nazis came to power, how they suppressed the Left, how they revived the economy, how the State was structured and functioned, how they made and waged war are...easily enough understood. But the Holocaust defies explanation.

To reduce the murder of six million people to an academic study may itself seem an obscenity. Even so, many historians as well as numerous psychologists and sociologists have attempted to provide an explanation for this twentieth century lapse into barbarism. Their views are often as contradictory as they are confusing. Hitler did not invent anti-Semitism nor was the Holocaust the first attempt to mass-murder Jews. In ancient times, the Babylonians, Egyptians and Romans all, in turn, oppressed the Jews. The wholesale slaughter of Jews was attempted at the time of the Crusades in the eleventh and twelfth centuries and, throughout the Middle Ages Jews were persistently persecuted across Europe. Jews were among the main victims of the Spanish Inquisition and, during the seventeenth century, half a million Jews fled from

TABLE 60
The fate of Jews in Germany and German-occupied Europe

Country	Jewish Losses	Percentage of Jews that survived
Poland	2,800,000	15
Czechoslovakia	260,000	18
Germany	170,000	19
Greece	60,000	20
Yugoslavia	55,000	27
Soviet Union	1,500,000	28
Austria	40,000	34
Netherlands	90,000	40
Romania	425,000	50
Hungary	200,000	51
Belgium	40,000	56
France	90,000	70
Italy	15,000	74
Bulgaria	7,000	86

Polish Russia to escape persecution. Anti-Semitism had been endemic in Russia for generations and pogroms, organised massacres of Jews, occurred during the nineteenth century. Russian Minister of the Interior, Konstantin Pobedonostev said 'One third of Jews must die, one third emigrate and one third assimilate'. Many of the measures taken against the Jews by the Nazis in the 1930s and 1940s had been taken against Russian Jews in the 1890s, including their forced settlement in ghettos. Were the Nazis simply conforming to a pattern already well established?

The intentionalists among historians see the Holocaust as a direct and logical outcome of a system of pre-existing ideas, namely Hitler's ideological hatred of the Jews which he made known in his writing and speeches. In *The War Against the Jews, 1933–45* Lucy Dawidowitz writes:

> The mass murder of Jews was the consummation of Hitler's fundamental beliefs and ideological convictions... For Hitler's ideas about the Jews were the starting place for the elaboration of a monstrous racial ideology that would justify mass murder.

Structuralist historians are of the view that the Holocaust came about, not as a result of the plans of one man, but as the consequence of a number of unco-ordinated developments. It happened, it wasn't designed. The German historian Martin Broszat comments that whilst Hitler's anti-Semitism played its part, it was but one contributory factor amongst many which led to the horror of the death camps. The Germans were in need of a scapegoat for their defeat in war and subsequent economic and political problems, and the Jews fitted the bill. It was helped by the inner momentum within the Nazi movement and, once in motion, it snowballed out of control. Do either the intentionalists or structuralists explain the Holocaust satisfactorily?

There are other questions to be answered. Why did the Nazi anti-Semitic programme intensify during the war? What part did Hitler play in these events? Did the German people know? Why did the Jews behave so passively? The German invasion of Russia gave Hitler the opportunity to achieve his twin aims of acquiring *Lebensraum* and destroying Russian Bolshevism. To him, the Slavs, Jews and Marxists were a threat to the proper development of the Aryan race. Jews and Slavs had to be eliminated before the programme of German resettlement could begin. As the fortunes of war began to change, so the urgency increased. The destruction of European Jewry was a cornerstone of Nazi ideology which, come what may, had to be completed even if the war was lost. Eichman spoke of the 'righteousness of the Final Solution' and Himmler described the Holocaust as 'a page of glory in our history'.

There can be little doubt that the German people knew, but how much they knew is a different matter. Even though they were told that German Jews were being resettled in the east, the method of their arrest and transportation, and general gossip, must have provided some evidence of what was really happening. In an interview, Richard Korherr, Himmler's statistician said, 'Everyone knew about the gassings. Good heavens, the sparrows were whistling it from the rooftops.' In his book, *Infiltrations*, Albert Speer wrote:

> When I think about the fate of Berlin's Jews, I am overcome by an unbearable feeling of failure and inadequacy. When I saw crowds of people on the platform, I knew this had to be Jews being evacuated. I had a feeling of unease... Perhaps, too, burying ourselves in work was an unconscious effort to anaesthetize our conscience.

There is no written evidence that Hitler ordered the Final Solution. He was not in Wannsee in 1942 and there is no record of him visiting the camps. This has led some apologists to express doubt about Hitler's direct involvement. In *Hitler's War* (Viking 1977), David Irving expresses the view that Hitler was not responsible. He maintains that the Führer was not aware that the Jews were being exterminated until 1943 and, afterwards, ordered the slaughter to end. Few accept Irving's conclusions. Although there may be some doubt if Hitler personally authorised the Holocaust, there is a mass of evidence to suggest that Hitler was well aware of what was going on. His own fanatical views were widely known and, in 1939, he prophesied that war would bring about the destruction of the Jewish race in Europe. As for the passivity of the Jews, it has to be remembered that they were victims of the worst extremes of barbarity. With numbers not names, the Nazis had attempted to dehumanise them and deprive them of normal human

KEY ISSUE

To what extent were the German people aware of what was happening to the Jews?

qualities. Caught between such brutality and the apparent indifference of the outside world, they had little choice other than to accept the hopelessness of their situation. Even so, there were instances when Jews organised revolts in the ghettoes and camps, but those who escaped were often handed back to the Nazis by the civilians with whom they had sought refuge. And the legacy of the Holocaust? For the Germans, a disturbed conscience which will endure for generations; for the rest of the world, moral outrage and a determination to ensure that such a thing will never happen again. As the German historian, Hannah Vogt, wrote in *The Burden of Guilt: A Short History of Germany, 1914–1945*:

> To the injustice committed in our name we must not add the injustice of forgetting. While relatives still mourn their dead, can we forget because the shadows of the past are so painful to us? There is no restitution for such enormous suffering. But by preserving the memory of the victims, we can perform a sacred duty imposed upon us by the guilt we bear towards our Jewish fellow citizens.

11 ⌁ THE FINAL COLLAPSE OF THE THIRD REICH

On 16 January 1945, the day before the Red Army liberated Warsaw, Adolf Hitler moved into a bunker beneath the Reich Chancellery in Berlin. Some 50 metres below the ground, the Führerbunker was to be Hitler's home and headquarters and provide refuge for Eva Braun and leading Nazis for the rest of the war. It was at the bunker that the Führer received news of the liberation of Budapest (13 February), the fall of Vienna (13 April) and that, on his 56th birthday, Soviet troops were entering the outskirts of his capital (20 April). A German officer was taken aback when he witnessed the wretched state of his leader (quoted in 'The End of the Dictators' by Alain Decaux in *Purnell's History of the Twentieth Century*):

> His head sways slightly. His left arm hangs down as if paralysed, his hand trembling all the time. His eyes shine in an indescribable way, suggesting almost inhuman anguish. His face and the pockets under his eyes show how tired he is, and how exhausted. He moves like an old man. His hair was grey and he walked with a stoop.

His behaviour was as bizarre as his appearance. When all others appreciated that the war was lost, he persisted in calling conferences and sending orders to non-existent armies. When he heard that Göring had suggested taking over the leadership, he ordered his arrest. He was equally upset when he discovered that Himmler was trying to make

peace with the Western Allies through a Swedish intermediary. The SS
chief's treachery came as a major blow. In a frenzy, he accused his generals of betrayal, claimed that the German people were unworthy of him
and began ordering the destruction of all German towns and cities and
any resource that would be useful to the enemy. In an unreal world, he
ordered the German army to counter-attack and drive the Russians
from Berlin. When told it was impossible, he burst into another rage.

On 29 April, Hitler married the faithful Eva Braun and after a brief
celebration, settled down to write his will and political testament. In
this lengthy document, he denied any responsibility for the war and
blamed the war and Germany's failures on international Jewry. He
expelled Göring from the Nazi Party and appointed Admiral Dönitz to
be his own successor with Goebbels as Chancellor. He stated that he
had 'decided to remain in Berlin and there of my own free will to
choose death at the moment when I feel the position of Führer and
Chancellor can no longer be held'. The following day, 30 April, with
Berlin engulfed in a sea of flames and Russian soldiers only a few
hundred metres away, he and his wife made their farewells and retired
to their quarters. At 3.35 pm he shot himself, whilst his wife preferred
to take poison. Previously he had asked that their bodies be burned so
that they could not be further mutilated by Russian soldiers. One week
later, on 7 May, Germany surrendered unconditionally to the Allies.

12 ⤳ BIBLIOGRAPHY

The history of the Second World War is excessively well covered in books and magazines as well as on film and television. Remember, however, there is always the need to distinguish between fact and fiction! Mark Arnold-Forster's *The World At War* (Collins 1973) provides a thorough and very readable account of the war. Also recommended are *A World in Flames: A Short History of the Second World War in Europe, 1939–1945* by M. Kitchen (Longman 1990) and *The Ordeal of Total War, 1939–1945* by G. Wright (Harper Torchbooks 1968). There can be no better coverage than that provided by the *History of the Second World War* published by Purnell in co-operation with the Imperial War Museum. *The Times Atlas of the Second World War* edited by John Keegan and the illustrated chronology *2194 Days of War* (Windward/WH Smith 1979) also provide very detailed accounts of the war. Books covering specialised topics include *The German Economy At War* by A.S. Milward (Athlone Press 1965), E.L. Homze's *Foreign Labour in Germany* (Princetown University Press 1967), *Hitler's War and the Germans: Public Mood and Attitude During the Second World War* by M. Steinert (Ohio University Press 1977), *The Bombing Offensive Against Germany* by Noble Frankland (Faber & Faber 1956) A. Werth's *Russia at War, 1941–45* (Barrie & Rockliff 1964) and *Hitler as Military Commander* by John Strawson (Batsford 1971).

Books covering the Nazi treatment of the Jews include *The Final Solution* by G. Reitlinger (Sphere 1971), *The Holocaust. The Destruction of European Jewry, 1933–45* by N. Levin (Cromwell 1968) and *The Scourge of the Swastika* by Lord Russell of Liverpool (Cassell 1954).

13 ⤳ DISCUSSION TOPICS AND ESSAY QUESTIONS

A *This section consists of questions that might be used for discussion (or written answers) as a way of expanding on the chapter and testing understanding of it.*

1. What would you say was the main motive behind Hitler's decision to invade the Soviet Union in June 1941?
2. 'The major turning point of the war.' How valid is this assessment of the Battle of Stalingrad?
3. To what extent can it be claimed Germany's alliance with Fascist Italy proved to be a liability?
4. Why did the Nazis' need to agree a 'Final Solution' to the Jewish question become more urgent after 1941?
5. Could contemporary Germans justifiably claim that they had no knowledge of what was happening to the Jews at the time of the Holocaust?

B *Essay questions.*

1. To what extent might Hitler's strategic blunders be held responsible for Germany's failure to win the Second World War?
2. How successful were the Nazis in imposing their New Order on the occupied countries during the Second World War?

14 ⌐ SINGLE SOURCE DOCUMENTARY EXERCISE ON THE BATTLE OF STALINGRAD

Read the following source carefully and then answer the questions based on it.

Stalingrad seems to have obsessed him [Hitler]... It lay more than 200 miles to the east of the direct route from occupied Poland to the Caucasus. It is true that it was a main centre of Russian industrial strength and that it lies on the Volga. The Volga <u>was one of Russia's main communication arteries</u>. Hitler seems to have feared that the Russians would defend Stalingrad at all costs and to the death.

...[Hitler] sacked generals mainly, it seems, because they were telling him things about Stalingrad that he did not want to hear. They told him, for example, that the German line was dangerously extended... They said that communications...were impossibly thin. Hitler did not want to hear this sort of news. Field Marshal List was sacked first. Halder followed him at the end of September. By this time General von Paulus had driven the Russians back into the city itself where the Russians under General Chuikov held on grimly to nine miles of river bank, sometimes by no more than a street or two... With the river behind them the Russians clung to every building, they defended the ruins of every factory, they regained by night the territory that the Germans, with their <u>superior fire power</u>, had gained during the day... By 22nd November...von Paulus and about a quarter of a million men were surrounded. Hitler told them not to surrender. Göring promised that the *Luftwaffe* would supply them by air. Nothing happened. Von Paulus remained encircled. The German position was now hopeless. Göring's promised airlift was a farce. Rations had to be reduced. Ammunition was running low. In January the Russians called on von Paulus to surrender. Hitler ordered him to refuse and made him a Field Marshal... on 2nd February von Paulus surrendered. By then 70,000 Germans had died in Stalingrad. The Russians took 91,000 prisoners including twenty-four generals.

SOURCE *From* The World At War *by Mark Arnold-Foster.*

(a) Explain the meaning of (i) *one of Russia's main communication arteries* and (ii) *superior fire power*.
(b) To what extent, does Hitler appear to appreciate the difficulties faced by von Paulus at Stalingrad?
(c) What evidence is there in the source to suggest that the Germans were outmanoeuvred and outfought by the Russians at Stalingrad?
(d) How valuable is the source to an understanding of the significance of the Battle of Stalingrad to the outcome of the war on the Eastern Front? (In your answer use your own relevant background knowledge as well as information derived from the source.)

15 ⌇ SYNOPTIC QUESTIONS

Read section 4 on page xxi in the *Preface: How to use this book*. Remember that in answering synoptic questions you should demonstrate an approach that draws together, whenever possible, the political, social, economic, religious and cultural aspects of the topic.

1. To what extent would you agree that, during the period 1919–45, Germany never experienced any form of democratic government?
2. 'Mainly aimed at revising the terms of the Treaty of Versailles.' How valid is this view of German foreign policy between 1919 and 1945?

16 Post-war Germany

INTRODUCTION

The immediate future of Germany was decided at two conferences – the Yalta Conference held in the Soviet Union in February 1945 and the Potsdam Conference that took place near Berlin six months later. The meeting at Yalta took place before the war was over and was attended by the so-called 'Big Three', Winston Churchill, the British Prime Minister, Franklin D. Roosevelt, the American President, and the leader of the Soviet Union, Josef Stalin. The implications of these conferences were to adversely affect the future relationship of the former wartime allies for the next 40 years.

1 ⌐ THE YALTA AND POTSDAM CONFERENCES, 1945

At the Yalta Conference, it was agreed that, until the treaty with Germany was finally settled, the country would be divided into four zones – British, American, Russian and French – and that Berlin would likewise be divided into four sectors. At Potsdam, held just after the war in Europe ended, only Stalin remained of the 'Big Three'. Roosevelt had died and been replaced by Harry S. Truman whilst Churchill, who was surprisingly beaten in the post-war elections, gave way to Britain's new Labour prime minister, Clement Attlee. The conference again considered the future of Germany and formalised the arrangements agreed at Yalta. Germany was to be administered by the Allied powers and divided so that Britain became responsible for the north-western provinces of Westphalia, Hanover and Schleswig-Holstein; the United States for the south-western provinces of Bavaria, and Württemburg; the Soviet Union for Brandenburg, Mecklenburg, Saxony and Thuringia; whilst the French were to occupy Baden and the Saar. At first, the wartime Allies managed the zones jointly under the Allied Control Committee but this was short lived. The fact that Berlin was situated in the Russian zone was to become the cause of friction between the occupying powers and a major factor in what was to become known as the Cold War. The future of Poland was another major issue to be considered.

Stalin made his position abundantly clear when he said, 'Throughout history, Poland has been the corridor through which the enemy has passed into Russia. Poland is a matter of life and death for Russia'. To

KEY ISSUE

The need to redefine Poland's frontiers.

ensure the future security of Russia, the Soviet leader insisted that his country's western frontier should be extended to include the land occupied following the Russian invasion of Poland in 1939 and that Poland should be compensated at the expense of Germany by moving her frontier forward to the banks of the rivers Oder and Neiße.

See page 397.

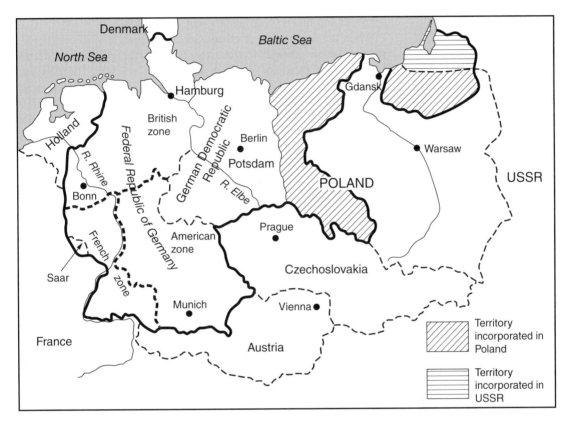

MAP 15
The post-war division of Germany and the revised frontiers of Poland

As the Russians were already in control of Poland, little could be done to challenge the Russian demands and this meant the enforced evacuation of some 3.6 million Germans from their former homes to the east of the rivers Oder and Neiße. Elsewhere in the liberated countries of Eastern Europe, Stalin agreed to free general elections as soon as it was possible. The Soviet leader had no intention of keeping his promise, however, since these countries were already occupied by the Red Army, within the Soviet sphere of influence, and were soon to have Communist-style **puppet governments** imposed on them.

As for reparations, it was agreed that:

puppet governments
governments under the control of and manipulated by others.

> Germany must pay for the losses caused by her to the Allied nations in the course of the war. Reparations are to be received in the first instance by the countries that bore the main burden of the war... The removal...from the national wealth of Germany of equipment, machine tools, ships, and rolling stock.'

Germany was also to make 'annual deliveries of goods from current production' and 'provide for the use of German labour'. German prisoners-of-war and Germans living in the Soviet zone were mobilised, transported to the Soviet Union and there used as forced or slave labour. Finally, Germany was to undergo the processes of demilitarisation and denazification so that the last vestiges of Hitler's Nazi Germany would be destroyed and former Nazi leaders were to face trial.

When the deportation of **ethnic** Germans began, it was badly organised and many starved or froze to death on the roads or in trains. Together with Germans expelled from Czechoslovakia, Hungary and Romania, on arrival at their destinations they were allocated to temporary camps where the appalling conditions and sanitary arrangements led to epidemics. With the young and the old being the most vulnerable, it is estimated that over 40,000 men, women and children died.

ethnic belonging to a particular racial group.

PICTURE 50
German families being expelled from their homes in Poland

There were several reasons why some nations decided to expel ethnic Germans. In the case of Poland, it was the enforced frontier changes that followed the end of the war. Elsewhere, in areas such as Czech Sudetenland, there was distrust of German minorities and a fear of possible ethnic violence, whilst in some cases it was simply a desire to punish Germans and avenge wartime atrocities.

2 ↬ THE CONDITION OF POST-WAR GERMANY

For ordinary people, the months following the German surrender in May 1945 proved horrendous. After 12 years of National Socialism, Germany was in ruins and facing humiliation and the ignominy of defeat. As a result of **carpet bombing** by the RAF and USAAF, German towns and cities had been reduced to rubble and their industries left in ruins.

carpet bombing the systematic and indiscriminate bombing of a whole area.

PICTURE 51
*Cologne cathedral stands
amongst the ruins of the city
following the first thousand
bomber raids carried out by the
RAF in May 1942*

The war-weary people tried the best they could to survive amongst the debris of their homes and cope with acute shortages of food, clothing and the simple necessities of everyday life. Since German money was worthless, cigarettes (*Zigarettenwährung*) and coffee became a form of alternative currency and, in desperation, many were forced to sell treasured possessions whilst some women turned to prostitution in order to survive. In addition to the five million Germans made homeless by the bombing, an influx of refugees, displaced persons, demobilised soldiers and survivors of the camps created an acute shortage of accommodation. In towns and cities, men and women formed chains to move bricks and roofing in order to build temporary shelters. Looting was commonplace, Russian soldiers were known to remove panes of glass and carpentry tools to send home and they also confiscated watches and valuables. In the British and American zones, wine cellars were robbed and Nazi memorabilia taken as souvenirs. Officially, servicemen were not allowed to **fraternise** with the civilian population, but this did not last long since soldiers could not resist giving chocolate to starving children any more than they could resist the attraction of beautiful German girls. In retaliation for the appalling crimes committed by the Germans in occupied Russia, during the latter stages of the war and the early months of occupation, Red Army soldiers raped an estimated two million German women. Made worse at the time by the lack of medical provision to treat venereal disease and perform abortions, the trauma of these experiences was to remain with many for the rest of their lives.

Any chances of steps being taken towards economic reconstruction were handicapped by a shortage of workers, machinery and raw materials. Some eight million German soldiers lost their lives during the war and few of those taken prisoner by the Russians were ever likely to return home. In addition, in the Soviet zone the region was quickly robbed of its wealth as factories and workshops were stripped of their assets. The Russians also carried out a search for German scientists and

fraternise mix with or come into friendly association with.

Q

How serious were the problems faced by German people after the Second World War?

scientific equipment that would help Operation Borodino, the development of a Soviet atomic bomb.

3 ⤳ THE PROCESSES OF DENAZIFICATION AND DEMOCRATISATION

Q

What methods had the Nazis previously used to indoctrinate the German people?

The aim of the denazification programme was to rid Germany of the remnants of the former Nazi regime and help bring about the country's rehabilitation. The process was to cover aspects of German political, social and cultural life and would be applied in different ways.

During the 1930s, over eight million Germans had joined the Nazi Party and been subject to the Party's indoctrination; now it was necessary to assess the true extent of their support for Nazi policies and their involvement in Nazi activities. In the American zone, individuals had to complete questionnaires, and former Nazis aged over 18 were listed in five categories – major offenders, offenders, lesser offenders, followers and exonerated persons. The media – the press, radio and film industry – were prohibited from producing pro-Nazi material and that already in existence was systematically destroyed. Books were vetted and over 30,000 titles, including a range of school textbooks, were banned. The Russians were far more rigorous in their approach. In the early days, former Nazi officials were often shot out of hand whilst ex-Nazi civil servants, teachers and lawyers were removed from their positions and placed in camps where thousands died. In place of National Socialism, the people were now to be instructed in the theories of Marxism.

As a step towards introducing democratic government, the zones were divided into *Länder*, each with its own form of elected government. During 1947, the British and American zones were brought together for economic purposes and became part of a Joint Economic Council. Since both feared the possibility of a resurgent Germany, France and the Soviet Union were against any form of union.

In 1945, an international military tribunal was set up to try individuals considered responsible for the outbreak of war and crimes committed by the Nazi regime. The trial of the 22 men regarded as the leaders was to be held in Nuremberg, formerly the site of elaborate Nazi political rallies.

4 ⤳ THE NUREMBERG TRIALS

A *The accused*

First, the leading Nazis had to be found. Adolf Hitler had already committed suicide, as had Joseph Goebbels. The Nazi propaganda minister's wife, Magda, first used morphine to put her six children to sleep and then poisoned them with cyanide before ending her own life. Heinrich Himmler, carrying false documents, wearing an eye-patch and with his moustache shaved off, was caught but immediately committed suicide. There were rumours that he was murdered by British Intelligence to prevent him disclosing details of his secret negotiations with the British government. Herman Göring gave himself up and was disappointed not to receive celebrity treatment, Arthur Seyss-Inquart was discovered by Canadian troops, whilst Alfred Rosenberg was arrested in Flensburg. Seemingly unconcerned by the turn of events, Joachim von Ribbentrop quite brazenly made an attempt to return to civilian life but was given away. Hjalmar Schacht, who had been interned in a concentration camp by the Nazis, was both surprised and annoyed to be arrested. The most audacious was Baldur von Schirach, who volunteered to work for the Americans as an interpreter until his true identity was discovered.

PICTURE 52
Cartoon from the St Louis Post-Dispatch *of April 1945,
'Witnesses for the prosecution'*

WITNESSES FOR THE PROSECUTION

State Historical Society of Missouri, Columbia

Others arrested included Hans Frank, Wilhelm Frick, Hans Fritsche, Walter Funk, Konstantin von Neurath, Franz von Papen, Ernst Kaltenbrunner, Fritz Sauckel, Albert Speer, Julius Streicher and the military leaders Karl Dönitz, Alfred Jodl, Wilhelm Keital and Erich Raeder. Rudolf Hess was returned to Germany from his place of internment in Britain, whilst Martin Bormann slipped away from the Berlin bunker and disappeared. Adolf Eichmann, the main architect of the Final Solution, escaped but was later found in Argentina by Israeli agents and smuggled back to Israel to face trial. He was hanged a year later.

See page 406.

B *The charges and the trial*

The 22 men (Bormann and Eichmann were tried in their absence) were indicted on four counts:

- planning or conspiring, with Hitler, to make war and commit war crimes
- committing crimes against peace – planning, preparing and initiating wars of aggression
- making war and committing war crimes
- committing crimes against humanity.

KEY ISSUE

The meaning of 'crimes against humanity'.

The trials were presided over by British, American, Soviet and French judges and each of the accused was represented by a defence counsel. The most condemning evidence against the defendants came with the showing of films of the concentration camps.

During the course of his trial, Göring, who appeared arrogant and the most outspoken, denied all the charges and tried to score points at the expense of the American prosecutor. An outraged Admiral Dönitz said:

> Politicians brought the Nazis to power and started the war. They are the ones who brought about these disgusting crimes and now we have to sit here in the dock with them and share the blame.

Like Albert Speer, who appeared to appreciate the enormity of the Nazi atrocities and made no attempt to evade his share of the guilt, Hans Frank showed remorse and said,

> Don't let anyone tell you they had no idea. Everyone sensed there was something horribly wrong with the system. Hitler has disgraced Germany for all time!

Joachim von Ribbentrop seemed the most resigned to his fate when he said,

> We are only living shadows, the remnants of a dead era, an era that died with Hitler. Whether a few of us live another ten or twenty years, it makes no difference.

The loathsome 'Jew baiter', Julius Streicher, remained menacing to the end:

> The Jews are making a big mistake if they make a martyr out of me, you will see. I am the only one in the world who clearly saw the Jewish menace as an historical problem.

Finally, the American prosecutor summed up:

> If you were to say of these men that they are not guilty, it would be as true to say that there had been no war, there were no slain, there has been no crime.

Herman Göring (53)	death		
Joachim von Ribbentrop (53)	death	Rudolf Hess (52)	life imprisonment
Wilhelm Keitel (64)	death	Walter Funk (56)	life imprisonment
Ernst Kaltenbrunner (53)	death	Erich Raeder (70)	life imprisonment
Alfred Rosenberg (53)	death	Baldur von Schirach (39)	twenty years
Hans Frank (46)	death	Albert Speer (41)	twenty years
Wilhelm Frick (69)	death	Konstantin von Neurath (73)	fifteen years
Julius Streicher (61)	death	Karl Dönitz (55)	ten years
Franz Sauckel (61)	death	Hjalmar Schacht (68)	acquitted
Alfred Jodl (56)	death	Franz von Papen (66)	acquitted
Arthur Seyss-Inquart (54)	death	Hans Fritsche (46)	acquitted

C *The verdicts*

TABLE 61
The verdicts on the leading Nazis tried at Nuremberg

Göring cheated the hangman by finding a means of committing suicide. The remainder of those sentenced to death were hanged on 16 October 1946 and afterwards their bodies were taken to Munich for cremation and their ashes 'scattered in a river somewhere in Germany'. Those sentenced to terms of imprisonment were sent to Spandau prison in Berlin, where some died before completing their sentences. In spite of numerous efforts to win his release, Rudolf Hess finally committed suicide in 1987.

Some have maintained that there is a mystery surrounding his death and question how it was possible for a 93-year-old man, who was nearly blind, suffering from a heart condition and unable to walk without the aid of a stick, to hang himself from a bar of a window using the electric cord of a reading lamp. After completing his sentence, Alfred Speer wrote and lectured about the Third Reich and was much in demand since he was one of the few who could claim to have known Hitler intimately. He died in 1981 at St Mary's Hospital, Paddington whilst working on a documentary for the BBC. Sometimes referred to as 'the good Nazi', it was later discovered that Speer did have knowledge of the atrocities carried out in the concentration camps, something that he had denied during his trial.

Q
At Nuremberg did all the defendants merit the verdicts they received?

THE FATES OF MARTIN BORMANN AND JOSEF MENGELE – SPECULATION AND RUMOURS

Martin Bormann, Hitler's secretary and Reichsminister, spent the last hours of the war with his Fuhrer in a bunker in Berlin. As the Russians closed in, it is claimed that he escaped, made his way through the ruins of Berlin and was never seen again. At Nuremberg, he was tried in his absence, found guilty and sentenced to death. His chauffeur claimed that he had been killed but no body was found. Instead there were rumours that, after plastic surgery, Bormann had made his way to South America and there were numerous unconfirmed sightings of him in Paraguay and Argentina.

Then in 1972 construction workers uncovered human remains in Berlin and, after extensive forensic research, the skeleton was proved to be that of Bormann and the West German government declared him dead. However, the controversy continued; there were rumours of further sightings and the reliability of the evidence used in the forensic examination was questioned. Bormann's son, Martin Bormann junior, became a convert to Roman Catholicism, entered the priesthood and worked as a missionary.

Known as the Angel of Death, **Josef Mengele** was the medical officer at Auschwitz concentration camp. There he used inmates for human experimentation and carried out experiments on twins, dwarves and those with physical abnormalities. He was known to kill victims merely in order to dissect them afterwards. The war over, using the name Fritz Hollamann, Mengele worked as an agricultural labourer but, aware that the net was closing in, he used the **ODESSA** network to escape to South America.

For a time, he lived in Argentina but later moved to Brazil and took up residence in Sao Paulo. Numerous sighting of him were reported but all attempts to track him down failed. In 1979, he suffered a stroke and died but it was not until 1992 that DNA testing finally confirmed his identity.

> **ODESSA** an organisation of former members of the SS that organised escape routes for wanted members.

D *The Nuremberg Trials – some considerations*

Criticisms were made of the Nuremberg Trials. Some Germans agreed with Göring's view that it was simply the case of the victors trying the losers and some lawyers questioned if 'crimes against humanity' was a viable charge. From an Allied point of view, the trials brought to justice major criminals and, through the exposure of the extent of Nazi atrocities, they hoped to influence German public opinion.

The Nuremberg Trials were the most famous of the many that took place across Germany. Elsewhere, those responsible for the management of the death camps, industrialists who employed slave labour and *Einsatzgruppen* commanders faced the courts.

The majority received prison sentences and only a few were executed. During 1950, the Allied authorities empowered German courts to take over the pursuit of the remaining Nazi war criminals. In addition, Simon Wiesenthal (1908–2005), an Austrian Jew who had survived four and a half years in concentration camps, devoted the remainder of his life to tracking down fugitive Nazi criminals. As for the guilt of the German people as a whole, Alan Bullock, in *Hitler, A Study in Tyranny* (Penguin 1962), has written:

See pages 436–7.

> Nazism was not some terrible accident which fell upon the German people out of the sky ... it is true that the majority of Germans never voted for Hitler, it is also true that 13 million did. Both these facts need to be remembered.

UNTER DEN LINDEN

State Historical Society of Missouri, Columbia

5 ⌐ GERMANY AND THE START OF THE COLD WAR

A *The collapse of the war-time alliance*

Disagreements over Germany between the former wartime Allies began even before the end of the war and developed apace afterwards. The basic difference between them was that whilst Stalin thought it essential to handicap Germany's ability to prepare for another war, the United States wanted to encourage German post-war reconstruction. The American view was based on the belief that German industrial recovery was essential to the stability of post-war Europe and this view strengthened as Soviet plans to extend their influence across Eastern Europe became increasingly obvious. America believed that if Stalin was opposed to the future reunification of Germany, then the United States, Britain and France should go it alone.

As the political situation worsened, so communications between the Western and Soviet controlled zones deteriorated to the point where, on the Russian side, the frontier was marked by a continuous line of minefields, barbed wire and electric fences. In a speech made at Fulton,

Missouri in March 1946, Winston Churchill summed up the situation in Europe and first used the term 'iron curtain' to describe the division between the Western powers and the area controlled by the Soviet Union:

> From Stettin in the Baltic to Trieste in the Adriatic an iron curtain has descended across the Continent. Behind that line lie all the capitals of the ancient states of Central and Eastern Europe – Warsaw, Berlin, Prague, Vienna, Budapest, Bucharest and Sofia; all these famous cities and the populations around them lie in what I must call the Soviet sphere, and all are subject, in one form or another, not only to Soviet influence but to a very high and in some cases increasing measure of control from Moscow.

In March 1946, Greece and Yugoslavia apart, Soviet influence had advanced unchallenged across the whole of Eastern Europe. To contain this, Harry S. Truman, the American president, issued a warning that the United States would support countries resisting outside interference in their affairs. The clear aim of the Truman Doctrine was to prevent further Communist infiltration. At the same time, George Marshall, the American Secretary of State, put forward a plan to assist the economic recovery of Europe, the European Recovery Programme, usually referred to as the Marshall Plan. His plan, described by Churchill as 'the most unsordid act in history', offered financial help to all the countries of Europe. Since Stalin was more interested in squeezing reparations from the defeated nations than helping their recovery, he regarded Marshall Aid as a devious, dollar-backed scheme to loosen the Soviet grip on Eastern Europe. He declined the offer of aid and his communist controlled east European satellites dutifully followed. Marshall Aid, administered by the Organisation for European Economic Co-operation (OEEC) was to bring immense benefit to the recipient nations and, of the money allocated, the Western zones of Germany received $1,000 million.

During the immediate post-war period, whilst the Western Allies allowed a speedy demobilisation of their servicemen, the Soviet Union maintained its armed forces at full strength. However, in the struggle to hold the balance of power, the US held a decisive advantage, the secret of the atomic bomb which it denied Russia. It was not until 1949 that Soviet scientists first tested an atomic bomb. During this period, the sectors of Berlin controlled by the West began to show evidence of rapid reconstruction that stood in stark contrast to the devastation that still existed in the Soviet sector. The apparent advantages of the capitalist system attracted large numbers of East Berliners and East Germans to West Berlin, where many found employment. This proved an embarrassment to Stalin and as relations between the Western democracies and the Soviet Union fell to an all time low, so the Cold War developed in earnest. During 1947, the American and British zones united for economic purposes to become Bizonia, though politically they remained separate.

This move, together with President Truman's refusal to allow the Soviet Union to receive reparations from the Western zones, so outraged

KEY ISSUE

The need of the Soviet Union to acquire reparations from the Western zones of Germany.

the Russians that they retaliated by harassing Western transport passing through their zone to West Berlin and trains, barges and vehicles were subject to lengthy delays at checkpoints. However, it was the Western plan to go ahead with currency reforms that proved the last straw and led to the first major crisis of the Cold War.

B *The Berlin blockade, 1948–9*

In June 1948, the three Western zones replaced the *Reichsmark* with the *Deutschmark*. Shortly afterwards, Soviet forces began to blockade the road, rail and canal routes across the Soviet zone of Germany that allowed the Western Allies access to Berlin. Whilst Stalin claimed that he was protecting the economy of the Soviet zone against the ruinous effects of the new currency, the West counter-claimed that the Soviets were trying to force them out of Berlin. The immediate reaction of the US commander, General Lucius D. Clay, was to threaten to send an armed column along the autobahn towards Berlin with orders to open fire if they were hindered. This was a dangerous ploy that might well have ended in war, and so instead it was decided to supply the Western sectors

Q

Were the Western powers or the Soviet Union the more responsible for the heightening of Cold War tension during this period?

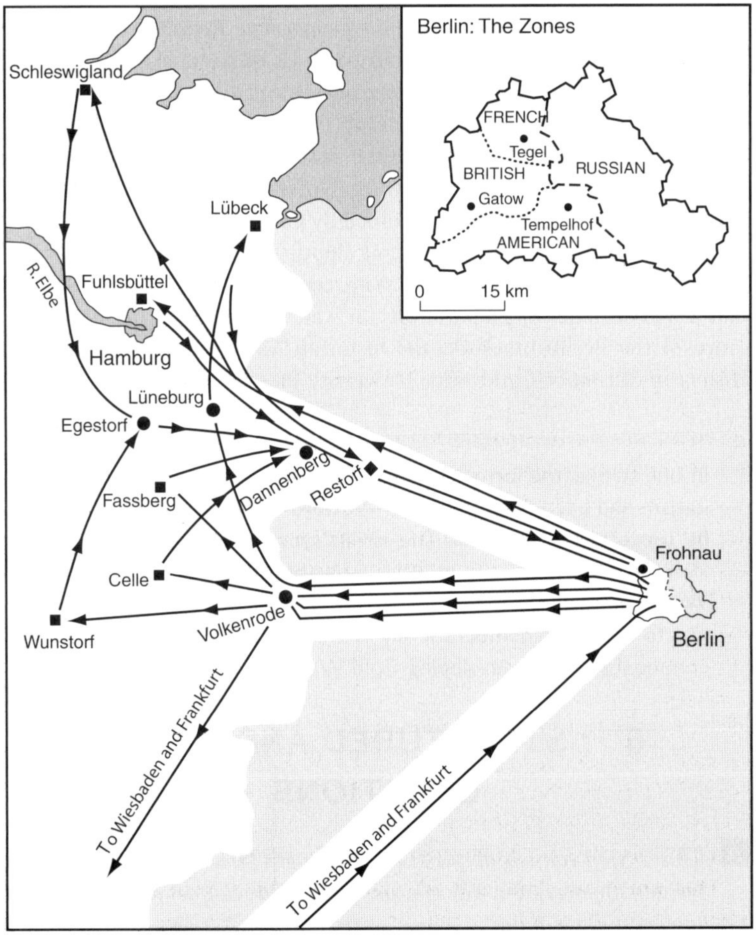

MAP 16

The map gives some idea of the intricate measures used by the Allies to ensure regular flights along the air-corridors into West Berlin

of Berlin by air. The plan, named 'Operation Vitals' by the Americans and 'Operation Plain Fare' by the British, aimed to use three air corridors to Berlin airfields at Tempelhof (American sector), Gatow (British sector) and Tegel (French sector). During a period of 321 days 278,228 flights were made carrying 2,363,628 tonnes of food, fuel, medical and other essential supplies. On the peak day, 16 April 1949, 1,398 flights carried 13,130 tonnes of supplies with an aircraft landing in Berlin every minute. West Berliners nicknamed the aircraft *Rosinenbomber*, 'raisin bombers'. The Russians tried to take advantage of the situation by offering rations to West Berliners who were prepared to register for the purpose; it says much for the determination of the people that less than 2 per cent of the population took up the offer.

The Russians also placed balloons in hazardous positions close to the flight paths and used MIG fighters to buzz the transport planes, but without shooting them down there was little they could do.

In May 1949, the blockade was finally lifted. The *Berlin blockade* made the Western powers even more mindful of the communist threat and this led to an increase in Cold War tension. In 1949, the Americans, British and French merged their zones of Germany to form the *German Federal Republic (BRD)* and before the end of the year the Russians had transformed their zone into the *German Democratic Republic (DDR)*. The blockade also encouraged the countries of Western Europe to draw closer together in a defensive alliance and in April 1949 they formed the *North Atlantic Treaty Organisation (NATO)*. The Organisation was made up of twelve countries – the United States, Britain, France, Canada, Belgium, the Netherlands, Luxemburg, Norway, Denmark, Iceland, Italy and Portugal. In 1952, they were joined by Greece and Turkey and, three years later, by the German Federal Republic. Stalin, alarmed at the prospect of an emerging German state, condemned NATO and claimed that it was evidence of preparations for war. Commenting on the significance of the Berlin blockade, the historian Mary Fulbrook (*A Concise History of Germany*, Cambridge University Press, 1990) has written:

> In one stroke, the former bastion of Prussian nationalism and Nazi militarism had become a symbol of Western freedom and democracy, to be protected at all costs. The air-lift symbolised the dramatic transformation of Western policies towards their part of Germany. Western Germany, no longer a defeated nation of despicable Nazis, was to become a democratic ally in the fight against totalitarianism and communism in the developing Cold War.

6 ⤺ STRUCTURED AND ESSAY QUESTIONS

A *This section consists of questions that might be used for discussion (or written answers) as a way of expanding on the chapter and testing your understanding of it.*

1. Why was the location of Berlin likely to become a cause of friction between the wartime allies?
2. What reasons did Stalin give to justify his proposals to change the Polish frontiers?
3. In the post-war situation, how did the German people cope with the lack of a worthwhile currency?
4. Explain the reasons for the influx of refugees into the Western zones of Germany during the immediate post-war period.
5. Why was Hjalmar Schacht 'surprised and annoyed' at his arrest?
6. Check the references made to Sauckel and Speer earlier in the book. Do you think their differing sentences were justified?
7. What exactly did Churchill mean when he referred to an 'iron curtain'?

B *Essay questions.*
1. To what extent were the decisions made at Yalta and Potsdam in 1945 in the best interests for the future peace in Europe?
2. Account for the chaotic state of Germany immediately following the end of the Second World War.
3. To what extent had a Cold War in Europe become inevitable by 1950?

7 ⌐ DOCUMENTARY EXERCISE ON THE NUREMBERG TRIALS, 1946

Study the following sources and then answer the questions based on them.

SOURCE A
From the opening address of Justice Robert Jackson, US Chief Prosecutor at the Nuremberg Trials.

We would make it clear that we have no purpose to incriminate the whole German people... If the German populace had willingly accepted the Nazi programme, no storm troopers would have been needed or concentration camps or the Gestapo... The Germans no less than the non-German world has accounts to settle with these defendants...

SOURCE B
From a statement made by Hermann Göring during his trial.

We had orders to obey the head of state. We weren't a band of criminals meeting in the woods at the dead of night to plan mass murders. The four real conspirators are missing – the Führer, Himmler, Bormann and Goebbels... This is a political trial by the victors and it will be a good thing when Germany realises that...

SOURCE C
From a statement made by Albert Speer during his trial.

I would like to sit down and write one final blast about the whole damn Nazi mess and mention names and details and let the German people see once and for all what rotten corruption, hypocrisy, and madness the whole system was based on! I would spare no one, including myself.

SOURCE D

The view of the British novelist, Rebecca West.

It was the virtue of the Nuremberg trials that it was conceived in hatred of war, and nurtured by those who strived for peace. Of course, the trial was botched and imperfect ... it had to deal with new crimes for which there was no provision in national law or international law.

1. *In Source A, what point does the US Chief Prosecutor imply about the guilt of the German people?*
2. *In Source B, what did Göring mean by 'a political trial by the victors'?*
3. *To what extent do the views of Göring and Speer (Sources B and C) differ regarding their responsibilities for Nazi crimes?*
4. *For what reasons might Rebecca West have considered the Nuremberg Trials to have been 'botched and imperfect'?*
5. *Overall, what impressions do the sources give of the attitude of the prosecutors and defendants at the Nuremberg Trials?*

The two Germanies and the events leading to reunification

17

INTRODUCTION

The creation of the German Federal Republic (BRD) and the German Democratic Republic (DDR) in 1949 in effect turned the former four zones of occupied Germany into two independent states, afterwards referred to as West Germany and East Germany. The status of Berlin remained the same and was to continue to cause animosity between the major powers. In both West and East Germany steps were taken to provide constitutions and hold elections.

1 ⌐ THE GERMAN FEDERAL REPUBLIC

A *A new constitution*

In 1949, the *Grundgesetz* (Basic Law), the constitution of the new German Federal Republic (BRD), was agreed. The parliament was to consist of two chambers – the *Bundesrat* and the *Bundestag*. The *Bundesrat* was the upper chamber that represented the interests of the German states, the *Länder*; members of the lower chamber, the *Bundestag*, were to be elected by universal suffrage by the German people and the seats allocated according to **proportional representation**.

The head of government, the Chancellor, would normally (though not always) be the leader of the largest party in the *Bundestag*. In all matters, the *Bundestag* held sway over the *Bundesrat*. The president of the Federal Republic, who was elected for one year only, was to be a non-political, nominal head of state who exercised no real power and whose functions were to be largely ceremonial. The Federal Constitutional Court was to fulfil the functions of the judiciary and be responsible for constitutional and legal matters. The constitution guaranteed basic human rights and liberties and equality before the law. The official seat of government was to be Bonn, a city on the River Rhine in North Rhine-Westphalia.

proportional representation system by which the seats are allocated according to the number of votes cast for each party.

B *Political parties and the outcome of the first post-war general election*

neo-Nazi parties new groups that embraced the ideas of the former Nazi Party.

West Germany saw the emergence of four major political parties and a host of smaller ones. In order to limit the influence of fringe parties, parties that received less than 5 per cent of the vote were not represented in the *Bundestag*. As we shall see, Germany was later to witness the re-emergence of several **neo-Nazi parties**.

TABLE 62
West Germany's major political parties

Christian Democratic Union (CDU)	Formed in 1945 from smaller Catholic and Protestant parties that had earlier resisted the Nazis. Whilst supporting private enterprise, it also believed in the need of the state to adopt measures to help the poorer members of society. The CDU did not exist in Bavaria.
Christian Socialist Union (CSU)	Established in 1946, the CSU was a Bavarian-based political party. Founded on Christian principles and conservative in outlook, it was affiliated to the CDU.
Social Democratic Party (SPD)	Germany's oldest political party and founded in 1875, the SPD was a moderate socialist party that maintained a high level of support during the 1920s and early 1930s. It was mainly supported by the working classes and trade unionists.
Free Democratic Union (FDP)	Founded by former members of the German Democratic Party (DDP), and liberal in outlook, the FDP was formed in 1948. It believed in a market economy and social welfare and drew most of its support from the middle classes and white-collar workers.

The smaller parties included the Communist Party, which collapsed with the coming of the Cold War and was banned in 1956, the German Party, a conservative party that drew most of its support from the northern states as well as the Coalition for Economic Reconstruction, the German Empire Party and the neo-Nazi National Democratic Party (NPD).

TABLE 63
West German election of August 1949 – result

Party	Percentage of vote	Seats won
Social Democratic Party (SPD)	29.2	131
Christian Democratic Union (CDU)	25.2	115
Free Democratic Party (FDP)	11.9	52
Christian Social Union (CSU)	5.8	24
Communist Party	5.7	15
All others	22.2	65

Of the 410 seats, eight were based in Berlin and not represented in the Bonn-based Bundestag. The first Chancellor of West Germany was Dr Konrad Adenauer and the first President, Theodor Heuss (1884–1963), a former liberal politician and historian.

Konrad Adenauer	1949–63	CDU
Ludwig Erhard	1963–66	CDU
Kurt Kiesinger	1966–69	CDU
Willy Brandt	1969–74	SPD
Walter Scheel	1974–74	FDP
Helmut Schmidt	1974–82	SPD
Helmut Kohl	1982–98	CDU
Gerhard Schröder	1998–2005	SPD
Angela Merkel	2005–	CDU

TABLE 64
Chancellors of the German Federal Republic

PROFILE

KONRAD ADENAUER (1876–1967)

The son of a civil servant, Konrad Adenauer was born in Cologne in 1876. After studying law and politics at Freiberg, Munich and Bonn universities, he became a lawyer in Cologne. A devout Roman Catholic, in 1906 he joined the Catholic Centre Party and was to remain a member of that party during the years of the Weimar Republic. Adenauer was elected to Cologne council and between 1917 and 1933 he was the mayor of his home town. After the Nazis came to power in 1933, he was subjected to persecution, dismissed from all his offices, and arrested. Once released, he lived in seclusion until 1944 when he was accused of being involved in the attempted assassination of Hitler and was arrested by the *Gestapo*. It is claimed that Hitler admired Adenauer but knew that his political views would naturally make him an opponent of the Nazi regime.

The war over, the US authorities once again installed Adenauer as mayor of Cologne but he was later dismissed by the British for incompetence. In post-war Germany, instead of withdrawing from public life, he worked hard to establish a new political party, the Christian Democratic Union (CDU) and tried to attract the support of both Roman Catholics and Protestants. After the elections of 1949, at the age of 73, he was appointed the first Chancellor of the German Federal Republic, a position he was to hold for the next 14 years. Amongst his many memorable quotes was 'An infallible method of conciliating a tiger is to allow oneself to be devoured'. As we shall see, Adenauer never proved an easy prey to those at home and abroad who sought to bring about his downfall.

C *The Adenauer years, 1949–63*

During his period as West German Chancellor, Adenauer experienced some difficult times in both domestic and foreign policy. Amongst his achievements were the establishment of a stable democracy in West Germany, reconciliation with France, winning trust so that West Germany was able to integrate and co-operate with the other Western powers and his contribution to *Wirtschaftswunder* – the West German 'economic miracle'.

KEY ISSUE

The BRD's integration with the rest of Western Europe.

In 1949, the BRD became a member of the Organisation for European Economic Co-operation (OEEC) that had been set up to encourage the growth of agricultural and industrial production in Western Europe. Two years later, West Germany became a member of the European Coal and Steel Community (ECSC), that established a single authority to encourage the development of these industries, and a full member of the Council of Europe. Events in the Cold War, particularly the outbreak of the Korean War in 1950, led the United States to press for the rearmament of West Germany so that, if it became necessary, the country could play a part in the defence of Western Europe. This did not meet with the approval of other countries and fears about the consequences of encouraging German militarism caused the French Prime Minister, René Pleven, to suggest the setting up of a European Defence Community (EDC) that would include France, Italy, the Benelux countries and West Germany. As a member of the EDC, West Germany's military commitment would be overseen by the other members. An agreement was signed in 1952 but, rejected by France, it came to nothing. Even so, in 1955 West Germany became a fully sovereign state and a member of the North Atlantic Treaty Organisation (NATO).

In 1950, Robert Schuman, the French Foreign Minister, said:

de facto in actual fact, even if not fully recognised.

> Europe will not be made all at once, or according to a single plan. It will be built through concrete achievements which first create a **de facto** solidarity. The coming together of the nations of Europe requires the elimination of the age-old opposition of France and Germany. Any action taken must in the first place concern these two countries.

It took time but gradually Franco-German relations improved and in 1963 Adenauer and the French President, Charles de Gaulle, signed the Elysée Treaty, by which both countries agreed to co-operate and work towards forging a close friendship. At the same time, the German–French Youth Association was set up to encourage exchanges and greater understanding between the young people of both countries.

In 1951, Adenauer took a step towards improving relations with Israel when he recognised his country's obligation to the Jews as a consequence of the Holocaust and subsequently paid £3,450 million as some recompense for their suffering. This led to an attempt on his life when a package addressed to him exploded in Munich Police Headquarters. An investigation proved that the would-be assassins were members of an Israeli extremist right-wing group, the Herut Party, and that a future prime minister of Israel, Menachem Begin, was involved. The Party was incensed by the fact that Adenauer's financial offer was made to the Israeli government and not as compensation to individuals who had suffered during the Holocaust.

What were the main aims of Adenauer's foreign policy?

The key principle in West German foreign policy during Adenauer's chancellorship was the Hallstein Doctrine. Named after a government minister, Walter Hallstein, the doctrine stated that the German Federal Republic had the exclusive right to represent the entire German nation and that, with the exception of the Soviet Union, the BRD would not establish diplomatic relations with any country that recognised East Germany. Adenauer resumed diplomatic relations with the Soviet Union and took steps to win the release of thousands of German prisoners-of-war still held in captivity ten years after the end of the war. In 1952, Stalin made a surprise offer to support the unification of West and East Germany on condition that the united country should not rearm or enter into alliances with other countries. In common with the leaders of the other Western powers, Adenauer, a staunch opponent of communism, saw the offer as a ploy to extend Russian influence over Germany and rejected it. 1957 saw the BRD become one of the signatories of the Treaty of Rome and so become one of the founder members of the European Economic Community. In 1956, the Saar, occupied by France immediately after the war, was reintegrated with West Germany following a plebiscite.

D Wirtschaftswunder – *Germany's economic miracle*

Undoubtedly, the greatest achievement of Adenauer's years was to oversee a period of unparalleled economic growth that led to the miraculous recovery of the German economy. The historian Mary Fulbrook has written (*A Concise History of Germany*, Cambridge University Press 1990):

> While Germany was thus in the process of being readmitted to the community of nations, it simultaneously experienced a remarkable economic recovery. From the ruins of a defeated and devastated nation grew a materialistic society witnessing astonishing rates of growth and productivity, and conveniently suppressing the past by focussing on the task of building a prosperous future. Former Nazis were relatively easily integrated into the new conservative Germany and its material successes giving a **pragmatic** legitimacy to the new democracy.

pragmatic more concerned with matters of fact than theories.

By 1961, the GNP had trebled, there was virtually full employment and German living standards had improved considerably.

There was also a boom in West German farming during this period. As the result of a minor agricultural revolution that involved the consolidation of small units into larger farms and the introduction of new technology, production increased substantially.

The good times were not to last indefinitely. During the mid-1960s West Germany entered a depression as production slumped and unemployment rose to 700,000. Their confidence shaken, many Germans feared a return to the economic disasters of the early 1930s. The situation was not helped by a further escalation in the Cold War when, in 1961, Walter Ulbricht, the East German leader, under instructions from Stalin's successor, Nikita Khrushchev, ordered the construction of a wall intended to isolate West Berlin from the remainder of Germany.

<table>
<tr><td>

HISTORIANS' DEBATE

</td><td>

The reasons for West Germany's remarkable economic recovery

- The policies of the West German Minister for Economic Affairs, who was responsible for the currency reform and the removal of price controls.
- Good industrial relations and the fact that organised labour was prepared to accept wage restraint in order to prevent inflation.
- The high morale of West Germans and their determination to accomplish a speedy recovery from the disaster of the war.
- The influx of relatively cheap labour from abroad – refugees and 'guest workers' from Turkey and Italy.
- The reconstruction of German industry, so badly damaged by Allied bombing during the war, was undertaken with the building of new factories and the introduction of the most modern machinery. This gave them an advantage over many of their rivals that still used outdated equipment.
- Booming exports – the German recovery was largely export driven. It was not long before cars produced by Volkswagen and Mercedes-Benz were available for export. 25,000 Volkswagens were produced in 1948, and by 1955 the best part of a million had been manufactured. In addition, products manufactured by such firms as Bosch, Siemens and Krupp appeared again. The Krupp family, Nazi Germany's leading manufacturers of armaments and members of which were tried as war criminals, changed from the production of weapons to the production of domestic appliances.
- Marshall Aid of course played a part, but it should be remembered that the amount received by West Germany was relatively small compared with Britain and France.

</td></tr>
</table>

E The Berlin Wall

The prosperity and political freedom evident in the West tempted an increasing number of East Germans first to cross from East to West Berlin and then to proceed to West Germany. The exodus of four million East Germans to the West, many of them well qualified and highly skilled workers, was something that the East German authorities could ill afford and had to be prevented. Known in East Germany as the 'Anti-Fascist Protective Rampart', the construction of the Berlin Wall began during August 1961. At first, it was no more than a wire fence but by 1965 it had become a concrete wall 3.6 metres high and 1.2 metres wide that stretched for a distance of 45 kilometres.

The wall caused considerable hardship and heartache since it separated families and friends and, for East Germans who had worked in West Berlin, a loss of jobs. It was manned by East German police, *VoPos* (short for *Volkspolizei*), and border guards, *GrePos* (short for *Grenzpolizei*), with orders to shoot to kill those who attempted to cross. During the lifetime of the wall, some 5,000 managed to escape East Germany but 263 were killed and many more injured. Many of the escapees jumped from windows or dug tunnels, whilst others drove reinforced vehicles at the wall and a few made daring escapes by means of hot-air balloons and light aircraft. Border crossings were set up that allowed West Germans with the necessary permits limited access to East Berlin. Unrestricted entry was allowed to American and British military personnel, officials and diplomats – the most famous point of entry being Checkpoint Charlie in the Friedrichstraße. A memorable moment occurred in June 1963 when the American President, John F. Kennedy visited the city and made a speech to an enthusiastic crowd of West Berliners:

> I am proud to come to this city as a guest of your distinguished Mayor, who has symbolised throughout the world the fighting spirit of West Berlin. And I am proud to visit the Federal Republic with your distinguished Chancellor who for so many years has committed Germany to democracy and freedom … Freedom is indivisible, and when one man is enslaved, all are not free. When all are free, then we can look forward to the day when this city will be joined as one … When that day finally comes, as it will, the people of West Berlin can take sober satisfaction in the fact that they were in the front line for almost two decades. All free men, wherever they may live, are citizens of Berlin and therefore, as a freeman, I take pride in the words '*Ich bin ein Berliner*' [I am a Berliner].

F *Adenauer – the final years*

In addition to the BRD's failing economy, various other difficulties contributed to Adenauer's declining popularity. Earlier, some of his critics

KEY ISSUE

The scandals that led to the downfall of Konrad Adenauer.

claimed that he had missed a golden opportunity to bring about the early unification of Germany when he rejected Stalin's offer in 1952. A man with a strong personality, he seemed determined to hang on to power and tended to treat his colleagues as inferiors and showed scant regard for the *Bundestag*.

After three periods in office, many, including some in his own party, regretted his decision to run for a fourth period as Chancellor in 1961 at the age of 85 and saw it as evidence of his increasingly authoritarian style of leadership. Some claim that his stubbornness was based on his hostility to Ludwig Erhard, whose achievements as Minister of Economics he envied. Adenauer was not helped by the activities of a students' movement led by Rudi Dutschke that, together with German trade unionists, organised demonstrations and protests. The last straw proved to be a political crisis caused by a scandal involving the weekly news magazine *Der Spiegel*. In 1962, the magazine published an article by Conrad Ahlers, in which he criticised the state of the *Bundeswehr*, the German army, and the fact that the defence of West Germany was dependent on the United States' nuclear deterrent. At the instigation of Franz Joseph Strauss, the Minister of Defence, the editor of the magazine was arrested and charged with high treason, whilst the Hamburg offices of *Der Spiegel* were raided and closed down. This led to widespread protests and the court refused to open the trial, claiming that the government's action was in breech of the freedom of the press. With the behaviour of Strauss appearing to be excessive and even absurd, Adenauer had no choice other than to dismiss his Minister of Defence. He himself retired the following year.

Whatever his critics may have said, it should be remembered that Konrad Adenauer established a stable democracy in the Federal Republic, took steps to achieve reconciliation with France, integrated his country within the Western community through membership of NATO and the EEC and, most importantly, created a situation in which most world powers came to trust Germany again. He once said, 'The art of politics consists of knowing precisely when to hit an opponent slightly below the belt.' It was an art in which he was well versed.

2 ⌁ THE GERMAN DEMOCRATIC REPUBLIC

As the war ended, Moscow-trained communists led by Walter Ulbricht (1893–1973) arrived in Berlin intending, with the support of the Russian authorities, to gain political control. In some ways the new constitution of the German Democratic Republic (DDR), said to be that of a 'republic of workers and peasants', followed a similar pattern to that of the Federal Republic. There were two elected assemblies, the *Länderkammer*, which represented the states, and the *Volkskammer*, the more important chamber whose members were to be elected by the people. The President, who had only limited powers, was elected by members of the largest party in the *Volkskammer*. Only one person was to hold this position, Wilhelm Pieck (1949–60). On his death the position was abolished and afterwards the effective head of state was styled the Chairman of the Council of State.

Although there were numerous political parties, the two most influential were the German Communist Party (KPD) and the German Social Democratic Party (SPD). Briefly the country was led by the leader of the SPD, Otto Grotewohl (1894–1964); but when the KPD and SPD joined together in 1948 to become a Stalinist-type Socialist United Party of Germany (SED), this was effectively the only political party in East Germany. Grotewohl, severely criticised by Soviet leaders for his failure to improve the economic condition of his country, was in declining health and resigned in 1964 to make way for the hard-line communist, Walter Ulbricht.

EAST GERMANY'S HARD-LINE LEADERS – WALTER ULBRICHT (1893–1973) AND ERICH HONECKER (1912–94)

Born in Leipzig, the son of a tailor and active member of the Social Democratic Party (SPD), the young **Walter Ulbricht** planned to become a carpenter. During the First World War, he served in the German army on the Eastern Front but in 1917 he deserted. During the upheavals of 1918, he became a member of the German Communist Party (KPD) and was elected to the regional parliament in Saxony. By 1928, he was a member of the *Reichstag* and the following year became the chairman of the KPD in Berlin. After the Nazis came to power in 1933, Ulbricht lived in exile in Paris and Prague and then moved to Spain at the time of the civil war. After the German invasion of the Soviet Union in 1941, Ulbricht worked for the Russians with other German communists, preparing propaganda material and interrogating prisoners. The war over, he was sent to East Germany and there worked to reconstruct the German Communist Party on Soviet lines. He was also largely responsible for making sure that the Socialist United Party (SED) dominated German politics.

Erich Honecker was born in the Saar, the fourth of the six children of a politically active coal miner, Wilhelm Honecker. At the age of ten, he joined the youth movement of the Communist Party, the Young Communist League, and trained as a roofer. Aged 17, he became a member of the Communist Party, went to Moscow to study at the International Lenin School and returned to Germany as a full-time politician. When the Nazis came to power, he joined the resistance and was arrested and sentenced to ten years' hard labour, spending much of his time in solitary confinement. He survived and at the end of the war went to Berlin to resume his party activities under Walter Ulbricht. In 1946, he became one of the first members of the Socialist Unity Party (SED), and after 1949 took his place amongst the leaders of the German Democratic Republic.

TABLE 65
DDR heads of state (1960–90)

Walter Ulbricht	1960–73	SED
Friedrich Ebert	1973–	SED
Willi Stoph	1973–6	SED
Erich Honecker	1976–89	SED
Egon Krenz	1989–	SED
Manfred Gerlach	1989–	LDPD
Sabine Bergmann-Pohl	1990–	

Q

To what extent had the DDR become a Soviet-style communist state by 1949?

Once in office, Ulbricht devoted himself to establishing a Stalinist-type regime. As part of his economic reforms, all estates of a hundred hectares or more were taken over and redistributed to the peasants. Large industries as well as mining and banking concerns were nationalised and even small private enterprises had ceased to exist by 1949. East Germany was now a fully fledged communist state controlled by the SED and watched over by the *Stasi*, a secret police that spied on the people and watched all areas of political and social activities.

A *The East German uprising of 1953*

The Soviet seizure of reparations and the drain of workers fleeing to the West led to major economic and social problems. In addition, there was an acute shortage of consumer goods in the shops and the people regularly suffered power cuts. This led to discontent which became open unrest when, in 1953, the government increased the production quota allocated to workers by 10 per cent. In reality this meant that East German workers would be expected to work harder but for no additional pay, a situation made worse by the threat that, if the new quotas were not fulfilled, there would be cuts in pay.

PICTURE 55
East German youths throwing stones at a Russian tank in 1953

The first unrest rose up amongst construction workers in East Berlin, where over 100,000 gathered to demonstrate and demand the resignation of the government. The disturbances spread rapidly from the city across the rest of East Germany and, in order to restore order, the government sought the aid of Soviet troops. The response was instant and severe as Soviet troops using T-34 tanks and supported by the *Volkspolizei*, the East German police, broke up strikes and riots. An estimated 260 were killed and over 1,800 injured. Afterwards, 105 leaders were executed and 5,100 arrested, of which 1,200 were sent to labour camps.

Ulbricht, considered inflexible, unapproachable and generally unliked, was not held in affection by Party members or the East German people. In true Stalinist style, he concentrated on heavy industry and, with consumer goods in short supply, living standards remained low. Manufactured goods were of very poor quality; this was well indicated by the Trabant and Wartburg cars that were part made of wood, badly designed, of poor comfort, and with high pollution outputs, and were considered indicative of the backwardness of East German industry. In 1966, Ulbricht introduced a New Economic System by which economic planning was to be decentralised. The change of policy led to greater efficiency but offended other hard-line Party members. The East German leader's fortunes changed when Leonid Brezhnev became the leader of the Soviet Union. As the relationship between the two men deteriorated, and facing the challenge of the scheming Erich Honecker, in 1973 Ulbricht resigned on grounds of poor health. He died two years later and was given the honour of an elaborate state funeral.

For a few months, Friedrich Ebert (1914–79), son of the first president of the Weimar Republic, stood in as acting head of state until the election of Willi Stoph (1914–99). Stoph, by any standards an unusual man, had, in spite of being a communist, served in the German army during the Second World War and been awarded an Iron Cross. He was to be the leader of East Germany between 1973 and 1976. No doubt embarrassed by the fact that, during his period in office, members of his family had fled to the West, he made an attempt to improve relations between their two countries by taking part in negotiations with the West German Chancellor, Willy Brandt.

see pages 477–478.

Stoph resigned in 1976 to be replaced by Erich Honecker (1912–94).

B *Honecker's leadership of East Germany, 1976–89*

Another hard-liner, Honecker remained totally loyal to Moscow. Earlier in 1961, he had made his reputation as the person directly responsible for the construction of the Berlin Wall and, intolerant of dissent, during his period in office over 120 East Germans were killed attempting to escape to West Berlin. For this, he was later to face charges as a **Cold War criminal**.

During his 13 years in office, the country's economy and the living standards of the people improved so that East Germany became the most prosperous country in Eastern Europe, but it still fell far short of those of the West. As consumer goods became more readily available, East

Cold War criminal a person held responsible for the shooting of those attempting to escape to the West.

glasnost and *perestroika* policies intended to make the Soviet Union more democratic and allow the people greater freedom.

See page 481.

German living standards improved further. At long last, Honecker put into practice plans to repair and remove what remained of the war-damaged buildings and introduced an accelerated programme of house building. In foreign policy, he continued to follow Soviet directives but was prepared to take advantage of the West German Chancellor, Willy Brandt's policy of *Ostpolitik* and agreed to economic co-operation between the two Germanies. In 1987 he became the first East German head of state to visit West Germany. However, he refused to introduce Mikhail Gorbachev's policies of **glasnost** and **perestroika** and as news of the greater freedoms being enjoyed by the Russian people reached East Germany, there followed a period of mounting civil unrest. Honecker was finally forced to give way and resigned in 1989.

He was replaced by Egon Krenz (1937–), who survived only 50 days before handing over to Manfred Gerlach (1928–). With East Germany at the point of collapse, in 1990 the conservative Sabine Bergmann-Pohl (1946–) very briefly held office. She was the only woman to hold this post; after German reunification, she became a member of the *Bundesrat*.

3 ∽ WEST GERMANY AFTER ADENAUER

Even though those who succeeded to the German chancellorship inherited a country with a stable, democratic government and one of the most prosperous economies in Europe, they had to face the ongoing problems of the re-emergence of Nazism and active left-wing terrorist groups.

A *The emergence of neo-Nazism and terrorist groups*

The emergence of low-key neo-Nazi groups first occurred soon after the end of the war. These extreme right-wing groups organised rallies during which skin-headed youths wearing brown uniforms chanted anti-Semitic slogans and carried banners bearing swastika-like emblems. They also resorted to attacking foreign workers, daubing graffiti on Jewish graves and memorials dedicated to the Holocaust and declaring former Nazi leaders to be cult heroes. The strong action taken by the government had little effect other than drive the movement underground. The period also witnessed the emergence of a new political party, the National Democratic Party of Germany, whose policies caused many to consider it neo-Nazi in outlook.

Far more serious were the activities of militant left-wing groups, particularly the *Rote Armee Fraktion*, the Red Army Faction (RAF). Originally called the Baader-Meinhof group and claiming to be anti-capitalist and anti-imperialist, its founding members were Andreas Baader (1943–77), a former college drop-out who had turned to crime, Ulrike Meinhof (1934–77), a journalist and daughter of an eminent historian,

PICTURE 56
The emblem of the Rote Armee Fraktion

and Gudrun Ensslin (1940–77), a pastor's daughter. With the revolutionaries Che Guevara, the South American revolutionary, and Ho Chi Minh, leader of the Viet Cong in the war against the US in Vietnam, as their icons, the movement turned to urban terrorism and committed numerous bombings, assassinations, kidnappings and hijackings, the most prominent targets often being Allied military bases in Germany. Some members of the RAF were trained abroad by the Palestinian Liberation Organisation (PLO). The leaders of the RAF were finally arrested and, in 1975, put on trial. Held at Stammheim prison, they went on hunger strike and had to be forcibly fed. During this time Meinhof committed suicide, whilst the remaining defendants were sentenced to life imprisonment. Later, both Baader and Ensslin committed suicide, although sympathisers claim that they were murdered by the authorities. This was not the end of the Red Army Faction, however, as a second movement later emerged to begin a wave of atrocities known as the 'German Autumn'.

> **Q**
> *What impact did the activities of terrorist groups have on the government of the BRD?*

B *The Chancellors of the Federal Republic, 1963–2005*

LUDWIG ERHARD (1963–6)

Born in Furth in 1897, for a time Erhard worked as an assistant in his father's grocer's shop. During the First World War, he served in the German army until he was wounded in 1918. After the war, he studied economics and then worked in market research. Erhard took no part in the Second World War but was known to have been in contact with German resistance groups opposed to the Nazi regime. After the war, he was employed by the American administration before being elected as a Christian Democrat to the federal parliament at Bonn.

KURT KIESINGER (1966–9)

Kiesinger was born at Ebingen in 1904. He studied at universities in Berlin and Tübingen and qualified as a lawyer. In 1933, he joined the Nazi Party and worked for the foreign ministry's radio propaganda department. Interned for two years after the war, he was eventually exonerated of war crimes since it was claimed that he used his position to hinder anti-Jewish measures being taken. He joined the Christian Democrats and in 1949 was elected to the *Bundestag.*

WILLY BRANDT (1969–74)

Born Karl Herbert Frahm at Lubeck in 1913, the illegitimate son of a store cashier, he was apprenticed to a shipping agent and joined the Social Democratic Party. A fervent anti-Nazi, he fled to Norway in 1933 and there changed his name to Willy Brandt in order to escape detection by Hitler's agents. He also took Norwegian nationality. After the war, Brandt returned to Germany and resumed his German citizenship. He joined the Social Democrats and from 1957 to 1966 was mayor of West Berlin. During this time, he was elected to the *Bundesrat*.

HELMUT SCHMIDT (1974–82)

The son of teachers, Schmidt was born in Hamburg in 1918. Conscripted into the army during the Second World War, he served with German air defences, briefly on the Eastern Front and then as an artillery officer in the West. In 1945, he was taken prisoner by the British. After the war, Schmidt studied economics and politics at Hamburg University. He joined the Social Democrats in 1946 and, in 1953, was elected to the *Bundestag*.

HELMUT KOHL (1982–98)

Born in Ludwigshafen in 1930 into a devout Roman Catholic family, Kohl was the third son of a civil servant. He was drafted into the German army during the Second World War, but did not see active service. After the war, Kohl studied history and politics at Heidelberg University and then entered business. A Christian Democrat, he was elected to the *Bundestag* in 1976, became leader of the opposition and was elected Chancellor in 1982.

GERHARD SCHRÖDER (1998–2005)

The son of a German soldier who was killed during the Second World War, Schröder was born in Mossenberg in 1944. After serving an apprenticeship in the retail trade, he worked as a construction worker before attending Göttingen University to become a lawyer. Schröder joined the Social Democrats in 1963 and was elected to the *Bundesrat* in 1980. Four times married, he earned the nickname 'Audi Man' after the four-ring symbol on Audi cars.

When Ludwig Erhard (1897–1977) succeeded Konrad Adenauer in 1963, he had already gained the reputation of being the man whose policies were largely responsible for the German economic miracle. His years as Chancellor were brief, since he became involved in a scandal when he was held responsible for a budget leak and this led to Free Democratic Union (FDP) members of the government resigning from their positions. In 1965, he was forced to resign and was succeeded by Kurt Kiesinger.

Following the collapse of Erhard's government, Kiesinger formed a grand coalition made up of members of the Christian Democrats, Social Democrats and Free Democratic Union. The main achievement of his chancellorship was the progress he made towards improving relations with members of the Soviet bloc, particularly East Germany, Czechoslovakia and Romania. Sadly, many in Germany could not forgive or forget his former membership of the Nazi Party and there were times when he faced public abuse. Following his resignation in 1969, he was succeeded by Willy Brandt (1913–92).

C *Willy Brandt and* Ostpolitik

Willy Brandt was arguably the most controversial of West Germany's post-war chancellors. Prior to 1969, he had twice unsuccessfully stood as a candidate for the chancellorship, and now in office he formed a coalition made up of the Social Democrats and the Free Democratic Union. At home, facing the threat of student riots and terrorist activity, he did not hesitate to grant the police additional powers and make those applying for employment as civil servants, including teachers, the subject of security checks. He also put forward an ambitious reform programme that, according to the historian William Carr, aimed 'to revitalise and democratise a society fossilised in the Adenauer era into stifling conformism and authoritarianism'. To some extent these measures appeased student and left-wing activists but they certainly did not win the approval of the older generations of Germans and they met with the resistance of state governments. Consequently, many members of the *Bundesrat* changed parties and joined the Christian Democrats. Additional problems faced by the government included a steep rise in unemployment and a massive rise in fuel prices caused by the Middle East oil crisis in 1973.

In foreign policy, Brandt aimed to bring about reconciliation between eastern and western Europe – *Ostpolitik*, literally translated as 'East politics' or 'Eastern policy'. After agreeing to accept the existing frontiers of Germany, including the Oder-Neiße Line and the division of Berlin, the East Germans made it possible for limited numbers of West Berliners to visit East Berlin.

In 1970, during a visit to Poland, he made his famous *Warschauer Kniefall*, when he spontaneously knelt before a monument to the victims of the Warsaw Ghetto, and the following year he was awarded the Nobel Peace Prize. In 1972, a Basic Treaty was signed by which the BRD and DDR committed themselves to developing normal relations. As a consequence

> **KEY ISSUE**
>
> *The exact meaning of the term 'Ostpolitik'.*

PICTURE 57
Willy Brandt paying homage to the victims of the Warsaw Ghetto

Q

Account for the downfall of Willy Brandt.

of *Ostpolitik,* the Federal Republic exchanged ambassadors with Poland, Bulgaria, Czechoslovakia, Hungary and the Soviet Union. However, *Ostpolitik* proved extremely controversial and was strongly opposed by the Christian Democrats as well as many members of Brandt's own party and in 1971 he was forced to face a vote of no confidence, which he survived.

Plagued by problems, in the end Brandt's downfall was brought about by a series of scandals. The first came when it was disclosed that the East German *Stasi* had secretly paid members of the government to vote for him and so keep him in office. Then it was discovered that one of Brandt's personal assistants, Günter Guillaume, was an East German agent, and this was followed by disclosures about his private life and his involvement with prostitutes. It is claimed that at this point Brandt contemplated suicide but instead accepted responsibility and resigned. Afterwards, he continued in politics and became involved in such causes as peace, Third World poverty and the reunification of Germany. In 1990, he flew to Baghdad to meet Saddam Hussein and negotiate the release of Western hostages.

After Brandt's departure, for nine days the Vice Chancellor, Walter Scheel, acted as Chancellor until Helmut Schmidt (1918–), the leader of the Social Democrats, was elected. Schmidt, who had already served as Defence Minister and Minister of Finance and Economics, was to serve three terms as chancellor. As he was quickly to learn, as leader of a coalition of Social and Free Democrats, he was not to enjoy an easy passage. In foreign policy, he tended to follow the policy of *Ostpolitik* and seek improved relations with East Germany and the Soviet Union. In 1979, together with the American President, Jimmy Carter, Giscard d'Estaing, the French President, and the British Prime Minister, James Callaghan, he attended a Summit of Four that was to consider the issue of a strategic arms treaty. The Strategic Arms Limitations Talks (SALT) resulted in a treaty being agreed between the Soviet Union and the United States that aimed to limit the production and testing of nuclear weapons. In 1982, the *Bundesrat* failed to agree the budget and the Social Democrats withdrew from the coalition. On failing to survive a vote of no confidence, Schmidt resigned.

D *The chancellorship of Helmut Kohl (1982–98)*

Helmut Kohl (1930–) first led a coalition of Social, Christian and Free Democrats but in order to make secure his position in 1983 he dissolved the *Bundesrat* and called a general election, which he won with a considerable majority. Like his predecessors, he continued to work vigorously for détente in Europe. In 1984, Kohl became the first BRD chancellor to visit Israel and in a speech to the Knesset he said that he had benefited from 'the grace of late birth', by which he meant that he was too young to have been involved in the crimes committed during the years of the Third Reich. Later that year, he met French President François Mitterrand at Verdun, where they commemorated the massive loss of life on both sides during the battle of 1916. Kohl claimed that the meeting was evidence of Franco-German reconciliation. The following year, he shook hands with the US President Ronald Reagan at a cemetery in Bitburg that contained the graves of SS soldiers, an act that led his critics to claim that he was insensitive to Germany's Nazi past. However, later that year he was offended when not invited to attend the fortieth anniversary of the D-Day landings in France.

In the elections of 1987, he was re-elected chancellor but with a reduced majority. Shortly afterwards, Kohl received a visit from Erich Honecker, the first leader of the DDR to venture to West Germany. In 1990, he began to take advantage of the changes taking place in Europe to press for the unification of Germany.

E *The coming of German reunification*

In 1985, Mikhail Gorbachev became the leader of the Soviet Union and introduced his policies of *glasnost* and *perestroika* that aimed to make government more democratic and allow greater freedoms to the Russian people. Naturally, events in the Soviet Union affected the attitude of the peoples of the Communist bloc countries, particularly when Gorbachev made it clear that he supported reformist movements. Events in the DDR unfolded with remarkable speed.

Early in 1989, thousands of East German tourists visiting Hungary and Czechoslovakia made their way to West Germany rather than return home. In the DDR, huge demonstrations began with 70,000 demonstrators taking to the streets in Leipzig; when Honecker ordered a clampdown, the armed forces refused to take action. Honecker had no choice but to step down. He was replaced by Egon Krenz (1937–), who was powerless to act when thousands of East Berliners approached the Brandenburg Gate, broke through the Berlin Wall and poured into West Berlin.

On 9 November 1989, the Berlin Wall was officially opened and East Germans allowed to proceed to the West unhindered. Although there remained obstacles, German unification seemed imminent. On 1 July

PICTURE 58

East Germans take to the streets to demonstrate against the DDR's communist government in 1989

1990, West Germany's currency was introduced to East Germany and three months later, on 3 October 1990, Germany was officially reunified with Berlin being named as the country's capital. Helmut Kohl, the West German chancellor, continued to serve as chancellor but now of a united Germany. His position was confirmed by the first national elections of 1990 when, after winning a landslide victory, he became leader of a coalition of Christian Democrats and Free Democrats.

PICTURE 59

East and West Germans meet on top of the Berlin Wall

F *Postscript*

Kohl again won the election in 1994 but against a background of increasing dissatisfaction with his policies. The merger of East and West Germany meant the bringing together of two different ideologies, two different systems of government and two very different economies. East Germans were very disappointed at the slow rate of economic progress which meant they still lagged well behind the prosperity enjoyed by West Germans; West Germans resented the imposition of higher taxes that reflected the spiralling cost of reunification. In former East Germany, workers were unhappy that unemployment was on the increase and their wages did not match those of their West German counterparts. The truth was that the entire **infrastructure** of former East Germany, its roads, railways and communications, was in need of a complete overhaul and modernisation. In addition, former East German industries were being transferred from state ownership to become part of a capitalist economy. Some former East Germans even began to regret reunification since they missed the state-guaranteed wages and benefits offered by the former communist regime.

> **infrastructure** all the component parts that make up the structure of a nation – industries, communications etc.

Helmut Köhl remained in office until he lost the election of 1998, when he was replaced by the Social Democrat leader, Gerhard Schroeder (1944–). After two periods as German chancellor, his party lost the federal election of 2005 and, unable to form a coalition, he stood down. Schröder was succeeded by Angela Merkel (1954–), a Christian Democrat and daughter of a Lutheran pastor, who was brought up in East Germany. She was the first woman to hold the position of chancellor of a reunited Germany.

As for the fates of the former leaders of the DDR, in 1990 the ailing 78-year-old Erich Honecker fled to Moscow to escape trial for Cold War crimes. After the collapse of the Soviet Union, he found refuge in the Chilean embassy but was finally caught and brought to trial. Released because of his ill health, he moved to live with his daughter in Chile and died there in 1994. Egon Krenz was not so lucky: charged with Cold War crimes, he was sentenced to a term of imprisonment. Then, on his release, he retired.

4 ⌁ BIBLIOGRAPHY

It is often the case that references to post-1945 Germany are to be found in the concluding chapters of modern histories of that country. Such books include *A History of Germany 1815–1980* by William Carr (Edward Arnold 1991) and Mary Fulbrook's *A Concise History of Germany* (Cambridge University Press 1990), and there is limited coverage in *Mastering Modern European History* by Stuart Miller (Macmillan Master Series 1988.). More detailed books dealing exclusively with this period are *West Germany: A Contemporary History* by M. Balfour (Croom Helm 1982), *The German Democratic Republic* by M. McCauley (Macmillan 1983), *Honecker's Germany* ed. D. Childs (Allen and Unwin 1985), *The Cold War* by S. Ball (Hodder & Stoughton 1995), *Germany Between East and West* by Edwina Moreton (Cambridge University Press 1987), *The Berlin Wall* by Ann and John Tusa (Hodder & Stoughton 1994), *Justice at Nuremberg* by Robert Canot (Farrar Straus Co, New York), and *The Baader-Meinhof Group* by Stefan Haust (The Bodley Head 1987).

5 ~ STRUCTURED AND ESSAY QUESTIONS

A *This section consists of questions that might be used for discussion (or written answers) as a way of expanding on the chapter and testing your understanding of it.*

1. In what ways did the new constitution of the German Federal Republic differ from that of Britain?
2. What is meant by the term 'Cold War'?
3. What measures did Konrad Adenauer take to improve the BRD's relationship with other West European countries?
4. Of all the reasons for West Germany's remarkable economic recovery, which was the most important?
5. Who were more badly affected by the building of the Berlin Wall, the East Germans or the West Germans? Give reasons for your answer.
6. With reference to the leaders of the German Democratic Republic, what is meant by the term 'hard-liner'?
7. Explain the reasons for the difference in the rate of economic growth between East and West Germany.
8. What were the aims of militant left-wing groups such as the *Rote Armee Fraktion*?

B *Essay questions.*

1. In 2003, a German television poll voted Konrad Adenauer 'the greatest German of all time'. To what extent did he merit this title?
2. 'Lack of a democratic government was the main reason for unrest in East Germany during the period 1950–99.' How accurate is this point of view?
3. How successful was Willy Brandt in implementing his policy of *Ostpolitik*?
4. What were the reasons for Germany achieving reunification in 1990?

6 ~ MAKING NOTES

Complete the following table to confirm your knowledge of the chancellors of the German Federal Republic.

Chancellor	Party	Years in office	Main achievements
Konrad Adenauer			
Ludwig Erhard			
Kurt Kiesinger			
Willy Brandt			
Helmut Schmidt			
Helmut Kohl			

7 ～ DOCUMENTARY EXERCISE ON THE BERLIN WALL

Study the following sources and then answer the questions based on them.

SOURCE A
From a 1962 brochure issued by the German Democratic Republic in 1962, explaining their reason for building the Berlin Wall.

It was the result of developments of many years' standing in West Germany and West Berlin. Let us recall preceding events: In 1948 a separate currency reform was introduced in West Germany and West Berlin – the West German reactionaries thereby split Germany and even West Berlin into two currency areas. The West German separatist state was founded in 1949 – Bonn therefore turned the zonal border into a state frontier. In 1954, West Germany was included in NATO. Thus did the aggressive NATO policy create the wall which today separates the two German states and also goes through the middle of Berlin. The Bonn government and the West German government have systematically converted West Berlin into a centre of provocation…

SOURCE B
From Berlin Memories, *by Ger Tillekens.*

The Wall proved to be not just a stone wall but a barricade, filled with concrete road blocks, rolls of barbed wire and with sand stripes between the walls. At night, the spotlights went on and we observed the *VoPo* making their rounds. At first, it gave us the feeling of being a city under siege but we soon got used to it. It seemed just like a play being performed on a large stage until, one night, we were awakened by the snarling sound of machine guns and suddenly it all became very real. The next morning we learned that a man had tried to climb the wall but was shot whilst crossing the sand stripes and had been left there, bleeding to death. … I still have a vivid memory of a Berliner standing on one of the wooden towers near the wall shouting 'Schiess denn!' (Come on, shoot!) to the guards on the other side.

Q

1 *How valid are the reasons given in Source A for the need to build the Berlin Wall?*
2 *What impression does Source B give of the attitude of those living in West Berlin to the construction of the Wall?*
3 *How valuable are Sources A and B to an understanding of the situation in Berlin during the 1960s?*

Glossary

Index